TechTV's
Upgrading Your PC

Second Edition

Mark Edward Soper and TechTV

*In memory of Harvey Humble,
history professor, Olivet
Nazarene University*

*With many thanks to Gunnell
Jordan, English professor, Olivet
Nazarene University*

*Their dedication to truth, wit,
and clear thinking have inspired
me for thirty years.*

TechTV's Upgrading Your PC

Copyright © 2004 by Pearson Education

Published by TechTV Press in association with New Riders Publishing, a division of Pearson Education.

New Riders Publishing
201 W. 103rd Street, Indianapolis, Indiana 46290

All rights reserved. No part of this book shall be reproduced, stored in a retrieval system, or transmitted by any means, electronic, mechanical, photocopying, recording, or otherwise, without written permission from the publisher. No patent liability is assumed with respect to the use of the information contained herein. Although every precaution has been taken in the preparation of this book, the publisher and author assume no responsibility for errors or omissions. Nor is any liability assumed for damages resulting from the use of the information contained herein.

International Standard Book Number: 0-7357-1360-X

Library of Congress Catalog Card Number: 2003101056

Printed in the United States of America

First printing: July, 2003

08 07 06 05 04   7 6 5 4 3 2 1

Interpretation of the printing code: The rightmost double-digit number is the year of the book's printing; the rightmost single-digit number is the number of the book's printing. For example, the printing code 04-1 shows that the first printing of the book occurred in 2004.

Trademarks

All terms mentioned in this book that are known to be trademarks or service marks have been appropriately capitalized. Pearson Education cannot attest to the accuracy of this information. Use of a term in this book should not be regarded as affecting the validity of any trademark or service mark.

Warning and Disclaimer

Every effort has been made to make this book as complete and as accurate as possible, but no warranty of fitness is implied. The information is provided on an as-is basis. The authors and the publisher shall have neither liability nor responsibility to any person or entity with respect to any loss or damages arising from the information contained in this book or from the use of the DVD or programs that may accompany it.

Bulk Purchases/Corporate Sales

The publisher offers discounts on this book when ordered in quantity for bulk purchases and special sales. For sales within the U.S., please contact: Corporate and Government Sales at (800)382-3419 or corpsales@pearsontechgroup.com. Outside the U.S., please contact: International Sales at (317)581-3793 or international@pearsontechgroup.com.

Publisher
Stephanie Wall

TechTV, Vice President, Strategic Development
Glenn Farrell

Production Manager
Gina Kanouse

TechTV Press Project Manager
Sasha Zullo

Acquisitions Editor
Wendy Sharp

Senior Project Editor
Sarah Kearns

Copy Editor
Jill Batistick

Indexers
Cheryl Lenser
Lisa Stumpf

Composition
Amy Hassos

Proofreader
Beth Trudell

Manufacturing Coordinator
Dan Uhrig

Interior and Cover Designer
Alan Clements

Media Developer
Jay Payne

Marketing
Scott Cowlin
Tammy Detrich
Hannah Onstad Latham

Publicity Manager
Susan Nixon

650 Townsend Street
San Francisco, California 94103

Table of Contents

Mark Edward Soper is president of Select Systems and Associates, Inc., a technical writing and training organization.

Mark has been in the computer industry since 1983, so this book commemorates his twentieth anniversary of coping with bits and bytes. His first technical writing project was a short instruction sheet for the 1541 disk drive used by the Commodore 64 home computer, establishing his philosophy of bridging the gap between technology and the non-technical user.

His formal technical writing career began in the late 1980s with a column for a local magazine. Since 1990, Mark has written more than 140 articles for publications such as *SmartComputing, PCNovice, PCNovice Guides,* and the *PCNovice Learning Series.* His early work was published in *WordPerfect Magazine, The WordPerfectionist,* and *PCToday.*

From 1992 to 1999, Mark taught computer troubleshooting and other technical subjects to thousands of students from Maine to Hawaii. He is an A+ Certified hardware technician and a Microsoft Certified Professional.

Although this is Mark's first book for New Riders, he's no stranger to the Pearson family of book imprints. Since 1999, he's written or contributed to many books published by Que, another Pearson imprint. He is the author of *The Complete Idiot's Guide to High-Speed Internet Connections* and *Absolute Beginner's Guide to Cable Internet Connections.* He is the co-author of the original edition of *TechTV's Upgrading Your PC,* and has also co-authored the first and second editions of *Upgrading and Repairing PCs, Technician's Portable Reference, Upgrading and Repairing PCs: Field Guide* (also available in various foreign-language editions), and *Upgrading and Repairing PCs, A+ Certification Study Guide, Second Edition.*

Mark has also contributed to *Upgrading and Repairing PCs, 11th, 12th, 13th, 14th,* and *15th Editions; Upgrading and Repairing PCs, 12th Edition, Academic Edition; Upgrading and Repairing Networks, Second Edition; Special Edition Using Windows Me; Special Edition Using Windows XP Home Edition; Special Edition Using Windows XP Professional, Bestseller Edition; Special Edition Using Windows XP Home Edition, Bestseller Edition; Special Edition Using Windows XP Professional, Bestseller Edition;* and *Platinum Edition Using Microsoft Windows XP.*

Mark welcomes your questions and comments at `mesoper@selectsystems.com`. See `www.selectsystems.com` for more information about his book and photo-archiving projects.

This reviewer contributed her considerable hands-on expertise to the entire development process for *TechTV's Upgrading Your PC*. As the book was being written, this dedicated professional reviewed all the material for technical content, organization, and flow. Her feedback was critical to ensuring that *TechTV's Upgrading Your PC* fits our reader's need for the highest-quality technical information.

Karen Weinstein is a computer consultant residing in North Potomac, Maryland. She has more than a decade of experience in PC sales and support. Karen has tech edited numerous computer books and online courses on topics including upgrading and repairing PCs, building a PC, high-speed Internet access, MS Office, and MS Visio. Karen is delighted to have had the opportunity to work with Mark Edward Soper on both the first and second editions of this book.

In addition to tech editing and tinkering with her own PC, Karen's favorite activities include spending time with her two daughters, her husband Mark, and her beautiful basset hound, Cleo.

Karen welcomes comments at kweinst565@aol.com.

The author gets the credit, but a lot of other people help the author to succeed. My thanks to all of them, especially:

First and foremost, Almighty God. "Whatever you do, do all to the glory of God." Writing about technology is what I do, and I do it to His glory.

My family: Cheryl, who appreciates my work (and appreciates it even more when it's finished!); Jeremy, whose quest for the fastest PC is still in progress; Kate and her husband Hugh, who have "upgraded" their family with the addition of Jarvis 1.0 this past winter; Ian, whose graphic arts skill I wish I could inherit; Edward and his wife Erin, who keep the computers and people at my old alma mater working and insured against disasters.

My father Stuart, my stepmother Elaine, and my mother-in-law Alice, for nodding and acting as if they understand what I'm doing and loving me anyway.

Wendy Sharp, for overseeing this book and for her patience with an author new to the ways of TechTV Press. Stacey Beheler, for keeping those advance checks coming on schedule. Jay Payne, for building the companion DVD.

Karen Weinstein, for improving the technical content and organization of both editions of this book.

The rest of the gang at TechTV Press, whose devotion to the artistic side of new media and graphic arts help technology have a heart.

Thanks also to Glenn Farrell, Sasha Zullo, and all the folks at TechTV for their hard work and dedication.

When I learned that this book was going to be one of the first TechTV books in a new series from TechTV Press, I realized it was one of those "twice in a lifetime" opportunities. As the co-author of the original edition, I now have the opportunity to create a new and even better book.

Eight Reasons You Need (and Will Love) This Book

Here's what makes this book uniquely valuable to you:

- **It helps you make the most of new technology**—Computer peripherals are getting faster and smarter, but if you can't plug them into your computer, they're useless. With coverage of hot technologies such as Serial ATA, USB 2.0, AGP 8x, Wi-Fi wireless networking, rewriteable DVD, and Bluetooth, this book helps you make your computer ready for the latest drives, cameras, devices, and gadgets.

- **It's practical**—Unlike some upgrade books, this one doesn't assume that you're trying to upgrade a PC that was born before Windows 98. Instead of trying to resurrect a computing dinosaur with a heavy dose of digital DNA, this book helps you take an "almost good enough" recent PC and make it the perfect PC for you.

- **It's fun**—Working on computers can be frustrating, but it can also be enjoyable. We've added a bit of humor to help you get through the pain to the gain of better performance. Don't miss our wise, witty, and occasionally wacky top-ten lists of reasons to upgrade major components of your system. They'll make you smile, think, and get busy making upgrades.

- **It respects your budget**—If you're like me, you get tired of reading computer books and magazines that assume that you're a millionaire. I know you can only spend so much every year on your PC, so why not make the most of it?

- **It recognizes that everyone's perfect computer is different**—Sure, I have favorite technologies and upgrades, but yours are different than mine. This book is designed to help you create the perfect computing environment for you. Whether you're a web addict, gamer, graphic artist, writer, photographer, telecommuter, or parent, my goal on every page is a simple one: to give you the help you need to get the speed, features, and reliability you want.

- **It won't put you to sleep**—This book is fast-paced and easy-to-understand to make the upgrading process enjoyable and absorbing.

- **It contains sharp, clear photos to instruct you**—I've been a serious amateur photographer for over thirty years, and TechTV Press's support of digital imaging artistry has inspired me to create better and more creative photographs and diagrams to guide you in your upgrade quest. I've even built a clear case PC to help you visualize the complete package of upgrades you can perform; see it on the companion DVD packaged with this book.

- **It's a TechTV book!**—Building from the knowledge base of the TechTV cable television network, TechTV Press is your trusted source for technology-related information. You can be assured that the information and advice you receive from a TechTV Press book is timely, easy to understand, and accurate.

Grab a Side(bar) of Help

TechTV provides fun, accessible, and informative tips in a variety of formats. In print, this book aims to do the same with these special features:

- **Read This Too**—These are the books that I've found to be useful for further research and for propping up my collection of computer magazines.

- **Stop, Look, Think!**—Your mother told you to "stop, look, and listen" before crossing the railroad tracks. This is our version, dedicated to keeping you out of the way of powerful computer foul-ups that can wreck your system, your data, and maybe even your day.

- **Analyze This!**—Get the real story on technology issues and avoid the personal confuser blues.

- **Mark's Tip Sheet**—If it's good advice, it's worth noting. You'll find a lot of advice here that's been field-tested by real computer users like you. This advice can help you out, in, or over some tricky PC problems.

- **On the Web**—Somebody's compared the World Wide Web to the world's finest library *after* somebody dumped all the books all over the floor. I've been rooting around to find the sites that help you go further in your quest for more computing power.

On the DVD

Check out the DVD packaged with this book for upgrade tips and tutorials straight from the TechTV vaults and from this author's own upgrading labs. Highlights include:

- A tour of a clearcase PC, making it easier than ever to see how PC upgrades fit into the big picture.

- How to connect monitors and TVs to a dual-display graphics card and configure the card in Windows.

- How to install a case fan for extra cooling.

- How to install a motherboard.

- How to connect an optical drive so you can use it for music playback and for data.

- How to use the connectors on a power supply.

- How slot-based and socketed processors compare.

- How to use the ports on the rear of a typical PC.

What's Covered in This Book

To help you get the most for your money, this book covers the entire upgrading process. It starts with evaluating the hardware and operating system in your current computer and continues by covering how to install upgrades for every major component in your system. Because your PC can be the hub of your digital entertainment, it also covers adding digital cameras, DV camcorders, and PDAs to your computer.

Along the way, this book helps you determine the best upgrades you need for particular computing tasks, the most cost-effective upgrades for any budget, the upgrades that are the best at making a middle-aged machine young again, and the upgrades that have little value.

The book is divided into eight parts:

- **Before You Upgrade**—Chapters 1 through 6

- **Upgrading for Performance**—Chapters 7 through 9

- **Upgrading for Greater Storage Capacity**—Chapters 10 through 12

- **Upgrading for Better Multimedia**—Chapters 13 through 15

- **Upgrading Connectivity**—Chapters 16 through 18

- **Input This! Output That!**—Chapters 19 through 21

- **Upgrading System Stability**—Chapters 22 and 23

- **Upgrading for Portability**—Chapters 24 and 25

In Chapter 1, "Making the Decision to Upgrade," you learn why PC upgrades make sense, how to turn a component failure into an upgrade, and how extended warranties can prevent upgrade opportunities. The chapter also provides a quick-reference to the most popular upgrades.

No matter what your budget, an upgrade can benefit your system. Chapter 2, "Upgrade Strategies," outlines common upgrade strategies, helps you find useful upgrades for any budget, and shows you how to make your system young again through carefully chosen upgrades.

If you're panicking because your system has failed before you're ready to perform major surgery on it, or you're trying to get your system in top-notch shape to make upgrades easier, be sure to read Chapter 3, "Alternatives to Upgrades," for maintenance and troubleshooting tips. Any part you don't need to replace saves money for the upgrades you want most.

Before you install any upgrade, you should find out what you already have. In Chapter 4, "Taking an Inspection Tour of Your System," you learn how to examine your system and use system analysis software to find the best place to start.

In Chapter 5, "Preparing for Your Upgrade," you learn how to take simple precautions and select the right tools to avoid problems during the upgrade process.

Getting the best upgrades for what you like to do is the focus of Chapter 6, "The Right Upgrades for You." This chapter also provides links to some of the more unusual upgrades on the market.

No matter how much you paid for your computer, chances are the vendor didn't install enough memory. In Chapter 7, "RAM Your Way to Faster Performance," you discover the different types of memory, how to find the right amount of memory for your needs, and how to add it.

The processor, or CPU, is the brains of your system. Chapter 8, "Speedy Computing with Processor Upgrades," helps you determine if your processor can be upgraded and shows you how to select and install the fastest processor suitable for your system.

An outdated motherboard stops processor upgrades cold and can force you to fill up your expansion slots with cards if you want to add the most popular port types. In Chapter 9, "Unlock Your System's Potential with Motherboard and BIOS Upgrades," you learn how to select and install a motherboard with the processor support and other features you want most.

No matter how big a hard disk you have, eventually you fill it up. In Chapter 10, "Adding a Huge Hard Disk," you discover how to select and install the big hard disk of your dreams, whether it's the first drive in a new system or an addition to the storage you already have.

Movable storage is a movable feast for your computers. Sit down at the table with Chapter 11, "Removable Storage to Go," and select from a buffet of magnetic and flash memory storage devices. Discover the perfect types to use for transporting data, backing up data, and hauling around your digital life.

Burn, baby, burn! Whether it's disco or Debussy, music or photos, rewriteable optical storage is a hugely popular upgrade. In Chapter 12, "A Burning Desire for Better Optical Drives," get up to speed on the latest rewriteable DVD and CD technologies, solve compatibility problems, and learn how to install internal and external models.

Whether you're fighting off zombies or editing digital photos, graphics card speed is critical. Chapter 13, "Extra Vroom with Faster Graphics and Bigger Displays," helps you fix slow display speeds and fuzzy monitors with the best upgrades that fit your computer.

Sick of listening to fuzzy stereo sound when your game or DVD has 5.1 surround sound capabilities? Get the sound you want with the help of Chapter 14, "PC Audio and More." Whether you'd prefer to specify better sound as part of a motherboard upgrade or you're looking to install the perfect sound card, here's sound advice.

Whether you're trying to rescue old slides, negatives, and prints from the ravages of time or swap film and videotape for pixels, Chapter 15, "Digital Imaging and Video," helps you select and install the best scanners, digital cameras, and DV camcorders.

The faster the Internet is, the more fun it is. If you're still stuck with a dial-up connection, Chapter 16, "Get Yourself Broadband—It's (Always) Going Fast!," is required reading. Learn how to choose and install the right broadband connection for your situation.

You learned to share in kindergarten. Don't stop sharing just because you have broadband, a new printer, or lots of extra storage. Chapter 17, "Share the Wealth with a Home Network," shows you how to choose and install popular home and small-office networks.

Want to surf the Internet inside and outside? Tired of cables? Chapter 18, "Wireless Wonders," has the solutions you need for Internet sharing and wireless networking.

Plug it in, plug it in. If you're out of places, or you don't have the right types of ports for today's hot new devices, Chapter 19, "Adding the Ports You Need for the Devices You Want," has the answers. From USB 2.0 and IEEE-1394a ports to hubs and converters, learn how to install the ports you need for today and tomorrow.

Keyboards, pointing devices, and game controllers can make work and play a pleasure or a pain. If you're getting more pain than pleasure out of your input devices, Chapter 20, "Selecting the Best Input Devices," has the answers you need.

If your current printer is costing a mint to operate but giving you dime-store quality, Chapter 21, "Output Unlimited with Printer Upgrades," shows you how to select and connect with the best printer for your print tasks.

A bad power supply makes any computer, old or new, a problem instead of a joy. Get back the joy and prepare your PC for power-hungry upgrades by reading Chapter 22, "Power Supply Upgrades."

Discover greater system stability and features without losing game-playing capabilities during your next Windows or Linux operating system upgrades. Read Chapter 23, "Winning Windows Upgrades," to learn how.

Want to take critical information everywhere? You're a candidate for mobile information devices. Chapter 24, "Upgrading to Mobile Information Devices," helps you choose from the major device types.

If you can't get information into your mobile device, it's not much good. Read Chapter 25, "Upgrading Your Portable's Connection with Your PC," to discover how the right software and hardware makes moving information to where you need it easier.

Each chapter includes explanations of unfamiliar terms, but if you need more help, there's also a glossary at the end of the book.

It's Your PC—Make It the PC You Need and Want

Whether you bought your PC two weeks ago or two years ago, you can make it better. You have the power, and my hope is that reading this book will help you enjoy and exercise the power you have to remake your PC. Thank you very much.

—Mark Edward Soper

Part I

Before You Upgrade

Chapter 1

Making the Decision to Upgrade

Upgrading your PC can be an adventure, but it offers you more: more performance, more versatility, more fun, and more enjoyment. In short, more of what you use a PC for.

If you're looking for more from your PC experience, you've opened the right book! In this chapter, discover the big three benefits of upgrading, find out how to turn a broken component into an upgrade opportunity, find out how extended warranties can prevent upgrades, and, if you're in a hurry to get upgrading, discover the fast track to the upgrades you need the most.

The Big Three Benefits of Upgrading

You might not need any reasons to upgrade your PC, but just in case you need to give your spouse, your roommates, or your conscience some justification (your kids will understand without a lot of explanations), there are three big reasons for upgrading your computer:

- Get the computer features you want whenever you want it.
- Play harder (and work better) with the system you know and love.
- Avoid the hassles of moving (to a new PC).

Let's look at each of these in turn.

Getting the Computer Features You Want—Now

Sure, it's fun to go shopping for a new computer—except that when you finally get it home, open it up, and discover that the vendor's idea of the hottest hardware isn't what you had in mind. Even if your new computer is a world-beater today, what about in six months? A year? That's when it's time to hit the upgrade trail.

Getting what you want when you want it is one of the biggest benefits of upgrading your own system. Even if you use a "build-to-order" service when you buy a computer, you must choose from the vendors that supply your computer builder. The advantage? A single call to a single vendor when things go wrong. The trouble, however, is that some vendors don't always have the latest, greatest stuff available when you buy. For example, some build-to-order vendors think that last year's 3D video card is good enough. However, if you want to be a world-beater, you want the latest, greatest card with the latest chipset from nVidia or ATI.

In the world of PC upgrades, though, you are the (re)builder. You choose the features you want and the price you want to pay for those features. Thus, if your video card is outdated or underpowered, you can choose the video card you want, at the price you want to pay.

From bigger monitors and hard drives to faster video cards and more comfortable pointing devices (consider the joy of the joystick!), when you get to decide what your computer uses, you're a happier and more productive PC user. However, remember that when you call the shots, you are also responsible for figuring out why device A and device B don't work together, or what to do if the power supply fails.

By controlling the upgrade process, you can turn a "jack-of-all-trades, master-of-none" PC into an optimized powerhouse for the computing tasks you perform most often. And, because you're calling the shots, you can skip often-useless software bundles or less-than-optimal hardware combinations present on many retail systems and put the money into the hardware or software you really need and want.

Here are a couple of the benefits of upgrading your system yourself:

- **You control how much of your operating system and software is retained in your upgrade.** You can move your old hard drive to a new motherboard, and if the motherboard recognizes your data, you can reinstall Windows so it finds your new hardware and get back to work while keeping your old programs intact. Prefer to start over? As long as you're not using the notorious restore CDs provided with some low-end computers, you can start with an empty hard disk, install your favorite flavor of Windows, install the programs you want to use, and get back to work with a stream-lined startup process. It's your choice.

JARGON

OEM products—These are the peripherals supplied with a computer that are usually not manufactured by the computer company itself. For example, some HP and Compaq computers have a basic, two-button mouse that was produced by Logitech, and an entry-level 10GB hard drive made by Seagate.

- **You can use the equipment you know and love.** If the user interface of the keyboard and mouse are major comfort factors for you, upgrading your existing system with the mouse and keyboard you choose is a much better option than putting up with the bottom-of-the-barrel Original Equipment Manufacturer (OEM) products that most vendors bundle with new systems.

Work Faster, Play Harder

No matter how much money you spend on your computer, if you use it for anything more than word processing and the odd game of Solitaire, you need to upgrade it to maintain its capability to do the jobs you need it to do. For example, if you do a lot of photo editing, you need a fast CPU, a big hard disk, and lots of RAM. If you're an online game player, your must-have list probably includes a fast 3D graphics card, a broadband Internet connection, a force-feedback game controller, and 5.1 sound for true 3D positional sound. And so it goes. As software adds features and more powerful hardware comes into view, your system needs upgrades just to keep up.

As a result of the industry's constant search for faster, bigger, and more feature-laden software and hardware, your efficiency and your enjoyment of leisure tasks with your computer drops over time when you stay with your system's out-of-the-box configuration. Ironically, the only way to *maintain* your ability to work and play with your PC is to *update* it at least once a year! Remember, it's cheaper to upgrade just the components that hold you back than to buy a brand-new computer every year or two.

ON THE WEB: Get Fresh Upgrade Ideas with Fresh Gear

Looking for the coolest upgrade ideas? Hit the Fresh Gear web site at www.techtv.com/freshgear for the latest reviews of software and hardware upgrades straight from the Fresh Gear show. Find out whether heavily hyped products match their publicity, or whether any overlooked products deserve a second look. Use the Archives link for shows you've missed.

Avoid the Hassles of Moving (to a New PC)

Do you love moving to a new home? Really? You must have forgotten the pain of wrapping dishes, labeling boxes, and lugging books and electronics equipment. Moving to a new computer is just about as painful. You need to:

- Figure out what files you really need.
- Transfer them to the new computer.
- Make sure you didn't lose anything along the way.
- Wipe out the hard disk on the old computer before you get rid of it so somebody can't dig through your old files.

It's a lot easier to add the stuff you want to your existing computer and simply avoid the agony of a virtual move.

Repairs as a Back-Door Way to System Upgrades

Sometimes an opportunity to upgrade your system comes disguised as a problem. If you have a major component failure, for example, you need to replace the component. Whether it's a monitor, hard drive, or whatever, you have two options:

- Buy an exact replacement.
- Buy an improved product as a replacement.

Any guesses as to which one I recommend?

Unless your component is covered by warranty, *never* settle for an exact replacement. Instead, always replace an existing component with a better, updated version. You have two major reasons to do so:

- If you take this opportunity to improve your component, you're really performing a system upgrade under the guise of a replacement. There's nothing like making the best of a bad situation!
- Most PC components aren't designed to be repaired; even if you send your sick PC to a repair shop, the tech is likely to repair it by sticking a replacement component in your computer.

In most cases, *you* can be the tech, save time and money, and get what you want instead of what the tech has on hand.

CAUTION: STOP! LOOK! THINK!

Nay, Nay, From These Components Stay Away!

Although most computer components can be repaired/replaced by intelligent folks like you and me (after all, that's why you're reading this book!), there are two major exceptions to the "open it up and change what's broken" rule:

- Power supplies
- CRT monitors

Unlike computers, which are safe to open and upgrade, both power supplies and monitors use dangerous and *potentially lethal* voltage levels to perform their work. Experienced monitor/TV techs must discharge the voltage retained by the picture tube inside the monitor's case even after it has been turned off before they can work on it, and power supplies are a "no user-serviceable components inside" item. Don't take chances! Consider both monitors and power supplies to be "no user-serviceable components inside" devices that must be swapped when they fail. Have a tech work on a broken monitor (if it's worth fixing), toss out a broken power supply, and get a decent one. Be safe—not dead!

How can you keep your options open? Stay away from extended warranties (which is where a lot of computer vendors make their money).

How Extended Warranties Can Prevent Upgrades

Extended warranties (extra-cost warranty plans that pay for repairs to covered products after the manufacturer's standard warranty has expired) might make sense for some products, but for computers, they make no sense at all—unless you're selling them. Salespeople who might not get a commission on computer sales often get a nice cut of the cost of the extended warranty. Is it any wonder why they're so eager to sell you one? Here's why:

- **Extended warranties cover only "like-for-like" repairs and replacements.** If your two-year-old system has a component failure, you're probably going to get an exact replacement instead of a faster, better component. Your chance to turn lemons into lemonade by getting a better product is gone (unless, by luck, the vendor has run out of two-year-old parts to use in your system).

- **Extended warranties cost too much for what they give you.** Because you get better components during repair *only* if an exact replacement is no longer available, the money you pay for an extended warranty guarantees that your computer remains stuck in the twilight zone of obsolescence instead of getting a shot of youth serum whenever something goes wrong.

- **Most components fail during the standard warranty, not later.** If you stress test your new computer during its first few days out of the box by using it heavily or by running system-testing software, you'll find most marginal components within the 14-day exchange period used by many retail stores. In addition, most other components will fail during the warranty period. If they fail post-warranty, well, that's your chance to upgrade to a better, faster component.

Here's the bottom line: Skip the extended warranty sales pitch, stick the money you'd spend on an extended warranty into your upgrade money bag, and fix repairs the right way—with a faster, better component.

CAUTION: STOP! LOOK! THINK!

Proprietary Designs Make for Upgrades That Don't Pay

Most of the time, it makes sense to upgrade your computer if it's just a year or so old. However, there are exceptions to every rule, and one of the biggest exceptions involves proprietary systems.

Many older low-cost systems such as IBM Aptivas, low-end HP and Compaq, Acer, as well as Packard Bell, Zenith, and NEC systems don't use standard motherboards. Instead, they typically feature a non-standard motherboard called an LPX (see Chapter 4, "Taking an Inspection Tour of Your System," for details), which restricts your upgrade options. One way to upgrade these systems is to buy a standard motherboard, case, and power supply and move your CPU, RAM, drives, and cards. However, if you need to work this hard to get a decent system, you might actually find it makes sense (and is cheaper) to start over and buy a new system. Memory and CPU upgrades are possible, but they might cost more than those with a standard system.

Most Popular Upgrades Checklist

What don't you like about your current system? What's too big, too small, or too old? If you're impatient, use this checklist to jump right to the chapter that covers your upgrade.

My computer is too slow	When I have a lot of programs open	When I edit videos or photos	When I play games
Read	Chapter 7	Chapter 7 and Chapter 13	Chapter 8 and Chapter 13
I'm running out of storage space	**For stuff I use every day**	**For digital music files (MP3 and WMA)**	**For downloaded movies and videos**
Read	Chapter 10	Chapter 10 and Chapter 12	Chapter 10 and Chapter 12

I can't connect my computer to	A broadband modem	A DV camcorder	My PDA
Read	Chapter 16	Chapter 15 and Chapter 19	Chapter 25
I want to use my computer to view	Photos taken with my digital camera	DVD movies	My family's old photographs
Read	Chapter 15 and Chapter 19	Chapter 12	Chapter 15
I want to hear	Music CDs	3D sound in games	Surround sound from DVDs
Read	Chapter 12 and Chapter 14	Chapter 14	Chapter 12 and Chapter 14
I want to create	Digital music CDs	DVD presentations	Digital photo albums
Read	Chapter 12 and Chapter 14	Chapter 12	Chapter 12 and Chapter 15
I'm tired of	My computer locking up and crashing	Tripping over network cables	Needing to reboot my computer several times a day
Read	Chapter 22	Chapter 18	Chapter 23
I want to add	Mobile access to my information	A second monitor	USB and IEEE-1394 ports
Read	Chapter 24	Chapter 13	Chapter 19

If you're not in such a hurry, or you have so many ideas that you don't know where to start, head over to Chapter 2, "Upgrade Strategies," and plan your upgrade strategy.

Chapter 2

Upgrade Strategies

When your computer is no longer getting the job done, it can be tempting to start throwing parts (and money) at it. But, if you take time to develop an upgrade strategy, you make the most of your time and your money.

In this chapter, you learn why you need an upgrade strategy, discover how to create task-based and budget-based upgrade strategies and how to avoid useless and overpriced upgrades, and explore how a sensible use of upgrades can transform an aging computer into a younger, more powerful model.

Why You Need an Upgrade Strategy

So, you've decided that your current PC just isn't cutting it anymore. You're ready to consider a PC upgrade. What's the best way to proceed?

The way I see it, there are two ways to plan an upgrade:

- You can upgrade based on the tasks you want your PC to perform (or perform more efficiently).

- You can upgrade based on your budget.

ANALYZE THIS

Price? Performance? It's Both!
Don't get caught in the "one way or the other" trap. Like most other issues in the computer business, you're probably making your upgrade decision based on both of these factors, even though they're covered separately here.

You want to get the most "bang for your buck" when you decide to retrofit your computer, so it pays to make a budget and decide which system upgrades can help you the most within the confines of your budget. As you'll see in this chapter, even if you can spend only $50, you can make a big improvement in your system.

Upgrading by Task

If you had unlimited funds at your disposal (I wish!), you could star in your own version of the old game show *Supermarket Sweep*. Instead of shoveling sirloin steaks into your shopping cart, you could roam the aisles of your favorite computer, electronics, or office-supply store and throw boxes of drives, memory, keyboards, scanners, and video cards into your shopping cart. If you wish you could shop like this, if you're frustrated because you have an upgrade budget, here's the good news: Having a budget means you need to *think* about what you need to make your computer faster, better, harder working, and more fun. Don't believe it? I could show you several computer upgrades in my office that I never should have bought. Instead of helping my computers to run better, run faster, work harder, or play better, they're gathering dust. What went wrong? As I look back on my upgrade misfires, it's obvious they have some factors in common:

- Some upgrades duplicate features and performance already in the system.
- Some are unproven gadgets instead of products that really enhance the system.
- Some simply won't fit into the target system.
- Some were purchased without enough thought about how they would be used; money was "burning a hole in my pocket" when I went to the computer store.

If you've ever bought a computer upgrade that you couldn't, or didn't, use, you know this can happen. One of the biggest reasons I wrote this book was to help you learn how to avoid upgrade blunders like these.

As you upgrade, look for upgrades that:

- Eliminate system bottlenecks.
- Enable your system to use new hardware and software.
- Improve your system's capability to perform certain tasks.

Generally, you can eliminate system bottlenecks with upgrades such as:

- Graphics (video) card
- More RAM
- Faster processor
- Broadband Internet

You can enable your system to use new hardware and software with upgrades such as:

- Motherboard with onboard AGP 4x and USB 2.0 ports
- Add-on USB 2.0 and IEEE-1394 ports
- 10/100 Ethernet card
- Windows XP or Linux operating system upgrade
- 2GHz or faster processor (might also require motherboard upgrade)
- More RAM (512MB or more)

To improve your system's capability to perform given tasks, you must do the following:

- Determine what tasks you want to perform.
- Evaluate your current hardware and operating system's capabilities.
- Upgrade components that are substandard.

See Chapter 6, "The Right Upgrades for You," for a detailed examination of the upgrades you might need for the most popular jobs (and fun) you want to have with your computer.

MARK'S TIP SHEET: How to Find the Bottlenecks in Your System

So what's slowing down *your* system? Until you know the answer to that question, you're really not ready to spend upgrade dollars intelligently. Of course, the answer depends on what you do most often. Here are just a few of the more common bottlenecks. Which one is most like what is happening on your system?

Is everything slow? If your system has less than 128MB of RAM, you've found problem #1. Upgrade to 256MB of RAM and do *everything* on your system a big favor.

Getting blown away in *Tribes*, *Quake Arena*, or some other 3D shoot 'em-up? If you're playing against the computer or on a local area network, it's time to find a faster video card with more 3D pixel-flinging magic. If you're playing against the world on the Internet, it's time for a faster Internet connection.

Running out of space for downloads, MP3s, and digital photos? It doesn't take a crystal ball to figure out that a bigger hard drive should be in *your* future.

You'll find the details later in this book, so be sure to figure out what you need *most* and buy it *first*. Otherwise, you'll be flushing your upgrade money away instead of getting a faster, better PC.

JARGON

Don't Get Baffled by What's Inside Your Box

It's hard to select upgrades for your system if you're not sure what's what. Here are some short definitions to keep you on the right track to upgrade success.

- **Motherboard**—The big circuit board that is the home for your system's RAM memory, expansion slots, and drive interfaces.
- **Video card**—The card your monitor plugs into; a lot of low-cost systems have built-in video on the motherboard. Almost all video cards speed up 3D games, but some are much better than others.
- **RAM**—Random Access Memory; your programs must be loaded into this to get any work done, and the more RAM you have, the more programs and information you can work with at one time.
- **CD-RW drive**—Lets you burn your own data and music CDs and read them too.
- **CPU**—Properly speaking, this is the processor (Pentium 4, Celeron, AMD Athlon, and so on), although some people call the box surrounding the CPU, RAM, and motherboard the CPU.
- **LCD display**—A flat-panel monitor that uses the same technology as a notebook computer screen.
- **Rewriteable DVD**—The CD-RW's newer sibling, it can do everything a CD-RW drive can do plus let you watch DVD movies and help you make your own DVD videos and slideshows.

Each of these technologies is covered in detail later in this book.

Upgrading by Budget

No one, not even yours truly, has an unlimited hardware budget. But by wise use of funds, I've kept some machines in service for up to six years or more, although they don't look like the same system anymore because of periodic upgrades. To keep a system running well for longer than the two or three years that PC makers seem to expect, you need to know what you can get for your money, as well as why you should spend your hard-earned cash on a given device. The previous section covered the why—now it's time for the what.

ANALYZE THIS

Prices Are Subject to Change—You'll Notice!

In this section, estimated prices based on typical products available in mid-2003 are used. Thus, one of two things is likely to be true by the time you read the book, count your money, and make your shopping list:

- Component shortages caused by anything from an earthquake, man-made disaster, or a buyer's miscalculation could make these price estimates look like the "good old days." In the late 1990s, an earthquake caused a RAM shortage and high prices that eventually dropped as the RAM shortage ended.

- With the daily changes in the computer industry, the price of major components seems to drop about as often. Six weeks after this book hits the street, these prices will look high...and that's normal. The longer you wait, the cheaper most things get. Of course, there will also be a pile of newer and faster things that sell for the old higher price. Yeesh!

Hey—it happens. However, you should at least be able to take the relative ranking of products in this section to the bank. No matter what happens to prices, in general some PC components cost less than others—and some cost more than others. So there.

Once you decide what you want to buy, you can use a web site like cNet's shopper (shopper.cnet.com), Idg.net's Price Finder (www.idg.net), Anandtech.com, Pricewatch.com, or TechTV's own link to Amazon.com to help you find the best deals online for systems, hardware components, and software.

So, what can you get for your money (more or less)? My recommendations are divided into four major categories to help you plan your upgrade. Here goes.

$50 or Less

If all you have to spare for a computer upgrade is what you saved by skipping a few lunches, you can still help your computer get better for an outlay of about $50 or less. Check out these options:

- **A new keyboard**—Let's face it, the keyboards shipped with most new systems these days are pretty lousy. Thanks to rampant cost-cutting to make computer systems cheaper, your hands and wrists might wind up paying the price for poor keyboard design and cheap construction. Get a decent keyboard (a lot of folks like the Microsoft Natural Keyboard series—and don't forget about the original IBM/Lexmark-style clicky-type keyboards sold by Unicomp); you'll get more work done with comfort.

- **A new mouse**—Take what I said about keyboards, and ditto it. Although some system vendors use OEM versions of Microsoft or Logitech mice (the best brands I know), others dredge up cheapjack mice with awkward shapes, buttons with little "click" mechanisms that are hard to keep clean, and outdated features. Want to get "mouse shoulder," that ache that makes you cringe at even the thought of starting up your system? Of course not, but using the typical brand X mouse is a great way to get it. For a lot less than $50, you can pick up a mouse (or other pointing device) to make web surfing, game playing, and even getting your work done a pleasure.

- **Need both?**—Look for mouse/keyboard bundles from Microsoft, Logitech, and other vendors, but make sure that both the keyboard and the mouse are what you want before you buy. If you're a good shopper, you might even find a wireless combo that cuts the cords for even more comfort for less than $80. (See Figure 2.1.)

Dedicated Internet
and multimedia keys

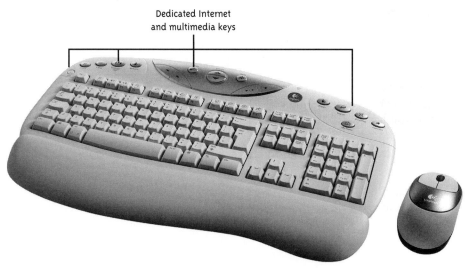

Figure 2.1

The Logitech Cordless Navigator Duo replaces your existing mouse and keyboard with an RF wireless model, which also offers dedicated web surfing and multimedia buttons. Photo courtesy of Logitech.

CAUTION: STOP! LOOK! THINK!

You're the Best Reviewer You've Got

Lots of people write reviews of computer products (and you'll find TechTV.com has lots of great reviews at your service), but when it comes to buying a new mouse or keyboard, you'd better save the final word for yourself. Because everyone wants different features, don't buy a new keyboard or mouse unless you can:

- **Try a friend's mouse or keyboard**—If you like theirs better than yours, get the brand and model number and go shopping.

- **Try your favorites at the store**—If not, buy from a store with a liberal return policy and give the favorites a good workout.

Trying before you buy is especially important if you're planning to switch to a completely different type of keyboard (such as an ergonomic unit) or pointing device (such as a trackball or trackpad touch tablet). One user's pleasure is another's torture. If you don't want your new keyboard or pointing device to wind up stuffed into a desk drawer or on the top shelf of the closet, try it first!

Other great review sites worth considering before you buy any upgrade include user reviews at Amazon.com and Epinions.com.

- **Game controller**—Whether your idea of fun is blasting aliens or blasting past other racecars, your game controller might be holding you back. If you're tired of staring at "game over," take a good look at your joystick, steering wheel, or game pad. If you think you can see your fingerprints permanently pressed into the buttons, it's time for a new one. Force feedback (which helps you forget it's just a game) and programmability to make finger-popping special moves much easier are just two of the benefits that a new game controller gives you, although better control is still the name of this game.

- **Memory (RAM)**—Thanks to that dreadful "improvement" called Unified Memory Architecture (an Unbelievably Miserable Achievement!), the so-called 128MB of RAM in a typical low-cost computer is about 16MB shy of a full load. Where's the rest of it? Running the built-in video, that's where.

  Even if your computer has a separate video card, the average computer still doesn't have enough RAM. What's "enough," you ask? More than you have, that's what, particularly if "what you have" is 256MB or less. Double your RAM and make every computer job you perform (or game you play) faster! Already have 512MB or more? Well, shucks, you can spend your hard-earned cash somewhere else!

- **Flash Memory Device**—If you're constantly moving around data that's too big for a floppy disk, but you don't want to lug around a CD-RW disc, consider one of the new, low-cost thumb-sized (keychain) drives. For $50 or so, you can get 32MB or 64MB sizes. Figure 2.2 shows a typical keychain flash memory device.

- **USB Hub**—Stop reaching around to the back of your computer to attach or remove USB keychain drives, flash memory card readers, drives, and other USB peripherals. As an alternative, some system vendors offer optional USB connectors you can slide into an empty drive bay.

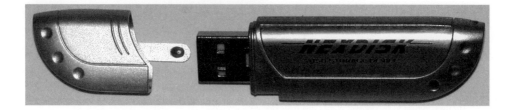

Figure 2.2

The NexDisk USB storage device plugs into a USB port for compact solid-state transportable data transfers.

Under $100

Find a whole Benjamin by counting the change under the couch cushions? Maybe you should post a warning sign: "Please Count Your Change After Watching TechTV!" Seriously, no matter how you come up with it, a hundred bucks can result in a serious improvement in the performance of your system. You can really get more work done in less time (or have more fun after work) with your choice of these upgrades:

- **A bigger hard drive**—When I bought my first "big" hard drive in 1990, I paid a thousand bucks for 200MB, and five dollars a megabyte was a good deal then. Today, we pay just less than a penny a megabyte, but no matter how much hard drive capacity you've got, those pesky freeware and shareware downloads, MP3 files, and miscellaneous web debris still fill up even the biggest drives in no time flat. If you run out of disk space (by the way, 15% or less free space on your drive is essentially out of space), Microsoft Windows will make life rough for you with (more) frequent system crashes and lockups. You can't get the biggest hard drives on the market for a Benjamin, but you can easily pick up a 40GB model and have a bit of change left over.

- **CD-RW drive**—CD-RW drives are among the most flexible storage devices you can buy. Feed them low-cost CD-R media and you can exchange data with virtually anybody with a CD-ROM, CD-RW, or DVD drive, make backups for pennies, and "burn, baby, burn" your own disco inferno mix CD. Switch to CD-RW media and you can save your work in progress and erase outdated files or the whole disc when you're done, or create temporary mix CDs that play in the latest portable CD and automotive players. Look for models with a CD-R burn rate of 40x or faster and a CD-RW rewrite speed of 10x or faster. For the best support and features, look for drives which include Nero Burning ROM, Nero Express, or Roxio Easy CD Creator CD-burning software. Some models come with no-name software that you'll need to upgrade, a hidden cost you don't need.

- **Combo CD-RW/DVD-ROM drive**—Want to create CDs and watch DVDs but don't want to spend a lot or buy two drives? The new combo CD-RW/DVD-ROM drives are two drives in one. The best models have recording features and speeds similar to the best CD-RW drives and read the most popular types of DVD media, including recordable, rewriteable, and movie DVDs.

- **Sound card**—Every computer made in the last few years has come with either built-in sound or a sound card. However, if you're looking to put DVD movies on your desktop, the cheap sound cards will let you down. Look for models that support Dolby Digital sound and support 5.1 speaker arrays if you want to enjoy the best in movies and games. Even if you think that DVD movies belong on your TV set, not on your desktop, a real sound card that plugs into the PCI slot is still a better deal if you listen to CDs or digital music. Compared to the old ISA sound cards that might be cluttering up your system, a PCI sound card provides better MIDI quality, 3D positional sound, and less drain on your CPU.

- **Speakers**—Another "cheap-it-out" feature of today's lower-cost computers is the speaker system. Whether you want to enjoy rock and roll, classical music, gaming, or DVD movies, toss your OEM speakers and get a decent set.

- **Wireless networking**—If you wish you could plunk down your notebook computer anywhere and still get on line, you need a wireless network card based on the 2.4GHz Wi-Fi (IEEE 802.11b or 802.11g) standards. More and more hotels, airports, and cafes offer wireless connections you can use, and if you already have a broadband network at home, you can connect to it anywhere in the house without a cable with a wireless network card and wireless router. Wireless networking also pays if you have a desktop computer and want to move it to a different room without rewiring your home.

- **Home/personal operating system**—You can achieve greater stability by upgrading to Windows XP Home Edition or add one of the exciting new desktop Linux distros. Either way, you open up new vistas for your existing hardware.

Under $200

Got a couple of hundred bucks handy? You can give your computer a huge boost in performance and comfort with one of these upgrades.

- **Motherboard and processor**—The motherboard is truly the "mother of all special features" on today's systems. What are you missing if your motherboard is not up-to-date? For starters, try this list: support for the latest, fastest AMD or Intel processors; support for IDE hard drives over 127GB; UDMA100 and faster IDE hard drives; enough PCI slots; USB 2.0 ports....You get the picture. If your processor is fast enough, keep it and reuse it. But if your current system has a processor under 1GHz, you can get a faster processor with your motherboard and still stay in budget.

- **Corporate operating system**—If your "personal" computer has to double as an outpost of the IT department, you can add Windows XP Professional and have some change left to spare. If your office prefers the Linux penguin, you can pick up the most high-end distro imaginable and also have change left to spare.

- **17- to 19-inch CRT monitor**—If you're still struggling with a 15-inch monitor, CRT monitor prices for high-quality 17-inch models are at rock-bottom now with the increasing popularity of larger CRTs. Look for a refresh rate of at least 72Hz at 1024×768, a dot pitch of .28 or smaller, and a flat picture tube for comfortable viewing. If you already have a 17-inch monitor but find that 1024×768 or 1280×1024 resolutions are fuzzy or flickery, get a better monitor at that size, or move up to a good 19-inch model.

- **Mid-range 3D graphics card**—Today's mid-range graphics cards based on ATI and nVIDIA chips are similar to yesterday's finest, and they're still a lot better than the motherboard-based video or low-end video card in many systems. If you're a "player," cards at this level can give you the high frame rates and realistic 3D textures your motoring, flying, and shooting adventures demand. Even if your idea of gaming is a quick hand of Windows Solitaire, today's fast video cards make web design, photo editing, and page layout a pleasure with support for faster flicker-free refresh rates, higher screen resolutions and color depths, and faster-than-ever screen redraws, especially with AGP cards. Want another reason to upgrade? Almost all mid-range models now have TV-out and dual monitor connections for more display goodness, as in Figure 2.3.

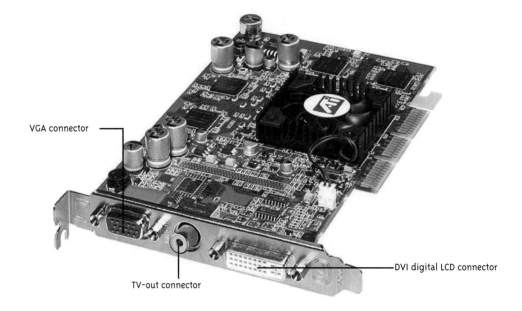

VGA connector

TV-out connector

DVI digital LCD connector

Figure 2.3

This ATI Radeon 9000 Pro video card features dual monitor display and TV-out connections. Photo courtesy of ATI Technologies.

More than $200

Got more than $200 to spend? You can pick up a couple of upgrades from the previous lists, grab a faster video card or processor than you planned, or go for one of the following:

- **Broadband Internet**—Even if you must pay up front for a broadband modem (and most providers waive or reduce equipment costs with a long-term contract), services like cable modem or DSL free up your phone lines and bring you all the Internet has to offer for about $40–$50 a month. Over a one-year period, typical broadband access runs you around $500, but believe me, it's worth it!

- **LCD displays**—More and more home and business users are trying LCD displays to save space, and LCD displays are getting better and better. Be advised that for best results you still need to spend around $250 to $300 for the typical 15-inch model (which is about like a 17-inch CRT monitor in usable screen display), and around $400 or more for the typical 17-inch model (about like a 19-inch CRT). Figure 2.4 shows you a typically sleek LCD display.

Figure 2.4

The KDS RAD 7m is a typical example of a 17-inch LCD display panel, which provides a screen display similar to a 19-inch CRT in far less space than a CRT requires. Photo courtesy of KDS.

- **Scanners, digital cameras, and inkjet printers**—Prices vary all over the map on these products, and so do their features. To get the most out of your purchases, make sure that you follow these guidelines:

  - *The more pixels, the better…up to a point.* Any photo scanned by a scanner or real-life scene captured by a digital camera loses some quality when reduced to pixels, and it loses even more quality when it's printed. Higher scanner, digital camera, and printer resolutions help avoid excessive loss of quality. But!!! If you're using digital images on the web, don't be duped into buying a super-expensive scanner or camera. You're going to lose all that resolution when you crunch the graphics to go on your web site. Buy more pixels if your digital pictures are headed for a printer or for publication, or if you're planning to crop most of your pictures.

  - *Share and share alike.* When you buy these devices, remember that they can be shared by multiple computers in your home or office. USB ports are the key to moving these and similar external devices around easily.

  - *Look at the quality, not the numbers.* Resolution numbers can lie, and nowhere is this clearer than with photography and printing. Because of differences in data compression, lens quality, and features, digital cameras with similar resolutions can produce drastically different image quality. Inkjet printers' output is affected by nozzle size, ink types, and how much ink the printer uses to make the picture, making for big differences in quality even with printers featuring the same print resolutions. Request print samples before you buy a printer, and read lots of reviews (preferably with actual scan/photo samples) before you buy your digital camera or scanner. See Chapter 15, "Digital Imaging and Video," for specific recommendations.

Deciding by Age: Three Years and Out

One of the easiest ways to evaluate a system for its suitability for upgrading is the "three years and out" rule. Simply put, this rule suggests that if a computer is at least three years old and has never had a significant upgrade during its history, it's probably too old to make upgrading economically feasible. Thus, any computer bought before 2000 that's never been upgraded before is probably too old to upgrade.

What about external peripherals such as printers, monitors, and so forth? Since part of a successful upgrade strategy involves reusing these devices as long as they're suitable, the "three years and out" rule doesn't apply to these components.

I'm not saying that you can't upgrade an older PC; after all, there are plenty of components around that can be successfully used to upgrade systems that are more than three years old.

However, I believe it makes more economic sense to start fresh with computers of this vintage. Perhaps it's time to get a new system and donate "old faithful" to the local school or non-profit or keep it as a second system for the kids, and here's why: A typical computer built in late 1999 has a slot-mounted processor with a clock speed of 700MHz or less, 64MB of RAM, no CD-RW drive, a 10GB hard disk, and a graphics card with little or no 3D capabilities. That's a lot of potential upgrades to make all at the same time, as Table 2.1 makes clear.

Table 2.1 Upgrading a Typical 1999 Vintage System		
Existing Component	**Upgrade**	**Upgrade Price**
Processor and motherboard	AMD Athlon XP 2100+ processor and motherboard	$200
CD-ROM or DVD-ROM drive	48x CD-RW drive (additional)	$80
Hard disk	40GB hard disk	$90
3D graphics	Mid-range 3D graphics card	$100
64MB RAM	256MB (additional)	$60
	Grand Total	**$530**

At $530, the cost to upgrade this computer is over half what a comparable new system would cost, and it might make sense to buy new.

However, if that same computer had been upgraded since it was built with a CD-RW drive, more memory, and a bigger hard disk, it would cost less than $300 to upgrade the motherboard/CPU and a newer, better 3D video card. That's a lot cheaper than buying a new system.

I've used this same philosophy in my office to gradually transform computers from aging wheezers into high-performance screamers. Although one of my systems was originally built more than three years ago, its *effective* age is much less.

Calculating the Effective Age of Your System

Some health experts like to calculate your "true age" by factors such as your blood pressure, cholesterol level, weight/height ratio, and family health background. Similarly, building inspectors take the condition and upgrades or damage to a building into account when calculating its effective age. Similarly, you can calculate the effective age of your system by determining whether your system still uses the original version any of these components:

- Motherboard/processor
- RAM
- 3D video card

Why these components? These are the "big three" that have the biggest impact on performance. Here's how it works:

Assume your system was built at the start of 2000. It has a calendar age of three and one-half years as of mid-2003. However, you can reduce the effective age of your system, as shown in Table 2.2.

Table 2.2   How Upgrades Reduce the Effective Age of Your System

Component	Upgrade Type	Reduces Effective Age (Months)	Upgrade Type	Reduces Effective Age (Months)	Chapter Reference
Processor and motherboard	2GHz or faster with support for DDR 333 memory, USB 2.0, AGP 4x	12	1GHz–2GHz with support for DDR memory	6	Chapter 8, Chapter 9
RAM	512MB or more DDR	6	256≤512MB DDR, 512MB or more SDRAM	3	Chapter 7
3D graphics (mid-range gamer)	High-performance 3D video chipsets ^	6	Mid-range 3D video chipsets#	3	Chapter 13
3D graphics (casual or non-gamer)	Mid-range 3D video chipsets#	12	Low-end 3D video chipsets*	6	Chapter 13

^ ATI 9600–9800 series; nVIDIA GeForceFX, GeForce 4 Ti4600
# ATI 9000–9500 series; nVIDIA GeForce 4 Ti 4400/4200
* ATI 8xxx series; nVIDIA GeForce 4 MX, GeForce 3, Matrox Parhelia

Thus, if you take a 2000 vintage system and upgrade it with a 2GHz processor and new motherboard, 512MB of DDR RAM, and a video card with a mid-range 3D graphics chipset, you can reduce the effective age of the system from 42 months to 6 months (see Table 2.3).

Table 2.3	Example of Reducing a System's Effective Age		
Effective Age Before Upgrade	**Upgrade**	**Reduces Effective Age By...**	**Effective Age Reduced to**
42 months	2GHz processor, motherboard with USB 2.0/DDR333 support	12 months	30 months
30 months	512MB DDR333 memory	12 months	18 months
18 months	nVIDIA GeForce 4 Ti4600	12 months	6 months

Thus, as Tables 2.3 and 2.4 make clear, hardware upgrades can make an older system comparable to a new system.

When Upgrades Don't Make Sense

Ever seen the studies that show that a typical $20,000 car will cost $60,000 when built from replacement parts? If you're not careful, the same thing (on a smaller scale) can happen to you as you put your system through its paces. I recommend the 50% rule to keep you from wasting your money.

MARK'S TIP SHEET: 50% Your Way to Upgrading Success!

Generally, for internal upgrades (such as CPUs, motherboards, memory modules, and drives), I recommend that you look at the 50% rule. This rule (which is also useful for deciding whether to repair or replace a computer) goes like this:

Add up the costs of the upgrade and compare your system's estimated performance (post-upgrade) to a similar new system. If you're about to spend more than 50% of the cost of that new system, you should save your money for the new system or scale back your upgrades.

The 50% rule of thumb is useful, but it can be tricky to apply because of the variables you need to use. To apply it correctly, make sure you are looking at similar or identical CPU types and speeds, memory types and speeds, and motherboard features when you compare the result of your upgrade to a brand-new system you can buy.

I don't count external devices such as external hard drives, printers, scanners, monitors, and digital cameras in the 50% rule because:

- External devices can be easily moved to another system when you finally decide to retire your current computer.

- Internal devices such as processors and memory are often difficult to "harvest" and move to another system because of compatibility issues. However, hard drives, video cards, and drives can be moved to another system.

So, now that you have an idea of what you can upgrade and how much it is going to cost, it's time to decide if you're ready to upgrade. To make sure an upgrade is the right move to make, or if you're having problems with your system, follow me to Chapter 3, "Alternatives to Upgrades."

Chapter 3

Alternatives to Upgrades

Before you slap down good money for a system upgrade, you'd better make sure that your PC is running as well as it can. Stuffing good hardware into a computer that isn't working well just complicates whatever problem your system is having. In addition, you might find out that the device you thought needed to be replaced just needs a bit of tweaking, enabling you to spend your hardware upgrade money where it really matters.

These are the major problem areas for a typical computer:

- Hardware problems
- Operating system problems

In this chapter, you learn how to handle the most common causes of problems in these areas to help assure a problem-free upgrade.

> **NOTE**
>
> **All About Troubleshooting**
>
> If you need more help in troubleshooting system problems of all kinds, check out my book *PC Help Desk in a Book* (Que, 2002), which is all about troubleshooting computer problems.

Fixing Common Hardware Problems

In this section, you learn how to fix common hardware problems that can prevent you from upgrading your computer. These include the following:

- Systems that won't start

- Systems that lock up

- Problems with loose cables

- Hardware driver problems

Fixing Systems That Won't Start

If you use your computer as much as I do, you probably feel like a "cyborg"—part human, part computer. When your computer stops working, it's like losing a vital part of yourself. And if, like most people, you're planning to back up your information later (a time that never seems to arrive for some of us), you are willing to pay any price to get your computer up and running. Well, put your wallet away. In this section, I cover some of the most common causes for computers that just won't get out of bed in the morning. I help you administer that first scalding cup of digital coffee to get your lazybones PC up and running.

Ever go out to your car, turn the key, and hear…nothing? No roaring engine, not even the radio? It's a chilling feeling, especially when you're already late for work. The usual cause for a "dead" car is a lack of power; you probably left the lights on and ran down your battery. Similarly, if your PC isn't getting any power, you're not going to be driving it anywhere. Put away the jumper cables, though. Unlike dead cars, dead computers don't need a jumpstart.

The most common causes for a dead system include the following:

- **No power reaching the system**—This can be caused by a surge protector that's unplugged or turned off, or by a loose power cable. As medieval philosopher William of Occam, computer tech ahead of his time, would say, check these simple causes first (his classic rule, Occam's Razor, states that the simplest answer that fits all the facts is the preferred one). If power appears to be getting to the system, but you're not seeing any signs of activity, check….

- **The AC voltage switch**—A sliding switch on the rear of the power supply (see Chapter 22, "Power Supply Upgrades") selects either 115V (volts) or 230V AC on most systems (some select the correct voltage automatically). In North America, 115V AC is the correct choice. Some digital jokesmiths like to fiddle with the voltage switch;

setting it to 230V is a harmless, though irritating, trick. Because your power supply is looking for double the voltage that is entering the power supply, it doesn't start your PC. The solution? Turn off the power, reset the switch to 115V, and restart your system. By the way, if you're reading this book where 230V power is the rule, *never* (and I mean *never*) flip the switch to 115V. As soon as you turn on the system, say goodbye to the power supply and maybe even the entire system.

- **Dead shorts inside the system case**—If you have eliminated the other reasons your system might not start, it's time to take a look inside. Check for loose card brackets, drive power connectors touching metal, loose screws, and so forth. See Chapter 4, "Taking an Inspection Tour of Your System," to learn how to open your system safely.

Unless the computer's taken a nasty lick from a power surge, you're likely to find the problems pretty quickly with this list.

ON THE WEB: Startup Help Is Just a Click Away

Baffled by a system that can't start correctly—or at all? Go to the TechTV web site (www.techtv.com) and enter "troubleshooting" or other terms into the search engine to find answers fast.

If your computer starts, but Windows can't start correctly, see the section "Fixing Problems with Windows" later in this chapter.

Fixing Systems That Quit

How many times has this happened to you? You're merrily typing and mousing away when the computer just stops. No words appear onscreen, no matter how hard you bang the keys. The mouse pointer seems glued to the menu bar. What happened? Your com-

> **NOTE**
>
> Hardware conflicts are covered in the "It's My IRQ—No, Mine! Stopping Hardware Conflicts" section later in this chapter.

puter's just decided to take a nap without asking permission. What causes it, and what can you do about it? System freeze-ups can be caused by loose components inside the case, hardware conflicts, and software conflicts. However, if you haven't added any new hardware or software to your system, the number one cause for a system freeze-up, ironically, is excessive heat.

What causes excessive heat buildup inside your PC? Here are the main culprits:

- Dirt and dust inside the computer
- Fan failure
- Inadequate cooling from working fans
- Inadequate airflow around the case (and under the unit if you use a notebook computer)

Here's how to cool down the inside of your box.

Clean Up and Cool Down

Did you know that the average PC does a full-time impression of a vacuum cleaner? It will never be good enough for the old *Amateur Hour* show, or even the *Gong Show*, but the vacuum cleaner schtick is how your PC keeps itself cool.

Here's what happens:

1. When you turn on your PC, the fan in the power supply begins to blow air out the rear of the system, creating a partial vacuum.
2. Air comes in through the cooling vents in the case to replace the expelled air. On most newer systems, additional case fans help bring the air in faster.

The result? A gentle breeze is cooling down the system all the time. However, because your computer has delusions of replacing your Dirt Devil, guess what comes in along with the air? Dust, dirt, and grime.

Over time, the parts inside your PC, and even the fans in the case and the power supply, all become coated with a thin layer of dust and gunk. This acts as an insulator. Unfortunately, the hot-running parts inside your PC don't need no stinkin' insulation! When memory, for example, gets too hot, its contents go south and your computer freezes up. Add animal hair or tobacco smoke to the normal indoor environment and you have a recipe for a system that will eventually get way too hot for its own good. So how do you solve the dirt dilemma? Get rid of the dust and dirt. The dynamic duo I recommend is compressed air and a computer vacuum cleaner. Use the compressed air to blow dust and dirt *out* of a system. Use the computer vacuum cleaner to pull dust and dirt out of components that can't be blown out, such as power supply fans.

CAUTION: STOP! LOOK! THINK!

If It's Not a Computer Vac, Keep It Away!
Conventional vacuum cleaners have static-prone plastic parts that can cause Electro-Static Discharge (ESD), which can fry chips inside your system, leaving you with a clean, but useless, personal confuser. Computer-grade vacuum cleaners are made especially for cleaning up your PC. They have no static-producing parts and are equipped with tiny extensions and brushes to clean tiny parts.

You can buy battery-powered or AC-powered versions. Stick with the AC-powered versions; the wall socket gives them the extra oomph you need to clean up the worst PC gunk.

Start with the computer case; if its airflow vents are gunked up, you'll still have an overheating problem even after you clean up the rest of the system. Next, move on to the fans (refer to Figure 3.2). Clean up the motherboard area, and wrap up your operation by vacuuming the power supply fan and the ventilator holes on the power supply case.

If the gunk your PC has dragged in is a bit on the sticky side, pick up a package of premoistened antistatic electronic cleaning cloths and clean the case vents inside and out. These cleaning cloths are also great for cleaning sticky keyboards and monitor screens.

MARK'S TIP SHEET: Closing Up the Gaps for Better Airflow

Part of your computer's cooling process, strangely enough, is the presence of the slot covers that close up the openings for empty card slots inside your PC.

If you've already been doing some upgrading and shuffling around, make sure every slot has either a card or a slot cover. If you find you're short a slot cover or two, check the spare parts kit you received with your system. Still come up empty? Check with friends or dip into the PC parts junk box at work. There must be millions of these covers floating around in desk drawers and shoeboxes. Don't forget to grab some screws while you're scrounging parts.

In addition, if you've reached the end of the line with an old PC that's about to be junked, take a few minutes and pull every screw, slot cover, and jumper block. These are some of the few parts that interchange among different brands, models, and generations of PCs. See Figure 3.1 for a closer look at empty slots and slot covers.

Slot covers (remove them to install expansion cards)

Screw holds slot cover in place

Screw holes

Figure 3.1

An outside (left) and inside (right) view of a system with open and closed card slots.

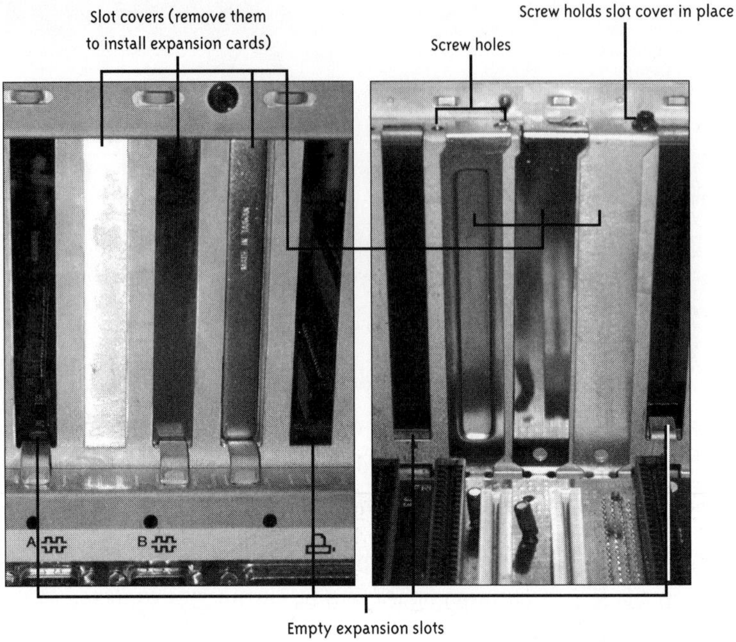

Empty expansion slots

Be a FANatic

When I first opened up a PC in the 1980s, the only fan in the system was the one built into the power supply. Times have changed. Today, that once-lonely power supply fan has a lot of company, including the following:

- CPU fan (also called an active heatsink)
- Case fan

And, on some systems, it also includes these:

- Drive bay fan
- Slot mounted fan
- Video card fan
- Chipset fan

> **JARGON**
>
> *Heatsink*—A finned aluminum or copper device that fits over a chip to transfer heat away from the chip. A passive heatsink doesn't include a fan; an active heatsink has a built-in fan.

These fans are essential. Running one of today's CPUs for even a few *seconds* without a cooling fan ruins it. And the other fans are just as important to keep your system in tip-top condition.

The first step is keeping the fans (and the heatsinks associated with them) clean. Use your vacuum/compressed air duo to perform that task. Step 2 is to make sure the fans are working properly. Leave the cover off the system and boot it up. Take a good look at the fans; are all of them spinning? Do you hear any unusual noise? Figure 3.2 shows you where to look for these fans.

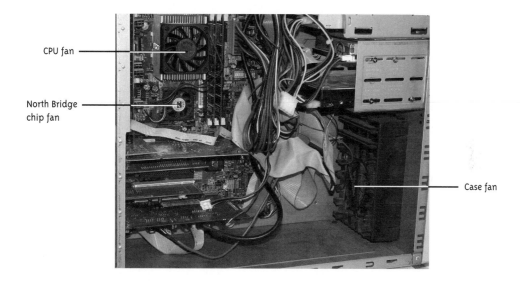

CPU fan

North Bridge chip fan

Case fan

Figure 3.2

Many recent systems have a power supply fan (not visible in this photo), a CPU fan, at least one case fan, and a fan on the motherboard's North Bridge chip (which connects the processor to memory and video).

The best fans use ball-bearing mechanisms, but a lot of cheap CPU fans use sleeve bearings, which depend on grease to keep them working. When the grease hardens or melts away, the fan starts sticking and slowing down, and eventually fails; a failing fan is usually noisier than normal. If you find fans that are noisy or slow, replace them.

READ THIS TOO

Many recent systems and motherboards have a fan-monitoring feature (sometimes called PC Health) that can warn you of fan problems. See Chapter 9, "Unlock Your System's Potential with Motherboard and BIOS Upgrades," for details.

If the fan on the video card is having problems, contact the video card manufacturer for a replacement. Case, CPU, and North Bridge fans can be picked up at many computer and electronics retailers.

MARK'S TIP SHEET: Chill Out with the Experts

The world's leading authorities on keeping systems cool are gamers and others who like to overclock their systems. *Overclocking*, in which users configure their CPUs and video cards to run at faster speeds than normal, puts extra stress on the cooling system. Get expert tips on keeping any system cool at www.overclockers.com.

If your fans are working properly but you're still concerned about heat, look carefully at your case to see if there are openings made for additional fans. Most cases have them, so you can install extra fans for extra cooling (see Chapter 9 for details). If you're using 10,000RPM or faster hard drives, these hot-rod drives need a drive bay fan (see Chapter 10, "Adding a Huge Hard Disk," for details).

Use Y-adapters to split the drive power connectors coming from your power supply if you don't have a spare power connector for a new fan. Case-mounted fans usually snap into place, but drive bay fans must be installed with screws and drive rails on some models.

JARGON

Y-adapter—A power cable extension that plugs into the end of the power connectors used by hard drives and enables two devices to use power from a single connector. See Chapter 4 for an example.

Loose Is Useless; Tighten Up Your Connectors

Cooling down the inside of your system reduces system lockups. However, poor electrical connections can still cause problems, so check the following:

- **Socketed chips on the motherboard and add-on cards**—The rectangular or square BIOS chips used on most motherboards and some add-on cards are vulnerable to a problem called *chip creep* if they are plugged into sockets. As the computer heats and cools, the differences in how parts heat (which expands the components) and cool (which contracts the components) causes socketed chips to slowly work loose. Eventually, loose chips can cause system lockups and failures. Push each end of the chip down into the socket with your thumb, as shown in Figure 3.3.

Figure 3.3

The system BIOS chip in many systems is a rectangular socketed chip. If your system won't boot, tighten the chip by pushing it into place.

- **Memory module contacts**—Gold is commonly used today on both DIMM memory modules and sockets. But, for older systems with SIMMs, both gold and tin are used for sockets and modules. Mixing metals can cause corrosion over time. Remove the modules and wipe the connectors clean with a soft cloth before you put them back into the sockets.

READ THIS TOO: For System Stability, Add Stabilant 22

From computer technicians to model train buffs, everyone who's used Stabilant 22 loves the way it improves the operation of electronic equipment. A few drops of Stabilant 22 on chip sockets, memory module connectors, and add-on card connectors enables even dirty contacts to work better; it's great for preventing contact problems as well.

Get more information about Stabilant 22 from its creator, D.W. Electrochemicals, at www.stabilant.com or by calling 905-508-7500.

Read *Scott Mueller's Upgrading and Repairing PCs* to learn more about how you can use Stabilant 22 to keep your system running reliably.

It's My IRQ—No, Mine! Stopping Hardware Conflicts

If your system works until you try to use a hardware device such as a modem or a sound card, and then it freezes, you might be having a hardware conflict.

Your CPU uses 16 Interrupt Request (IRQ) lines to communicate with components. The IRQs that are used by motherboard components and add-on cards are listed in Table 3.1.

Table 3.1	Typical IRQs and Their Uses
IRQ	**Typical Use**
2/9	Varies
3	COM 2, COM 4 (serial ports)
4	COM 1, COM 3 (serial ports)
5	LPT 2, sound cards
6	Floppy drive controller
7	LPT 1 (printer port)
10	Varies
11	Varies
12	PS/2 mouse
14	IDE host adapter #1
15	IDE host adapter #2

IRQs 3 through 7 are sometimes called ISA IRQs because they are used by older components that can't share IRQs. Even though some IRQs (3, 4, and 5) are listed for two different devices, this really means that the IRQ could be used by either device but not by both at once. See Chapter 4 to learn about ISA cards and slots.

JARGON

ISA—Industry Standard Architecture, the prevailing standard expansion slot design from 1984 to the mid-1990s. Serial and parallel ports are considered ISA devices, even though they are built into the motherboard on recent systems. Most systems built in recent years don't have ISA slots anymore.

A common cause for a hardware conflict happens when a modem (which uses a COM port) is installed in a system that has COM 1 and COM 2 ports. If the modem uses the ISA connector, it uses COM 3 or COM 4. If the user has a mouse on COM 1, and COM 3 is used for the modem, using the modem interferes with the mouse and locks up the system.

> **CAUTION: STOP! LOOK! THINK!**
>
> **Stop with the ISA Cards, Already!**
> The easiest way to avoid these kinds of conflicts is to vote ISA cards off your PC "island." PCI cards *can* share IRQs from 3 through 12, avoiding conflicts that crash your system, as seen in Figure 3.4.

If your system has ISA slots (see Chapter 4 for an example) and you must use an ISA card rather than a PCI card, use the Windows Device Manager to make sure the IRQ you choose for the card isn't already in use, or configure the ISA card to work in a Plug-and-Play (PnP) mode (PnP mode allows Windows to configure the card).

To open the Windows Device Manager with Windows 9x, Windows Me, or Windows 2000, do the following:

1. Click Start.
2. Click Settings.
3. Click Control Panel.
4. Double-click System.
5. With Windows 2000 only, click Hardware.
6. Click Device Manager.

To open the Device Manager with Windows XP, do the following:

1. Click Start.
2. Click Control Panel.
3. Click Switch to Classic View if Category View is displayed.
4. Double-click System.
5. Click Hardware.
6. Click Device Manager.

With the Device Manager, you can see the specific driver and hardware settings for any device, or the hardware resources already in use for the entire system.

Figure 3.4 shows you the Device Manager in Windows 9x/Me. A yellow "!" indicates a device that is having a conflict or other problem. After the Device Manager is open in Windows 9x/Me, double-click the computer icon at the top of the screen to display IRQ or other hardware usage; click the hardware setting you want to see.

Figure 3.4

Use the Windows Device Manager to see if any devices, like the 3Com Etherlink III network card shown here, have problems before you install new hardware or software.

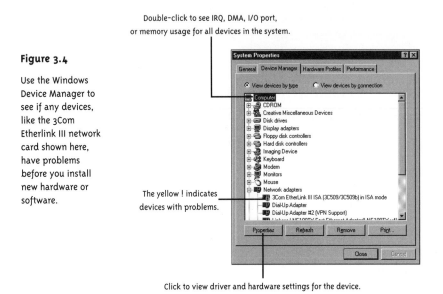

Double-click to see IRQ, DMA, I/O port, or memory usage for all devices in the system.

The yellow ! indicates devices with problems.

Click to view driver and hardware settings for the device.

With Windows 2000/XP, click View, then Resources by Type, and then select the resource you want to see. See Figure 3.5. Note that Figure 3.5 shows how well Windows 2000 and Windows XP can manage IRQ sharing, enabling all PCI IRQs (as well as ACPI power management) to share the same IRQ (9).

Click + to display resource usage in each category.

Click View to change how Device Manager displays information.

Figure 3.5

Use the Windows
Device Manager to
see the hardware
resources in use by
all devices. With
Windows 2000 or
Windows XP, click
the + next to each
resource category to
see the settings
already in use.

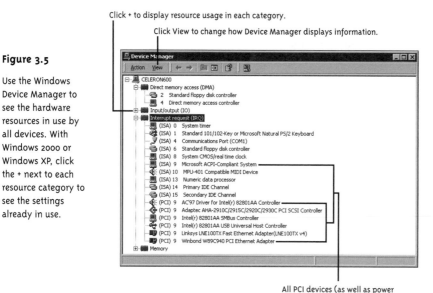

All PCI devices (as well as power
management) share IRQ 9 without conflicts.

Fixing Other PC Annoyances

After you've learned how to keep your system from walking off the job, you can turn your
attention to other PC annoyances that can spoil your day. In this section, you learn how to
deal with problems caused by:

- Keyboards
- Mice
- Printers
- Monitors
- Floppy drives
- CD and DVD drives
- Video cards
- Damaged cables

If the fixes outlined in the following sections don't improve how these devices work, consider
buying better devices as upgrades.

Dealing with a Balky Keyboard

Your keyboard is the primary user interface you have with your PC. To keep it working properly, follow these tips:

- Keep food and liquids away from it.

- Use the dynamic duo of computer vacuum and compressed air to remove dust, dirt, and gunk from the keyboard. Even if your keyboard is fairly well-sealed against contamination, the keys can still get sticky.

- If you can remove the keycaps from the keyboard (IBM/Lexmark/Unicomp keyboards and some others have this feature), do it before you clean. The chip puller included in most PC tool kits works very nicely. See Figure 3.6.

- Use antistatic electronics cleaning wipes (many different brands are available) to clean off the keycaps, and use cleaning wands to remove debris between keys.

DRIVER DETAILS: Keyboards Have Drivers, Too

Many keyboards today have additional keys for quick Internet access, multimedia, and fast scrolling. Download and configure the latest version of the keyboard driver software to keep these extra keys working correctly. See Chapter 20, "Selecting the Best Input Devices," for more information.

Figure 3.6

Removable keycaps on some keyboards make it easier to use a computer-grade vacuum cleaner to remove dust and crumbs.

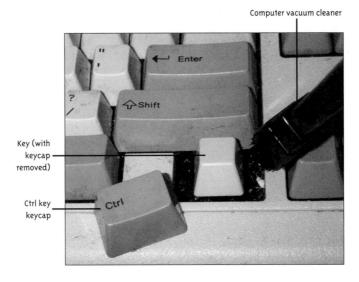

Computer vacuum cleaner

Key (with keycap removed)

Ctrl key keycap

Improving Mouse and Pointing Device Performance

One of the best ways to cure a sticky, skipping mouse pointer is to dump the conventional ball and roller mouse mechanism for an optical mouse, which uses sensors to detect motion. However, if you prefer a mechanical mouse, cleaning the mouse mechanism and keeping it clean is essential.

Does your mouse need a trip to the washroom? Take off the ball retaining mechanism, remove the ball, and look at the rollers. If you see dirt and gunk along the middle of the rollers, the rollers are dirty.

You can use a mouse cleaning kit (which uses a special cleaning pad and cleaning ball with a liquid cleaner) to remove the gunk. Prefer the DIY approach? Use isopropyl alcohol (*not* rubbing alcohol) and lintless swabs to *gently* wipe away the dirt and dry the rollers.

If your mouse pointer is still acting jerky as you move it around the screen after you clean the mouse, use the Mouse icon in the Windows Control Panel to adjust acceleration and speed.

CAUTION: STOP! LOOK! THINK!

No Erasers, Please

Use the *minimum* force possible to clean the mouse rollers. Years ago I ruined a mouse by trying an ink eraser to clean metal mouse rollers; I wore the plating off the rollers and the mouse got dirtier even faster. Today's mechanical mouse devices use relatively soft plastic parts, so even excessive scraping can cause similar problems.

DRIVER DETAILS: Install the Latest Drivers

To finish up the process of getting your mouse into shape, be sure to download and install the latest drivers for your mouse.

To minimize the need to clean your mouse, stop using the normal cloth-covered mouse pad. As the pad sheds fibers, the ball on the mouse picks up these fibers (and any dirt on the surface) and transfers them to the rollers. Non-shed mouse pads like the Precise Mousing Surface from 3M and various plastic-based mousepads can help out.

ON THE WEB: A Precise Mouse Pad from 3M

Whether you prefer the classic mechanical mouse or the newer optical mouse, 3M has a Precise Mousing Surface for you. Get more information at www.3m.com/ergonomics/precisemousepads.jhtml.

Making a Better Impression with a Clean Printer

It's amazing—no matter how dirty the inside of the printer gets, we expect it to produce perfect-looking printouts. What are we thinking? If your printouts are coming down with a case of the measles, the printer needs a good cleaning.

Toner cartridges used in laser printers tend to leak toner, which is a very fine powder. Because toner is so fine, most computer-grade vacuum cleaners can't handle it. Instead, you need to do the following:

1. Turn off the printer and unplug it.
2. Open the printer and remove the toner cartridge.
3. Use a soft lint-free dampened cloth to remove spilled toner.
4. Read the printer's instructions to learn how to clean other problems such as fuser rollers or the paper path.

You can improve the cleaning process by purchasing a product such as KleenLaser, which contains several sheets of a special cloth-like substance. Use a sheet in place of paper to print a short document. The cleaning cloth cleans the rollers and paper path.

To prevent print-quality problems with an inkjet printer, turn it off with its own power switch. When you do this, the printer caps the cartridges before turning itself off to avoid ink drips and clogged cartridges.

If you are having problems with uneven printing due to nozzle clogs, you can remove the printheads on some printers, such as the HP DeskJet and Canon BubbleJet series (they're part of the ink cartridge), and clean the printheads with a special kit. For Epson printers and others with built-in printheads, buy an inkjet printer cleaning kit that uses a liquid cleaner and special printing sheets. Moisten the sheet, insert it in place of paper, and print a few lines of text. As the sheet passes through the printer, it cleans the printheads and the rollers.

If you can see the rollers, you can clean them yourself. Turn off the printer and unplug it. Then, use premoistened antistatic electronics wipes to clean off the rollers. Dirty rollers leave marks on the paper.

> **DRIVER DETAILS: Use the Vendor's Drivers for Best Printer Control**
>
> The inkjet printer drivers supplied with Windows might not support the display of cartridge ink levels or provide you with a way to clean the cartridge. To get these features, use the driver CD included with the printer, or download the latest driver and utility software from the printer vendor's web site.

Fixing Murky Monitors

Serious monitor problems such as shaky screen displays and uneven image sizes may require a trip to the repair shop or to the store for a replacement. However, some problems are easy to fix, including the following:

- Fuzzy or low-contrast picture
- Occasional loss of color
- Color fringing
- Geometry problems

If the display isn't as sharp and clear as it once was, try cleaning the monitor glass. Premoistened antistatic electronics or eyeglass tissues remove dust and fingerprints, and can also reduce static buildup, so that dust won't be attracted to the surface. You can use the same cleaning method with either CRT or LCD displays, but CRTs have more problems with static buildup.

Some cheap monitors lose focus with age; check the rear of the monitor and see if there's a focus knob or a recessed hole marked Focus.

If you share the system with other users (especially kids), take a careful look at the toolbars and desktop icons. If they look smaller, it's likely that somebody's been changing the screen resolution. Many monitors don't perform very well at the highest resolution they're made to provide.

MARK'S TIP SHEET: Monitor? Video Card? Cable? Here's How to Tell

There are actually three parts to your video subsystem. While a shaky screen display or uneven image sizes (the image enlarging and shrinking) might seem serious enough to indicate a major problem with the monitor, the cause could be bent pins in the monitor cable or a bad video card. Before you go to the repair shop or start shopping for a new monitor, turn off both monitor and computer, unplug both, unscrew the monitor cable from the video connection and give it a good eyeballing. If you see bent pins, *carefully* use a small set of needle-nose pliers to straighten out the bent pins. If the cable is too badly damaged, you might be able to replace it if you can remove it from the monitor. Note that I'm talking about a monitor cable that uses thumbscrews; if the monitor has a fixed cable, the monitor needs to be repaired or replaced by professionals. Tighten the cable to avoid intermittent problems.

If you have a spare working monitor (raid the kids' computer!), try it to see if the same picture flaws happen. If the picture is seriously messed up no matter what monitor you attach to your system, your video card or circuit is to blame. If a different monitor plugged into the same video card performs flawlessly, repair or replace your monitor.

CAUTION: STOP! LOOK! THINK!

Fiddling Inside the CRT Isn't for Fun
If your monitor can be refocused, but the focus control is recessed, take it to a technician who works on TVs or CRTs for help. Focusing should be done while the display is turned on, and the inside of the monitor contains dangerously high voltage. Technicians use special plastic wands instead of metal screwdrivers to make adjustments, avoiding electric shock.

To check resolution settings, open the Display properties sheet in Control Panel (or right-click the desktop) and click the Settings tab. Choose the options you want there, and confirm (or reject) the settings. I recommend 1024×768 on a 17-inch monitor and 800×600 on a 15-inch monitor, but a lot of eagle-eyed kids prefer the next higher setting.

The 15-pin VGA cable that attaches your monitor to your video card can get loose very quickly if you don't use the thumbscrews to lock it into place. Loose cables can cause color and picture flickering, so do your eyes a favor and tighten up.

MARK'S TIP SHEET: Making Desktop Peace

Here are some ways to avoid the desktop wars:

- If you have Windows 98/Me/2000/XP, try the Advanced options under the Effects tab in the Display properties sheet; you can access the Display properties sheet from the Control Panel. The Use Large Icons option increases the size of desktop icons without changing the resolution.

- In the Settings tab, check the Advanced button and then the Adapter tab. Try adjusting the refresh rate. Some monitors set for very high refresh rates give you better-looking screens if you reduce the refresh rate. However, to avoid flicker, don't go below 70Hz unless your monitor won't support higher refresh rates.

- Enable Multi-user settings with the Users icon in Control Panel. Each user needs to log on, but each user then gets a customized desktop and resolution settings.

CAUTION: STOP! LOOK! THINK!

Too Much Power

It's tempting to use an electric screwdriver to tighten cables with thumbscrews. After all, you don't need to crawl as far under the desk as you would if you used your hands. However, you should avoid this temptation. The torque is so high on even the low-cost electric screwdrivers that using one damages the card. Use your fingers, or, at most, a tiny straight-blade screwdriver to tighten or remove video, printer, and serial-port cables.

Most recent monitors have the correct picture dimensions for different screen resolutions memorized into their non-volatile memory. However, if you're trying a different resolution than usual or you're trying to change the vertical or horizontal size or position, you might find various problems with your picture also result.

Look for the display adjustments on the front of your monitor for the solution. In addition to controlling picture size and position, most adjustment features also enable you to fine-tune the edges of the picture to fix geometry problems, such as pincushion or barrel distortion, or to degauss the picture tube to fix color fringing. LCD displays don't have problems with screen geometry, but can have problems with color, contrast, and vertical/horizontal size, and pixel positioning.

JARGON

Degauss—To demagnetize the shadow mask inside the picture tube, which returns the display to normal appearance. Some monitors automatically run a degaussing operation when you turn them on, while others have a separate button or menu option in their on-screen controls.

Pincushion distortion—On-screen geometry problem with CRT displays in which the sides of the picture are curved toward the middle of the picture tube.

Barrel distortion—On-screen geometry problem with CRT displays in which the sides of the picture are curved outward.

Don't Let Your Floppy Drives Be a Flop

Floppy drives don't seem very important until you need to transfer a file from home to work, or from home to school, or you need to use the Windows 9x/Me Emergency Disk to fix a problem. Then, disk-read problems can ruin your day.

The read-write heads on the floppy drive make direct contact with the disk surface. So, dirty heads can not only cause problems reading the disk, but also damage the disk so that you can't use the information in the future.

Use a wet-type head cleaning kit to clean the heads every six months or so. It contains a special disk with cloth in place of media and a bottle of cleaner. Apply the cleaner to the disk, insert it in the drive, open a command prompt session, and type this command to try to read the contents of the cleaning disk:

```
DIR A:
```

You should get a General Failure error because the cleaning disk contains no media. Repeat this two or three times to move the heads around. Remove the disk and wait five minutes before you use the drive to allow the heads to dry.

Even if the read-write heads are clean, problems with disk alignment and disk speed can also prevent reliable disk-based data transfers between PCs. Here's a reliable way to see if your disk drive is working:

1. Use the Unconditional Format option in the Windows Explorer on an empty disk; this rewrites the magnetic structure of the entire surface instead of just erasing the data.

2. Copy 1.3MB or more of files from your system to the disk; Windows Explorer shows you the size of the files you select at the bottom of the screen. Copy text files so that you can open them elsewhere.

3. Try to read the disk on a different computer. If you can open all the files, your drive is working properly. If you can't, the problem could be with your drive or the other computer's drive. Repeat on different PCs at home, at school, or the office. If you can't read the disk anywhere but in the original PC, the drive is no good. Replace it.

Keep Your CD or DVD Drive from Acting Seedy

The CD or DVD drive is the primary method most people use for installing software. In addition, if you have a CD-RW or rewritable drive, it's the major way you have of transferring information *out* of your computer. Keep it in tip-top shape by doing the following:

- Use a cleaning CD to wipe dust away from the laser lens. Music CD cleaners work fine.

- Use CD media cleaner to remove dust, dirt, and fingerprints from the media surface before you insert CDs in the drive. To avoid scratching the CD and ruining its contents, make sure you wipe from the center of the CD to the edge; *don't* wipe in a circular pattern.

- Avoid sticky labels that don't cover the entire label surface of the drive; high-speed drives become unbalanced and might vibrate.

- Use My Computer or Windows Explorer to verify that data was transferred correctly to your drive; if a CD-RW disc overheats, the writing feature won't work until the disc cools down.

Destroy Damaged Cables Before They Destroy Your Data

If any of your internal drives are connected to damaged ribbon cables, sooner or later you could experience data loss. Replace damaged, dented, or cut cables immediately. For extra reliability, use the newer 80-wire Ultra-DMA cables for all IDE-based drives and devices. See Figure 3.7.

If you use external USB or IEEE-1394 drives, keep in mind that damaged cables can also cause these drives to fail or corrupt data. Replace any damaged or cracked cables on these drives.

Bad cables can also cause dial-up and broadband Internet connections to fail. If the plastic clip that locks RJ-11 (telephone/modem) or RJ-45 (Cat 5 Ethernet) cables into the sockets won't lock or is broken off, replace the cable. If the shielding is damaged or the clear plastic end of the cable is cracked, replace the cable.

Figure 3.7

Even a slight nick,
ding, or dent in the
ribbon cable used
by a hard drive or
floppy drive could
result in data loss.

Cable damage (dent in cable)

Markings
for pin 1

Don't Be a Video Card Victim

If you're having problems with running a particular program or if your system locks up or
the screen is corrupted when you move your mouse, the problem might actually be with
your video card's driver software. Windows handles video cards, like other hardware, through
driver software. Upgrading video card drivers can solve a lot of problems, such as these examples from ATI's web site:

- 3D compatibility problems with DirectX games
- Open GL game graphics problems
- DOS mouse pointer problems

To find the solutions, go to the tech support area of your video card maker's web site,
Microsoft's Knowledge Base, or the application or game software's web site.

For Windows-based programs, you might be able to work around video problems until you
can install a new driver by adjusting the acceleration option for your video card:

1. Right-click the desktop and select Properties.
2. Click the Settings tab.
3. Click Advanced.
4. Click the Troubleshoot tab (Windows XP) or Performance (other versions).
5. Adjust the slider all the way to the left to disable all video acceleration. With Windows
   XP, you should also clear the Enable Write Combining checkbox (see Figure 3.8).
6. Click OK repeatedly to close the Display properties dialog.

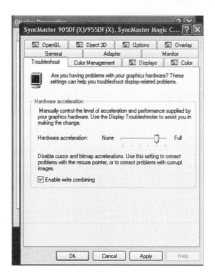

Figure 3.8

The Windows XP
Advanced Graphics
Settings properties
sheet. Two clicks left
from Full accelera-
tion is the suggested
setting if you're
having problems
with program errors
or crashes.

Use Table 3.2 to determine the best setting to use for the display problem you're having with
Windows XP. With other Windows versions, use Table 3.3.

Table 3.2	**Using Graphics Acceleration Settings to Troubleshoot Windows XP**				
Acceleration Setting	**Left**	**One Click From Left**	**Two Clicks From Left**	**Two Clicks From Right**	**One Click from Right**
Effects of Setting	No acceleration	Disables all but basic acceleration	Disables DirectX, DirectDraw, and Direct 3D acceleration (mainly used by 3D games)	Disables cursor and drawing accelerations	Disables mouse and pointer acceleration; Enables full acceleration
Long-Term Solution	Update display, DirectX, and mouse drivers	Update display, DirectX, and mouse drivers	Update DirectX drivers	Update display drivers	N/A

Table note: Disable write combining, a method for speeding up screen display, whenever you select any setting other
than full acceleration to improve stability. Re-enable write combining after you install updated drivers and retry.

Table 3.3	Using Graphics Acceleration Settings to Troubleshoot Windows 9x/Me			
Mouse Pointer Location	Left	One Click From Left	One Click From Right	Right
Effects of Setting	Disables all acceleration	Basic acceleration only	Disables mouse pointer acceleration	Full acceleration
Long-Term Solution	Update display and mouse drivers	Update display and mouse drivers	Update mouse drivers	N/A

If you're not certain of which setting is the best for your situation, use this procedure:

1. Start the computer.
2. Open the Troubleshooting or Performance dialog box, as described in the previous section.
3. Slide the acceleration pointer one notch to the left from its current position.
4. Click Apply, OK, and OK again to close the Display properties dialog.
5. Use your normal software and perform typical tasks.
6. If the computer now performs acceptably, continue to use this setting until you can obtain and install updated drivers. If the computer continues to have problems, repeat Steps 2-5 and move the pointer one step to the left each time until the problems go away or until you can install updated drivers as specified in Tables 3.2 or 3.3.

For 3D accelerated cards in Windows versions prior to XP, use the card's own properties sheet to make adjustments in 3D card features required by some games. Check for driver updates for a definitive solution, because workarounds frequently slow down video.

Drivers Aren't Just for Drives

Most of this chapter so far has focused on mechanical or electronic solutions for common hardware problems, but don't forget that your hardware is operated by driver software. If the cables and other physical properties of your hardware appear to be OK but you're not getting satisfactory results from your hardware, download and install new device drivers. Use the Windows Device Manager to view the properties for your device; in Windows 9x/Me, click the Driver tab to see the current driver file and install a new driver, as shown in Figure 3.9.

Windows 2000 and XP also provide a Reinstall Driver button on the General tab of a device's properties; use this button to reinstall the existing driver file, rather than a new driver.

Figure 3.9

The Driver tab in Windows 9x/Me's Device Manager properties sheet for the currently selected device. Click Update Driver to install new driver files.

Fixing Problems with Windows

Remember the old saying "If Momma ain't happy, ain't nobody happy?" Replace "Momma" with "Microsoft Windows" and you'll understand how important a correctly running Windows is to your system. It's pointless to perform hardware upgrades if Windows is malfunctioning. After all, Windows is what controls and configures virtually any hardware you'd care to add to a system these days. Even if you are planning to upgrade to a new version of Windows, it pays to get your current version of Windows working as well as possible first.

All recent versions of Windows offer the aspiring PC doctor a bagful of diagnostic tools. In the following sections, I focus on using the system tools provided with Windows 98 and Windows XP Home Edition, the most popular home and small-office versions of Windows.

> **ON THE WEB: Surf a Wave of Windows Tips**
>
> You can "hang ten" with your fingertips by searching the TechTV site for Windows tips. And, you'll also find live video clips of Windows tricks that make using Windows a lot easier. For a short cut directly to the favorite Windows tips of Patrick and the rest of the Screen Savers team, head on over to www.techtv.com/screensavers/.
>
> Click the Windows Tip link for the current tip featured, and follow the sidebars to many, many more.

continues

CONTINUED

Other great Windows sites online include the following:

- ZDNet's Windows discussion forums—www.zdnet.com/community

- *PCWorld*—www.pcworld.com

- *PC Magazine*—www.pcmag.com

- Microsoft's official Windows site—www.microsoft.com/windows

Keeping the Windows Registry in Shape

The Windows Registry is a master listing of everything that's unique about your system. Even if your computer began its "life" as one of a thousand identically configured PCs sold during a busy week at Joe's Computer Shack, by the time you're ready to upgrade it, the Registry is no longer the way it was when Windows was first loaded on the system.

Every time you install a new program, uninstall an old one, install or remove a piece of hardware, or even open a file, the Registry changes to reflect the current condition of your system. The Registry is read every time you start your system so that Windows knows what your favorite font, preferred screen colors, and folder options are.

To keep the Registry working properly, make sure you do the following:

- **Use the Add/Remove Programs icon in Control Panel to remove any programs, instead of deleting the folder containing the program**—Uninstalling the program removes the files *and* removes Windows Registry pointers to the program.

- **Use the Device Manager to remove hardware you no longer use**—This provides accurate hardware information to Windows so that it can install new hardware without trying to avoid conflicts with non-existent hardware.

- **Shut down programs and your system properly**—Windows records information about your programs' and system's settings to the Registry during the shutdown process. When you cut off the power, the information isn't recorded.

"That's great," you might be thinking, "but I've already broken every one of those rules—just today!" What happens if you've hosed the Registry? For example, you start getting error messages when you start Windows or programs don't work anymore.

ANALYZE THIS

The Registry's Secret Identity

Windows 9x and Windows Me store the Registry as two hidden files in the Windows folder:

- **User.dat**—User-specific information

- **System.dat**—System-specific information

If you want to make backup copies of these files, change the default settings in Windows Explorer to display all files:

1. Open Windows Explorer from the Start, Programs menu or right-click My Computer and select Explore.

2. Navigate to the C: drive and open the Windows folder.

3. Click View, Folder Options.

4. Click the View tab.

5. Select Show All Files.

6. Click OK.

You can then copy these files to a CD-RW, CD-R, or removable-media drive (they're normally too big to be stored on a floppy drive).

The worst thing you can do if you think your Registry is broken is to reboot your system *if* you still use Windows 95. Here's what I mean. Windows 95 replaces the old Registry with a new copy it creates when you reboot the normal way. However, if you have a big problem with your system and then reboot, your old Registry becomes a backup copy (User.da0 and System.da0). Reboot again and Windows 95 performs the same process again, moving a possibly bad Registry to backup, replacing it with another bad Registry, and throwing out a possibly good Registry.

If you reboot after having problems with Windows 95, make a backup copy of User.da0 and System.da0 as soon as you finish booting to the Windows Desktop (these are your old User.dat and System.dat files). You may need to replace faulty User.dat and System.dat files with these copies.

Windows 98 is a lot smarter. It stores five older versions of the Registry in a folder called Sysbckup. The backup files are called RB*xxx*.cab, where *xxx* is a number from 000 on up. A Windows program called Scanregw makes the backups automatically. Click the Details button in Windows Explorer to see the dates when the Registry backups were made.

For example, if today is August 3 and your system is spitting out error messages like crazy, but the system worked fine on July 31, look for a RB*xxx*.cab file dated 7/31 or earlier. The most recent RB*xxx*.cab file will be called rb000.cab, and the oldest is called rb005.cab. To restore the Registry to the date you select, follow this procedure:

1. Start Windows in MS-DOS mode: use the Emergency Boot Disk, select Restart in MS-DOS mode from the Shutdown menu, or boot the system to the Windows 98 startup menu (press Ctrl or F8 at system startup and select Command Prompt Only).

2. Type this command: `scanreg /restore`

3. Choose the date you want to restore from the list of Registry backups. In this example, you'd want a Registry copy dated July 31.

4. Press Enter to reset the Registry to the condition it was on the date you chose.

5. Restart your computer.

6. After you restore the Registry, you need to determine what caused your system to go down.

If you installed a new program or new hardware, the newly installed item could be the cause. By restoring an older Registry, you've prevented Windows from using the new hardware or software, even though the files may still be on the system. Before you reinstall it, better check the vendor's web site or readme files to figure out why you had a problem. You might need to get newer drivers or a revised installation program before you try to reinstall the program or hardware.

MARK'S TIP SHEET: Windows Me and XP Home Do It Better with System Restore

The System Restore feature in Windows Me and Windows XP Home is an even handier way to send your system "back, back in time" to when it worked. Click Start, Programs, Accessories, System Tools to start and configure System Restore. System Restore removes Registry entries after the date selected to undo the changes made by new hardware or software. With Windows XP only, select "Last Known Good Settings that Worked" from the Windows XP startup menu to revert to the last working configuration.

However, data files you created after the date you select for Registry or System Restore stay on the system.

When Windows Won't Start

Not to be paranoid or anything, but did you ever notice how Windows likes to stop working right before you decide to make improvements? Spooky, isn't it? It's especially annoying if Windows decides it won't restart right before—or right after—you decide to install new hardware or software. What can you do about it? Use Windows' Safe Mode, the startup menu, and Windows' MSConfig tool to fight back!

READ THIS TOO: Troubleshoot Windows and Get Promoted at the Same Time!

If you work with Windows on the job as well as at home, you can brush up on your troubleshooting skills and maybe get yourself a promotion if you pick up some industry certifications. A great place to start is the A+ Certification, which covers hardware and operating system troubleshooting and repair topics. Get ready for the tests and pick up lots of practical information by reading *Upgrading and Repairing PCs: A+ Study Guide, Second Edition*, by Scott Mueller and Mark Edward Soper (Que, 2001). Que also publishes the Exam Cram series of certification guides for Microsoft Certified System Engineer exams.

Make Safe Mode Work for You

It's never pleasant to see the Safe Mode message come up when you start your system. To use it effectively, it's best to understand what triggers Safe Mode, what Safe Mode can (and can't) do, and when you should start Safe Mode deliberately.

Windows 9x/Me automatically start in Safe Mode if the system didn't start successfully on the previous startup. This could be caused by a system problem or by an accidental reboot of the system partway through the startup process. If there's no real problem with your system, you can shut down your computer with Start, Shut Down. Then, wait about fifteen seconds and restart it. You should be able to restart normally.

MARK'S TIP SHEET: Manually Starting Windows in Safe Mode

You can also start Windows in Safe Mode manually, which is useful if Windows starts but can't finish; press F8 or Ctrl to bring up the Windows startup menu, and select Safe Mode from the startup menu.

However, if Safe Mode is the only way Windows will start, there's something more seriously wrong with your Personal Confuser. Put on your detective's thinking cap (I prefer a deerstalker, myself) and ask yourself the following question: *Did I just install something new?*

In many cases, that's the cause of the problem. Be glad that Safe Mode exists as a fallback. Why does a Safe Mode startup work when normal modes fail? Safe Mode uses a minimal set of drivers (for example, VGA instead of chipset-specific, 3D-accelerated, video drivers) and services; it doesn't load any legacy drivers in Config.sys and Autoexec.bat, and it skips over the Startup group and Registry-based load on startup programs and utilities. Because Safe Mode uses only the minimum drivers and services to start your system, it bypasses potential conflicts that can prevent the system from starting.

After Safe Mode has started Windows, what's next? If you think that the last piece of hardware you installed might be the culprit (and this is a good place to start), the Device Manager is ready and waiting to help you remove the offending device. When you use the Device Manager in Safe Mode with Windows 9x/Me, it shows you *all* the device drivers installed on the system, including device drivers that are part of a pre-installed standard disk image or are leftovers from previous installations (see Figure 3.10). I like to use Device Manager to remove these phantom devices as well as any device that I installed that appears to be malfunctioning.

Current and duplicate Epson
USB printer installations

Figure 3.10

In Normal Mode (left), the Windows 9x/Me Device Manager shows you only currently installed hardware, but in Safe Mode (right), you can see duplicate hardware installations and devices that may no longer be present.

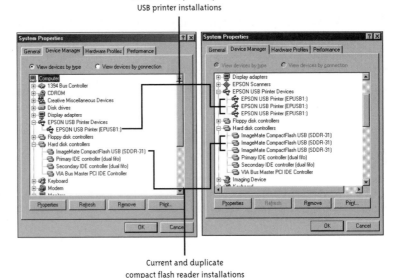

Current and duplicate
compact flash reader installations

What about IRQ conflicts? Unfortunately, you can't see IRQ or other hardware configuration details in Windows 9*x* or Me Safe Mode, although you can see this information when Windows XP is started in Safe Mode.

Think software's to blame? You can open the Control Panel and use the Add/Remove Programs icon to ditch an offending program. Safe Mode's also handy for using ScanDisk or Defrag disk tools with Windows 9x/Me (covered later in this chapter) because other programs that might interfere with their operation aren't started in Safe Mode.

READ THIS TOO: Getting Deeper into Windows

For more details about stomping startup or shutdown problems in Windows Me, pick up a copy of *Practical Microsoft Windows Millennium*, by Faithe Wempen (Que, 2000). Prefer Windows 98? Faithe's also got you covered with *Practical Microsoft Windows 98 Second Edition* (Que, 1999), and Ed Bott comes to your rescue with *Practical Microsoft Windows 2000 Professional* (Que, 2000). Jim Louderback is at your service with *TechTV Microsoft Windows XP for Home Users* (Que, 2001).

Making the Startup Menu Work for You

You can start your PC in Safe Mode anytime you want by displaying the Windows startup menu. In Windows 9*x*, press the Ctrl key (or F8 on some systems) as soon as the system's Power-On Self Test (POST) is complete. Windows 2000 and Windows XP also use the F8 key; press it when prompted on-screen.

The Startup menu for Windows 9x lists these options (Windows Me lists the ones marked with an asterisk ★):

- Safe Mode★
- Safe Mode with Network Support
- Safe Mode Command Prompt
- Command Prompt
- Step-by-Step Confirmation★
- Logged★
- Normal★

What can you do with them?

Safe Mode you already know about; Safe Mode with Network Support enables you use your Internet or other network connection to get the files or information you need to find your problem.

Safe Mode Command Prompt boots the computer to a command prompt *without* peeking at the Registry or the Config.sys/Autoexec.bat duo. It's like using a boot disk to start your system. Use this when you need to start the computer without loading any drivers into memory, which can be useful for troubleshooting.

Command Prompt does load the Registry and Config.sys/Autoexec.bat but never gets around to starting the Windows GUI. Use this mode to start the system in a DOS-like mode if you need to run a DOS-level troubleshooting program or run a game program that can't run under Windows.

Step-by-Step Confirmation provides a way to troubleshoot startup problems by letting you skip over programs and configuration files you suspect are causing problems for your system. If you're using Windows 98, forget about this option and use MSConfig instead; it's easier.

Logged creates a hidden file called Bootlog.txt in the root folder (C:\). You can view it with the DOS program Edit and see what's happening when you start Windows. If Windows seizes up before finishing, the last line in Bootlog.txt usually tells you what program or device is malfunctioning. Then, you can use Safe Mode to remove it or reconfigure it.

To open Bootlog.txt, boot the machine to a command prompt, type `Edit bootlog.txt`, and press Enter. Edit will retrieve bootlog.txt and display it on-screen.

Normal starts Windows as it normally runs.

Windows XP Home adds the following startup options:

- **Enable VGA mode**—Uses a VGA driver in place of a normal display driver, but uses all other drivers as normal. Useful for solving display problems without the slowdowns caused by Safe Mode.

- **Last Known Good Configuration**—Starts the system with the last configuration known to work; useful for solving problems caused by newly installed hardware or software.

- **Debugging Mode**—Enables the use of a debug program to examine the system kernel for troubleshooting.

Using MSConfig to Stomp Startup Bugs

After a while, the average Windows computer becomes clogged with programs and utilities that load at startup. Windows 98/Me and XP users can fight back with the System Configuration Utility, better known as MSConfig.

Don't bother looking through your Start menu to find MSConfig; Microsoft doesn't want you to know about it. Just click Start, Run, type MSConfig, and click OK to get started.

The General tab works like Step-by-Step Confirmation if you select Interactive startup. You can also select what startup files to run and which to skip. To get rid of programs that are cluttering up your system tray and taskbar, click the Startup tab and uncheck programs you no longer want to load at Startup. See Figure 3.11.

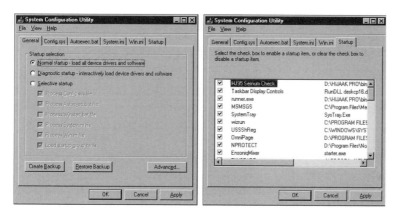

Figure 3.11

MSConfig's General tab (left) for Windows 98 enables you to start the system by skipping over specified configuration files. The Startup tab (right) helps you stop programs from loading into your system tray or toolbar.

The Windows Me and Windows XP versions of MSConfig are generally similar to Figure 3.11. You can change options anytime you like by running MSConfig. The changes you make take effect the next time you boot your system if you apply the changes or save them when you exit the program.

Be Your Own Sherlock Holmes with Dr. Watson

One of the banes of any Windows 98/Me user's life at the keyboard is the Illegal Operations message. When you see one of these, your first thought might be the same as when you see the police car lights in your rear-view mirror: "What did I do this time?" Fortunately, Windows isn't tattling on you. This message really means that Windows itself (or a program running under Windows) has broken some rule about memory usage (General Protection

Fault), run out of memory resources, run out of virtual memory (Page Faults), or committed some other serious problem. You're not the problem, but with Dr. Watson at your side, you could get closer to a solution.

JARGON

Illegal operation—An instruction that can't be performed by the operating system or processor, and normally causes the program that tried the illegal operation to be terminated. These can be caused by disk errors, running low on system resources, incompatible programs in memory at the same time, and memory errors.

General Protection Fault (GPF)—An error caused by a program trying to use memory that isn't assigned to its use. To prevent crashes, 32-bit versions of Windows will close the program that triggered the GPF. Buggy or out-of-date software can cause GPFs, so you should note the name of any program that causes GPFs on a regular basis and check into patches or updates for it.

To have Dr. Watson run automatically with Windows 98/Me, add it to your startup group as described in the following tip. The good Watson will capture a large amount of information about your system when a GPF or other illegal operations error takes place. Dr. Watson can also generate a snapshot of your system whenever you want. Want to try it out first? Click Start, Run, type drwatson, and click OK. The good doctor jumps into the system tray; double-click the icon to get started.

MARK'S TIP SHEET: Making Sure the Doctor Is Always On Call

Once you've tried Dr. Watson, you will probably want to have the doctor on call whenever you start your system. To add Dr. Watson to your Windows startup group with Windows 98/Me, do the following:

1. Right-click the Taskbar.
2. Select Properties.
3. Click the Advanced tab.
4. Click Advanced to open up the Windows Explorer and display Start menu shortcuts.
5. Open Programs (click the plus sign) and scroll down to StartUp.
6. Open StartUp; the contents of the folder appear in the right window.

7. Right-click in the right window and select New, Shortcut.

8. Click Browse and move to C: drive, Windows folder, and highlight Drwatson.

9. Click Open.

10. The path to Drwatson.exe is displayed in the Create Shortcut window; click Next.

11. Click Finish to take the default name (drwatson.exe), or enter a different name, such as Dr. Watson, and then click Finish.

12. The shortcut is now in your StartUp group; the next time you start Windows, Dr. Watson will run automatically in your system tray.

The Diagnosis tab (see Figure 3.12) shows you any problems with your system. To see other options, click View and select Advanced View. Use the arrows at the right to scroll through other options for a complete look at your system.

When you enable Advanced View, you can also see the following information:

- **System tab**—Displays operating system version, processor type, on-board RAM memory, free system resources, swapfile location, and temporary files location. This tab can help you find problems caused by running short of system resources or other resources.

- **Tasks tab**—Lists all programs running in memory when the system snapshot was taken. This tab can help you find programs that cause problems when they are run at the same time.

- **Startup**—Lists all programs and routines that start automatically when the system starts, and whether they are found in the Startup group or are started from the Registry.

- **Patches**—Lists programs that have been modified in memory.

- **Hooks**—Lists programs that control (hook) various parts of the system. For example, the mouse will be hooked by a mouse driver.

- **Kernel drivers**—Lists the routines that are essential to the operation of your copy of Windows, including operating system files and hardware driver files.

- **User drivers**—Drivers used by power management and sound cards.

- **MS-DOS drivers**—Drivers used by MS-DOS mode (Windows 9x only).

- **16-bit modules**—Drivers that run in 16-bit mode.

Use the File menu to save log files as normal log files or as text files, to open an old log file for viewing or printing, or to take a new system snapshot. Use the Options selection in the Advanced menu to specify where Dr. Watson log should be stored and what view to use as the default.

Figure 3.12 also shows the System tab within Dr. Watson, which shows the Windows version, Internet Explorer version, memory size, CPU type, and memory resources in use.

Figure 3.12

Take a look at Dr. Watson's Diagnosis view (left) and System view (right) of a typical system.

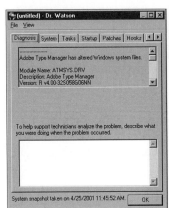

ON THE WEB: Bringing GPFs to Justice

Dr. Watson helps you grab the details about problems such as GPFs, but that's only half the battle. Fire up your browser and go to Microsoft's search site (http://search.Microsoft.com) and search the Knowledge Base for illegal operations and GPFs. Be sure to enter the program name that Dr. Watson has identified in your search to find the answer faster.

For more help, check out The PC Guide's Troubleshooting Run-Time Error Messages site at www.pcguide.com/ts/x/sys/operr.htm.

If you use Windows XP, it also contains its own version of Dr. Watson (drwtsn32.exe). The Windows XP version of Dr. Watson runs automatically when a program error occurs, and stores information in a log file, which is useful primarily to Microsoft support technicians. To see this log file, use this procedure:

1. Click Start, Run.

2. Type drwtsn32 and click OK.

This starts Dr. Watson and displays a list of recent program crashes. If the same program causes frequent program crashes, you should check with the program vendors for updates and solutions.

Solving Hardware and Software Problems with System Information

To help you stomp out hardware and software problems, the ultimate Microsoft research tool is Microsoft's System Information program. To start it with any recent version of Windows, click Start, Run, type `msinfo32`, and click OK.

Use the Explorer-like menus at the left side of the System Information window to explore both hardware and (Microsoft) software details about your system. It takes a few moments to gather information, so be patient when you click a category. Windows XP displays complete information about each device at all times. However, with Windows 9x/Me, the hardware categories list hardware settings and drivers for each device in Basic view. If you're really curious, use the Advanced view to see Registry keys, driver file dates, times, and versions (see Figure 3.13). To change views with the Windows Me version of System Information, click View, Advanced from the top-level menu.

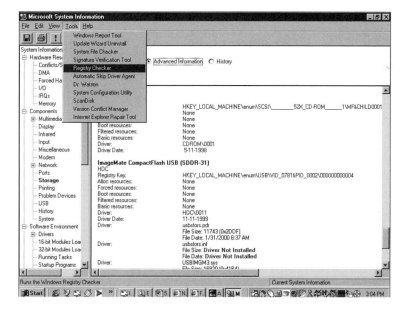

Figure 3.13

The Microsoft System Information tool for Windows 98. The Tools menu is open and advanced information about removable storage devices is displayed behind the menu.

Wondering how your Microsoft applications are configured? Check each major setting for your favorite installed application. For example, I learned that my copy of Microsoft Word XP is configured to open certain types of files to which it can't save, and vice-versa. This is handy to know when you're trying to share files with another user. You can rerun the Office XP installation program and select additional file converter settings to solve this problem.

System Information Tools

Use the tools drop-down menu to launch the following Windows fix-ups, which vary by Windows release, as shown in Table 3.4.

MARK'S TIP SHEET: Know What's Wrong? Skip System Information and Fix It!

Most of the programs on the System Information Tools menu can be run without starting System Information first. Just use the Find command in your version of Windows to find the program listed in Table 3.4 and double-click it to start your fix-up project.

Table 3.4 System Information Tools

Tool Name	Use	Windows Versions	Program Name
Windows Report Tool	Stores information about your system in a form you can send to Microsoft.	98	winrep.exe
Update Wizard Uninstall	Have fixes made by Windows Update gone bad? This fix uninstalls updates to Windows performed by the online Update Wizard.	98, Me	upwinun.exe (98)
System File Checker	Verifies system files and replaces corrupt or damaged files from the originals stored in compressed .CAB files.	98	sfc.exe
Signature Verification Tool	More and more files of all types (such as driver files) use digital signatures to verify their authenticity. Search your system for your choice of signed or unsigned files.	98, Me, XP	sigverif.exe
Registry Checker	This fix runs the Registry replacement program discussed earlier in the chapter.	98, Me*	scanreg.exe
Automatic Skip Driver (ASD)	Agent Use this program to list the devices that are being skipped, and then let it help you re-enable the device and give it another try.	98, Me	asd.exe

Tool Name	Use	Windows Versions	Program Name
Dr. Watson	Captures details about system configuration.	98, Me, XP	drwatson.exe (98, Me) drwtsn32.exe (XP)
System Configuration Utility	Configures system startup.	98, Me, XP	MSConfig.exe
ScanDisk	Checks for disk errors and repairs them.	98, Me	scandisk.exe
Version Conflict Manager	Sometimes newer isn't better when it comes to system files. Use VCM to list the system files that have been replaced with newer versions, and restore the old reliable version from a backup.	98	vcmui.exe
Internet Explorer Repair Tool	Break your IE? This fix replaces missing or corrupt Internet Explorer or Outlook Express files.	98	N/A
Network Diagnostics	Displays and tests network configuration and hardware, including network cards and modems.	Me, XP	N/A
System Restore	Runs the System Restore feature, which allows you to roll back your system configuration in case of problems.	Me, XP	N/A
DirectX Diagnostics	Checks DirectX drivers and tests operation (DirectX is Microsoft's support for 3D audio, video, and gaming features in Windows).	Me, XP (98)*	dxdiag.exe
WMI Control	Configures Windows Management settings on this or another specified computer	Me	N/A

*With this version of Windows, click Start, File, Run, enter the name of the program in the last column, and click OK to run the program

Using Windows Hard Disk Tools

The continued good health and prosperity of your hard disk is important to you—and it's just as important to Windows. Because every upgrade you make to your system involves copying some type of file to your hard disk, and because your hard disk volunteers to help out whenever you run short of real RAM (a technology called virtual memory), keeping your hard disk working properly and as fast as possible is something both you and your operating system agree is important.

The major Windows hard disk tools include the following:

- **ScanDisk/Chkdsk**—Use it for disk surface testing and logical structure repairs. ScanDisk is used by Windows 9x and Me; Chkdsk is used by Windows XP.

- **Defrag**—Aligns files for faster reading.

- **File system properties**—Controls your swapfile size and makes sure your drives are using 32-bit access.

- **FAT32 Converter**—Switches old FAT16 drives to the more efficient FAT32 file system.

Here's a short course in how to use these tools to keep your hard disk working properly.

Fix Disk Problems with ScanDisk and CheckDisk

The old CHKDSK (checkdisk) program used by generations of MS-DOS users was replaced by ScanDisk, a smarter and more powerful disk fix-up utility in Windows 9x and Me; Windows 2000 and XP call their error-checking program ChkDsk, but it's very similar to ScanDisk. ScanDisk runs automatically with late versions of Windows 95 and by newer versions of Windows when the system is not shut down properly.

What can ScanDisk and Chkdsk fix?

- They read the entire surface of your disk and note areas that cannot be read; these areas are marked as bad.

- They copy readable portions of files from bad areas to good areas of the disk.

- ScanDisk also displays disk usage information, such as how many files and folders are stored on a drive, at the end of its run.

The best way to run ScanDisk is to right-click a drive in the Windows Explorer, select Properties, select Tools, and click the Error-Checking button. Windows 9x and Me know the last time you ran the utilities on this tab and display the days elapsed since the last time you used these utilities. Windows 2000 and XP's Chkdsk can be run the same way, but Chkdsk doesn't display the elapsed time since you last checked your drive for errors. Also note that Windows 2000/XP don't run Chkdsk automatically if the system shuts down improperly or locks up. In those cases, run Chkdsk yourself from the Tools menu and select the option to fix errors automatically. Chkdsk must have exclusive access to the drive to perform those tests, so they take place during the next startup process.

You can also run ScanDisk from Start, Programs, Accessories, System Tools, ScanDisk. Running ScanDisk or CheckDisk about once a week is sufficient unless you're having serious disk problems, such as frequent disk read errors.

CAUTION: STOP! LOOK! THINK!

Don't Take a ScanDisk Aspirin If You Have Digital Cancer

ScanDisk and Chkdsk are adequate disk fix-up tools, but if you are running into frequent disk-read errors, don't settle for using them to repair whatever they can. Today's hard disks are generally very reliable, but if you need to run
ScanDisk or Chkdsk daily because one file after another isn't reading properly, you could have a very sick hard disk
on your hands. Use ScanDisk or Chkdsk like the proverbial canary in the mineshaft: Miners knew that if the canary
keeled over that they'd be next. If you keep encountering disk-read errors, your hard disk is getting ready to do its
own canary impression. Download and run the drive vendor's own disk-testing software. If it determines your drive
is bad, back up vital data, call your vendor for an Return Merchandise Authorization (RMA) if the drive is still under
warranty, and get a replacement *before* you lose everything.

If you need more thorough disk testing than what ScanDisk and Chkdsk can do for you, I recommend Norton Utilities
or Norton System Works (www.symantec.com) for use with both Windows 9x/Me and Windows 2000/XP drives running any file system, or SpinRite 5 (www.grc.com), which runs on FAT16 or FAT32 file systems only.

Figure 3.14 shows the drive Tools display for
Windows 98 (other versions have similar displays).
It's no accident that error checking (ScanDisk) is
listed first; you should use it before you make backups of your drive or defragment the files. Other
versions of Windows also lists error checking before
defrag for the same reason.

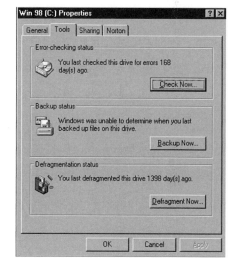

Figure 3.14

This is a typical C: drive that might be suffering from neglect; it's
been months since it was checked for errors and much longer since it
was defragmented. However, the Norton tab suggests this user
might be using Norton's superior disk tools instead.

Maximize Useful Space with Defrag

Hard drives are amazing little devices: If we have to store something, it has to fit into a single
location. However, your computer can store a huge file in lots of small areas on the disk and,
presto, reassemble them into a working unit whenever you retrieve the file. Windows prefers
to store a file in a single chunk of disk space, but if it must, it uses its digital jigsaw to cut the
file into pieces that occupy the empty bits of space around the disk. The problem of frag-
mented files (files stored in multiple locations) gets worse the longer you use your system.

The cure for slow disk saves and slow disk reads? Defrag! Defrag puts the pieces of each file together into a single chunk, switches all the files into a single area of the disk, and leaves the rest of the disk empty for faster storage of future files. The first time you use Defrag (which you can access by right-clicking the drive in Windows Explorer and choosing the Tools or Properties menu), start watching your *War and Remembrance* video tape set or throw a Mahler symphony into your CD player; it's gonna take a long time to get your files reorganized. Later, you'll just have time for a segment of *20/20* on TV or a couple of Top 40 pop hits on the radio before Defrag's done—*if* you do it every week.

> **MARK'S TIP SHEET: Let Windows Do It for You with Scheduled Tasks**
>
> Use the Task Scheduler feature in Windows to tell Windows to run error checking, defrag, or other utility tasks. Windows 98 displays the Scheduled Tasks folder in My Computer; Windows Me and XP use a Scheduled Task or Add a Scheduled Task icon in Control Panel.
>
> Schedule ScanDisk to run one evening a week, followed by Defrag. Add other programs to the list and relax—you've just taught Windows how to take care of itself.

Fine-Tuning the Windows Swapfile and File System

No matter how much RAM you have (and I remember when 4MB was awesome—I even remember when 640KB was all you'd ever need), Windows finds a way to use it up. When you have used all the physical memory in your system, your hard disk (with a little prompting from Windows) steps forward and unselfishly offer some megabytes of disk space as a substitute called *virtual memory,* which is managed as a special file called a *swapfile* in Windows 9x/Me or a *paging file* in Windows XP.

> **JARGON**
>
> *Virtual memory*—Disk space that is treated as an extension of RAM; programs can be swapped to and from virtual memory to actual RAM memory as needed if there are too many programs to fit into available system memory.
>
> *Swapfile*—A special file (called Win386.swp with Windows 9x and Me) that contains the contents of virtual memory.
>
> *Paging file*—The Windows XP term for a swapfile. The paging file can be distributed across more than one drive.

By default, Windows uses whatever space is remaining on the C: drive to use for a swapfile. How smart is Windows? Not very. Let's say that you have a 10GB C: drive and you've used all but 20MB of it. Then, you add a 40GB D: drive. Will Windows wake up and say, "I'd better start swapping to the D: drive?" Don't kid yourself; it keeps using the C: drive until your system is totally out of space and crashes almost before you've started it. By the way, if you have less than 15% of your disk space available, you're essentially out of disk space on any drive up to 40GB. This isn't enough free space to defrag your drive and can be exhausted by a couple of large print jobs (which are also stored on disk).

If you have more space somewhere else, Windows needs a hand in finding it. To help out Windows 98/Me, open the System properties sheet in Control Panel and click Performance. Then, click Virtual Memory (Windows 9x/Me). With Windows XP, open the System properties sheet in Control Panel, click Advanced, click the Settings button in the Performance section, click the Advanced tab, and then click Change.

The default is to let Windows "manage" (Microsoft's word, not mine) its own virtual memory. As you've already seen, Windows mismanages it. Specify your own location if you have a *hard drive letter* (not floppy, CD-RW, flash memory, or anything else) with more room than the C: drive. See Figure 3.15.

If you have more than one physical drive with similar amounts of empty space but one is faster than the other, put your swapfile on the faster drive.

With Windows XP, you can also set up multiple drives to use for the paging file (Figure 3.15), and adjust the system performance according to whether the computer is used as a server or to run applications.

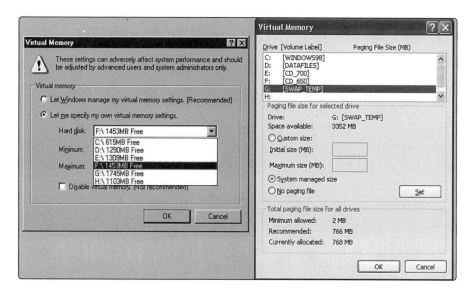

Figure 3.15

No matter which drives have more space than the C: drive, Windows uses C: for the swapfile until you select a better location (98/Me version on left, XP version on right).

If you change the location or size of the swapfile, you need to reboot for the changes to take effect.

Troubleshooting Call for Help

Don't even *think* about other upgrades until you're sure that Windows is working properly. Use this section to help you get your system into tip-top working order before you start your next software or hardware upgrade.

Help! I'm trying to restore my Windows 98 or Me Registry, but I can't find the Sysbkup folder. What's wrong?

Your system is OK—it's just that Microsoft likes to hide folders and files it doesn't think you are smart enough to work with. To be able to see system and hidden files and folders (so you can fix problems), do this:

1. Open Windows Explorer.
2. Click View, Folder Options (Windows 98) or Tools, and then Folder Options (Windows Me).
3. Click the View tab.
4. Under Hidden Files, click the radio button that enables you to see the hidden files.
5. Click OK.

The Sysbckup folder inside the Windows folder is now visible so that you can restore the Registry.

Help! I'm trying to defragment my hard disk in Windows 98, but I keep seeing a disk write message and Defrag restarts. I'm not using any other programs. Do I have a virus?

No, but what you do have is a classic symptom of a not-too-bright built-in Microsoft utility program. Defrag gets worried and restarts the system with *any* disk change, including the little change to your system that says, "It's time for the screen saver." You can turn off the screen saver and empty your system tray and task bar to stop the background activity that's upsetting (and resetting) Defrag, but it might be easier to restart the system and go into Safe Mode to use Defrag (not necessary with Windows XP).

Help! I'm defragging my C: drive and after it finishes, I still see small areas all over the disk marked as unmovable. What's going on? This unmovable thing is pretty badly fragmented itself!

The Unmovable areas on your drive are almost certainly the Windows swapfile. As you've already guessed, the drive isn't really defragmented unless the swapfile is. Unfortunately, Windows 98 and Me can't defragment their own swapfiles, but Norton Utilities and Norton System Works can.

I recommend the latest release (2003 or above) of Norton System Works; I use its Disk Doctor in place of ScanDisk and SpeedDisk in place of Defrag. System Works also includes Norton Antivirus and lots of other great utilities.

Help! I'm trying to change my swapfile location in Windows 98/Me, but when I look at the file system properties, it lists some drives as running in MS-DOS compatibility mode. I've also noticed that the system seems slower lately. What's up?

Something is preventing your system from using 32-bit drivers to run your drives. As a result (especially if the hard disk or CD-ROM drives are affected), your system is much slower because Windows has to ask the system ROM BIOS to move the disk heads around to read or write data (the BIOS is much slower than Windows is at controlling the drive).

What are the usual suspects? Lots of possibilities; take your choice and start investigating the following:

- **A damaged or erased ESDI_506.pdr driver file (if the hard disk or CD-ROM is affected)**—This file runs IDE devices. You might be able to fix it with the Windows 98 System File Checker, or you might want to try the Update Driver button on the standard hard disk controller's properties sheet in Device Manager.

- **MS-DOS CD-ROM drivers in Config.sys and Autoexec.bat (Windows 9x only)**—Windows 9x has its own 32-bit drivers for CD-ROM drives, so you don't need to load CD-ROM drivers in Config.sys and Autoexec.bat. Put a REM in front of the line installing the CD-ROM driver in Config.sys and the MSCDEX.EXE command in Autoexec.bat. You can open these files with Notepad or with the DOS Edit program.

To open Config.sys for editing with Notepad:

1. Click Start, Programs, Accessories, Notepad.

2. Click File, Open.

3. The contents of C: drive are displayed; type `Config.sys` for the File name and click Open.

4. Type `REM` and a space at the beginning of the line containing the CD-ROM device driver, as shown in Figure 3.16.

5. Click File, Save, and then File, Exit.

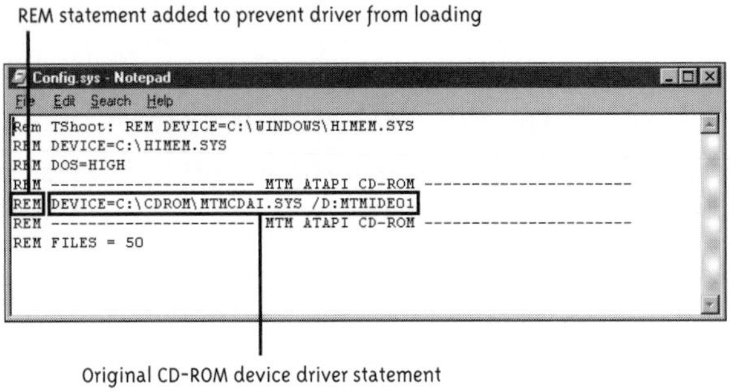

REM statement added to prevent driver from loading

Figure 3.16

A typical Config.sys file after putting a REM statement in front of the CD-ROM driver.

Original CD-ROM device driver statement

To open Autoexec.bat for editing with Notepad:

1. Click Start, Programs, Accessories, Notepad.

2. Click File, Open.

3. The contents of C: drive are displayed; type `Autoexec.bat` for the File name and click Open.

4. Type `REM` and a space in front of the line containing MSCDEX unless the line containing MSCDEX starts with IF EXIST, as in Figure 3.17. IF EXIST will run MSCDEX only if the CD-ROM device driver is started in Config.sys, so there's no need to REM it out (you already prevented the CD-ROM device driver from starting by adding a REM statement to Config.sys).

5. Click File, Save (if you made changes in Step 4), and then File Exit.

Restart the system. Windows should run the CD-ROM drive with its 32-bit device drivers (you might need to reboot again after it detects the drive and installs driver software).

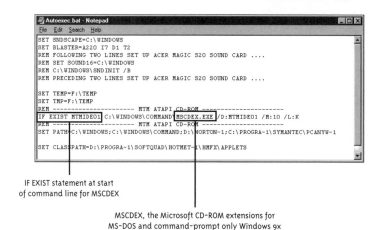

IF EXIST statement at start
of command line for MSCDEX

MSCDEX, the Microsoft CD-ROM extensions for
MS-DOS and command-prompt only Windows 9x

Figure 3.17

An Autoexec.bat file
that uses the IF EXIST
conditional
statement to load
MSCDEX only if the
CD-ROM driver
is loaded in
Config.sys. This file
needs no editing if
Config.sys has
already been edited
to prevent the CD-
ROM device driver
from loading.

- **You might have a boot-sector virus**—Use an up-to-date antivirus program to find and repair the problem.

- **You might need to install bus-mastering drivers for your motherboard chipset**—Windows 98 and newer versions provide high-speed drivers for many motherboard chipsets, but if your motherboard comes with a CD or diskette with drivers, you may need to install them manually. If these drivers aren't installed, your IDE host adapters for your hard disk won't work properly.

To see if you need to install motherboard chipset drivers manually with Windows, click Start, Settings, Control Panel, System, and click the Device Manager tab (click Hardware, and then Device Manager with Windows 2000/XP). Open the Hard disk controllers section and see if any IDE devices have a yellow "!" (exclamation mark) listed next to them. If they do, install the drivers you received with your motherboard or system or check the motherboard maker's web site for updated versions.

You may need to get the drivers from the chipset manufacturer in some cases. For example, Via Technologies (a popular motherboard chipset maker) has a listing of motherboard drivers on its web site, categorized by chipset name and operating system. Read the instructions on-screen very carefully, because if you install the wrong drivers for your chipset or operating system, your system will run even worse. You will need to reboot after installing bus-mastering drivers.

For more details, causes, and cures for MS-DOS compatibility, enter MS-DOS Compatibility Mode (exact phrase) into the Search Microsoft web site (http://search.Microsoft.com).

Chapter 4

Taking an Inspection Tour of Your System

In Chapter 2, "Upgrade Strategies," you received an overview of the major upgrades you can add to your system in approximate terms of how much they'll empty your wallet. Knowing what you can buy is only half the battle when it comes to upgrading a computer system; the rest of the battle comes from figuring out what you need (or really ought) to buy.

Three Methods for Evaluating Your System

To determine what you really need to buy, you need to take a close look "under the hood" of your system. There are three ways to evaluate your system:

- Evaluating startup hardware information display
- Using system reporting software
- Performing a physical examination of your system

In this chapter, you learn how to use each method because some systems provide more information in some ways than others.

In Chapter 2, you learned that you can evaluate a system by its age and its onboard equipment. However, regardless of how impressive (or unimpressive) your system's specifications might be if boiled down to a fact sheet, the bottom line is this: Can your PC do the jobs you want it to do now?

Basically, this point means this: "If you can't get your work (or play) done comfortably and efficiently with your system's current configuration, it's time for a change!" In an era of ever-increasing performance and ever-dropping component costs, it's easy to overlook the wisdom of personal computing pioneer Adam Osborne: "Adequacy is sufficient." Your definition of adequacy might be different than mine, but fortunately, we can both reach the results we want the same way—by upgrading our systems.

MARK'S TIP SHEET: Making a (Task) List and Checking It Twice

Before you go any further down the road marked "Faster, Better PCs Through Upgrading," take a few minutes and make a list of the tasks you want your computer to do. Then, as you compare your computer's current features to this list, you can see at a glance which jobs your computer handles nicely, and which ones require you to shell out for an upgrade. Don't be afraid to be specific. Table 4.1 provides a simple example:

Table 4.1   Evaluating Your Computer by Sufficiency to Task

Tasks	Upgrade Needed?
View full-motion video from the Internet	Yes
Store work files larger than a floppy can hold	No
Write CDs for use with portable CD player	Yes
Print photo-realistic photos	No

How do you decide when an upgrade is needed? If you're not satisfied with how well or how fast your system does the tasks you care about most, it's time for an upgrade. If you don't care about a particular task, don't worry about it. If you share the computer with others, be sure to get everybody's input to make the list complete. Once you identify the tasks you're most concerned with, be sure to see Chapter 6, "The Right Upgrades for You," for a detailed exploration of the upgrades I recommend for the most popular computing tasks.

> **ON THE DVD: What Does This Stuff Look Like?**
>
> As you read the rest of this chapter, you might experience a bit of "MEGO" (My Eyes Glaze Over) as I discuss various system components. The illustrations in the book are helpful, and you will also find live video of typical systems on the DVD to help you understand what's what.

Potential Upgrade Traps

It's a lot easier to upgrade some systems than others. Here are some of the traps lying in wait for you as you plan a computer upgrade strategy:

- Proprietary system designs
- Obsolete motherboard types
- Lack of slots and drive bays
- Obsolete memory types
- Obsolete processor types
- Not enough PCI slots

Proprietary System Designs

Although much of the computer industry now uses industry standards such as ATX for case, motherboard, power supply, and other components as shown later in this chapter, there are quite a few systems that use proprietary designs and components. These include the following:

- **Systems using LPX riser-card motherboards**—These computers, which include most Acer and Packard-Bell models and some older IBM, Compaq, and HP models, use a riser card for expansion slots. Because the LPX standard never specified a location for the riser card, computers using these motherboards can't use motherboard upgrades. You can see examples of these dead-end systems later in this chapter.

- **Motherboards with first-generation SDRAM-DIMM memory**—The characteristics of early SDRAM modules are different than those for more recent systems; they require special (and more expen$ive!) memory upgrades.

- **Dell Dimension computers built from September 1998 until 2000**—Most of these systems use a different pinout for the power supply and motherboard than normal systems. They use the same physical connector for the power supply as older systems, but the voltages carried by a given pin are different than on standard systems. This means you need to buy special Dell-compatible power supplies for upgrades. If you want to upgrade the motherboard, you must also replace the power supply with a standard model.

ON THE WEB: The Best Power Supplies and Information

The PC Power and Cooling web site offers the best power supplies around, and its interactive power supply selector helps you determine if your Dell computer needs a special Dell-compatible power supply or can use an off-the-shelf ATX model. Go to www.pcpowerandcooling.com to get started.

JARGON

Pinout—The voltage and signals carried by a particular connector.

LPX—Refers to motherboards with a riser card that holds expansion cards. LPX doesn't officially stand for anything, but my unofficial suggestion is "Limiting Possible Expandability."

CAUTION: STOP! LOOK! THINK!

Don't Get "Burned Up" by a Bad Upgrade!
How big a deal is the pinout change on some Dell motherboards and power supplies? Put it this way: If you ever wanted to replicate humorist Dave Barry's burning toaster experiment, but with a PC instead of a toaster, mismatching a standard motherboard with a Dell power supply will do it—flames and all! You might not get flames if you use a standard power supply and a Dell motherboard—but you still get a fried system. You have been warned.

- **Motherboards with motherboard-based video**—While some systems with integrated video have AGP slots for adding faster video, many others force you to use the older PCI slot design for video upgrades. The result? You might wind up with a video downgrade instead of an upgrade.

Although systems with these characteristics can still be upgraded, these issues can limit your options or raise the price of the upgrades you want to perform.

- **Direct 3D video**—Means the video is built into the motherboard chipset. If no AGP slot is mentioned, your upgrade options are limited to the slower PCI slot type. Although there are still a few PCI-based video cards, these cards normally use low-end chipsets, not the superfast chipsets available on AGP video cards.

ANALYZE THIS

How to Avoid Buying a Dead-End System
Thanks to the Internet, it's easier than ever before to find out about a particular computer model before you buy it. Here are some of the terms to watch for in specification sheets and ads; if you see these terms, your upgrade options are limited at best.

- **Integrated video**—Means the video might have its own chip on the motherboard instead of being part of the main chipset. But, if no AGP slot is mentioned, you're still stuck with slower PCI slot video upgrades.

- **All-in-one system**—Could mean the system uses an LPX (non-upgradable) motherboard or its successors, the upgradable NLX, flexATX, or mini-ITX form factors, which, while standard, aren't easy to find at your local or online PC parts emporium.

- **Slimline system**—Very limited space inside the case for upgrades of any kind, and often means an LPX or NLX motherboard's inside. Bring bandages and gauze if you go inside the case, as you're liable to draw blood.

- **Legacy-free system**—Doesn't use serial or parallel ports (and might not have PS/2 keyboard/mouse ports) and depends on USB (and sometimes IEEE-1394) ports for expansion. Usually lacks more than one or two card slots for interior upgrades. Sometimes lacks empty drive bays, too. A legacy-free system is a good idea if you use only USB or IEEE-1394 (FireWire) peripherals. However, if you still use PS/2 mice and keyboards, serial-port PDA cradles, and parallel printers and scanners, legacy-free isn't the way to go.

Lack of Slots and Drive Bays

Today's smaller computer cases can make internal upgrades tricky. Make sure that your system has room for the add-on cards or drives you want to install.

MARK'S TIP SHEET: Multifunctional Peripherals and USB Ports Can Save the Day!

Running short on internal space? Use these space-saving tips to save the day:

- Instead of adding a second hard drive, buy a bigger drive to replace the capacity in the original unit; because hard drives are cheaper per GB as they get larger, it won't cost much more to buy a unit with more capacity.

- Use an external CD-RW or rewriteable DVD drive with a USB 2.0 port instead of replacing your existing CD-ROM drive; this enables you to copy CDs without writing their contents to the hard disk first. It's faster and easier. Be sure to add a USB 2.0 port if your system has only USB 1.1 ports.

- Look at multi-functional cards. You can add two types of ports in many cases by installing a single card, such as USB 2.0 and IEEE-1394, or IEEE-1394 and SCSI. However, some multifunction boards don't work very well; be sure to look very carefully at user comments and detailed reviews before you buy.

---

continues

CONTINUED

- If you run out of space on the inside, don't forget about USB ports, which can be used for many different types of drives, as well as printers, mice, scanners and much more. Although the slow speed of USB 1.1 exacts a performance penalty from hard drives and CD-RW drives, it's more than fast enough for smaller removable-media drives; many recent systems now have USB 2.0 ports, which are much faster. You can also add USB 2.0 ports to desktop and portable systems. Also, remember that USB devices can be moved from system to system without shutting down or rebooting your computer. USB peripherals can follow you to your future systems, unlike serial and parallel devices, whose ports are being phased out and being replaced by USB.

JARGON

USB—The Universal Serial Bus; this very flexible port is found on most systems built from 1997 to the present; can handle printers, scanners, web cameras, small removable-media drives, keyboards, mice, and digital camera readers on a single port when a USB hub is used. The original version is called USB 1.1; a faster version called USB 2.0 or High-speed USB is common in systems built in 2002 or later.

IEEE-1394—Also called FireWire or i.Link, this faster rival to USB is a great choice for mobile hard drives, interfacing with DV camcorders, and other devices that pump a lot of data; you must add a card to most systems to use IEEE-1394 devices. Most systems have IEEE-1394a (FireWire 400); IEEE-1394b (FireWire 800) ports and cards were introduced in early 2003 and can be adapted to work with FireWire 400 devices.

SCSI—Small Computer System Interface; this is a long-lived, very flexible interface for drives and scanners. It's much faster than USB 1.1 and most versions are as fast or faster than IEEE-1394 and USB 2.0. You'll also need to add a card to most systems if you want to use SCSI devices, but since SCSI devices are very expensive and don't support hot-swapping, you might prefer to skip it.

Obsolete Designs for Memory and CPUs

If the biggest gripe you have with your computer is a lack of performance for business applications, memory and CPU upgrades are the one-two punch that can bring you the speed you need. But, watch out for these potential problems:

- **Slot-based processors**—Both AMD and Intel have returned to socket-based processors in their latest designs. Although you can sometimes use a slot-to-socket adapter (also called a slotket) to add a newer socket-based Intel Pentium III or Celeron processor to an older system, the AMD Slot A design doesn't offer a conversion to the newer Socket A CPUs. Bottom line: if your current motherboard has a slot-based CPU and you need a faster processor, it's time for a new motherboard as well.

- **Pentium, K6, or older processors (486 and earlier)**—A Pentium III, Celeron or Athlon/Duron-based system is the minimum system worth upgrading today. Systems with older processors can't be upgraded to meet even minimum speed standards unless you're willing to throw out everything but the case and power supply.

- **SIMM memory modules**—Once the king of memory, SIMM modules have been replaced by DIMM modules on newer systems. Even though SIMMs are still on the market, they can cost twice as much per megabyte as their newer, faster siblings. Virtually any system that uses SIMMs also uses obsolete 486, Pentium, AMD K6, or very early Pentium II/Celeron processors that have limited or no CPU upgrade paths.

If your system has any of these outdated components, consider looking at a motherboard plus a CPU upgrade to speed things up, or consider a replacement PC.

Recording Your System Information

Before you can make sensible decisions about what you need to upgrade, you need to know what's inside your system. The following methods can be used to get the inside story about your computer's components before you look at actual components, as you'll see later in this chapter:

- Watch the computer's configuration display at startup.

- Use Windows' own utilities.

- Use third-party system reporting programs such as Norton System Information, AMIDiag, or SiSoftware Sandra.

- Check your system's vendor-supplied specifications.

To get the most complete picture of your system, use as many of these methods as you can.

Use the checklist in Table 4.2 to record your findings.

Table 4.2 Recording Your Equipment			
Equipment	**Examples**	**Your PC**	**Where to Find Information**
PC manufacturer (brand name)	HP, Joe's Computer Shack	_____	Case front, Case rear, invoice

continues

CONTINUED

Equipment	Examples	Your PC	Where to Find Information
Model name/ number	Pavilion 5300, Pentium Special	_____	Case front, Case rear, invoice
Form factor (shape and size of motherboard)	ATX, micro-ATX, Baby-AT, LPX, notebook	_____	Compare to Figures 4.12—4.16
Case type	Desktop, tower, mini-tower	_____	Most microATX systems use a mini-tower case, while flexATX systems might use a mini-tower or slimline/desktop case and full ATX systems use a mid-tower or full-size tower case. FRANKENPC uses a mid-tower case.
CPU type	Pentium MMX Celeron	_____	Startup display, System reporting software
CPU clock speed	667MHz, Celeron, 1400MHz, 2GHz	_____	Startup display, System reporting software
BIOS manufacturer and date or version	AMI: 03/07/00, Award: v.4.50G	_____	Startup display, System reporting software
Operating system	Windows 98 Windows 98SE Windows XP Windows Me	_____	Windows system properties, System reporting software
Network card type*	10Base2 100BaseTX Token ring	_____	Windows Device Manager
Network card brand	Linksys, 3Com	_____	Windows Device Manager
Network card model	LANCard II EtherExpress III	_____	Windows Device Manager
Quantity of RAM	64MB 128MB	_____	Startup display, Windows system properties
Type of memory	184-pin RIMMs 168-pin DIMMs 184-pin DIMMs	_____	SiSoftware Sandra, examination of memory modules

Equipment	Examples	Your PC	Where to Find Information
Maximum installable RAM	512MB, 1GB	_____	System documentation
Storage device interface	IDE, SCSI	_____	Windows Device Manager
Hard disk model	WD Caviar 33100, Maxtor Diamond Max 4320	_____	Windows Device Manager, SiSoftware Sandra
Hard disk capacity	6.0GB, 20GB	_____	System reporting software, Windows Explorer, Startup display
Second hard disk model*	(same)	_____	Windows Device Manager, SiSoftware Sandra
Second hard disk capacity*	(same)	_____	System reporting software, Windows Explorer
Disk drive A size	3 1/2" 1.44MB	_____	Startup display, System reporting software
Disk drive B size*	(same)	_____	Startup display, System reporting software
Number of "half-height" drive bays		_____	Examination of system case
Number of 3 1/2" drive bays		_____	Examination of system case
CD-ROM model & speed	NEC Multispin 6x, AOpen 36x CD-936E	_____	Windows System properties sheet, Physical examination of drive
Removable media drives*	Iomega Zip 100, LS-120	_____	Windows System properties sheet
Monitor model and size	Magnavox Enhanced VGA 15", Mag Innovision DJ700 17"	_____	Physical examination of monitor
Monitor maximum resolution	800h x 600v, 1280h x 1024v	_____	Monitor documentation, SiSoftware Sandra

continues

Table 4.2   Recording Your Equipment (Continued)

Equipment	Examples	Your PC	Where to Find Information
Number of ISA expansion slots		_____	Look inside case
Number of PCI expansion slots		_____	Look inside case, SiSoftware Sandra
AGP slot type	AGP 2x, AGP 4x	_____	SiSoftware Sandra, system documentation
Other slot type	CNR, ACR	_____	Look inside system
Number of USB ports		_____	Examine rear and front of system, Check system documentation
Type of USB ports	1.1, 2.0 (both)	_____	Check system documentation, SiSoftware Sandra
Number of COM (serial) ports		_____	Examine rear of system, check system
Video card model	ATI All-in-Wonder 128, Creative Graphics Annihilator Pro	_____	Windows Device Manager, System reporting software
Video card max. resolution	1024h x 768v, 1280h x 1024v	_____	Card documentation
Video card RAM	8MB, 16MB, 32MB	_____	SiSoftwarec Sandra, Dxdiag.exe, card documentation
Sound card model*	Sound Blaster AWE32, AOpen AW35Pro	_____	Windows Device Manager
Modem model, speed, and fax support*	US Robotics Sportster 56K, Supra 56K Fax	_____	Windows Device Manager, physical examination of modem
Power supply size	200W (watt), 300W	_____	Examine power supply
Mouse model and interface	Logitech M-RR63, Microsoft mouse port, USB port	_____	Physical examination of mouse and port

Equipment	Examples	Your PC	Where to Find Information
Keyboard model and interface	Microsoft Natural Keyboard USB port, PS/2 keyboard port	_____	Examine keyboard and port
Printer type*	Laser, color inkjet, dot matrix	_____	Identify from brand and model
Printer brand*	Hewlett-Packard, Epson	_____	Examine printer
Printer model*	LaserJet 6P, Stylus Color 600	_____	Examine printer
Maximum printer resolution and features	1200dpi, photo-realistic prints	_____	Check printer documentation
Scanner model*	Epson Expression 600, HP ScanJet 5300	_____	Examine scanner
Maximum scanner resolution and features	1200dpi, slide/filmstrip option	_____	Check scanner documentation
Other internal components*	Game adapter, SCSI port, fan card	_____	Windows Device Manager, SiSoftware Sandra, look inside system
Peripherals*	Digital camera, microphone, joystick	_____	Windows Device Manager, examine system

*Indicates optional component or accessory

What Your System Tells You at Startup

Some systems display a *Reader's Digest* condensed book-sized guide to their configuration when you turn them on. This information tends to flash by pretty quickly, but if you press the Pause button or Ctrl+S on your computer keyboard, you can usually stop the display and digest the contents.

MARK'S TIP SHEET: Coaxing System Information Out of Hiding

The latest PC design recommendations from Microsoft require system vendors to hide the configuration information so that the system boots up a few seconds faster. If your computer doesn't display any hardware information when you turn it on, you may need to press the key specified by your system's BIOS setup program to start setup and enable this option.

For example, to see hardware information when I start my HP Pavilion computer, I had to press F1 to start the BIOS setup program, move to the Boot menu, and enable the Boot-time Diagnostic Screen. After I saved the changes and exited the BIOS setup program, I see my system's onboard hardware every time I turn on the computer. Check your system documentation for details. On some systems, the default is "quiet boot"; disable quiet boot to see configuration information.

Figure 4.1 is the startup configuration screen from one of my systems.

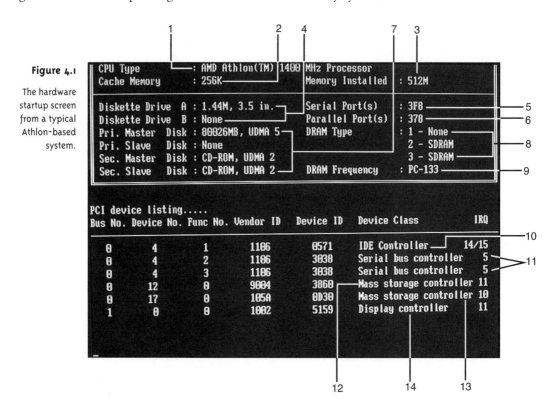

Figure 4.1

The hardware startup screen from a typical Athlon-based system.

This display might be a little cryptic, but it shows you much of what you need to know if you're considering a system upgrade. Here's an explanation in plain English (the numbers in parentheses are keyed to Figure 4.1):

- **CPU Type (1)**—The CPU type, such as Pentium III, Celeron, Athlon and so on. If you see 386, 486, K6 or Pentium displayed here, it's time to buy a new computer, or at least a new motherboard, processor, and RAM. Some systems, as in this case, also list the CPU speed (Athlon 1.4GHz).

- **Cache Memory (2)**—This is an area of memory that is faster than normal memory; it holds recently used information for fast reuse. The Pentium II and newer processors have this type of memory (also called L2 or Level 2 cache) built into the processor, but older systems mounted this on the motherboard.

- **Memory Installed (3)**—This system has 512MB of memory. Some systems list base (first megabyte) and extended (memory above one megabyte) separately.

- **Diskette Drives (4)**—Also known as floppy drives. Some systems support only one floppy drive.

- **Serial port(s) (5)**—Listed by their I/O port addresses; this system has one serial port; others would be listed as 2E8, 3F8, and 3E8. Serial ports are used for older mice and modems.

- **Parallel port(s) (6)**—Listed by their I/O port addresses; this system has one parallel port; others would be listed as 278 and 3BC. Parallel ports are used for printers, scanners, and some external drives.

- **Pri/Sec Master/Slave Disk (7)**—Drives connected to the motherboard's dual IDE/ATA controllers. This system has one 80GB hard disk and two CD/DVD drives. Regardless of type, the BIOS lists them as CD-ROM drives. The UDMA number next to each drive indicates its Ultra-DMA transfer rate (higher is faster; see Chapter 11, "Removable Storage to Go," for details).

- **DRAM Type (8)**—Type of memory installed in each socket. Most systems today use SDRAM (as here) or DDR SDRAM. This system has two memory modules installed and one free socket.

- **DRAM Frequency (9)**—The speed of the memory. This system uses PC-133 memory. A system that uses DDR SDRAM might use PC1600, PC2100, or PC2700 memory (higher number means faster memory). New memory should match or exceed the speed of already-installed memory.

- **PCI devices (10-14)**—This section provides general information about some of the PCI devices in this system. These include two IDE host adapters (10), two USB controllers (11), an Adaptec SCSI host adapter card (12), a Promise Technology RAID adapter (13), and an ATI Radeon-based VGA card (14). This list of devices isn't always complete. For example, this list doesn't include the 10/100 Ethernet card and Creative Labs sound card installed in this system.

> **ON THE WEB: Discovering Device and Vendor IDs**
>
> Did you ever wonder how diagnostic and reporting software programs "know" what's in your system? They look up the device and vendor IDs of your hardware in their PCI device database! By looking up the vendor ID and device ID numbers displayed by some systems at startup, you can identify the PCI hardware in your system, as in Figure 4.1. One of the most up-to-date online resources for this information is located at www.yourvote.com/pci/vendors.txt.

> **JARGON**
>
> *BIOS*—The Basic Input-Output System; the BIOS chip contains firmware (software on a chip) that allows different types of computers to use the same operating system (such as Windows or Linux) and the same programs.
>
> *PCI*—Peripheral Component Interconnect; the smaller white slots inside your PC that handle most add-on cards. PCI pioneered easier (Plug-and-Play) installations.

As you can see, the system configuration screen tells you a lot of information about your system, but it doesn't tell you everything you want to know. For example, what type of video card do you have? How fast is your CD-ROM drive? What brand (and speed) of Ethernet card do you have? To learn details like these, you need to go a step further and try system-reporting software.

Using Software to Evaluate Your System

To get additional information about your system, you can use software that digs into your system to find out the nitty-gritty about components that the system BIOS just doesn't know (or care) about. Built-in tools found in Windows include the Windows Microsoft System Information (MSinfo32), and DirectX Diagnostics. The Device Manager provides detailed hardware information, but Microsoft System Information and DirectX Diagnostics are also useful because they provide different types of information.

Third-party tools I've found useful include SiSoftware Sandra, Norton System Information, and the Belarc Advisor. Table 4.3 provides a quick reference to each tool to help you determine which tool is best for determining what you need to know about your system.

Table 4.3   System Reporting Software Compared

Program Name	Obtain From	Types of Information	Best Use
Windows Device Manager	Built into Windows 9x/Me/XP	Physical drives, ports, and resources	Identifying problem devices and specific models of hardware
Windows System Information	Built into Windows 9x/Me/XP	Hardware and software overview and details	Identifying Registry keys for devices and programs
DirectX Diagnostics	Built into Windows 9x/Me/XP	DirectX video and audio information, including memory	Video memory and settings, audio and video tests
Norton System Information	Part of Norton System Works and Norton Utilities	Quick overview of hardware and settings	Capabilities of printers and display
SiSoftware Sandra	Download from vendor (free and commercial versions available)	Complete hardware information, benchmarks, and burn-in testing	The most information you can get without opening your system

To determine the brand and model of your CD drive, for example, right-click My Computer on the Windows desktop and select Properties (or open the System icon in Control Panel), and then click the Device Manager tab, as seen in Figure 4.2.

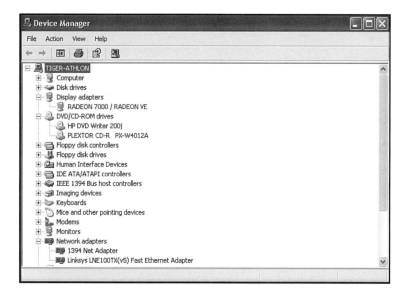

Figure 4.2

Access the Windows Device Manager through the System properties sheet. Click the plus (+) sign next to a device to see the brand and model, as seen here for the CD-ROM/DVD drives and display adapter (video card) in Windows XP.

To use Microsoft System Information, click Start, Programs, Accessories, System Tools, System Information to start the program. To get information on the components in your system, click the plus (+) sign next to Components and then click on each component you are wondering about, as in Figure 4.3.

Figure 4.3

Microsoft's System Information basic information display about the IDE host adapters used for hard drives and CD/DVD drives. Note that this system uses a bus-mastering IDE host adapter from VIA (top).

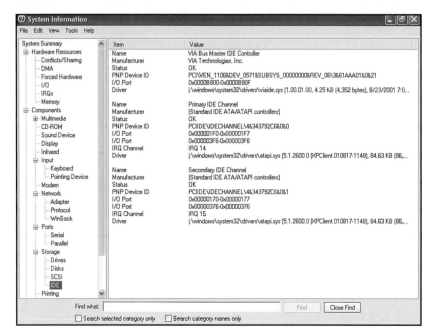

The advanced option also lists Registry keys and driver file versions; you won't need this level of information most of the time, but if you are having problems getting a device working and need to manually update driver files or Registry entries, it's handy to know. You can also use System Information to display most of the basic information that the system configuration display at bootup shows (click View, Advanced for the most complete information) in the System Summary. However, to get details about drive letter, physical hard disks, and other information, you will need to dig into the components listing. System Information doesn't provide details about rewriteable drives (they're all just CD-ROM drives as far as it's concerned) or their speed.

Although the Device Manager and Microsoft System Information (as well as Norton System Information and DirectX Diagnostics) all provide useful basic information about your system, details such as video card memory, motherboard chipset type, and main memory configuration are missing. If you want this level of system information, you need to download a copy of SiSoftware Sandra, available from SiSoftware at www.sisoftware.demon.co.uk.

SiSoftware Sandra, which is free for personal and educational use (more powerful versions are available for as little as $29), provides a staggering level of detail about your system, including video card memory sizing, motherboard chipset maker and model, PCI and AGP slot usage, CD-ROM drive benchmarking, and more (check out Figure 4.4). Sandra can even identify your DIMM memory modules, so you can find out if your system uses any unusual varieties! About the only things that Sandra can't tell you about your system is how many drive bays you have and whether you have any of the now–obsolete ISA slots on-board.

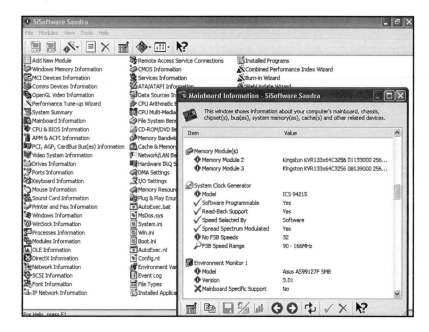

Figure 4.4

SiSoftware Sandra offers a staggering number of system identification and benchmarking modules (background) that offer impressive detail, such as the memory module identification and other information in the mainboard (motherboard) module (foreground).

Wondering what upgrades would serve you best? Use SiSoftware Sandra's Performance Tune-Up Wizard to get tips on what hardware upgrades and Windows configuration tweaks are best for you (see Figure 4.5).

ON THE WEB: Get Great Advice from Belarc Advisor

Belarc, Inc. makes the BelManage and beITsmart PC management system used by major corporations to keep watch over their systems' components, condition, and on-board software. However, you don't need to be a major corporation to benefit from their knowledge of what's under the hood of a PC. Send your browser to www.belarc.com and click the Free Download link to try the Belarc Advisor on your own system. It displays what's in your system right in your web browser (see Figure 4.6).

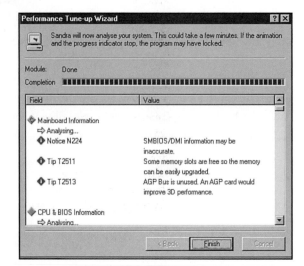

Figure 4.5

On this system, SiSoftware Sandra suggests switching to an AGP video card for faster performance and points out that empty memory sockets on this system's motherboard make for easy system memory upgrades.

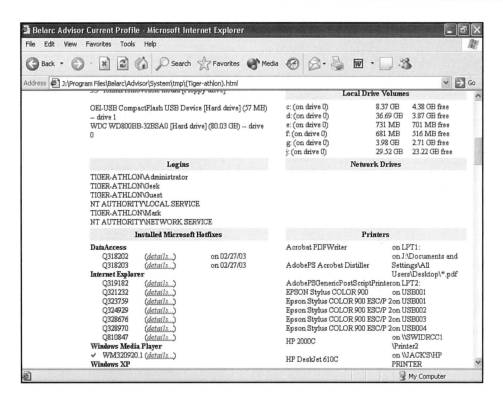

Figure 4.6

A portion of a typical system report created by the Belarc Advisor. Unlike other system reporting products, it also identifies Microsoft Windows hotfixes and usernames.

Based on what you discover by reading your startup screens and using reporting software, you might be ready to make some upgrades. However, if you want to add drives, add cards, replace your CPU, or upgrade your power supply, you need the inside story.

Taking a Look Inside Your System

Even if you run a top-notch reporting utility like SiSoftware Sandra through its paces, you still need to take your screwdriver in hand to finish your system configuration listing, especially if you are planning a power supply, internal drive, memory, or CPU upgrade.

> **CAUTION: STOP! LOOK! THINK!**
>
> **Look, But Don't Fry, Your System**
>
> If you've never been inside your PC before, you'll want to head over to Chapter 5, "Preparing for Your Upgrade," first and check out my suggestions on toolkits and ESD (Electrostatic Discharge) protection. Be sure you unplug the system, take precautions against ESD (don't touch cards or chips) and use the correct tools to open the case and look inside. You can hurt the PC if you're not careful, but it can't shock you if it's unplugged.
>
> However, the insides of the monitor and system power supply *are* dangerous. They retain high voltage for long periods of time even after they're unplugged, and you might need a *life* upgrade if you try fiddling around with their innards. Stay out and stay alive!

When you open up your system, look carefully at the following components:

- Power supply
- Motherboard form factor
- Number and types of expansion slots—in use and free
- Memory types and open sockets
- Types of drive bays—in use and free
- CPU form factor—slot or socket
- The location of fans

Use the figures in this chapter to help you determine what type of a system you have.

Looking Around the System

Many system upgrades these days don't require you to lift a screwdriver. Thanks to the wide-spread popularity of USB ports and devices and built-in networking and sound, you can attach a lot of different devices to your computer, as you will learn in later chapters. If you are thinking about adding a scanner, digital camera, printer, or external drive to your computer, it pays to take a tour of the outside of your system before you worry about the interior.

Figures 4.7 and 4.8 show you the exterior of my beloved FRANKENPC, the computer I'll be upgrading throughout this book. It's a typical example of a computer that can benefit a lot from various upgrades.

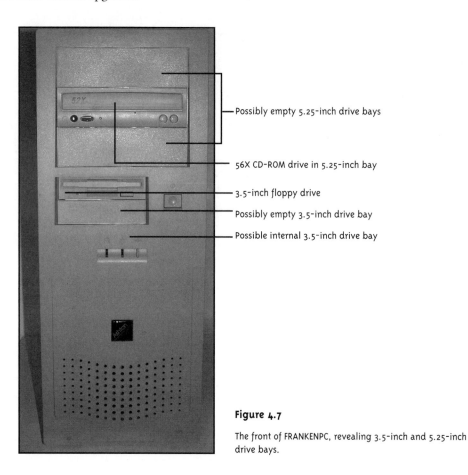

Possibly empty 5.25-inch drive bays

56X CD-ROM drive in 5.25-inch bay

3.5-inch floppy drive

Possibly empty 3.5-inch drive bay

Possible internal 3.5-inch drive bay

Figure 4.7

The front of FRANKENPC, revealing 3.5-inch and 5.25-inch drive bays.

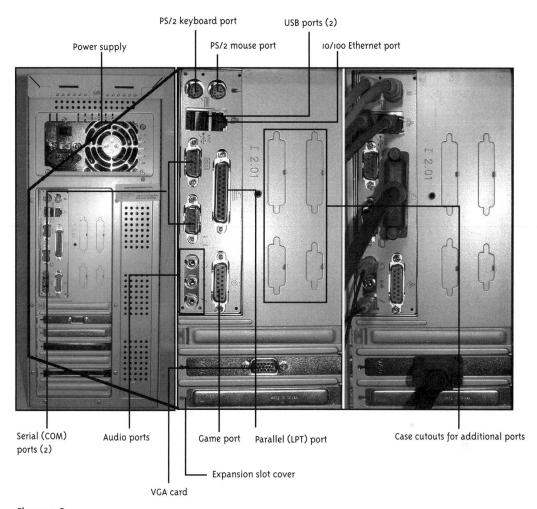

Power supply · PS/2 keyboard port · PS/2 mouse port · USB ports (2) · 10/100 Ethernet port

Serial (COM) ports (2) · Audio ports · Game port · Parallel (LPT) port · Case cutouts for additional ports · Expansion slot cover · VGA card

Figure 4.8

Overall (left) and detail views (center, right) of the rear of FRANKENPC. Center detail view shows the rear panel and VGA card connectors, while the right view shows the same connectors with cables connected.

In Figure 4.7, note that some of the drive bays are labeled as possibly empty. Since it's possible to install a 3.5-inch hard disk into a 5.25-inch bay with an adapter kit, and since some 3.5-inch drive bays are internal bays with no front opening, the only way to tell for certain which drive bays are available is to open the system. FRANKENPC is an example of a mid-tower case. A mini-tower case usually has only two drive bays (one 3.5-inch and one 5.25-inch), while a full tower case has room for as many as nine or ten drives.

Opening Up Your System

Cases vary—and some are *very* difficult to pop open. But in general, the following things are generally true (note the word "generally"—I'm covered in case you have a bizarre example of the case maker's art):

- Lower-cost and older systems (those with Baby-AT or LPX motherboards, many micro-ATX systems, and most desktop systems) have slide-off cases.

- Systems with ATX motherboards typically have modular cases and removable side panels.

Look for the screw locations to tell which you have. If you have a one-piece case with screws along the rear edge, you slide the cover off the rear of the system (see Figure 4.9). Desktop machines whose cases don't overlap the rear of the system have hidden screw sockets; you slide this type off from the front of the system (see Figure 4.10). If you have removable panels, you can remove the front panel and the left side panel (as viewed from the front) to add drives; just remove the left side panel to add memory or upgrade the CPU or motherboard (see Figure 4.11).

CAUTION: STOP! LOOK! THINK!

Don't Remove the Cover Until You Pull the Plug
Most recent systems aren't really *off*, regardless of how firmly you pushed the on/off switch on the front of the case. Usually, this switch just puts systems into a deep sleep and still allows a small amount of power to move through the system. Fiddling with a system that still has power flowing through it is a great way to fry a component (or yourself!). Unplug the system before you open it.

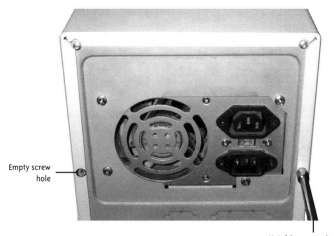

Empty screw hole

Nut driver removing screw

Figure 4.9

Removing the screws on a one-piece case. After the screws are removed, the case is lifted off to the rear.

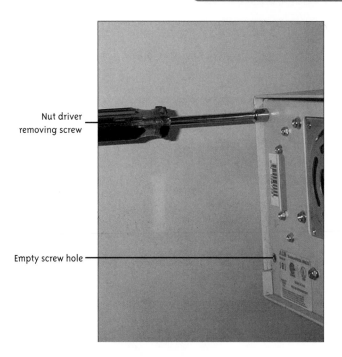

Figure 4.10

Removing the screws on a slide-off tower computer case. After the screws are removed, the case slides forward.

Nut driver removing screw

Empty screw hole

Screws holding top panel in place

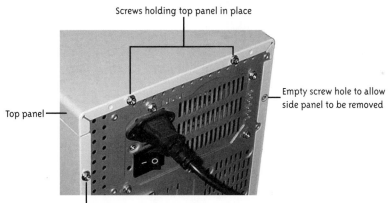

Figure 4.11

Removing the side-panel screws on an ATX case. The top, left-side, and right-side panels can be removed independently.

Empty screw hole to allow side panel to be removed

Top panel

Screw holding side panel in place

CAUTION: STOP! LOOK! THINK!

Before You Break It, Read About It

What do you do if your computer case doesn't resemble any of the ones shown? When opening cases, as with any other computer activity, it pays to read the manual. Every computer case that is intended to be opened by ordinary mortals has instructions on how to do it—somewhere. Check your computer vendor's company web site for information if the manual is missing. Keep in mind that some companies such as Acer use separate component manuals (yes, the case is considered a "component"), so you might need to find the model number of your case—or cross-reference your system model number to the case component number to get instructions.

Eyeballing Your System

If you're a "newbie" to computer upgrading, the first time you open your computer case could be an overwhelming experience. Don't get rattled! Figures 4.12 and 4.13 introduce you to the many components "under the hood" of a typical PC.

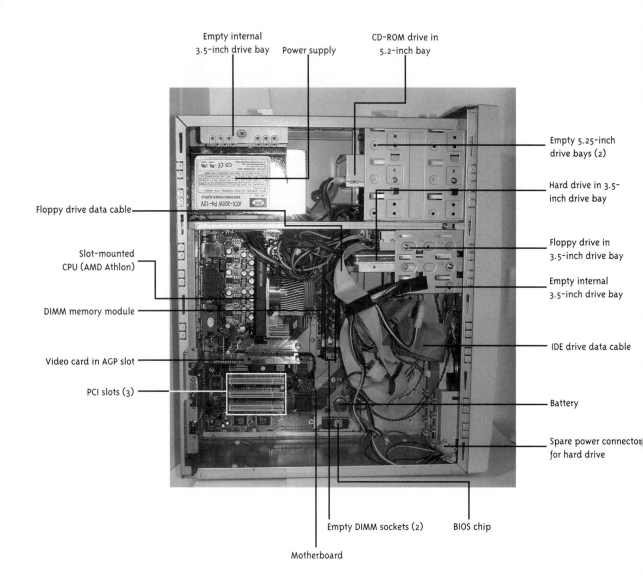

Figure 4.12

Inside FRANKENPC, the main subject of the upgrades covered in this book.

Figure 4.13 shows a section of a typical system with a socketed processor.

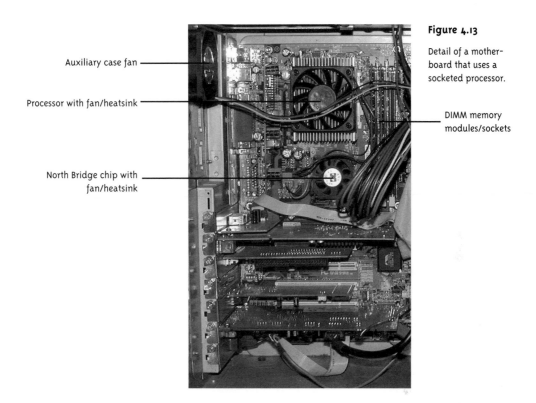

Auxiliary case fan

Processor with fan/heatsink

North Bridge chip with
fan/heatsink

Figure 4.13

Detail of a mother-
board that uses a
socketed processor.

DIMM memory
modules/sockets

Later in this chapter, you'll be seeing these parts "up close and personal," but Figures 4.12
and 4.13 are typical of what you'll find inside upgrade-worthy systems.

CAUTION: STOP! LOOK! THINK!

Look, But Don't Touch (Much)

As you look around inside your system, you might need to touch the stuff inside the case, but be careful! If the term
ESD looks like just another set of letters to you, skip to Chapter 5 to bone up on *electrostatic discharge*, which can
hose your motherboard, CPU, drives, RAM, and anything else that has computer chips on-board. Buy an ESD wristband, touch the case to ground yourself, don't touch chips or connectors, and be careful while you look around.

As you look around inside your system, the most critical factors to look for as you consider internal upgrades include the following:

- The motherboard form factor
- The number and type(s) of open expansion slots
- The number and type(s) of memory modules and open sockets
- The number and type(s) of open drive bays
- The size of the power supply

Motherboard Form Factor

A *form factor* is just a fancy way of saying what shape and size a device is. Because hammering a wrong-sized motherboard into place is *never* a good idea, use this section to find out what kind of motherboard your system uses. Your replacement motherboard (which is essential for making upgrades to the fastest CPUs and providing memory possible) needs to fit into your case the way your current model does.

There are four major form factors for motherboards:

- ATX
- Baby-AT
- LPX
- NLX

Figures 4.12 and 4.13 are two different examples of the most popular (and easiest to upgrade) motherboard form factor, ATX. ATX comes in three sizes, ATX, microATX, and flexATX. Full-size ATX motherboards have five or more expansion slots, while microATX motherboards have three or four expansion slots. The newest ATX sibling, flexATX, typically has only one expansion slot if any. Most systems use cases in proportion to the motherboard size. MicroATX motherboards are found in many low-cost mini-tower systems built by Compaq and HP that are popular at electronics superstores. FlexATX motherboards are found primarily in corporate small form factor/slimline systems. A full-size ATX case can handle the smaller sizes, but with the lack of slots, you probably wouldn't want to use the smaller boards. Compare Figures 4.12 and 4.13 to Figure 4.14, which shows the older Baby-AT motherboard design.

ATX-series motherboards (ATX, microATX, and flexATX) all use similar rear panels for their built-in ports. Refer back to Figure 4.8. If you have an ATX-family motherboard in your computer, you can easily upgrade the motherboard, which opens the door to most other system upgrades you want to make. However, if you have one of the other form factors, your upgrade options are very limited unless you want to move parts to a new case.

The Baby-AT motherboard shown in Figure 4.14 is a descendent of the original IBM PC motherboard from 1981! Because it was originally developed long before the current trend towards integrated ports, Baby-AT motherboards place the CPU in line with the expansion slots and use clumsy cables (not shown) to route built-in serial, parallel, PS/2 mouse and USB ports to external connectors. Although a few vendors built Baby-AT motherboards for Pentium II, Pentium III and Celeron-based processors, these motherboards are hard to find and are rapidly disappearing.

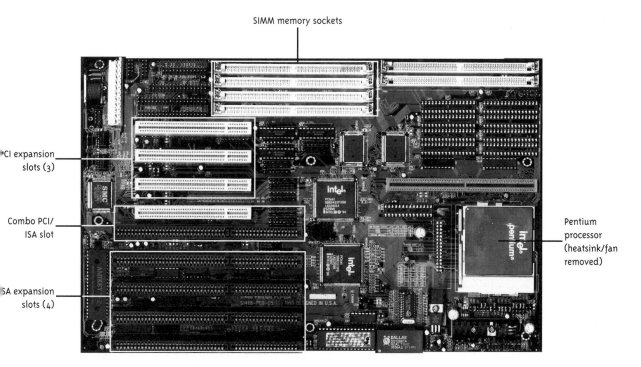

Figure 4.14

A typical Baby-AT motherboard. When a cooling fan (not shown) is added to the top of the CPU, three expansion slots are partially blocked.

A system with a Baby-AT motherboard has a rear panel similar to Figure 4.15. Note that the only port at the motherboard level is the keyboard port; other external device ports must be connected with ribbon cables and typically use brackets in unused card slots.

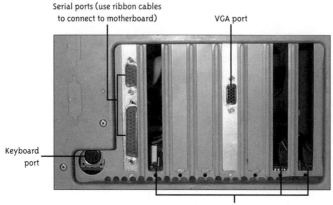

Serial ports (use ribbon cables to connect to motherboard)

VGA port

Keyboard port

Empty card slots (can be used for additional ports from motherboard or add-on cards)

Figure 4.15

Rear view of a typical system using a Baby-AT motherboard.

Before the microATX design became popular for low-cost "mass-market" computers, most of these computers used a type of design called LPX. LPX motherboards (see Figure 4.16) don't have built-in expansion slots. Instead, they use a riser card located near the middle of the motherboard for expansion slots. Because the riser card can mount the expansion slots at a 90-degree angle to the motherboard or can raise the expansion slots to a "double-deck" second level, there is no uniformity in motherboard design and therefore no motherboard-level upgrades. Although LPX motherboards, like ATX, have built-in ports, LPX ports attach to the rear edge of the motherboard, as seen in Figure 4.16.

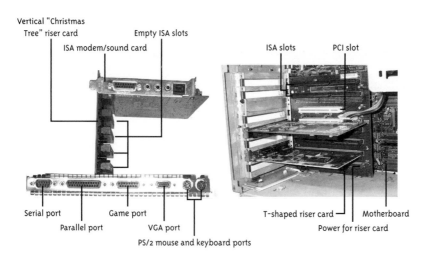

Vertical "Christmas Tree" riser card

ISA modem/sound card

Empty ISA slots

ISA slots

PCI slot

Serial port

Parallel port

Game port

VGA port

PS/2 mouse and keyboard ports

T-shaped riser card

Motherboard

Power for riser card

Figure 4.16

The figure shows two examples of the many variations in LPX-based systems. On the left is a motherboard with a vertical riser card; this system has one ISA card installed on the riser card. On the right is a double-deck LPX motherboard/riser card with ISA and PCI cards installed.

As seen in Figure 4.16 (left side), LPX motherboards always have a single row of built-in ports along the back side of the motherboard, although they differ in their specific arrangement. Don't confuse LPX motherboards with a much different riser card design, the NLX. The NLX motherboard also uses a riser card, but with three major differences:

- The NLX motherboard plugs into the riser card, not the other way around. This enables the motherboard to be pulled out of the system quickly for fast repairs in the field, and also allows a true standard for replacements.

- The riser card plugs into the side of the motherboard.

- The ports on the rear of the NLX motherboard are clustered in two rows somewhat similar to the design used by ATX systems (refer to Figure 4.8).

Although NLX systems, unlike LPX systems, use a standardized design that enables motherboard upgrades, they are cramped and limit room for expansion—and few third-party motherboards exist.

Rating Motherboard Designs by Their Upgrade Potential

The motherboard inside your system has an enormous impact on your ability to upgrade the system. Which motherboards offer you the best options, and which ones are better left alone?

- Best bets for upgrading: full-size ATX

- Doable, but not your best value: microATX and flexATX

- Can be done, but products are scarce and don't support new processors: NLX and Baby-AT

- Don't bother, almost impossible: LPX

Expansion Slots

Two computers can have identical motherboards, processors, and RAM, but the add-on cards installed in expansion slots can drastically affect how each system performs a given task. Your ability to upgrade your system with new ports and faster video is affected by the type(s) of expansion slots you have and how many you have.

How many do you have? What kinds? Which ones are still open? Before you buy an add-on card, you need answers to these questions. The most common expansion slot designs today include the following:

- **PCI**—An all-purpose expansion slot
- **AGP**—Designed strictly for high-performance video

Older systems might have one or more ISA slots, but with no recent add-on cards made in this design, ISA slots are practically useless for most upgrades.

Refer to Figure 4.14 to see how PCI and ISA slots compare to each other. Typically, the newer the motherboard, the fewer the ISA slots you will see (current systems have none).

JARGON

PCI—Peripheral Component Interconnect, a 32-bit wide, 33MHz slot developed in 1993 by Intel. Can also be used for video, but AGP slots are faster.

AGP—Accelerated Graphics Port, available in four speeds (1x, which is twice as fast as PCI; 2x, 4x, and now 8x).

ISA—Industry Standard Architecture, a slow and narrow (16-bit) slot design originating with the IBM PC and AT of 1981 and 1984.

Combo slot—Also called a shared slot, this is two physical slots that share a single-slot cover. You can use one slot or the other, but not both at once.

Figure 4.17 shows how AGP slots differ from PCI slots: The AGP slot is offset toward the middle of the motherboard and is normally made from dark-brown plastic. There can be only one AGP slot per system, so Figure 4.17 illustrates two different systems.

Note that AGP comes in four flavors: 1x, 2x, 4x, and 8x. Most recent motherboards are designed for AGP 2x/4x, but the newest AGP flavor, AGP 8x, can work in AGP 4x slots. If you have the original AGP 1x slot, you need to stick with AGP 1x or 2x cards only. Read your system documentation to figure out which types of AGP cards you can accept. Some systems use an AGP Pro slot. The Universal version of the AGP Pro slot (shown in Figure 4.17) will accept the widest variety of AGP cards, including lower-voltage high-speed cards that won't work in AGP 2x or AGP 1x slots. AGP 4x/8x slots are longer than original AGP slots, but are shorter than AGP Pro slots.

Figure 4.18 shows typical AGP video cards; one is designed for the original AGP slot, and the other is designed for the faster AGP slots.

r of motherboard

slots

Figure 4.17

AGP 1x/2x and AGP Pro slots compared to PCI slots.

AGP 1x/2x slot

AGP Pro slot

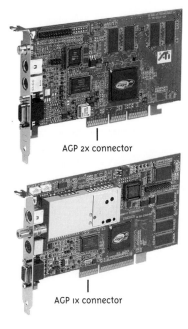

AGP 2x connector

AGP 1x connector

Figure 4.18

ATI's Rage Fury (top) uses the AGP connector typical of 2x and faster AGP cards. Compare the four-part connector on the bottom of the card to the three-part connector used on the earlier ATI All-in-Wonder 128 (bottom), which supports the original AGP 1x slot. Photos courtesy of ATI Technologies.

MARK'S TIP SHEET: When AGP Isn't Really AGP

One of the many reasons for going "under the hood" with your PC is to find out exactly what your friendly computer vendor actually means by AGP. AGP video can be built into your motherboard, but if it is, you're usually stuck with a low-end chipset-integrated solution that will get you killed right away in your next LAN party death-match. However, if you have an AGP slot, you can toss the system vendor's (usually) cheapjack AGP card and put a fire-breathing, hardcore card in there. Some systems have both on-board AGP and an AGP slot—but you don't know until you take a look.

ISA slots have been around in their current form since 1984 (the IBM PC used a single-connector 8-bit version of this slot back in 1981!). This slot design is too narrow (at only 16 bits of data), too slow (it runs at just 8.33MHz), and too stupid (it can't share IRQ settings) to be useful today. None of the popular add-on cards on the market today use this design. It's dead, Jim! Figure 4.19 compares ISA and PCI cards. Note that the cards face different directions, which makes the combo card slot seen in Figure 4.14 possible.

Figure 4.19

A typical ISA card (top) is compared to a typical PCI card (bottom). Both cards have two connectors, but the PCI card's connectors are smaller and have more "teeth."

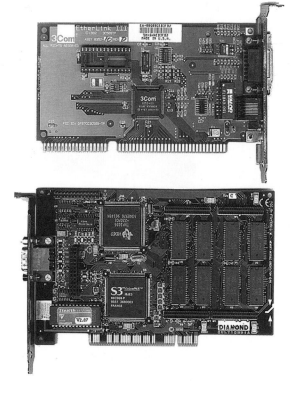

ANALYZE THIS

Why Counting the Slots from the Outside Is Misleading

You might figure you can just count the card bracket covers on the back of your system to figure out how many slots your motherboard has. Unfortunately, all you're really counting is how many slots your *case* supports. System manufacturers of all kinds, ranging from the big boys like HP to the corner "Joe's Computer Shack," frequently drop small motherboards into bigger cases. The system shown in Figure 4.12 is no exception; the case has seven slots, but the motherboard only has five slots. How can you use this annoyance to your advantage? If you're planning a motherboard upgrade, look for motherboards that provide the largest number of useful slots (AGP and PCI) that can fit into your case.

If all you have on your motherboard are ISA and PCI slots, use the PCI slots first. However, if you're looking for a video card upgrade, you really need to use the AGP slot if it's present. If your motherboard doesn't have an AGP slot, consider upgrading to a motherboard that does.

Rating Expansion Slots by Their Upgrade Potential

Your expansion slots control the kinds of card-based upgrades you can perform. Here's how to rate them:

- Best bet for video card upgrades: AGP

- Best bet for other devices: PCI

- Obsolete and basically worthless: ISA slots

Memory Types

Before you can add memory to your system (one of the best upgrades there is!), you need to find out what kind(s) of memory your system can handle, as well as what memory sockets are still available for upgrades.

These are the major types of memory on Pentium-class and newer systems:

- **168-pin DIMM**—Dual Inline Memory Modules are the leading memory type in use today, although DDR SDRAM is the most common type of memory in the newest systems. Almost all DIMMs use SDRAM (Synchronous Dynamic RAM) chips; very few DIMMs use the slower EDO memory chips. Because SDRAM DIMMs have been the most common type of memory for several years, expect your best memory deals to be on SDRAMs.

- **184-pin DDR SDRAM**—This type of DIMM uses double-data-rate (DDR) memory that can transfer twice as much data in a single clock cycle. The latest systems use DDR SDRAMs, but they're still a bit more expensive than standard 168-pin SDRAM modules.

These types of memory have completely replaced the once-common 72-pin SIMM (Single Inline Memory Module) memory devices. See Figure 4.20 for a comparison of SIMM and 168-pin DIMM memory. SIMM sockets can be seen in Figure 4.14.

Figure 4.20

The 168-pin DIMM (top) has replaced the 72-pin SIMMs (bottom) in recent systems. DIMMs can be added one at a time to most systems, unlike SIMMs, which must be added in pairs on Pentium-class and faster processors.

If you have a recent or a high-performance system, you might see one of these memory types instead:

- **184-pin DDR SDRAM**—This faster form of SDRAM memory (see Figure 4.21) costs a bit more than regular SDRAM; it's the new mainstream memory for systems 2GHz and faster.

- **RDRAM RIMM**—Rambus Dynamic RAM comes in a special memory module called a "RIMM" (Rambus Inline Memory Module), but if you look at the price tag you might suspect that RIMM really stands for "Really Impacts My Money!" RIMMs (see Figure 4.22) are about two to three times as expensive as DDR-SDRAM DIMMs, but some of the pricier Intel-based Pentium III and Pentium 4 systems require this so-called "Richie Rich" memory. Don't say I didn't warn you. Oh, and pay attention if you have a system that requires pairs of identical RIMM modules. Ouch—and double-ouch! RDRAM is faster in some benchmark tests, but most of us will notice the extra money it costs more than the performance gain.

Figure 4.21

A typical DDR (Double-Data-Rate) SDRAM module, designed to support the 1GHz and faster CPUs now available from Intel and AMD. Photo courtesy of Micron Technologies.

Figure 4.22

A typical RIMM module, required by several high-end chipsets that support the Pentium 4 processor. RIMM-using systems with dual-channel memory must use identical pairs, but others can use single or mix-and-match RIMMs. Photo courtesy of Micron Technologies.

Best Bets for Upgrading Memory

Your memory sockets (and motherboard/chipset features) dictate how much and what kind of memory you can use:

- Best bet for fast, economical memory upgrades: DDR-SDRAM or standard SDRAM (depends upon motherboard)
- Best bet for a new motherboard: specify a motherboard that uses DDR-SDRAM, particularly 333MHz DDR memory (also known as PC2700 DDR memory)

- Fast but overpriced: RDRAM

- Obsolete and expensive: 72-pin SIMM memory; any system that uses this memory isn't worth upgrading

Drive Bays

Although there are more and more external drives of all types on the market, you have to pay a hefty premium for the privilege of connecting a removable-media, rewriteable CD or DVD drive or a hard drive to an IEEE-1394 or USB cable. If you're mainly concerned about the best "bang for the buck," internal drives rule! However, if you want to add an internal drive, it needs an empty drive bay.

ANALYZE THIS

Internal Versus External Drives

Most removable-media drives are available as either internal or external forms, and hard drives are now available as IEEE-1394 and USB external drives as well as their normal internal IDE and SCSI forms. When you want to add a drive, which is better? These guidelines can help you sort out the best answers:

- **Speed**—Internal is faster. IDE (sometimes called ATA) provides a hefty improvement over USB 1.1. Most SCSI versions, USB 2.0, and IEEE-1394 are much faster than USB 1.1, but still lag behind IDE.

- **Cost**—Internal is cheaper *if* you need a drive for just one system. Internal drives don't need expensive cables, enclosures, or power supplies, enabling you to save quite a few bucks on your next drive purchase. However, if you need a particular drive type only occasionally and have more than one system, consider a USB 2.0 or IEEE-1394 external drive (but be prepared to add a card providing the port you prefer to systems that lack these ports).

- **Flexibility**—Externals are preferred. With USB or IEEE-1394 ports, you can hot-swap drives from system to system, allowing multiple computers to share a single drive for easy data transfer.

Speed? Cost? Flexibility? You decide which factors are more important to you and choose wisely.

JARGON

Hot-swap—A device that can be connected and disconnected from the system without shutting down the system. Windows 98SE and later versions of Windows allow you to hot-swap IEEE-1394 and USB devices. You can also hot-swap PC Card (PCMCIA) devices. Note that if the Eject/Safely Remove Hardware icon in the Windows toolbar lists the device, you should stop it with this dialog before you remove it.

There are two types of drive bays:

- **3.5-inch**—Use this type of drive bay for hard drives, floppy drives, and ZIP/SuperDisk removable media drives.

- **5.25-inch**—Use the larger drive bays for CD-ROM, CD-RW, and similar drives. You can also install high-capacity removable-media drives, such as the Castlewood ORB, into this size of drive bay.

Depending on the case, a varying number of drive bays are internal (hidden), meaning that there is no cutout on the front panel to give you access to the drive. The more removable-media drives you want to install, the more external (visible) drive bays you need. Figure 4.23 gives you an inside view of these drive bays on a typical ATX-based system. Some systems also have another hidden 3.5-inch drive bay located over the power supply (not visible in this picture).

Empty 5.25-inch drive bays   CD-RW drive in 5.25-inch drive bay

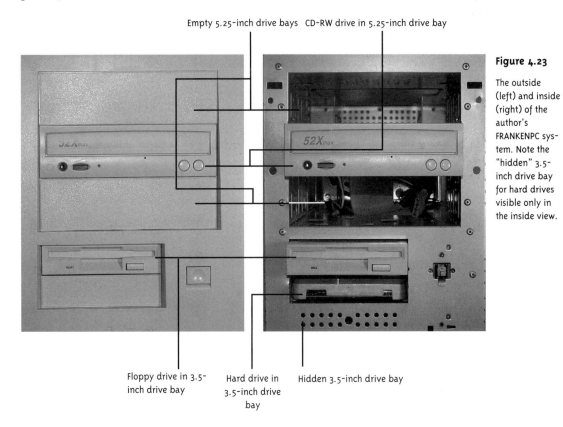

Figure 4.23

The outside (left) and inside (right) of the author's FRANKENPC system. Note the "hidden" 3.5-inch drive bay for hard drives visible only in the inside view.

Floppy drive in 3.5-inch drive bay

Hard drive in 3.5-inch drive bay

Hidden 3.5-inch drive bay

Some computers use plastic or metal drive rails to secure the drives into the 5.25-inch drive bays; make sure you have spares. Extra sets are usually provided by the system or case maker.

While you're at it, check to see if you have any unused power leads, and note whether they're for hard drives and CD-ROMs (large connector, often called the Molex connector after its manufacturer) or floppy drives (small connector). See Figure 4.24. If you don't have the right type of connector for your next drive (or for some power-hungry expansion cards), you can buy a Y-splitter and attach it to the end of a Molex power connector. The Y-splitter is an extension cable that has two Molex, two small connectors, or one of each connector on the arms of the "Y," enabling you to run two drives from a single power cable.

Figure 4.24

Small (top) and Molex (bottom) power connectors; the typical power supply has two or three of each type of connector.

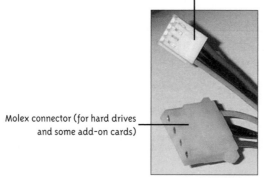

Small connector (for floppy drives)

Molex connector (for hard drives and some add-on cards)

MARK'S TIP SHEET: Shrinking the Big Drive Bay Down to Size

If you have a 5.25-inch drive bay available but want to add a 3.5-inch drive, don't panic. Many of these drives come with an adapter kit that enables you to put a small drive into a big bay (see Chapter 10, "Adding a Huge Hard Disk," for details). If your cheapjack bulk-packaged drive lacks this hardware, you can buy a separate adapter kit to do the trick. Don't ask about shoehorning a 5.25-inch drive into a 3.5-inch bay; I wore out a set of "as seen on TV" knives last time I tried that one.

Best Bets for Upgrading Internal Drives

The number and size of empty drive bays (or drive bays with drives you plan to replace) control whether you can use low-cost internal or must switch to higher-cost and often lower-performance external drives to add additional storage. Note the following:

- Best bet for adding rewriteable CD or DVD storage: a 5.25-inch drive bay with a removable panel.

- Best bet for adding a hard drive: a 3.5-inch drive bay (internal or external) is OK.

- No empty drive bays: Replace an existing drive or add external storage if you have (or plan to add) a USB 2.0 or IEEE-1394 port.

Power Supply Size

The capacity of your power supply (measured in watts and amps) has a direct effect on how much internal hardware you can safely install in your system. If the power supply doesn't have enough capacity, adding one of today's fastest (3GHz-class and faster) processors is off the table until you upgrade it.

To find out how much "oomph" your power supply has, don't bother whipping out your tape measure. Instead, look at the label on the drive. If you have a 4-bay midsize tower case (my favorite for balancing upgrade options and space), your power supply should have a rating of *at least* 300 watts (more is better), and it should always have safety certification indications from the major organizations, such as CSA and UL (see Figure 4.25).

Overall wattage rating

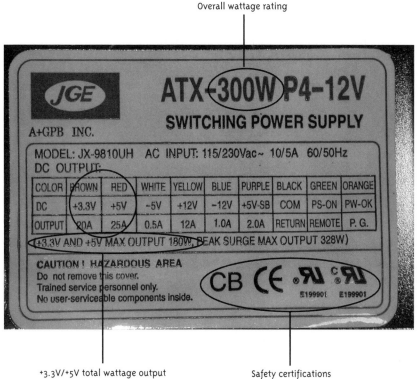

Figure 4.25

This is a 300-watt power supply, but the most important voltage levels on today's systems are the +3.3V and +5V ratings, which are used by the processor and PCI/AGP slots.

+3.3V/+5V total wattage output

Safety certifications

Mid-tower systems with power supplies under 300 watts might fall prey to lockups and crashes if you stuff the system full of cards and drives or add a faster processor. Why? Every component takes a slice of the wattage (see Chapter 22, "Power Supply Upgrades," for details). If the devices in your system and so-called "bus-powered" external devices (also powered by your system) ask for more wattage than your power supply puts out, or if the amperage needed by a particular device exceeds the power supply's rating, one or more of the following disasters is right around the corner:

- The power supply overheats when it tries to provide power beyond its specified output; overheating increases the temperature of other components in the case, causing CPU and memory failures.

- The voltage going to the motherboard goes out of the normal range under heavy loads, causing an immediate reboot.

- An overloaded power supply sends poor-quality power to your motherboard and attached components, causing the contents of memory modules to become corrupted and causing your system to lock up.

Bottom line? Think big (in watts, I mean). If you need to replace the power supply on your system, buy one that's at least 50 watts higher than the one in your existing unit; 100 watts or more higher is even better if you can afford it. There's no such thing as too much power.

But before you can buy a power supply, make sure you find out what type of motherboard connector it uses. The major types of power supply connectors to the motherboard are shown in Figure 4.26; some motherboards also require auxiliary 4-pin and 6-pin connectors (see Chapter 22 for details) to provide adequate power for the CPU and expansion slots.

JARGON

20-pin ATX power connector—Used by virtually all current systems that have ATX, Micro-ATX, and NLX motherboards, this connector is keyed to prevent incorrect power supply attachment.

6-pin auxiliary power connector—Some motherboards require this extra connector along with the standard ATX power connector to provide enough voltage for thirsty CPUs and peripherals.

4-pin ATX12V connector—The Pentium 4 requires extra 12V power, so its motherboards have a 4-pin connector as well as the standard ATX power connector.

Figure 4.26

An ATX motherboard uses the 20-pin power connector seen at left. Now-obsolete LPX and Baby-AT motherboards use the twin 6-pin connectors shown at right. If the black wires are not attached next to each other as shown, motherboard or power supply damage can result. See Chapter 22 for the gory details.

Best Bets for Upgrading Power Supplies

Your choices for upgrading your power supplies are determined by your motherboard. Buy a UL-listed power supply with the same form factor and connector type used by your system. Buy a high-quality unit with at least 50 watts higher rating than your current power supply. Note the following:

- ATX power connector: Clear sailing to bigger power supplies.
- LPX power connectors: Should you add a new power supply to an obsolete unit? Only do it if you can't upgrade to a new system.
- Dell computer built September 1998–2000: Find out from Dell or the power supply vendor if you need a Dell-compatible model before you buy it and plug it in.

Practicing: Some Upgrade Scenarios

All right, you've done your research and you're *almost* ready to start upgrading your own system. However, why not practice on one of these first?

Here, for your upgrading pleasure, are three systems crying out for upgrades:

- An AMD Athlon 600MHz system with an 13GB hard drive, a 32X CD-ROM drive, a 16MB VGA card, 64MB of RAM, a 56Kbps V.90 modem, Windows 98, AGP 2x, and PCI slots.
- A Celeron 700MHz with an 8GB hard drive, a 12X CD-ROM drive, integrated video with 32MB of RAM, a 33.6Kbps modem, Windows 98, and PCI slots only.

- A Pentium 4 1.5GHz system with a 20GB hard drive, a rewriteable (CD-RW) drive, 128MB RAM, a 56Kbps K56flex modem, Windows Me, and an AGP 4x slot.

All three of these machines are "behind the curve," but the extent to which they lag current products varies a lot. You'll note that no Pentium-based or earlier systems are listed. Although they can be upgraded, they're generally so far behind that virtually *everything* would need to be replaced, as you learned in Chapter 2 with the "three-years-and-out" rule. If you need to replace everything, guess what? You need a new computer. My goal is to help you make the changes you need most *without* buying a new PC.

Assume that you have a $300 upgrade budget to work with. With this play money, you can fix the most pressing problems these systems have.

Upgrading the Athlon 600MHz System

If you wanted to install a faster processor in this system, you're looking at a motherboard/processor upgrade ($200 to $250) because the 600MHz Athlon uses the now discontinued Slot A interface. However, if you're not using the system for gaming, you can get more for your money with a couple of other upgrades.

- **Boost the memory to 512MB**—Remove the 128MB module and stick in a couple of 256MB modules. Why not leave the 128MB module in and have 768MB of RAM? Windows 98 (and Windows Me as well) has a problem with memory addressing when you mix AGP video with more than 512MB of RAM.

- **Add a combo CD-RW/DVD drive**—So you can create your own music and data CDs and watch DVDs.

- **Add a 40GB hard drive**—So you can store more information and not need to erase files as often.

These upgrades create a much more productive (and enjoyable) system. See how this group of upgrades comes out, price-wise, in Table 4.4.

Table 4.4	Upgrading the Athlon 600MHz System		
Upgrade Rank	**Upgrade**	**Benefit**	**Estimated Cost**
1	512MB RAM (remove 128MB)	Speeds up system performance	$90 (2×256MB)
2	Combo CD-RW/ DVD drive	Backs up home and business data, plays DVDs	$125
3	40GB hard drive	More storage for data	$85
		Total	**About $300 (or less)**

Upgrading the Celeron 800MHz

First, forget about turning this aging beast into a game player's dream; without AGP slots it ain't gonna happen! However, you can get more out of this system without spending a bundle. Here are the most urgently needed upgrades for this system:

- **More RAM**—Any system running Windows 9x/2000/Me needs at least 128MB of RAM to do it right. At today's prices, 512MB of RAM makes sense. Depending upon the exact type of integrated video in the system, upgrading main memory might also make more memory available for the display to improve color quality at high resolutions and performance.

- **A bigger hard drive**—Before you go to the store to pick up a multi-gigabyte monster on a system with an 8GB or smaller drive, check your BIOS limitations; you might need to install a BIOS upgrade *first* to allow you to get a bigger drive. 40GB is a great size to upgrade to, since it's five times larger than the original drive, but is about the smallest drive on the market today. To learn how to tell if your BIOS has a problem with bigger drives, see Chapter 10.

- **Add a CD-RW drive**—Not only is the CD-ROM drive too slow in this system, but it can't read increasingly popular CD-RW media. A CD-RW drive can read any type of CD media.

- **Download faster**—A 33.6Kbps modem will drive you crazy with its slow, sloooow downloading of today's media-rich web sites and bigger music, operating system, and graphics files. If you can't get a broadband connection, consider getting a 56Kbps mode.

- **Upgrade the processor**—A 1.3Hz Celeron processor will boost overall speed, including video performance, and can be grabbed for a song if your motherboard is designed to handle it.

- **Upgrade to Windows XP Home Edition**—If you're more concerned about system stability than adding a bit more speed, this is a better upgrade than changing out the processor.

Table 4.5 shows how the upgrade costs work out for this system.

Table 4.5	Upgrading the Celeron 800MHz System		
Upgrade Rank	**Upgrade**	**Benefit**	**Estimated Cost**
1	256MB RAM (plus 128MB= 384MB total)	Speeds up system performance	$45
2	40GB hard drive	More room for data and applications	$80
3	CD-RW drive	Backs up home and business data	$75
4	56Kbps V.90 modem	Faster Internet surfing and downloading	$25
5 (tie)	Celeron 1.3GHz processor	Improves overall system and video performance	$55
	Windows XP Home	Better system stability	$95
		Total (with 1.3GHz processor)	**About $280**
		Total (with XP Home)	**About $320**

These five upgrades will make the system a much better performer.

Upgrading the Pentium 4 1.8GHz System

This computer has the most potential for upgrades, and is the best candidate of the three for broadband Internet. Consequently, I'd suggest:

- **More RAM**—Upgrading to 512MB of RAM makes sense with any recent version of Windows. If Windows XP Home is part of the upgrade process, keep the existing memory module. Otherwise, remove it to keep the system at 512MB of RAM for compatibility with AGP video and Windows Me.

- **Mid-range 3D graphics card**—Most system vendors use the cheapest 3D graphics card available; some still use two-and-three-year-old models to reduce costs. Consequently, even a low-cost card based on a current 3D chipset such as the ATI Radeon 9000 Pro will boost performance and visual quality. However, a small business user might prefer....

- **Windows XP Home**—I'm not crazy about Windows Me, folks (ironic, isn't it, since I helped write one of the standard references to it). However, the best parts of Windows Me (better driver installation, System Restore, and better multimedia features) are alive and improved in Windows XP. Best of all, an end to rebooting the computer almost daily!

- **Cable modem**—I *love* my cable modem, even though when I got my service I couldn't buy one outright the way you can now. While the cost listed in Table 4.6 doesn't include monthly Internet service, if you spend a lot of time online, that $40 or so (less if bundled with cable TV and phone) is a great deal.

Table 4.6 shows how these upgrades add up.

Table 4.6 Upgrading the Pentium 4 1.8GHz			
Upgrade Rank	**Upgrade**	**Benefit**	**Estimated Cost**
1	512MB of RAM	Speeds up system performance	$90 (2×256MB)
2	Mid-range 64MB 3D video card	Faster 3D graphics	$100
3 (tie)	Windows XP Home	Better system stability	$95
	Cable modem	Faster Internet connection	$75
		Total (with ATI Radeon 9000 Pro)	**About $265**
		Total (with Windows XP Home)	**About $240**

How about the K56flex modem? It's not the current standard, but if you're moving to broadband Internet, who cares? You might be able to get a free upgrade from the modem vendor for those occasional cable outages when you need to go online.

CAUTION: STOP! LOOK! THINK!

Jack of All Trades, Master of None?
Because computers are so versatile, it's way too easy to throw a bunch of mediocre components into a box and say you're ready to take on any computing job. What I've learned (often the hard way!) is that it's better to spend a bit more to get components that work the way you do. If you're a hardcore 3D gamer, you won't be satisfied with a $75 video card; likewise, if you want the security of being able to back up your data in a hurry, an old-school 12X CD-RW drive will leave you drumming your fingers waiting for the backup. It's up to *you* to figure out what jobs are most important to you. And it's also up to you to buy quality components that are fast enough and reliable enough to get the job done, whether it's blasting the bad guys or blasting through leftover work from the office. If you need to leave an upgrade off your list until later, it's usually worth it to spend a bit more to get a better, faster device that's important to what you do on a PC. Be sure to see Chapter 6 for a detailed list of upgrades by major computing task.

So far, you've learned what upgrades can do for you and how to find out what's in your computer, and you've practiced a few upgrade calculations on paper. But before you do anything else, you need to take some precautions. Follow me to Chapter 5, where you'll learn how to prepare for your upgrade.

Chapter 5

Preparing for Your Upgrade

Upgrading your computer is a big deal. You're investing some money, some time (unless you get your kids to do it for you), and some thought in return for transforming your old computer into a better, faster model. Do it wrong, and you have a big problem. Use this chapter to make sure you're ready for any problems you might encounter before you start the upgrade process.

Don't Upgrade Without a Net

Here's a scary thought: During your computer upgrade, your system is inoperable until you finish the upgrade process. Until you get everything back together, your computer is just a pile of parts and your data is locked away in various magnetic and optical bits and bytes.

What happens if things go wrong? Instead of wishing you'd been prepared, it's much better to prepare for the worst, and be pleasantly surprised when it doesn't happen.

Before you remove the first screw from your computer's case, take a little time to make sure you've created a safety net for your system—and your data—in case something goes wrong.

Your digital "safety net" should include the following steps:

1. Make a Windows Emergency (startup) Disk.

2. Back up your system.

3. Enable and use System Restore.

4. Record system (CMOS/BIOS) information.

5. Build and buy a computer toolkit.

Each of these issues is covered in detail in this chapter.

Because the exact steps you need to take vary with the version of Windows you use, Table 5.1 provides a quick-reference to the preparations needed for each version of Windows.

Table 5.1 Upgrade Preparations by Windows Version			
Windows Version **Upgrade Steps**	**Windows 9x**	**Windows Me**	**Windows XP**
Windows Emergency Disk	Yes	Yes	N/A
System restore	N/A	Yes	Yes
System backup	Yes	Yes	Yes
Record BIOS/CMOS information	Yes	Yes	Yes
Build/buy computer toolkit	Yes	Yes	Yes

Creating Emergency Disks

The Windows Emergency Disk (also called the Emergency Boot Disk, Emergency Startup Disk, or Startup Disk) is an essential part of every Windows 9x/Me user's software collection, yet many people don't consider this issue until their systems no longer start and it's too late to make one. Don't let this happen to you!

The Windows Emergency Disk for Windows 9x and Me is a bootable floppy disk that contains various command-line programs, such as hard disk preparation, used for system repair and special functions.

MARK'S TIP SHEET: The Windows XP CD Is the Emergency Disk

If you need to reinstall Windows XP, you can boot your computer with the Windows XP CD-ROM and repair your installation or reinstall Windows if necessary. Thus, there's no need to create an emergency disk. However, you'd better keep your Windows XP CD-ROM safe!

Why You Need the Windows 9x/Me Emergency Disk

The Windows Emergency Disk for Windows 9x/Me can be used to start your system in Command Prompt (DOS prompt) mode, transfer boot files to your hard drive to fix boot problems (with the Sys command) if your system fails to start, and prepare a hard drive for use (with Fdisk and Format). With Windows 98 or Windows Me, the Windows Emergency Disk can also be used to start the system with CD-ROM support (enabling you to reinstall Windows) and to display built-in help.

You are prompted to make the Emergency Disk during Windows installation, and that's the best time to do it. However, if you skipped that step, read on to learn how to create this essential protection for your system.

How to Make the Windows 9x/Me Emergency Disk

Whether you are running Windows 95/98 (9x) or Windows Me, open the Control Panel, click Add/Remove Programs, and click the tab called Startup Disk (see Figure 5.1). Provide a blank, formatted disk for drive A: when prompted and label it as prompted when done.

After the disk is completed with Windows 98 and Windows Me, write-protect the disk by sliding the write protect tab toward the top of the disk. When the write-protect hole is visible, the disk can't be changed, erased, or infected by a virus.

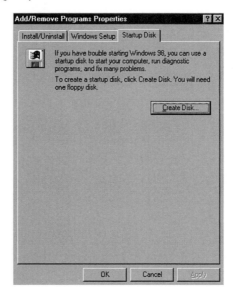

Figure 5.1

Making the Windows Emergency Disk in Windows 98.

Testing Your Emergency Disk

To make sure your Windows Emergency Disk works:

1. Leave the disk in drive A:.

2. Restart your computer from the Start, Shutdown menu.

3. Press the correct key to go into your computer's BIOS setup program. Look on the screen for a prompt indicating what key to press, or check your system manual. Some common keystrokes include Del, Esc, F1, F2, or F10.

4. Go to the Advanced Setup options and check the boot sequence or boot order; set the A: drive as the first bootable device *if* it's not already the first bootable device.

5. Save any changes and exit the BIOS setup program. The onscreen menu will display the correct keystrokes you need to save your changes.

6. Your computer should boot to an A:\> prompt.

If you have the Windows 98 or Windows Me version of the Emergency Startup Disk, you see a prompt to enable CD-ROM support during the boot process. Select this option, and then make sure you can read your Windows 98 or Windows Me CD-ROM in your CD-ROM drive after your system finished booting. Use the DIR *X*: command (replace *X*: with the actual drive letter used by your CD-ROM drive and displayed on the screen); if you see the contents of your Windows CD, your Emergency Disk is working correctly.

Enabling CD-ROM Support with Your Windows 95 Emergency Disk

Windows 95's Emergency Disk lacks built-in CD-ROM support, which is a big shortcoming if you need to reload Windows 95. However, you can add it if you know which file your system uses for command-prompt (also called *real-mode* or *16-bit*) CD-ROM device support. Open your computer's Config.sys or Config.dos file (located in the root folder of the C: drive—C:\) with Notepad or with the DOS-mode Edit program. Then look for a line similar to the following (this example uses MYCDROM.SYS as the name for the CD-ROM device driver; the actual name will be different, but usually has CD or ATAPI in the name):

```
DEVICE=C:\CDROM\MYCDROM.SYS /D:DRIVE01
```

You also might instead see a line resembling the following:

```
REM DEVICE=C:\CDROM\MYCDROM.SYS /D:DRIVE01
```

The REM (short for REMark) prevents the CD-ROM device driver from loading; Windows 9x adds the REM to the device driver line if the drive can be operated entirely by Windows.

Note the name of the folder (in this case, C:\CDROM) and the name of the file (MYC-DROM.SYS). The /D: option (/D:DRIVE01) names the device; this can be any name you like (how about Charley?), but it must match the option used by the Mscdex.exe program run in AUTOEXEC.BAT to finish setting up CD-ROM support. You need to create a file on the Emergency Disk, called Config.sys, to contain a reference to the CD-ROM device driver file, and you need to copy the CD-ROM device driver file to the Emergency Disk.

MARK'S TIP SHEET: Solving the Mystery of the Missing CD-ROM Drivers

What if you *don't* have MS–DOS-style CD-ROM drivers on your Windows 95 system? Here are some of my favorite ways around the problem:

- **Check your system recovery CD-ROM for drivers**—Look for a folder called CDROM or something similar, or for a filename containing CD and ending in .SYS.

- **"Borrow" a Windows 98 Emergency Disk for use in reinstalling Windows**—If you need to reinstall Windows, you can boot with the Windows 98 Emergency Disk and then rerun the Windows 95 SETUP program from the Windows 95 CD-ROM.

- **Contact the maker of your drive for compatible CD-ROM drivers**—Use the Windows Device Manager to display the brand name and model number of the drive, then check on the drive manufacturer's web site for an MS-DOS/Windows 3.1 driver. Despite the name, this driver also works with the Windows 95 Emergency Disk.

- **Find a compatible "generic" driver on the web**—The following web site offers a compressed archive of popular "generic" drivers: www.gcscanada.com/support/download/cdrom/generic/any_cdroms.htm.

Try each driver in your Config.sys to see which one works the best for you. On my systems, which use a variety of different brands of drives, I find that the Aoatapi.sys driver made by Oak Technologies works quite well.

Here's how to add a Config.sys file that adds CD-ROM support to the Windows 95 Emergency Disk. If your system lacks a reference to the CD-ROM driver in Config.sys, skip Steps 3–6.

1. Make sure the Windows 95 Emergency Disk is placed in drive A:. Close the write-protect slider if needed so that you can copy new files to the disk.

2. Start Notepad; click Start, Run, and type Notepad; click OK or click Start, Programs, Accessories, Notepad.

3. Open Config.sys or Config.dos; these are located in the root folder of C: drive (C:\).

4. Highlight the line containing the CD-ROM device driver and select Edit, Copy from the Notepad menu.

5. Select File, New from the Notepad menu to create a new file; do not save any changes to the previous file.

6. Select Edit, Paste to place the CD-ROM device driver line into the new (blank) document window in Notepad.

7. Edit the line with Notepad to resemble the following:

```
DEVICE=MYCDROM.SYS /D:DRIVE01
```

Note that, if it's present, the path to the driver file should be removed from the command because the driver file you will use to start your system will be copied to the Emergency Disk later. Also, remove REM from the start of the command so that the command will run when you start the system with the Emergency Disk. Use the actual name of your CD-ROM device driver in place of MYCDROM.SYS.

8. Add the following two lines to the Notepad document:

```
DEVICE=HIMEM.SYS
DOS=HIGH
```

9. When you are finished, the document window in Notepad should resemble the following:

```
DEVICE=HIMEM.SYS
DOS=HIGH
DEVICE=MYCDROM.SYS /D:DRIVE01
```

10. Select File, Save As and type the following for the filename:

```
A:\Config.sys
```

See Figure 5.2 for a typical example of Config.sys before and after editing.

By itself, the CD-ROM device driver does not enable you to use your CD-ROM drive when you boot the system. You also need to add a standard Windows command-line program called MSCDEX.EXE (which stands for Microsoft CD-ROM Extensions) to a separate file called Autoexec.bat. Here's how to use Notepad to create Autoexec.bat:

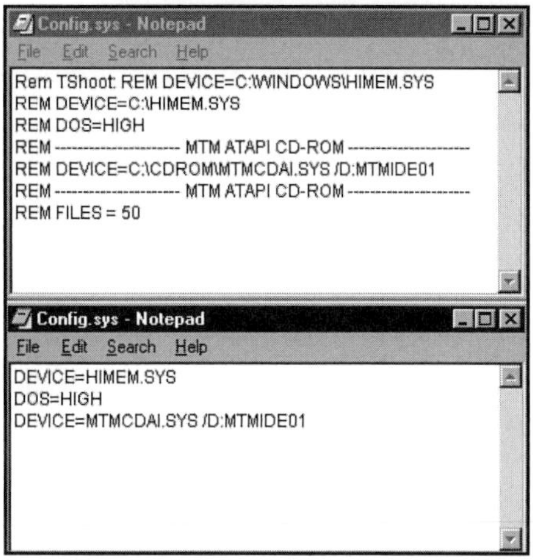

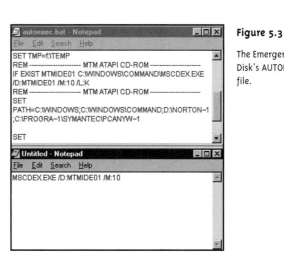

Figure 5.2

A typical example of Config.sys from the C: drive (top window) and the same file on the Emergency Disk after editing (bottom window).

1. Make sure the Windows 95 Emergency Disk is inserted into Drive A:.

2. Select File, New from the Notepad menu.

3. Type a line resembling the following into the blank document window:

```
MSCDEX /D:DRIVE01 /M:10 /L:X
```

   (The /D:*devicename* statement must match the /D:*devicename* statement used in Config.sys for the CD-ROM device driver. The /L:*driveletter* should use the same drive letter you normally use for your CD-ROM drive. For example, if your CD-ROM drive is normally G:, use /L:G.)

4. Select File, Save As and type the following as the filename:

```
A:\Autoexec.bat
```

See Figure 5.3 for a typical example of Autoexec.bat.

Next, use the Windows Explorer's Find command to locate the CD-ROM device driver, the Himem.sys memory manager, and MSCDEX.EXE. After you locate each file with Find, right-click the file and select Send to Drive A: to copy the file to the floppy drive. See Figure 5.4.

Figure 5.3

The Emergency Disk's AUTOEXEC.BAT file.

After you have copied all three files to the Windows Emergency Disk, shut down Windows and restart it with the disk still in drive A:. If A: is the first boot device, your system should boot *and* install CD-ROM support; change the boot order in your computer's BIOS setup program as described earlier to make the floppy drive first if the floppy disk is ignored at boot time. Test the CD-ROM drive to make sure you can access the Windows CD-ROM drive.

Now that you have a working Windows Emergency Disk with CD-ROM support, you have *part* of what you need to recover from an emergency. Next, you need backups of your data—or your entire system, if possible. If you're a Windows Me or XP user, though, go to the next section first.

Figure 5.4

Use the right-click Send To menu to copy the CD-ROM driver to the Windows 95 Emergency Disk in drive A:.

Using the System Restore Feature in Windows Me or Windows XP

System Restore, while not a replacement for system backups, is a great safety net for users of Windows Me or Windows XP. How does it work?

System Restore allows you to make a snapshot of your system state before you install a new hardware upgrade or software program. If the upgrade or installation backfires, you can roll back your system to its pre-upgrade or pre-installation condition. System Restore won't remove any data you create with the new hardware or software (or the program and driver files installed), but it will remove Registry settings created by those installations, essentially resetting your system to its previous condition.

System Restore automatically sets restore points, but I recommend you set a restore point yourself before you install new hardware or software.

To set up a restore point with Windows Me, do the following:

1. Click Start.

2. Click Programs.

3. Click Accessories.

4. Click System Tools.

5. Click System Restore.

If the computer indicates that System Restore has been turned off, click Yes to enable it.

Select Create a Restore Point to take a snapshot of your system. To roll back your system to its condition at an earlier time, select Restore My Computer to an Earlier Time, and choose the desired restore point from the calendar (see Figure 5.5).

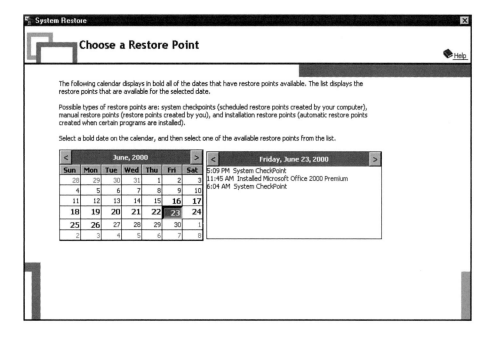

Figure 5.5

The Choose a Restore Point menu. On the date selected, two system checkpoints and a software restore point are available for rollbacks. Dates in boldface indicate other available restore points.

To set up a restore point in Windows XP, do the following:

1. Click Start.

2. Click All Programs.

3. Click Accessories.

4. Click System Tools.

5. Click System Restore.

The remainder of the process is similar to that used by Windows Me.

If the computer indicates that System Restore has been turned off when you start it, click Yes to enable it.

With Windows XP, Windows displays the System Restore tab of the System properties sheet if you need to enable it. Clear the checkmark next to Turn off System Restore on all drives to start System Restore (see Figure 5.6). By default, the system uses up to 12% of the space on each drive for restore points. To reduce the amount of space used for each drive, highlight a drive and click Settings, and then use the slider to adjust the disk space setting.

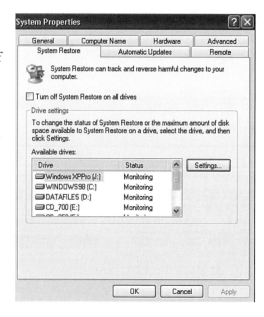

Figure 5.6

Enabling System Restore in Windows XP.

Making Backups

Why are backups so important? If you calculated the value of your computer based on how hard it would be to replace, your computer hardware would be worth very little. After all, as this book is telling you, hardware upgrades and even "build-it-yourself" solutions abound. Computer software is worth more because, in many cases, despite the improvements made in data import and export, it's still difficult for Program A to work with data created by Program B. Your library of computer software might easily cost more than your computer.

But what's at the top of the value list—literally priceless? Your data! After all, you can go to a store and buy hardware and software, but there's *never* any data for sale. Let's say you made a terrific digital photo, a figure-perfect family budget, the next Great American Novel, or a killer business plan. Great! Guess who's responsible for keeping it around? *You are!*

There are three considerations to making backups:

- **What** you back up
- **Where** you create your backups
- **How** your backups are stored on the media

ON THE WEB: Backup Help Is Just a Click Away

The TechTV web site is stuffed with backup tips, tutorials, and reviews of backup devices. Just use the Search tool on the TechTV home page (`www.techtv.com`) and specify Backup to find the information you need. If you're new to making backups, Leo Laporte's article "Backup Basics" at `www.techtv.com/callforhelp/howto/story/` `0,24330,2162034,00.html` is a great place to start.

What You Need to Back Up

At a minimum, you should back up your data *before* you perform an extensive upgrade that could affect your access to the hard drive. In addition to the hard drive itself, the CPU, BIOS, and motherboard could also decide to say "No data for you!" if something goes wrong during the upgrade. By backing up your data, you can resume work with a different computer if necessary after reloading your operating system and application programs. (Ugh!)

Table 5.2 lists the types of upgrades that are most likely to put your data at risk if anything goes wrong.

Table 5.2   Upgrades That Put Your Data at Greatest Risk

Upgrade Type	Risk to Data	Why
Motherboard	High	New motherboard's IDE host adapter might not be able to read the drive's data, especially if the BIOS or the IDE host adapter is different on the new motherboard.
Hard disk replacement	High	If data is not copied correctly to the new hard disk, you will lose it when the old hard disk is discarded or recycled into a different computer.

continues

Table 5.2 CONTINUED

Upgrade Type	Risk to Data	Why
Additional hard disk	Moderate	If you prepare the wrong hard disk, you could lose your data.
BIOS upgrade	Moderate	A failed BIOS upgrade renders your computer useless until you get a replacement BIOS chip or use the BIOS recovery feature on some systems.
Other upgrades	Slight	If you're upgrading an internal component, be sure to note any cables you need to remove and be sure to reattach them properly.

MARK'S TIP SHEET: In Search of Data

Wondering where your computer is stashing the letters, budgets, and cool digital images you've been making? Microsoft tries to make it easy to find them with Windows 9x and newer versions by creating the My Documents folder on C: drive for the files you make; many (but not all) Windows programs use this folder by default. If you have enabled user profiles on your system, you will have a folder for each user beneath the Profiles folder (Documents and Settings folder in Windows XP) instead. However, if you've gone your own way on storage, I hope you've had some kind of a plan and used some sort of a folder organization system for your files. If you're clueless about where your data and downloads are stored, you can:

- Open your applications and look at the Preferences, Tools, or Settings menu (names might vary) to see if your programs have default (normal) locations for files. If you're a cheapskate getting by with Windows' own WordPad and Paint, that folder is normally the Windows folder itself.

- Use Find to locate typical files by their extension (that three-character part of the filename that Windows likes to hide), such as .doc (Word files); .bmp (Paint files); .wpd (WordPerfect files); .xls (Excel files); .pcx, .tig, .gif, and .jpg (graphics files); .mp3 (MP3 music files); and so on. The Find option works well when you can't find what you're looking for in the program menu. After you've found your files, get organized! Use the Windows Explorer to create folders and subfolders in which to store your files to make them easier to back up.

Read "Backup Basics" on TechTV's web site to learn more places where data files such as saved games, email, and others like to hide:

http://www.techtv.com/callforhelp/howto/story/0,24330,2162034,00.html

If you have access to larger backup devices such as CD-R or CD-RW drives, high-capacity removable-media drives, or tape drives, consider backing up your entire system. This enables you to start working in just a couple of hours if you need to replace your hard drive when your existing drive stops working.

Where to Create Your Backups

The most convenient way to create your backups is to send backup files directly to some form of removable media. Several different types of media and technologies are available for you to use for backup storage, including the following:

- Floppy disks
- Super floppy (100MB and beyond) disks
- CD-RW/CD-R media
- Tape drives
- Hard disk-performance removable media drives
- External hard drives
- Online storage

Except for the floppy disk and online storage, each of the backup methods on the preceding list requires a special drive you might not already own. Be sure to consider the cost of the drive or service and how it connects to your system before you decide which backup solution is the best for you.

Now, let's see how these storage options compare to one another.

Floppy Disks

Everybody has a floppy drive. And floppy disks are cheap—*really* cheap (ever buy floppy disks and get more than you paid back as a rebate?). And so, everybody has a low-cost backup drive. So what?

Floppy disks have been a complete flop as a backup medium for some time. Even if you have only a 10GB drive to back up, it will take you over 6,000 1.44MB floppy disks to back up its contents! Even if you grab a few rebates along the way, you could have bought a much better backup drive long before you pay for 6,000 floppy disks. Installing and removing 6,000 floppy disks during the course of a single backup is a recipe for insanity unless you're tuned into

TechTV. In addition, floppy disks are also a flop when it comes to long-term durable storage; they're awfully good at developing bad sectors and taking your data with them. My advice? Forget floppies.

Even though backup software such as Windows Backup and third-party solutions enable you to use multiple disks for a single large file you're backing up, the notion of juggling hundreds or thousands of floppy disks is ludicrous. Any of the following options are better—but some are *much* better than others.

"Super Floppies" Aren't Super When It Comes to Big Backups

If you're content to back up just your data, the so-called "super floppy" drives such as the Imation LS-120 SuperDisk (120MB), rare second-generation SuperDisk LS-240 (240MB), or Iomega Zip drives (100MB, 250MB, and 750MB) are better than a floppy; if you need to back up a more-modest 4GB of data, however, you're still juggling anywhere from six (750MB Zip) to as many as 40 (100MB Zip) of these disks. The least expensive of these solutions, the 750MB Zip, will set you back about $80 per backup, while the Zip 100 will set you back about $90 per backup. SuperDisk media is even more expensive. If you don't have a Zip drive, you need to buy one at a cost of anywhere from about $70 (Zip 100) up to as much as $150 (Zip 750).

I've used my trusty Zip 100 frequently over the years for works in progress. But backing up a few book chapters or technical graphics is a far cry from saving your entire hard drive. With hard drive capacities climbing, there are better solutions.

Tape Drives

Low-cost tape drives, whose major advantage is the capability to store an entire multi-gigabyte drive on a single tape, are hard to find these days. Given a high-capacity tape drive's "one tape does it" capability, why don't more people use tape drives? Why did I get rid of *my* old tape drive?

First, unlike CD-RW and CD-R media, which are standardized and easy to find, even at your local drug store, it seems as if there are about a zillion different incompatible standards for tape drives (Travan, DAT, QIC-Wide, OnStream, VXA, and so on) that make it hard to find compatible media. When you add common media problems such as tape stretching and broken tapes (both of which destroy your backup), it's easy to see why the lower-cost standards, such as Travan, aren't as popular as they used to be. Tape still has its place, but the higher cost of reliable drives ($500 and up) has meant that tape has largely been relegated to network file servers used by companies who can afford the more durable tape cartridge designs built for automated insertion and fast overnight backups.

High-Capacity Removable Media

Looking for a hard-disk sized removable cartridge for backups? This once-thriving segment of the marketplace is now about extinct. Iomega's two ventures into this market, the older Jaz (1GB and 2GB) and newer Peerless (10GB and 20GB) are now discontinued, while Castlewood's Orb drives (2.2GB and 5.7GB) are hard to find at most computer stores.

Although these units boast performance similar to hard drives and can even be used as primary (boot) drives, their cartridges are far more expensive per MB/GB than even floppy disks. For example, an Orb 2.2GB cartridge costs about $30 each in three-packs, and a Jaz 2GB cartridge is about $100 each in three-packs. With prices like these, you can go broke in a hurry by using them for hard disk backup.

External Hard Drives

If you're looking for primary storage that can also double as backup, the new breed of large USB 2.0, FireWire/IEEE-1394, or combo USB-FireWire drives are a great choice. Available in capacities from 20GB to over 200GB, these drives can be moved from one computer to another in just a minute or two, and some include backup features such as one-button launching of backup programs.

The only drawbacks to this technology are price ($150 to $300 or more per drive) and the question of long-term storage of data you might want to keep. Even a 250GB behemoth is eventually going to run out of capacity. However, you can always move data to one of the following backup methods: CD-R/RW or rewriteable DVD.

Fast, Cheap, and Reliable—Why CD-R and CD-RW Rule!

From the standpoint of low operating costs for backups, it's hard to beat today's CD-RW drives, especially when you use them with CD-R media. What's the difference? The shiny smooth silvery CD-RW (CD ReWritable) surface can be written to, erased, and rewritten up to 1,000 times, whereas the gold-, green-, or blue-surfaced CD-R (CD Recordable) is a write-only (no rewrite) medium. However, you can buy high-quality CD-R media from major vendors for as little as $20 for a *cakebox* container of 50 or more 700MB platters. Even if you need to use several to back up your system, at a cost of about 40 cents (or less) per

CD-R platter, there's very little to complain about. In addition, CD-R media can be read by almost any CD-ROM drive, old or new.

If you'd rather rewrite and erase the contents of the media after awhile, you have to pay more for rewriteable media, but in quantities, you're still looking at under 60 cents a platter. CD-R/RW is the best backup deal around for making backups up to 3GB or so, especially if you already have the drive and backup software (included with more and more drive models).

Rewriteable DVD (DVD+R/RW, DVD-R/RW, DVD-RAM)

Everything you like about CD-R and CD-RW backups is also true about rewriteable DVD, plus more—more capacity, that is. Instead of stopping at 700MB per disc, rewriteable DVD drives store up to 4.7GB (over $6^1/2$ times more data!) per disc. While drive prices are still about three times higher than for high-speed CD-RW drives, you can get your choice of models for around $300 each. The biggest debate? Which rewriteable DVD standard to choose! I'll give you my 2 cents worth about that issue in Chapter 12, "A Burning Desire for Better Optical Drives." I use rewriteable DVD and CD-RW drives in my systems, and they're a great way to back up the data I care about.

Online Storage

As many people are fond of noting, the Internet has changed everything, including where people back up information. Online storage now makes it possible for you to back up information from one web-enabled computer and access it from another web-enabled computer anywhere in the world.

There are two types of online storage worth considering:

- Those that treat the online storage location like an additional disk drive, such as Xdrive Plus (www.xdrive.com), SwapDrive (www.swapdrive.com), and others.
- Those that automatically back up data for you, such as Connected TLM from Connected Corporation (www.connected.com), @backup from SwapDrive (www.backup.com), and others.

These services don't require a special drive and let you get to your data from anywhere. However, three big limitations: cost, capacity, and backup speed might mean that these aren't the best solutions for you.

Cost and capacity are directly tied to each other: the more data you want to store online, the more it will cost you each month. For example, SwapDrive lets you store 300MB online for $22.50/month; get two months free with a yearly contract for $225.00. At first glance, Connected offers a much better deal at 4096MB (4GB) of backup for $14.95/month. However, Connected is a background service that backs up files automatically after your initial setup, so that 4GB of storage could encompass a lot of changes to existing files rather than new files.

Naturally, all this takes time. Don't even *think* about online backup/storage services unless you have a broadband Internet connection. And, be sure to try the free trial offers most companies provide before you pay your money. You might discover that online backup is painless, or you might prefer the additional capacity and control of backup media you can see and touch.

Which Upgrade Should You Make First?

My advice? If you don't already own a *reliable* CD-RW drive with at least 40X write and 10X rewrite, no matter which other upgrade you are considering, make a CD-RW or rewriteable DVD drive the *first* upgrade you buy. When system failure or user error wipes out your data, you'll thank me for suggesting it.

How to Record Your Data

The simplest way to "back up" your data is to copy the files directly to the media. This is the approach taken by Iomega's Automatic Backup software, which enables you to use any removable media drive as an automatic backup device. If you need the file, just drag it from the drive and you can use it instantly.

If you don't mind doing a bit of work, you can do the same thing yourself with most types of drives (except for some tape drives and CD-R drives). Just open Windows Explorer and drag and drop the files and folders you want to back up onto the icon for the removable drive of your choice. This works fairly well for data-only backups that aren't too large, but it doesn't work with files that are larger than your backup media or for complete system backups.

To back up large files or your complete system, you need a true backup program that compresses your files (if desired) to save space on the media and that allows you to "span" a large file or backup across multiple disks or CD-R/CD-RW platters. Because the data is no longer in its original form, you must use the backup program's restore function to retrieve your files to a drive for use.

MARK'S TIP SHEET: Beating the Backup Blues

If you've never used a backup program before, here are a few tips to help you out, no matter which backup program you use.

- **Make sure a full backup is a *full* backup**—Probably the easiest way to do this is to use the backup wizard feature provided with many backup programs. For example, when you start the Stomp Back Up My PC program, select Back Up My Computer, All Selected Files, and then select where to store the backups and accept the defaults for compression and comparison, you can start the back up your entire drive with just a few mouse clicks! (Note that by selecting My Computer, you back up files on all local drive letters.)

  If you run backup programs manually, make sure you select the drives you want and that you back up the Windows Registry (and System State with Windows XP). After all—no Registry or System State equals no working system!

- **Don't forget to use safety options**—Although the verify step might double the total backup time with most types of backup drives, it's worthwhile to use this option with any backup. If verify fails, you're notified and the data can be backed up again. It's cheap insurance against making "backups" that don't really back up anything.

JARGON

Full backup—A backup of all files and folders on the system.

Differential backup—A backup of only the files and folders that have changed since the last full backup.

Verify—Compares the data on the backup device with the data on your hard drive.

Compression—Storing information in less space than normal. Already-compressed data, such as archive files, and graphics files, such as .jpg, .gif, and some types of .tif files, are stored without additional compression.

Figure 5.7 shows you one of my favorite backup programs, Stomp's Back Up My PC, in operation.

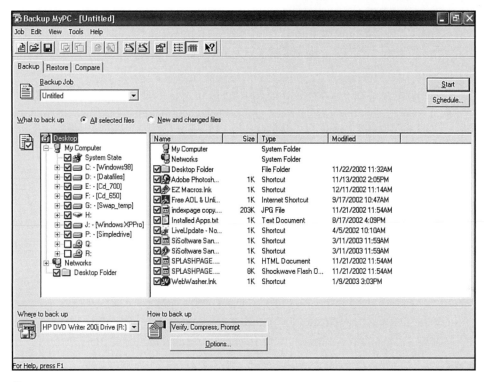

Figure 5.7

Manually selecting which drives to back up gives you more control, but it also means that you must verify that options such as backing up the Windows Registry (9x/Me) or System State (XP, shown here) are set correctly.

There are a lot of backup programs on the market, not to mention those included with Windows, so which ones will work best for you?

First, consider the backup programs provided with Windows; after all, they're free!

- Windows 95's built-in backup program works with only a few outdated tape drives and the humble (and outdated!) floppy disk.

- The built-in backup programs included with Windows 98, Windows Me, and Windows XP are a little better, because they work with most recent tape backups and non-floppy removable media, such as LS-120 SuperDisk and Zip drives.

Unfortunately, none of these backup programs is designed to work with CD-R or CD-RW media. The Windows 98, Me and Windows XP backup programs will copy compressed files to a CD-RW or CD-R drive set up as a removable drive with a program such as Roxio's DirectCD. However, they don't support backup spanning (which enables you to switch to another disk when the first one is filled up) with CD-R or CD-RW drives. When you run out of space on your first CD-R or CD-RW disc, your backup grinds to a halt with an "out of space" error message and can't be restored. This reminds me of one of my favorite ways to refer to not-very-useful, but free programs: "It's worth every penny I paid for it."

A truly useful backup program lets you back up data to your choice of tape, CD-R, CD-RW, rewriteable DVD, external hard drive, other removable media drives, or network drive and also supports a feature called *disaster recovery*. The disaster recovery feature enables you to start a computer from a special set of bootable floppy disks or a bootable CD and restore your system from the backup media without reinstalling Windows and your backup software. Although Windows' own backup programs don't work this way, most backup programs you can buy from third-party vendors provide this as either a standard or extra-cost feature, including such programs as NovaStor's NovaBackup, Stomp's Back Up My PC (based on Veritas Backup Exec), Dantz Restrospect, NTI Backup Now Deluxe, and others.

If your backup program doesn't support CD-R/CD-RW drives, you can use a program such as PowerQuest's DriveImage or Norton's Ghost (also part of the Norton System Works Professional program) to create a compressed file for backup. The latest versions of these programs record directly to CD-R media (Ghost also supports DVD media). Because many backup programs are included with tape or CD-RW drives or may be included as part of a software suite, you may already have a suitable backup utility right under your nose.

Did Your Backup Work?

There are three kinds of users:

- Those who don't back up their information.
- Those who back up their information and then can't retrieve it.
- Those who back up their information and retrieve it when they need it.

ON THE WEB: Better Backup Software Is a Click Away

Learn more about major third-party backup solutions from the vendors' own web sites:

- **Dantz (Retrospect, Retrospect Express)**—www.dantz.com
- **Stomp (Back Up My PC, Simple Backup)**—www.stompinc.com
- **NovaStor (NovaBackup for Disk/CD-RW, DVD; NovaBackup for Tape)**—www.novastor.com
- **New Tech Infosystems (NTI Backup Now! Deluxe, Backup Now!)**—www.ntibackupnow.com
- **PowerQuest (DriveImage)**—www.powerquest.com
- **Symantec (Norton Ghost)**—www.symantec.com

Guess which group you want to be in?

How can you avoid that "I'm dead" feeling when you try to restore information from a backup—and can't? Test your backup process. What does "test" mean?

1. Make a backup of the information you want to save (just your data or your entire hard disk).
2. Restore a few files to a different folder or (for a full system backup) to an empty hard disk.
3. If you can restore the files, your backup works!

Remember that if you want to test a "disaster recovery" backup, you need to start out with an empty but formatted hard drive (*not* your existing drive full of information) for testing the restore function. This is a perfect use for an older "spare" drive you might have lying around.

If you can't read your backup or you can't restore any or all of the backed-up files, contact the backup software vendor for help. Be sure to write down any error messages you see and make sure you have installed the latest patches and updates for the program. Try it again after you've gotten updates or other help. After your backup works, go on to the next step: recording your BIOS setup information.

Recording System Information

The system BIOS controls many parts of your computer, but it doesn't store the settings you make for such items as hard drive and floppy drive types, parallel and serial port settings, and so forth. Another chip on the motherboard called the *CMOS* (for its Complementary Metal-Oxide Semiconductor design) or, more properly, the *RTC/NVRAM* (Real-Time Clock/Non-Volatile RAM) is responsible for remembering your menu selections from Cafe BIOS.

The most important reason to record your BIOS/CMOS settings is in case you lose access to your hard drive or need to use your hard drive on another machine. Each hard drive uses a series of numerical settings called its *geometry*, and if the drive geometry isn't set exactly the same way on a new computer as on the old one, or isn't reset after being changed, you aren't able to access data on the drive.

However, the hard drive isn't the only setting you need to record. Port settings, IDE performance settings, boot order, and many more should also be recorded. Why should you record this information?

- If a battery failure, user error, or computer virus wipes out these settings, you won't be able to access your system until they're restored.
- If your upgrade strategy includes a motherboard upgrade, you'll need to provide these settings to the new motherboard's BIOS setup program to enable your new motherboard to read your current drive's contents.

To access the BIOS/CMOS program's menu, you normally press a specified key displayed onscreen when you start the computer. Figure 5.8 shows a typical BIOS standard setup screen, while Figure 5.9 shows a typical boot-sequence screen.

When the BIOS has a main menu, use the arrow keys to select the menu to view; some BIOS versions display the standard menu as the initial menu, and use a top-level menu or function keys to move to other screens.

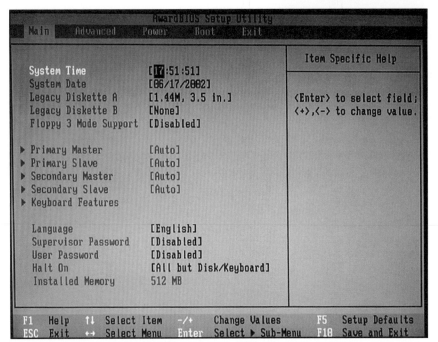

Figure 5.8

A typical BIOS standard setup screen; access to other screens is available through a top-level menu.

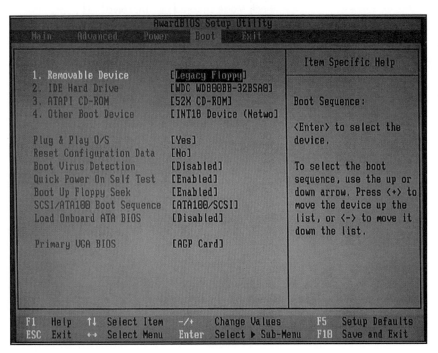

Figure 5.9

A typical BIOS screen, which lets you adjust the boot sequence of your drives.

Use the worksheet shown in Table 5.3 to record your system's settings. This worksheet is based on recent versions of the AMI and Award BIOSes, which are popular choices in the industry. Option names and menus might vary between BIOS versions and BIOS brands. Not all BIOS options are listed, such as Memory (Advanced Chipset) options, because these affect relatively few users. Use the additional blank lines for less-important BIOS options you decide to record.

Table 5.3 CMOS/BIOS Information

Date ___/___/____   **System Name** _____

Standard CMOS Settings

Floppy Drive A: _____   Floppy Drive B: _____

First IDE drive

Auto? _____ (If yes, skip other items.)

Heads ____ Sectors per track ____ Cyl _____

LBA Mode (a.k.a. DOS Mode) _____

CD-ROM ____ LS-120/ZIP/Other ____

Block Mode Enabled ____ Disabled ____

PIO Mode _____ UDMA Mode _____

Second IDE drive

Auto? _____ (If yes, skip other items.)

Heads ____ Sectors per track ____ Cyl _____

LBA Mode (a.k.a. DOS Mode) _____

CD-ROM ____ LS-120/ZIP/Other ____

Block Mode Enabled ____ Disabled ____

PIO Mode _____ UDMA Mode _____

Third IDE drive

Auto? _____ (If yes, skip other items.)

Heads ____ Sectors per track ____ Cyl _____

LBA Mode (a.k.a. DOS Mode) _____

CD-ROM ____ LS-120/ZIP/Other ____

Block Mode Enabled ____ Disabled ____

PIO Mode _____ UDMA Mode _____

Fourth IDE drive

Auto? _____ (If yes, skip other items.)

Heads ____ Sectors per track ____ Cyl _____

LBA Mode (a.k.a. DOS Mode) _____

CD-ROM ____ LS-120/ZIP/Other ____

Block Mode Enabled ____ Disabled ____

PIO Mode _____ UDMA Mode _____

Boot Sector Virus Protection

Enabled ____

Disabled _____

(Use the following rows for additional settings.)

_____   _____

_____   _____

_____   _____

Advanced CMOS Settings

First Boot Device _____   Second Boot Device _____

Third Boot Device _____   Fourth Boot Device _____

Boot Up Num Lock _____   PS/2 Mouse Support _____
Enabled?

Display Type _____   Check Password? _____

Internal (L1) Cache _____   External (L2) Cache _____

USB Ports Enabled? _____   USB Legacy Support _____
                                     Enabled?

ECC Memory In Use? _____   _____ _____

(Use the following rows for additional settings.)

_____   _____

_____   _____

_____   _____

_____   _____

Power Management

APM Power Management _____   ACPI-Aware OS _____
Enabled?   (Win98/ME/2000/XP)

Power Button Use   Suspend ____   Ports Monitored? _____

Shut Down ____

(Use the following rows for additional settings.)

_____   _____

_____   _____

_____   _____

_____   _____

Plug-and-Play and PCI Settings

Plug-and-Play _____   Use IRQ for PCI VGA? _____

Operating System?

(Use the following rows for additional settings.)

_____   _____

_____   _____

_____   _____

Peripheral Settings

Floppy Controller _____   Primary IDE Enabled? _____

Enabled?

Secondary IDE _____   Parallel Port Type _____

Enabled?

Parallel Port Setting _____   ECP Mode Type _____

Parallel Port IRQ _____   Parallel Port DMA _____

Serial Port 1 Setting _____   Serial Port 2 Setting _____

(Use the following rows for additional settings.)

_____   _____

_____   _____

_____   _____

Password Settings

User _____   Supervisor _____

Remember, if you upgrade your BIOS chip or move your drive to another system, you might need to reset the hard drive information in the BIOS. Settings such as boot order, plug-and-play, power management, peripheral settings, and so forth can affect how fast and how reliable your system is.

CAUTION: STOP! LOOK! THINK!

Look, But Don't Change the BIOS Settings

Be sure to choose the Exit, Discard Changes, or Exit, Don't Save Changes option when you're through writing down BIOS setup information. Because it's easy to change a setting by mistake as you move through different menus, and changing a setting could cause system problems, exit in a way that disregards any changes you might have made by mistake. Save changes only if you are working in the BIOS to make changes on purpose.

Building or Buying Your Toolkit

If you plan to perform even one internal PC upgrade, you ought to buy a set of computer-specific tools instead of rooting around in your household toolbox for a chewed-up Phillips screwdriver and a battered pair of pliers. Why? As with any task, computer upgrading is easier to do if you have the right tools. You don't need to spend a mint, but you do probably need to add a few tools to the typical low-cost PC toolkit available at stores.

CAUTION: STOP! LOOK! THINK!

Why Not Just Raid Your Toolbox?

Computer toolkits can be a little more expensive than ordinary tools from the hardware store, but there are some good reasons to pay more, including the following:

- **Demagnetized tools**—Although you can't damage the data on a hard disk with the weak magnetism used by some screwdrivers to hold screws in place, floppy disk and removable media such as Zip and SuperDisks might not survive a close encounter. If you do use magnetized tools (which are handy for working with screws), keep them away from your magnetic media.

- **Specialized tips**—Whenever possible, you should use a hex driver to insert or remove hex-shaped screws commonly used in computers. Why? Hex drivers don't slip off the screw the way that Phillips and straight-bladed tools will. If your screwdriver slips when you're installing a motherboard, you've probably ruined it if you scratch the wire traces on the top of the motherboard. The most common hex sizes are part of any computer tool kit, along with very small screwdrivers useful to tightening cable thumbscrews and star-shaped Torx drivers used on some Compaq models.

- **ESD protection**—Computer tools are designed to reduce the possibility of ESD discharge.

All in all, it pays to pick up a computer toolkit before you dive inside your PC.

What's in the Typical PC Toolkit?

Belkin's F8E060 11-piece tool kit is a typical example of a low-cost (around $15) computer toolkit. It contains the following items:

- Two nut drivers (1/4" and 3/16")
- Two slotted screwdrivers (3/16" and 1/8")
- Two Phillips screwdrivers (#1 and #0)
- One TORX screwdriver (T15)
- One three-pronged parts retriever
- Tweezers
- One chip extractor
- One zipper case

What Else Do You Need?

The Belkin kit (and its similar rivals) provides a good start, but these low-cost kits are usually missing a few items, including needle-nose pliers (great for straightening bent pins at the end of a cable), a magnifying glass (useful for us over-40 types who like to perform our own upgrades), a flashlight (great for working inside a case under the desk), interchangeable-tip screw/nut/Torx driver, and electro-static discharge (ESD) protection devices to prevent you "frying" your computer parts while you're working. Some vendors offer kits with some of these additional tools, or you can build the perfect kit by buying what you need separately.

ON THE WEB: Ultimate PC Toolkit

Check out the TechTV web site article, "Ultimate PC Toolkit," for additional tools to add to your system, as well as spare parts to have on hand. Find it fast by entering the article title (including quotes) into the TechTV search engine at `http://cgi.techtv.com/search` or use the following URL:

`http://www.techtv.com/screensavers/answerstips/story/0,24330,5812,00.html`

Why ESD Protection Is Important

If you've ever had a shocking experience from touching a doorknob on a winter day or almost blown your lips off from kissing your sweetheart (my wife and I still have it!), you've experienced electro-static discharge (ESD). ESD takes place when two items with different electrical potentials come close to each other or touch each other. The results aren't always visible (miniature lightning) or detectable (ouch!), but it takes very little ESD to damage or destroy computer parts.

How much is "not very much," you ask? Consider this: It takes about 800 volts of ESD for you to get a tingle or shock. It takes less than 100 volts (an amount you can't even feel) to ruin a CPU, memory module, or other computer part. Low-power construction makes these parts very vulnerable to ESD.

You can sometimes find ESD protection devices such as wrist straps (see Figure 5.10) and antistatic mats at a local electronics store, computer store, or Radio Shack. If you can't find the toolkits you want locally, one of many good online sources for anti-static grounding straps and work area mats is e-Mat (www.anti-staticmat.com/). Look for field service kits, which combine a grounding strap for your body with a grounded parts mat for components you are removing (or installing).

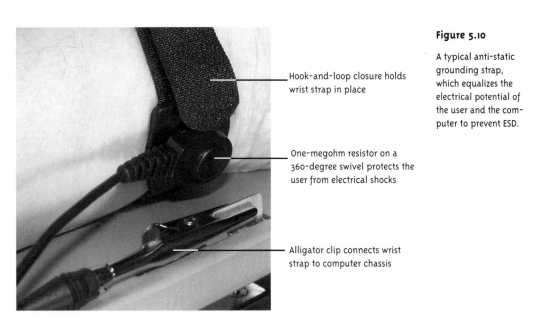

Figure 5.10

A typical anti-static grounding strap, which equalizes the electrical potential of the user and the computer to prevent ESD.

Hook-and-loop closure holds wrist strap in place

One-megohm resistor on a 360-degree swivel protects the user from electrical shocks

Alligator clip connects wrist strap to computer chassis

Help minimize ESD both while you work inside the computer and with your computer by taking the following steps:

- Use anti-static wipes and cleaners to clean cases and monitors.

- Dress in cotton or other natural fibers when you work on your PC; if you're working at home, ditch those synthetic-soled shoes and work in your stocking feet. You'd be amazed how much ESD you can generate with just a few steps of the "synthetic shuffle."

- If you absolutely *can't* get an ESD protection kit before you open your PC, be sure to touch the case of your PC while it's *unplugged* to help reduce ESD buildup.

- Hold components by the case or card bracket, never by the circuit boards or data/power connectors.

Now that you've backed up your system's information and selected your tools and ESD protection, you're ready to start upgrading the right way.

TIP

Don't Forget to Clean Up After Your PC!

No matter the reason for opening up your PC (upgrades, maintenance, or just looking around), you may encounter dust, dirt and grime. Refer back to Chapter 3, "Alternatives to Upgrades," for tips on cleaning the interior of your computer

Chapter 6

The Right Upgrades for You

If you have unlimited money, you can upgrade your computer until it's a master of everything. However, let's get real. You don't have unlimited money. That's why I helped you create an upgrade budget in Chapter 2, "Upgrade Strategies." This chapter is designed to help you focus on the upgrades that offer the biggest payoff for what you want your PC to do best.

Upgrades for Gaming

If you shun the console gaming systems for the multipurpose world of the PC, you've got to admit that the typical off-the-shelf PC isn't the world's greatest gaming platform. However, with some carefully chosen upgrades, you can transform your box into a winner.

Game Controller

You *can* play most games with a keyboard and mouse, but that's a sure formula for defeat if you're up against opponents with better controllers than you. Fortunately, you can add anything from a gamepad that's practically a twin of a console controller to highly specialized control panels. The only considerations are your taste and budget. If you prefer to play games that are designed to work with a mouse, some mice are much better than others for gaming. The USB interface means you can install and remove your favorite controllers at will, so choose the right controller for your game. See Chapter 20, "Selecting the Best Input Devices," for details.

ON THE WEB: TechTV's Game Central

If you're a PC gamer, be sure to start exploring the TechTV game product reviews page for the fastest access to our evaluations of games and game hardware. For more information, go to www.techtv.com/products/games/.

Display

You can't beat what you can't see, and there are two ways to improve your ability to see your foes:

- Larger monitor
- Faster graphics card

Add a 19-inch CRT monitor to your computer, and you improve your ability to see your opposition in two ways: You can keep your screen resolution the same and see larger images, or you can use the larger screen real estate with a higher resolution and see wider vistas in all directions. With a high-quality 19-inch CRT, you can use resolutions up to 1,600×1,200. Compared to 1,024×768, that's a lot more pixels. Because some popular games are very dark, look for monitors with dual brightness levels.

If your idea of gaming involves fast-action combat or racing, you live (or die!) by frame rates. Most off-the-shelf computers ship with integrated video or a low-cost graphics card based on old technology; these are sure losers in a death match.

The best 3D graphics adapters today use high-end chipsets, such as the ATI Radeon 9600, 9700 (see Figure 6.1), and 9800 chipsets, and the nVIDIA GeForce FX chipsets. Get a video card based on one of these powerhouses, and you can crank up your resolution, select high-quality antialiasing for smoother graphics, and still have frame rates that help you win. See Chapter 13 for upgrade details for monitors and video cards.

Figure 6.1

The ATI Radeon 9700 Pro is one of TechTV's favorite video cards for gamers. Photo courtesy of ATI Technologies.

Processor/Motherboard/RAM

Next to the video card, the speeds of the processor and motherboard are the most important factors in fast-action gameplay. If your current processor runs at a speed of less than 2GHz, you should consider upgrading to a faster processor. See Chapter 8, "Speedy Computing with Processor Upgrades," for details.

Because of differences in voltage requirements, pinouts, and improved internal design, the latest Pentium 4 and AMD Athlon XP processors (see Figure 6.2) often require different motherboards than those used by earlier Pentium 4 and Athlon models. A motherboard upgrade can enable you to use the newest AGP 8x video cards at top speed. Such upgrades provide USB 2.0 and IEEE-1394 ports for high-speed external devices and other features. See Chapter 9, "Unlock Your System's Potential with Motherboard and BIOS Upgrades," for details.

If you need to upgrade the motherboard, you might also need to upgrade your computer's memory to match the motherboard's requirements. Most current high-performance mother-boards use DDR333 memory instead of the slower DDR speeds or PC-133 memory used by older motherboards. See Chapter 7, "RAM Your Way to Faster Performance," for details.

Figure 6.2

The AMD Athlon XP is a popular choice for cost-effective gaming PC upgrades. Photo courtesy of ABD.

Cooling

Whether you run your components at recommended speeds or, as many gamers do, over-clock the processor, motherboard, memory, and graphics card, keeping your system cool is more critical than ever. Thermal tests prove that high-performance 3D games raise processor, memory, and video card chipset temperatures, and if your cooling doesn't keep up with the demand, your system's in trouble.

JARGON

Overclocking—Configuring a component to run faster than its rated speed.

Heatsink—Copper or aluminum assembly that radiates heat away from a hot component. Often includes a fan to improve airflow.

Heat spreader—Copper or aluminum cover for memory modules that radiates heat away from the memory chips on the module.

Overheated components fail, and if your RAM or processor overheat, they can corrupt your data when they fail. How can you fight back? Improve your current system's cooling capabilities with the following upgrades:

- **Case fans**—Although the latest systems typically include front and rear case fans, older systems might not have a rear case fan. Add one to help keep your system cool. See Chapter 9 for details.

- **Cooling for your motherboard**—The motherboard has two built-in chips—the North Bridge and the South Bridge—whose cooling needs are often neglected. If your motherboard's North Bridge chip doesn't have a fan, or the fan starts to fail, install a new one. The South Bridge chip doesn't get as hot as the North Bridge chip, but it can also overheat, and it often has no cooling provisions at all. You can add a stick-on passive heatsink to the South Bridge to keep it cool. Keep in mind that if either chip fails, you need a new motherboard. See Chapter 9 for details.

- **Memory cooling**—Your system never works harder than when you're playing a high-speed 3D game, and your video card and system memory get very hot as a result. Although improving case cooling helps reduce overall heat buildup, these components need extra help to keep cool. Heat spreader plates help radiate heat away from memory so case fans can move the heat out of the system. See Chapter 7 for details.

- **Graphics card cooling**—One of the ways you can tell a low-end card from its faster siblings is the lack of a cooling fan over the graphics chip. Many low-end cards use a cheaper passive heatsink instead. If you overclock your card for faster performance, you should replace that passive heatsink with a fan. See Chapter 13 for details.

  High-end graphics cards often feature finned heatsinks on the memory to help dissipate heat. You can add them to the memory chips on any video card to help keep your card flinging pixels faster and longer. See Chapter 13 for details.

  Of course, keep in mind that these types of changes to your video card void the warranty, but if it keeps the card from a meltdown, it might be worthwhile.

- **Hard disk cooling**—Today's hard disks are another heat source that's easy to overlook. Current 7,200-RPM and the newest 10,000-RPM ATA and Serial ATA drives run much hotter than the slower 5,400-RPM drives that many older systems use. However, drive manufacturers have left the issue of cooling these drives to third-party companies. Many high-end cases provide hard drive mounts next to the front cooling fan, as was the case with the clear-case PC we built for this book. You can also install your 3.5-inch drives into 5.25-inch drive bays with a combination drive bay adapter and cooling fan. Some drive coolers also add a heatsink to further improve drive cooling. See Chapter 10, "Adding a Huge Hard Disk," for details.

ON THE WEB: Cool and Quiet the TechTV Way

Fans are noisy, but they're not the only way to keep your system cool. Check out Patrick Norton's "World's Quietest PC" article to learn how to keep your system cool the quiet way. You can read the article at www.techtv.com/screensavers/answerstips/story/ 0,24330,3338992,00.html.

Audio

3D sound is just as important a part of gameplay as 3D video. Although some recent systems now offer six-channel integrated sound with Dolby Digital 5.1 support, others continue to offer only stereo or four-speaker sound. If your computer falls into the latter category, you should upgrade to a sound card with six-channel or greater audio support.

A six-channel sound system won't do you any good without upgrading your speaker system. Upgrade your speakers to add surround sound so that you can hear all the action. See Chapter 14, "PC Audio and More," for details.

Optical Storage

If you use an optical drive with a maximum CD-ROM read rate of 24x or slower or a DVD-ROM drive with a 10x DVD maximum read rate, your game loading and access time suffers. Save time installing games and playing games that use the game CD by upgrading to today's faster drives. As a bonus, you can also add rewriteable CD or DVD capabilities along with greater speed. See Chapter 12, "A Burning Desire for Better Optical Drives," for details.

Upgrades for Video Editing and Playback

If your idea of a good time is becoming the Martin Scorcese of the desktop, you're looking for upgrades that will help you get video into your computer, edit it into a masterpiece, and output it to your adoring fans (also known as your family and friends).

DV Camcorder

Sure, you *can* convert analog video from an old-school camcorder into digital form, but you're better off starting with digital. Any camera you choose should have an IEEE-1394 port so that you have a direct connection to your PC. Consider adding an external hard disk for storage or editing. See Chapter 15, "Digital Imaging and Video," for details.

IEEE-1394 Port

Born for DV image capture, this port is also the gateway to high-speed high-capacity external hard drives. Some computers already include a couple of these ports, but if not, you can add them to almost any desktop or notebook computer. See Chapter 19, "Adding the Ports You Need for the Devices You Want," for details.

Analog Video Capture Hardware

If you're trying to bring old-school analog camcorder or VHS video into the 21st century, you need to convert it into a digital form. Many different types of devices have video input jacks. These devices include some high-end webcams, video cards (such as the ATI All-in-Wonder series), and dedicated video capture devices (see Figure 6.3). Add one to your system to grab analog video and transform it. See Chapter 15 for details.

Figure 6.3

The Dazzle Digital
Video Creator 100
captures analog data
from TV or video
sources for editing
with the bundled
MovieStar 5 software.
Photo courtesy of
Dazzle Multimedia.

Video-Editing Software

Although some recent versions of Windows, such as Windows Me and Windows XP, contain
a low-end video editor (Microsoft MovieMaker), it's hardly the tool of your video-editing
dreams. You can purchase video-editing software separately, it's often bundled with DVD creation software or video capture hardware. You might prefer to try the bundled software to see
if it's adequate before opting for an upgrade. See Chapter 15 for details.

Rewriteable DVD Drive

After you create your digital masterpiece, don't leave it trapped inside your computer. With a
rewriteable DVD drive, you can share it with others. See Chapter 12 for details.

Operating System

Digital video editing takes a lot of system resources. If you don't want to spend as much time rebooting your computer as you do editing your work, consider upgrading to Windows XP. Its stability and improved user interface make video capture and editing a pleasure, no matter which devices or software you use. See Chapter 23, "Winning Windows Upgrades," for details.

Upgrades for Digital Imaging

Want to see family and friends groan and nervously slip out of the room? Set up a slide projector and reach for the light switch. Instead, turn old photos into modern digital masterpieces and shoot with pixels instead of film by upgrading your computer.

Scanner

There are two benefits from converting your old photos into digital images: you can use them for the web, print them, and display them on a monitor. At the same time, you can crop them and repair the ravages of time or bad exposure. Choose a flatbed scanner if you're a print maven, and look at adding a film scanner if you also have a collection of slides and negatives. See Chapter 15 for details.

Display

If you're struggling with photo editing on a 15-inch CRT, it's time to get a 17-inch or larger model so that you can see more of your image at one time. Although LCD displays are thinner and lighter, most are not quite up to the job of displaying the full range of brightness needed for photo editing. However, adding an LCD monitor as a second display lets you drag floating menus away from your working space so that you can see even more of your picture. It also enables you to preview some photos while you edit others. See Chapter 13 for details.

Digital Camera

If you want to skip the scanning stage and go straight to digital, a digital camera is what you need. Don't worry about prints: You can take flash memory cards or CDs to most camera shops or camera departments and get high-quality snapshots of your work or you can make great prints from the latest inkjet printers when you use photo paper. Even if you prefer a 35mm single-lens reflex camera for your serious work, a digital camera's great for family snapshots. See Chapter 15 for details.

ON THE WEB: TechTV's Digital Camera Headquarters

Check out our reviews of the coolest digital cameras and DV camcorders at
www.techtv.com/products/digitalcameras/.

Storage

You should scan at high resolutions to capture the full detail in your original photos and create reduced-size images for use on the web or in slideshows. All those pictures take up a lot
of disk space, so consider adding a rewriteable CD or DVD drive to store them and to help
you create digital photo albums you can share with others. See Chapter 12 for details.

If you opt for a digital camera, don't settle for using a serial or USB cable connection to
transfer your photos. They're too slow. They also tie up your camera so that you can't take
pictures until the photos are copied, and they eat batteries. Instead, add a flash memory card
reader and buy additional flash memory cards (see Figure 6.4); when you fill one up, interchange it and keep shooting. See Chapter 11, "Removable Storage to Go," for details.

Figure 6.4

Lexar Media's USB 2.0
Multi-Card reader
handles five popular
types of flash memory
cards used in digital
cameras. Photo cour-
tesy of Lexar Media.

Input Devices

If you're already developing a case of "mouse shoulder" with what you do on the PC, digital imaging will make matters worse. Get a better mouse (I love wireless models), or add a graphics tablet to make photo editing easier and less painful. See Chapter 20 for details.

Printer

If it's been more than two years since you last bought an inkjet printer, or you're using a cheapjack model whose cartridges cost almost as much as the printer, you're overdue for a change. For less than $150, you can pick up a general-purpose printer with terrific photo and text quality. For around $200 to $300, you can have your choice of very competent multi-function models or dedicated photo printers that trade slow text printing speeds for even better photo printing. See Chapter 21, "Output Unlimited with Printer Upgrades," for details.

Processor/Motherboard/RAM

If you want to edit several photos at the same time, make sure you have at least 512MB of RAM installed. If you don't, you'll spend almost as much time waiting as editing. See Chapter 7 for details.

A sub-1GHz processor is marginal for most tasks, but completely outclassed for photo editing. A 2GHz or faster processor with 512MB of RAM is a great combination. If your current motherboard isn't ready for a processor that fast, you need a motherboard upgrade as well. See Chapter 8 for processor upgrades and Chapter 9 for motherboard upgrades.

Operating System

Photo editing takes a lot of system resources. If you don't want to spend as much time rebooting your computer as you do editing your work, consider upgrading to Windows XP. Its stability and improved user interface make video capture and editing a pleasure, no matter which devices or software you use. See Chapter 23 for details.

Upgrades for Broadband Internet

Instead of kicking your dial-up modem across the room (it's downloading as fast as it can!), spend your energy on adding upgrades for broadband Internet to your computer.

Network Adapter

You *can* attach a broadband Internet adapter to your computer through the USB port, but if all you have are USB 1.1 ports, you're creating a bottleneck. If you don't have a 10/100 Ethernet port in your computer, add one and improve your broadband throughput and leave your USB ports free for other devices. See Chapter 17, "Share the Wealth with a Home Network," for details.

Home Network

If you have more than one computer in your home or office, but only one broadband Internet connection, you have two choices: share your computer or share your connection. You're better off sharing your connection with your choice of wired or wireless connections (see Figure 6.5). See Chapter 17 for details.

Figure 6.5

Build a wireless network with an access point/router/switch (left) and a network interface card (right) for each computer. Photo courtesy of Linksys.

Broadband Internet Service

There are several different choices on the market: cable modem, DSL, and satellite are the most popular. Any of them make the Internet an always-on, easy-to-use, fast resource for fun and education. One of them is right for you. See Chapter 16, "Get Yourself Broadband—It's (Always) Going Fast!," for details.

Upgrades for Digital Music

If you're hankering to take your music collection with you without lugging around a stack of CDs, these upgrades will fill the bill.

Storage

There are lots of low-cost and free programs that can turn your CD collection into digital music files. However, they depend on how fast and how accurately your current optical drive can read a music CD for conversion, a process called "ripping." If your current drive takes almost as long to rip a CD as it does to play it, it's time to look for a drive with fast and accurate digital audio extraction (DAE). Get a fast rewriteable CD or DVD drive and burn your collection faster than ever before. See Chapter 12 for details.

Portable MP3 Player

You won't need a computer to play your digital music with a portable MP3 player. Despite the name, most of these players can also play WMA (Windows Media Audio) files if you prefer that format. Some use flash memory, but the best ones have on-board hard drives that can store hundreds of songs. Need even more reasons to try one? Some models can also be used as an external hard drive for your computer and can capture and display digital photos (see Figure 6.6). See Chapter 14 for details.

ON THE WEB: MP3 Players the TechTV Way

Discover the latest digital audio device reviews on the TechTV web site at www.techtv.com/products/consumerelectronics/.

Figure 6.6

The Archos Jukebox Multimedia 20 plays back still images, MPEG-4 video, and MP3 audio; it can also be used as a 20GB USB 2.0 hard drive. Photo courtesy of Archos.

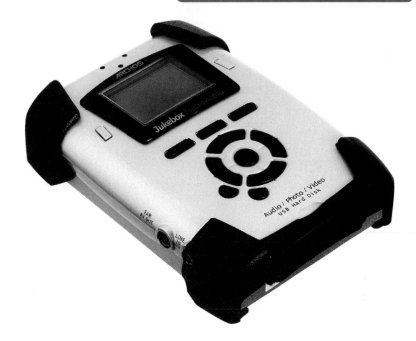

Sound Card and Speakers

The higher the sampling quality of the sound card you use to record digital audio, the better the music sounds when you play it back, especially with a 5.1, 6.1, or 7.1 sound card and speaker system. See Chapter 14 for details.

Upgrades for Education

Computers can be an exciting way to help your child learn. However, it can be frustrating to make a preschool or young elementary-age child try to use the same devices and software older children and adults use. Try these upgrades to help make the kids' computer truly child-friendly.

Input Devices

Child-sized input devices aren't easy to track down, but smaller buttons and kid-friendly colors and designs help children use computers more easily. Because these use the USB port, you can easily interchange them with grownup-sized keyboards and mice.

Mice

KidzMouse from KidzMouse.com (also sold under the IBM brand name) is a friendly mouse in design and color. Available in your choice of Nickelodeon, Disney, Sesame Street, cute insect, or design-it-yourself themes, it's shaped for small hands and features left and right mouse buttons; squeeze to click both buttons. See Chapter 20 for installation details.

ON THE WEB: TechTV Loves the KidzMouse

Check out our four-star review of the KidzMouse line at www.techtv.com/products/ consumerelectronics/story/0,23008,3354758,00.html. Go directly to the Kidzmouse web site at www.kidzmouse.com.

Keyboards

Imagine your keyboard is 50 percent wider than it normally is. Now, imagine trying to touch-type. Frustrated? So are your kids. The DataDesk Technologies LittleFingers keyboard (see Figure 6.7) has the same QWERTY layout as a normal keyboard, but reduces the size of the keys to a scale comfortable for kindergarten through sixth-grade students. Get it with a choice of trackball ($70) or number pad ($50), and with the traditional PS/2 or USB interface. If you want to type along with the youngsters, you can plug in a standard-size PS/2 keyboard into the LittleFingers PS/2 version using its pass-through connector. The USB version has an extra USB port for adding a full-size USB keyboard.

Figure 6.7

The Datadesk Technologies LittleFingers keyboard (right) compared to a standard PC keyboard (left). Photo courtesy of Datadesk Technologies.

ON THE WEB: TechTV Loves the Datadesk LittleFingers Keyboard

Check out our review of the LittleFingers keyboard at `www.techtv.com/freshgear/`
`products/story/0,23008,2216615,00.html`. Go directly to the LittleFingers keyboard web
site at `www.datadesktech.com/education_base.html`.

Operating Systems

Windows XP Home Edition, with its easy multiple-user setup, is the perfect upgrade if you
need to share the computer with young children. You can use a picture of your little darling's
favorite toy or cartoon character on the login screen (logging in can be done with a click of
the mouse), and by using a password on the older children's and adults' logins, you can keep
the little ones from hosing the system. Each user gets a unique desktop and access to only
their programs.

Upgrades for Web Site Building and Programming

Have something to say? The Internet is your printing press. Whether you want to express
yourself through blogging or a personal web site, or to make a living through coding, here
are the upgrades you need to make your work (or play) easier and more productive.

JARGON

Blogging—Popular term for creating a web log, or blog. Blogs are used by everyone from journalists to students to
provide a running commentary on life, the meaning of the universe, and what's on TV. Free software for blogging is
available from `www.blogger.com`, and many blogs are hosted by `www.blogspot.com`.

Display

If you already have a dual-display capable video card but have only one monitor connected
to it, you're really missing out. Add a second monitor and watch your productivity go up as
you preview your site on one display and create updates on the other display. If you're a web
site builder, use a CRT display for previewing your work because it handles many different
resolutions. LCD displays work at just one or two resolutions, but are great for text editing. If
your video card's a one-monitor type, it's time for an upgrade. See Chapter 13 for details.

Programmable Keyboard or Keypad

If you're tired of typing the same code sequences over and over again, consider a programmable keyboard. One keystroke can replace dozens. You won't find these at your local computer store, but some specialized online vendors offer several different models. Look for a model with a USB connection, and you can interchange it with a normal model the easy way.

If you don't want to learn a new keyboard or you're worried about pressing the wrong key and accidentally programming a macro into your keyboard, you can get programmable keypads that plug into the USB or PS/2 ports. See Chapter 20 for installation details. See Figure 6.8.

Figure 6.8

The P.I. Engineering X-Keys Desktop USB keypad has 20 programmable keys. Larger models are also available. Photo courtesy of P.I. Engineering.

Part II

Upgrading for Performance

Chapter 7

RAM Your Way to Faster Performance

As you might remember from Chapter 6, "The Right Upgrades for You," one of the most important considerations in any computer upgrade strategy is RAM. Why? Well, RAM, which is short for random-access memory, is the workspace used by your computer's CPU. Whether you're blasting away in a death match, writing the next Great American Novel, or digitizing a photograph, the information that eventually gets transmitted to the Internet or saved to your hard drive is originally created in RAM.

Note, however, that RAM isn't just for your data. RAM is also used by your operating system, your applications, and all those useful, annoying, or mildly interesting icons that wind up in your system tray as you start the computer. Computer programs help you create data, and to do it, they need RAM. In addition, if that wasn't enough, your system also uses RAM to speed up two distinctly different types of operations:

- Disk access
- Data manipulation

So, if you're looking for a big boost in performance, a RAM upgrade could do more for you than you could imagine. At today's prices, it's about the first upgrade you should perform to any system. In this chapter, I help you do the following:

- Learn what RAM can do for your system
- Discover the different types of RAM
- Install and troubleshoot RAM upgrades

Ten Reasons to Upgrade Your RAM

If you're not sure you need to upgrade your system's RAM, check out our "top ten" list of reasons you might need to install more RAM. If you recognize yourself (or your system) in this listing, keep reading the chapter.

1. Your Windows 98/Me system has less than 128MB of RAM installed.
2. Your system slows down when you open three or more programs at the same time.
3. You're tired of waiting while you switch between open programs.
4. You're starting to edit high-resolution (two-megapixel or higher) digital photos.
5. Your computer has integrated video.
6. You're editing digital video.
7. You want faster system performance.
8. Your system has less than the amount of memory recommended for a program you want to run.
9. Your Windows XP system has less than 256MB of RAM installed.
10. Your computer is still running with its original amount of memory.

How Your Computer Uses RAM

RAM is an essential upgrade for almost any system because of the many ways it is used by your computer:

- RAM holds the running programs and operating system components that are in use at any one time.

- RAM is used for a temporary workspace for data before it is stored on disk.
- RAM is used by the operating system to boost the read/write performance of storage devices (a feature known as disk caching).

RAM and Disk Caching

When PCs were new (over 20 years ago), the CPU communicated directly with the disk subsystem; as soon as you typed the command or selected the menu option Open File, the disk drive began to transfer the file from your storage device, a dog-slow floppy disk at the time, to RAM so that your system could work on the file. During the file retrieval process, your computer couldn't do anything else but get the file.

Even after floppy drives were replaced by hard drives, the process worked in a similar fashion for several years. Eventually, though, software companies created a feature called *disk caching*, which allowed data that is being read—or will be read—to be temporarily stored in RAM before being used by the CPU. Later this *read caching* process was supplemented by *write caching*, which uses RAM to hold data on its way to your hard disk. Windows has incorporated disk caching for a number of years now.

Adding RAM makes it possible for your system to hold more data in its disk cache, thus enabling you to get more done while the system takes care of reading the data and saving it. Basically, disk caching lets the CPU hand off information to the RAM and assume that everything's gonna be all right. As long as you don't do something dumb like turn off your computer without shutting down Windows first, the disk cache will make sure the data gets where it belongs.

RAM Versus Virtual Memory

RAM is also used by your system for data-manipulation chores of all types. Whenever you type within a word processing program, resort the rows in your budget, or apply a special-effects filter to a digital photo, you're manipulating the data in RAM to (hopefully) improve the final result.

However, what if you need *more* RAM than what's installed in your system to perform a given task? Does a little sign pop up with a message like "LOCAL P4 ON STRIKE—MORE RAM OR LESS WORK!"? Nope. Like a clever office manager, your computer looks for a RAM substitute called *virtual memory*. In addition, just as Jim Phelps on the old *Mission: Impossible* TV show used to choose the same operatives for any mission no matter how many pictures he flipped through, your PC chooses the same source for virtual memory every time: your hard disk.

Your hard disk is a complex, mechanical device that spins one or more round platters at a high speed to store and read information. RAM is electronic and has no moving parts. Guess which one is faster? That wasn't hard, was it? Your hard disk is rated in milliseconds (thousandths of a second) access time; memory is rated in nanoseconds (millionths of a second). It isn't even close. If your system is short on RAM, you'll wind up spending a whole lot of time drumming your fingers, watching the disk access light on your computer flicker away while you wait for operations that would take only a few seconds if you added more RAM. Besides, everybody knows that virtual anything is never as good as the real thing.

Types of RAM

"Rose is a rose is a rose." I still don't know what Gertrude Stein meant by that, but I can tell you that thinking that "RAM is RAM is RAM" can prevent you from getting anywhere with a memory upgrade.

From 1981 through 1985, every memory upgrade required installing a handful of individual memory chips; there's no telling how many memory chips were destroyed by ESD (static electricity) or by being stepped on, dropped, or bent. The modern memory module period began in 1986, when IBM introduced its XT/286 computer along with the 30-pin SIMM, a type of memory that attaches memory chips to a more-durable miniature circuit board. Although the 30-pin SIMM and its newer 72-pin sibling are now obsolete, current memory modules such as DIMMs and RIMMs use a similar construction method.

Here's what you need to know to get a RAM upgrade for your system:

- How much RAM your system already has.
- How many open memory slots your system has.
- The physical memory types (or *form factors*) supported by your system.
- The memory chip types supported by your system. In most cases, you can't mix chip types because of how they are accessed by your system.
- The speed of the memory used by your system. You can normally add memory that's faster, but not slower, than what is already in your system.
- The width (in bits) of memory modules supported by your system.

- The sizes of memory modules supported by your system.
- Whether parity checking or ECC error-correction is used by your system.

MARK'S TIP SHEET: Hit the Books Before You Upgrade

If you took the "grand tour" of your system described in Chapter 4, "Taking an Inspection Tour of Your System," you should already know the amount of RAM your system has and the number (and type) of memory sockets available. If you used SiSoftware Sandra as part of your system analysis, you also know the type and speed of installed memory as well.

However, to dig out information such as supported memory module types, speeds, sizes, and ECC/parity compatibility, get your system manual or motherboard manual and do some reading. If yours is buried in a box (or a landfill) somewhere, go to your system vendor or motherboard vendor's web site to find out these details.

If your system uses standard memory modules (also called *generic memory*), these eight factors will point you in the right direction. However, because of proprietary differences in some major brands of computers, you might need to specify the brand and model number of your system instead to be assured of getting the correct memory.

ON THE WEB: Feeling Wrung out by RAM? Just Ask Us!

You can search the TechTV web site (www.techtv.com) for "RAM" to find lots more tips, tricks, and tutorials on RAM.

The Alphabet Soup of Memory Form Factors

The major memory form factors in use on upgrade-worthy systems include the following:

- **DIMMs**—Dual Inline Memory Modules are available in both 168-pin and 184-pin forms. Although the 168-pin SDRAM module is used in many recent systems, almost all brand-new systems and new motherboards use the faster 184-pin double-data rate (DDR) variety.

- **RIMMs**—Rambus Inline Memory Modules are 184-pin modules used by motherboards using some of Intel's 8xx-series chipsets, including the Intel 820, 820E, 840, and
850 series and some third-party chipsets. These chipsets are used in some systems running the Pentium III or Pentium 4 processors. Although Rambus memory is theoreti-
cally faster than the DDR SDRAM memory used by most systems, the difference in
practice is small. The major real-life differences are in price; when you compare identically sized DDR SDRAM DIMMs and RIMMs, the RIMMs cost two to three times
as much.

DIMMs and RIMMs are also available in reduced-size versions called SODIMMs (Small
Outline DIMMs) and SORIMMs (Small Outline RIMMs) that are primarily designed for
use in notebook computers. Figure 7.1 compares three types of DIMMs (SDRAM, DDR
SDRAM, and SDRAM SODIMM) to the 72-pin SIMM memory module popular in the
mid-1990s and a proprietary notebook memory upgrade from the same period.

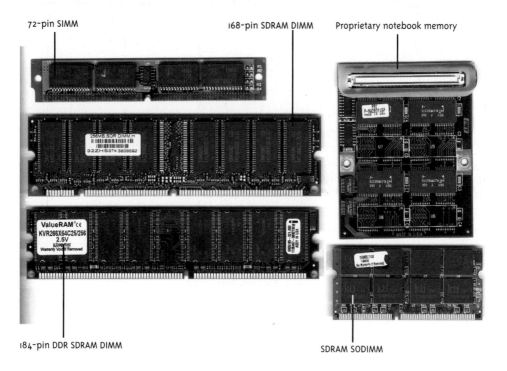

72-pin SIMM   168-pin SDRAM DIMM   Proprietary notebook memory

184-pin DDR SDRAM DIMM   SDRAM SODIMM

Figure 7.1

Obsolete desktop and notebook memory modules (top left and right) compared to current desktop and notebook DIMM
memory modules (middle and bottom left, bottom right).

Compare these memory modules to the RIMM module shown in Figure 7.2.

A RIMM resembles a DIMM, but has metal covers called heat spreaders over the memory chips on the module.

Figure 7.2

A typical PC800 RIMM module used by some high-performance Intel and third-party chipsets for the Pentium 4 processor.

What Kind of Memory Is That? Types and Speeds

In some ways, buying memory for upgrade-worthy systems today is simpler than it was a few years ago. If you buy a 168-pin DIMM module, you have SDRAM. If you buy a 184-pin DIMM module, you have DDR SDRAM. If you buy a RIMM module, you have Rambus RDRAM. There's no longer the confusion caused by multiple memory types using a single form factor. However, it's still important to understand how different types of memory chips affect memory performance if you're planning to upgrade to a new motherboard (which probably uses different memory than your current motherboard) or to add memory to an existing system.

The major memory chip types used on recent systems include the following:

- Synchronous DRAM (SDRAM)
- Double-Data-Rate SDRAM (DDR SDRAM)
- Rambus DRAM (RDRAM)

Although some early DIMM modules used a now-obsolete type of memory called EDO, all DIMMs used in recent and current systems use either standard or DDR SDRAM chips. SDRAM derives its name from its being synchronized with the memory access speed (also called the motherboard or Front-Side Bus [FSB] speed) of the CPU. For this reason, SDRAM-based DIMM modules are referred to by MHz ratings. SDRAM modules are available in three speeds:

- 66MHz (PC66)
- 100MHz (PC100)
- 133MHz (PC133)

PC133 modules can be used with most lower-speed motherboards as well; thus, you can usually standardize on PC133 SDRAM DIMMs for systems that use standard SDRAM DIMMs.

CAUTION: STOP! LOOK! THINK!

Have One of These Chipsets? PC100's the Limit
Motherboards and systems that use the Intel 440BX, 810, or 810e chipsets are *not* compatible with PC133 memory. Use only PC100 memory with these chipsets. To determine the chipset your system contains, check your system documentation or use SiSoftware Sandra. See Chapter 4 for details.

The newer DDR SDRAM chips are used on 184-pin DIMMs. DDR SDRAM DIMMs are sometimes identified by the FSB speed of the CPU, but now most often use the throughput of the memory to identify each type. The most common types include the following:

- PC1600 (1.6GB/second) modules run at 200MHz and are also referred to as DDR200 modules.

- PC2100 (2.1GB/second) modules run at 266MHz and are also referred to as DDR266 modules.

- PC2700 (2.7GB/second) modules run at 333MHz and are also referred to as DDR333 modules.

- PC3200 (3.2GB/second) modules run at 400MHz and are also referred to as DDR400 modules.

As with conventional SDRAM DIMMs, you can use faster memory in place of slower memory. Thus, you can use PC2700 memory in place of PC2100 memory.

RAMBUS RDRAM modules, called RIMMs, are referred to by the internal speed of the RDRAM chips. Current speeds include the following:

- 800MHz (also called RIMM3200 or PC800 RIMM)
- 1066MHz (also called RIMM4200)

You should *not* mix different RIMM speeds on the same system, and you should verify which RIMM speed your system is designed to use.

Your system or motherboard manual is the authority on what you can use, but if you can't locate your manual—even online—here's a rule of thumb that almost always works: Buy another DIMM or RIMM module just like the one(s) you already have if you have open slots. Motherboards can get fussy about mixing and matching sizes, but almost any system will accept more of the same.

MARK'S TIP SHEET: Stick a Label on It!

Memory module packages are clearly marked with their contents, but some modules aren't marked nearly so well. If your memory isn't clearly identified, attach a paper sticker to it and write the speed and size of the module on the sticker. It will make life easier at upgrade time.

How Wide (and How Large) Is Your Memory?

Most current memory modules (DIMMs, RIMMs, and compact SODIMM and SORIMM versions) contain 64 bits of data, regardless of their size in megabytes. Modules that support ECC error correction contain 64 data bits plus 8 bits used for error correction, for a total of 72 bits.

JARGON

Know Your Bits and Bytes

If you want to have a clue about memory, you need to understand the difference between bits and bytes. A *byte* is the basic unit of data storage, and 1 byte equals one character stored in a plain-text file. However, although memory is sized in byte-sized units, each *byte* contains 8 bits. Modern memory modules, such as DIMMs, are constructed with memory chips that contain multiples of 8 bits. The number of bits in a memory device helps determine how many devices must be added at a time to expand a system's memory.

Each type of memory module can be purchased in a variety of sizes. SDRAM DIMMs are available in sizes ranging from 32MB to 1024MB (1GB), with 64MB, 128MB, and 256MB being the most popular. DDR SDRAM modules are available in sizes ranging from 128MB to 2GB. RIMMs are available in 128MB, 256MB, and 512MB sizes.

Which size is right for you? The manual knows! Check your system documentation to determine which sizes of memory modules are acceptable.

Avoiding the Data Bus Blues

Time to go to the bank! The memory bank, that is. Before you add RAM to your system, you need to understand the concept of a memory bank. Memory is always added in memory banks, which equal the number of data bits in a CPU's data bus. For example, a Pentium III, Pentium 4, or AMD Athlon CPU has a 64-bit data bus. Thus, these processors have a 64-bit memory bank. You must add memory in 64-bit wide units.

At one time this always required calculations on your part before ordering memory because of the differences in data bus width and memory device width. Today, in most cases, the match up is easy. Because any system with a Pentium CPU or better (Pentium II/III/Celeron, Pentium 4, AMD K6, Athlon, Athlon XP, Athlon 64, or Duron) has a 64-bit data bus and DIMMs and RIMMs that are 64 bits wide, you can generally add memory one module at a time.

To Every Rule There's an Exception...

Pick a pair! If your system uses dual-channel memory, you need to add identical pairs of modules, even though the CPU and the memory module have the same width in bits. This improves performance.

Some systems offer dual-channel support as an option. If you install a matching pair of memory modules, dual-channel support is enabled. If you mix and match memory sizes, it isn't. Check your system or motherboard manual for details.

Using Your Memory Sockets Effectively

When you add memory, you should strive to add the most memory possible using the smallest number of memory sockets on the motherboard. This is relatively simple if your system uses DIMMs, because this type of memory is usually added one module at a time. Wondering what empty and full DIMM sockets look like? Take a look at Figure 7.3.

Let's assume, for example, that your system has 64MB of memory on board and of the three DIMM sockets on the motherboard, one is in use. Thus, you have a 64MB DIMM installed. If you want to have at least 256MB of RAM, you could use any of the following options to get there:

- Add a 64MB DIMM and a 128MB DIMM (256MB total onboard memory)
- Add two 128MB DIMMs (320MB total onboard memory)
- Add one 256MB DIMM (320MB total onboard memory)

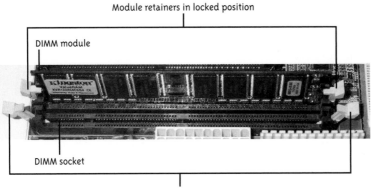

Module retainers in locked position

DIMM module

DIMM socket

Module retainers in unlocked position

Figure 7.3

A 168-pin DIMM module (top) and an empty DIMM socket (bottom).

But which option makes the most sense? I hope you chose option three (add one 256MB DIMM) because that's the best answer! Here's why: If you install two DIMMs, you use up all your memory sockets and have no room for the inevitable future memory upgrade unless you remove one of your existing memory modules. Don't think you'll ever need more memory? Join the millions who have believed the same thing! Can't find the rest of the "No More Memory Club" members? That's because they're all out buying more memory!

Avoiding Memory Upgrade Pitfalls

Before you determine exactly how much RAM you need to buy, it's time to learn about hidden "gotchas" that can prevent you from using all the RAM you're installing, make it way too easy to add too much RAM to your system, or trick you into buying more expensive types of memory than you need. Consider these pitfalls:

- Built-in video that steals system memory
- Chipset limitations on useful memory size
- Windows limitations on useful memory size
- Parity and ECC—when to buy it, and when to skip it

Each is discussed in the following sections.

Fighting the Invisible Memory Thief—Built-In Video

It's time for a trick question. How much usable memory does a system have if it has a 128MB memory module installed?

Is the correct answer:

A.   128MB of course!

B.   Let me ask my accountant.

C.   A lot less if the video is built into the motherboard.

The correct answer is C. Why? Most recent systems that feature motherboard-based video use a design called Unified Memory Architecture (UMA), a fancy way of saying this: "I'm video, and I'm taking a cut of the motherboard memory. If you don't like it, tough!" Systems with UMA use the same memory for both main memory and video memory to save money. However, UMA has its own price, not in money but in lower system performance—and at the cost of reducing the system memory actually available for uses other than video.

How much of a "cut" does your built-in video take out of your system's total memory? It varies with the system. For example, motherboards based on the Intel 845G-series chipsets use 8MB of RAM at all times for video, and varying amounts of additional RAM, depending on the graphics requirements of the program(s) that are running. With 128MB of RAM installed, the maximum amount of memory used is 32MB. With more than 128MB of memory installed, the maximum amount of memory used is 48MB or 64MB, depending on the version of the Intel Extreme Graphics Driver in use. The maximum amount of RAM is most likely to be used when you are editing photos or playing games using 32-bit color settings. In these cases, a system with 256MB of RAM could have as little as 192MB (256-64) of RAM available for Windows and applications.

You can fight back by doing the following:

- **Adding more RAM than you were planning to add**—Add a 256MB module rather than a 128MB module, for example. Even with the additional video memory usage that is triggered by increasing RAM beyond 128MB, you're still ahead of the game.

- **Disabling on-board video and installing a video card**—This enables you to reclaim all the memory used by onboard video. This provides a double-barreled boost in performance when you install an AGP video card because the AGP card is also faster than onboard video. However, if your system lacks an AGP slot, I don't recommend using a PCI video card. These are often no faster than onboard video and use low-end or obsolete graphics chipsets. If you need to manually disable onboard video before installing an external video card, follow the instructions carefully. If you make a mistake, you might wind up with no video at all!

Too Much RAM? How to Avoid Getting Burned

You've probably heard that you can never be too rich, too thin, or have too much RAM. Unfortunately, only the first part of this cliche is really accurate. You can be too thin and—believe it or not—you can add too much RAM! There are two reasons why this might happen:

- Older motherboards sometimes can't handle today's larger memory modules.
- Windows versions can have limitations in the total amount of memory they can use.

Could these problems cause you problems? Absolutely! Before you run to the store (physical or online) and buy your RAM upgrade, you need to find out the facts.

Old Motherboards Don't Understand New Memory

When a motherboard is designed, the manufacturer normally tries to make sure that it can use the standard memory modules available *at the time*, and in some cases, the manufacturer might be able to design the motherboard to support some upcoming larger memory modules. For example, many older motherboards can't use 1GB or 2GB modules.

Sooner or later, the newest, biggest memory modules might actually be too big for a given motherboard. Could it happen to you? To avoid problems, check your system or motherboard manual *before* you buy RAM that won't work.

Windows Doesn't Like Too Much RAM, Either

If you use Windows 9x or Windows Me, don't try to use more than 512MB of RAM on your system if you have an AGP video card or integrated AGP video. Why? The 32-bit memory cache driver called Vcache runs out of address space it needs to start Windows or to open MS-DOS prompt sessions; see Microsoft Knowledge Base article #253912 for details. This isn't good news if you are planning to take advantage of the 1.5GB or higher total memory sizes supported by many recent systems and the low prices on 256MB and 512MB DIMM modules. However, look on the bright side: After you have 512MB of RAM installed, you can upgrade something else!

JARGON

Knowledge Base—The Microsoft Knowledge Base is a fancy term for the reams and reams of information Microsoft has accumulated on the good, bad, and ugly behaviors (and misbehaviors) of Windows. If you need help with Windows, it's a great place to start! Send your browser to http://search.Microsoft.com. You can enter search terms to locate articles, or enter the number of a Microsoft Knowledge Base article (such as 253912) that you want to read.

ON THE WEB: How Much RAM Is Enough?

I like to recommend at least 256MB with any operating system, and up to 512MB if you can afford it. You get the biggest benefits with 512MB or more of RAM if you work with large data files such as print-quality digital photographs or big databases, or if you run many programs at the same time. How much RAM does your favorite program need to run well? Check out Crucial.com's software guide at www.crucial.com/library/softwareguide.asp. Crucial also offers a memory calculator to show you how different motherboard, processor, and memory combinations perform. The calculator is at www.crucial.com/calculator/. Kingston analyzes the effect of both the operating system and the work and play you do with its Memory Assessor at www.kingston.com/tools/assessor/default.asp.

Parity and ECC—Expen$ive and Not Always Useful

From the memory used in the first IBM PC introduced over twenty years ago through the early 1990s, memory chips, and later memory modules, added an extra memory bit to each group of 8 bits used to create memory banks. This extra bit is called a *parity bit*, and it was used to help your system determine if the contents of memory were reliable or had been corrupted. If the parity check failed, indicating the contents of memory were corrupted, you'd see a "parity error—system halted" message on the screen. Your system would stop, requiring you to reboot your computer, and any unsaved information in RAM was lost. Sooner or later, you'd turn off a system that wasn't working anyway, but parity checking tells you right away that you need to start over.

Eventually, the extra money that parity-checked memory required didn't seem worthwhile to system designers because parity checking couldn't do anything about memory errors but tell the user to start over. Most desktop computers made from about 1994 onward have used chipsets that don't support parity checking. Without parity checking, a system with corrupt memory just locks up without any onscreen error messages. You still lose your unsaved data, but don't know why.

However, memory made for parity-checked systems can also be used by a special chipset feature called ECC (Error Correcting Code), which can use the parity bit to correct some types of memory errors. Obviously, this is useful, but parity/ECC memory is more expensive, and it doesn't do you any good if your system doesn't support ECC operation.

MARK'S TIP SHEET: Parity or Not? Count the Chips!

Wondering if you have parity-checked memory installed in your system? The easiest way I know to tell is to use what I call the "count and divide" method. Memory modules that support parity-checking have an odd number of memory chips on board, and non-parity modules have an even number of memory chips. Do you *need* to install (expensive) parity-checked memory in your system? Not necessarily. Read on to find out how to tell if the parity bits are actually being used.

If you can't enable ECC in the system configuration, don't bother buying parity/ECC-compatible memory, even if your system already has parity/ECC memory installed. A good way to find out if your system supports parity or ECC operation is to view the Advanced and Advanced Chipset configuration screens in your system BIOS. On systems that support parity or ECC operation, an option to enable or disable this feature is displayed. If your BIOS shows nothing about these options or if parity/ECC is disabled, it's a safe bet that lower-cost non-parity memory will work.

CAUTION: STOP! LOOK! THINK!

Cheap or Safe? You Can Choose Only One

Although parity-checking by itself does nothing to keep the contents of memory working correctly, ECC-compatible chipsets use parity bits for error correction. If you are performing critical work with your computer *and* your computer supports ECC, it might be worth the extra money to switch to ECC-compatible memory. If you want to save money, you can leave ECC/parity checking disabled, but you should determine how often lockups (often caused by corrupt memory) occur and how costly it is to you to recreate lost data.

Buying Your RAM

To get the correct memory for your system, you need to specify it accurately. Some vendors allow you to specify memory like this: "I want a 128MB PC100 DIMM module." However, if your motherboard needs a less common version of memory, or you want to avoid any mis-understanding about what you're getting, it pays to learn exactly how to specify memory.

CAUTION: STOP! LOOK! THINK!

Don't Try to Outsmart the Memory Vendor
Because more and more systems are designed to use memory modules that vary from so-called generic memory, most major memory vendors now feature interactive buying guides on their web sites for both name-brand systems and popular motherboard brands and models. Because choosing memory can be tricky, these buying guides are your best bet to getting the right memory. Some vendors might give you a hard time with returns if you skip the buying guide and try to guess the memory you need, so use the guide if you can!

Use the following sections to specify memory if your system can use standard memory modules and you can't use the interactive buying guide to determine the correct part number because your system or motherboard isn't listed.

Buying Standard SDRAM DIMMs

To specify standard SDRAM DIMMs, you *must* specify the following:

- Size (MB)
- Non-parity (64-bit) or ECC (72-bit)
- Motherboard speed (66MHZ, 100MHz, or 133MHz)
- Voltage (3.3 volts for PCs—Macs use 5 volts)
- Buffered, unbuffered, or registered (PCs use unbuffered or registered memory)
- CAS Latency (CL2 and CL2.5 are faster than CL3)

Multiply the first number listed in the standard designation by 8 to get the actual size of the module.

JARGON

CAS latency—How quickly a memory module can prepare data for use by the PC. Some systems require a particular CAS latency factor, while others can adjust automatically.

Registered memory—Uses special circuits on board that amplify memory signals and are required by some systems; you cannot mix registered and unbuffered modules on a system.

Wondering which one you need? Repeat after me: "Read the manual!" Check the system documentation to determine the specific SDRAM memory modules needed for a given system.

Table 7.1 provides some examples of how to specify standard SDRAM DIMMs.

Table 7.1	Specifying SDRAM DIMMs				
Size	**ECC**	**Speed**	**CAS Latency**	**Registered**	**Standard Designation**
32MB	No	66MHz	CL3	No	8M×64 66MHz
128MB	Yes	133MHz	CL2.5	No	16M×64 133MHz ECC CL2.5
512MB	Yes	100MHz	CL2	Yes	64M×72 100MHz Registered ECC CL2

CAUTION: STOP! LOOK! THINK!

Stop Me Before I Buy the Wrong Memory!
DIMM modules in particular are really confusing to specify, but here's a couple of secrets I find to be really, really useful:

- If your system is specifically listed on a memory vendor's database, ordering the specified memory is the safest way to go. Why does your system require "special" memory? Is it faster than normal? Slower than normal? Use purple chips? Who cares? Just order it and know that it will work.

- If your existing memory has a label on it indicating a model number (see Figure 7.4), look up the model number on the vendor's web site to figure out what it is. If you're adding DIMMs, you don't need to buy the same size or speed in most cases (you can use PC133 with most older PC100 or PC66 systems), but knowing the model number will tell you if it has unusual characteristics, such as a faster CAS latency rating (such as CL2 in place of the more common CL2.5 or CL3 timings) or is registered.

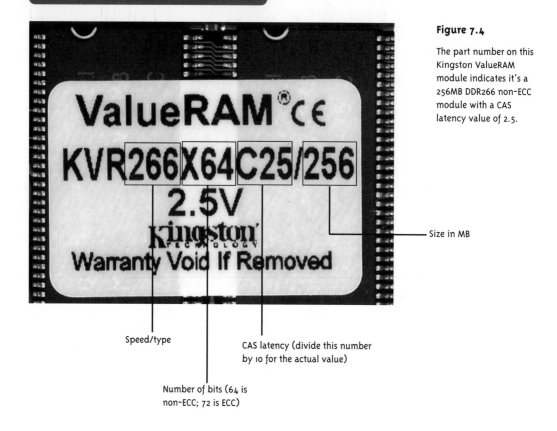

Figure 7.4

The part number on this Kingston ValueRAM module indicates it's a 256MB DDR266 non-ECC module with a CAS latency value of 2.5.

Speed/type

Number of bits (64 is non-ECC; 72 is ECC)

CAS latency (divide this number by 10 for the actual value)

Size in MB

Buying DDR SDRAM DIMMs

To order a DDR SDRAM DIMM, you need to specify the following:

- Size
- Speed
- ECC or non-ECC
- CAS Latency
- Standard (184-pin) or small outline (SO) form factor

Table 7.2 provides some examples of how to specify DDR SDRAMs.

Table 7.2	Specifying DDR SDRAM DIMMs					
Size	ECC	Speed	PC Type	CAS Latency	SODIMM	Standard Designation
128MB	No	266MHz	PC2100	CL2.5	No	DDR266 PC2100 128MB non-ECC CL2.5
256MB	Yes	400MHz	PC3200	CL3	No	DDR400 PC3200 256MB ECC CL3
512MB	No	333MHz	PC2700	N/A	Yes	DDR333 PC2700 512MB SODIMM

Note that you don't need to specify CAS Latency values for SODIMM memory.

Buying a RIMM Module

To order a RIMM module, you need to specify the following:

- Memory speed (800 or 1066MHz)
- Memory size
- ECC or non-ECC

Each "device" in the standard designation equals 16MB. Multiply 16MB by the number of devices to determine the actual size of the RIMM module in megabytes.

Table 7.3 provides some examples of how to specify RIMM modules.

Table 7.3	Specifying Rambus RIMMs		
Size	ECC	Speed	Standard Designation
128MB	No	800MHz	128MB 800MHz non-ECC four-device RIMM
256MB	No	1066MHz	256MB RIMM4200 1066MHz eight-device RIMM
512MB	Yes	800MHz	512MB PC800-40 ECC sixteen-device RIMM

Leave no socket unfilled! When you install RIMMs, you cannot leave any RIMM sockets empty on your motherboard. Instead, sockets that aren't being used for memory modules must be occupied by a continuity module, which resembles a standard RIMM module but has no memory chips on board. If you need additional continuity modules, also called *Continuity RIMMs* or *C-RIMMs*, you can order them from the memory suppliers who sell RIMM memory modules. Because a C-RIMM or memory RIMM must occupy each RIMM socket, you'll need to remove C-RIMMs before you add additional RIMMs.

MARK'S TIP SHEET: Getting the Best Deals on Memory

Because memory is such an important part of your system, the lowest price on memory isn't necessarily the best deal. However, I can tell you, without hesitation, where you can get the worst deal on memory: your system vendor!

With few exceptions, your computer's manufacturer doesn't make memory, but has to buy modules made for the system from a supplier. If you buy from your system vendor, you're buying memory with an extra markup. Instead of spending the extra money, use reliable memory vendors such as Kingston, PNY, Crucial.com, Viking Components, and others. Look for a lifetime warranty, and try to get the best direct price. Beware of retail stores' memory "specials"; the low prices you often see advertised in Sunday-newspaper fliers often include a rebate you have to wait weeks to get—if it comes at all.

Memory Installation—Pop 'Em in and Power Up Your System!

You've paid your money and made your choices; now it's time to install your memory. To prepare for the memory upgrade, do the following:

1. Shut down your system.

2. Unplug your system's power cord.

3. Remove the side cover or top cover to gain access to the inside of the system.

4. Locate the memory modules and empty sockets. Check the system manual to determine which memory socket should be used for the new memory module. In some systems, memory must be added in a particular order.

5. Ground yourself against the power supply or attach a ground strap to your wrist.

6. Remove the memory module from its packaging. Don't touch the connector on the module because you could damage it.

7. Align the module with the slot, push down firmly on the module until the locks at each end of the module swivel up to hold the module in place, and you're done. See Figure 7.5.

Figure 7.5

Installing a DIMM. Move the module locking levers into the open position (top) *before* putting the DIMM into place (middle). Then, push down on the DIMM until the locks swivel into place (bottom).

Most recent systems automatically recognize the additional memory when you restart your computer. However, if your system displays a "memory size mismatch" or similar memory error after you restart it, start the BIOS setup program, go to the Standard Setup screen, note the new memory size reported, and save the changes. When you exit the BIOS setup after saving the changes, your system reboots without any other errors.

After Windows starts, you can also use the System properties sheet to determine if the memory has been recognized (see Figure 7.6). Note that if your computer has a UMA design in which video memory is borrowed from main memory, the memory shown in the System properties sheet is less than the total amount installed.

Figure 7.6

This computer has 256MB of RAM installed, but only 224MB of memory is recognized by Windows because 32MB of RAM is used by the onboard video.

Amount of memory recognized by Windows XP

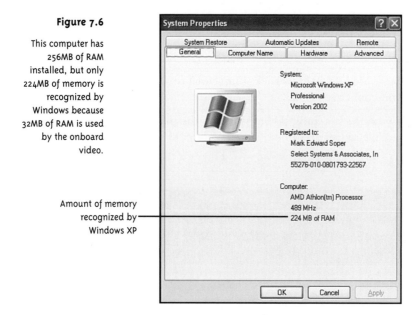

The missing memory can be detected with the DirectX Diagnostics (DXDIAG) program. To run DXDIAG:

1. Click Start, Run.

2. Type DXDIAG and click OK.

3. Click the Display tab to see the amount of video memory in use (see Figure 7.7).

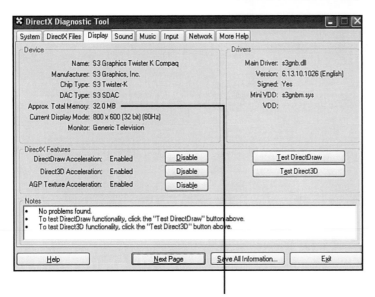

Amount of memory used by video

Figure 7.7

DirectX Diagnostics detects the memory used by onboard video. This amount plus the memory amount seen in Figure 7.6 adds up to 256MB (224+32).

Memory Upgrades for Notebook and Portable Systems

The process of selecting and installing memory for portable computers is quite a bit different than for desktop computers. The major differences include the following:

- **Differences in form factor**—Depending on the computer, a memory upgrade might be made in the form of a credit card with edge connectors, a flat module with a single plug-in connector on the bottom of the module, or another non-standard device. Although recent portables use SODIMM or SORIMM modules, older models you might wish to upgrade often use a proprietary module.

- **Higher cost for proprietary modules**—Because some notebook computers require memory made in a proprietary form factor, memory manufacturers must charge more to offset the higher development and manufacturing costs of proprietary modules.

- **Differences in installation**—Many notebook computers have only a single socket for memory upgrades, making it critical that you buy the largest memory upgrade possible. However, most notebook computer memory can be added by removing a small external cover, rather than partially disassembling the system. See Figure 7.8.

Figure 7.8

A typical SODIMM memory module after installation in a notebook computer.

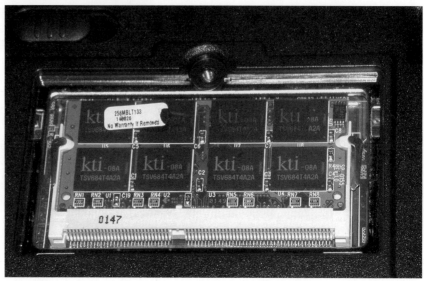

If your notebook computer's documentation doesn't offer detailed installation instructions for memory upgrades, contact your memory vendor. In particular, Kingston (www.kingston.com) offers excellent online documentation for most proprietary notebook computer memory upgrades.

When You Need to Upgrade Other Components First

A memory upgrade can significantly boost system performance, but if you're planning any of the following upgrades, you should consider how these upgrades might affect the amount and type of memory you need to buy:

- Motherboard upgrade
- Processor upgrade
- Graphics (video) card upgrade

How a Motherboard Upgrade Affects Memory Upgrade Plans

If you've decided you need a new motherboard, it's very likely that you also need new memory to fit that new motherboard. This is particularly likely if you are replacing a motherboard in a major-brand (IBM, HP/Compaq, Gateway, and so on) computer. Frequently, name-brand computers use proprietary memory that might not work correctly in a third-party replacement motherboard.

If you're replacing a third-party motherboard with a newer third-party motherboard, you might also need new memory, unless that motherboard is very recent. A couple of years ago, PC133 memory was the most popular. Today, DDR266 or DDR333 are tops in popularity because they provide the faster performance needed by newer, more powerful processors. As you learned earlier in this chapter, PC133 and DDR memory aren't interchangeable. The bottom line? If your motherboard's getting replaced, count on replacing your memory too.

How a Processor Upgrade Affects Memory Upgrade Plans

If you're planning to upgrade your processor, don't perform a memory upgrade first. Although your system might have a motherboard that can handle a significantly faster processor, a lot of motherboards can't. Thus, odds are pretty good that you will also need a motherboard upgrade to support the faster processor. As you learned in the previous section, a new motherboard usually means new memory is also needed.

How a Graphics Card Upgrade Affects Memory Upgrade Plans

If you're replacing an older graphics card with a brand-new screamer, this type of upgrade has no effect on memory. However, if you're moving from onboard video to a separate graphics card, good news! You're actually getting a "free" memory upgrade as a result. Because your system will no longer be using onboard video, the memory used by onboard video will be available for system use. Thus, you might be able to use a smaller memory upgrade to reach your desired usable memory size.

Troubleshooting Your Memory Upgrade

If your memory upgrade didn't work, use this section to determine what went wrong and get your system up and running.

Help! I just installed memory and now my system won't boot!

If you had to disconnect drive or power cables to access your memory sockets, chances are you didn't reattach the cables or didn't reattach them properly. Make sure that you reattach power cables to all drives and that the colored stripe on the data cables runs between pin 1 on the motherboard or add-on card connectors and pin 1 on each drive.

It's also possible you didn't lock the module in place. Turn off and unplug the system and verify that the module is locked in place; compare the installation to Figure 7.5 or Figure 7.8. If the module isn't locked down, press carefully on both ends of the module until it locks into position.

If the module is installed correctly, but doesn't work, you might have installed a dead module or an incorrect module type. Turn off the system, remove the module you just installed, and turn the system back on. If the system boots when you remove the new memory, you either have a dead module or you bought the wrong type. Put it back in the anti-static package, find your receipt, and go back to the store. Before you put on your best "help me" face to see if you can persuade the store to let you return or exchange your memory, better take another look at your system manual or existing memory to make sure you're getting the right type, size, and speed.

Now you know why I don't close up the case until I'm sure the system is working!

Help! I just spent good money on memory that my system doesn't recognize! What's wrong?

If none of the memory is being detected, you probably didn't lock the memory in place when you installed it. Go back and take a careful look at Figure 7.5 or 7.8. The locks used on DIMM and SODIMM modules help assure that the connector on the memory module is up close and personal with the motherboard's memory socket.

If the memory is properly locked into place, you might have installed the wrong type of memory. If you bought memory that has a higher capacity than your motherboard was designed to use, some of the memory (but not all) might be detected. In either case, try to return it, but make sure you verify the correct memory type before you return it.

Help! My system keeps locking up, and it's actually gotten worse since I added memory.

More memory requires more power (and creates more heat), so cleaning the cooling vents and fans on your system can't hurt. If you're running DDR memory, especially if you're overclocking it, your memory might be overheating. Take a tip from memory makers such as Corsair Memory (www.corsairmemory.com). Corsair's XMS (Xtreme Memory Speed) modules are designed for overclocking and feature heat spreaders over the memory chips to help keep them cool at high speeds.

Other vendors have also developed overclock-friendly memory with heat spreaders, but you don't need to replace your memory to benefit from heat spreader technology. You can purchase aftermarket heat spreaders from companies such as Vantec Thermal. For about $10–$12 per module and a few minutes of installation time, you can keep your current memory cool. Figure 7.9 shows how a Vantec Thermal Iceberg DDR copper heat spreader fits on an off-the-shelf DDR266 memory module.

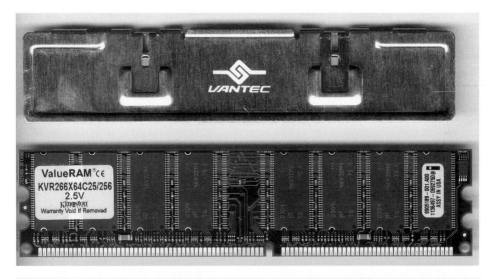

Figure 7.9

A Vantec Iceberg DDR copper heat spreader (top) before installation on a DDR266 memory module (middle) and after installation (bottom).

However, if your system still uses SIMMs, it's also possible your existing memory and sockets are corroded. This can happen if you mix tin and gold contacts; some SIMM memory and sockets are tin and others are gold. Corrosion can result when dissimilar metals are in contact over long periods of time. Dampness in the air can accelerate this process. Be sure to buy tin-connector SIMMs for motherboards with tin (silver-colored) SIMM sockets, and gold-connector SIMMs for motherboards with gold SIMM sockets. Newer memory types, such as DIMMs and RIMMs, all use gold connectors and sockets.

READ THIS TOO: Much, MUCH More About RAM

If this chapter has just whetted your appetite to learn about RAM, check out the following resources.

Books

Upgrading and Repairing PCs, 15th Edition, by Scott Mueller (Que, 2003). Scott's work has been a constant inspiration to me since the first edition was published in 1988. I've also been privileged to work on the 11th and newer editions with him. Check out the chapter on memory for lots more about older memory technologies and the newest RIMM and DDR SDRAM modules.

How Computers Work, Sixth Edition, by Ron White (Que, 2001) helps you visualize how memory works with other computer components, thanks to terrific, imaginative, full-color illustrations.

Web Site

Kingston's Ultimate Memory Guide (available from www.kingston.com) provides what I consider the best single online guide to memory technologies.

Chapter 8

Speedy Computing with Processor Upgrades

No matter what you add to your system as an upgrade, whether it's AGP 8x graphics or a rewriteable DVD, your friends are *most* impressed by how fast a processor your computer has. Naturally, the computer with the fastest processor is the "best"—but note the quotation marks.

A faster processor is only part of the equation for superb PC performance. Couple a fast processor to slow memory, graphics, or hard disk, and it's like watching an Autobahn-ready BMW sports sedan stuck in rush-hour traffic. However, there's never been a better time to unleash the performance of your PC by combining fast memory, high-performance 3D graphics, and fast hard-disk performance with a fast processor. A processor upgrade is more complicated than most other upgrades, but sometimes it can be the missing link between your current hardware and supercharged computing.

In this chapter, you learn to determine which processors can be upgraded, when you also need to replace the motherboard and memory as part of the upgrade process, and how to find out what your upgrade options are for your system.

Ten Reasons to Upgrade Your Processor

A processor upgrade is about as close to brain surgery as the average non-medical person is going to get. It can be expensive, requires opening up a mysterious enclosure, and can take a long time if things don't go well. It's no wonder that some people put it off as long as possible. Maybe our top-ten list will inspire you to see things differently.

1. Your computer's running the slowest processor on the list of supported models.
2. You bought a Duron when you really wanted an Athlon XP.
3. You bought a Celeron when you really wanted a Pentium 4.
4. Your processor plugs into a slot instead of a socket.
5. Your computer thinks that the Pentium ends with II.
6. Your Athlon doesn't have XP in the name.
7. You're running DDR memory with a processor that can't appreciate the speed.
8. You promised yourself *last* year you'd upgrade the processor.
9. The fan on your processor has so much gunk on it, it's growing crops.
10. You've upgraded the motherboard and RAM, so it's time to do the processor.

Recognize yourself or your computer? Keep reading!

Processors 101

It's a lot easier to understand why the processor (also called the *Central Processing Unit (CPU)*) should be upgraded if you know what it does. The CPU has been called the "brain" of the computer. The CPU is used to create, manipulate, and send commands to other peripherals used to store, transmit, or print data. It coordinates the operation of most types of peripherals, and it has a high-speed direct connection to RAM.

Because the CPU performs the most critical tasks in the computer, the design of the CPU (which influences how efficiently the computer works with information) and its *clock speed* (which measures how quickly the computer performs tasks relative to other CPUs with similar designs) are two important measures of the relative speed of a computer.

Major Features of Modern CPUs

All modern CPUs have the following features:

- **A high-speed data bus to memory**—The speed of the CPU to memory bus is often referred to as the *front-side bus* (FSB). The faster the FSB, the faster the access to memory and the faster your system performance. Because of the wide range of FSB speeds, you must make certain you buy the correct memory speed for your system and adjust the FSB setting to match the correct speed used by your processor.

- **A 64-bit wide memory bus**—Although all desktop CPUs (except the new 64-bit Athlon 64) process data internally only 32 bits at a time, using a 64-bit memory bus enables the CPU to work more efficiently.

- **Internal cache memory**—Cache memory inside the CPU's core (Level 1 or L1 cache) retains a copy of data recently retrieved from main memory, enabling the system to reuse that information without another fetch from main memory. L1 cache is always accessed at full processor speed. All modern processors also have a larger Level 2 (L2) cache built into the processor that is accessed if L1 cache doesn't have the requested information. Main memory is accessed only if L1 and L2 cache don't have the required information. In otherwise similar systems, larger L1/L2 cache sizes produce better system performance.

- **Multimedia extensions**—Additional instructions (such as Intel's MMX, SSE, and SSE2, AMD's 3D-Now! and 3D-Now! Professional) improve video and multimedia performance when software is written to work with these instructions.

- **Efficient design**—The latest processors (Intel Pentium 4 3GHz and above, Athlon XP, and Athlon 64) have various design features that enable them to perform more operations than previous designs in the same time.

The "perfect" processor upgrade for you is the one that significantly enhances performance over your current processor at a cost that is a lot less than getting a new system. "Significant" in this case means at least a 50 percent improvement in performance in processor-intensive functions such as 3D gaming and digital media creation and playback. Keep in mind that if you use your PC primarily for checking email and word-processing or other functions that aren't processor-intensive, you won't see much benefit from a processor upgrade.

In some cases, the fastest processor your system can use might be priced out of your budget, but if you wait a few months or set your sights a bit lower, you can still improve system performance at a significant savings. Sometimes, a processor upgrade might also require a motherboard and memory upgrade to get the full benefit of a new processor or to enable your system to handle a different type of processor.

ON THE WEB: Tom's Hardware Puts Them All to the Test

In early 2003, the Tom's Hardware web site tested 65(!) processors with speeds from 100MHz all the way to over 3GHz. You can use these test results to help choose upgrades that will make the biggest difference in performance. Note that motherboard and RAM differences also impact performance. See "Benchmark Marathon: 65 CPUs from 100 MHz to 3066 MHz" at http://www6.tomshardware.com/cpu/20030217/index.html.

MARK'S TIP SHEET: How Fast Is Your Current Processor? Here's How to Find Out

If you're not sure about your processor type, clock speed, and cache sizes, go back to Chapter 4, "Taking an Inspection Tour of Your System," and review the methods for finding out this information. Some systems will display this information when you start them up, but for others, you may need to use reporting software such as SiSoftware Sandra to get the information you need. You can't make an intelligent decision about processor upgrades until you know what you already have.

Processors at the End of the Trail

No matter how much you paid for your current computer, it will be outdated sooner or later. It's not a big deal as long as you make periodic upgrades every year or so, but sooner or later, you wind up throwing out so many components that you might as well buy a new PC and start over.

If your computer has one of the following processors, let me suggest you find a good home for it and start with a new one:

- 486 (any speed)
- Pentium (any speed)
- Pentium MMX (any speed)

Here's why:

- There are no cost-effective upgrades that can plug into the sockets used by these old processors, or the upgrades available can't reach speeds above 400MHz or so.

- The other features of these systems (memory, power supply, drive size, and so forth) aren't adequate to support a processor plus motherboard/memory upgrade.

Newer processors (Pentium II, Celeron, Pentium III, Athlon, and Duron) as well as current processors (Athlon XP and Pentium 4) have a wide variety of upgrade options. However, some systems are more upgrade-friendly than others.

Socket to Me! How Sockets, BIOS Chips, and Chipsets Determine Your Options

Your processor upgrade options are limited by several factors, including the following:

- **The processor socket on your motherboard**—You can use only processors that are designed for your motherboard socket or ones that can be adapted to your motherboard socket/slot.

- **The processor settings supported by your motherboard**—Clock multiplier, FSB, and voltage settings must support the processor you want to install. If you want to install a CPU that is not supported by your motherboard, you need to use a special (and more expensive!) upgrade version of the CPU. In some cases, you might need to install faster memory to enable the motherboard to run at the FSB speed needed to support a faster processor.

- **BIOS compatibility**—Because the BIOS is the bridge between your system's hardware and software, you might need to upgrade the BIOS on some older systems before you can install a faster CPU.

ON THE WEB: Get Your Processor Tips Right Here!

The TechTV web site has lots of processor tips, advice, and reviews. Just search for your favorite processor at http://cgi.techtv.com/search.

Want to talk about your favorite processor or other upgrade issue with other users? Try the TechTV message boards at http://cgi.techtv.com/messageboards/.

Socket/Slot Overview

The connection between your processor and the motherboard is a critical factor in determining your processor options. Table 8.1 provides an overview of the CPUs that work in each slot and socket (starting with the 486) and notes the basic options for upgrading each processor. Earlier processors (8088, 8086, 286, and 386) didn't use named socket types.

Table 8.1   Processors, Slots, and Sockets

CPU Type	Socket Type	Slot Type	Upgrade Options
486	Socket 1, 2, and 3	N/A	Obsolete; replace the system
Pentium	Socket 4	N/A	Obsolete; replace the system
Pentium	Socket 5	N/A	Obsolete; replace the system
Pentium-MMX	Socket 7	N/A	Obsolete; replace the system
AMD K5	Socket 7	N/A	Obsolete; replace the system
AMD K6, K6-2, and K6-III	Socket 7	N/A	Obsolete; replace the system
Cyrix 6x86, 6x86MX, and MII	Socket 7	N/A	Obsolete; replace the system
Pentium Pro	Socket 8	N/A	Third-party upgrades to Socket 370 processors via adapter available
Pentium II and Celeron	N/A	Slot 1	Third-party upgrades to Socket 370 processors via adapter available
Celeron and Pentium III	Socket 370	N/A	Varies by motherboard and installed memory
Pentium III	N/A	Slot 1	Third-party upgrades to Socket 370 processors via adapter available
AMD Athlon	N/A	Slot A	Replace motherboard and processor
AMD Athlon, Duron, and Athlon XP	Socket A	N/A	Varies by motherboard and installed memory
Pentium 4	Socket 423	N/A	Third-party upgrades to Socket 478 processors via adapter available
Pentium 4, Celeron	Socket 478	N/A	Varies by motherboard and installed memory

> **READ THIS TOO: Digging Deeper into CPUs? Read This!**
>
> When I want more information about CPUs in an easily digestible form, I turn to the CPU chapter in the latest edition of Scott Mueller's *Upgrading and Repairing PCs* from Que. Over the years, Scott's done an amazing job of digging through the mounds of technical data produced by Intel (http://developer.intel.com), AMD (www.amd.com), and smaller players in the CPU biz to help the vast amounts of information out there make sense. If you need more details than there's room for in this chapter, Scott's book is my final answer!

Where Is the Socket Information?

Although the sockets for the now-obsolete 286, 386, and early 486 processors didn't have labels, processor sockets starting with Socket 3 (used for the last 486-based systems produced) have been labeled and this practice has continued to the present. The socket identification is found on the face of the socket itself, as shown in Figure 8.1. If you're wondering where the CPU socket is on your computer, take a look at your motherboard's documentation. Chapter 9, "Unlock Your System's Potential with Motherboard and BIOS Upgrades," has sketches of typical motherboard types and their CPU socket locations.

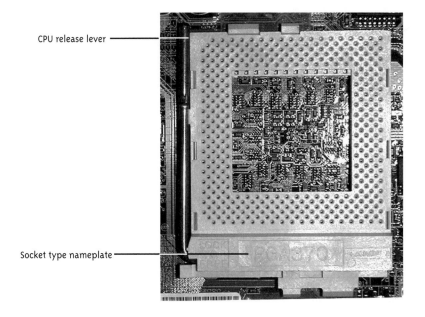

CPU release lever

Socket type nameplate

Figure 8.1

Socket 370 is used by some Pentium III and Celeron processors. It is identified as PGA370 on the nameplate.

Early socket names (refer to Table 8.1) were based on the order in which the sockets were introduced. Starting with Socket 370, the socket name refers to the number of pins in the socket.

MARK'S TIP SHEET: Shining a Light on Sockets

It can be hard to read the name on some sockets inside your computer. Use a flashlight held at an angle to add cross-lighting to make reading the name easier if you're having problems or use a reporting program such as SiSoftware Sandra (see Chapter 4 for details) to identify the socket and processor.

Most sockets starting with Socket 370 are identified as PGA(*socket number*) on the faceplate. In the computer business, PGA doesn't refer to golf; it means *Pin Grid Array*, referring to the pins on the bottom of the CPU that correspond to holes in the CPU socket. See Figure 8.2 for an example of a PGA-type CPU, the AMD Athlon.

Figure 8.2

Bottom (left) and top (right) views of an AMD Athlon, which uses a PGA-type connector.

As you can see from Figure 8.2, CPUs don't have markings to identify the socket type they're designed to use.

Table 8.2 lists the popular names for sockets used by recent upgradable processors, as well as the label actually found on each socket.

Table 8.2 Current CPU Socket Names and Labels

Popular Name	Labeled on Socket As	Number of Pins	CPU Types Using Socket
Socket 370	PGA-370	370	Pentium III and Celeron
Socket A	PGA-462	462	Athlon, Duron, and Athlon XP
Socket 423	PGA-423	423	Early Pentium 4
Socket 478	mPGA-478B	478	Current and future Pentium 4 and Celeron
Socket 754	Socket-754	754	Athlon 64

See the pattern? Although you still need a guidebook to remember which socket works with which CPU (the details about this are contained in subsequent sections in this chapter), at least the name on the socket tells you the number of pins.

How about slots? Although slots don't have nameplate arrangements, it's *much* easier to keep them straight:

- All Intel desktop-type CPUs that use a slot use Slot 1. Intel also makes the Xeon series of server CPUs that use Slot 2 and Socket 603.

- All AMD CPUs that use a slot use Slot A.

Pentium II, Pentium III, Pentium 4, and Celeron Upgrades

So, you found out that your current processor is one of these models. What are your upgrade options? Figure 8.3 provides a brief overview of the possible options. Later in this section, you learn the details.

1. Pentium III (Slot 1)
2. Pentium II
3. Celeron for Slot 1; rear view
4. Slot 1
5. Pentium III/Celeron
6. Pentium III Tualatin
7. Socket 370
8. Pentium 4 Willamette
9. Socket 423
10. Pentium 4 Northwood
11. Celeron Northwood
12. Socket 478

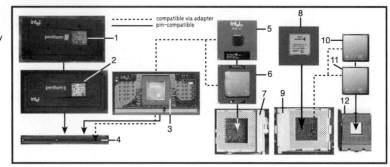

Figure 8.3

Slot and socket compatibility of recent Intel processors.

As Figure 8.3 shows, there are four distinct slot/socket designs used by recent Intel processors. Of these, only Socket 478 is in current production on new systems. In most cases, if you have a Celeron or Pentium 4 motherboard using Socket 478, you can do a direct chip upgrade to a faster processor. A BIOS upgrade might be necessary in some cases.

Table 8.3 provides a capsule summary of the processors shown in Figure 8.3.

Table 8.3	Intel Processors from Pentium II to Pentium 4				
Processor	**Connector Type**	**Clock Speed Range**	**L2 Cache**	**FSB Speed**	**Code Name and Notes**
Pentium II	Slot 1	233–400MHz	512KB*	66 or 100MHz	Deschutes
Celeron	Slot 1	266–300MHz	0KB	66MHz	Covington; based on Deschutes
Celeron	Slot 1	300–433MHz	128KB	66MHz	Mendocino; based on Deschutes
Celeron	Socket 370	300–533MHz	128KB	66MHz	Mendocino; based on Deschutes
Pentium III	Slot 1	450MHz–1GHz	512KB* or 256KB	100 or 133MHz	Coppermine
Pentium III	Socket 370	500MHz–1.1GHz	256KB	100 or 133MHz	Coppermine
Celeron	Socket 370	533MHz–1.1GHz	128KB	66 or 100MHz	Coppermine-128 based on Pentium III Coppermine

Processor	Connector Type	Clock Speed Range	L2 Cache	FSB Speed	Code Name and Notes
Pentium III	Socket 370	1.133–1.4GHz	256KB or 512KB	133MHz	Tualatin
Celeron	Socket 370	900MHz–1.4GHz	256KB	100MHz	Tualatin-256 based on Pentium III Tualatin
Pentium 4	Socket 423	1.3–1.8GHz	256KB	400MHz#	Willamette
Pentium 4	Socket 478	1.8GHz–3.06GHz and higher	256KB or 512KB	400MHz# or 533MHz# or 800MHz#	Northwood
Celeron	Socket 478	1.7–2.4GHz	128KB	400MHz#	Willamette-128 based on Pentium 4 Willamette

*Cache runs at half processor speed.

#Actual FSB speed is one-fourth this value; computer performs four operations per clock cycle to reach this speed.

Here's how to read Table 8.3: If your motherboard currently uses a processor that's based on the same design as a faster model *and* uses the same processor socket (or slot), you can probably do a processor swap. You might also need to install a motherboard BIOS upgrade. However, if the processors are based on different designs, there could be differences in pinouts or voltages that could prevent a direct processor swap. A third-party adapter kit can be used in some cases, but it adds to the expense of the upgrade.

Determining Your Processor Upgrade Options (Overview)

To determine whether you can upgrade to a faster processor without the expense of a third-party kit, follow this procedure:

1. Determine what motherboard and processor type/speed you are currently running. See Chapter 4 for details. I recommend downloading and using SiSoftware Sandra for the greatest detail.

2. Check with your motherboard or system vendor to determine the fastest processor you can use. Even if you have your original system manual, the vendor usually has updated information on the web site that indicates the BIOS updates needed to use faster processors. Some vendors have a quick processor lookup chart for any given motherboard to show all the processors supported at a glance, along with the BIOS updates needed to use a particular processor.

3. If you cannot install a processor faster than 1GHz, consider a third-party upgrade kit or a processor/motherboard/memory upgrade.

4. If you can install a processor faster than 1GHz, look at the speed of your onboard memory as determined by SiSoftware Sandra (refer to Chapter 4 for details). If your onboard memory is not fast enough for the processor speed you want to use, you need to upgrade the memory or consider a processor/motherboard/memory swap. Depending on the motherboard and processor, you might need to move to a faster memory type than what is installed to use a faster processor.

5. Try to get a processor upgrade that is at least 50 percent faster than your current processor's clock speed. Smaller increases in clock speed are usually not worthwhile.

See the following sections for details.

ON THE WEB: Upgrading Help for Dell Computer Fans

If you want to upgrade the processor in a Dell Dimension PC, stop by Robert Hancock's Dell Dimension Processor Upgrade FAQ web site (`http://www.roberthancock.com/dell/`) for a useful overview of your options.

Upgrading Slot 1 Systems

Slot 1 has been out of date for several years. In fact, a system with a Slot 1-based processor must use an adapter (sometimes referred to as a slotket) to allow a Socket 370 processor to plug into Slot 1 to move to faster processors because Slot 1 processors have been out of production for several years.

If you want to keep your current motherboard, the safest way to upgrade Slot 1 systems is with an upgrade processor assembly. See the "Processor Upgrade Kits" section later in this chapter for details. Because of the relatively high cost of high-quality upgrades, I would recommend alternatives such as a motherboard/processor/memory upgrade or using the computer for less strenuous tasks.

Upgrading Socket 370 Systems

At first glance, an upgrade from a slow Socket 370 processor to a fast one looks simple. Unfortunately, Socket 370 (see Figure 8.4) has gone through three variations:

- When Socket 370 was first introduced, Intel positioned it as an economy product. Its flagship Pentium III was still being produced in the bulky cartridge form shown in Figure 8.3, and the Socket 370 Celeron was designed to be sold to the low-cost market.

- Later, Intel redesigned the Pentium III, moving the L2 cache memory that had once been inside the cartridge into the processor itself, creating a new Pentium III design that was the same size as the Socket 370 Celeron. Unfortunately, the Socket 370 version of the Pentium III, also known as the Coppermine, has a different pinout than the Celeron. Thus, early Socket 370 motherboards designed for the Celeron might not work with Pentium III processors.

- The last versions of the Pentium III used an improved design code named Tualatin; Tualatin-based Celerons were also produced before the Celeron switched to Socket 478. Processors based on the Tualatin design used lower voltages than previous Pentium III and Celeron processors, and once again, motherboards built before Tualatin might not work with it.

Figure 8.4

Pentium III processor (top) and Socket 370 (bottom).

If you want to continue to use a pre-Tualatin motherboard but upgrade to a processor running at 1GHz or higher, the safest way is with a pre-built processor upgrade kit from companies such as PowerLeap (www.powerleap.com) or Evergreen Technologies (www.evertech.com). You can also buy adapters that correct voltage and pinouts for use with processors you purchase separately. See the "Processor Upgrade Kits" section later in this chapter for details. However, because of the relatively high cost of these upgrades, I recommend considering a motherboard/processor/memory upgrade or using the computer for less strenuous tasks.

Table 8.4 compares some possible upgrades.

Table 8.4 Examples of Socket 370 Celeron Upgrades				
Current Processor	**Front Side Bus**	**Suggested Upgrade**	**Front Side Bus**	**Notes**
600MHz	66MHz	1.2GHz, 1.3GHz, or 1.4GHz	100MHz	Upgrade to PC100/133 memory if necessary
667MHz	66MHz	1.3GHz or 1.4GHz	100Mz	Upgrade to PC100/133 memory if necessary
766MHz	66MHz	1.4GHz	100MHz	Upgrade to PC100/133 memory if necessary
800MHz	100MHz	1.4GHz	100MHz	No memory upgrade is necessary

If your Celeron processor is running faster than 800MHz, the value of an upgrade to a 1.4GHz Celeron is marginal.

You can buy a 1.4GHz Celeron processor for about $60. A cooling fan is about $10. Pentium III processors running at 1.4GHz cost over $200, making them a significantly poorer value.

Upgrading Socket 423 Systems

Often, the computer business punishes early adopters of new technology: they pay too much, get too little in return, and sometimes wind up with an orphan with limited upgrade potential. If you bought an early Pentium 4-based system (which used Socket 423), Intel has *no* processor upgrade options for you at all. Fortunately, Socket 478 Celeron and Pentium 4 processors can be adapted to plug into Socket 423 by third-party vendors. See the "Processor Upgrade Kits" section later in this chapter for details.

Upgrading Socket 478 Systems

Current Pentium 4 processors and Celeron processors use Socket 478 (see Figure 8.5). Socket 478 is a micro-PGA design that uses connectors that are much closer together than with previous processors. This is why the socket and processor are smaller than Socket 370.

Figure 8.5

Pentium 4 processor
(top) and Socket
478 (bottom).

Upgrading a Socket 478-based system to a faster processor is relatively simple. You can do
one of the following:

- Choose a processor that is significantly faster than your old processor *and* uses the same
  FSB speed.
- Adjust the FSB speed (if possible) to use even faster processors.

The first generation of Pentium 4 processors and Celeron processors have a 400MHz FSB.
Figure 8.6 shows how they compare in features and demonstrates some suggested upgrades.

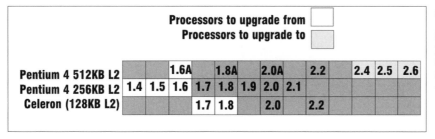

Figure 8.6

Suggested upgrades
for Socket 478
Pentium 4 and
Celeron processors
with 400MHz FSB.

	Processors to upgrade from								
Pentium 4 512KB L2		1.6A	1.8A	2.0A	2.2	2.4	2.5	2.6
Pentium 4 256KB L2	1.4 1.5	1.6 1.7	1.8 1.9	2.0 2.1				
Celeron (128KB L2)		1.7 1.8		2.0	2.2			

If your motherboard can be adjusted to use the 533MHz FSB speed supported by faster
processors, this opens up additional upgrade options, as shown in Figure 8.7.

Figure 8.7

Suggested upgrades for Socket 478 Pentium 4 and Celeron processors with 400MHz and 533MHz FSB.

							Processors to upgrade from ☐					
							Processors to upgrade to ☐						
Pentium 4 512KB L2 533MHz FSB								2.26	2.4	2.53	2.66	2.8	3.06
Pentium 4 512KB L2 400MHz FSB		1.6A		1.8A		2.0A		2.2	2.4	2.5	2.6		
Pentium 4 256KB L2 400MHz FSB	1.4	1.5	1.6	1.7	1.8	1.9	2.0	2.1					
Celeron (128KB L2 400MHz FSB)			1.7	1.8		2.0		2.2					

AMD Athlon, Athlon XP, and Duron Upgrades

The AMD Athlon was originally introduced in the Slot A form factor, which, like Intel's Socket 8 and Socket 423, has become an orphan with no other processors using this form factor.

Later Athlons, all Durons (a now-discontinued economy version of the Athlon with a 128MB L2 cache), and all models of the Athlon XP, AMD's current 32-bit processor, use Socket A. This is a 462-pin socket (see Figure 8.8) also known as Socket 462.

Figure 8.8

AMD Athlon processor (top) and Socket A (bottom).

Although all Durons and all Athlon XPs use the same Socket A used by late-model Athlons, internal differences between models (such as voltage requirements and memory types supported) mean that you need to check the manual for your system or motherboard to determine what processors you can install as upgrades.

AMD processors for Socket A use three different FSB speeds:

- **200MHz**—Supported by all Duron processors and most Athlon processors up to 1.4GHz; most systems use PC100 (168-pin DIMM) memory with this FSB speed.

- **266MHz**—Supported by newer Athlon processors from 1GHz up to 1.4GHz and by Athlon XP processors up to some models of the 2600+. Depending on the motherboard, systems typically use PC133 (168-pin DIMM) or DDR2100 (184-pin DIMM) memory with this FSB speed.

- **333MHz**—Used by the latest Athlon XP processors, starting with some versions of the 2600+ and higher. Systems typically use DDR2700 (184-pin DIMM) memory with this FSB speed.

Newer motherboards offer more FSB setting options than older processors, which is why two computers with the same processor installed might have significantly different upgrade paths.

To get the latest information about which Socket A processors can be installed on your motherboard, check your vendor's web site.

ANALYZE THIS

What Makes an Athlon XP Xtra Special?

The "XP" in Athlon XP, according to AMD, indicates that Athlon XP processors have "extreme performance" to better support Windows XP, as well as previous versions of Windows. Although low-end Athlon XP processors have clock speeds similar to the fastest conventional Athlon processors, the XP versions have better overall performance because of improved internal designs.

The model numbers of different Athlon XP processors *don't* reflect the actual clock speeds of the processor. Instead, they reflect how the processor compares in overall performance to a particular Pentium 4 processor. Although Athlon XP processors have significantly *slower* actual clock speeds than Pentium 4 processors, AMD's model numbering scheme is fairly accurate because of the advanced internal designs used by AMD.

Table 8.5 shows the actual clock speeds of Athlon XP processors compared to the clock speeds of the fastest non-XP Athlons. All processors run at 266MHz FSB unless noted.

Table 8.5   Athlon and Athlon XP Compared

Processor Type	Model Number	Actual Clock Speed	Clock Multiplier	L2 Cache Size	Notes
Athlon	1200	1200	4.5x (266FSB)	256KB	Some models have 200MHz FSB; they use 6x clock multiplier
Athlon	1333	1333	5x (266FSB)	256KB	
Athlon	1400	1400	5.5x (266FSB)	256KB	Some models have 200MHz FSB; they use 7x clock multiplier
Athlon XP	1500+	1333	5x	256KB	
Athlon XP	1600+	1400	5.25x	256KB	
Athlon XP	1700+	1466	5.5x	256KB	
Athlon XP	1800+	1533	5.75x	256KB	
Athlon XP	1900+	1600	6x	256KB	
Athlon XP	2000+	1666	6.25x	256KB	
Athlon XP	2100+	1733	6.5x	256KB	
Athlon XP	2200+	1800	6.75x	256KB	
Athlon XP	2400+	2000	7.5x	256KB	
Athlon XP	2500+	1833	5.5x	512KB	333MHz FSB
Athlon XP	2600+	2083	6.25x	256KB	333MHz FSB
Athlon XP	2600+	2133	8x	256KB	
Athlon XP	2700+	2167	6.5x	256KB	333MHz FSB
Athlon XP	2800+	2083	6.25x	512KB	333MHz FSB
Athlon XP	3000+	2167	6.5x	512KB	333MHz FSB
Athlon XP	3200+	2333	7x	512KB	333MHz FSB

If your motherboard can run with a 333MHz FSB, get the biggest boost in performance by moving to an Athlon XP processor model featuring 512KB of L2 cache. This design, code-named "Barton," is likely to be used in lower-speed models as time passes.

OEM Versus Boxed Processors

If your motherboard can be configured to use the processor speed you prefer, you can often buy the processor in two forms:

- OEM
- Boxed

Which one is better for you? Read on.

OEM Processors

An *OEM (Original Equipment Manufacturer)* processor is sold by its manufacturer in groups, packaged in anti-static trays, and is intended to be integrated (a fancy name for assembled) into a finished product such as a PC or an upgrade CPU. Because the CPU manufacturer doesn't know how the CPUs will be used (or abused) by the OEM vendor, these CPUs have two major characteristics you need to understand:

- No fan or heatsink is provided by the CPU vendor.
- They have *very* limited warranties. These are often as little as 30 days. In addition, the warranties are handled by the vendor from which you bought the CPU, rather than from the CPU's actual manufacturer.

If you buy an OEM processor, don't be fooled by the lower price you pay compared to a boxed processor. If the vendor doesn't provide you with at least a one-year warranty, think again. And remember that if you don't buy a bundle containing a fan/heatsink combination, you need to buy the fan/heatsink yourself. OEM processors aren't bad to buy—*if* you are an experienced CPU upgrade jockey and get the right aftermarket warranty and correct heatsink.

CAUTION: STOP! LOOK! THINK!

Don't Be a Heatsink Cheapskate

You might be wondering why a reputable vendor often insists on selling a matched heatsink with an OEM processor. It's because too many users try to get by with reusing the heatsink off the old processor. *Unless* you chose a heatsink for the old processor that is also designed to work with the new processor, don't reuse it. Here's why:

- Some heatsinks are designed for chips with a different thickness than the chip you're installing. For example, if you try to use a heatsink for Socket 7 with a Socket 370 CPU, you could crush the processor core (the small area at the center of the chip that contains the integrated circuits).

- As clock speeds rise, processors get hotter. AMD now requires a copper heat transfer surface on heatsinks for its newest processors instead of aluminum because copper transfers heat better. Use an aluminum heatsink instead of a copper model, and you could literally fry your processor. Figure 8.9 compares all-aluminum and copper-surface heatsinks.

- Older heatsinks usually move less air than newer ones do and often have less efficient designs.

The bottom line? Pay the money and get a heatsink that protects your processor.

The main reason to get an OEM processor and heatsink? Overclocking. If you're not satisfied running your system at standard settings, you need an OEM processor and the most powerful heatsink you can buy. Some heavy and high-dollar models have huge fans and all-copper construction to move massive amounts of air and heat away from your processor. See Figure 8.9.

If you'd rather have the processor vendor worry about matching up the parts *and* you're not interested in overclocking, buy a boxed processor instead.

Figure 8.9

An all-aluminum heatsink (left) for processors under 2GHz clock speeds compared to a heatsink with a copper contact surface (right) for use with faster processors.

CAUTION: STOP! LOOK! THINK!

Overclocking Pros and Cons

Overclocking refers to configuring a PC component so that the processor, memory, or graphics card runs faster than specified. Economy-minded gamers and digital media fans love overclocking because it enables them to use lower-rated (and lower-cost) components to achieve performance similar to higher-rated (and more expensive) components.

You can overclock the processor and the memory in many recent systems by adjusting the BIOS settings; some processors also allow you to adjust the clock multiplier. Some graphics cards include overclocking utilities.

I have to admit I'm *not* a big fan of overclocking, even though I like a bargain as much as the next PC user. Here's why:

- Overclocking can damage components unless they can be adequately cooled.

- Overclocking voids manufacturers' warranties.

- Overclocking can be a false economy because of the extra time needed to find stable settings and because of the additional expense of auxiliary fans and more powerful replacement processor and graphics card heatsinks.

If you want to try overclocking, be sure to check the experts for tips and cautions:

- See TechTV's article, "Overclock Your Processor," at www.techtv.com/screensavers/answerstips/story/0,24330,2119488,00.html.

- Tom's Hardware (www.tomshardware.com) typically overclocks processors as part of its normal test procedures.

- Overclockers.com (www.overclockers.com) offers user reports of overclocking experiences. The OverClock Intelligence Agency web site (www.ocia.net) offers links to other overclocking web sites. Both offer their own articles and reviews of case, cooling, and other products you need to successfully overclock your system.

Boxed Processors

A *boxed* processor comes in a retail box and features niceties you really need, including the following:

- **An integrated fan and heatsink**—These usually feature ball-bearing construction to make sure they last throughout the warranty period and provide adequate cooling.

- **A long warranty**—Three years is typical, although you might be looking for another upgrade in less time.

You have to spend more for a boxed processor than an OEM processor, but you have fewer worries during installation—and later. Just remember that if you're looking for the bleeding-edge latest CPU, the OEM vendors get them before your friendly boxed version is ready for store shelves. In addition, if you're hot to trot with overclocking, you can find lots of high-performance (expensive) active heatsinks available for your extreme-performance cooling pleasure and ready to attach to a OEM processor. A factory-provided heatsink provides adequate cooling for the processor, but isn't designed to handle overclocking.

Processor Upgrade Kits

In the days of the Pentium and K6 series of processors, installing a processor meant that you needed to adjust switches or jumper blocks on the motherboard to configure the front-side bus speed, voltage, and processor clock speed. It was easy to make mistakes, and a mistake could mean that you could damage or destroy your processor.

Most recent systems automatically set the voltage for you and use a BIOS configuration utility to set the other options. However, if your motherboard isn't designed to provide the correct voltage for the processor you want to install or lacks the correct bus speed or processor clock speed options for the new processor, you can't install an OEM or boxed processor. Instead, you have to install an upgrade processor.

An upgrade processor of a given speed performs *identically* to its OEM or boxed retail sibling. So, what's the difference? The upgrade CPU can be plugged into systems that could never handle the standard OEM or boxed versions of the CPU because of differences in the physical connector, the voltage requirements, or the clock multiplier. Thus, upgrade CPUs can provide faster CPUs for motherboards that, based on their normal CPU options, have already reached their top CPU speed.

How Upgrade Processors Differ

Compared to a normal CPU, an upgrade CPU sometimes resembles a "Dagwood sandwich" of additional components needed to bridge the technological gap between the motherboard and the whizz-bang CPU of your dreams. Additional components such as voltage regulators, clock control circuitry, pinout adapters, and a customized heatsink are typically used along with an off-the-shelf processor to create a customized processor upgrade.

Processor upgrades are available for the following:

- Slot 1 motherboards (adapts Socket 370 processors and adjusts voltage).
- Pre-Tualatin Socket 370 motherboards (adjusts voltage and pinouts to use Tualatin Socket 370 processors).
- Socket 423 motherboards (adjusts pinouts to use Socket 478 processors).

As long as power, logic, and data signals can be properly converted, an upgrade processor can be used in place of a normal processor.

With the increased standardization of processor designs (Socket 478 works with all current Intel processors), the upgrade processor business is not as popular as it once was. Several years ago, Intel made a line of OverDrive processors for upgrading older systems, but the last products made supported the long-outdated Pentium MMX and Pentium Pro processors. The major vendors today include PowerLeap (www.powerleap.com) and Evergreen Technologies (www.evertech.com).

Note that there are *no* upgrade processors made for AMD Athlon, Duron, or Athlon XP processors. Because AMD's processors are less expensive than comparable Intel processors and most Athlon-based systems have highly configurable motherboards, you can often do a direct chip upgrade or you can afford to replace your motherboard and processor.

Is an Upgrade CPU Worth It?

Although real-world results vary, you can see overall performance boosts of 30 percent to as much as 60 percent on some tasks if you make a significant upgrade (double or faster than the original CPU clock speed), depending upon how slow your original CPU was and how much faster your new CPU is.

An upgrade processor can be an attractive alternative to a motherboard plus processor upgrade if you don't want to wrestle with the motherboard, or if your system doesn't have an ATX or microATX motherboard. However, in many cases, a motherboard plus processor upgrade is a better long-term solution.

ON THE WEB: Putting Upgrade Processors to the Test

Find out whether upgrade processors are worthwhile and learn more about them with these links:

- **Duh Voodoo Man's PowerLeap Upgrade Guide**—Hands-on reviews of PowerLeap's Slot 1, Socket 370, and Socket 423 upgrades are at http://duhvoodooman.com/powrleap/PLmain.htm.

- **Upgrade an Older PC**—*PC Magazine* tests a PowerLeap upgrade processor for Slot 1 systems at www.pcmag.com/article2/0,4149,896096,00.asp.

Protecting Your New Processor

If you opt for one of AMD's or Intel's fastest processors, it could be one of the most expensive upgrades you can make. Here's how to protect your processor investment before you install it:

- **Make sure your power supply is ready**—See Chapter 22, "Power Supply Upgrades," to learn how to evaluate your current power supply. If your power supply doesn't put out enough watts or supply adequate amperage for your new processor, you could damage it.

- **Watch the power supply**—If you've decided you need to change motherboards as well, make sure your power supply has the right connections. For example, if you're opting for a Pentium 4 processor, your power supply needs to have an ATX12V connector as well as the normal 20-pin ATX connector to supply correct power levels. You can buy an adapter if your power supply is otherwise suitable, but if not, figure on a new power supply.

- **The heatsink's important**—The fan on the heatsink supplied with your boxed or upgrade processor (or selected by you or your vendor if you buy an OEM processor) moves heat away from the processor. However, if you have a case without a rear fan, the heat may stay inside the case and cause stress for other components. Figure 8.10 shows a typical 80mm case fan you can install in a case that doesn't have one.

Figure 8.11 shows an interior view of the case before and after fan installation. In this example, the fan was connected to a three-pin chassis fan connection on the motherboard. Connecting the fan to the motherboard enables the BIOS to display fan rotation speed. Note that many newer cases use larger fans.

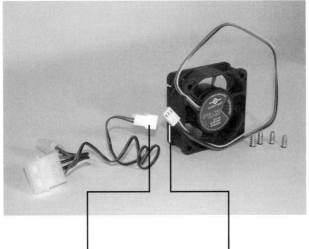

Figure 8.10

An 80mm case fan that can be plugged into the mother- board or into a 4-pin hard drive power cable. The adapter has a pass- through connector, so it can be used to power the fan and a drive.

Adapter for use with 4-pin power cable   3-pin connector to motherboard

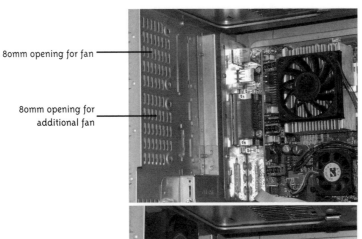

Figure 8.11

The interior of a computer before (top) and after (bottom) the instal- lation of a rear case fan.

80mm opening for fan

80mm opening for additional fan

Case fan after installation

Out with the Old, In with the New

The CPU replacement process involves the following steps:

1. Selecting a CPU that works with your system (as discussed earlier).

2. Making sure your system is ready for the new CPU.

3. Removing your old CPU and heatsink.

4. Installing your new CPU and heatsink.

5. Configuring your system for the new CPU.

Before you can remove your old CPU, you need to do the following:

1. Record your CMOS/BIOS information, as discussed in Chapter 4.

2. Shut down and unplug the system.

3. Remove the cover, as discussed in Chapter 4.

4. Take anti-static precautions, as discussed in Chapter 5, "Preparing for Your Upgrade."

5. Remove the motherboard (see Chapter 9 for details).

Removing the motherboard seems like a lot of extra trouble to take for a processor upgrade. However, there are good reasons to do it:

- If you are installing an upgrade for a Socket 370, Socket A, or Socket 423 motherboard, the spring clips that hold the heatsink in place require lot of downward pressure to remove and re-engage. Combined with the weight of today's heatsinks and the possibility the motherboard might not be adequately supported, you could crack your motherboard if you don't remove it. What about Socket 478? It uses a heatsink support that uses the case instead of the motherboard to handle the weight.

- If you don't connect the fan to a proper power connector, you could destroy your processor in a few seconds if it runs without cooling. This is especially true with AMD Athlon, Duron, and Athlon XP models. To allow for fan monitoring, you should attach the fan to the motherboard if it's designed to do so. The CPU fan connector is very close to the processor socket. Consequently, it's easier to connect the fan if you remove the motherboard to work on the processor.

MARK'S TIP SHEET: Make It a Kodak Moment Before You Take It Apart!

Whether you prefer film or pixels or videotape, you should whip out your favorite type of camera and document the inside of your system before you disconnect cables and start the upgrade process. It's way too easy to forget which cables go where. Just make sure you're close enough to see the components clearly, but don't get *too* close. A lot of cheap 35mm, digital, and pocket cameras can't focus closer than about three feet or so, so if you have a camera with a macro feature, now is the time to use it.

If you don't have a suitable camera, use stickers to label the cables attached to the motherboard before you disconnect them.

Removing and Replacing Socketed CPUs

Before you remove the old CPU, determine which corner of the CPU socket marks Pin 1. Depending on the model, the corner of the CPU might be beveled off, marked with a round or square dot, or marked with a triangle. Because the CPU has a heatsink mounted on it, you might need to look for a Pin 1 marking on the motherboard instead. It's critical that you note which corner is Pin 1. There are at least four ways to mount a square CPU into a square socket, but only one way is correct; the others turn your screaming CPU into a useless hunk of silicon as soon as the power comes on.

CAUTION: STOP! LOOK! THINK!

Don't Touch That Processor Without Protection!
The processor can't hurt you, but if you don't take the ESD precautions outlined in Chapter 5, you can destroy your new processor before it has a chance to boot.

Figure 8.12 compares the most common CPU sockets on systems you might want to upgrade. Note each processor type has a different location for Pin 1 relative to the locking lever, and also note that Socket 423 has the locking lever on the opposite side of the socket from the other socket types. Pin 1 on the new CPU must correspond with Pin 1 on the old CPU.

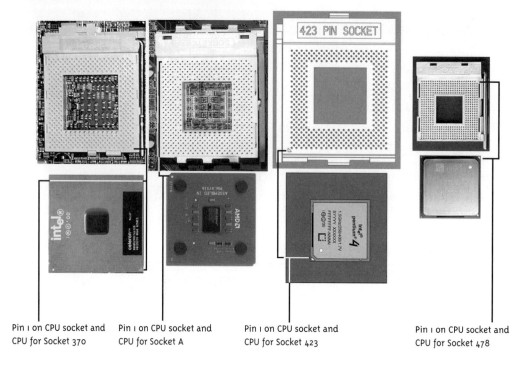

Pin I on CPU socket and CPU for Socket 370

Pin I on CPU socket and CPU for Socket A

Pin I on CPU socket and CPU for Socket 423

Pin I on CPU socket and CPU for Socket 478

Figure 8.12

Socket 370, Socket A, Socket 423, and Socket 478 motherboard processor sockets and processors compared.

Removing the Old Heatsink and Processor

If the heatsink is attached directly to the processor (Socket 370, Socket A), you must first remove the heatsink before you can remove the old processor. Unplug the heatsink's fan from the motherboard or power supply connector before continuing.

Most CPUs have a spring-loaded metal retainer clip that lies across the heatsink and clips it to brackets that extend from opposite sides of the CPU socket. To release the retainer clip, push down and in on the taller side of the clip until the clip is free from the retainers. Then, swing or pry the clip away from the CPU socket. After the taller side is released, push the clip toward the other side of the processor to release it. Then, lift off the heatsink. Don't scratch the motherboard or damage the CPU or socket! See Figure 8.13.

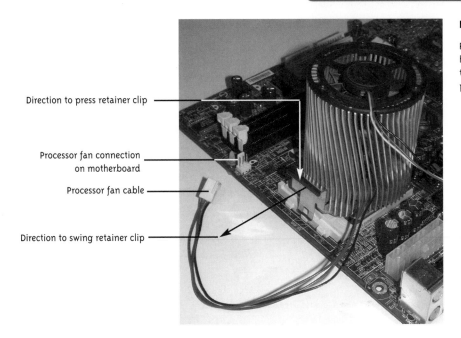

Figure 8.13

Removing the heatsink from a typical Socket A processor.

Direction to press retainer clip

Processor fan connection on motherboard

Processor fan cable

Direction to swing retainer clip

After the heatsink is released from the CPU, lift it off carefully. Many motherboards have delicate capacitors and other circuitry near the CPU socket; damage them and you'll become an unwilling candidate for a motherboard upgrade.

Virtually all processors using modern socket designs use the ZIF (Zero-Insertion-Force) socket design developed late in the 486's lifespan for Socket 3. To remove a CPU mounted in a ZIF socket, push the handle slightly away from the socket, and then rotate it straight up to release the clamp holding the CPU in place. The CPU will lift away freely (see Figure 8.14). Place the old CPU on anti-static material and continue with the new CPU.

If you are installing an upgrade for a Socket 478 processor, the procedure is different because the heatsink is connected to an external frame and a bracket. With these processors:

1. Release the pressure levers that hold the bracket in place over the processor and heatsink.

2. Release the bracket's clips from the frame.

3. Remove the bracket, heatsink, and processor.

4. Remove the frame if the new processor uses a heatsink that requires a different frame.

Direction of movement to release CPU

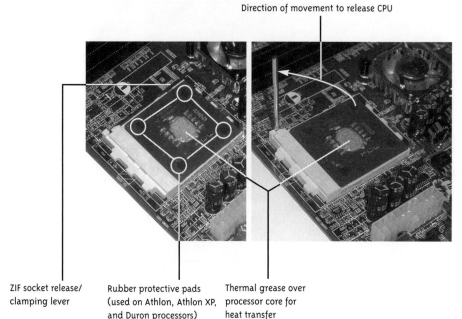

Figure 8.14

After you release the ZIF socket lever (left), raise it (right) to release the CPU for removal.

ZIF socket release/ clamping lever

Rubber protective pads (used on Athlon, Athlon XP, and Duron processors)

Thermal grease over processor core for heat transfer

ON THE WEB: Upgrading a Socket 478 Processor

If you didn't get detailed instructions with your new Socket 478 processor and heatsink, go to `www.quietpcusa.com/rfp4binstall.html`. This set of instructions is specific to the QuietPC-USA Radial Fin CPU cooler, but is also a useful resource for any Socket 478 upgrade process.

Installing the New Processor and Heatsink

You need the following items available before you can install your new CPU:

- The CPU with heatsink.
- A power source for the heatsink's fan; this might be a motherboard connection or a spare drive power connector, depending on the fan type.
- A Y-splitter if your heatsink fan is powered from a drive connector and you have no empty connectors.
- Thermal transfer material, such as thermal grease or thermal tape as recommended by the heatsink and processor vendor; some may be supplied with the heatsink.
- A nutdriver or other tool to push the new heatsink's attachment clip into position.

To install the new CPU and heatsink in a system that uses Socket 370 or Socket A, do the following:

1. Align Pin 1 on the CPU with Pin 1 on the CPU socket.

2. Gently place the CPU into position and make sure all CPU pins are lodged in the correct socket holes; no pins should be bent or out of a mounting hole.

3. Rotate the ZIF socket lever back down to the motherboard and snap it into place parallel to the motherboard.

4. If the heatsink has a thermal pad already applied to it, be sure to remove the protective covering before attaching the heatsink. If you must apply thermal material separately, place a small amount of thermal grease or a thermal pad in the center of the heat spreader plate on the top of the processor to better conduct heat from the CPU to the heatsink. If the CPU uses a flip-chip pin grid array (FC-PGA) design (has a small rectangular metal slug over the processor core in the middle of the CPU), place the thermal grease across the metal slug (refer to Figure 8.14).

5. Follow the manufacturer's directions for placing the heatsink on the processor. AMD Athlon XP processors are very thin, so the bottom of the heatsink is thicker on the side that fits over the label area of the socket. It is also thinner over the processor and its protective rubber pads (refer to Figure 8.14).

6. Position the top end (the end away from the locking handle) of the heatsink clip around the retainer, as shown in Figure 8.15 (see your heatsink's instructions for details).

7. Push the other end of the heatsink clamp down to line up with the mounting lug on the other side of the CPU socket, and then swing it into place (see Figure 8.15). A great deal of force is required, so be sure that you have the heatsink properly positioned. If it's crooked, it could damage the processor.

8. Examine both ends of the clip to make sure they're in place.

9. Plug the heatsink's fan into the correct power supply connector; it might be on the motherboard or might require a connector from the power supply itself.

If you are installing a socket-type CPU into an adapter for use with a slot-type motherboard, the process is similar to the preceding, except that the CPU socket is on the adapter.

Figure 8.15

Positioning the heatsink and retaining clip on the new processor.

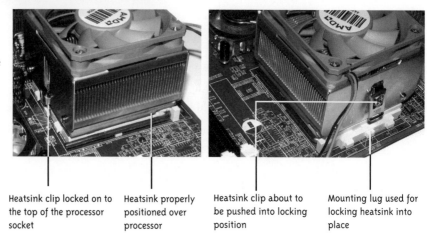

Heatsink clip locked on to the top of the processor socket

Heatsink properly positioned over processor

Heatsink clip about to be pushed into locking position

Mounting lug used for locking heatsink into place

If you are installing a processor on a Socket 478 motherboard, follow these steps:

1. Align Pin 1 on the CPU with Pin 1 on the CPU socket.

2. Gently place the CPU into position and make sure all CPU pins are lodged in the correct socket holes; no pins should be bent or out of a mounting hole.

3. Rotate the ZIF socket lever back down to the motherboard and snap it into place parallel to the motherboard.

4. Attach the replacement frame to the motherboard if necessary. Use the same mounting holes used for the original frame.

5. If the heatsink has a thermal pad or transfer compound already applied to it, be sure to remove the protective covering before attaching the heatsink. If you must apply thermal material separately, place a small amount of thermal grease or a thermal pad in the center of the heat spreader plate on the top of the processor to better conduct heat from the CPU to the heatsink.

6. Attach the heatsink to the frame according to the manufacturer's instructions. Some heatsinks screw into place, while others clip into place.

7. Tighten the heatsink until it makes contact with the heat-spreader plate on top of the processor.

8. Plug the heatsink's fan into the correct power supply connector; it might be on the motherboard or might require a connector from the power supply itself.

After the processor and heatsink are locked into place and the processor fan is connected to the motherboard, reinstall the motherboard into the computer, as described in Chapter 9.

Removing and Replacing Slot-Type CPUs

If you choose to buy an upgrade processor as a replacement for your Slot 1 processor, you need to remove the old processor first. Although lower force is required to perform this upgrade, you should still remove the motherboard first.

Fortunately, upgrading a slot-type CPU is considerably simpler than installing one for the first time on a new motherboard because you can reuse the existing guideposts and heatsink support used by the old CPU.

Although there are no upgrades available for Slot A processors, the removal process is the same as for Slot 1 processors.

Removing the Old Slot I Processor and Heatsink

To remove the old CPU and heatsink, do the following:

1. Unplug the heatsink's fan power connector from the motherboard or power supply.

2. Push the retention clips on both support arms away from the CPU to release it.

3. Lift the CPU up and away from the slot (see Figure 8.16).

4. Place the old CPU on anti-static material.

Direction of CPU removal after
release from retention clips

Support arms with
retention clips

Figure 8.16

Removing a Slot I
Celeron CPU from the
motherboard.

Installing the New Processor and Heatsink

You need the following items available before you can install your new processor:

- The processor with heatsink.

- A power source for the heatsink's fan; this might be a motherboard connection or a spare drive power connector, depending on the fan type.

- A Y-splitter if your heatsink fan is powered from a drive connector and you have no empty connectors.

- A power source for the adapter's voltage regulator (if necessary); this might require another Y-adapter purchase.

- Thermal grease or a thermal pad as recommended by the heatsink vendor if you are attaching the new processor to an adapter yourself; thermal material may be supplied with the heatsink.

If you purchased an upgrade processor, the heatsink is already attached. However, if you purchased a converter kit that requires assembly, apply thermal grease or a thermal pad to the processor as directed by the heatsink vendor before attaching the heatsink. Then, attach the heatsink before you install the processor.

Depending on the CPU/adapter type and heatsink type, this might require clipping the heatsink to one side of the CPU or securing the heatsink to the CPU with bolts. See the heatsink's documentation for details. See Figure 8.17 for an example.

Figure 8.17

The author's Athlon 800MHz OEM processor with a Thermaltake heatsink installed. The retaining clips engage holes on the rear of the processor cartridge. A similar method is used with most Slot 1 heatsinks.

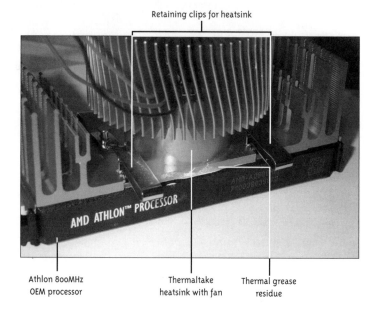

Retaining clips for heatsink

AMD ATHLON™ PROCESSOR

Athlon 800MHz OEM processor

Thermaltake heatsink with fan

Thermal grease residue

To install the CPU after the heatsink is installed, do the following:

1. Look at the bottom of the CPU cartridge or card to note the orientation of the connector; the CPU slot has two different-sized connectors that correspond.

2. Hold the CPU over the CPU slot and move it downward between the support arms.

3. Push the retention clips away from the CPU (if needed) to enable the CPU to be lowered into place.

4. Gently push the CPU into place until the retention clips click into place on both ends of the CPU card or cartridge.

5. Attach the CPU's heatsink fan to the correct power supply connector or motherboard power connection.

Double-Checking Your Installation

After your CPU is installed *and* before you reinstall the motherboard and start the system, double-check the processor installation for the following:

- Is the CPU securely seated in the slot or socket?

- Did you close the ZIF socket lever to secure a socketed CPU?

- Is the heatsink securely positioned onto the CPU?

- Has the heatsink fan been connected to a working power source?

- If the motherboard is an older type that uses switches or jumpers for processor configuration, has the motherboard been properly configured for the new CPU speed, voltage, clock multiplier setting, and FSB? If the motherboard uses a switchless (BIOS-controlled) configuration, you configure the processor after you restart the system.

If you are satisfied that your newer, faster, and better processor is properly installed, plug the system back in and restart your computer. Don't close the case just yet; watch the CPU's heatsink fan to make sure it's turning, and keep your hand on the power switch. Many of today's hot CPUs can ruin themselves in just a few seconds if they are run without active cooling!

Configuring Your Processor in the System BIOS

Although some motherboards automatically detect the necessary settings for your processor, others default to very low settings that will work but might not use your processor to its full capabilities. Therefore, as soon as you start your system, press the key that starts your computer's BIOS setup program (see your motherboard or system documentation for details).

The exact steps needed to configure your new processor vary with the motherboard and processor type. Figure 8.18 shows a typical configuration screen for a system running an AMD Athlon, Athlon XP, or Duron processor.

Figure 8.18

Configuring the clock multiplier, DRAM (memory) frequency, and CPU bus frequency on a typical Athlon-based computer.

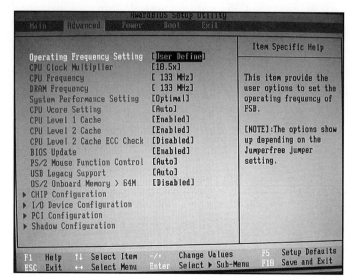

```
                    AwardBIOS Setup Utility
   Main    Advanced   Power    Boot    Exit
                                              ┌──────────────────────┐
                                              │    Item Specific Help │
   Operating Frequency Setting  [User Define] │                       │
   CPU Clock Multiplier         [10.5x]       │ This item provide the │
   CPU Frequency                [ 133 MHz]    │ user options to set the│
   DRAM Frequency               [ 133 MHz]    │ operating frequency of │
   System Performance Setting   [Optimal]     │ FSB.                  │
   CPU Vcore Setting            [Auto]        │                       │
   CPU Level 1 Cache            [Enabled]     │ [NOTE]:The options show│
   CPU Level 2 Cache            [Enabled]     │ up depending on the   │
   CPU Level 2 Cache ECC Check  [Disabled]    │ Jumperfree jumper     │
   BIOS Update                  [Enabled]     │ setting.              │
   PS/2 Mouse Function Control  [Auto]        │                       │
   USB Legacy Support           [Auto]        │                       │
   OS/2 Onboard Memory > 64M    [Disabled]    │                       │
 ▶ CHIP Configuration                         │                       │
 ▶ I/O Device Configuration                   │                       │
 ▶ PCI Configuration                          │                       │
 ▶ Shadow Configuration                       │                       │
                                              └──────────────────────┘
   F1   Help   ↑↓ Select Item   -/+  Change Values    F5   Setup Defaults
   ESC  Exit   ↔  Select Menu   Enter Select ▶ Sub-Menu F10  Save and Exit
```

Understanding Clock Multipliers

Although early processors ran internally at exactly the same speed as they processed data externally, processors have not worked this way since the Pentium 75. To properly configure your new processor, you need to know the CPU and memory (DRAM) frequency and

> **JARGON**
>
> *DRAM*—Dynamic RAM. General term for memory that requires frequent recharges of electricity to retain its contents. Main memory in almost every PC ever built is DRAM.

what clock multiplier to use. This information can be obtained from the memory and processor maker, but it isn't always easy to understand.

Table 8.6 shows how to configure a system that has been upgraded from an Athlon 1.4GHz (266FSB) processor to an Athlon XP 2500+ (333FSB) processor. The values used in this example are derived from those in Table 8.5.

Table 8.6 Adjusting System Settings After a Processor Upgrade			
Processor	**Processor Clock Speed=**	**FSB Setting in BIOS**	**Clock Multiplier Setting in BIOS**
Athlon 1.4GHz	1400MHz	133MHz (266/2)	10.5 (5.25×2)
Athlon XP 2500+	1833MHz	166MHz (333/2)	11 (5.5×2)

It's necessary to divide the processor's rated FSB speed by two and multiply the clock multiplier from Table 8.5 by two when configuring the system BIOS. Here's why: the Athlon processors (including the Athlon XP and Duron) perform two operations per clock cycle. However, the BIOS wants the actual FSB speed, not the effective speed. Similarly, the clock multiplier (which is used along with the FSB speed to set the processor clock speed) is based on multiplying the actual, not effective, FSB speed. Thus, instead of using an FSB speed of 333MHz and a clock multiplier of 5.5 when configuring the BIOS for the new processor, use 166MHz and 11.

Other processors work in a similar fashion, such as Intel's Pentium 4 and Socket 478 Celeron. The 400MHz, 533MHz, or 800MHz FSB speeds are due to quad-pumping (four operations per data cycle). So, divide the effective FSB speed by four when configuring the BIOS.

Troubleshooting Your Processor Upgrade

Because the CPU is the heart and brain of your system, nothing happens if your CPU isn't working. Check out the following to help troubleshoot your system.

Help! My system won't start! All it does is beep!

Take it easy. The fact the system beeps is good news. If you'd really killed it, nothing would be happening. Count the beeps. If you counted five, you probably have an AMI BIOS—and the BIOS is trying to tell you that your CPU is defective with its own five-beep call for help. Is it time to call the vendor to arrange replacement? Maybe not yet, but keep your receipt handy while you double-check your CPU socket and connections.

If your system's not beeping, take a look at where you attached the fan for the processor. Many motherboards made by Gigabyte Technology, for example, include the Guardian feature (it's controlled with a jumper). When Guardian is enabled, it prevents the system from starting if you don't have your processor fan plugged into the processor fan connector on the motherboard. Before he discovered this setting, my son Jeremy spent six frustrating weeks trying to figure out why the vendor could make his motherboard work and he couldn't. Disable this feature if you attach the fan to a drive power connector instead of the motherboard.

Help! My CPU fan won't turn!

First (forgive the yell), *turn off your system—now!!!* (Now back to normal voice.) System off? Okay, I yelled at you (nothing personal) because running your computer without the processor fan working is a great way to fry the processor in just *seconds*. Next, it's time to determine *why* the fan isn't working. Check these possibilities:

- **The fan's getting no power**—Maybe you forgot to plug it into a spare power supply connector or the motherboard? Nobody's perfect, but CPUs aren't very tolerant of forgetfulness.

- **The fan's trying to turn, but can't**—Hmm, I hope you didn't buy one of those cheapjack sleeve-bearing active heatsinks. Those break down very easily. However, if you spent a few extra bucks for the good ball-bearing model, maybe something is blocking your fan. It might be something like an extra power supply connector or ribbon cable. Use a twist tie and move whatever it is out of the way.

Help! My system is crashing faster than ever after my processor upgrade!

Ouch! I know you didn't install a CPU upgrade to get that kind of result. Check the following:

- Make sure the motherboard is set to use the correct FSB speed, clock multiplier, and voltage. A brand-new CPU is no time to fiddle around with overclocked settings.

- Never try hot-rodding your new processor until you are sure—really sure—that it runs correctly in stock configuration using the default settings.

Let me ask you, are you using an adapter to connect your CPU to the motherboard? If so, the settings on the adapter need to be checked as well.

Help! My system thinks I've installed a downgrade!

You say your system is now so slow you think the CPU is installed backward? The last thing you'd expect with a new CPU is a slowdown, right? Check the following:

- Did you install the accessory software supplied with the CPU upgrade (if any)? Some CPU upgrades need a boost from special device drivers to run at full speed.

- How about BIOS settings? If your CPU manual says to make changes and you haven't made them yet, reboot your system, jump into the BIOS setup program, and tweak away as directed. While you're looking at the BIOS setup, make sure that both the internal (Level 1) and external (Level 2) cache settings are enabled.

- Wondering if you're getting a bit more speed—but not enough to matter? You should install the speed-testing software provided with some upgrades and check your system before and after the upgrade. If you didn't get any speed-checkers in the CPU package, you can use SiSoftware Sandra, Norton System Works/Norton Utilities System Information, or similar utilities mentioned in Chapter 4 to check your before and after results.

- And don't forget to double-check the clock-multiplier and FSB settings on your motherboard or in your system's BIOS configuration screens. Did you make the changes needed for maximum speed with your new CPU? Remember: Although overclocking can be risky on some systems, I've yet to see a system complain about *underclocking*, which is what you have when you leave your FSB, clock multipliers, or both set to the pedestrian values of your old CPU. Some systems revert to a fail-safe speed if they don't boot successfully. For example, my computer uses a 1.4GHz Athlon XP. The normal setting is a clock multiplier of 10.5 with an FSB frequency of 133MHz. If I turn off the system before it finished booting, it reverts to a multiplier of 10.5 with an FSB frequency of 100MHz; in other words, it underclocks itself to 1.05GHz!

Chapter 9

Unlock Your System's Potential with Motherboard and BIOS Upgrades

If you can upgrade your memory, your CPU, and your video card on your current system, should you bother with a motherboard upgrade? Absolutely! Here's why a motherboard upgrade makes so much sense:

- A new motherboard helps you get the most out of the fastest new processors (Athlon XP and hyperthreading Intel Pentium 4) and memory types (DDR400).

- It's the only way to try a brand-new processor design like the Athlon 64.

- A new motherboard can incorporate advanced port types such as USB 2.0, IEEE-1394, and Serial ATA, so you don't need to clutter up your expansion slots with add-on cards to enjoy the benefits of these new ports.

- A new motherboard includes a new BIOS chip so that you can overcome hard disk size limits and use features like the new hyperthreading mode in the latest Intel Pentium 4 processors.

- A new motherboard cranks up your graphics potential with support for AGP 4x and 8x.

Of course, there are all types of motherboards on the market: brand new, recent, and (ahem…) mature products that aren't any better than the one you're trying to replace. In this chapter, you learn how to find the right motherboard, and then you learn about the care and feeding of the motherboard's most important and invisible component, the system BIOS.

So, if you're about to order an upgrade or two for your existing system, take a break and digest this chapter first. You might change your mind about what to upgrade next.

Ten Reasons to Upgrade Your Motherboard

Don't let anybody kid you: A motherboard upgrade might be the single most complex upgrade you perform on your system. It can trigger a domino effect of processor and memory upgrades, and it often requires you to perform a repair (re)installation of Windows XP. Thus, it's not surprising if you're thinking twice about doing it. Check out our list of top-ten reasons to take the big step, and you might recognize yourself or your situation. If you do, keep reading!

1. The fastest processor your current motherboard supports doesn't even break the 1GHz barrier.
2. Your motherboard is so old you remember being worried about how it would handle Y2K.
3. Your motherboard has several empty slots, but they're all ISA slots.
4. Your motherboard thinks that Pentium III is as high as Intel can count.
5. Your motherboard thinks that XP and Athlon don't go together.
6. Your motherboard can't work with socketed processors.
7. Your motherboard doesn't have any USB 2.0 ports.
8. Your motherboard doesn't have an AGP slot for fast video.
9. You can't find BIOS upgrades for your motherboard anymore.
10. Your motherboard can't use DDR memory.

If you're considering a motherboard upgrade, you'll find that the entire process makes more sense if you understand what the motherboard does.

What the Motherboard Does

As you saw in Chapter 4, "Taking an Inspection Tour of Your System," virtually everything in your computer is connected to the motherboard. No wonder its name suggests it's the "mother of all boards!" The features built into your motherboard control the following options on your system:

- **CPU type and speed**—Motherboards are designed to handle only particular CPU models in a specified speed range. For maximum flexibility, you want to choose a motherboard that can also accept processors that are substantially faster than the model you plan to install today.

- **Memory form factor and size**—Make sure your motherboard uses the most popular types of memory and can use the high-density memory modules on the market, or you'll severely limit your system's current and future performance potential.

- **Expansion slot types and availability**—Even with the large number of built-in ports on today's motherboards, having four or more PCI slots on a full-size motherboard is critical to full expandability for networking, adding forthcoming high-speed ports such as IEEE-1394b, and other uses.

- **Integrated or add-on video options**—A motherboard that offers both integrated video and an AGP 4x or faster slot enables you to save money initially and upgrade to faster video later. Otherwise, you should insist on an AGP 4x or 8x slot instead of integrated video without an AGP upgrade.

- **Speed of IDE host adapters**—Although current hard drives don't use the full bandwidth of ATA/100 or ATA/133 interfaces, future drives are likely to do so. Serial ATA (SATA) offers even greater bandwidth, along with smaller cables.

- **Hi-Speed USB (USB 2.0)**—Although USB 1.1 is a capable replacement for legacy ports (such as serial, parallel, and PS/2 mouse and keyboard ports), Hi-Speed USB, also known as USB 2.0 (which is backward-compatible with USB 1.1) manages multiple low-speed devices better and provides a fast connection for external drives and high-performance scanners.

- **Chipset and BIOS options**—The more options for boot sequence, bootable drives, drive capacity, drive types, peripheral management, CPU and motherboard speeds, and other features your BIOS provides, the more versatile your system is. However, your BIOS can only maximize the potential of your motherboard's chipset. Choose a motherboard with a chipset that offers the features you need now and in the future (faster CPU and AGP support, and so forth).

If any of these features aren't adequate in your current system, a motherboard is a one-stop solution, and the more items on the list you believe need attention, the higher a motherboard upgrade should climb in your to-do list.

Selecting the Right Motherboard

What's the right motherboard for you? The answer depends in great measure on your answers to these questions:

- What kind of case do you have?
- How large is your power supply?
- Do you want to reuse your existing CPU? If not, what CPU type(s) do you want to install?
- Do you want to reuse your existing memory modules? If not, what memory type do you want to install?
- How many slots do you need altogether?
- Do you have (or plan to get) AGP 8x video?
- What other features do you need that you don't have now?
- How much can you afford to spend for a motherboard upgrade (especially if you also need to upgrade your processor and memory)?

Obviously, your definition of the perfect motherboard is different from mine, and anyone's definition is likely to change over time. However, I'd like to suggest a philosophy of motherboard selection that will serve you well regardless of the specifics of your answer:

- Although a motherboard upgrade often requires you to upgrade your processor and memory, it's a worthwhile investment to make to enhance system performance and useful life.
- If you opt for a motherboard that enables you to reuse your current processor or memory, you save money now but you might also limit the future expandability of your system. This approach makes sense primarily if the components you want to reuse can be used with a motherboard that can also use much faster versions of the same components.
- Mid-size and larger ATX-format cases provide you with the greatest range of upgrade options; micro-ATX and flex-ATX provide you with fewer options. Other types of motherboards (Baby-AT, NLX, and LPX) can't be upgraded because of a lack of readily available replacements that offer current technology.

So, the perfect motherboard upgrade is a balancing act among the following:

- What your case allows
- What your budget allows
- What components you plan to reuse

Even with these limiting factors, you can usually find a motherboard that will provide you with a solid boost in improved performance and features now and more "headroom" for future upgrades down the road.

ON THE WEB: Extreme Web Sites for Extreme Speed Fans!

If you're looking for reviews and news about the fastest motherboards and other extreme gear, be sure to check out these web sites:

- `www.tomshardware.com`—The single best site for coverage of motherboards and chipsets (which make the motherboards do what they do) as well as all the other components in modern PCs.

- `www.maximumpc.com`—The pioneer of sky's-the-limit power computing in its print magazine, the companion web site offers capsule reviews of motherboards and other hardware. Use its rankings as a quick shopping list if you're looking for the best of the best.

- `www.theregister.co.uk`—Wondering what's happening on the other side of the pond (Brit-speak for the North Atlantic)? Stop by the Register and find out why this informative, hard-hitting, and very funny web site truly lives up to its motto: "Biting the hand that feeds IT." Because tech news, like technology itself, has no borders, what's news there is news wherever you are.

Motherboard and Case Form Factors

As you learned in Chapter 4, the most desirable case form factor is ATX, because of its versatility. A mid-sized or larger ATX case can handle any motherboard in the ATX family:

- ATX
- Micro-ATX
- Flex-ATX

A micro-tower ATX case can handle a micro-ATX or flex-ATX motherboard, which offer fewer slots and less potential for high-end performance. Most computers sold at retail since the late 1990s are based on the ATX or micro-ATX designs.

Figure 9.1 shows side views of typical systems with ATX and micro-ATX motherboards. The case with the ATX motherboard has more slots and more drive bays than the case with the micro-ATX motherboard.

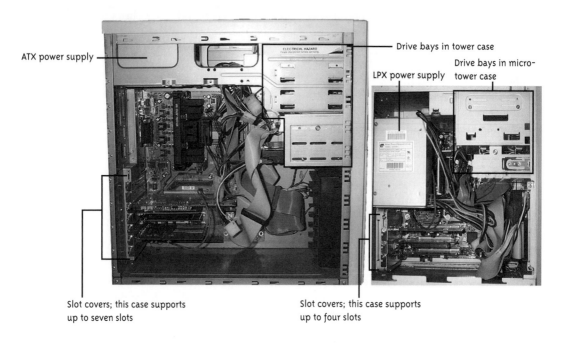

ATX power supply

Drive bays in tower case

Drive bays in micro-tower case

LPX power supply

Slot covers; this case supports up to seven slots

Slot covers; this case supports up to four slots

Figure 9.1

A typical system with a full-size ATX motherboard (left) compared to a system with a micro-ATX motherboard (right). The case at left can support more expansion cards and more internal drives than the case at right.

Figure 9.2 is a simplified comparison of typical ATX and micro-ATX motherboards without case, installed components, or cables.

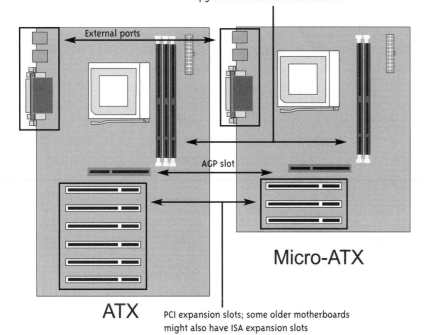

Memory upgrade slots; most micro-ATX
motherboards have fewer memory
upgrade slots than ATX motherboards

External ports

AGP slot

Micro-ATX

ATX

PCI expansion slots; some older motherboards
might also have ISA expansion slots

Figure 9.2

Major features of an
ATX motherboard (left)
compared to a micro-
ATX motherboard
(right). Many micro-
ATX motherboards
installed in low-cost
computers don't have
AGP slots, but replace-
ment motherboards
often do.

As you compare your system and motherboard to Figure 9.2, you might notice that your
motherboard has fewer slots than those pictured in Figure 9.2; this sketch was designed to
show the maximum number of slots possible. Look at the general location for components
and the proportions of the boards to determine which type of motherboard your system uses.

As Figures 9.1 and 9.2 make clear, micro-ATX–based systems limit your upgrade options in
two ways:

- Fewer expansion slots for add-on cards that you might want to install in the future
- Fewer drive bays for high-speed, low-cost internal drives

Although some computer vendors install micro-ATX motherboards in cases that can also be
used with the larger ATX motherboard design, most do not. There are two ways to deal with
the limits that a small case imposes:

- **Install the most advanced, most highly integrated micro-ATX motherboard
  you can afford**—Make sure it has USB 2.0, IEEE-1394, AGP 8x, Serial ATA, and
  other advanced features so that you don't need to use up your expansion slots.

- **Buy a larger case and matching power supply that can support a full-size ATX motherboard**—A new case and power supply could also support smaller motherboards.

> **ON THE WEB: Surfing for a Bigger, Better Case**
>
> If you're looking for a huge variety of system enclosures (the more elegant way to refer to your computer's case), check out the following vendors:
>
> - **Antec, Inc (bundles Chieftec cases with its own power supplies)**— www.antec-inc.com
> - **WaveSonic Technology (US distributor of Enermax)**—www.wavesonic.com
> - **Chieftec**—www.chieftec.com
> - **Atech Flash Technology (best known for card readers)**— www.atechflash.com

The type(s) of motherboard your case can handle determines the options you have for upgrade considerations. The options include the following:

- Total number of slots and slot types
- CPU types
- Memory expansion

Let's look at each of these in turn.

Slots and Slot Types

Expansion slots enable you to add ports, devices, and features to your motherboard, enabling it to work (and play!) harder for you.

The total number of slots a motherboard can have is controlled by the motherboard form factor. In addition, it is controlled by the case into which you want to install it.

As Figure 9.2 demonstrated, an ATX motherboard can have up to seven slots, and the smaller micro-ATX motherboard has a limit of just four slots. Wondering how many your case can hold? Look at the rear of the case and count the card brackets you see. Don't be surprised if your case can handle more slots than your current motherboard does.

Table 9.1 compares typical values for the most popular motherboard types.

Table 9.1 Card Brackets and Slots Available by Motherboard Type		
Slots and Card Brackets	**ATX**	**Micro-ATX**
Number of card brackets available on case	Seven	Four
Maximum number of slots supported by motherboard	Seven	Four
Typical number of slots on board	Six to seven	Three to four

As you can see, your case might support more slots than your current motherboard does. On today's ATX and micro-ATX motherboards, board makers decide whether you get the full number of slots your case can support, or if you're left a slot short. Micro-ATX motherboards frequently feature only three slots, especially those with built-in video, and ATX motherboards often feature only six slots.

If you choose a motherboard with a high degree of port integration, the total number of slots on the motherboard is less important than it once was. However, you should still want to have one or two PCI slots available for future upgrades, even if you choose a motherboard with all your favorite technologies already included. After all, you never know what Silicon Valley will think up next!

There are two major types of expansion slots on motherboards today:

- PCI
- AGP

Older motherboards might also have a third type of expansion slot, called ISA.

See Chapter 4 for illustrations of all three slot types.

ANALYZE THIS

What's in a (Slot) Name?

Expansion slots are almost always referred to by their acronyms, but you might find it useful to know what the names behind the acronyms are and to get a bit of extra history about the slots:

- **ISA**—Industry Standard Architecture is a Compaq-coined name for what is also called the "AT" slot after IBM's now-ancient IBM PC/AT, the first computer to introduce this slot type (in 1984!). The ISA slot spawned two short-lived variations over the years. The first of these was the EISA (Extended Industry Standard Architecture) slot, which was a double-deck version of ISA that could also accept 32-bit cards; the second was the VESA Local-Bus (VL-BUS), an ISA slot with an extra two-part connector at the front end, designed originally for fast 32-bit video cards, but also used for dual-channel multiple I/O cards with IDE, floppy, serial, and parallel ports on board. There have been no new ISA, EISA, or VL-Bus cards made for several years, so these slot designs are obsolete.

- **PCI**—The Peripheral Component Interconnect was developed by Intel in 1993. This jaw-breaking slot type is a fast 32-bit design, but uses a much smaller connector than ISA or its kin. Servers often use longer versions of the PCI slot that can run at 66MHz and support either 32-bit or 64-bit PCI cards.

- **AGP**—The Accelerated Graphics Port was also developed by Intel in 1996 (no wonder they say "Intel Inside!"). This slot is strictly for video. At a minimum (AGP 1x), it runs twice the speed of the PCI slot, and recent versions are several times faster than PCI (see Chapter 13, "Extra Vroom with Faster Graphics," for details).

The typical motherboard today has mostly PCI slots; one AGP (4x or 8x is preferred) for high-speed video. ISA is nowhere to be found on recent motherboards.

PCI Slots—The More the Merrier

Of the three types of expansion slots, the PCI slot is the workhorse, capable of accepting add-on cards that can perform any type of task you can imagine. A typical Micro-ATX motherboard has three of these and an ATX motherboard has five or six. The ATX motherboard thus has more than enough PCI slots for virtually any need.

AGP Slot—One to a Customer

The AGP slot is used only for high-speed graphics and comes in four major varieties:

- **AGP 1x**—Obsolete.

- **AGP 2x**—Obsolete.

- **AGP 4x**—Currently the most popular; most cards can be installed in AGP 1x or 2x slots as a stopgap until the motherboard is updated.

- **AGP 8x**—Available on some of the newest motherboards and graphics card designs.

JARGON

Obsolete—Outdated; not currently in production and completely replaced by newer, faster versions.

Obsolescent—A device that is being replaced by newer, faster versions, but is not yet obsolete.

Stopgap—A temporary solution that works, but not as well as the ideal solution would.

The AGP slot is frequently omitted from Micro-ATX systems and less-expensive ATX systems that have integrated video. Even if you want to save money now by upgrading to a motherboard with integrated video, I urge you to choose one that also has an actual AGP slot (4x or 8x) so that when you grow tired of the mediocre performance of integrated 3D video, you can upgrade to something better.

CPU Types

As you learned in Chapter 8, "Speedy Computing with Processor Upgrades," socket-based CPUs have completely replaced slot-mounted CPUs in recent systems. Although some earlier types of socket-mounted CPUs can be adapted to motherboards with a CPU slot, the latest socketed processors work only in a compatible motherboard.

If your system uses a socketed processor (such as a Socket A [Socket 462] Athlon, Duron, or Athlon XP, a Socket 478 Pentium 4 or Celeron, or a Socket 370 Pentium III or Celeron), it might be able to handle a significantly faster processor without a motherboard upgrade. However, older systems that use socketed processors such as the Intel Pentium, MMX Pentium, AMD K5 or K6 series, or the Cyrix 6x86 series cannot be upgraded to a modern (1GHz or faster) processor.

The slot-based AMD Athlon processors can't be upgraded past 1GHz, but slot-to-socket adapters can be used to upgrade some motherboards with slot-type Pentium II, Pentium III, and Celeron processors. See Chapter 8 for details.

If you want to enjoy a significant performance upgrade from a processor upgrade, your motherboard should be able to handle a processor that is at least 50 percent faster in overall performance than the processor you currently use. If you can make only a modest performance boost because your motherboard can't handle the processor you want to install, replace the motherboard.

Memory Types

Many two- and three-year-old systems use 168-pin PC100 or PC133 SDRAM, but this memory slows down the latest 2GHz-class and faster Pentium 4 and Athlon XP processors. A much better match for these processors is 184-pin DDR266 or DDR333 SDRAM. Although a few motherboards can use both types, changing to faster memory almost always dictates swapping motherboards.

A few Intel Pentium III and Pentium 4 systems use Rambus RIMM memory, which is more expensive than DDR333 memory. The earlier PC600-700-800 types use a different socket than the latest PC1066 RIMM modules do.

Thus, moving to faster memory requires a motherboard upgrade. Even if your older motherboard can handle a 2GHz-class or faster processor, if it uses PC133 memory, you should upgrade to a motherboard that uses DDR266 or DDR333 memory so that you get the best performance. See Chapter 7, "RAM Your Way to Faster Performance," for details about memory modules and installation.

Chipsets and Your Motherboard

It can be mind numbing to read over pages and pages listing motherboards for sale. The acronyms start to blur together after a while, and it can be very difficult to remember what you've read. Here's an easier way to cut to the chase on motherboards: As hardware superstar Scott Mueller says, "The chipset *is* the motherboard."

To understand what the author of the long-running *Upgrading and Repairing PCs* book series from Que means, you need to understand what chipsets do. When I first began to work with PCs in the early 1980s, the motherboards were so crowded with individual chips that there was barely room for the expansion slots, memory chips, memory module sockets, and the CPU socket. And this was long before today's design trend of building hard drive host adapters, floppy drive controllers, and add-on ports into the motherboard.

Take a look at a current motherboard (any motherboard maker's web site has plenty of pictures you can admire) and count the chips—you'll be lucky if you can find more than 15. In addition, remember that today's motherboards include built-in features that the computer users of the 1980s either installed through add-on cards or didn't even imagine.

What happened? The development of complex, multi-functional chips called chipsets, that's what happened.

What Bridge and Super I/O Chips Do

Today, the I/O functions of a motherboard are typically handled by as few as two or three chips:

- The *North Bridge* connects the CPU's FSB (front-side-bus) or system bus to the bus used by expansion slots such as AGP and PCI; systems with integrated chipset-based video integrate video into the North Bridge.

- The *South Bridge* runs the IDE hard drive, USB ports, and other high-speed ports.

- The *Super I/O chip* runs the floppy drives, serial, and parallel ports; this function might be built into the South Bridge instead of into a separate chip.

Although some vendors use different names for these chips to reflect how the chips are connected to each other (many now bypass the PCI bus for a separate bus), the chips still serve these basic functions.

Because many chipsets are modular, enabling different North Bridge and South Bridge chips to be used together, and because the Super I/O and South Bridge chips might be separate or combined, many feature variations are possible.

ANALYZE THIS

Similar Chipsets Make for Lookalike Motherboards

How important are chipsets to a motherboard? The chipsets control just about everything; that's how important they are. Don't believe me? Try this experiment:

1. Find any two motherboards in a magazine ad, at a motherboard makers' web sites, or anywhere else that use the *same* chipset.

2. Compare major features, such as the following:

   - CPU types and speeds supported

   - Maximum memory and memory types supported

   - IDE/ATA interface speeds

   - AGP speeds

I bet you find them to be almost identical.

After you figure out which chipset has the features you like (CPU type and speeds supported, memory speeds and types supported, and so on), you can concentrate on just the motherboards that use that chipset. Want to dig deeper into chipsets? Check the following web sites:

- **developer.intel.com**—This is the "techy" side of Intel's web site. Search for IA-32 chipsets (IA-32 is Intel's term for its 32-bit CPUs such as the Celeron and the many members of the Pentium family) to see details about current and past Intel chipsets.

---

continues

CONTINUED

- **www.viatech.com**—Via Technologies is the leading developer of chipsets for the AMD Athlon and Athlon XP, and it also develops advanced Pentium 4-compatible chipsets.
- **www.amd.com**—To help improve the popularity of its Athlon and Duron CPUs, AMD sells its own chipsets for these CPUs.
- **www.aliusa.com**—Ali Corporation's Aladdin, AliMagiK, and CyberMagiK series (for Athlon and Duron CPUs) are also very popular with motherboard makers.
- **www.sis.com**—Silicon Integrated Systems offers some of the highest-performance Pentium 4-compatible chipsets as well as Athlon XP-compatible models.

Comparing Your Old Motherboard to a New One

You can help your shopping process immensely if you create a table like Table 9.2 to compare the features of your old motherboard to a particular motherboard you're considering. A comparison like this will help you find motherboards that have as many of the features lacking in your current motherboard as possible.

The data in Table 9.2 is based on FRANKENPC's current motherboard and the motherboard I'm using as a replacement. Use the motherboard or system manual and the information you gathered in Chapter 4 to fill in the values for your current motherboard, and use the vendor's information to fill in the values for the new motherboard you're considering.

Table 9.2   Comparing Current and New Motherboards

Feature	Old Motherboard	New Motherboard
Brand and model	PCChips M800LMR	MSI KT4 Ultra-SR
Chipset	VIA KX133	VIA KT400
Processor type/speeds supported	Athlon Slot A 500–850MHz	Athlon XP up to 3000+, also Athlon and Duron Socket A
Memory types supported	PC100 SDRAM	DDR200, 266, 333, and 400 SDRAM
Number of memory slots	3	3
Maximum memory size	768MB	3GB
AGP type	2x	8x
Number of PCI slots	4	6

Feature	Old Motherboard	New Motherboard
Number of ISA slots	0	0
ATA IDE	ATA-100	ATA-133
SATA	No	Yes
RAID	No	SATA RAID
Ethernet	10/100	10/100
USB version	1.1	2.0
Number of USB ports	2	6
IEEE-1394a	No	No
Audio	C-Media analog stereo	C-Media six-channel analog and digital
Wireless networking	None	Bluetooth ready
BIOS brand	Award	AMI
PC Health monitoring	Yes	Yes

As Table 9.2 makes clear, FRANKENPC will be immensely better after the upgrade in almost every way and will also be ready for future expansion.

Deciding Between Similar Motherboards

Because only a few companies make motherboard chipsets, many, many motherboards are similar. How can you decide which one of a dozen or so similar boards to buy?

- **Read the reviews**—Print sources such as *MaximumPC* and *Computer Shopper* publish motherboard reviews, but check out the links to many other print and online sites at the motherboard vendor's own page. Of course, these reviews are the most favorable available, so don't hesitate to search for other reviews online that may provide a more balanced view. Some of my favorite sources include www.motherboards.org, www.maximumpc.com, www.extremetech.com, and www.tomshardware.com. When you read the review, be sure to look for the reviewer's own biases and compare them to your own. Gaming web sites and magazines tend to be very impressed by overclocking capabilities, but most reviewers also discuss stability and compatibility with a wide range of hardware.

- **Spend some time at the manufacturer's web site *before* you buy**—Can you locate BIOS upgrades and online documentation easily? Is there a US office and telephone number for technical support? What about email support options? Because the motherboard essentially *is* the computer because so many components are built into it, you might feel as though you're really buying the motherboard *vendor* when you buy the motherboard.

- **Check the warranty**—You should have at least a one-year warranty, and longer is better. Find out what provision the vendor has for sending you a replacement; after all, the warranty *doesn't* cover lost time while you hang around the mailbox waiting for a replacement motherboard to be returned to you. Also, find out what issues are excluded. For example, will you void the warranty if you overclock the board?

- **Make sure you understand *all* the motherboard's features**—Even though the chipset is the primary control over a motherboard's major feature set, some vendors add refinements such as switchless BIOS-controlled configuration to make overclocking speed adjustments easier. They also might add bundled software, support for a wider range of CPU speeds, and additional support chips to enable integrated USB 2.0 or IEEE-1394 ports, ATA RAID, or digital audio.

- **Stick with a BIOS you know and trust**—BIOS brands and versions might vary, as might motherboards with similar or identical chipsets. If you're accustomed to a particular BIOS's functions and operation, you'll prefer a board that uses a BIOS brand and version similar to what you're accustomed to.

How to Read a Motherboard Ad

After you decide that a new motherboard is just what you need to breathe new life and possibilities into your system, you're confronted with a bewildering number of motherboard models for sale from local retailers, online specialty and superstores, and from the e-stores run by motherboard makers themselves. These ads are sometimes almost as terse as apartment ads are reputed to be. In this section, you learn how to decipher some typical examples.

Table 9.3 provides a detailed examination of a brief description of a Soyo P4X400 Dragon Ultra motherboard from a typical online retailer, Insight Components (www.insightcomponents.com).

Most sites that provide such shorthand listings also provide a button you can click for additional details. Use this option to view a more complete description of the motherboard and a photo of the board. Take advantage of this option before you buy. Note that serial, parallel, PS/2 mouse, keyboard, and USB ports are nearly universal on motherboards, and often aren't mentioned specifically. If USB ports aren't identified as USB 2.0, assume they're USB 1.1.

Table 9.3	Soyo P4X400 Description Analysis		
Feature	Explanation	Additional Information You Need	Where to Find the Information
Socket 478 interface	Socket used for current Pentium 4 processors	What processor speeds are supported?	Visit motherboard vendor web site (www.soyousa.com)
VIA PX400 chipset	VIA chipset for Pentium 4	Major chipset features	Visit chipset vendor web site (www.viatech.com)
3.0GB	Total amount of memory supported	Memory types supported	
PC3200, PC2700, and PC2100 DDR memory supported	Types of memory supported	Total number of modules	
3 DIMMs	Total number of modules	Any particular memory configurations required?	Visit motherboard vendor web site
1 AGP (8x/4x, 1.5v only)	Type of AGP slot		
5 PCI expansion slots	Number of PCI expansion slots		
Onboard HiPoint ATA133 IDE RAID	Built-in ATA RAID controller	What RAID configurations are supported?	Visit motherboard vendor web site
Onboard 10/100 LAN	Built-in 10/100 Ethernet LAN controller	What chipset is used?	Visit motherboard vendor web site

Take a look at the other terminology you might run into as you look for your best deal:

- **AMR**—The Audio Modem Riser slot is a small expansion slot designed to enable a special AMR modem and audio device to be plugged into the motherboard. Although a number of motherboards have the AMR riser, it's much more difficult to find modems that use the AMR slot than conventional PCI or ISA internal modems. In addition, because an AMR-based modem must use the CPU and the operating system to control its operation, you're better off with a conventional internal or external modem. Avoid boards that have an AMR slot if possible, because the AMR slot reduces the number of PCI slots available on your motherboard.

- **CNR**—The Communications Network Riser slot is similar to the AMR, but it has a newer design that's intended to handle home networking as well as the audio and modem features of its predecessor, the AMR. Although many companies announced support for CNR when it was introduced in 2000, this slot, like the AMR, also appears to be largely useless because of a lack of riser cards. One benefit of CNR is that it can be part of a combo CNR/PCI slot arrangement, so you can use a PCI card in the same slot if a CNR riser card is not installed.

- **AC97 audio**—This term refers to motherboards that have built-in support for Microsoft's Audio Codec '97, a standard for digital and analog audio. Although separate sound cards provide superior support for wavetable MIDI sounds and 3D positional audio, AC97 is adequate for casual sound and gaming users.

The Motherboard Upgrade Process

After you select a motherboard that fits into your case and provides the performance and features you need, it's time to perform the upgrade process. The upgrade process includes the following steps:

1. Removing the old motherboard.
2. Inserting the new motherboard.
3. Starting the system.
4. Configuring the motherboard through its setup screens.
5. Installing new drivers required by the new onboard hardware (this might require you to reinstall Windows, particularly if you use Windows XP).

Because the old motherboard might still be useful in another system or as a spare, you should be careful during both the removal and insertion processes.

Before you start, be sure to take the ESD precautions described in Chapter 5, "Preparing for Your Upgrade." For extra safety, use a hex driver rather than a screwdriver to remove and insert screws into the motherboard if your motherboard uses hex screws. Screwdriver damage to the motherboard will void your warranty, and a hex driver is far less likely to slip than a screwdriver.

Running Windows XP? Read This Before You Install Your New Motherboard.

Unfortunately, Windows XP has complicated matters for the motherboard upgrader. Unlike Windows 9x/Me, which can usually boot and then detect new motherboard hardware, Windows XP isn't designed to handle this type of upgrade. Here's what I recommend:

- If you are planning to upgrade to Windows XP, wait until *after* your new motherboard is up and running with your existing Windows version. It's easier for Windows XP to detect hardware that's already being controlled by a previous version than it is to force Windows XP to cope from scratch with a brand new motherboard.

- If you already installed Windows XP with the old motherboard, you need to perform a *repair installation* to get Windows XP to install the drivers needed by the new motherboard. Boot from the Windows XP CD, select Repair Install, select the current Windows XP installation, and press R to start the installation. See the web site "Moving XP to new MB or Computer" at www.michaelstevenstech.com/moving_xp.html for details and warnings.

- Do *not* continue with the installation if the Repair Install option is not listed; your Documents and Settings folder, Windows folder, and Registry keys for applications will be nuked if you keep going.

Step-by-Step Motherboard Removal

To remove an ATX motherboard from a standard case, follow these steps to make the upgrade process as painless as possible. Keep in mind that these instructions assume that the motherboard is attached directly to the case. If the motherboard is attached to a removable tray, follow the instructions provided by the system or case maker to remove the tray from the case before you remove the motherboard. Be sure to take the ESD precautions listed in Chapter 5.

1. Shut down and unplug the computer.

2. Disconnect all external and internal cables attached to add-on cards after labeling them for easy reconnection. Use stickers to identify the card to which each cable attaches.

3. Disconnect all ribbon cables attached to built-in ports (I/O, storage, and so on; refer to Figure 9.3) after labeling them for easy reconnection.

4. Disconnect all cables leading to internal speakers, keylocks, speed switches, and so on (refer to Figure 9.3) after labeling them for easy reconnection. The easiest way to do this is to look at your motherboard or system manual's diagram of front panel connectors, which are usually grouped together near the front edge (the side away from the expansion slots) of the motherboard. Again, use labels to mark which cables perform what task. If you don't have the manual for your old motherboard and the motherboard isn't labeled, go to the manufacturer's web site and download the manual to determine which cables are used for what purpose.

5. Disconnect power cables running to the motherboard or components, such as fans, on the motherboard. All these cables must be removed before the motherboard can be removed.

6. Remove all add-on cards and place them on an anti-static mat or in anti-static bags. (See Chapter 5 to learn why you don't want your parts to have a "shocking" experience.)

7. Disconnect the power-supply leads from the motherboard (see Figure 9.4). The new motherboard must use the same power-supply connections as the current motherboard. See Chapter 22, "Power Supply Upgrades," for current information about power supplies.

Figure 9.3

Drive cables (top) and motherboard front-panel cables (bottom) must be disconnected before the motherboard can be removed.

— Drive cables

— Front panel cables

Figure 9.4

An ATX power supply is usually connected to the edge of the motherboard. To remove it, unlatch the lock and pull the power connector toward you.

Screw holding motherboard in place

Power connector lock

Power connector

8. Wondering what's keeping your motherboard in place? Look carefully. There are screws around the edges of your motherboard (Figure 9.5 shows a typical location for one of them) and two in the middle. Unscrew the motherboard mounting screws and save them for later. Take a good look around and make sure you've removed all the screws. Figure 9.5 shows an ATX motherboard with typical screw hole locations. Use this as a guide to locating all the screws. On some boards, plastic standoff spacers might be used instead of screws for some screw holes.

Figure 9.5

Screw holes in a typical ATX motherboard. The inset shows that screw holes have a metal reinforcing ring.

1. Screw hole positions
2. Detail of screw hole with metal reinforcing ring
3. Hole for plastic standoffs, not screws

9. After the screws have been removed, lift the motherboard out of the system and place it on an anti-static mat. Remove the I/O shield around the ports at the back of the system and store it with the old motherboard. Refer to Figure 9.6.

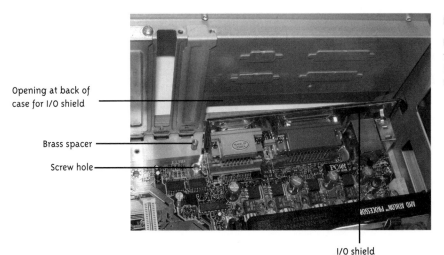

Opening at back of case for I/O shield

Brass spacer

Screw hole

I/O shield

Figure 9.6

Removing the old motherboard and I/O shield from FRANKENPC.

10. Use a pair of pliers to squeeze together the tops of any plastic spacers used on the old motherboard. Then, push them from the top until they fall out of the motherboard. They can be inserted into the new motherboard. These spacers come in different heights for use with different types of cases.

CAUTION: STOP! LOOK! THINK!

You Break It—You Buy It (and Cry!)

You might be impatient to take your old motherboard for a one-way trip and install a better model, but don't get hasty. Some classic ways to mess up the installation include the following:

- **Using too much force before you're ready**—If you forget to unscrew the motherboard all the way before you start pulling, tugging, or pushing on it, you might crack it. Cracked motherboards are worthless (unless you want to make a clock out of the remains).

- **Oops, I slipped!**—Screwdriver damage caused by the screwdriver slipping and scratching the motherboard (old or new) is another sure-fire way to ruin your computing day. If your motherboard is secured with hex screws, use a hex driver instead of a screwdriver for extra safety.

- **Yes, it's heavy, it's my heatsink**—One of the best reasons to install RAM and the CPU *before* the new motherboard goes into the system is because of the increasing weight of the heatsink. Although the Socket 478 Pentium 4 and Celeron processors use an improved heatsink design that takes the weight off the motherboard, the Athlon XP continues to use the motherboard to support the weight of the heatsink. Today's heavy (sometimes all-copper construction) heatsinks can crack a motherboard if you're not careful. Worried about it? Fold a few sheets of paper or a bit of cardboard into a shim and place that under the motherboard beneath the CPU and heatsink.

Make sure you're taking your time and doing it right.

Step-by-Step Motherboard Installation

All right, you're halfway there. The old motherboard is out. It's time to get the new one in place.

Before you install the new motherboard into the computer, take a moment and install your memory and CPU on the motherboard; if you're moving these from the old motherboard, don't forget to ground yourself before you remove these parts; fry them, and your motherboard upgrade suddenly becomes a lot more expensive.

If you're fuzzy on the details of how to install the processor or RAM on your new motherboard, check out Chapter 8 (for the CPU) and Chapter 7 (for RAM). Also, pull out the manual for your new motherboard (or if you don't have the manual, go to the manufacturer's web site) and see if you need to set the CPU speed, multiplier, type, and voltage settings on the motherboard. Most new motherboards use BIOS-based controls rather than switches or jumpers. If you need to set jumpers, it's much easier to do before the motherboard goes down into the depths of the system; you might find it's tough to see (or fiddle with) the motherboard after it's installed.

To install the motherboard, follow these steps:

1. Place the new motherboard over the old motherboard to determine which mounting holes should be used for plastic standoffs (if needed) and which should be used for brass spacers. Matching the motherboards helps you determine that the new motherboard will fit correctly in the system. To avoid damaging your new motherboard, place it on the insulating foam or bubble-wrap in which it was shipped and pick up the board with this material as insulator. Hold your new board by the edges only.

2. If the new motherboard's mounting holes are in different locations than the old motherboards, look at the case or motherboard tray to determine if you can use brass spacers in their current positions, or if you need to move them. Use pliers to unscrew and reattach the spacers or to install additional ones if needed. Figure 9.7 shows a brass spacer and the variety of mounting hole positions that can be used.

   Some motherboard trays or cases have markings similar to the ones shown in Figure 9.7. The B marking (not visible in Figure 9.7) means that a mounting hole can be used with old Baby-AT motherboards.

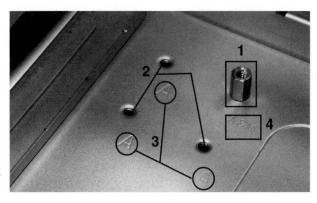

1. Brass spacer
2. Alternative mounting holes for spacer
3. A legend (indicates hole is usable with ATX motherboards)
4. A & M legend (indicates hole is usable with ATX and micro-ATX motherboards)

Figure 9.7

A brass spacer inserted into a mounting hole usable by both ATX and micro-ATX motherboards. Other mounting holes are designed for use by ATX motherboards only.

3. Use the plastic stand-off spacers you removed from the old motherboard and push them through the bottom of the appropriate holes on the new motherboard. The spacers prevent the motherboard from shorting out on the bottom of the case.

4. When you place the new motherboard into the case, position the I/O shield and connector at the back of the case (see Figure 9.8); make sure the labels for the port types are visible out the rear of the case. Some systems use only brass spacers; line the mounting holes on these motherboards up with the spacers.

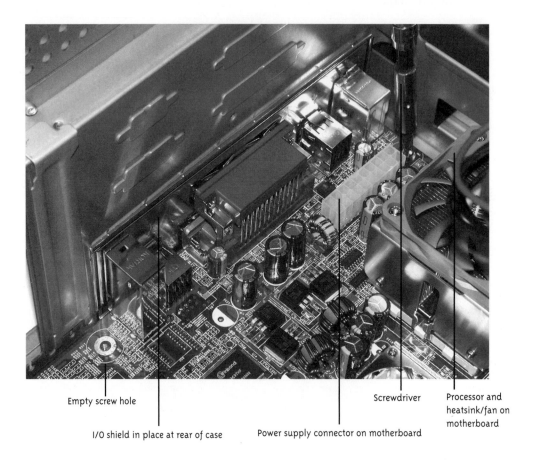

Empty screw hole

Screwdriver

Processor and heatsink/fan on motherboard

I/O shield in place at rear of case

Power supply connector on motherboard

Figure 9.8

Lining up the I/O shield and mounting the new motherboard.

5. Reattach the wires to the speaker, and then reset the switch, the IDE host adapter, and the power lights.

6. Attach fans on the case and processor to the motherboard or power supply if not already connected. If case fans are monitored by the PC Health feature in the system BIOS, they must be connected to the motherboard for monitoring to take place.

7. Reattach the ribbon cables from the drives to the motherboard's IDE and floppy disk drive interfaces. Match the ribbon cable's colored side to pin 1 on the interfaces.

8. Reattach the power supply connector to the motherboard.

9. Insert the add-on cards you removed from the old motherboard; make sure that your existing cards don't duplicate any features found on the new motherboard (such as sound, USB 2.0, and so on). If they do, and you want to continue to use the card, you must disable the corresponding feature on the motherboard. Use the new motherboard's BIOS setup program to disable these features. See the motherboard manual or motherboard vendor's web site for details.

Starting the System

Double-double-check everything: Make sure you've put all the screws back into the motherboard, plugged everything back in, turned on the monitor, and then the system. Keep your hand on the power switch. If you don't see BIOS status messages in just a few seconds, turn off the power and check your drive and power cables. But if you do see the messages, smile and say, "I'm good! I'm really good!"

Configuring the New Motherboard

The BIOS chip on the new motherboard has a menu of allowable settings. However, on a new motherboard, the menu defaults to settings that might not work with your hardware. To start the BIOS setup process, press the key displayed onscreen or specified in the user manual and go through each screen as directed in the manual.

Depending on your motherboard and BIOS design, you might need to do the following:

- Configure hard drive settings
- Configure the floppy drive type
- Configure memory timing
- Configure built-in ports and devices
- Select the correct settings for the processor, memory type, front-side bus, and voltage

After making the changes needed, save the changes, and restart the computer.

Installing New Drivers

When you restart your system, you better have your Windows CD-ROM handy, as well as any driver disks provided with the motherboard. Because Windows uses 32-bit drivers for both add-on cards and motherboard-based features, Windows busily detects your motherboard's new features as it starts.

MARK'S TIP SHEET: Making Life Easier for Windows and You

Windows has its hands full after you swap motherboards because of the new chipset and other new features on your new board. To help make Windows' job easier (and help prevent nasty lockups and crashes), use these tips:

- If your new motherboard has built-in video, start Windows in Safe Mode the first time and select VGA as the video type. When you restart the computer in Normal mode, Windows detects the correct video type and prompts you for drivers.

- If Windows' .cab and driver files are stored on the hard disk (common with pre-installed versions), you don't need the Windows CD. Look for a folder called CABS (often stored in the Windows\Options folder). However, if you're using an upgrade version, you need to keep the Windows CD handy so that drivers can be installed from the CD to your computer.

- When Windows detects and installs support for a device, it usually prompts you to restart. Take its advice, and you might find yourself rebooting five or six times before it finds all your hardware. You're better off to select No and let Windows keep looking for new hardware. Don't forget to reboot after Windows stops looking and displays the desktop. In addition, don't be surprised if Windows finds a few more new components next time you start up.

- If you're still using Windows 95, it's advisable to upgrade to Windows 98SE or Windows Me *before* you install the new motherboard. Windows 95 has a hard time coping with AGP slots, bus-mastering IDE hard disk host adapters, and other features that are now common. See Chapter 23, "Winning Windows Upgrades," for details.

- If you're running Windows XP, make sure you review the "Running Windows XP? Read This *Before* You Install Your New Motherboard" section in this chapter.

Making Sure Your New Motherboard Is Working Properly

Just because your system boots doesn't mean it's working as well as it should. Many recent systems have a built-in BIOS feature that can help you keep an eye on your system performance. It's called the Hardware Monitor.

To use the Hardware Monitor feature in the BIOS, do the following:

1. Start the system and press the key(s) that activate the BIOS setup program. F1, F2, Esc, Del, and F10 are some common choices; watch onscreen or see your system manual for the correct keystrokes.

2. Use the BIOS menu to select the Hardware Monitoring screen. It will resemble Figure 9.9.

CPU fan is working correctly

Both should remain below
110° F to avoid overheating

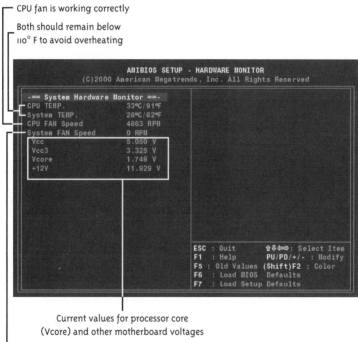

Figure 9.9

A typical BIOS's hardware monitoring display. Voltage levels are within limits, and the CPU fan is running. However, there is no speed given for the system (case) fan.

Current values for processor core
(Vcore) and other motherboard voltages

System (case) fan is either not present,
is not being monitored by motherboard,
or has failed

On this motherboard, the nominal value for Vcc is 5 volts; for Vcc3, it is 3.3 volts, and for +12v, it is 12 volts. Vcore for this computer's Athlon 800MHz Model 4 (Thunderbird) processor is 1.75 volts. As you can see from Figure 9.9, all values are very close to the nominal values; this motherboard's electrical signals are working properly.

To use the hardware monitor as a sort of burn-in test, you can leave your system overnight on this screen, turn off the monitor, and return in the morning to see how the temperature and other values are doing.

Barebones PCs Are an Easier Way to Upgrade

If you're not crazy about wrestling your old motherboard out of its case, or if you're trying to upgrade a microATX or other case type with limited upgrade options, consider the easy way to upgrade: a barebones system.

Barebones systems typically include the following preassembled components:

- Case
- Motherboard
- Power supply

Some might also include CD-ROM and floppy drives.

Although a barebones system can save you time and effort, it might not be right for you. Before you buy one, make sure you know what you're getting. Ask questions like these:

- **What brand and model of motherboard is included?**—The answer to this question can be used to determine the motherboard form factor as well as the processor, RAM type and size, AGP card type, and other components you can install. Look up the motherboard specifications on the vendors web site for details.

- **What size is the power supply?**—For a mid-tower case, I recommend 300 watts or more. Small cases can get by with less.

- **Is the power supply UL approved?**—Don't even *think* about buying a non-UL power supply.

- **What brand and model of power supply is included?**—Don't be surprised if you find out it's a non-name brand. However, once you know, you can compare its specs to my recommendations in Chapter 22.

- **What type of case is included?**—A slimline or micro-tower case limits your future expansion options.

- **How many 5.25-inch drive bays?**—These are the drive bays you need for DVD-rewritable and CD-RW drives.

- **How many 3.5-inch drive bays?**—Use these drive bays for hard drives, a floppy drive, and other small removable-media drives, USB hubs, and card readers.

- **What other components are included?**—If you need a keyboard, mouse, floppy drive, or other components, getting them included might be OK if you're not fussy about what you get.

- **What type of warranty is included?**—If you get a warranty with on-site service or an instant exchange via UPS or FedEX, you won't have much downtime in case of problems. However, if you must wait until your system is tested and repaired before you get it back as a replacement, this type of warranty isn't much help if your system fails. Also ask about the length of the warranty—the longer the better.

Many vendors sell barebones, but I like the wide range of models and prices available at Tiger Direct (www.tigerdirect.com). To find others, use a search engine such as Google.

Five Reasons to Upgrade Your BIOS

The basic input/output system (BIOS) chip is a small rectangular or square chip on the motherboard. But don't let its small size fool you; the BIOS is in charge of interfacing hardware and software and specifying the hardware options your motherboard can use.

Because the BIOS is in charge of the hardware/software interface (both of which are constantly being changed and improved), and because it's firmware (software on a chip), it can be upgraded. Fortunately, you can put your wallet away this time because this is one upgrade that's a freebie *if* you can get it from your motherboard or system vendor's web site. How can you tell if you need a BIOS upgrade? Check out our top-five list to see if you qualify!

1. Your brand new CPU doesn't work at all or doesn't run at the correct speed.
2. You're not happy with how the motherboard performs power management.
3. You're having problems with motherboard features such as USB 2.0.
4. You can't install an ATA hard disk without using a host adapter with a built-in BIOS.
5. You can't boot from a CD-ROM to install Windows.

These problems aren't limited to older motherboards. Brand-new motherboards often need BIOS upgrades so that they can work with hardware (such as faster processors) introduced after the motherboard was designed. They also might need upgrades to work better with the latest version of Windows.

Upgrading the BIOS Chip

The BIOS is a small chip on your motherboard with a big job to do: managing your basic system hardware during the boot process until Windows shows up to take over. Wondering who made your BIOS? Watch your system startup screens; they usually display the BIOS brand and model number. However, as you learn later in this chapter, knowing whose name is on the BIOS isn't all that useful when it comes time for a BIOS upgrade.

Because your BIOS is designed to work with existing hardware, and new CPUs, add-on cards, and hardware standards are continually reaching the market, it's likely that you'll need to upgrade the BIOS chip in your system at least once during the life of a given motherboard.

Where Is the BIOS Chip?

The BIOS chip is typically a socketed chip about 1.5 inches long located in various places on the motherboard. (Basically, it's wherever the designer could jam it into place!) On older systems, the BIOS chip has a label indicating the manufacturer and model number. The same label is now often applied to the outermost expansion slot on a lot of new systems, although the BIOS chip is still present on the motherboard—someplace. On some new systems, the BIOS chip isn't socketed anymore, but is surface-mounted. Does it matter? Nope, because in almost every case, you upgrade the *contents* of the BIOS chip, not the BIOS chip itself.

See Figure 9.10 for typical examples of BIOS chips and motherboard batteries. The battery is used to maintain settings you make from the menus displayed by the BIOS chip during hardware configuration.

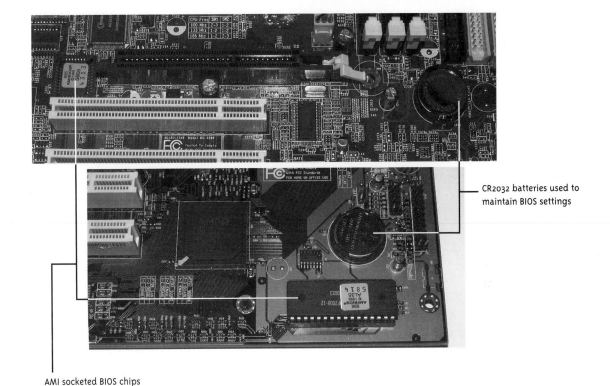

CR2032 batteries used to
maintain BIOS settings

AMI socketed BIOS chips

Figure 9.10

Typical examples of socketed BIOS chips made by American Megatrends (AMI) and motherboard batteries. The top motherboard uses a PLCC (plastic leaded chip carrier) style used on recent motherboards, and the bottom motherboard uses the DIP
(dual inline package) style used since the first IBM AT was introduced almost 20 years ago.

Who Made Your System BIOS?

Originally, BIOS chips were made by the same companies that made the first PCs, and they
were made only for that company's PCs. If this were still true, you'd be able to choose from
only a few name brand PCs, such as Compaq, IBM, and Acer, all of whom have made their
own BIOS chips in the past.

Today, though, regardless of the name on the outside of the box, the BIOS is far more likely
to come from one of these major BIOS developers:

- **AMI (American Megatrends)** — www.ami.com

- **Award Software (originally an independent BIOS maker, but now part of
  Phoenix Technologies)** — www.phoenix.com

- **Phoenix Technologies** — www.phoenix.com

ANALYZE THIS

How Phoenix and Rivals Make Cheap Computers Possible

Why are there so many different brands (and white-box no-brands) of PCs available today? It wouldn't be possible without third-party BIOS vendors. Here's why.

BIOS development is extraordinarily difficult, and early companies just stole other companies' BIOS routines. But after they got caught, good-bye!

You'd have only a few brands to choose from if Phoenix hadn't come along. Phoenix deserves the credit for figuring out how to create a BIOS chip that would use the same MS-DOS operating system and application software and run the same peripherals as the Compaq and IBM systems did back in the 1980s. Phoenix has never put its name on a single computer, but it licensed its BIOS to PC makers large and small, inspiring AMI and Award Software (now owned by Phoenix) to do the same. Thus, you can buy computers from Joe's Computer Shack, IBM, Compaq, Dell, Gateway, and a host of other vendors and be assured that they all run Windows and work with virtually any whiz-bang gizmo available at your friendly neighborhood computer store.

When it comes time for a BIOS upgrade, though, you need to understand that the BIOS on your system is no longer really an AMI, Phoenix, or Award BIOS. Because different motherboards have different chipsets, use different CPUs, and are made to handle different generations of peripherals, the BIOS code, menus, and options must be modified for each motherboard.

In essence, your BIOS resembles the stock BIOS originally created by the BIOS vendor the same way that a custom van resembles the stripped-down cargo van purchased by the customizer for modification. Who provides the warranty for a tricked-out, raised-roof custom van? The custom van producer or dealer, not Daimler-Chrysler, Ford, or GM—it's not their product anymore. Similarly, your system or motherboard vendor, not the BIOS creator, is responsible for upgrades to the BIOS. Keep in mind that, just as you can get *some* technical support for the parts of the custom van that are still factory spec (such as the engine and the drivetrain), BIOS vendors can answer *general* questions such as the beep or onscreen error codes used to report problems. But that's about it; for details about specific BIOS screens or options, ask your motherboard or system vendor.

BIOS Chip Types

BIOS chips come in two forms:

- **Flash BIOS**—Uses flash memory
- **ROM BIOS**—Uses permanent read-only memory (ROM)

The Flash BIOS chip can be upgraded with software; the older ROM BIOS chip must be physically removed from the motherboard and replaced with an improved model. Almost any system made since the mid-1990s has a flash BIOS; even though the BIOS chips on most of these motherboards are socketed, you can change their contents by downloading and installing a BIOS upgrade. About the only time that you'd need to remove a socketed flash BIOS chip is when you've tried to install a flash BIOS upgrade that failed and the BIOS chip doesn't have a built-in recovery option.

Upgrading the Flash BIOS

Because the motherboard or system maker customizes your motherboard's BIOS chip, that's the logical place to go for a BIOS upgrade. With major brands of systems, it's pretty easy to locate the BIOS upgrade. Just go to the web site and look up your system. You usually find a link to the downloadable file and update instructions. Typically, the process works like this after you locate the upgrade:

1. Download the BIOS upgrade file to your computer. A BIOS upgrade is usually stored as a self-installing program (.exe) file.

2. Run the program you downloaded and insert a blank, formatted floppy disk into your computer's drive A: when prompted. The actual BIOS code and loader program are written to the floppy disk.

3. Before you upgrade your BIOS, make sure you have noted the major BIOS settings (see Chapter 5, "Preparing for Your Upgrade," for details); note especially hard disk settings. In some cases, you might need to reset the new BIOS with the correct settings.

4. To update your BIOS, boot with the disk you made and follow the onscreen instructions. The process of changing the BIOS chip's contents takes about three minutes; if the cat pulls the power cord out of your system or an approaching thunderstorm takes out your power before the upgrade is finished, you're left with a system that can't boot. See "Recovering from a Blown Upgrade" later in this chapter for help—or wait until the cat's away and it's a sunny day!

The process is similar with a white-box generic PC that's assembled from parts by a local vendor after you get your hands on the BIOS upgrade. Do you take a blank floppy disk back to Joe's Computer Shack and ask for a BIOS upgrade? No; instead, you need to figure out what motherboard Joe was using the week you bought your computer and download the BIOS upgrade from the motherboard maker.

How do you know whose motherboard Joe was using? Some systems indicate the maker during bootup. Others display only a mysterious series of numbers. Fortunately, you can decode these numbers to get the motherboard's maker.

ON THE WEB: Surf the Web to a BIOS Upgrade

These web sites cross-reference the ID numbers displayed by some systems at startup time with the actual motherboard maker:

- **Wim's BIOS page**—www.wimsbios.com/
- **Phoenix Technologies' Award BIOS Vendors**—www.phoenix.com/en/ customer+services/bios/awardbios/award+bios+vendors.htm
- **American Megatrend's BIOS Support page**—www.ami.com/support/bios.cfm

To download the correct BIOS upgrade for your system or motherboard, links to the motherboard vendor's sites are a big help. Try these sources:

- **Wim's BIOS page**—www.wimsbios.com/
- **MicroFirmware's BIOS products catalog page**—www.firmware.com
- **eSupport's BIOS upgrade page**—www.esupport.com
- **Motherboard HomeWorld**—www.motherboard.org

MARK'S TIP SHEET: Hooray for BIOS Upgrade Companies

You might figure that if your computer has a flash BIOS that you'll never need to check out BIOS upgrade companies such as MicroFirmware or eSupport. Think again! Here are some of the other ways they can help you out:

- **Useful utilities**—Find programs to test your system for compatibility with greater-than-8.4GB hard drives *before* you buy, clear your CMOS, and more.
- **Motherboard-specific tech support**—Look up your motherboard and find links to the vendor's web site and the cost and benefits of a BIOS upgrade.
- **BIOS and motherboard "helper" cards**—Can't get a BIOS upgrade to handle large hard drives? Looking for additional IDE ports? These companies have put their BIOS expertise to work to provide add-on cards that do what your BIOS can't do for itself.

- **Hardware testing products**—From diagnostic software to POST-code cards, you can get help with difficult system problems.

- **Motherboard identification software**—Their upgrade wizards can identify who made your motherboard and what chipset it has.

These companies have recently upgraded their sites to make them more useful and easier to navigate. Stop by today before you have problems.

Recovering from a Blown Upgrade

Did the cat yank out the power cord or did some joker turn off the circuit breaker right in the middle of your BIOS upgrade? You now have a system that won't boot. In many cases, it's time to use an old-fashioned technical support device called a telephone (you might have heard of it) and call the motherboard or system vendor for help. You might be standing in line the next day at your local shipping office to return your system for BIOS surgery. However, that won't necessarily be the case. Some BIOS chips have an automatic recovery feature built-in; systems with the feature have a motherboard jumper called the flash recovery jumper. BIOS chips with this feature contain a mini-BIOS that can be reinstalled from a reserved part of the chip.

To find out if you're one of the lucky owners of a BIOS with this feature, take a look at the MicroFirmware web site, which lists popular motherboards using Phoenix BIOS chips that have this feature.

To use flash recovery, follow this basic procedure:

1. Download the correct flash BIOS file to a working computer and use the file to make a bootable floppy disk. You might need to download a separate loader program with some BIOS versions. See the vendor's web site for details.

2. Take the floppy disk to the computer with the defective BIOS.

3. Open the system and locate the jumper that controls the BIOS recovery feature. Set the jumper for recovery.

4. Insert the floppy disk and rerun the BIOS install process.

5. Listen for beeps and watch for the drive light to run during this process, because the video won't work.

6. Turn off the computer, reset the jumper to Normal, and restart the computer.

What if you *don't* have a BIOS with this feature built in? If your system has a dual BIOS feature, read the manual to determine how to activate the second BIOS chip.

If you don't have a BIOS recovery feature or a dual-BIOS option on your motherboard, here are some other options to try:

- Contact MicroFirmware (www.firmware.com) for details about their disaster recovery and replacement BIOS services. With prices from $35 to $45 for a replacement BIOS (which sometimes has more features than your original), MicroFirmware's replacement (which you can install yourself) is a better deal than sending your fried system back to the vendor.

- Contact eSupport (formerly called Unicore; www.esupport.com) and use their BIOS wizard to identify your system and receive a customized price quote on a replacement BIOS.

- BIOSWorld (www.biosworld.com) downloads the latest BIOS from the motherboard vendor and uses it to create a BIOS chip for you for about $30. This site also offers information regarding motherboard manufacturers that are no longer in business.

If the BIOS update can't be installed, your motherboard might have a jumper that write-protects the flash BIOS. Check the manual to see if your system has this feature. To update a BIOS on a system with a write-protected jumper, you must do the following:

1. Disable the write-protection—yes, you need to open the system—find the jumper, and move it.

2. Perform the update.

3. Make sure you re-enable the write-protection to keep unauthorized people, viruses, and assorted bad stuff from changing the BIOS.

Replacing a Damaged ROM BIOS Chip

If your BIOS is damaged during the upgrade process, or if your BIOS cannot be upgraded with a download, you need to remove it and replace it. Should you? Well, consider these issues before you place your order:

- BIOS chip upgrades cost $30 to $45 or more; this is about halfway to the cost of a new motherboard in many cases. A new motherboard provides an updated BIOS "for free" along with other updated features.

- Although the BIOS will be updated, the rest of the system might still be out of date.

If you still need to update the BIOS chip itself, make sure that the vendor has the *correct* BIOS chip replacement. Don't be alarmed if you might wind up with a different brand of BIOS than your current BIOS. Just make sure that you have recorded your hard drive information before you pull your old BIOS chip, because you need to reenter this and other manually configured options (such as boot order) into the new BIOS's setup program.

The vendor identifies the BIOS chip you need by the motherboard ID information displayed at bootup. eSupport offers a free download utility called the BIOS Wizard to display this information for you. MicroFirmware has the most popular systems and motherboards listed by brand and model. To replace the chip, follow these steps:

1. Locate the BIOS chip on your motherboard after you open the case to perform the upgrade. It usually has a sticker listing the BIOS maker and model number.

2. Use the BIOS extraction tool provided by the upgrade vendor to remove your old BIOS chip.

3. Gently rock the ends of the chip to free it, and straighten any bent pins when you finish removing it.

4. Remove the existing BIOS chip carefully and put it on anti-static material in case you need to reuse it in that system.

5. Follow the instructions provided with the upgrade to install the new BIOS chip; some chips are rectangular and others are square.

6. Make sure the BIOS chip is mounted correctly in the socket; if the legs are misaligned or if the chip is installed backward, you'll fry the BIOS as soon as you turn on the computer. See Figure 9.11.

7. Turn on your system, and use the new BIOS's keystroke(s) to start the setup program to reenter any information. You might get a CMOS error at startup, which is normal with a new BIOS chip. After you reenter the BIOS data you recorded earlier and save the changes, the system will run without error messages.

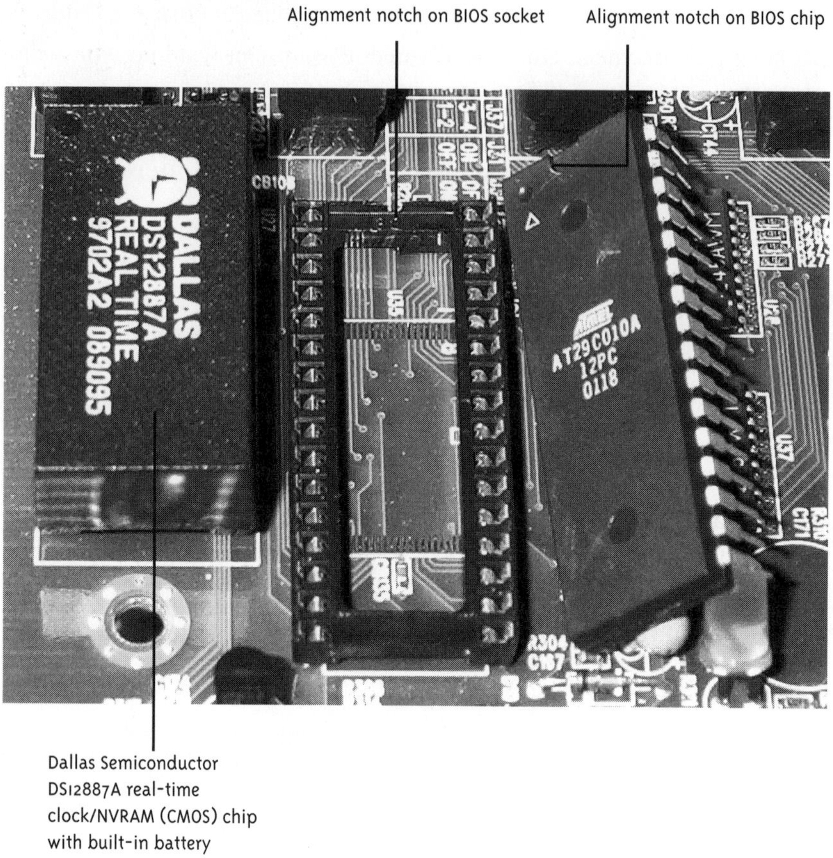
Alignment notch on BIOS socket
Alignment notch on BIOS chip
DALLAS
DS12887A
REAL TIME
9702A2 089095
AT29C010A
12PC
0118
Dallas Semiconductor DS12887A real-time clock/NVRAM (CMOS) chip with built-in battery

Figure 9.11

A socketed BIOS chip (right) and its socket (center). Use the alignment notches to properly orient the BIOS chip in the socket.

Troubleshooting Batteries and CMOS Issues

As you learned in this chapter and elsewhere, the BIOS chip contains all kinds of options for configuring your system. However, the BIOS chip itself doesn't store the options you choose; instead, it functions something like a restaurant menu and lists the choices you have. Where are the options you select stored for use? At a restaurant, it might be a touch-screen computer at a fast-food restaurant, an order pad, or, at the finest restaurants, the memory of a very alert waiter or waitress. Now, even if you're hungry, you won't find a waiter or waitress in your computer, but you will find a chip which takes your digital order for BIOS selections: the CMOS chip.

The Complimentary Metal-Oxide Semiconductor (CMOS) chip receives this name from its construction, which requires very little power to maintain its contents. In fact, on most recent systems, a small 3V DC watch battery (a CR2032 or equivalent) is all you need to maintain its contents for several years. See Figure 9.12 for examples of typical motherboard batteries.

Dallas semiconductor DS12887A
(combines CMOS, clock, and battery)

Sony CR2032 (3-volt lithium)

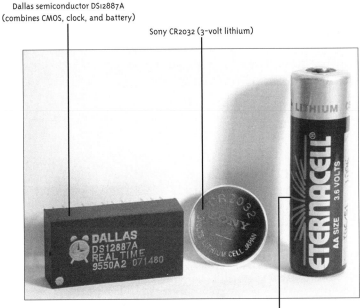

Eternacell 3.6-volt AA-size (normal AA is 1.5 volts)

Figure 9.12

The Dallas Semiconductor chip on left combines CMOS, clock, and battery into a single unit. The CR2032 battery in the middle is the most common battery in use today, and the 3.6-volt AA-sized battery at right was used on some older Compaq and Zenith systems.

Another, less common but more accurate name for this chip is the non-volatile RAM/Real-Time Clock (NVRAM/RTC) chip. Whew, what a mouthful! Whether you call it Ray, or Jay, or CMOS, or NVRAM/RTC, it does the same job: It stores the options you choose for drive types, boot sequence, power management, and other BIOS options.

The CMOS is an unsung part of the startup process; in fact, I wouldn't be surprised if you'd never given it a thought until this chapter—*unless* you've seen an error such as CMOS corrupted or CMOS checksum error at boot time. Panic city!

However, you don't need to panic, especially if you see a message like this after you perform a pull-and-reinsert chip BIOS upgrade or install a new motherboard. In both cases, your CMOS doesn't have a valid record of BIOS settings. Fixing this problem is simple: Just enter the BIOS setup program, detect your drives, and set other options such as power management, boot order, and port configurations. Then, save the changes. If your battery is working properly, you won't see this message again for a very long time.

But what if you see the same or similar message again? Check the following:

- **Worn-out battery**—The battery connected to the motherboard won't last forever; about two to three years is typical. Install a replacement battery and restart your system; reset your BIOS options, save them, and reboot.

MARK'S TIP SHEET: Your Battery's Days Are Numbered When...

- Your computer loses a significant amount of time; if your PC clock is hours, months, or years off and continues to lose time after you reset it, your battery is dying.

- You must reset the CMOS every time you turn on your computer; your battery is probably already dead.

If you see symptoms like this, it's time to get to the store and buy a new battery.

- **Viruses**—The CMOS has been targeted by a number of viruses, including AntiCMOS, Stoned.Azusa, and The Exe_Bug/CMOS Killer—to name just a few. Using up-to-date antivirus software can prevent infection. If your system starts reporting that there are no floppy or hard drives present, suspect a virus.

- **Power surges**—The CMOS can be corrupted, or even "killed" by power surges (after all, it's a low-power chip). Save the CMOS and the rest of your system from getting clobbered by using a decent surge protector.

- **CMOS clear jumper set**—To prevent you from using a new motherboard with the hardware test configuration stored at the factory, some vendors ship their motherboards with this jumper enabled so that any previous settings are wiped out. You can't store CMOS settings until you disable this jumper.

Resetting Passwords

Most BIOSes have two password options:

- A power-on password that must be provided before you can turn on the system

- A supervisor password that must be provided before you can enter the BIOS

These passwords can help keep your system secure, but they can also cause big problems. Want to outsmart yourself? Use the BIOS options to set up passwords for both options, enable these options—and then *lose* the passwords. Guess what? You're locked out of your system without a digital coat hanger.

Your only recourse? Clear the CMOS memory to make your computer have CMOS amnesia. Instead of forgetting about its first love or the last time it saw Paris online, a computer with an erased CMOS forgets these passwords—and every *other* BIOS setting. Hope you recorded them first! You can't access the data on the hard disk until you restore correct BIOS settings.

To clear the CMOS, look for the following options:

- Most recent motherboards have a "clear CMOS" jumper installed, usually near the battery. Place a small plastic jumper block (it has metal inside to make a connection) over the correct pins, turn on the system power for a few seconds, turn off the power, and your system's CMOS will be thoroughly flushed. You'll probably see one of those CMOS errors when you restart, but you know how to fix those.

- Some motherboard designers ask you to use a screwdriver or tweezers to clear the CMOS by shorting across the battery connectors. Ouch! It works, but don't get heavy-handed while you're down in Motherboardland or you might damage something.

- A few older systems require that you remove the battery and wait, and wait, and wait for the CMOS to lose its information. This can take several hours.

Troubleshooting Motherboard Problems

Motherboard upgrades might go smoothly, but Murphy's Law suggests you'll have a few bumps along the way. Use these tips to get through this task with minimal pain.

Help! I've installed my new motherboard and nothing happens when I turn on the power!

Chances are you've missed one or more of the following; make sure you *turn off and unplug* the system before you check and fix these items:

- **You didn't push the ZIF (Zero Insertion Force) socket lever down to clamp the CPU in place**—If the system doesn't know the CPU is present, you can't boot. Look for this one with any socketed CPU. See Chapter 8 for examples.

- **You forgot to attach a power cable to the motherboard**—No power, no boot!

- **You didn't install the memory correctly**—You can't boot without memory. See Chapter 7 for examples.

- **You didn't connect the ATA/IDE cables properly**—Some systems can't display anything onscreen until the drives spin up, and if the cables are reversed, the drives can't get the command.

Help! I've installed my new motherboard and the memory and CPU are working, but it's not booting!

Chances are you forgot to connect power to the drives or forgot to define the drives in the BIOS setup program. You need to do the following:

- Check the power cables to the drives; replace any broken or worn Y-adapters with new ones.

- Restart the system and make sure the drives are properly identified in the BIOS setup. Use the Auto-detect feature to set your hard drives, CD-ROM, and other IDE devices. You might need to change the floppy drive default to the correct value; some systems select 3.5-inch 1.44MB for drive A: by default, but others don't.

Help! My system is running slower after the motherboard or BIOS upgrade. What's wrong?

If your system is booting up more slowly, you probably have the hard drives set to Auto-Detect in the BIOS. Use the auto-detect feature in most recent BIOS chips to determine the size and settings for each drive, and then store those settings as user-defined drive types. You can waste several seconds on every bootup if you let the BIOS search for the drives every time you start the system.

If your system is running slower after it boots, check the following:

- Make sure the clock multiplier and FSB speeds are set correctly for your CPU. Multi-speed motherboards are often factory-set to the slowest FSB speed for safety. Make sure you set the board correctly for your CPU.

- If you are mixing memory speeds (DDR266 and DDR333, or PC100 and PC133 SDRAM, for example), some systems run all memory at the speed of the lowest memory, while others can change access speeds on a module-by-module basis. If your CPU supports faster FSB speeds than your memory does, your memory is slowing down the system. Upgrade to modules as fast as (or faster than) your CPU requires.

- Check your BIOS configuration. Many BIOS chips offer automatic configuration, but if you choose the wrong options, you slow down memory access, disable CPU caching, and more. Choose turbo or optimal on BIOS chips that offer a range of automatic configurations. Avoid BIOS defaults or Power-On defaults unless you are troubleshooting a system that won't run with faster settings. Check your motherboard manual or online help to see which settings are the fastest for your motherboard. Make sure you double-check the settings after you finish. I've seen some motherboards that disable external cache with some settings, and disabling external cache will really slow down your system.

Part III

Upgrading for Greater Storage Capacity

Chapter 10

Adding a Huge Hard Disk

Since the development of the first hard disks for PCs in the early 1980s, one of the most common upgrades to perform on any computer has been, and continues to be, a hard disk upgrade.

Although programs at one time fit on one or two floppy disks that contained less than a megabyte of information, hard disks became a way to avoid the floppy disk shuffle. Today, a single high-end program installation, such as Adobe Photoshop 7, can use about a hundred megabytes of disk space. Install an office suite, such as Microsoft Office, and kiss about 200MB of disk space goodbye. As you might expect, the latest version of Microsoft Office, Microsoft Office XP, wants even more space: 250MB. In addition, Windows XP needs a *minimum* of 1.5GB just for installation.

Obviously, you need only combine today's huge programs, enormous office suites, and space-gobbling operating systems with the popularity of MP3 downloads, high-speed web surfing (which makes downloading programs, movie trailers, and digital audio even easier), digital imaging, and online gaming, and most users are on the verge of a storage crisis every time they turn on their computers.

What happens if you run out of disk space? Besides the obvious problems such as no room to install new programs and no room to save new or changed documents, Windows also begins to malfunction because there is not enough room to store temporary files created when you browse the web, print documents, or use the hard disk as virtual memory. No matter how big your current hard drive is, sooner or later, you will be performing a hard drive upgrade.

In this chapter, you learn about AT Attachment (ATA) and Integrated Drive Electronics (IDE), Serial ATA (SATA), and SCSI hard drives and how to install them in your system. You also learn about external drives that use IEEE-1394a or USB 2.0 interfaces.

Ten Reasons to Add a Huge Hard Disk

You're probably thinking about installing a bigger hard disk, or you wouldn't be reading this chapter. If you're not sure you need one, check out this top-ten list of reasons for installing a bigger drive. If you recognize yourself or your computer somewhere in this list, you're ready to get a bigger hard drive.

1. You're tired of deleting programs so that you can install more programs.

2. You have two or more small hard disks already installed, and you're still out of space.

3. You have less than 15 percent of your hard disk space left.

4. You keep choosing the minimal install feature when you install new programs because there's not enough room to install all the features.

5. You need more space for digital photos.

6. You need more space for MP3 music downloads.

7. You need more space for program downloads.

8. Windows keeps displaying the Disk Cleanup wizard.

9. You're tired of running the Disk Cleanup wizard.

10. You need more space.

What to Do Until the New Hard Drive Arrives

If you're in a panic because you're short of hard disk space *now* and the drive you ordered won't arrive until tomorrow, take it easy. There are several ways you can get rid of excess or junk files to buy yourself a little time until you can upgrade your storage space. You might even be able to put off a hard drive upgrade for a little longer.

I mentioned the Windows Disk Cleanup Wizard in the previous section. Although it runs automatically whenever your computer runs short of space on a particular drive, you can start it manually whenever you would like to free up space on a particular drive letter.

To view the amount of free space on a drive and run Disk Cleanup:

1. Right-click the drive letter in Windows Explorer.

2. Select Properties, and the General tab displays a pie chart reflecting the amount of used and free disk space. If the drive has less than 15% free space remaining, click the Disk Cleanup button to see if any free space can be created on that drive.

3. Disk Cleanup calculates how much free space can be created if old files are compressed (with NTFS drives only), if temporary Internet files are deleted, if the contents of the Recycle Bin are discarded, and if index files are deleted. After calculating this information, the total savings are displayed, and you can choose to accept or reject each of the suggested changes.

4. Click the More Options tab to see a dialog that allows you to free up more disk space by removing Windows components, programs, or old System Restore points.

Other ways to enhance available storage space include the following:

- Copy old data files to recordable or rewriteable DVD or CD media, and then delete the files from the hard drive. See the next tip for details.

- Deleted files go to the Recycle Bin and continue to use disk space unless you hold down the Shift key when you delete them. Make sure you have backed up the files you delete because if they aren't in the Recycle Bin, you must use a third-party file recovery tool such as Norton Utilities to retrieve them.

- Run Defrag from the Tools menu for a particular drive, or use a third-party defragging tool. Defrag doesn't create any additional space on a drive, but it puts empty space on the drive into contiguous locations so that it's used more efficiently.

ATA the Traditional Way

Drives based on the IDE interface began to replace older drive interfaces starting in the late 1980s. ATA is the preferred name for the most common type of IDE interface, but because some vendors prefer to use the terms IDE or Enhanced IDE, I use ATA/IDE in this book to refer to the ATA version of the IDE interface. The ATA/IDE interface continues to be, by far, the most popular drive interface used today; nearly every system you use or can buy has at least one ATA/IDE hard disk installed.

CAUTION: STOP! LOOK! THINK!

What's in a Name—An ATA Would Be Just as Cheap

ATA/IDE is the current version of IDE, but at one time, there were two other IDE versions:

- **XT IDE**—A version of IDE that supported 8-bit systems that used the long-outdated 8088 or 8086 processors. XT IDE also used a 40-pin connector identical to ATA IDE.

- **MCA IDE**—A version of IDE that supported the now-obsolete Micro Channel Architecture (MCA) slot found in some IBM PS/2 models; it used a 72-pin interface.

Because these other versions of IDE have been obsolete for years, IDE now equals ATA.

The PCGuide web site has a detailed history of ATA/IDE standards at www.pcguide.com/ref/hdd/if/ide/std.htm.

An ATA/IDE hard drive can be recognized by its 40-pin connector, which connects to a 40-wire or 80-wire cable. Two drives can be connected to each cable, and the cable normally connects to an ATA/IDE host adapter on the motherboard. Most systems have at least two host adapters on the motherboard. If the drive is larger than the system BIOS can manage, the drives might be attached to a separate host adapter card.

Some advanced motherboards now feature four ATA/IDE host adapters, with the latter two offering a feature called *Redundant Array of Inexpensive Drives (RAID)*, which means that data is automatically copied to both drives (drive mirroring) or that both drives are treated as part of one big drive (data striping).

JARGON

Striping—Two drives are treated as a single drive, with both drives used to simultaneously store different portions of the same file. Also called RAID Level 0. Data striping boosts performance, but if either drive fails, all data is lost. Don't using striping for data drives.

Mirroring—Two drives are treated as mirrors of each other; changes to the contents of one drive are immediately reflected on the other drive. Also called RAID Level 1. Data mirroring provides a built-in backup method.

ATA/IDE Isn't Just for Hard Drives

ATA/IDE was originally designed for hard drives, but in the last few years, several other types of storage devices have been adapted to it, including the following:

- Optical drives (including CD-R, CD-RW, and DVD drives)
- Removable-media drives, such as ZIP and LS-120
- Tape backup drives
- Magneto-optical drives

These drives are sometimes referred to as *AT Attachment Packet Interface (ATAPI)* drives, and they use the same master/slave/cable select jumpers and data cable as standard ATA/IDE drives do. You can connect an ATAPI and ATA hard disk to the same cable, if necessary. You can learn more about how these drives work in Chapter 11, "Removable Storage to Go," and Chapter 12, "A Burning Desire for Better Optical Drives." A removable-media drive is sometimes also referred to as an *ATAPI removable media drive (ARMD)* .

ATA/IDE Variations

The simple term "ATA/IDE" conceals a huge number of variations in performance and capacity. To make sure you understand the maximum performance and limitations of a given IDE device, use this section to learn about the most significant ATA/IDE standards, speeds, and technologies.

READ THIS TOO: Paying More Attention to ATA

To learn much more about the history and features of different ATA/IDE drives and standards, I recommend Scott Mueller's *Upgrading and Repairing PCs, 15th Edition* (Que, 2003). Older editions also cover the very early history of hard drives such as the ST-506 and ESDI interfaces.

For a great visual treatment of drive operation, be sure to take a look at Ron White's *How Computers Work, Sixth Edition* (Que, 2001).

ATA/IDE drives are sometimes categorized by their speeds or by their compatibility with a particular ATA standard. Table 10.1 lists the major ATA/IDE standards.

Table 10.1 ATA/IDE Standards and Features

ATA Specification	Major Features
ATA-1 (original)	Standardized master/slave jumpers
	IDE Identify command for automatic configuration and detection of parameters
	PIO modes 0–2
	CHS (standard cylinder-head-sector) and LBA (logical block addressing, sector-translated) parameters
ATA-2	PIO modes 3–4
	Power management
	CHS/LBA translation for drives up to 8.4GB
	Primary and secondary IDE channels
	IDE block mode
ATA-3	S.M.A.R.T. self-diagnostics feature for use with monitoring software
	Password protection
	Improved reliability of PIO mode 4
ATA-4	UDMA/33
	ATAPI support
	80-wire/40-pin cable
	BIOS support for LBA increased to 136.9GB
ATA-5	UDMA/66
	Required use of 80-wire/40-pin cable with UDMA/66
ATA-6	UDMA/100
	Increased capacity of LBA to 144 PetaBytes (PB; 1 PB = 1 quadrillion bytes)

An ATA-7 standard is currently in draft form. It is expected to provide standards for external hard drives and for the Ultra ATA-133 transfer rate (FastDrive) developed by Maxtor and available in current Maxtor drives.

ON THE WEB: For ATA, Go to T13

What's T13? T13 is the American National Standards Institute (ANSI) technical committee responsible for maintaining and developing the ATA standards listed previously in this chapter and related BIOS and interface standards. If you need more detailed technical information on the ATA/IDE standard, go to the T13 web site, located at www.t13.org.

Enhanced IDE is a marketing term used by some vendors to refer to the enhancements listed as ATA-2 in Table 10.1. Some vendors prefer to use the term "EIDE" for their drives rather than "IDE" or "ATA/IDE."

Virtually any drive you can buy today is compliant with at least the ATA-5 standards, and most now support ATA-6. If your system lacks support for the advanced features of ATA-5 or newer versions, your new drive can still be used, but its performance (and possibly its capacity) will be reduced.

In the following sections, you learn more about terms such as PIO (programmed input/output), UDMA, block mode, and LBA (Logical Block Addressing).

ANALYZE THIS

What You Need to Know to Configure an ATA/IDE Drive

To install an ATA/IDE drive into your system, or move it from one system to another, you might need to know the following:

- **The drive geometry**—The cylinders, heads, and sectors per track values specified by the manufacturer or used when the drive was prepared.

- **The translation scheme**—As you see later in this chapter, you need to use a feature called LBA to trick a system into recognizing the capacity of any drive you buy.

- **Support for IDE block mode**—All recent drives support this mode, but some systems require you to enable this option manually and specify how many blocks the drive supports.

- **PIO or UDMA mode supported**—Using the wrong data transfer rate setting can corrupt data or cause data to be transferred more slowly than the drive requires.

If your system has an Auto setting for configuring hard drives, this information is set automatically. However, you might need to set these values manually on some systems.

Wondering what these terms mean? Read on!

PIO and Ultra DMA Modes

Programmable Input/Output (PIO) and UltraDMA (UDMA; also called UltraATA) both refer to how quickly data is passed from the hard disk to the host adapter. The simplest way to set your system for the correct values is to use the BIOS's Auto setting, which queries the drive for the correct values. However, in some cases, you might need to select the proper setting manually.

As you can see from Table 10.1, the first ATA/IDE hard drives were designed to run at one of several PIO modes. Most recent systems automatically select the correct speed for the combination of ATA/IDE host adapter and drive, but some older systems require you to set the PIO mode manually in the system BIOS configuration.

Recent drives have abandoned PIO mode for UltraDMA for faster data transfer. However, no matter which transfer type a particular hard drive uses, selecting transfer rates too fast for the drive can cause data corruption, and selecting rates that are too slow can slow down the system.

How fast can you transfer data to your drive? If your system supports only PIO modes, check out Table 10.2. Although recent hard drives use even faster UDMA transfer speeds, some CD-ROM drives still use PIO modes.

Table 10.2	PIO Peak Transfer Rates
Mode	Peak Transfer Rate
PIO 0	3.33MBps
PIO 1	5.22MBps
PIO 2	8.33MBps
PIO 3	11.11MBps
PIO 4	16.67MBps

Current ATA/IDE drives have left PIO modes behind for the even faster performance of UDMA modes, as you can see in Table 10.3.

JARGON

Direct Memory Access (DMA)—A high-speed data-transfer method that moves data directly between a device and memory without continuous CPU control. Was used by a few hard drives as an alternative to PIO (which is controlled by the CPU).

Ultra DMA (UDMA)—A faster and more reliable version of DMA that provides cyclic redundancy checking (CRC) error correction for data transferred to and from the drive.

Table 10.3 UDMA Peak Transfer Rates

Mode	Also Called	Peak Transfer Rate
UDMA 2	UDMA 33, ATA/33, Ultra ATA/33	33.33MBps
UDMA 4	UDMA 66, ATA/66, Ultra ATA/66	66.66MBps
UDMA 5	UDMA 100, ATA/100, Ultra ATA/100	100MBps
UDMA 6	UDMA 133, ATA/133, Ultra ATA/133	133MBps

What do you do if you bring home a brand-new UDMA/133 drive from the store and your motherboard can't run any faster than UDMA/66? No problem—ATA/IDE drives are backward compatible; you can select a slower DMA mode than the drive supports if your system doesn't support the correct DMA mode. If you have a really old motherboard, you can even use PIO modes if that's all you have. Performance will be slower, but the drive will still work.

Most UDMA 4 and faster drives are packaged with a utility program that should be used if the drive needs to be configured to run at a slower UDMA speed. This is necessary if the ATA/IDE host adapter's maximum speed is slower than the speed of the drive's UDMA interface. These programs can also be downloaded from the drive vendors' web sites. See the vendors' web sites for details.

ANALYZE THIS

Special Cables for Speed and Reliability

Drives that support UDMA mode 4 (also called Ultra ATA/66) or faster modes require (and usually are shipped with) a special cable. The cable has a 40-pin connector like normal ATA/IDE cables, but it has 80 wires—40 for data and signals, with each wire alternating with a ground wire. Figure 10.8 later in this chapter compares the 40-wire and 80-wire cables. One end of the cable is made of blue plastic. This blue connector must be attached to the host adapter on the motherboard or PCI host adapter card. The Ultra ATA/66 cable uses cable select. The master drive must be attached to the end of the cable opposite the blue connector, the slave drive must be attached to the connector near the middle of the cable, and both drives must be jumpered to use cable select.

By the way, it's perfectly all right to use these cables with slower ATA/IDE devices for added reliability. Just make sure that you re-jumper devices as Cable Select when you use the UDMA/66 cable.

To get the maximum benefit out of any UDMA-compatible drive, you also need to install the correct bus-mastering drivers for your motherboard, as discussed in Chapter 9.

ON THE WEB: Get the Real Facts About Your Drive

Although today's systems make installing a drive very simple (just select Auto in the BIOS and it's all done for you), older systems might force you to know more about your drive. If you're coming up empty in the facts department about block mode, UDMA or PIO support, or even your drive's geometry, don't panic! Go to the drive maker's web site and get the straight story. Here are the web sites for the "big four" disk drive makers:

- For Seagate and Conner Peripherals, go to www.seagate.com.
- For Maxtor and Quantum, go to www.maxtor.com.
- For Western Digital, go to www.wdc.com.
- For IBM or Hitachi, go to www.hgst.com.

ATA/IDE Block Mode

ATA/IDE block mode refers to an improved method of data handling designed to—what else?—speed up your drive. Originally, a hard drive was allowed to read only a single 512-byte sector before the drive sent an IRQ to the CPU. Early in their history, some ATA/IDE hard drives began to use a different method called *block mode*, which enabled the drive to read multiple sectors, or blocks, of data before an IRQ was sent. Drives that support block mode (they all do today) run more quickly when block mode is enabled in the BIOS.

Recent systems automatically determine block mode capability when they auto-detect the drive. Older systems might require that you enable or disable block mode manually, and still others enable you to select the number of blocks the drive can read. If you must set block mode manually, check with the drive vendor to see whether the drive supports block mode and what options to select if it does. What happens if you set block mode incorrectly? Fortunately, you can't hurt your data, although you can slow down your system.

See Figure 10.1 for a typical example of an ATA/IDE hard disk BIOS configuration screen. Figure 10.2 is a typical example of an optical (CD-ROM/CD-RW/DVD) BIOS configuration screen.

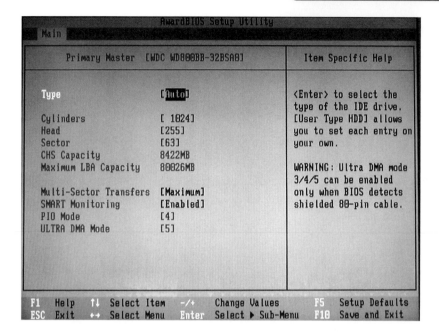

Figure 10.1

A typical peripheral configuration screen with automatic configuration of PIO, UDMA, and block modes for ATA/IDE hard drives. These options can be set manually if necessary.

```
                    AwardBIOS Setup Utility
  Main

      Primary Master  [WDC WD800BB-32BSA0]        Item Specific Help

  Type                   [Auto]            <Enter> to select the
                                           type of the IDE drive.
  Cylinders              [ 1024]           [User Type HDD] allows
  Head                   [255]             you to set each entry on
  Sector                 [63]              your own.
  CHS Capacity           8422MB
  Maximum LBA Capacity   80026MB           WARNING: Ultra DMA mode
                                           3/4/5 can be enabled
  Multi-Sector Transfers [Maximum]         only when BIOS detects
  SMART Monitoring       [Enabled]         shielded 80-pin cable.
  PIO Mode               [4]
  ULTRA DMA Mode         [5]



  F1   Help   ↑↓  Select Item   -/+  Change Values    F5   Setup Defaults
  ESC  Exit   ↔   Select Menu   Enter Select ▶ Sub-Menu F10  Save and Exit
```

Figure 10.2

A typical peripheral configuration screen with automatic configuration of PIO and UDMA modes for an optical (CD-ROM, CD-RW, DVD) drive.

```
                    AwardBIOS Setup Utility
  Main

    Secondary Master  [PLEXTOR CD-R  PX-W4012A]    Item Specific Help

  Type                   [Auto]            <Enter> to select the
  PIO Mode               [4]               type of the IDE drive.
  ULTRA DMA Mode         [2]               [User Type HDD] allows
                                           you to set each entry on
                                           your own.

                                           WARNING: Ultra DMA mode
                                           3/4/5 can be enabled
                                           only when BIOS detects
                                           shielded 80-pin cable.



  F1   Help   ↑↓  Select Item   -/+  Change Values    F5   Setup Defaults
  ESC  Exit   ↔   Select Menu   Enter Select ▶ Sub-Menu F10  Save and Exit
```

Logical Block Addressing and Drive Translation

ATA/IDE drives go back far enough that I once owned an "enormous" 200MB drive that cost "only" $1,000 (in 1989). Quite a lot has changed since then, including the cost versus capacity curve. The way I figure it, as drive sizes increase and the cost per GB (formerly the cost per MB) keeps dropping, you'll eventually be able to buy a hard disk of infinite capacity for zilch! Wonder how Western Digital will make money on that deal?

Seriously, though, when you buy one of today's big hard drives, you'd like to use every giga-byte of storage you paid for. However, if you try to install that big hard disk into some sys-tems, you could be in for a shock if you're unaware of the built-in disk-size limitations. As this section shows, a feature called "drive translation" must be present to enable drives to work at their full capacity.

CHS and LBA

When you install an ATA/IDE drive in your system, you must configure the BIOS to prop-erly recognize the drive by specifying the drive's geometry, which comprises the following:

- The number of cylinders
- The number of read/write heads
- The number of sectors per track

These values are sometimes called the *Cylinder-Head-Sector (CHS)* values for the drive, and they are usually printed on the drive. Although you could enter these values manually in the system BIOS setup, the easiest and best way to feed these values into the system BIOS is to use the Auto setting shown in Figure 10.1.

By using Auto, you also enable another important setting: drive translation. Without drive translation, your large hard disk is recognized as a tiny fraction of its actual size.

When the ATA/IDE interface was developed in the late 1980s, several limitations on the total capacity of an ATA/IDE hard disk existed:

- A MS-DOS limitation of 1,024 cylinders per drive
- An ATA/IDE limitation of 63 sectors per track
- A BIOS limitation of 16 heads

These limitations resulted in a total capacity of approximately 528 million bytes. However, when a "big" drive was just 200MB, who cared? Nobody cared until late 1993 and early 1994 when drives began to surpass this limit. To solve this problem the right way, a feature called *Logical Block Addressing (LBA)* began to show up in BIOS configurations.

What does LBA do? LBA mode alters how the drive is accessed internally by changing the BIOS limit to 255 heads (instead of 16) and dividing the cylinders and multiplying the heads by the same factor to reduce the cylinder count below the 1,024 cylinder MS-DOS limit. The result? The CHS limitations are done away with, your drive has a completely different logical geometry, and you can use the full capacity you paid for. LBA's geometry changes are also referred to as "drive translation."

How does it work? Let's assume you want to install a 6.4GB hard disk with a geometry of 13,328 cylinders, 15 heads, and 63 sectors per track. The first (and only) problem is the cylinder count. If LBA mode isn't enabled, the cylinder count is reduced to 1,024, and presto!— your 6.4GB drive has an effective capacity of just 528MB.

Enable LBA mode, however, and the following mathematical magic takes place:

Original Cylinders	Divisor	Result	Under Limit?
13328	15	952	Yes
Original Heads	**Multiplier**	**Result**	**Under Limit?**
15	15	225	Yes

Table 10.4 shows how the original and new LBA geometry compare to each other.

Table 10.4	Sample LBA Geometry Conversion		
Geometry	Cylinder	Heads	Sectors per Track
Original CHS	13328	15	63
LBA	952	225	63

MS-DOS and Windows are incapable of using more than 528MB of any ATA/IDE hard drive unless LBA mode is enabled. The Award BIOS also supports a different translation method called *LARGE*, but this method is not used by other BIOS makers and should be avoided. LBA mode is supported by all major BIOS and system makers, although there are variations in how different BIOS types and motherboards perform the translation.

Some BIOS types show you the actual normal (CHS) and translated (LBA or LARGE) geometry values when the drive is configured, but others don't. How do you know it's working? When your disk preparation software (Fdisk with Windows 9x/Me or Disk Management with Windows 2000/XP) can access the entire capacity of the drive, your translation works! If Fdisk or Disk Management claims that your big drive is only 528MB in size, LBA mode is not enabled in the BIOS.

> **JARGON**
>
> *FDISK*—The Windows 9x/Me hard disk partitioning program.
>
> *Disk Management*—Part of the Microsoft Management Console (MMC) that is used to prepare drives for use in Windows 2000/XP.

> **CAUTION: STOP! LOOK! THINK!**
>
> **It's Not Nice to Play with LBA**
>
> What happens if the LBA mode is disabled after the drive is configured using LBA mode? The drive will not work properly.
>
> With MS-DOS, the system at some point might try to write to data stored on areas past the barrier of 1,024 cylinders that LBA mode overcomes. Without LBA mode to translate the drive's full capacity, the system loops back to the beginning of the drive and overwrites the partition table and file allocation table, destroying the drive's contents. Ouch!
>
> Fortunately, however, systems running Windows 9x, Me, 2000, or XP will be incapable of booting, so your data is safe, but the drive can't be accessed until LBA mode is enabled.
>
> It would be a dumb human trick to turn off LBA mode on purpose, but you could turn it off by accident. Some of the earlier AMI BIOS versions that supported LBA mode put this setting into one of the advanced BIOS setup screens rather than on the drive configuration screen. The result? If you reset the BIOS with one of the default options, the LBA mode got turned off. Now there's a dumb BIOS trick for you!

Think your system is A-OK because you're using a drive bigger than 528MB and you know how to set LBA mode? Think again. Some systems have a few other problems you should know about.

Overcoming Drive Size Limitations

On any system built from 1999 to the present, there are no capacity problems caused by limitations in BIOS support as long as you use Windows 98 or later and install an ATA/IDE drive that's no more than 120GB in size.

> **ON THE WEB: Drive Size Limitations on Older Systems**
>
> Pre-1999 systems often have various BIOS-based limitations for drive size. The Windows 95 upgrade has a maximum drive size of 8.4GB (caused by the limitations of MS-DOS), and the Windows 95 full version has a maximum drive size of 32GB. To learn more about dealing with BIOS and Windows-based limitations in older systems, check out the excellent discussion provided by DEW Associates Corporation's Knowledge Center at `www.dewassoc.com/kbase/hard_drives/` `drive_size_barrier_limitations.htm`.
>
> See also Seagate's "Why can't I see the full capacity of my drive?" page at `www.seagate.com/support/kb/disc/capacity/index.html`.

However, you should note the following glitches with Windows 98/98SE and drives greater than 64GB:

- Fdisk doesn't properly report the size of drives greater than 64GiB. Microsoft Knowledge Base article number 263044 provides a downloadable fix. Search for this article at `http://support.microsoft.com`.

> **JARGON**
>
> *GiB*—Gibibyte, term for what was formerly known as a binary gigabyte (GB). One decimal GB is one billion (1,000,000,000) bytes. One gibibyte is 1,073,741,824 bytes. Some vendors use the term GB to refer to both decimal gigabytes and binary gigabytes (gibibytes).

- Format doesn't display the correct size of a formatted drive over 64GiB at the start of the formatting process. This doesn't affect the operation of Format, and there is no fix required. Learn more from Microsoft Knowledge Base article number 263045.

However, if you're planning a much larger drive upgrade, such as an upgrade beyond 120GB, you must deal with the limitations of the ATA interface. Unless your computer's BIOS fully supports the new 48-bit LBA mode translation supported by ATA-6, you can't use a drive larger than 137GB without providing your system some help:

- If your computer has an Intel 8*xx*-series chip set, download and install the Intel Application Accelerator (IAA) driver from the Intel web site. IAA also provides faster ATA/IDE drive performance.

- With other chipsets, install an ATA/IDE host adapter with 48-bit LBA support (also known as "greater than 137GB support") and connect the drive to it.

Note that the only versions of Windows with official support for 48-bit LBA drives include Windows XP (with Service Pack 1) and Windows 2000 (with Service Pack 3); Windows 2000 also requires manual changes to the Windows Registry. Windows 98 and Windows Me can use 48-bit LBA drives safely when the IAA driver or a 48-bit LBA host adapter is used.

ON THE WEB: Conquering the 137GB ATA Barrier

Download the IAA driver from `www.intel.com/support/chipsets/iaa/`.

If you're wondering if your system has 48-bit LBA support in the BIOS, download the 48-bit LBA test program from `www.intel.com/support/chipsets/iaa/lba_test.htm`.

Seagate provides an excellent operating system-specific guide to using greater-than-137GB hard disks at `www.seagate.com/support/kb/disc/capacity/index.html`.

What to Do When Your BIOS Can't Cope with a Big Drive

The best solution for any problem caused by an out-of-date BIOS—including disk-size limitations—is to upgrade the BIOS! Chapter 9, "Unlock Your System's Potential with Motherboard and BIOS Upgrades," covers the process in detail.

However, what should you do if you find out that your system or motherboard maker has voted your system off the island and left you stranded without any BIOS updates to solve this problem and you can't find a third-party BIOS upgrade solution either? Well, you *can* upgrade your motherboard (also covered in Chapter 9) and get a new, up-to-date BIOS in the bargain, but a faster and more cost-effective solution (assuming you have a spare expansion slot) is to pop in an ATA host adapter card with a BIOS capable of handling greater-than-137GB hard disks.

You can get cards that offer Ultra ATA-133 support, SATA support, combo cards that provide both port types (sometimes with FireWire or USB 2.0 ports as well), or RAID controllers. To determine if a particular ATA card can break the 137GB barrier, be sure to check the card's documentation carefully.

The following vendors offer ATA, SATA, and ATA or SATA RAID cards with greater-than-137GB (48-bit LBA) support:

- **Maxtor**—www.maxtor.com; Ultra ATA/133.
- **SIIG**—www.siig.com; Ultra ATA/133 and SATA cards as well as ATA RAID and combo cards with various combinations of ports.

- **Promise Technology**—www.promise.com; various SATA RAID and ATA RAID cards.

- **HighPoint Technologies**—www.highpoint-tech.com; various SATA RAID and ATA RAID cards.

You should install your choice of card and driver *before* you install the new drive that requires updated BIOS support. If you install the drive first, you will either be able to use only a part of the drive's capacity or the drive maker's disk setup program will install a software driver to enable you to use the full capacity. Although the software driver solution is free, boot-sector viruses could corrupt your drive. BIOS is best!

Serial ATA—The New Kid in Town

Although Serial ATA (SATA) has been on the horizon since 2001, the first SATA drives hit the marketplace in early 2003. What's special about SATA, and what do you need to know about upgrading to an SATA drive?

- A single four-wire cable up to one meter (over three feet) long; a longer, thinner cable than ATA drives use (80-wire ATA cables are 18 inches long). Figure 10.3 compares these cables.

- Direct one-to-one connection between SATA drive and host adapter; no need to jumper drives for master and slave.

- Low-cost adapters enable existing ATA drives to connect to a SATA cable (Figure 10.4).

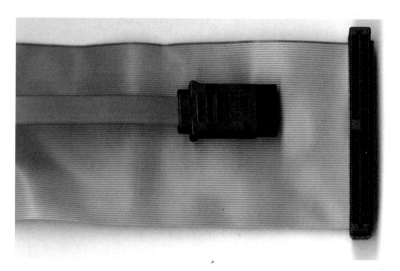

Figure 10.3

An SATA cable (foreground) compared to an 80-wire UltraATA/66 cable (background).

Compared to standard ATA drives, SATA has a higher theoretical transfer rate (150MB/sec) when compared to 133MB/sec for Ultra ATA/133 drives. However, neither current ATA nor first-generation SATA drives achieve these maximum transfer rates in real-world situations.

Figure 10.4

An ATA/IDE drive with normal power and data cables (left) compared to an ATA/IDE drive with an SATA adapter (right).

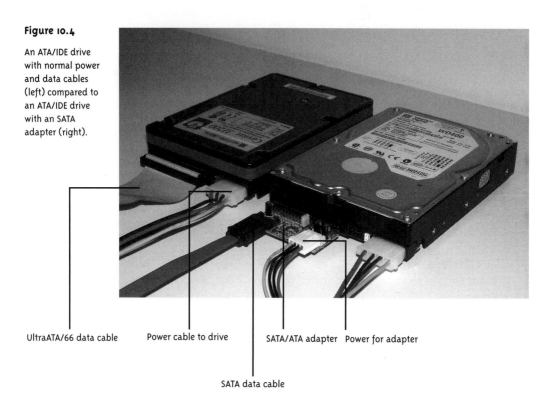

UltraATA/66 data cable   Power cable to drive   SATA/ATA adapter   Power for adapter

SATA data cable

Although SATA promises higher speeds in the future and offers easier cabling and configuration, it also has some disadvantages for the economy-minded upgrader. SATA drives have capacities starting at 80GB and are more expensive than Ultra ATA/133 drives with similar capacities. Unless your motherboard has an SATA host adapter, you also need an SATA host adapter card similar to the one shown in Figure 10.5 to add a SATA drive to an existing system.

Although SATA isn't for everyone right now, sooner or later it will replace the conventional ATA interface. Because SATA is based on ATA, its BIOS configuration and setup is similar to ATA.

Figure 10.5

A typical SATA host adapter; plug it into a PCI slot to support up to two SATA drives.

ON THE WEB: The Official Story of SATA

Get the latest information on the SATA standard direct from the Serial ATA Working Group at www.serialata.org.

Plug It in, Plug It in—USB and IEEE-1394a Drives

If you don't want to worry about fiddling with the inside of your computer, just plug an external drive to your computer's USB 2.0 or IEEE-1394a ports to add more free space in a few seconds.

Although these drives are more expensive than internal ATA/IDE or SATA drives and require a USB 2.0 or IEEE-1394a port (not included in all systems), they offer several advantages:

- **Portable and sharable**—You can move the drive between desktop and portable computers and have immediate access to lots of data.

- **No need to worry about disk preparation**—An external drive is preformatted at the factory for immediate use.

- **No installation worries**—If you want more storage without wrestling with the system case or ribbon cables, an external drive is the answer. Plug it in, and you're ready to go.

To learn more about these drives, see Chapter 11.

SCSI—Fast, Powerful, but Unfriendly

The SCSI interface is used for many different types of devices, as I discuss in Chapter 19, "Adding the Ports You Need for the Devices You Want." However, its original use was as a high-performance, hard-drive interface, and it is still used this way by many people who are dissatisfied with limitations of ATA/IDE. Some of the limitations of ATA/IDE include the following:

- There is a limitation of two drives per ATA/IDE host adapter.
- ATA/IDE can't work with devices other than drives.
- ATA/IDE devices don't support command queuing; each command must be given by the CPU to the drive only after the previous command has been completed.

SCSI hard drives make sense when you:

- Need high performance in a multitasking environment or for A/V editing and production.
- Need drives for a server or want a single interface card for as many as fifteen different devices.

If you want SCSI that truly is faster than ATA/IDE, you need to buy a high-performance SCSI host adapter as well as fast SCSI drives. The bottom line is this: SCSI done right is going to cost you a lot more money than ATA/IDE drives.

To attach a SCSI hard drive to your system, you need the following:

- A BIOS-equipped SCSI host adapter that supports the SCSI standard used by your hard drive (see Figure 10.6)
- A matching SCSI hard drive and cable

Although a number of 7,200 RPM Ultra SCSI hard drives are available from several different vendors, these drives aren't likely to perform much better than 7,200 RPM UDMA-66 or faster ATA/IDE drives unless you do a lot of multitasking operations. To reach significantly better performance than ATA/IDE that's worth paying for, you need to take a deep breath, check your wallet, and consider 10,000 RPM and 15,000 RPM drives. The latest versions of these drives require Ultra 160 or Ultra 320 interfaces. These interfaces can also be used with devices that support slower versions of SCSI.

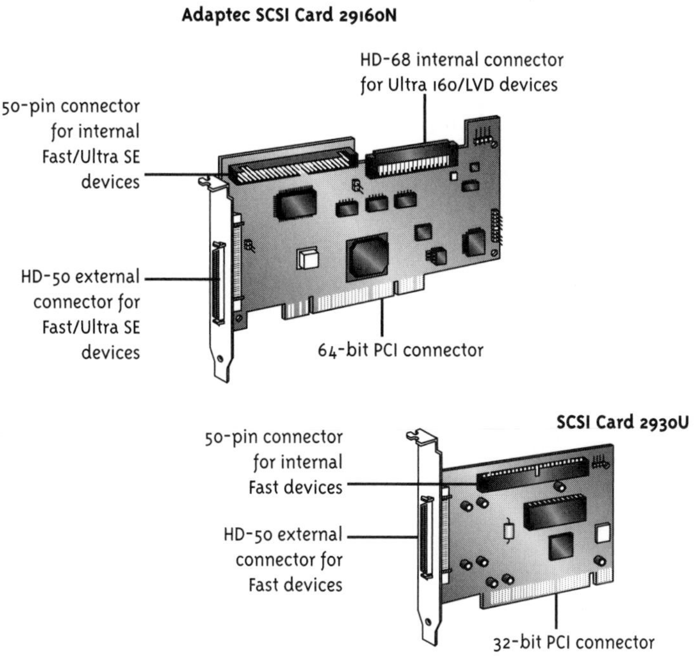

Adaptec SCSI Card 29160N

HD-68 internal connector
for Ultra 160/LVD devices

50-pin connector
for internal
Fast/Ultra SE
devices

HD-50 external
connector for
Fast/Ultra SE
devices

64-bit PCI connector

SCSI Card 2930U

50-pin connector
for internal
Fast devices

HD-50 external
connector for
Fast devices

32-bit PCI connector

Figure 10.6

The Adaptec SCSI card 29160N (top) can support up to fifteen different devices and SCSI speeds up through 160MBps (Ultra-3 SCSI/Ultra 160), while the Adaptec SCSI card 2930U (bottom) supports up to seven different devices at speeds up to 20MBps (Ultra SCSI). Both cards support hard drives as well as other SCSI devices.

Keep in mind that Ultra 160 and Ultra 320 SCSI drives and host adapters, although breathtakingly fast, are designed for and priced for business use. For example, an 18.4GB Maxtor Atlas 10K (10,000 RPM) III drive with an Ultra 320 SCSI interface sells for about the same price as a Maxtor 120GB UltraATA/133 drive (about $170). An Adaptec 29320 host adapter kit that supports Ultra 320 and slower SCSI devices is about $310. An Ultra 160 version of the same 18.4GB drive is about $120, or about the same price as an 80GB UltraATA/133 drive. An Adaptec 19160 host adapter kit (including cables and software) for Ultra 160 and slower SCSI devices is about $240.

Although some SCSI devices, such as scanners and optical drives, can use a 50-pin/50-wire cable, most SCSI hard drives require a 68-pin/68-wire cable.

Selecting the Right Hard Disk for You

Now that you have learned about the different types of hard disks, it's time to hit the web sites and catalogs or jump in the car and go shopping for your hard disk upgrade.

First, you need to decide which type of hard disk you want to get. I recommend the following choices, based on what is most important to you.

ATA/IDE Benefits and Drawbacks

I'm 99% sure without using a crystal ball that your system contains an ATA/IDE drive. What are the benefits of sticking with what's already in your system?

- Lowest cost per GB
- Fast performance with ATA-100 and ATA-133
- Can replace your existing drive

However, there are some potential drawbacks you should think about:

- Requires opening your system
- Might require changing cable and jumper settings on already-installed drives
- Drive must be prepared before use with operating system or vendor-provided utilities

If you want to save money and don't mind working inside your system to add huge amounts of storage, stick with ATA/IDE.

SATA Benefits and Drawbacks

SATA is the newest drive interface, but it might be the best for you because it does the following:

- Uses small, easy-to-route data cables.
- Will have potentially higher speeds in the future.
- Easier configuration (no jumpers or cable positions to worry about).
- Can be used with existing ATA devices.
- Longer cable (1 meter versus 18-inch cable used by latest ATA/IDE drives) makes it easier to install the drive in a large case in any drive bay desired.

However, consider these drawbacks:

- Higher cost per GB than with ATA/IDE.
- Most systems require an SATA host adapter card.
- Requires opening your system.
- Drive must be prepared before use with operating system or vendor-provided utilities.

Choose SATA to reduce cable clutter and be ready for the future of low-cost, high-performance drives.

External IEEE-1394/USB 2.0 Drive Benefits and Drawbacks

External drives with an IEEE-1394 or USB 2.0 interface offer the following advantages:

- Ready to work as soon as you attach them to your system.
- Can be shared between systems.
- Some offer both types of interfaces for maximum flexibility.

However, keep in mind the following drawbacks:

- Much higher cost per GB than with ATA/IDE or SATA.
- USB 1.1 interface severely lowers performance; should be used with a USB 2.0 interface (not present on all systems).
- Might require installation of a USB 2.0 or IEEE-1394a interface.
- Most systems can't boot from external drives.

Choose IEEE-1394a or USB 2.0 external drives when convenience and drive sharing between systems are your most important requirements.

SCSI Benefits and Drawbacks

Wondering if SCSI drives are right for you? They are if you value the highest performance while performing heavy multitasking. However, SCSI drives have several drawbacks for the average user:

- Highest cost per GB, even higher than external drives
- Must add expensive host adapter
- Must open system to install host adapter

SCSI is the way to go if performance is your sole criterion, but keep in mind that the latest 10,000 RPM SATA drives come close to 10,000 RPM Ultra 160 SCSI performance for a lot less money.

Shopping for a New Hard Disk

Alrighty, then! You understand more about the whys and wherefores of hard drives than you did before you started this chapter, so it's time to go shopping for your next drive. Here are some checklists to help make sure you make the right choice.

For ATA/IDE drives:

- What brand and model do you currently have installed?
- How large a drive (in GB) do you want?
- Are you adding this drive to your system or replacing your existing drive?
- What size drive bay do you have available?
- Do you want a retail pack or bulk drive?
- How fast a drive do you want?

For SATA drives:

- How large a drive (in GB) do you want?
- What size drive bay do you have available?
- How fast a drive do you want?
- How will you connect your drive to your system?

For external drives:

- How large a drive (in GB) do you want?
- How will you connect your drive to your system?

For SCSI drives:

- How large a drive (in GB) do you want?
- Do you have other SCSI devices already installed?
- Can you use an existing SCSI host adapter for your drive?
- Do you have an open PCI slot you can use for the SCSI host adapter?

Before you head to the store, to the phone, or to a web site to buy your new hard drive, take some time to find out why these questions are important.

Why You Need to Know Your Current Drive's Brand and Model

When the IDE drive interface was first developed, there were no official standards for IDE. The ATA/IDE standards you learned about came after quite a few IDE drives had already been built. As a result of this "build it now and standardize it later" philosophy, there can still be lingering problems with trying to connect two brands of ATA/IDE drives on the same cable. However, since the hard drive in your current computer is probably made by one of the major drive vendors (Seagate, Maxtor, IBM/Hitachi, or Western Digital), you should be able to find a drive that meets your needs and is made by the same company that built your original drive. By buying a new drive made by the same company as your current drive, you are assured of compatibility.

What brand and model of drive do you have? To find out, you can either use diagnostic software as discussed in Chapter 4, "Taking an Inspection Tour of Your System," or just open up your system and take a look.

Why Size Matters—A Lot!

The questions of how large the drive should be and whether you are adding the drive to your system or replacing an older drive are closely related. If you are replacing an existing drive, the new drive you purchase should be at least double the capacity of your old drive. If you face a drive-size limitation caused by an old version of Windows, consider upgrading to Windows XP before you install your new drive. As you learn later in this chapter, it's easy to transfer the entire contents of your existing hard drive to your new hard drive if you are replacing the old drive.

If you're installing a drive over 137GB in size, make sure you get a compatible host adapter, upgrade your system BIOS to obtain 48-bit LBA support, or install the IAA driver as discussed earlier in this chapter before you perform the drive installation.

Where Will You Install Your Drive?

If you are planning to add the drive to your system, you need to have an empty drive bay if you want to use an internal drive. Your new hard drive will probably be 3.5 inches wide. What if the only drive bay you have is 5.25 inches wide? In that case, you need to attach an adapter to the sides of the drive to make it wide enough to fit into the larger drive bay. The easiest way to get the adapter kit made for your drive is to purchase a retail-packaged drive. If you don't have an empty drive bay, check to see if you have a USB 2.0 or IEEE-1394 port; either port type supports high-speed external hard drives.

> **MARK'S TIP SHEET: Don't Forget About Power**
>
> Even if you buy a retail-packaged drive with what the manufacturer calls all the goodies, there's one important option that usually gets left out: a Y-splitter power cable. Believe it or not, just because you have six drive bays in a particular machine is no indication of the number of actual power connectors you have. In most cases, you wind up needing at least one Y-splitter to enable the last power connector left in your system to run two drives. Even if you don't need to split power now, the Y-splitter also makes a dandy cable extender to make plugging the power to the drive a lot easier!

Retail or Bulk-Pack? More Than the Box Is at Stake

There are two ways in which hard drives are sold:

- Retail
- Bulk

Bulk-packaged drives are less expensive for stores to purchase and are therefore less expensive for you to buy. The reason? The only thing you get is the drive.

On the other hand, a retail-boxed drive includes the following:

- The drive
- Complete installation instructions

- Mounting hardware

- Data cable matching the requirements for the highest transfer rate supported by the drive

- Drive installation and diagnostic software

- Eligibility for special rebate and bonus offers (check the store for the current details)

In my opinion, the extra goodies you receive with the retail–packaged drive more than make up for the small extra cost of the drive, especially if your ATA/IDE drive is designed to run at UDMA/66 or faster speeds; these speeds use a more expensive cable than older ATA/IDE drives. If this is your first drive installation, it's also handy to have instructions and setup software. My advice is this: Unless you're an old hand at hard drive upgrades, get the retail-packaged box.

Measuring Hard Drive Speed

There are four ways in which hard drive speed is measured:

- **The UltraDMA rating**—Measured in megabytes per second (MBps). This rating is used by ATA/IDE drives to measure the maximum burst rates at which the drive can transfer data and is seldom achieved for long periods of time. Larger is better. See Table 10.5.

- **The drive's spin rate**—Measured in *revolutions per minute (RPM)*. A drive that spins faster can access data faster than a drive with a slower spin rate, even if both drives have the same UDMA rating. Faster is better.

- **Seek time**—Measured in milliseconds (ms); the average time it takes for a drive's read-write heads to move to a specified location. This factor is affected by spin rate and by the drive's internal design. Shorter is better. ATA/IDE drives have seek times from around 13ms down to 8.5ms, and high-performance SCSI Ultra 160 and Ultra 320 drives have seek times as low as 3.6ms.

- **Buffer size**—Measured in megabytes (MB); all hard disk drives contain memory that is used to store data being transferred between the computer and the drive. Larger is better. Typical sizes for ATA/IDE drives include 2MB and 8MB.

Table 10.5 shows the UltraDMA (also known as UltraATA) speeds supported by recent and current ATA/IDE drives. Note that this rating alone doesn't necessarily reflect real-world performance. However, drives with UltraDMA/100 or UltraDMA/133 interfaces, which also feature fast spin rates, fast seek times, and an 8MB buffer, can be expected to outperform slower drives with slower interfaces. Currently, only Maxtor produces UltraDMA/133 drives, but all other major vendors produce UltraDMA/100 drives.

Table 10.5   UltraDMA Ratings

UltraDMA Speed	Also Known As	Maximum Transfer Rate	Cable Types Supported
UltraDMA/33	UDMA2	33MBps	40-wire or 80-wire
UltraDMA/66	UDMA4	66MBps	80-wire
UltraDMA/100	UDMA5	100MBps	80-wire
UltraDMA/133	UDMA6	133MBps	80-wire

Table 10.6 shows the spin rates used by various types of internal drives. Generally, if two drives have otherwise similar features (same number of disk platters, same interface, and same buffer size), the drive with the faster spin rate provides better performance.

Table 10.6   Typical Spin Rates by Interface Type

Spin Rate	ATA/IDE	SATA	SCSI
5,400 RPM	Yes	No	No
7,200 RPM	Yes	Yes	Yes
10,000 RPM	No	Yes	Yes
15,000 RPM	No	No	Yes

SATA drives designed for desktop computers feature 7,200 RPM spin rates, but enterprise-class SATA drives designed for use in servers feature the same 10,000 RPM spin rates used by many high-performance SCSI drives.

Generally, 5,400-RPM drives have the slowest seek times, and 15,000-RPM drives have the fastest seek times.

ON THE WEB: Surf the Reviews Before You Buy

Wondering whose drives are *really* the fastest? Looking for a great review source for hard drives, optical drives, and interface cards? Click on over to Storage Review at www.storagereview.com. Storage Review's Leaderboard gives you quick summaries of the drives that currently lead the pack in performance.

Because the hard drive's performance has a huge impact on system performance, I recommend drives with the fastest spin rate and seek time available for your interface type—unless cost is an issue. When cost is an issue, look for the best-performing drive in the next lower RPM range.

If you're looking at external USB 2.0 and IEEE-1394 drives, keep in mind that the more compact models use 2.5-inch wide drives originally developed for notebook computers. These drives usually have spin rates of around 4,200RPM. More bulky external drives use the same 3.5-inch drives found in desktop computers and offer better performance because of a faster spin rate and larger buffer.

CAUTION: STOP! LOOK! THINK!

Don't Fry Your Data: Keep Your Drives Cool
Keep in mind that hard drives become very hot at 10,000 RPM and higher spin rates, so you should install drive bay cooling or install your drives where existing cooling is most effective. Although first generation hard disk coolers required a 5.25-inch drive bay, newer models can fit into a 3.5-inch drive bay. Thermaltake (www.thermaltake.com) and Vantec Thermal (www.vantecusa.com) are two good sources to try.

Installing an Internal Drive

If you've decided your perfect hard disk is an internal model, use the following sections to help you install an ATA/IDE, SATA, or SCSI hard disk and host adapter card. First, I describe the process for installing an ATA/IDE drive, and then I cover the differences you will encounter with the other drive types.

Installing Your New ATA/IDE Drive

Before you start the installation process, be sure to take the electrostatic discharge (ESD) precautions described in Chapter 5, "Preparing for Your Upgrade." The process of installing your ATA/IDE hard drive includes the following steps:

1. Setting the drive selection jumper.

2. Placing the drive into the drive bay.

3. Connecting the drive to the data cable.

4. Connecting the drive to the power cable.

5. Adding a drive bay adapter and rails (if required).

6. Setting up the drive in the system BIOS.

Each of these steps is discussed in detail in the following sections.

> **READ THIS TOO**
>
> If you need to install an ATA/IDE host adapter, see the "Installing a Host Adapter" section later in this chapter.

Master, Slave, or Cable Select?

The ATA/IDE interface can accept up to two drives on one data cable. Because of this, there needs to be a way to distinguish which drive is which. Traditionally, this task was performed by the master and slave jumpers on the rear or the bottom of ATA/IDE drives. When you use the standard 40-pin, 40-wire ATA/IDE host adapter cable, it does not matter which drive is at the end of the cable and which drive is connected to the middle of the cable. The drive you want to be bootable must be set to master, and the other drive must be set to slave. The bootable drive needs to be connected to the primary ATA/IDE host adapter on the motherboard. Depending on the type of drive you are installing, you might use one jumper that is moved to different sets of pins, or you might use two jumpers in different combinations to set master or slave. See Figure 10.7 to see the jumper locations used on different types of ATA/IDE drives.

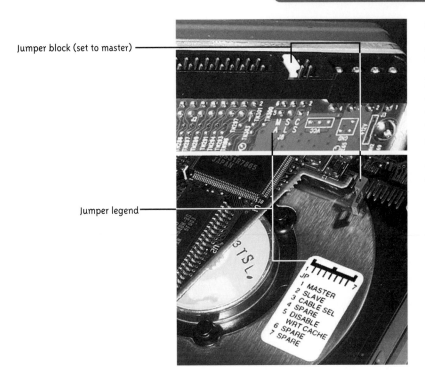

Jumper block (set to master)

Jumper legend

Figure 10.7

Most ATA/IDE drives use drive-select jumpers located on the rear of the drive near the data and power cable connectors (top); a few use drive-select jumpers located on the bottom of the drive (bottom).

In Figure 10.7, the top drive uses the abbreviations MA for master, SL for slave, and CS for cable select.

When both drives are compatible and properly jumpered, the system should be able to distinguish between the master and slave. A clear sign that the drives cannot coexist with each other on the same cable is when the system is unable to determine master and slave when the drives are detected later in the installation process, even though they are properly jumpered.

The third option, cable select, is used when 80-wire, 40-pin cables are used. Because this type of cable is required when UltraDMA/66 and faster ATA/IDE drives are used, cable select is now replacing traditional master/slave jumper settings. When a cable-select compatible data cable is used, the blue-colored end of the cable is designed to be plugged into the ATA/IDE host adapter on the motherboard, the far (black) end of the cable is used for the master drive, and the middle connector (gray) is used for the slave. Thus, cable select eliminates concerns about setting one drive as master and one drive as slave; simply set both drives to cable select and position drives on the cable according to which one you want as master and which as slave. Figure 10.8 shows typical 80-wire and 40-wire ATA/IDE cables.

Figure 10.8

A standard ATA/IDE data cable (left) and the master end of an UDMA/ATA-66 data cable (right). The UDMA/ATA-66 has a smoother appearance because of the extra wires it uses to produce a higher-quality signal.

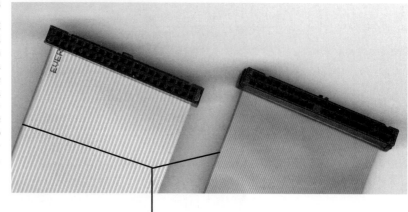

Pin 1 side of cable (solid or dotted red markings)

Connecting Power and Data Cables

To properly connect the data cable to your drive, locate pin 1 on the drive's data connector and match the colored stripe on the cable (see Figure 10.8) to that end of the data connector. Repeat the process for other drives connected to the ribbon cable and the host adapter.

Because the distance between the master and slave drive connectors is not very long, I recommend (if you are attaching two drives to the ATA/IDE cable) that you disconnect the ATA/IDE connector from the motherboard so that you can connect the cables to the new drive before you slide it into the drive bay.

The power cable is keyed to attach only one way. If you are using a Y-splitter to borrow power from an existing drive, connect one end of the Y-splitter to the new drive and connect the data cable to the rear of the drive, as in Figure 10.9, before you install the drive into the computer. This makes it easier to finish the installation process after the drive is inserted into the drive bay.

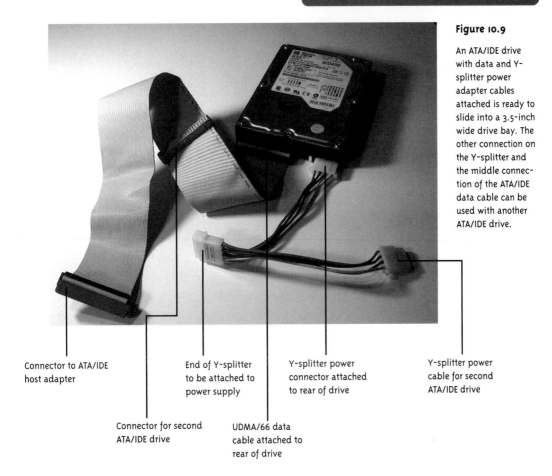

Figure 10.9

An ATA/IDE drive with data and Y-splitter power adapter cables attached is ready to slide into a 3.5-inch wide drive bay. The other connection on the Y-splitter and the middle connection of the ATA/IDE data cable can be used with another ATA/IDE drive.

Connector to ATA/IDE host adapter

End of Y-splitter to be attached to power supply

Y-splitter power connector attached to rear of drive

Y-splitter power cable for second ATA/IDE drive

Connector for second ATA/IDE drive

UDMA/66 data cable attached to rear of drive

Using an Adapter Kit to Install the Drive

You need to use the drive bay adapter shown in Figure 10.10 only if you have decided to use a 5.25-inch wide drive bay with your new hard drive. Some cases also require the use of special rails supplied with the case for any drives installed in the 5.25-inch drive bay. Check the spare parts kit supplied with your system or your case for these rails, which are screwed to the sides of the frame adapter. Most recent rail designs snap into place to hold the drive securely in the case, but some older ones might require you to screw them in place to secure the drive in the case; this varies by case.

Figure 10.10

An ATA/IDE drive adapted for use in a 5.25-inch drive bay that uses rails.

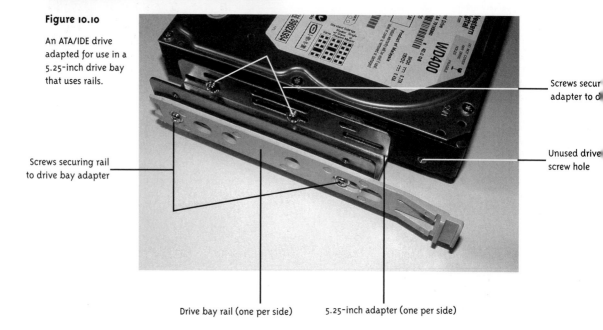

Screws securing rail to drive bay adapter

Screws secur adapter to d

Unused drive screw hole

Drive bay rail (one per side)   5.25-inch adapter (one per side)

Into the Case You Go

With most systems, the drive bay adapter kit shown in Figure 10.10 is not necessary. The drive is inserted directly into the drive bay. Depending upon the system, you might use one of the following methods after you remove the system cover:

- On systems with a removable drive cage, press the button to release the cage. It might swing out or slip out of the front of the system.
- On other systems, slide the drive into the drive bay.

After you slide the drive into the drive bay, secure it on both sides with four screws, two per side. See Figure 10.11.

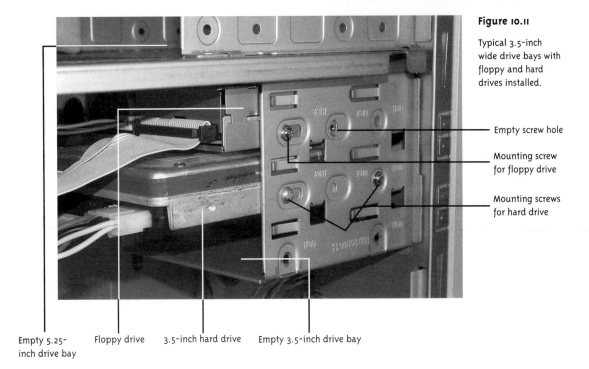

Figure 10.II

Typical 3.5-inch
wide drive bays with
floppy and hard
drives installed.

Empty screw hole

Mounting screw
for floppy drive

Mounting screws
for hard drive

Empty 5.25-   Floppy drive   3.5-inch hard drive   Empty 3.5-inch drive bay
inch drive bay

Connecting the ATA/IDE Data Cable to the Motherboard

After you have secured the drive, make sure the power and data cables are connected properly. Then, if necessary, reconnect the power and data cables to the other drive and to the motherboard's ATA/IDE host adapter (see Figure 10.12).

If you use an ATA/IDE or ATA RAID add-on card instead of the motherboard's ATA/IDE connector, connect the drive to the host adapter instead. Note that both motherboard and card-based host adapters have primary and secondary ATA/IDE channels. Be sure to connect your cable to the correct channel. For the only hard drive in the system or a bootable hard drive, use the primary channel connector. For additional drives, use the primary or secondary connector as available.

Figure 10.12

Connecting an 80-
wire UltraATA cable
to the ATA/IDE host
adapter on the
motherboard.

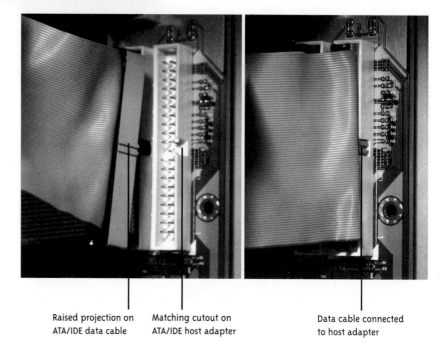

Raised projection on   Matching cutout on   Data cable connected
ATA/IDE data cable   ATA/IDE host adapter   to host adapter

It's Showtime! Boot Up and Detect Your New ATA/IDE Drive

After the drive is physically installed and properly cabled, restart the system and press the correct key to access the BIOS setup program.

If the drive is new, the best way to set up and to verify that it works is to use your BIOS's
auto-detection feature. Depending on the BIOS, the auto-detection feature may be performed on the standard BIOS/CMOS setup screen or with a separate menu item such as
IDD HD Auto Detect or Auto-Detect Drives. See Figure 10.13 for a typical example. The
BIOS auto-detection feature works with a command built into your drive called Identify
drive; your drive tells your computer how it is to be configured.

Most systems list the drive as Auto and don't show the exact CHS or LBA parameters when
you use the auto-detect function. Don't forget to manually enable LBA mode if necessary; if
LBA mode is not listed on the standard drive setup screen seen in Figure 10.13, look for the
LBA option on the advanced setup screen or peripheral setup screen. Some BIOS versions
call this option Greater than 504MB or DOS mode. After you save your changes and restart
the system, you can use the operating system disk setup programs to finish getting your drive
ready for use.

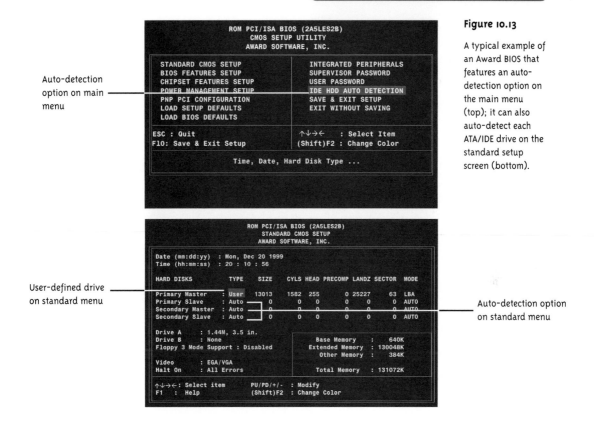

Figure 10.13

A typical example of an Award BIOS that features an auto-detection option on the main menu (top); it can also auto-detect each ATA/IDE drive on the standard setup screen (bottom).

Installing Your New SATA Drive

Before you start the installation process, be sure to take the ESD precautions described in Chapter 5. The process of installing your SATA hard drive includes the following steps:

1. Installing an SATA host adapter if your computer doesn't have onboard SATA.

2. Placing the drive into the drive bay.

3. Connecting the drive to the data cable.

4. Connecting the drive to the power cable.

5. Adding a drive bay adapter and rails (if required).

6. Verifying the drive has been detected by the SATA host adapter BIOS or setting up the drive in the system BIOS (depending upon how the drive is connected to your system).

Each step is discussed in detail in the following sections.

Installing a Host Adapter

Because the first SATA hard disks didn't hit the market until the spring of 2003, it's likely that you need to install an SATA host adapter before you can install a SATA drive. Make sure you have an open PCI expansion slot you can use.

CAUTION: STOP! LOOK! THINK!

Make the Most of a Single PCI Slot

If you're concerned about running out of expansion slots, consider a multi-function host adapter card. SIIG (www.siig.com) offers a wide variety of multi-function cards that combine ATA/IDE or SATA ports with USB 2.0, IEEE-1394a, and other port types.

To install an SATA host adapter with recent versions of Windows, follow these steps:

1. Shut down your system.

2. Disconnect the power cable from the outlet to cut all power to the system.

3. Use ESD protection equipment, such as a wrist strap and work mat, if available (see Chapter 5 for details).

4. Open your computer and locate an unused PCI slot.

5. Remove the slot cover; save the screw for use in reattaching the new card.

6. Insert the SATA card into the slot.

7. Secure the card into place with the screw removed from the slot cover.

8. Reconnect the power cord and restart the computer.

9. Install drivers when prompted.

10. Restart your computer if prompted.

11. Open the Windows Device Manager to verify that the SATA host adapter is working. It should be listed under the category SCSI Controllers, SCSI Adapters, or SCSI and RAID Controllers. See Figure 10.14.

Figure 10.14

The Windows XP
Device Manager view
of a typical SATA
host adapter after
a successful
installation.

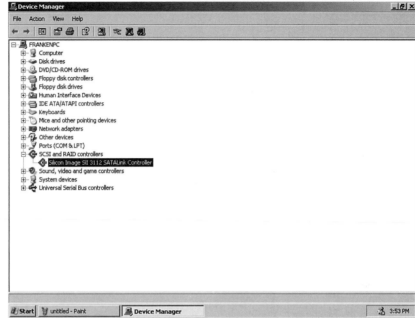

Use a similar procedure to install an ATA RAID or ATA/IDE host adapter card with an onboard BIOS.

Connecting SATA Power and Data Cables

The data cable used for SATA drives is a thin cable that is keyed to connect only one way. Because SATA drives also use a new type of keyed power connector, they are usually shipped with an adapter that converts the standard four-wire Molex connector used on ATA/IDE drives to the smaller size used by SATA. Figure 10.15 shows the rear of a typical SATA drive before and after data and power cables are connected.

Mounting the SATA Drive in Your System

Because SATA drives are built in the same 3.5-inch form factor used by ATA/IDE drives, they are mounted in the same way. See the sections "Using an Adapter Kit to Install the Drive" and "Into the Case You Go" earlier in this chapter for details.

Figure 10.15

Connecting power and data cables to a typical SATA drive.

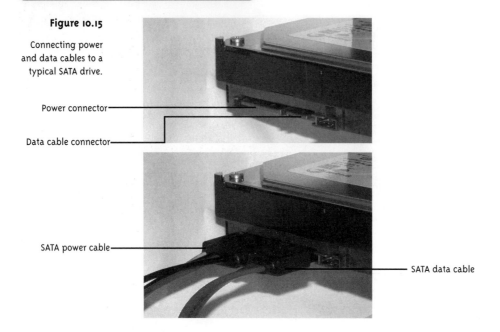

Power connector

Data cable connector

SATA power cable

SATA data cable

Connecting SATA Power and Data Cables to the System

After you have secured the drive, connect the power cable adapter to a four-wire Molex power connector and connect the SATA data cable to the SATA host adapter card (see Figure 10.16) or motherboard-based SATA connector (see Figure 10.17).

PCI slot used by SATA host adapter card   Empty PCI slots

Figure 10.16

Connecting the SATA data cable to a typical SATA host adapter card.

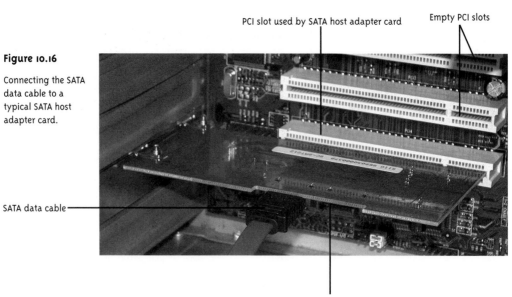

SATA data cable

Connector for additional SATA drive

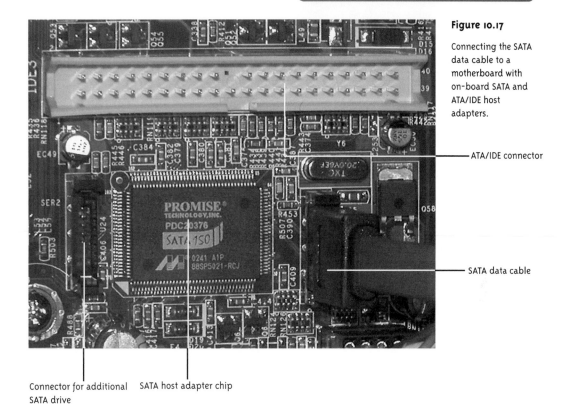

Figure 10.17

Connecting the SATA
data cable to a
motherboard with
on-board SATA and
ATA/IDE host
adapters.

ATA/IDE connector

SATA data cable

Connector for additional   SATA host adapter chip
SATA drive

Detecting Your New SATA Drive

After the drive and host adapter card are physically installed and properly cabled, restart the
system. If the SATA drive is connected to a SATA card, the card should display a message at
startup indicating the drive has been detected.

If the SATA drive is connected to the motherboard, verify that the SATA host adapters on
the motherboard are enabled in the system BIOS. Then, use the BIOS auto-detect feature, as
described in the "It's Showtime! Boot Up and Detect Your New ATA/IDE Drive" section
earlier in this chapter.

Installing a SCSI Hard Disk

Before you start the installation process, take the precautions against ESD detailed in Chapter 5. The process of installing a SCSI hard drive includes the following steps. If you need to
install a SCSI host adapter, see Chapter 19 for details.

1. Set the drive ID or enabling SCAM support.

2. Set the termination.

3. Connect the drive to the data cable.

4. Add a drive bay adapter and rails (if required).

5. Place the drive into the drive bay.

6. Connect the drive to the power cable.

Steps 1 and 2 are different on SCSI drives than on ATA/IDE drives, but the other steps are similar to those outlined for ATA/IDE earlier in the chapter. Therefore, the following sections cover only the areas where SCSI differs from ATA/IDE.

Configuring Device IDs

Each SCSI device connected to the same host adapter must have a unique device ID, whether it is a hard drive, a scanner, or another type of device. To determine the available device IDs, use a SCSI investigation program supplied with your host adapter, if possible. For example, with Adaptec SCSI host adapters, the program is called SCSI Interrogator (see Figure 10.18). If you do not have a similar program, you need to examine each SCSI device connected to your host adapter, determine which device IDs are in use, and then select one of the unused device IDs for your drive.

SCSI hard drives use jumper blocks to set the device ID. If the drive is connected to a 50-pin (Narrow SCSI) cable, you can select device IDs from 0 to 7. Wide SCSI devices use a 68-pin cable and have device IDs from 0 to 15. If you plan to boot from your SCSI hard drive, use device ID 0 or 1 for the drive.

To simplify installation, some drives and some host adapters support a feature called SCSI Configuration Auto Magically (SCAM). SCAM, when enabled, automatically selects a working device ID.

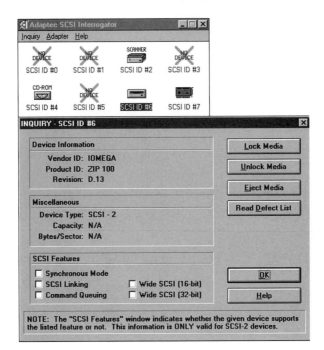

Figure 10.18

The Adaptec SCSI Interrogator program displays the used and available SCSI IDs (top) and can also provide details on each connected device (bottom).

SCSI Termination

Any type of SCSI installation is, in essence, a small network on your desk. The last internal SCSI device on a ribbon cable must be terminated, and the last external device in a daisy chain must also be terminated; otherwise, the SCSI devices will not work correctly. Depending on the speed of the SCSI drive you are using, the termination might be done by setting jumpers or by attaching a small device to your drive. Figure 10.19 shows you how the devices to be terminated change as more devices are added to a SCSI daisy-chain. If you have only internal or only external SCSI devices, you do not need to terminate the SCSI host adapter; it is self-terminating.

Connecting SCSI Power and Data Cables

Internal SCSI power and data cables attach the same way that ATA/IDE cables do. However, SCSI cables are either 50-pin or 68-pin. The 50-pin cables used by Narrow SCSI devices are wider than ATA/IDE cables, but 68-pin cables use smaller-diameter wires similar in size to those used in 80-wire UltraDMA/66 cables. Thus, a 68-pin cable is narrower than a 50-pin cable. See Figure 10.20 for a comparison of SCSI and ATA/IDE cables.

Figure 10.19

A simple SCSI daisy-chain (1) compared to the same system after additional internal and external devices are added (2). Note the last device in the daisy-chain is always the device to be terminated.

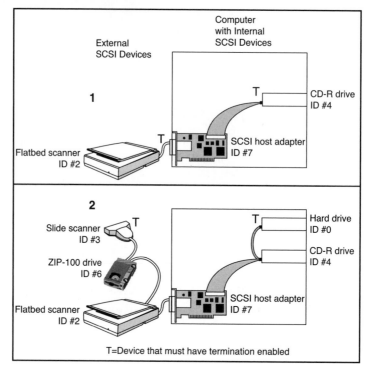

T=Device that must have termination enabled

Figure 10.20

A 50-pin SCSI internal ribbon cable (rear) is wider than, but otherwise similar to, the 40-pin/40-wire ATA/IDE ribbon cable (front).

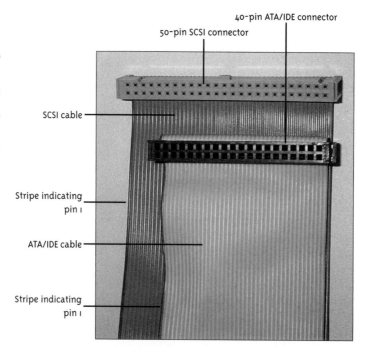

Booting Up and Setting Your SCSI Host Adapter

After you have installed the SCSI host adapter (if needed) and attached the SCSI hard drive to the host adapter and to the power supply, you can start your system.

Watch for the SCSI BIOS message to be displayed on your screen during boot and press the key specified to start the SCSI BIOS configuration process. You need to perform the following steps to make your hard drive ready for your operating system's disk preparation process:

1. Enable the BIOS on the SCSI host adapter card.
2. Enable Extended BIOS support and Int13h extensions for hard drives over 1GB.

Check the documentation for your SCSI drive to see if you need to run a low-level format on the drive before using your operating system's disk preparation programs. In most cases these days, you won't.

MARK'S TIP SHEET: Get That ATA/IDE Out of My Way!

If you are booting from a SCSI hard disk as described in this chapter, don't forget to set the boot sequence in your system BIOS to indicate SCSI (if available). If SCSI doesn't show up as a bootable device, then make sure that ATA/IDE drives (which are either not present or are not bootable) are *not* specified in the boot sequence. If you have no ATA/IDE drives, make sure the drive type for all ATA/IDE connections listed is set to None.

Installing an External Drive

If you've decided to install an external drive that connects to the USB 2.0 or IEEE-1394a interfaces, you've chosen the easiest installation possible. As soon as the drive has been detected and drivers installed, it's ready to work. If you need to install a USB 2.0 or IEEE-1394a port, see Chapter 19 for details.

If you are installing an external SCSI hard drive, the same steps listed earlier for internal SCSI drives apply. The only difference is that you connect the drive to the external SCSI port on the rear of the SCSI host adapter card and you must turn on the drive and wait about five seconds before turning on the system.

Replacing Your Old Hard Disk with a New Drive

If you are installing a new hard disk as a replacement for your existing drive, you don't need to use the normal disk-preparation tools provided with Windows. Because you want to migrate your operating system and all your information to the new hard disk, you should use one of these options:

- A disk-preparation tool provided by the hard-drive vendor *if* it supports your version of Windows; these might be provided with the drive or be downloadable from the vendor's web site.

- A third-party drive migration tool, such as Drive Copy from PowerQuest (www.powerquest.com) or Disk Manager from Ontrack (www.ontrack.com). Drive Copy supports all versions of Windows up through Windows 2000 Professional. Disk Manager 4.0 supports all versions of Windows through Windows XP.

These programs can perform the following tasks for you:

- Provide a guided step-by-step installation process depending upon whether you plan to use your new drive as a replacement drive or an additional drive, as in Figure 10.21.

- Create disk partitions and file systems on your hard disk (replacing FDISK/FORMAT or Disk Management).

- Copy data from the old drive to the new drive.

- Test old or new drives for errors.

- Determine if a malfunctioning drive needs to be replaced.

The latest versions of drive installation software provided by these major drive vendors work with Windows XP as well as with Windows 9x/Me:

- **Western Digital** (www.wdc.com)—Use Data Lifeguard v10.0 or higher.

- **Seagate** (www.seagate.com)—Use DiscWizard 2003 or newer or DiscWizard Online.

- **Maxtor** (www.maxtor.com)—Use MaxBlast 3 or newer.

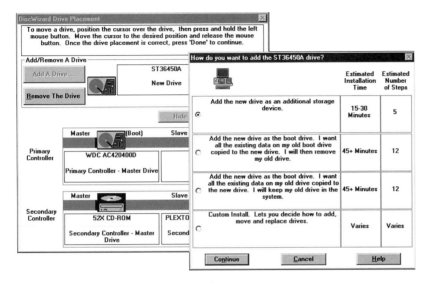

Figure 10.21

Seagate's DiscWizard program provides step-by-step instructions and guidance for any installation type you select.

MARK'S TIP SHEET: All You Need Is One (Drive, That Is)

If your new drive's vendor doesn't offer a fast installation tool, you might be able to use the installation tool provided by the old drive's vendor to copy files from the old drive to the new drive. In most cases, the only requirement is that at least one drive in the system be made by the company providing the setup software.

Even if you're familiar with the normal disk preparation process for your version of Windows, there are two benefits from using a drive setup tool:

- They supply graphical configuration options and guided installation to help you avoid making mistakes (see Figure 10.21 for an example of the Seagate DiscWizard program).
- They usually supply a drive-copying utility to make replacing your old drive easier.

These programs vary by drive manufacturer. To learn more about them, check the drive manufacturer's web site.

MARK'S TIP SHEET: Try Them, You'll Like Them!

I admit it: I haven't always been happy with drive vendor-supplied utilities. However, the latest versions of the tools I mentioned earlier in this section really do work. It doesn't surprise me that Drive Copy, a tool I have used with great success several times over the years, hasn't been updated for Windows XP because the latest versions of free vendor-supplied utilities work about as well for copying drives and do it free of charge.

Even if you've been disappointed with older versions as I was, try these new setup tools and save yourself some time and trouble. They also work well for installing an additional drive with any recent version of Windows.

Here's how to use disk-installation software to set up a new drive as a replacement for an existing drive, using Western Digital Data Lifeguard Tools v10.0 as an example:

1. Shut down and unplug the computer.
2. Connect the new hard disk to the computer as discussed earlier in this chapter. It is not necessary to install it in a drive bay if you are planning to remove the old hard disk. Instead, carefully place the drive on top of a box (such as the box provided by the drive vendor) and run data and power cables to it.
3. Plug the computer back in.
4. Insert the drive installation program floppy disk into the floppy drive.
5. Start the computer and allow the computer to boot from the floppy disk. Select the option to install the new drive.
6. Select Drive to Drive copy and click Next to continue.
7. Select Entire Drive.
8. Select your original drive (Primary Master) as the source drive (drive to copy from).
9. Select your new drive as the destination drive (drive to copy to).
10. If you want to leave space on the new drive for another operating system (such as Windows XP or Linux installed to dual-boot with your current operating system), select Manually adjust destination partitions. If you plan to install Windows XP as a replacement for your current version of Windows, select Automatically resize partitions.
11. If you chose Manually adjust destination partitions, adjust your current Windows partition so that it's large enough to handle future programs. For example, if your Windows 98 system's current C: drive uses 4GB (4096MB), set the partition to about 8GB

(8192MB) so that you have room to install more games. The rest of the drive will be left empty (Windows XP or Linux will use the empty space when you install either operating system).

12. Click Finish to start the copying process.

13. After the copying process is over, remove the installation disk from drive A: and restart the computer.

14. After Windows boots, you can view the new drive with Windows Explorer.

15. Shut down the computer, unplug the power supply, and disconnect the old drive.

16. Install the new drive where the old drive was connected, connect power and data cables to it, plug in the computer and restart the system. After the system boots and the Windows desktop is displayed, you can install Windows XP or Linux into the unpartitioned space.

Disk Preparation with Windows XP

All versions of Windows XP are based on Windows 2000, and as a consequence, system management, including hard disk partitioning and formatting, are performed similarly in Windows 2000 and Windows XP. The Computer Management tool is used for hard disk preparation, as well as for other system management issues.

To start the Windows XP Computer Management tool:

1. Click Start.
2. Right-click My Computer.
3. Select Manage.

In the following sections, I describe the process of installing the new hard disk as an additional drive for Windows XP to use. If you want to replace your existing hard disk, use the tools discussed earlier in this chapter in the "Replacing Your Old Hard Disk with a New Drive" section.

Partitioning the Disk with Disk Management

Disk Management is one of the many system management tasks you can perform with Computer Management. To partition the new hard disk with Disk Management, do the following:

1. Click Disk Management in the left window of Computer Management; the Disk Management main menu appears similar to the one displayed in Figure 10.22.

Figure 10.22

The new hard disk is displayed as Unallocated space in the Disk Management screen display.

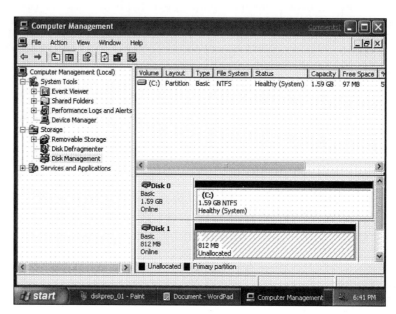

2. Right-click the new disk.

3. Select New Partition to start the New Partition Wizard.

4. Click Next.

5. Click Extended partition to create a non-bootable drive; click Primary partition to create a bootable drive. Unless you are planning to run multiple operating systems, you should select Extended partition, as in this example.

6. Click Next.

7. Accept the full capacity listed; you will subdivide it into logical drives later. Click Next.

8. Click Finish.

9. The Disk Management menu appears again; the new disk is now listed as free space.

Creating and Formatting Logical Drives with Disk Management

An extended partition cannot be used as disk space until it contains one or more logical drives. To create logical drives with Disk Management, do the following:

1. Right-click the free space disk and select New Logical Drive to restart the New Partition Wizard; click Next.

2. Logical drive is already selected for you; click Next.

3. To use the entire available extended partition space as a single drive, click Next; to sub-divide it into two or more drives, enter a smaller value and then click Next. In this example, the default (entire extended partition as a single drive) is used.

4. To use the default drive letter, click Next. You can also select a different drive letter, mount the drive so that it appears to be part of an existing (empty) folder on a current NTFS file system drive, or not assign it a drive letter or path. Click Next.

5. Select the Format options desired; the default file system is NTFS (compatible with Windows 2000), but you can also select FAT (compatible with MS-DOS and early Windows 95), FAT32 (compatible with Windows 95B and Windows 98/Me), or skip formatting the partition. You can also enable file and folder compression to save space and provide your own volume name. See Figure 10.23. Click Next.

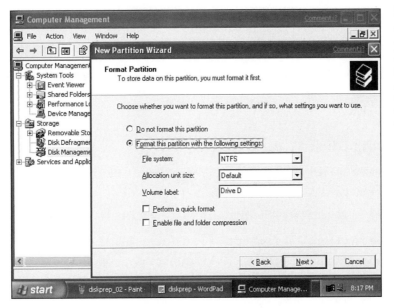

Figure 10.23

The default values for file system and allocation unit size have been retained, but this user has entered a different volume label than the default for this logical drive.

6. Click Finish to complete the format process.

7. The main Disk Management menu appears again and displays the progress of the Format command; it takes varying amounts of time, depending on the size of the logical drive and the speed of the drive and your computer.

8. The drive will display its name, size, file system, and condition (Healthy) when the format process is complete. You can use the new drive immediately.

9. To close Computer Management, click File, and then click Exit.

Disk Preparation with Windows 98/Me

After you've started your computer with your new drive, you're halfway to using it. In this section, I discuss setting up your drive with the Windows 98 Fdisk and Format programs. Windows Me prepares drives in a similar fashion to Windows 98. I call out differences between versions when necessary.

Unlike Windows XP's Disk Management, Windows 98/Me use two different programs descended from MS-DOS to prepare a hard disk:

- Fdisk creates or destroys disk partitions and logical drive letters.

- Format prepares drive letters created with Fdisk.

The process that follows is almost identical in any recent DOS or Windows version that uses Fdisk. Fdisk is a text-mode program, but Format can be performed from a command prompt or from within Windows Explorer.

Partitioning with Fdisk

Depending on whether the drive is being added to your system or is the first drive in an empty system, you can start Fdisk with Start, Run in Windows or by starting your computer with the Windows emergency boot disk, typing Fdisk, and pressing Enter.

By default, Fdisk enables Large Disk support so you can create FAT32 partitions. Press Enter after Fdisk starts to accept this default. If you answer No, any partitions you create are FAT16 and are limited to a maximum size of 2047MB (2GB). Use FAT16 *only* if you need to access the drive with an MS-DOS or early-release Windows 95 boot disk.

If you have one physical hard disk installed, the main Fdisk window resembles Figure 10.24.

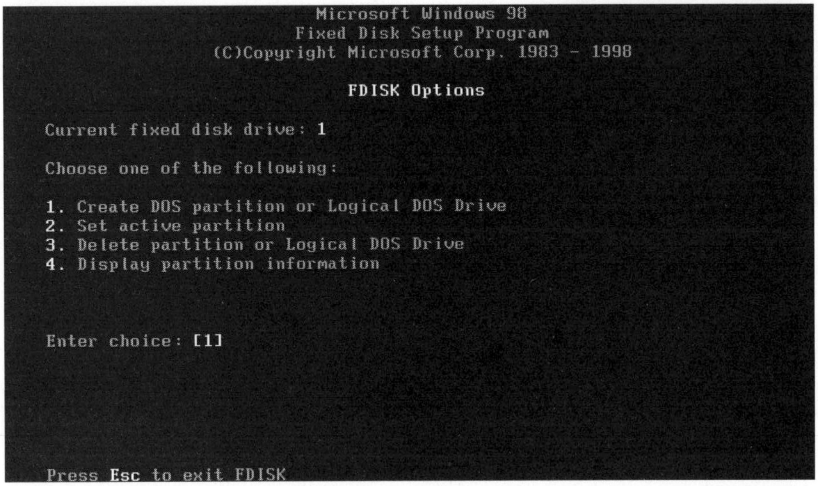

```
                    Microsoft Windows 98
                   Fixed Disk Setup Program
                (C)Copyright Microsoft Corp. 1983 - 1998

                         FDISK Options

Current fixed disk drive: 1

Choose one of the following:

1. Create DOS partition or Logical DOS Drive
2. Set active partition
3. Delete partition or Logical DOS Drive
4. Display partition information


Enter choice: [1]



Press Esc to exit FDISK
```

Figure 10.24

The Windows 98
Fdisk main menu
screen for single-
drive systems.

When two or more physical disks are installed, Fdisk lists a #5 option: Change Current Fixed
Disk Drive.

Primary Versus Extended Options

Of the many different ways to use Fdisk, only a few options make logical sense in this
situation:

- If you are installing the first hard drive in your system, and if you want only one drive
  letter, create a primary partition for the entire disk.

- If you are installing the first hard drive in your system, but want two or more drive letters, create a primary partition (which becomes drive C) from part of the drive. Then,
  create an extended partition for drive D and beyond. The extended partition can hold
  one or more logical drive letters.

- If you are adding this drive to a system that already has a hard drive you are keeping,
  create an extended partition from the entire disk.

Here's why:

- A primary partition can be bootable; it can be used to start your system.

- An extended partition cannot be bootable, but it enables you to create multiple logical
  drive letters inside it.

- Primary partitions are assigned lower drive letters than extended partitions, and they
  take over existing drive letters on extended partitions.

For example, if your original drive contains drive letters C: and D:, D: is in the extended partition. If you prepare your new drive with a primary partition, it becomes D: and the logical DOS drive in the extended partition becomes E:. Any programs or data references to D: are completely mixed up!

Creating a Primary (Bootable) Partition

If you're installing the first hard drive on an empty system, follow this procedure:

1. Choose Enable Large Disk Support when prompted.

2. Select #1, Create DOS Partition or Logical DOS Drive from the main menu.

3. From the Create DOS Partition or Logical DOS Drive menu, press Enter to select #1, Create a Primary DOS partition.

4. Next, it's decision time:

   If you want to use the entire drive as C:, press Enter to accept the default (Yes). Follow the prompts to shut down your system and restart it. See "Finishing the Job with the Format Command" later in the chapter for the rest of the process.

   If you want to create at least two drives, type N (no) when asked if you want to use the entire capacity of the drive.

5. Enter the amount of space you want to use for the primary partition in either MB or percentages. For example, to use 6GB, enter 6144 (1024MB=1GB); to use 50 percent of the drive, enter 50% and press Enter (see Figure 10.25).

Figure 10.25

The primary partition on this 1.2GB drive is being set as 800MB by Fdisk.

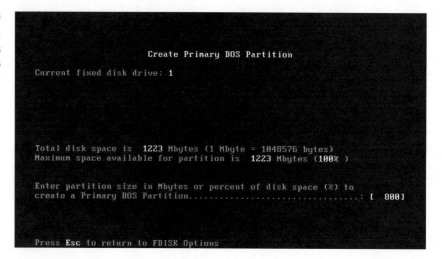

```
                          Create Primary DOS Partition

Current fixed disk drive: 1




Total disk space is  1223 Mbytes (1 Mbyte = 1048576 bytes)
Maximum space available for partition is  1223 Mbytes (100% )

Enter partition size in Mbytes or percent of disk space (%) to
create a Primary DOS Partition....................................: [  800]



Press Esc to return to FDISK Options
```

6. Press Esc to return to the main Fdisk menu.

7. Because you created a primary partition using only a portion of the disk space, a warning appears to remind you that the primary partition is not yet active; it must be marked active to be bootable.

8. To mark the primary partition as active, type 2 (Set Active Partition) and press Enter to display the Set Active Partition menu.

9. Type the number of the partition you want to make active (normally 1), and press Enter. The status column displays an A for active partition, as in Figure 10.26. Press Esc to return to the main Fdisk menu.

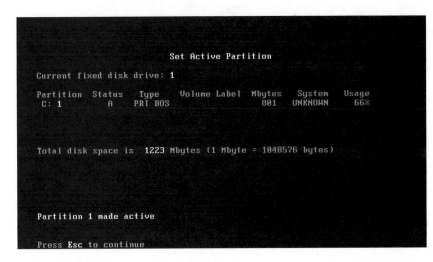

Figure 10.26

The 800MB primary partition after Fdisk sets it as Active. To be bootable, this partition must also be formatted with the /S (system) option.

10. To prepare the rest of the drive for use by Windows, select #1, Create DOS Partition or Logical DOS Drive.

11. From the Create DOS Partition menu, select #2, Create an Extended Partition.

12. Press Enter to accept the default (the remaining capacity of the drive); the logical drives are stored in the extended partition.

13. Create one or more logical drives when prompted, specifying the size you want for each letter. The drive letter for each logical drive is listed; note the letters because you need to format each logical drive after you finish using Fdisk and reboot.

14. When the entire capacity of the drive is used, the Fdisk display resembles Figure 10.27. Press the Y key to view the logical drives stored in the extended partition.

15. After you press Enter again to accept these changes, you're prompted to shut down the system and reboot it. If you ran Fdisk from within Windows, close the Fdisk window, shut down Windows, and reboot. See the "Finishing the Job with the Format Command" section to complete the process.

The file system is listed as
Unknown until the drive is formatted.

Figure 10.27

This drive contains
both a primary and
an extended parti-
tion; logical drives
in the extended
partition make this
entire drive avail-
able to Windows 98.

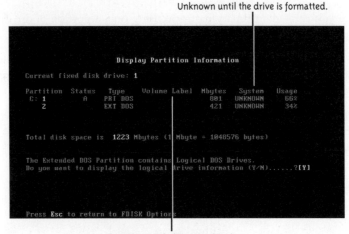

The Volume Label remains blank
until the drive is formatted.

Creating an Extended Partition with Fdisk

Follow these steps to install a fixed disk with an extended partition as an addition to a system
with one or more existing drives:

1. Select #5 from the main menu.

2. Select the drive you want to change from the drives listed. For this example, Disk #2
   would be selected, as in Figure 10.28.

3. From the main Fdisk menu, select #1, Create DOS Partition or Logical DOS Drive.

4. From the Create DOS Partition menu, select #2, Create an Extended Partition.

5. Press Enter to accept the default (the entire capacity of the drive); the logical drives are
   stored in the extended partition.

6. Create one or more logical drives when prompted, specifying the size you want for
   each letter. Note the drive letters that you need to format later are listed.

7. When the entire capacity of the drive is used, you should see a message similar to
   Figure 10.29.

8. Exit Fdisk, close Windows if you ran Fdisk from within Windows, and restart the
   computer.

Existing
disk partitions
on Disk #1

Free space
(no disk partitions)
on Disk #2

Figure 10.28

Hard disk #2 (a
2014MB drive) has
no disk partitions.
Type 2 and press
Enter to select it and
continue.

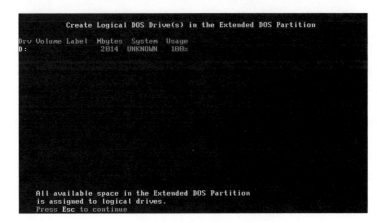

Figure 10.29

Hard disk #2 now
has a single logical
drive occupying
100% of its extended
partition.

Finishing the Job with the Format Command

The Windows Format command finishes the disk preparation process you started with Fdisk.
You can use the Windows Explorer to format drives or command-line options.

The command-line options listed in Table 10.7 are used with hard disks. Format offers additional options that work with floppy disks only.

Table 10.7   Format Options for Hard Drives

Format Command	Meaning	Used for...	Example
Format x:/s	Formats x: drive with system (boot) files	Any bootable drive (normally C:)	Format C:/s
Format x:	Formats x: drive without system files	Any non-bootable drive (D: or higher)	Format D:

To format the hard disk from a command (MS-DOS) prompt, follow these steps:

1. Click Start, Run, Command to open up a command-prompt window.

2. Start the format process with the correct command from Table 10.7. The system displays a warning of possible data loss and enables you to stop if you are about to format the wrong hard disk.

   If you continue, a progress indicator is displayed. If your hard disk has any surface damage, a message of `Trying to recover allocation unit number xxxxx` appears as the system marks the damaged area as a "do not use" area. Because modern hard disks have built-in defect management, you should not see any bad allocation units displayed during format. If you do, use the disk manufacturer's own diagnostic utility to replace bad sectors with spare sectors, or to determine if the drive needs to be returned for repair.

3. At the end of the format process, you can add a volume label (up to 11 characters) and see the disk statistics listed, including the drive's total size and the allocation unit size and number available.

4. To format the drive in the Windows 9x/Me explorer, right-click the drive and select Format from the menu. Figure 10.30 explains the options you can select.

Now your drive is ready to use. If it's the first drive in your system, you're ready to install Windows. See Chapter 23, "Winning Windows Upgrades." If it's an additional drive, you can make folders on it and start storing programs or data there.

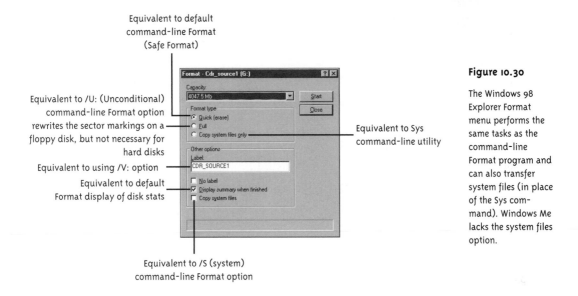

Equivalent to default
command-line Format
(Safe Format)

Equivalent to /U: (Unconditional)
command-line Format option
rewrites the sector markings on a
floppy disk, but not necessary for
hard disks

Equivalent to using /V: option

Equivalent to default
Format display of disk stats

Equivalent to Sys
command-line utility

Equivalent to /S (system)
command-line Format option

Figure 10.30

The Windows 98
Explorer Format
menu performs the
same tasks as the
command-line
Format program and
can also transfer
system files (in place
of the Sys com-
mand). Windows Me
lacks the system files
option.

Troubleshooting Your Hard Disk Upgrade

You might never have installed a hard drive before, or it might be something you do for your own systems, for work, or for friends on a regular basis. It doesn't matter; Murphy's Law can strike at any time. Tell Murphy to take a hike with these solutions.

Help! My system manual says it supports UDMA/100 drives, the drive says it's UDMA/100, but the BIOS detects my drive as a UDMA/33. Have I been ripped off?

Your hardware, believe it or not, is probably working *exactly* the way it's supposed to. Some UDMA/66 or faster drives are shipped out with the support for UDMA speeds over UDMA/33 disabled. You need to connect the drive to your system and run a special software program to enable the drive's UDMA feature. For example, Western Digital calls their program Ultra ATA Manager. You might find the program on your drive's setup disk, or you might need to download it from the vendor's web site. Make sure you also use the 80-wire cable needed for UDMA/66 or faster drive.

Help! I prepared my hard disk with a drive setup program instead of using the operating system tools because my BIOS couldn't handle the full capacity of my drive. Now I've installed a BIOS update, but I can't get the drive to work correctly when I detect the full capacity in the BIOS. What do I do now?

Your system's doing its own version of the "War Between the States"—not North and South, but software-controlled versus BIOS-controlled. Because the drive setup program is using a different method for accessing the drive than an LBA/Int13h, extension-aware BIOS will, you're having problems. Unfortunately, the solution I have for you isn't much fun. Ready? Here goes:

1. Back up *everything* with a file-by-file backup program. As an alternative, at least back up your data files and be prepared to reinstall your programs. This would be a great time to buy a fast CD-RW or rewritable DVD drive with backup software and a cakebox of CD-R or recordable DVD media. Don't do an image backup, because you need to change your drive's configuration and reload Windows and applications before you can restore your backup.

2. Check the backups to make sure you can access your information.

3. Follow the software vendor's directions for removing the drive setup program BIOS override software from your system; don't do it *until* you're sure you have a good, working, complete backup. In some cases, you might get lucky and find that your system works after the software is removed without any additional steps because your BIOS can take over immediately. If not, follow steps 4–9.

4. Restart your system and set up the BIOS to use the full capacity of the drive.

5. Prepare your drive again; you can use your operating system's partitioning/disk formatting software or the drive's own setup software if it supports your version of Windows. The BIOS replacement feature provided with the drive's own setup software isn't used because your BIOS can now access the entire drive.

6. Reinstall Windows.

7. Reinstall your applications.

8. Restore your backups.

9. Promise yourself you'll *never* use BIOS replacement software again (this part's easy)!

Help! I cheaped out and decided to put Brand A hard disk on the same cable with Brand B because Brand A was cheaper than Brand B this week. They don't like each other. I want to use both drives!

I feel for you. And I've been there and had trouble doing that. What saved me was using the second ATA/IDE host adapter. Sure, it's better if you can put both drives on the same cable, but it's okay to make each one the master of its domain. If you're still using 40-wire cables, just keep in mind that with some brands you mount the jumper sideways when the drive is the only one on the cable rather than jumper it as a master; check the drive vendor's web site for details. Put your CD-ROM drive on the slower drive's cable as a slave. If you already have both a CD-ROM and a DVD or CD-RW drive, maybe it's time to invest in an additional ATA/IDE host adapter—or look for a really good deal on a drive that matches one of your existing drives. Don't forget that if you're using an 80-wire UDMA/66 cable that you will now use Cable Select for the drives on that cable.

Help! I just installed my new ATA/IDE drive, turned on my machine, and nothing! I can hear the fans running but there's no boot, no beep, and no picture. I can't believe I fried my machine!

I bet you a beat-up floppy disk your computer's just fine—*except* for how you attached the ATA/IDE host adapter cable to either the drive or to the motherboard. Some ATA/IDE cables have a plugged pin to correspond with a missing pin on some adapters, and others have a raised section on one side to correspond to a cutout in the connector. Guess what? Because of these competing ways to key the ATA/IDE connector, a lot of cables don't bother with either keying type!

An unkeyed ATA/IDE cable can be attached *backward* to either the drive or motherboard's host adapter. A lot of systems won't boot when an ATA/IDE drive is connected until they send the "spinup" command and the drive responds, "spinning." Your system sounds like it's stuck waiting for a response to a spinup command that never reached the drive. Shut down the system, fix the incorrect end of the cable, and try it again. If your data cable is plugged in correctly, check the power cable going to the drive. And, if you performed some other upgrades, make sure they are installed correctly too.

Help! I just bought a wide SCSI type of host adapter for my 68-pin drive and realized that my other SCSI devices are 50-pin. I have only one expansion slot I can use for my host adapter. What do I do now?

Adapt, not to circumstances, but to new cables. You can get a cable adapter to adapt your internal SCSI devices to attach to a 68-pin Wide SCSI ribbon cable. For external devices, welcome to the world of SCSI ain't SCSI. Every time I buy a new SCSI device, it seems I have to buy a new cable with different connections on each end. Adaptec's Cable Selector utility (www.adaptec.com) has answers for you, but better take some nerve pills before you check out the prices. SCSI cables and adapters are expensive. Of course, you can return the SCSI host adapter and buy a model that supports both 50-pin and 68-pin devices.

Keep in mind that unless you need the screaming speed of Ultra 160 or Ultra 320 SCSI(and don't mind paying through the nose for drives and host adapters), you're probably better off with high-speed interfaces such as IEEE-1394a (FireWire 400) and USB 2.0 instead. They can do what older versions of SCSI can do at about the same speeds (or faster) and support popular upgrades such as external drives, high-speed scanners, and DV camcorders without all the fiddling needed to get SCSI working.

Help! I can't format my new hard drive with Windows Explorer. Windows keeps telling me to stop viewing its contents—what contents?!?

This is a common problem with Windows Explorer. It might be that you're running some utility such as Norton Utilities or System Works in the background. Its monitoring of all drives is stopping Format from working. The best solutions I know include the following:

- Restart your Windows 9x/Me computer in Safe Mode (press F8 or Ctrl when the system starts and select Safe Mode from the menu) and try either the command-line Format or Windows Explorer.

- Restart your computer in Safe Mode command prompt and use the command-line Format (with Windows 9x only, not Windows Me). To format a floppy disk, type `Format A:`.

Either way, you're not loading up any programs that could interfere with Format.

Chapter 11

Removable Storage to Go

Removable storage provides you with a way to have your data and retrieve it too. Removable storage spans the gamut of capacities from 1.44MB floppy disks to multi-gigabyte tape back-ups. The newest types of removable storage don't use a disk or tape at all; instead, they use the same flash memory used in digital cameras.

Use this chapter to learn about the different types of removable storage and how to add your favorite to your system.

Ten Reasons Why Removable Storage Still Makes Sense

In an era of 200GB hard drives and 4.7GB rewriteable DVD drives, you might be wondering, "Who needs removable storage?" Wonder no more. Peruse the following reasons to use removable storage, and prepare to select the best types for you:

1. Your boss wants you to work at home but you don't want to take your computer home to do it.
2. You finally have the next Great American Novel ready to send to the publisher, and you don't want to lose it.
3. You're taking a trip and you want to take your favorite web site URLs along.
4. You want to carry your work with you everywhere.

5. Your boss lets you use the office computer, but you'd rather not store your files on that machine's hard drive.

6. You share information with another user who has a removable-media drive.

7. You need a storage device that you can plug into any computer.

8. You want to stick a bunch of information into your shirt pocket.

9. You want a drive that's cooler than a floppy drive.

10. You've always wanted to back up your big drive with a single cartridge.

Admit it; you *do* want removable-media storage. However, let's face it: If you haven't been shopping for removable-media drives lately, you might be surprised to find that things have changed—a lot. Entire product lines have come and gone in the last couple of years, so join me for a survey of the current crop of drives and their uses.

Thumbs Down! on Floppy Drives

The venerable (a polite way of saying *really, realllly old*) floppy drive has been around in some form since the first IBM PC showed up back in 1981. The current 1.44MB 3.5-inch models date back to the late 80s. Is it any wonder that this "universal" removable-media drive is out-dated by almost any standard? It is too small for making backups of anything bigger than a few reports or emails, is painfully slow to read from or copy to, and has a bad habit of going bad and losing your data.

I'll admit floppy drives aren't completely useless (yet). After all:

- If your system gets hosed, the humble floppy disk can restart your system and help you reinstall a real operating system if you use Windows 9x/Me. No wonder the floppy disk is the emergency disk used by these Windows versions. The Windows XP CD-ROM works as a bootable disk, so this latest version of Windows doesn't need a floppy disk for emergencies.

- The retro, tiny floppy disk might not hold much, but it's the one type of removable storage that everybody has.

However, floppy drives are just about extinct. Some vendors have stopped putting them in their latest systems (although you can always plug in a USB external floppy drive if you need one), and others are likely to follow. The main virtue of a floppy disk is that almost every computer has a floppy drive, and every store stocks floppy disks. Thus, it's a universal storage standard. However, given the fact that floppies can fail and aren't large enough to hold some types of data, it's time for a replacement. So, the next question is , what kind of a replacement is best?

Data Backup or Data Sharing?

Until recently, the floppy drive was unique in its ability to be used for both data backup (making a spare copy of data in case the original gets hosed) and data sharing (making a copy of data to pass along to another user). Low-cost and the universal availability of floppy drives made data backup and sharing with a single device a reality.

However, the floppy drive is no longer alone. Rewriteable CD and DVD drives using recordable CD (CD-R) media make sharing large amounts of data as low-cost and universal as floppy disks and drives have made sharing small amounts of data. However, this combination isn't perfect:

- CD-based media can be fragile. Have you ever run over a CD with your desk chair? It's not a pretty sight.

- Although almost every CD-ROM drive can read a CD-R, using rewriteable CD-RW media with different CD-RW creation programs can be difficult. Differences in how different programs create and change CD-RW contents can trip you up.

- Reading CD-RW media on a CD-ROM drive requires the user to install a special reader program.

- CD and DVD media are relatively bulky; unless you use the small credit-card size media, it's too big for your shirt pocket.

As you can see, there's still a place for removable-media drives that don't use CD or DVD technologies. As you search for a floppy drive replacement, think *universal, low-cost, compact,* and *more storage than a floppy* as your watchwords.

> **MARK'S TIP SHEET: How to Avoid Getting Burned by a New Drive Technology**
>
> Everybody gets excited about new technologies; I've broken out in a sweat a time or two just thinking about 3.2GHz CPUs myself. However, when it comes to my data, I have a "take no chances, take no prisoners" attitude. I remember reading about how IBM's brand new PC/AT's 20MB hard disks were dropping like flies back in 1984, and I've seen a lot of other problems with data storage since then. Do yourself a favor before you buy your next new storage device:
>
> - **Don't stand in line at midnight to buy the first one**—And don't buy pre-releases either. You're buying blind—and that's just dumb.
>
> - **Read real reviews, not just press releases**—If you buy a drive when it's first introduced, all the information that's available is rehashed press releases. Wait until somebody has a real drive in hand and has copied data to it, erased data from it, restored backups with it, and used it the way you and I do in the real world.
>
> - **Check forums and message boards**—Sure, you'll read messages from people who can't type or spell (and maybe can't even think!). However, you'll also read some insightful comments from pioneers who *did* stand in line at midnight to buy the new drive. What's good and what's bad? How's the company's tech support? How's the *reliability*? Remember, it's your data. Check www.epinions.com and user feedback at Amazon.com for user reactions.
>
> - **Wait for .1**—There's a saying in this business that you should never buy .0 anything. It applies to hardware too. All drives can have their behavior changed through driver updates, and a lot of them have updateable firmware as well. Again, let the impatient find out what's wrong before you buy.

Magnetic Alternatives to Floppy Drives

Several vendors have tried to create so-called "super floppy" drives that have the floppy drive's combination of low cost, shirt-pocket size, and easy media availability—all the while increasing drive capacity.

The leading vendors in the floppy replacement game include the following:

- Iomega
- Imation

Iomega's entry is the Iomega Zip, now in its third generation; Imation's SuperDisk, on the other hand, is in its second generation. Let's find out how these drives compare with each other and how good they are as a potential replacement for the 3.5-inch floppy drive.

SuperDisk and Son of SuperDisk

Because the floppy disk is so old, so small in capacity, and so slow, the ideal replacement would have a higher capacity, be faster, and be compatible with existing media. The Imation LS-120, better known as the *SuperDisk*, has been the most popular of these potential floppy replacements. The SuperDisk uses its own 120MB LS-120 media, and, unlike Zip drives, can also read and write standard 3.5-inch 1.44MB and 720KB floppy disks.

Unfortunately, the LS-120 SuperDisk arrived several years after the Iomega Zip drives were introduced, and it was never able to overcome the substantial lead that the Iomega Zip had in both retail sales and OEM pre-installations. This was despite the fact that the LS-120 works with regular floppy media and the Zip drive doesn't. As a result of disappointing sales, LS-120 SuperDisk drives have been discontinued by Imation and most other vendors, although you can still buy LS-120 SuperDisk media.

An improved SuperDisk, the LS-240, was introduced a couple years ago. As the name implies, the LS-240 uses LS-240 240MB floppy disks, LS-120 floppy media, and regular floppy media. It also adds a bonus: the ability to format regular 3.5-inch 1.44MB media to hold up to 32MB of data. Unfortunately, the LS-240 flavor of SuperDisk also showed up too late to beat the Zip drive or the increasingly popular CD-RW drive in the US market. As a result, USB-interface versions from various vendors were quickly discontinued in the US market. If you have a Hewlett-Packard or IBM notebook computer with an interchangeable drive bay, you're still in luck—at least for now. LS-240 drives are still available in Asia and Australia.

Is SuperDisk Super Enough?

SuperDisk drives are much harder to find than other types of removable-media drives, but they can be located with some effort. Should you buy one? I recommend a SuperDisk drive if you:

- Already share data with someone who has one
- Prefer magnetic media over flash memory
- Want magnetic media you can give away

The floppy drive and floppy disks provide a universal, low-cost, compact storage solution. How does SuperDisk compare?

- **Universal?**—A long way from it. Zip is much more common.

- **Low-cost?**—Not really; LS-120 disks are about $9 each and LS-240 disks are about $10 each, and the HP/IBM notebook drives are around $200 or more. USB drives are about $150—if you can find them.

- **Compact size?**—Yes; because SuperDisk drives are also compatible with floppy drives, the media fits into a shirt pocket.

- **More storage than a floppy?**—Absolutely.

The SuperDisk is a suitable choice if you need to interchange data with other SuperDisk users and can locate a drive, but it's too hard to find media for it. There are better choices.

Zipping Along with Iomega Zip Drives

The Iomega Zip drive beat the Imation SuperDisk to market by about two years, and it looks as if it will outlive both versions of the SuperDisk. Although Zip drives have had their share of problems over the years, newer models use more durable media and the drives are cheaper than older models. Unlike SuperDisk, Zip is much more likely to be installed in (or connected to) your friend's and co-worker's computers. Zip attaches to almost any port (IDE/ATA, USB, SCSI, parallel, PC Card (PCMCIA), IEEE-1394/FireWire and proprietary notebook drive bays), so it's easy to install it.

Zip drives come in three sizes:

- **100MB**—Read/write 100MB media

- **250MB**—Read/write 250/100MB media

- **750MB**—Read/write 750/250MB media; read 100MB media

Although Zip drives hold as much or more than SuperDisk drives, they have one significant drawback compared to SuperDisk: Zip drives work only with Zip media. Thus, if you're hoping that a Zip drive will let you yank out your old floppy drive and toss it, it won't.

However, there are millions of Zip drives in use, so it's more likely you can interchange Zip disks with other users than any other type of magnetic media except for floppies. So, should you pick up a Zip drive? Look at the drive models and interfaces available before you decide.

Zip Drive Models and Interfaces

Although Zip drives connect to almost any external interface, including USB 1.0, USB 2.0, FireWire (IEEE-1394), SCSI, parallel port, and the ATA/IDE internal interface, I recommend using USB unless you're planning to transfer very large files between the Zip drive and your PC. The Zip 750 can use Hi-Speed USB (USB 2.0) and FireWire, but Zip 250 and Zip 100 support the slower USB 1.1 standard. How much faster are the USB 2.0 and FireWire versions than USB 1.1? The Zip 750 has a maximum data transfer rate of 7.3MB/sec when attached to USB 2.0, FireWire, or ATA/IDE interfaces. Connect the USB 2.0 drive to a USB 1.1 port, and the data transfer rate sinks to just 900KB/sec (eight times slower!). The Zip 100's USB version has a data transfer rate of just 700KB/sec, while the ATA/IDE version has double the transfer rate of USB 1.1 (1.4MB/sec).

If you're trying to avoid additional cables, keep in mind that the latest versions of the Zip 100 and Zip 250 drives that use the USB 1.1 interface are powered by the USB port; no extra transformer is necessary. However, all Zip 750 external models require an AC power source.

ON THE WEB: All the Zip Stats in One Place

Check out all the vital statistics on current models of Iomega Zip drives at this URL:

`www.iomega.com/zip/zip_comp_chart.html`

To Zip or Not to Zip

Although Zip drives and media are sold in most electronics and computer stores, that's no guarantee that anybody you want to trade data with already has a Zip drive. A second problem is that the latest Zip drive, the Zip 750, can read Zip 100 media, but can't write to it. Because the most popular size of the three is the Zip 100, this is a big problem. In addition, although Zip 250 and Zip 750 can read/write the next smaller size of media, both drives slow down drastically when they do so.

I recommend a Zip drive if you:

- Already share data with someone who has one
- Prefer magnetic media over flash memory
- Want magnetic media you can give away

If you compare the features of Zip to the benefits of a floppy drive and floppy disks, you can see why the Zip drive, although useful, is no longer on my "must-have" list.

- **Universal?**—There is no guarantee, but they are far more popular than SuperDisk.
- **Low-cost?**—Not really; Zip disks sell for $8 to $13 each, and the drives are between $70 and $150 or so.
- **Compact?**—Yes; although Zip disks are a bit thicker than SuperDisk or conventional floppies, they still fit comfortably into your shirt pocket.
- **More storage than a floppy?**—Absolutely.

You'll have no problem tracking down a Zip drive, but it's mighty expensive to buy a bunch of Zip media for backups. If you're primarily concerned about toting around work (or play) in progress instead of a full system backup, let me introduce you to a much more compact product.

Thumbs Up! for USB Thumb Drives

USB flash memory storage devices (better known as USB thumb drives or USB keychain drives) aren't exactly new. However, they're quickly becoming the most popular way to move data amounts that fall between the capacities of a floppy disk (1.44MB) and an optical drive (650MB or more).

A USB thumb drive is about the size of your thumb (drive sizes, like thumb sizes, might vary; consult your hand for details)—hence the nickname. Another popular nickname for this device is "keychain drive." No points for guessing why.

How do they work? These devices contain flash memory chips, which are a special type of memory chip also used in digital cameras and digital music players. Flash memory, unlike conventional memory, can retain its content without power and can have its contents changed thousands of times.

Typical capacities range from 32MB up to 2GB. Prices start at around $1/MB and drop to around $.60/MB in larger sizes. When a thumb drive is plugged into a computer's USB port, it works just like any other removable drive. You need to install drivers (a one-time job) with Windows 98, but later versions of Windows (or Mac OS) recognize the device immediately. USB thumb drives are self-contained. Because they plug into a USB port (available on almost any computer built since about 1998), they're practically universal.

Here's how USB thumb drives compare to floppy drives and disks:

- **Universal?**—They plug into any 1998 or newer PC, making them about as close to universal as you can get.

- **Low-cost?**—Initial cost similar to or higher than a Zip drive at comparable capacities, but no media cost means that there are no ongoing costs.

- **Compact?**—They really are no bigger than a thumb or a keychain. Some models even have pocket clips and lanyards so that you won't lose them.

- **More storage than a floppy?**—Absolutely.

Unlike floppies, Zip, or SuperDisk media, you won't want to give your USB keychain drive to anybody else. They're 100 percent intended for small-scale backup and data transport, not data sharing. However, for backup and data transport, they are just about perfect.

Figure 11.1 compares typical 1.44MB floppy, 100MB Zip, and LS-120 SuperDisk media to a 128MB thumb-sized USB storage device.

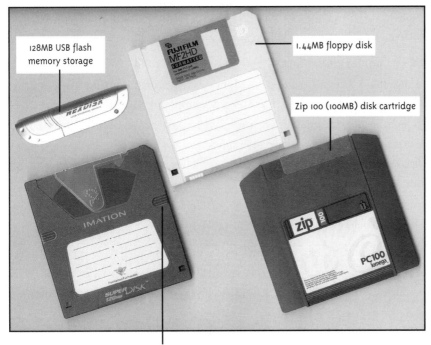

128MB USB flash memory storage

1.44MB floppy disk

Zip 100 (100MB) disk cartridge

LS-120 SuperDisk media

Figure 11.1

Four generations of removable media: 1.44MB floppy, Zip 100MB, LS-120 SuperDisk, and Jungsoft NexDisk 128MB USB keychain drive.

Removable and External Hard Drives

What if you need to carry more storage with you than a USB thumb-sized drive or Zip drive can hold, and you want more speed than a CD-RW or DVD rewriteable drive provides? What do you really want? You want a hard disk you can take with you.

The easiest and most versatile way to add a removable hard drive to your system is to choose an external model that plugs into the USB 2.0 or IEEE-1394 ports found in most recent computers.

> **READ THIS TOO: Don't Have USB 2.0 or IEEE-1394 Ports? Let Me Help**
>
> Flip over to Chapter 19, "Adding the Ports You Need for the Devices You Want," to learn how to add either type of port to your system.

External Hard Drives

External hard drives range in capacity between 20GB and 250GB, with prices ranging from about $150 up to $400, depending on capacity and physical size. Because of the high transfer rates of USB 2.0 and IEEE-1394, drives connected to either of these ports are about as fast in real-world performance as drives connected to the IDE/ATA interface used by most internal drives.

External drives can use the 3.5-inch hard disks used in most PCs, or the smaller (and more expensive per GB) 2.5-inch hard disks used in notebook computers. External drives, which use desktop drive mechanisms, are larger and heavier (but less expensive per GB) than those that use notebook drives. Some external drive assemblies that use notebook drives might not need external power sources in some cases, but drive assemblies based on desktop drives do need external power. You can even build your own external drive from a spare 3.5-inch or 2.5-inch drive with enclosures from companies such as ADS Technologies (which also makes USB and IEEE-1394 external hard drives).

Because you might prefer to use an external hard drive with a wide variety of systems, I recommend a combo model such as the SimpleTech SimpleDrive Deluxe shown in Figure 11.2. This drive includes both USB 1.1/2.0 and IEEE-1394a interfaces for maximum versatility.

MARK'S TIP SHEET: Checking Out the Latest Portable Drives

We *love* portable drives at TechTV. Check out these recent Roundups:

- **Roundup: Portable Data Storage Devices**—Robert Heron's take on both USB flash drives and portable hard drives is at www.techtv.com/callforhelp/products/story/0,24330,3406604,00.html.

- **Roundup: Small Storage Media**—Han Choi pits 1GB flash memory-based storage devices against the Hitachi (originally IBM) Microdrive (which fits into a Compact Flash+ slot) at www.techtv.com/products/hardware/story/0,23008,3381659,00.html.

- **Roundup: Removable Storage Options**—Greg Melton provides a quick review of both removable drives and interface options at www.techtv.com/callforhelp/products/story/0,24330,3368547,00.html.

Follow these links straight to the manufacturers of leading portable hard drives:

- **Maxtor**—www.maxtor.com

- **Western Digital**—www.wdc.com

- **Simple Technologies**—www.simpletech.com

- **ADS Technologies**—www.adstech.com

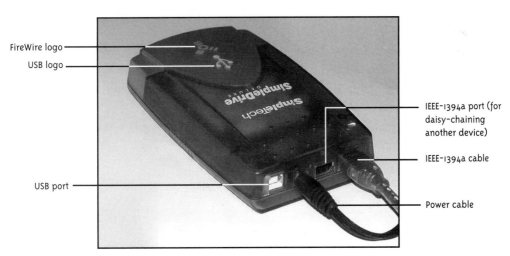

FireWire logo
USB logo
USB port
IEEE-1394a port (for daisy-chaining another device)
IEEE-1394a cable
Power cable

Figure 11.2

This 20GB external hard drive from SimpleTech includes both IEEE-1394a and USB ports.

External drives like the ones mentioned in this section are great for both large-scale backup and for adding extra primary storage to systems. They're available from many vendors, including Simple Technologies, Maxtor, Western Digital, Pocketec (a favorite at TechTV for USB 2.0 ports), and others.

That's the good news. What's the bad news? These drives have fixed media; they aren't removable cartridge drives. High-capacity removable-cartridge drives aren't as popular today as they were a few years ago.

Iomega introduced its much-touted modular 10GB and 20GB Peerless drive system about two years ago, but it never became popular and has been discontinued. The remaining quantities of drives, interface modules, and data cartridges are vanishing quickly. If you want hard disk-like performance and removable media, the Castlewood Orb is a possibility.

Castlewood Orb Drives

The Castlewood Orb features 2.2GB and 5.7GB hard disk-style cartridges that plug into both internal (IDE/ATA) and external (SCSI, USB, and IEEE-1394) drives. With the demise of Iomega's Jaz and Peerless lines of high-capacity removable-media hard disk drives, the Castlewood Orb is the only major removable hard disk drive on the market today. It's in a class by itself.

Originally introduced with a capacity of 2.2GB, the Orb is also available in a 5.7GB capacity. Table 11.1 provides details about Orb drives by capacity and interface type.

Table 11.1   Castlewood Orb Selection Matrix

Drive Size	Ultra SCSI	UltraWide SCSI	IEEE-1394a	USB 1.1	IDE	USB 2.0
2.2GB	Y*	Y	Y	Y*	Y	N
5.7GB	N	N	Y	N	Y	Y

*Also available in a USB 1.1/SCSI combo drive
^USB 2.0/FireWire (IEEE-1394) combo drive only

Note that the 5.7GB versions of the Orb drive can read, but not write, the 2.2GB Orb cartridges.

As with any other drive, the interface type has a huge impact on the Orb's performance. Table 11.2 gives you the stats for the 2.2GB version.

Table 11.2   Castlewood 2.2GB Orb Drive Speeds by Interface Type

Interface	Location	Speed Average/Burst
UltraWide SCSI	Internal	12.2MB/sec—40MB/sec
Ultra SCSI	External	12.2MB/sec—20MB/sec
IEEE-1394a	External	12.2MB/sec—20MB/sec
IDE	Internal	12.2MB/sec—16.6MB/sec
USB 1.1	External	1.0MB/sec

The 5.7GB EIDE version of the Orb is faster than any 2.2GB version, offering a sustained data transfer rate of 17.35MB/sec and a 66MB/sec burst transfer rate.

Drive prices vary by interface and capacity, as shown in Table 11.3.

Table 11.3   Castlewood Orb Drive Pricing

Drive Type/Capacity	Direct Price*
2.2GB EIDE/ATA^	$195
2.2GB Ultra-Wide SCSI^	$195
2.2GB Ultra SCSI#	$195
2.2GB SCSI/USB 1.1#	$280
2.2GB Ultra SCSI/USB 1.1#	$280
2.2GB IEEE-1394a (FireWire 400)#	$250
5.7GB IEEE-1394a/USB 1.1#	$400
5.7GB EIDE/ATA^	$300

*Prices from Castlewood direct, rounded to nearest dollar
^Internal
#External

2.2GB cartridges are about $40 each, and 5.7GB cartridges are about $60 each.

Figure 11.3 shows a Castlewood Orb in its 2.2GB USB version and Orb media.

Figure 11.3

The Castlewood 2.2GB Orb is available in a transparent-cover USB version (right), but most external versions are the same basic-black color as the media (left). Photo courtesy of Castlewood.

Although the Castlewood Orb offers a wide variety of interfaces and two different sizes, the Orb isn't a flawless choice. Early adopters often had reliability problems, but the hardware has been redesigned. However, technical notes on the Castlewood web site (www.castlewood.com) indicate that the 2.2GB USB/SCSI version doesn't work as well with Windows XP as with older versions of Windows.

Current and Future Removable Hard Disk Alternatives

If you prefer to use an off-the-shelf hard disk as a removable device, you can install a removable hard disk rack into your system to create a "do-it-yourself" removable hard disk system. These racks enable you to insert and remove an off-the-shelf 3.5-inch hard disk. Note that you need to attach a protective tray to each drive you want to interchange and you also need to use the larger 5.25-inch drive bays to accommodate the rack. You must also shut down the system before you switch drives; this is definitely not a Plug-and-Play (PnP) system. Some of the nicest ones are made by Vantec Thermal Technologies. However, this type of system is more for the enthusiast than the everyday user.

A better solution is being developed in Japan, where the members of the Information Versatile Disk for Removable Usage (iVDR) consortium have adapted 2.5-inch and 1.8-inch ATA and Serial ATA drives to a new hot-swappable interface. They aren't shipping products yet, but early buzz looks impressive. Unlike other types of removable storage, iVDR is designed to work in non-PC applications such as video recorders.

If you want more durability than DVD or CD-RW media provides but still want shirt-pocket portability for media and you want it right now, there is one more solution and it's easy to overlook. Magneto-optical (MO) drives have been popular for years in Europe, but aren't as popular here. 3.5-inch MO drives are now available in capacities up to 2.3GB, and they can also use smaller-capacity 3.5-inch cartridges in sizes ranging from 128MB to 1.3GB. These drives are available as internal IDE/ATA or SCSI drives or USB external drives, so they attach to the most popular interfaces.

3.5-inch MO drives are relatively expensive, with prices ranging from about $250 to $350. However, media costs are less expensive than Zip, ranging from around $7 each for 128MB cartridges up to about $20 each for 2.3GB cartridges. Other sizes available include 230MB, 640MB, and 1.3GB, which enable you to choose the size you need for your data. MO drives are faster than Zip, but slower than a hard disk.

ON THE WEB: Keeping an Eye on the Removable Storage Biz

If you're interested in Iomega's Peerless or Zip, get info from Iomega's web site at `www.iomega.com`.

Get more information about Vantec Thermal Solutions's ezswap line of removable hard disk adapters at `www.vantecusa.com`.

What does TechTV like to use for backing up? Find out at `www.techtv.com/screensavers/answerstips/story/0,24330,3301514,00.html`.

Check out the future of removable hard disk storage at the iVDR web site at `www.idvr.org`.

Fujitsu is the leader in 3.5-inch MO drives. Get more information at `http://us.fujitsu.com`.

Flash Memory and Your PC

Many PC users have been working with flash memory long before encountering the first USB thumb-sized drive; they've been using it to capture images taken with digital cameras. However, if your PCs are equipped with flash memory readers, there's absolutely no reason why you can't use the same flash memory cards used by digital cameras and music players to transfer data between computers. Data is data, and if you think USB keychain drives are small, you'll be amazed at how small flash memory cards are.

Figure 11.4 compares the sizes of common flash memory cards with the USB keychain drive originally shown in Figure 11.1.

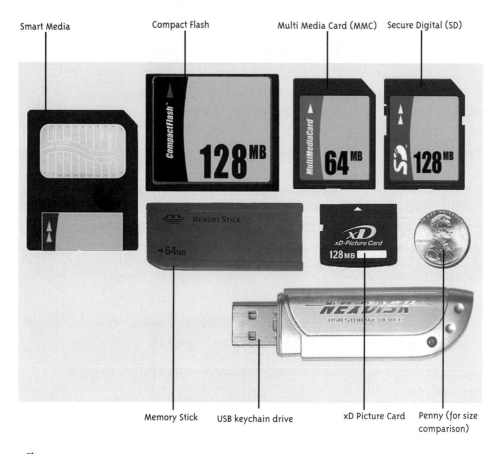

Figure 11.4

A USB keychain drive (lower right) compared to flash memory cards used in digital cameras, music players, and a U.S. penny.

Unlike the USB keychain drive, flash memory cards can't be plugged directly into a USB port. However, if you already have a flash memory card reader that also has write capabilities, you can copy data to a card as easily as you can read a card. Some recent computers include a flash memory card reader built into the front of the computer. In addition, you can always connect one to a USB hub, as shown in Figure 11.5.

MARK'S TIP SHEET: All Readers Read, But Only Some Can Write

Before you buy a new flash memory card reader, check the documentation to see whether it can also write to your media. If you already have a card reader, check its documentation, or try to copy some files to an empty flash memory card to see whether it can both read and write.

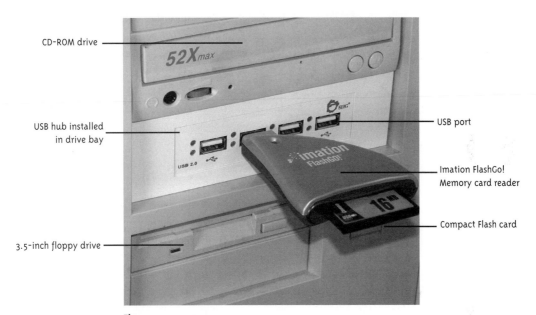

CD-ROM drive

52X*max*

USB hub installed in drive bay

USB port

USB 2.0

Imation FlashGo! Memory card reader

Compact Flash card

3.5-inch floppy drive

Figure 11.5

A USB hub is a convenient place to attach a small flash memory reader such as the Imation FlashGo! This setup makes it easy to treat a flash memory card as another disk drive.

Even when you factor in the cost of a flash memory card reader, the total cost of a flash memory card-based storage solution is usually even less expensive per MB than a USB keychain drive. As with USB keychain drives, however, they're too expensive to pass along to other users, but they pack durable backup and low long-term costs into a tiny space. In addition, it's a perfect way to get more use out of flash memory cards between photo expeditions.

What flash memory standard should you use, if you decide flash memory is the best way to transport data? You can decide by answering the following questions:

- What flash memory cards do your digital cameras and other devices already use?
- Which cards offer the highest capacity?
- Which cards are most durable?

Table 11.4 provides you with capacity information about the flash memory cards shown in Figure 11.4, as well as an enhanced version of Memory Stick called Memory Stick Pro (not shown in Figure 11.4).

Table 11.4 Flash Memory Cards Comparison				
Device	**Minimum Capacity**	**Maximum Capacity**	**Notes**	**Typical Price (128MB)**
Compact Flash	16MB	512MB (Type I) 1GB (Type II)	Lexar Media and SanDisk also make faster versions of CF media; Lexar Media also makes USB-enabled CF media.	$55
SmartMedia	16MB	128MB	Most digital camera vendors are switching to the xD-Picture Card.	$55
MMC (MultiMedia Card)	16MB	128MB	May be interchanged with SD cards on many systems.	$70
SD (Secure Digital)	16MB	1GB	May be interchanged with MMC cards on many systems.	$75
Memory Stick	16MB	128MB	Developed by Sony; licensed to Lexar Media.	$70
Memory Stick PRO (also known as Memory Stick Magic Gate)	256MB	1GB	Enhanced high-speed version of Memory Stick with digital rights management support.	$150 (256MB)
xD-Picture Card	16MB	128MB	Match brand of media and digital camera for best results, because different brands of xD-Picture Card media are optimized for different camera brands' features.	$80
USB keychain drive	16MB	2GB	Some include password-protection and write-protect features.	$100

The most durable and highest-capacity flash memory card is the Compact Flash card. USB-enabled Compact Flash cards can be connected to the USB port with a low-cost cable instead of a bulkier card reader. Secure Digital and Memory Stick PRO are also available in 1GB capacities, but aren't as durable. Note it is sometimes less expensive to buy two lower-capacity cards than a single high-capacity card.

Back Up Your Digital Life with Tape

Given the enormous disparity between even the biggest removable-media drive's capacity and the size of your hard disk (40GB is common, and stores now sell drives as large as 250GB), it's safe to say that if you want to make periodic backups of everything on your drive, you really need a tape drive. A tape drive big enough to back up the typical hard disk isn't cheap, but losing months (or years) of data is a lot more costly.

Comparing Tape and Other Removable-Media Drives

Tape drives differ from other removable-media drives in a number of ways, including the following:

- **Capacity**—The capacity of tape drives is measured assuming 2:1 compression during the backup process. This tends to overestimate the actual capacity of the drive. Media of other types use the actual capacity.

- **Data access**—Tape drives are streaming media and must be read from one end to the other, just like music cassette tapes. Other types of removable media use random access, enabling you to locate any file in just a few moments, just as with music CDs.

- **Backup versus file copy**—Tape drives are designed to use special backup software (which might be included with the drive or might be an extra-cost item). Backup software changes data into a form that can be compressed and split across multiple tapes or cartridges, and it must be restored before it can be used. Although other types of removable drives can be used for backup, they are more often used for file copy (drag and drop) operations through Windows Explorer. Drives that use file-copy procedures enable you to read the file from the media and use it immediately, just as if it's on a floppy disk or CD-ROM.

- **Interfacing**—The highest-performance and largest-capacity tape drives traditionally use SCSI interfacing, but given the cost and complexity of SCSI connections and the lack of hot-swap capabilities, I don't believe that SCSI tape drives are a suitable choice for most users. Instead, I would focus on IDE/ATA internal tape drives and USB 2.0 and IEEE-1394 external tape drives. These choices offer the performance, capacity, and easy interfacing most home and small-office users want and need.

> **MARK'S TIP SHEET: Lowering Your Expectations for Tape Drives**
>
> Tape drives lie! I remember how shocked I was to discover that the supposed 2:1 compression ratio was more like 1.5:1–1.75:1 when I used my tape drive to make backups.
>
> Why does this happen? Tape backups assume that all data can be compressed and that all data can be compressed by the same factor. If you use WinZip, PKZIP, or similar compression utilities, you know how incorrect these assumptions are.
>
> Text files and some types of bitmap graphics files, such as the popular .BMP file created by Windows Paint, can be compressed to one-tenth their original size or less. However, program files often shrink by only 30 percent when compressed. The worst-case situation is when you try to compress files, such as Zip or .CAB archive files, or .GIF or .JPG (JPEG) graphics files, that are already compressed. These files don't compress, and they use the same space on the tape as on the hard disk.
>
> What's your *real* compression rate? Use the report prepared by your backup program to see how you're doing. If you're shopping for a tape drive, assume that the drive will perform at a 1.5:1–1.7:1 compression ratio. These figures are based on my experience with typical real-world compression ratios with tape and other types of compressed backups.
>
> To determine the real size, divide the claimed (2:1 compression) size of the drive by 2 and multiply by 1.5 or 1.7. For example, a so-called 40GB tape backup (2:1 compression) has a native capacity of 20GB (40/2 equals 20). If you assume a 1.5:1 compression ratio, the drive has a capacity of only 30GB. If you assume a 1.7:1 compression ratio, the drive has a capacity of 34GB.

The major types of tape backups suitable for home and small-office users include the following:

- Travan
- OnStream ADR and ADR2

Travan: 40GB Is the New Limit

Travan drives descended from the longtime favorite QIC-80 tape backup used on PCs for a number of years.

Travan drives have been around in various capacities for a number of years, but the current models are available in two sizes:

- **Travan 20**—20GB (2:1) 10GB (native capacity)
- **Travan 40**—40GB (2:1) 20GB (native capacity)

ANALYZE THIS

Travan and QIC Origins
QIC stands for "Quarter Inch Committee," a trade group that has put forth many different standards for tape backups. Ironically, Travan is actually based on a wider version of QIC called QIC-Wide (which is .315 inches)!

CAUTION: STOP! LOOK! THINK!

Travan 20? Too Small for Today's PCs
Nothing personal, but Travan 20 (more like Travan 15 or 17 using my formula) is too small for today's systems. With entry-level computers now featuring 40GB hard drives, a Travan 20 drive would need two or more cartridges to back up the system after it's been in use for awhile creating data. Take it from somebody who has watched backups become ruined because one tape in a multiple-tape backup failed: it's *much* better to use one tape to back up your system if possible. A 40GB (2:1) drive is the *smallest* tape drive I'd consider today.

Travan Performance

The performance of any drive is controlled by two factors: the speed of the interface used to connect the drive to the computer and the design of the drive. Table 11.5 provides this information for current Travan tape drives.

Table 11.5	Travan Drive Performance by Interface	
Drive Type	**Interface**	**Maximum Speed**
Travan 20	IDE and SCSI	120MB/min (2MB/sec)
Travan 20	USB 1.1	85MB/min (1.42MB/sec)
Travan 40	IDE/ATA	240MB/min (4MB/sec)
Travan 40	USB 2.0	240MB/min (4MB/sec)

As you can see from Table 11.5, Travan 40 drives are both larger and much faster than Travan 20 drives, making them a better choice. Figure 11.6 shows the contents of a Seagate TapeStor Travan 40 USB 2.0 kit.

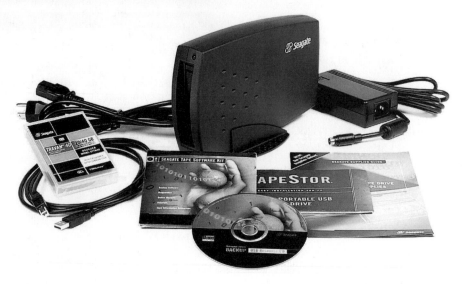

Figure 11.6

Seagate's TapeStor Travan 40 USB 2.0 drive kit also contains backup software (center) and a Travan 20/40 tape cartridge
(left). Photo courtesy of Seagate Removable Storage Solutions.

Travan Costs

Travan 20 drives have prices between $230 (IDE/ATA) and $360 (USB 1.1). SCSI drives are
about $290, and Travan 40 drives have prices between $370 (IDE/ATA) and $500 (USB 2.0).
TapeStor Travan drives include backup software and a tape cartridge, and Seagate's Hornet
"bare" drives without backup software or tape media are less expensive.

Because of the design of Travan media, it's more expensive than some other tape media per
GB. Travan 20 (TR-5) media sells for around $35–$40 per cartridge. Travan 40 (TR-7) media
sells for around $44–$47 per cartridge.

OnStream ADR2: Up to 120GB

OnStream's ADR (Advanced Digital Recording) technology was initially developed by
Philips Electronics. It uses an eight-channel array to read and write error correction code
(ECC) information within eight data tracks at the same time. The drive uses a variable-speed
mechanism to reduce tape wear and to enable the drive to work in better coordination with
the speed of the system to which it's connected. An advanced servo system keeps the tape
heads aligned with the data tracks. This enables the drive to reach an amazing level of data

reliability: only one unreadable bit out of every 10^{19} bits recorded. In plain English, this means that you'll get your data back. I recommend the second-generation ADR2 drives in ATA/IDE and USB 2.0 configurations:

- **ADR2.60 internal IDE**—60GB (2:1) 30GB (native)
- **ADR2.60 external USB 2.0**—60GB (2:1) 30GB (native)
- **ADR2.120 internal IDE**—120GB (2:1) 60GB (native)

ADR2.60 IDE version has a price of about $470, while the USB 2.0 version has a price of about $670. ADR2.120 IDE (which also supports ADR2.60 cartridges) has a price of about $750. 60GB cartridges (2:1 compression) are about $60 each, or about $52 each in quantities. 120GB cartridges (2:1 compression) are about $83 each, or about $75 each in quantities. Cartridges are made by both Onstream and Verbatim. Figure 11.7 shows the ADR2.60 IDE drive, while Figure 11.8 shows the ADR2.60 tape cartridge.

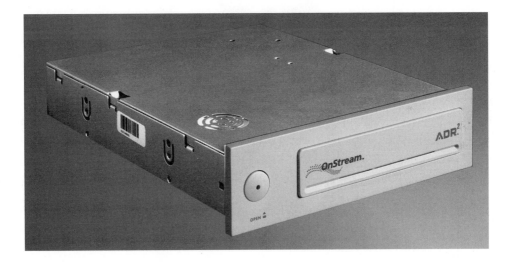

Figure 11.7

OnStream ADR2.60 internal IDE tape drive. Photo courtesy of OnStream Data BV.

Figure 11.8

OnStream ADR2.60
tape cartridge. Photo
courtesy of OnStream
Data BV.

Is a Tape Drive Right for You?

Many PC owners see a tape drive as a hard expense to justify. After all, it doesn't provide any increase in performance, and a tape drive usually costs more than many low-end systems. The value of a tape drive is in the protection it gives your data. After all, although computers and upgrades are easier and cheaper than ever, data is literally priceless and can't be bought at any store. If you lose it, it's gone.

To help you decide if a tape drive, rather than CD-RW or rewriteable DVD, is the best back-up type for you, ask yourself these questions:

- **How much data on your system changes every week?**—If the answer is less than 1GB, a couple of CD-R or CD-RW discs will do the job. If the answer is less than 10GB, a couple of rewriteable DVD or recordable DVD discs can do a suitable job. However, if the answer is more than 10GB, or if you want a single-cartridge backup solution, you need a tape backup.

- **How easy would it be to recover from a crash?**—If you can reload your system from a system image on CD or DVD media back to a specified point, it's easy to recover from a crash. However, if your current backup system requires you to reinstall Windows, reinstall your backup software, and then restore your information, you could lose the better part of a day to a crash. A tape backup with disaster recovery could reduce a lost day to a couple of hours.

If you decide that your data changes frequently enough or that a system crash is a big enough problem to justify a tape backup, the other decision to make is what interface to select:

- ATA/IDE is cheaper, but it can back up other systems only through the network.
- USB 2.0 is more expensive, but it lets you share the backup device with any computer with a USB 2.0 port.

I recommend a USB 2.0 tape drive that supports disaster recovery, especially if you have more than one computer. To help you decide which model is the best choice, consider the compressed/native capacity of the drive, drive cost, media cost, and estimated cost per GB.

Calculate the cost per GB by dividing the cost of a tape cartridge by the estimated capacity of the cartridge. For example, a Travan 40 tape cartridge has an estimated capacity of 35GB, assuming a 1.5:1 compression ratio. The price of a Travan 40 cartridge averages about $45. 45/35 = about $1.28/GB.

CAUTION: STOP! LOOK! THINK!

Consider Software as Well as Hardware

When you make your choice of tape drive, make sure that the software included with the drive:

- Works with your operating system
- Supports disaster recovery, which lets you create bootable media that can be used to reinstall Windows and your backup to an empty drive
- Enables one drive to back up systems on a network

If the backup software provided doesn't support the features you need, consider buying a bare drive and getting the backup software you prefer, or factor in the cost of buying suitable backup software for the drive. You can often upgrade bundled backup software to full versions for much less than buying the full version outright.

Installing a Removable-Media Drive

All the removable-media drives in this chapter attach to various external or internal interfaces. Internally mounted removable-media and tape drives considered in this chapter connect to the same IDE/ATA connector used for hard, CD-ROM, and other optical drives. See Chapter 10, "Adding a Huge Hard Disk," for details.

Externally mounted removable-media and tape drives can connect to IEEE-1394, USB 1.1, or USB 2.0 ports found on the rear or front of a computer. To install drives using these interfaces:

1. Check the drive's documentation to determine if driver and utility/backup software (if any) should be installed before or after the drive is connected to the system. Install driver and software as directed.

2. Plug the drive into a working power source if necessary.

3. Connect the data cable to the drive.

4. Connect the data cable from the drive to the port on the system.

5. The drive should be recognized. If the drivers are not already installed per the device documentation, install them now.

When a removable-media, flash memory, or Zip drive is installed, it has a drive letter like any other drive on your system. It might have a unique icon, or it might use the generic removable-media icon.

Most tape drives are invisible to the system until the tape backup software is started. A few tape drives support drive-letter access, but most do not. The following sections provide a detailed pre-installation checklist for each interface type discussed in this chapter.

Internal IDE

Here's what's required for an internal IDE drive:

- **Interface**—Included in system.

- **Connection**—Empty 40-pin connection on IDE cable.

- **Configuration**—Set jumper to master, slave, or cable select; 80-wire cable is required to use cable select.

- **Drive bay**—Some can use 3.5-inch; others require 5.25-inch. Check drive documentation for details.

External (USB)

Here's what's required for an external USB drive:

- **Interface**—USB 1.1 or 2.0, depending on the drive; a USB 2.0 drive can be connected to a USB 1.1 port, but performance will be much slower and isn't recommended. Plan to install a USB 2.0 port if your drive specifically supports it and your system doesn't have one. See Chapter 19.
- **Connection**—USB device cable (included).
- **Configuration**—Verify USB port on system is enabled and USB-compatible operating system is in use; be sure to install USB 2.0 drivers to enable USB 2.0 ports to work at full speed.

External (IEEE-1394)

Here's what's required for an external IEEE-1394 drive:

- **Interface**—IEEE-1394; if not present, it must be added.
- **Connection**—IEEE-1394 six-pin device cable; if your system has an IEEE-1394b (FireWire 800) port instead of an IEEE-1394a port, use a converter cable to connect your device.
- **Configuration**—Verify IEEE-1394-compatible operating system is in use and port is enabled.

Flash Memory

Here's what's required for a flash memory device:

- **Interface**—A compatible flash memory card reader with read/write capability.
- **Connection**—Most card readers plug into a USB port; see the "External (USB)" section above for details.
- **Configuration**—Verify USB port used by flash memory card reader is enabled and working; install any drivers required by flash memory card reader.

Troubleshooting Call for Help: Removable Storage

Use this section to fix a balky drive and get back to normal—or hopefully *better* than normal.

Help! I'm having trouble reading data from my Zip drive. It's the only place I have my backups!

Zip drives are wonderful when they're working (which is most of the time, to be honest), but it's certainly scary when they decide to take a dive. Here's what I'd suggest:

- If you think your drive is exhibiting the "click of death" (repeated clicking), *don't* try to read disks with backup data in the drive. If the drive has a problem, it could damage your data.

- Check the drive with the Iomega diagnostics software included with the latest versions of IomegaWare (you can download it from `www.iomega.com`). Also check it with Steve Gibson's terrific freeware *Trouble in Paradise* program, available from `http://grc.com/tip/clickdeath.htm`. Use a blank Zip disk or one with out-of-date information to perform these checks.

Trouble in Paradise can tell you immediately if your drive is healthy. If you're experiencing the "click of death," follow the "How can I cure it?" link at the bottom of the `http://grc.com/tip/clickdeath.htm` page to learn how you can request a replacement for your drive and damaged media from Iomega, regardless of how long you've had the drive. Other links on the page provide additional help.

If you have data trapped on a bad Zip disk, Gibson's SpinRite 5 program, an outstanding deep-analysis disk testing program, can recover data in marginal areas of a still-readable Zip, floppy, hard, or other removable-media drives. Get more information and pricing at `http://grc.com`.

You can also use Ontrack's Easy Recovery data recovery programs to locate and retrieve lost data from Zip, hard, or other types of removable-media drives, even if the disk or drive has been formatted or suffered other major damage. Download the free version (which displays the data files that can be recovered) to see if Easy Recovery can help you. Get more information and pricing at `www.ontrack.com/easyrecovery`.

Help! I've just installed my new drive, but I can't get my system to recognize it.

Depending upon the interface and drive type, check the following:

- **Jumpering**—You need to set an IDE drive to master or slave unless you are using the 80-wire cable; the 80-wire cable uses cable select, so both drives must be jumpered to cable select.

- **Patches and drivers**—Tape backup programs might need a bit of software encouragement to recognize a new tape backup model. Check the backup drive maker's web site for a list of supported programs and information about any needed patches.

Help! I've just installed a new tape backup and I can't find the drive letter in Windows Explorer!

Repeat after me, please: A tape backup is *not* a random-access device. Unless the drive includes software that lets the drive emulate a hard disk, it's not going to act like a drive letter.

Help! My tape backup drive is too large for my hard disk. I'm tired of paying big bucks for a tape cartridge that's only partly used. Should I cheap out and put multiple backups on a single cartridge?

No, absolutely not! After all, the reason to have a backup is to keep your data safe. Odd things can happen if you try to put a second backup on a drive. You're better off using smaller cartridges if you can. Note that ADR2.120 can also use ADR.60 cartridges. Buy the cartridge size that matches your actual backup needs. Just make sure the drive has *read and write* compatibility with smaller sizes. Some drives can use only one size of tape for creating backups, although they can read older, smaller sizes for restoring an old backup.

Chapter 12

A Burning Desire for Better Optical Drives

Optical drives rule! Whether you're looking for a fast, low-cost way to back up important information, convert your CD collection into customized mixes with the song sequences you want, or archive old photographs, today's rewriteable optical drives are the perfect solution.

In addition, because the current crop of rewriteable optical drives are faster, cheaper, and more reliable and because they store more than drives available just a couple years ago, it pays to consider replacing an older drive. It also pays to move from the venerable CD-R/RW formats to one of the higher-capacity rewriteable DVD formats.

In this chapter, you learn how to tell when it's time to bid farewell to your old optical drives and when it makes sense to add a new drive type. You also learn how to select the best drive interface and how to install the right optical drive for you.

Ten Reasons You Might Need a New Optical Drive

Even with the tempting array of high-speed, high-capacity rewriteable optical drives on the market, you might not be ready to upgrade yet...or are you? Check out my top-ten list of reasons for installing a new optical drive. If you recognize yourself or your computer, it's time to make a move.

1. You're sick of making data backups with floppy disks.

2. You'd like to watch movies on your computer.

3. Your collection of CD-shaped drink coasters created by buffer underruns is now complete.

4. You want a faster way to create music-mix CDs.

5. Your DVD player is getting tired of playing *The Simpsons* and *Star Trek*.

6. You've created the greatest home movie of all time—and won't be content until all your friends have a copy.

7. There's an empty 5.25-inch drive bay in your computer whispering, "Install something!"

8. It takes your computer more time to burn a CD than it takes to eat breakfast.

9. You're a digital packrat who's run out of ways to save every bit (and byte) you've ever downloaded.

10. You don't want to be the last person on earth without a CD or DVD burner.

Types of Optical Drives and Interfaces

An optical drive works on the same principle as a CD player or DVD player: it reads a single spiral data track that starts at the hub of the media and works its way to the end of the data. The media might contain only a few megabytes of data, or as much as 650MB (original 74 minute CD/CD-R), 700MB (80-minute CD-R), or 4.7GB (DVD). The data is stored in alternating high and low areas called *pits* and *lands*. DVDs use a different frequency laser than CD-ROM, CD-R, and CD-RW drives and can read a narrower track than the other types of optical drives can. Figure 12.1 compares the data tracks of a CD with those of a DVD.

Commercially produced
CD-ROM, music CD, and
DVD movies are pressed
from an original source, and
user-created CD-R, CD-
RW, recordable DVD, and
rewriteable DVD discs are
made with a laser beam
that is powerful enough to

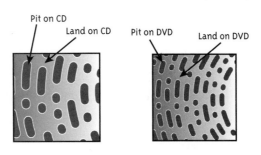

Pit on CD Land on CD Pit on DVD Land on DVD

Figure 12.1

Data on a CD (left)
uses wider data
tracks, more spac-
ing, and larger pits
and lands than data
on a DVD (right).
The DVD can store
more data in the
same-sized media
for this reason.

change the data surface. This process is often called *burning* a CD.

You can still buy and install read-only CD (CD-ROM) and DVD (DVD-ROM) drives, but
with the extra versatility of rewriteable drives available for a relatively small price premium,
you should opt for rewriteable drives. A rewriteable drive can create new data as well as
retrieve user-recorded or commercially recorded data.

The major types of optical drives worth considering include the following:

- CD-RW

- Combo CD-RW/DVD-ROM

- DVD-R/RW

- DVD+R/RW

- DVD-RAM/R

These drives get their names from the type of media with which they work and the tasks
they can perform with that media. ROM stands for read-only memory (contents cannot be
erased), and RW stands for rewriteable (contents can be changed and erased). Thus, a combo
CD-RW/DVD-ROM drive can read, write, and rewrite CD-RW media, but can only read
DVD media.

All drives listed here can read CD-ROM and music CD media, and CD and DVD rewriteable drives can also use low-cost CD-R recordable media. DVD-RAM is also rewriteable,
but works in a different fashion than other types of DVD rewriteable drives and media.

Use the following factors when you evaluate your current optical drives or evaluate possible
upgrades; they can help you determine the best choices for your needs:

- **Interface type**—This determines how you connect the drive to your computer and the speeds you can expect to reach.

- **Speed**—Generally, newer drives are faster than older drives.

- **Buffer underrun protection**—Older rewriteable drives lack this feature, but all current drives offer this option to prevent making useless CD coasters.

- **Media compatibility**—You want to be able to read both pre-recorded and user-recorded CDs.

- **Digital Audio Extraction (DAE)**—Fast speeds put MP3 creation from your own CDs closer than ever before.

ON THE WEB: Optical Drives the TechTV Way!

Looking for TechTV's extensive coverage of rewriteable CD and rewriteable DVD drives? Use our search engine (or use Google's Advanced Search) to look for "rewriteable DVD" or "CD-RW" to find news, reviews, and how-tos.

Where to Plug It in? Interface Types

Until recently, the ATA/IDE interface built into every desktop computer (see Chapter 10, "Adding a Huge Hard Disk," for more information) was the only place to connect an optical drive if you wanted high performance and maximum economy. Now, thankfully, other high-speed interfaces and the proliferation of portable computers that need to use external drives for expansion have made this question a bit more complicated. Or, in other words, you have choices. The leading choices for today's and tomorrow's computers include the following:

- **USB 2.0**—The Hi-Speed USB port, covered in detail in Chapter 19, "Adding the Ports You Need for the Devices You Want," is very versatile, like its USB 1.1 predecessor, and adds speed to that versatility. With a top rate of 480Mbps (about 60MBps), USB 2.0 ports offer theoretical performance similar to the UDMA/66 (66MBps) flavor of ATA/IDE ports (real-world performance is somewhat slower).

- **IEEE-1394a**—This interface (also called FireWire 400 or i.LINK) has a top speed of 400Mbps (50MBps), which is comparable to mid-range SCSI devices and just a tad slower than USB 2.0.

In practical terms, these interfaces have about the same real-world performance. The main reason to choose one or the other should be based on the ports available in your system. Many brand-new systems have USB 2.0 ports, but relatively few include IEEE-1394a ports. However, many vendors of external CD-RW and rewriteable DVD drives support both port types, so you can use either port.

MARK'S TIP SHEET: Back to the Future: Supporting Legacy Systems

Although most external drive vendors have forgotten about older computers, MicroSolutions (www.micro-solutions.com) still offers various models in its Backpack line of external optical drives that support legacy ports as well as USB 2.0. The Model 212010 drive shown in Figure 12.2 includes parallel and PC Card (PCMCIA) interfacing and features CD-RW and DVD-ROM compatibility. They also produce CD-RW and CD-RW/DVD-ROM drives that feature USB 2.0/parallel and USB 2.0/parallel/PC Card interfaces.

Expect a price premium of $100 or more above the price of a comparable ATA/IDE drive if you opt for an external drive. However, if you're planning to share the drive between two or more computers, buying a single external drive is much less expensive than

Figure 12.2

MicroSolutions' Model 212010 includes PC Card, parallel, and USB 2.0 interfaces (lower right). It offers 24x CD read and write, 10x CD-Rewrite, and 8x DVD write. Photo courtesy of MicroSolutions.

buying two or more internal ATA/IDE drives, especially rewriteable DVD models.

The X-Factors: Understanding Optical Drive Speeds

The x-factor is used to rate optical drives' performance. What does it mean? When used with CD-ROM and CD-RW drives, or with DVD drives working with CD-type media, "x" refers to the data transfer rate used for the original 1x CD-ROM drives, which is 150Kbps; music CDs are played at a 1x speed. Read, write, and rewrite operations are multiples of this speed.

For example, a 52x maximum CD-ROM drive is able to transfer data from the CD surface at a maximum of 7,500Kbps (52×150). CD-RW speeds are generally given like so:

Write×Rewrite×Read

Thus, a 52x×32x×52x drive, such as the new PX-Premium drive from Plextor (www.plextor.com), writes to CD-R media at up to 52x (7,500Kbps maximum), rewrites CD-RW media at up to 32x (4,800Kbps maximum), and reads CDs at up to 52x (7,500Kbps maximum).

When used to describe DVD speeds, DVD drive speeds are expressed as a multiple of 11.08Mbps, the speed of a 1x DVD drive. Thus, a 12x DVD drive has a maximum DVD transfer rate of 132.96Mbps (12×11.08). Unlike CD-ROM and CD-RW drives, in which faster disk performance improves real-world usage, faster DVD speeds don't improve the viewing quality of DVD movies. Faster DVD drive speeds do, however, enable you to locate chapters and other bonus content more quickly, and it also translates into faster CD reading/writing speeds.

Note that the speeds given for drives are almost always expressed as maximum (up to) speeds. This is because most drives use a mechanism called *constant angular velocity (CAV)*. Although CAV drives have high-speed ratings such as 40x, 48x, or 52x, the speed rate is misleading. These drives spin the CD at a constant speed, no matter what part of the CD is being read.

What's wrong with that? CDs are recorded from the center outward. Because CDs store much more data on the outer areas of the CD (which is used less often than the inner tracks), the drive actually has a variable speed rate as far as data transfer is concerned. How much of a difference is there? A typical 40x maximum CD-RW drive records or reads the innermost tracks at around 10x! Speed increases gradually as the drive reads or writes to outer tracks, but with so many prerecorded CDs being only half-full, and many users creating a CD that uses less than the full capacity of the media, these drives seldom give you the full benefit of the rated speed. CAV mechanisms are used in most drives with CD read or write rates above 16x.

A very small number of drives use a more expensive mechanism called *Constant Linear Velocity (CLV)*, which varies the speed of the drive to provide more consistent performance across the entire surface of CD media. *Partial-CAV (P-CAV)* drives use a mechanism with characteristics of both CLV and CAV. In the real world, there's not much you can do about drive designs. However, if you see significant benchmark performance differences between drives with similar speed ratings, you might be seeing the impact of different drive mechanisms.

> ### READ THIS TOO: CAV, CLV, and P-CAV Fully Revealed!
>
> Check out Scott Mueller's *Upgrading and Repairing PCs, 15th Edition* (Que, 2003) for more about optical drive mechanisms.

Buffer Underrun Protection

What's a buffer underrun? A buffer underrun happens when a rewriteable CD or DVD drive runs out of data during the recording process. Because optical drive data is recorded in a continuous spiral, any interruption in the recording process ruins the media. You might as well throw it away, play catch with your dog (as shown in a Plextor CD-RW drive ad), or make a drink coaster out of it.

Buffer underruns were a problem ever since the first 2x (37 minutes to record a 650MB CD) CD-R drives were developed. As drive speeds have increased (the fastest CD-RW drives now write to CD-R media at maximum speeds above 50x), buffer underruns have become more of a problem than ever.

In the past, several methods and technologies were tried to keep data flowing to the drive:

- Let your PC run *only* the CD-mastering task, turning off all other processes (even screen savers).

- Create a CD disk image of the information you want to store on a CD and transfer the image to the CD; a CD disk image puts all the files into the same temporary location and organizes them the same way they will be placed on the CD. This option is available with most CD mastering programs.

- Buy a drive with a larger buffer (8MB instead of the more common 2MB).

Although these solutions help prevent some buffer underruns from taking place, they create big losses in convenience. Most people don't want to put the world on hold for 20 minutes or longer to make a CD. Creating a disk image can double the amount of time it takes to make a CD, and increasing buffer size might only delay—and not prevent—a buffer underrun.

The best single reason to replace your old CD-RW drive with a new model, even if you opt for a relatively slow drive (32x or less write speed), is the development of true buffer underrun protection. The first of these was Sanyo's BurnPROOF, first licensed by Plextor. BurnPROOF has lots of company today, as other vendors such as Ricoh (JustLink),

WasteProof and Safeburn (Yamaha), and Superlink (Mediatek) have introduced their own buffer underrun protection technologies.

All CD-RW drives on the market today use some sort of a buffer underrun protection method. They work by suspending disk writing when the drive is out of data and continuing when the drive's data buffer has been refilled. The drive places the writing laser very precisely so the gap between writes is small enough to appear to be a continuous burn.

I use Plextor CD-RW drives with BurnPROOF. Originally, I had a 12x write—10x rewrite—32x read ATA/IDE model. I now use a 40×12×40 ATA/IDE model. I've never made a coaster with either drive, even when performing several disk-intensive jobs at once. In my opinion, it's foolish to use any CD-RW drive that lacks buffer underrun capability, especially with many drives available for well under $100. In addition to extra reliability, you get faster burn performance, faster rewrite performance, and better *Digital Audio Extraction (DAE)* when you replace your old CD-RW drive with a new one.

Media Compatibility

Another reason to look at upgrading your existing optical drive is media compatibility. One of the major reasons for the decline in popularity of high-capacity floppy drives such as the LS-120 and LS-240 SuperDisk drives you learned about in Chapter 11, "Removable Storage to Go," is the rise of a CD technology called CD-RW.

CD-RW media can be rewritten, just as floppies can (although the principle is optical, not magnetic), but the lower reflectivity of CD-RW media prevents older CD-ROM or CD-R drives from reading CD-RW disks. Optical drives had to be redesigned to handle CD-RW media, and such drives are called *MultiRead* drives. Because more and more people are using CD-RW media in place of CD-R media to distribute information to other users, it makes sense to have an optical drive that can read any type of CD media.

How can you tell if you already have MultiRead capability? Generally, MultiRead drives run at 24x or faster and usually have a MultiRead logo or MultiRead-compatible sticker or marking on the front of the drive.

JARGON

MultiRead—Term used to denote CD-ROM drives that can read CD-RW media as well as normal CD-R, CD-ROM, and music CD media.

MultiRead2—Term used to denote DVD-ROM drives that can read CD-RW and DVD-RAM media as well as normal DVD-Video, DVD-Audio, CD-R, CD-ROM, and music CD-media.

Even if you already have a MultiRead CD-ROM drive or a CD-RW drive, you're missing out on DVD content (movies and multimedia productions) unless you also have a DVD-ROM drive. Instead of using two drive bays (one for CD-RW and one for DVD-ROM), for about $100 to $130, you can buy a combo CD-RW/DVD-ROM drive for your desktop computer. Pop the popcorn—it's time for PC Movie Night!

Have a Better DAE with Faster Digital Audio Extraction

DAE is the latest benefit of recent optical drives. DAE is a feature prized by people who create their own MP3-based mix CDs from their personal music collection (a process called *ripping*). In the early days of MP3 rip-

> **JARGON**
>
> *Digital Audio Extraction (DAE)*—High-speed digital extraction of CD audio music tracks; a faster DAE rate enables you to create MP3 or Windows Media Audio (WMA) digital music files more quickly from your own CDs.

ping, tracks had to be extracted at the normal CD read speed of 1x for music. In other words, it would take three minutes to read a three-minute song you wanted to convert into MP3 format. If you wanted to convert a 70-minute album into MP3 format, you needed an hour and ten minutes. Ouch!

Optical drives featuring DAE enable music tracks to be read digitally at higher speeds and with more accuracy. Although most recent CD-RW drives feature high-speed DAE, if you want to read several tracks from your own CD and transfer them immediately to a CD-RW, it's handier to have a CD-ROM or DVD drive with a high DAE rating instead of flipping the music CD in and out of the CD-RW drive.

If you're tired of KaZaa and other music file-trading software dumping loads of spyware on your computer, optical drives with fast DAE ratings take a lot of the pain out of creating MP3 files yourself.

Now that you understand the basic technology behind optical drives, it's time to determine whether you need to upgrade or add a new drive to your system.

ON THE WEB: No DAE Rating? No Problem!

Although DAE capability has been around for awhile, it isn't always easy to find out how quickly or how well a particular optical drive can perform DAE. If your drive vendor doesn't list a DAE speed for your model or you're wondering which drives have the fastest and most accurate DAE performance, check out Erik Deppe's CD Speed 2000 web site at `www.cdspeed2000.com`.

This site provides data-read, DAE extraction speed, and DAE quality test results for over hundreds of drives. Don't see your drive listed? You can also download a copy of CD Speed so that you can do your own benchmark and media tests and read useful tips on CD recording.

Reading the Riot Act to Read-Only Drives

Back when rewriteable CD drives cost hundreds of dollars, it made sense to install less expensive CD-ROM or DVD-ROM drives. Although you can still buy both CD-ROM and DVD-ROM drives, I recommend skipping them in favor of their rewriteable siblings, even if you already have a rewriteable drive. Here's why:

- You can buy advanced CD recording software that can record to two or more drives at the same time.

- Rewriteable drives generally have faster and better DAE than read-only drives, improving MP3 creation speed and quality.

- You can purchase a single drive that incorporates DVD reading or DVD recording/rewriting, as well as full CD-RW rewrite capabilities.

Because of the huge speed improvements in read, write, and rewrite rate with late-model rewriteable CD and DVD drives alike, there's no longer any discernable benefit to using a read-only drive. Leave them on the shelf and move on.

ON THE WEB: Burn Two (or More) at One Time!

Want to make the most of multiple rewriteable drives? Check out programs like these:

- **Disc Juggler**—Padus, Inc (www.padus.com); Disc Juggler Professional adds support for rewriteable DVD drives and burning over networks.

- **Nero Burning Rom 5.5 or higher**—Ahead Software (www.nero.com); standard version supports up to two drives; optional extra-cost plug-ins available to support up to seven or up to 32 drives depending upon version.

- **RecordNow Max! 4.0 or higher**—Stomp, Inc (www.stompinc.com); developed by Veritas Software and supports up to 64 recorders. Sold separately or as part of the RecordNow Max Platinum suite.

Discover the results of TechTV's experiments with multiple-drive mastering. Read Yoshi DeHerrera's "Burn Multiple CDs on a PC" at www.techtv.com/screensavers/answerstips/story/0,24330,3325099,00.html.

Rewriting the CD Way

CD-RW drives are becoming one of the most sought-after storage upgrades on the market today. They're so important to computer use that if you don't have one already, it's high time you got one! As you have already learned, it might also be time to move up to a faster model.

A CD-RW drive is a development from the CD-R drives of the late 1990s. CD-R drives were the first popularly-priced drives able to write to special CDs that contained a recordable layer made from various types of colored dyes. The data areas of pressed CDs look silver; the data areas of CD-Rs appear blue, gold, green, or other colors because of the dye layer.

CD-Rs can be written to in either a single session or in multiple sessions, enabling you to add content to the CD until you fill it up. A CD-RW drive differs from a CD-R drive in that it has the ability to use both CD-R media (which can be added to but not deleted) and CD-RW media, which can be changed, erased, and rewritten up to 1,000 times.

From Backups for Pennies to Making Your Own CDs

Because CD-RW drives give you the ability to make your own CDs, the possibilities they offer are almost endless:

- Use DAE to extract music tracks from your own CDs and make MP3 mix CDs you can play on your computer.

- Combine music tracks from your favorite albums into a single "Best of Me" album you can play on car or home stereo systems.

- Convert older music sources in your library, such as cassette, 8-track, and vinyl, to CD for personal use.

- Archive photos of all types and create self-running slide shows and digital photo albums.

- Store compressed backups of your hard disk or make duplicate copies of the day's work.

- Create business-card sized presentations on smaller CD media that can be self-contained or combined with web-based content.

You get the idea. If you have room for only one optical drive in your system, make sure it has CD-RW capabilities.

CAUTION: STOP! LOOK! THINK!

Don't Burn a Bunch of Music CDs Without Testing the Media
Although the latest auto and portable stereo systems are designed to read both CD-R and CD-RW media, older audio systems aren't designed to work with CD-RW media (it has lower reflectivity than CD-R or pressed CD media), and they could also have problems with CD-R media. Before you create a huge stack of music-mix CDs for use on non-computer CD players, better make just one first with your favorite brand of CD-R media and try it on your different CD players. If you have problems with a particular type of media, try a different brand with a different type of dye.

CD-RW Versus CD-R—Which Media Is Best?

A CD-RW drive can use either CD-R or CD-RW media. It's important to choose the right media, and that depends on the recording tasks you have to perform.

Use CD-R media for the following jobs:

- Full system backups

- Sending media to others when you don't know what type of drive they are using

- Creating music CDs for older car audio players and stereo systems

Use CD-RW media for these jobs:

- Making temporary backups of selected files

- Sending files to others who also have CD-RW drives and will return the media with changes

- Creating temporary music mixes for CD-RW compatible car audio players and stereo systems

The bottom line? Use CD-R when you want compatibility with virtually any CD-ROM or music CD device; use CD-RW for data you will change and when the receivers also have a compatible drive. When in doubt, use CD-R.

Mastering Software Versus Packet-Writing Software

There are two ways to send files to a CD-RW, DVD-RW, or DVD+RW rewriteable drive:

- Mastering software such as Nero and Easy CD/DVD Creator

- Packet-writing software such as DirectCD, inCD, or Drag and Drop

What's the difference? Mastering software requires more effort on your part because you must open up a special program, drag files and folders into a layout window, and then start the recording process. Packet-writing software enables you to treat a rewriteable drive as a big floppy: you drag and drop files using the Windows Explorer to the CD media instead of taking time to create a CD layout; packet writing uses the Universal Disk Format (UDF) standard, version 1.5. Packet-writing was originally designed to support rewriteable CD and DVD media, but some packet-writing programs, such as Roxio's DirectCD and Drag and Drop, can also write to CD-R media.

At first glance, it would seem that packet writing is a whole lot easier than using mastering software. Up to a point, that's true. However, packet-written CDs can be read only by other systems that are running Windows, unless you change the disk format when you close the packet-writing session. Also, the other computer must have a UDF-compatible reading program, such as Adaptec's DirectCD reader. For example, when you create a packet-written CD with Adaptec's DirectCD, DirectCD puts a copy of the DirectCD Reader program on the CD-RW media to enable other Windows-based computers to read the media. Note that because of differences in the way that packet-writing programs work, you might need to install more than one reader program on a PC that works with media created by more than one packet-writing program.

CAUTION: STOP! LOOK! THINK!

Ejecting the Media the Right Way
The safest way to eject packet-written media is
with the right-click Eject option in Windows
Explorer. In some cases, you need to follow
onscreen prompts to make the CD readable on
other systems.

If you create a CD to be used on both Windows and other systems such as Macs, Linux, or MS-DOS, you should use the mastering software included with your drive and create the appropriate multiplatform layout called ISO 9660. Mastering software also gives you more control over the CD you create and typically lets you run the full speed of your high-speed drive.

The short take? Use packet writing to make quick backup copies for yourself, but if the CD is going somewhere else, take time to use the mastering software so that the receiver can read it reliably.

Rewriting the DVD Way

If you love the rewritability of CD-RW drives, but wish they held more information, your wish has been granted. In fact, there are three different rewriteable DVD standards from which to choose, all of which hold at least 4.7GB of data (equal to about two hours of DVD movie-quality video):

- **DVD-RAM**—The oldest and most durable (100,000 rewrite cycle) CD rewriteable standard, but not compatible with set-top DVD players or most DVD-ROM drives. No special drivers are required for drag-and-drop file copying or selective erasure. Some recent models also use DVD-R recordable media and a few can also support CD-R/RW media. DVD-RAM media is also available in double-sided varieties, which can hold 9.4GB (4.7GB per side).

- **DVD-RW**—The first to reach 4x DVD writing speeds, but media contents can't be modified without a full erasure. It is compatible with many, but not all, set-top DVD players and most DVD-ROM drives. All DVD-RW models also use DVD-R recordable media and can also support CD-R/RW media.

- **DVD+RW**—Also similar to CD-RW, but unlike DVD-RW, DVD+RW supports selective erasure and editing of contents. DVD+RW media can be formatted in just a few seconds, unlike first-generation DVD-RW media. It is compatible with many, but not all, set-top DVD players and most DVD-ROM drives. First-generation DVD+RW drives could not use DVD+R recordable media, but all current drives do. The latest models also support 4x DVD writing speeds. All DVD+RW drives also support CD-R/RW media.

Confused yet? Me too. There are two industry groups that create and support DVD recordable/rewriteable standards. The DVD Forum created and manages DVD-RW, DVD-R, and DVD-RAM standards, while a second group called the DVD+RW Alliance created and manages the DVD+RW and DVD+R standards.

ON THE WEB: Get Your DVD Standards Here!

Check out the DVD Forum at www.dvdforum.org.

The DVD+RW Alliance is online at www.dvdrw.com.

Why I Prefer DVD+RW Drives

Which standard do I recommend? My PC has an HP 200i DVD+RW/R drive installed. I use it just like an overgrown CD-RW, which I couldn't do with DVD-RW. It takes me just a minute or so to format a blank DVD+RW disc for drag and drop (CD-RW drives can take 25 minutes or longer, while first-generation DVD-RW drives took about an hour). I can drag and drop files to a DVD+RW disc at any time using the same DirectCD software I use with my Plextor CD-RW drive. I can also delete any files I choose any time I want.

If I used one of the latest second-generation DVD-RW drives instead, I would enjoy formatting times comparable to the minute or two it takes to format a DVD+RW disc. Unfortunately, that's where the similarities end. I would need to unfinalize a DVD-RW disc to add additional contents to it, and edits to content already on the disc would require me to copy the contents of the media to hard disk, erase the disc, and copy back the changes. Although in some cases DVD-RW and DVD-R media are more compatible with older DVD players, most of the latest DVD players can work with either format.

Solutions to the DVD Format Wars

Although some writers have referred to the DVD format wars as the equivalent of the VHS-Betamax war of the 1970s and 1980s, this comparison is overblown. VHS and Betamax used fundamentally different tape sizes and cartridge designs, making cross-compatibility impossible. Fortunately, DVD drives all support DVD-ROM media, making cross-compatibility possible.

There are now increasing numbers of rewriteable DVD drives that can handle the many different flavors of DVD media. Sony pioneered the trend with its Dual RW series of DVD±R/RW drives. These drives work with DVD+R/RW, DVD-R/RW, and CD-R/RW media. Sony offers internal ATA/IDE and external IEEE-1394a (i.Link)/USB 2.0 models. Hitachi/LG offers a drive to OEM customers that supports the same media types as the Sony Dual RW series and also supports DVD-RAM; look for this drive to appear under a variety of brand names. LG also produces a DVD-R/RW/RAM drive called the GMA-4020B Super-Multi. Drives like these can help you meet the challenges of sharing your DVD creations with others.

ON THE WEB: Keeping on Top of the Latest DVD News

Learn more about Sony's DR series of DVD±R/RW drives at www.storagebysony.com.

Track the latest news about DVD rewriteable drives, standards, and software at these sites:

- www.DVDplusRW.org (DVD+RW news and utilities)

- www.dvd-cd-r.com (new products for DVD-R/RW and CD-R/RW formats)

- www.cdrwcentral.com (reviews and news about rewriteable CD and DVD drives)

- www.cdrlabs.com (reviews and news about rewriteable CD and DVD drives)

Combo Drives

If your heart says "DVD," but your budget says "CD-RW," a CD-RW/DVD-ROM combo drive might be just the ticket for your next optical drive. Combo drives are extremely popular in notebook computers, enabling busy business travelers to sneak in a DVD movie between meetings and save their valuable documents at meetings. They're also available for around $100 to $130 or so for desktop computers.

Although early desktop combo drives required a big sacrifice in CD write and rewrite speeds, the latest models can read CDs and record CD-R media at 48x speeds and rewrite CD-RW media at 24x speeds. These speeds are just a bit slower than the fastest CD-RW drives without DVD compatibility.

Even if you already have a rewriteable DVD drive, a combo drive makes a good second drive for a couple of reasons:

- You can use it to read DVD media you want to back up with your rewriteable DVD drive.

- A high-speed combo drive often offers faster CD-R/RW writing/rewriting speeds than some rewriteable DVD drives.

Choosing the Best Optical Drive for You

Which drive is the best for you? Even after you decide whether you want CD-RW, some type of rewriteable DVD, or a combo CD-RW/DVD-ROM drive, it's still not an easy question. To narrow down your choices, use the following checklist:

- Are you replacing an existing drive, or adding a new drive?
- Do you want to share the drive with another computer?
- What media type(s) do you need to support?
- What types of data do you want to create?
- What CD/DVD creation software do you prefer?

Replacement Versus Additional Drive

If you're replacing an existing optical drive, you should buy the same form factor/interface as your current drive. In most cases, you're going to be replacing an ATAPI (ATA/IDE interface) drive, so you need an ATAPI drive as a replacement. ATAPI (ATA/IDE) drives provide the widest choice of brands and models and the lowest cost.

If you're adding a drive, you can use ATAPI, or you could consider USB 2.0 or IEEE-1394a drives for more flexibility. See Chapter 19 for details about these port types and how to add them to your system.

Sharing the Drive

You can't share an ATAPI drive with another computer except through a network connection. Unless you plan to use a specialized CD/DVD creation program such as DiscJuggler, this won't work as a viable way to make CDs or DVDs. Instead, look at drives with USB 2.0 or IEEE-1394a interfaces. These drives cost more because of the enclosure, the power supply, and more expensive cabling, but they make sharing very simple.

Media Types to Play Back

If you want to view DVD-based content, you need to choose a drive with DVD-ROM and DVD-Video capability, such as a rewriteable DVD or a combo CD-RW/DVD-ROM drive. If you aren't concerned about DVD capabilities, any decent CD-RW drive will work.

CAUTION: STOP! LOOK! THINK!

Make Sure You Have the Right Stuff for DVD Moviemaking

Most DVD-ROM, combo CD-RW/DVD-ROM, and rewriteable DVD drives include a DVD player program so that you can watch movies on your computer. With a 1GHz or faster processor, playback is as smooth as if you were using one of the DVD decoder cards that were common a few years ago. However, if you buy a lower-cost OEM drive instead of a retail-box drive, the decoder software might not be included.

If you didn't receive DVD playback software with your drive, it's not a big deal if you already have DVD playback software included with your video card, as many recent cards do. However, if you don't have a DVD playback program of some kind, you need to buy one.

Similarly, if you are buying a rewriteable DVD drive, make sure it has video-editing software if you're planning to use it to create or edit digital movies. Retail-box drives usually include this, but an OEM drive might not. Check to be safe instead of sorry. In addition, don't forget that you need an IEEE-1394 port to get digital video from a DV camcorder and a video capture device to grab analog video from existing videotapes (Dazzle makes several nice models; see their web site at www.dazzle.com).

For best sound quality, consider upgrading your playback software to support Dolby Digital sound if your sound card and speaker array support 5.1 or better configurations. See Chapter 15, "Digital Imaging and Video," for details.

Data You Plan to Create

Both CD-RW and DVD rewriteable drives offer huge possibilities for the creative computer user. Whether you're interested in music, photography, graphics, or video, these drives can help you archive, edit, and share your work—if you have the software you need for the job.

When you evaluate the drives that have the interface and media compatibility you like, don't forget to consider the bundled software. An inadequate software bundle limits your potential until you purchase upgrades or replacements.

What types of software are included with drives? The following list is a compilation of typical software titles included with leading drives. Check this list against the specific software bundles provided with a specific drive.

CD and DVD drives typically include the following:

- Basic CD (DVD) mastering software, such as Nero Express, Roxio Easy CD/DVD Creator Basic, Veritas Record Now, and others.
- Drag-and-drop file copying software for CD-RW and rewriteable DVD media, such as Nero InCD, DirectCD, Drag and Drop, DLA (Drive Letter Access), and others.

Some might also include the following:

- MP3 ripping software, such as Music Match Jukebox.
- Backup software, such as Dantz Retrospect Express or Simple Backup (a Veritas product relabeled by various vendors).

DVD drives also typically include the following:

- DVD video creation software, such as Sonic MyDVD, ArcSoft ShowBiz DVD, DVD Movie Factory, Pinnacle Studio, and others.
- DVD playback software, such as CyberLink PowerDVD, Sonic CinePlayer, and others.

Keep in mind that most bundled software lacks the full set of features available with a separately purchased version of the software. Upgrade pricing might be available to get the full packages.

Your Preferred CD/DVD Creation Software

If your next rewriteable drive isn't your first model, chances are you already have a preference for a particular program's features and user interface. Do you need to switch to the bundled software to use your drive?

The answer is "maybe not." If you purchase a drive that's been on the market for a few months, odds are pretty good that your software vendor has created an update to support your newly purchased drive. Unlike floppy and hard drives, which are supported by the operating system, rewriteable drives require special software to work and use different write and rewrite commands so that software patches are necessary to support new drives as they are developed. Check the vendor's web site to download the updates needed.

The story's different if you can't wait to be the first kid on the block with a brand-new CD-RW or rewriteable CD drive model. Unless your vendor has worked closely with major third-party software vendors to support that new drive from day one, you might have to wait for awhile to use your old software with your new drive.

Even if your preferred software already supports your new drive, give the software bundle provided with your new drive a try. At the very least, it might introduce you to some new uses, and in some cases, certain drive utilities are provided only through the drive vendor's software bundle. After you work your way through the checklist, it's time to install the drive you prefer and get burning!

Installing an Internal Optical Drive

The process of installing an internal optical drive includes the following steps:

1. Finding a drive bay to use for your new drive.

2. Inserting the drive into the drive bay.

3. Connecting the drive to your sound hardware.

4. Installing the vendor's software bundle.

Making Sure You Have Room for Your New Drive

Internally mounted optical drives must use a 5.25-inch drive bay. The drive bay needs to have a removable panel to enable the optical drive's tray or slot-loading mechanism to receive media. Figure 12.3 shows empty and full 5.25-inch drive bays in a typical system.

Figure 12.3

An empty 5.25-inch drive bay is ready for an optical drive.

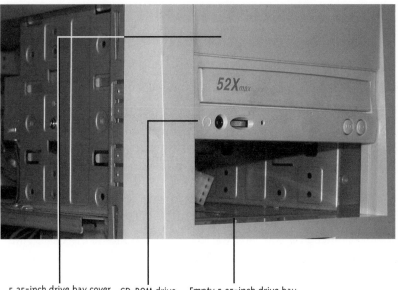

5.25-inch drive bay cover   CD-ROM drive   Empty 5.25-inch drive bay

MARK'S TIP SHEET: Make Room with the Drive Bay Shuffle

If you can't find an available drive bay to use for your new optical drive, see if you can move a drive located in an external bay to an internal bay to free up space. For example, if one of the 5.25-inch drive bays shown in Figure 12.3 contained a 3.5-inch hard drive, it could be moved to a 3.5-inch bay. If you can't come up with an available drive bay (a big possibility if you upgrade a low-cost microtower or slimline system), install the most versatile drive you can, or choose an external drive instead.

Configuring Drive Jumpers

An ATAPI optical drive, like any other ATA/IDE device, has a three-position jumper:

- Master
- Slave
- Cable Select

Although new ATA/IDE hard drive installations use the 80-wire cable discussed in Chapter 10 and as a consequence use Cable Select for both drives, most optical drives are shipped with the older 40-wire cable that supports master and slave jumpers.

Here's how to configure these jumpers (refer to Figure 12.4):

- Only drive on the cable: Master
- Adding the drive to an existing drive already plugged into the cable: Slave

The drive jumper block is very small and hard to reach after the drive is installed, so you should configure the drive jumper before you slide the drive into the drive bay.

MARK'S TIP SHEET: 80-Wire Cables Work for Optical Drives, Too!

Although optical drives usually support UltraATA/33 speeds (which is why a 40-wire cable is sufficient), there is no reason you can't use an 80-wire cable if you have one. Just keep in mind that 80-wire cables are sometimes shorter than 40-wire cables, so you should make sure that the cable can reach from the drives to the ATA/IDE connector on the motherboard. If you use the 80-wire UDMA/66 cable, be sure to set the jumper on each drive connected to the cable as Cable Select.

Connecting Cables to the Optical Drive

Although you might be able to connect cables to the optical drive after it's installed, it's usually easier to connect the audio cables to the drive before you install it. In addition, if the optical drive doesn't share the ATA/IDE data cable with another drive, you should connect it first as well. If you have an unused power connector, connect it to the drive after you install it. However, if you need to share an existing power connector to support two devices, attach the Y-splitter to the rear of the drive before installing it.

Figure 12.4 shows the rear of a typical ATAPI optical drive before and after audio, data, and power cables are installed.

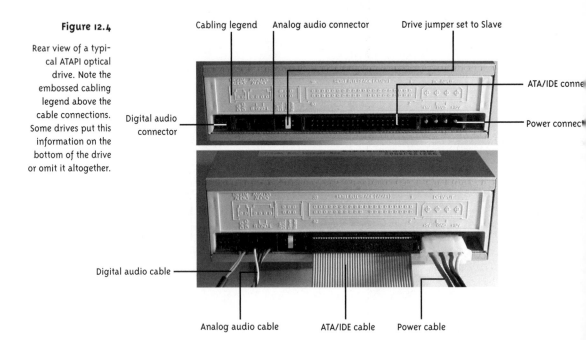

Figure 12.4

Rear view of a typical ATAPI optical drive. Note the embossed cabling legend above the cable connections. Some drives put this information on the bottom of the drive or omit it altogether.

Cabling legend   Analog audio connector   Drive jumper set to Slave

Digital audio connector

ATA/IDE conne

Power connect

Digital audio cable

Analog audio cable   ATA/IDE cable   Power cable

Installing the Drive into a Drive Bay

After removing the drive bay cover as shown in Figure 12.3 and attaching the cables as
shown in Figure 12.4, you can slide the drive into the drive bay. After the drive has been
installed, secure it in place. Although a few systems require you to attach rails to the drive
before you install it (see Figure 12.5), most systems use screws supplied with the drive to
secure it in place (see Figure 12.6).

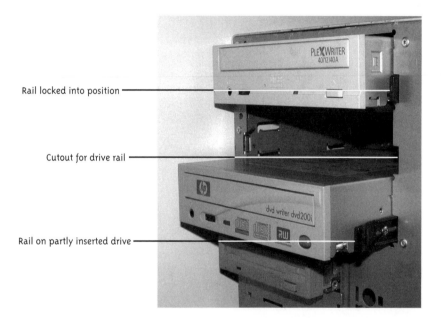

Rail locked into position

Cutout for drive rail

Rail on partly inserted drive

Figure 12.5

Inserting an HP
DVD200i drive (bot-
tom) into a drive
bay that uses rails.
The Plexwriter
40/12/40A drive
(top) is locked into
position.

Screw holding
existing CD-ROM
drive in position

Screwdriver

Figure 12.6

Inserting an HP
DVD200i drive into a
drive bay that uses
screws to secure
the drive.

Connecting the Optical Drive to Your Sound Hardware

Virtually all sound cards (and motherboards with built-in sound) can accept the four-pin analog connector and enable you to hear CD music though the speakers or headphone jacks attached to your sound card. For better quality, use the digital connector between the optical drive and sound card or motherboard if both are so equipped. You can also connect one optical drive to the analog jack and another to the digital jack on your sound card if you have two drives you want to use for CD music. Figure 12.7 shows you how the four-pin analog cable and two-pin SPDIF digital cable connect between the optical drive and the sound card.

Figure 12.7

Analog and digital cabling between a typical optical drive and sound card.

Digital sound cable

Analog sound cable

Analog output (CD In) on sound card

Digital input (CD SPDIF) on sound card

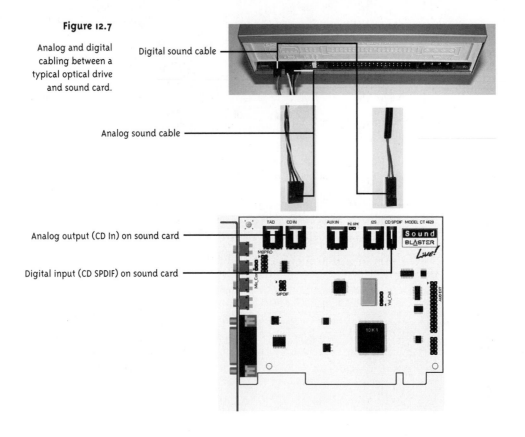

Install or Update Your CD/DVD Writing Software

Without software, your rewriteable CD or DVD drive is just an overpriced CD-ROM or DVD-ROM drive. If you are installing your first rewriteable drive, you must install the software supplied with the drive (or compatible third-party software) before you can use the drive's writing features with most versions of Windows.

Windows XP has very limited CD-creation features, and they pale in comparison to even the most limited CD-mastering or packet-writing program supplied with a rewriteable drive.

If you already have CD or DVD mastering and packet-writing software installed, check the vendor's web site to see if your new drive is supported. Install any patches needed to support your drive.

Installing an External Optical Drive

Single-connector external drives are installed like any other device using the same connector:

1. Connect the drive.
2. When the drive is detected by the system, install the drivers (unless directed otherwise for a particular device).

If the external drive has multiple connectors (such as the MicroSolutions BackPack drive shown earlier in Figure 12.2), make sure you use an interface supported by the operating system used on the computer. See Table 12.1 for information about external ports used by optical drives. Note that you should *never* move any external drive while it's operating.

Table 12.1	External Port Support by Operating System					
Port Type	Windows NT 4.0	Windows 95	Windows 98	Windows Me	Windows 2000	Windows XP
Parallel	Yes	Yes	Yes	Yes	Yes	Yes
USB	No	No*	Yes	Yes	Yes	Yes
PC Card	Yes	Yes	Yes	Yes	Yes	Yes
IEEE-1394	No	No	Yes	Yes	Yes	Yes

* Although some late versions of Windows 95 OSR 2.x include USB support or can use add-on USB drivers, most USB devices require Windows 98 or above. Consult the device manufacturer for details.

ANALYZE THIS

How External Optical Drives Play Your CDs

You can use an external optical drive to play your music CDs, even though it doesn't use the two-wire or four-wire patch cables shown in Figure 12.7. Here's how it works:

- You must use a program, such as Windows Media Player, that can digitize music CDs, or you must use an application bundled with your sound card.

- When you start to play the CD, there's a short delay while the program converts the data into digital form for playback.

After the drive is connected to the computer and has been recognized, install the software supplied with the drive unless you already use compatible software. See the "Install or Update Your CD/DVD Writing Software" section earlier in this chapter for more details.

Troubleshooting Optical Drives

Optical drives are no longer a gadget; they're a necessity...and we computer geeks need our necessities. If your optical necessity has rendered itself useless, check this section for solutions and get back to work (or play).

Help! I'm trying to install my new IDE/ATA CD-RW drive and I'm out of places to connect it!

This can easily happen when you have a couple of IDE drives, a CD-ROM or DVD-ROM drive, and an IDE ZIP or LS-120 drive already installed. You have these options:

- Install a secondary IDE host adapter card in an empty PCI slot. It has two IDE host adapter connections on board, enabling you to run your new CD-RW drive plus three more drives.

- Replace your current CD-ROM or DVD-ROM drive with the CD-RW/DVD-ROM optical drive or a rewriteable DVD drive. However, you're really better off with two (one from which to read originals and the second for copying the originals for safe-keeping).

Help! I've installed a high-speed IDE/ATA CD-RW drive and my write speeds are pathetic! I feel like I've been ripped off!

Make sure the following settings are correct. They can help you get maximum speed from your CD-RW drive:

- You need to have the bus-mastering drivers for your IDE host adapter correctly installed. Go to your motherboard vendor's web site and download the appropriate bus-mastering driver and the installation instructions.

- You also need to enable DMA for your CD-RW drive; do it for your CD-ROM drive as well to improve its read performance. Use the Settings tab in the Device Manager properties sheet for the drive.

Figure 12.8 displays typical Device Manager screens after IDE bus-mastering drivers are installed and DMA is enabled for the drive. If you see a yellow ! sign next to your IDE host adapter, you need to install the correct drivers.

Bus-mastering controller
listing in Device Manager

DMA enabled on CD-RW
drive's Settings properties sheet

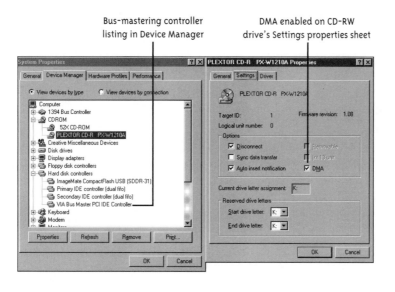

Figure 12.8

The left window displays IDE host adapters after the VIA bus-mastering drivers have been installed; the right window shows the DMA setting for IDE CD-ROM and similar optical drives.

The drive might also be optimized for a different type of media than what you're using. For details, see the following section.

Help! The store ran out of my favorite brand of CD-R media, and my write speeds have plummeted with the new brand. Any ideas?

CD-RW and rewriteable DVD drives can be very picky about the types of CD-R media they use. Many drives are optimized for particular dye colors and speeds. For best results, follow these suggestions:

- Follow your drive vendor's recommendations for media brands and speeds. Although a lot of media on the market now is designed to run at 40x or faster recording speeds, some low-cost brands or old inventory might be approved for slower speeds. If your recorder is designed to evaluate the media and adjust its write speed accordingly (a feature called SafeBurn, Intelligent Burn, PowerRec, and so on), using unapproved or slow-spec media is sure to slow down your recording times.

- Check your drive vendor's web site for a firmware upgrade for your drive. My Plextor 40x drive would record at only 13x maximum with some media types before I installed the latest firmware; after the firmware upgrade, I hit speeds above 40x!

Help! My external drive isn't being recognized by Windows!

There are a bunch of possible causes for this problem. Let's look at a few of the most likely causes, broken down by interface:

- **SCSI**—Drive not powered up before starting system, incorrect (conflicting) device ID, incorrect termination of daisy-chain, or cabling problems.

  Keep in mind that if the new drive is the last drive in the SCSI daisy-chain, the termination must be turned off for the device to which the drive is attached and turned on for the drive (because it's now the last device). Cabling problems don't necessarily mean loose or damaged cables. The 25-pin SCSI cable used by some low-cost SCSI devices (such as my Zip SCSI drive) does not do an adequate job of passing signals through to other devices if it's used before my scanners in the daisy-chain. So, I always place this drive at the end of the SCSI daisy-chain.

- **USB**—Incorrect operating system, port not enabled, device pulls too much power to be used with a bus-powered hub, or loose cables.

  Review the USB setup and troubleshooting tips in Chapter 19. Remember that if you insist on using a so-called USB-enabled version of Windows 95, a lot of devices aren't going to cooperate. It's time to upgrade to Windows XP already!

- **IEEE-1394**—Incorrect operating system, loose cables, or host adapter not powered up.

Review the IEEE-1394 setup and troubleshooting tips in Chapter 19. If you just installed the IEEE-1394 host adapter, use the Device Manager to be sure it's working properly.

- **PC Card**—PC Card not plugged into socket all the way, no Card and Socket Services loaded, or can't use CardBus device in normal PC Card socket.

  Drives with PC Card adapters work in either PC Card or CardBus-enabled slots. However, USB and IEEE-1394 PC Cards require CardBus slots to work.

Remember that if you're using a drive with multiple interfaces, make sure you've *tightly* attached the interface to the drive and to your PC.

Help! I can't hear any music through my optical drive when I use the Digital CD (SPDIF) cable!

You need to make sure your sound card mixer control is set up to handle this signal. Open the volume control (in Control Panel or the system tray) and make sure that SPDIF-IN or Digital CD is listed and that the volume is turned to an acceptable level (it might even be muted). Also, make sure you have connected the cable properly at both ends; if you have pin 1 talking to pin 2 because the cable was twisted, it won't work.

Help! I left my rewriteable CD or DVD disc in my notebook computer, and now I can't save anything to it!

Portable computers are notorious for running hot—very hot. (I'm glad they're not called laptop computers anymore, because I'm not sure my lap could stand the heat!) Excessive heat can cause rewriteable CD or DVD media to malfunction (temporarily). My advice? Insert the disc, read the disc's contents, eject the disc so that it stays cool, and insert the disc again only when you need to re-read it or drag and drop data to it.

Fortunately, desktop computers and drives typically don't have this problem. To help keep your notebook computer cool, try the following tips:

- Check the computer vendor's web site for firmware or driver upgrades. An updated BIOS or keyboard controller driver update could improve power management and system cooling.

- Use an auxiliary cooling device that fits beneath the notebook computer. Most models use fans that plug into the computer's USB or PS/2 port for power, but a few use passive cooling technologies. Coolers are available from various vendors, including Bytecc (www.byteccusa.com), Nexus Technology (www.nexustek.nl), and Zerus (www.zerus.com).

Help! I turned off my computer with an optical disc in the drive, and now I can't eject the media!

Most optical drives have a small hole in the front cover, which is for the "universal emergency optical disc ejection device." If you didn't get one of these with your drive, don't worry: You probably know it better as a jumbo paper clip.

Straighten out the paper clip and push it through the hole. Push hard, and the optical drive's tray is ejected so you can get to your media. Note that if you use a slot-loading drive that you must restart the computer and use the eject button on the drive.

Keep in mind that you can also open Windows Explorer, right-click on the drive, and select Eject if the other methods listed here don't work.

Part IV

Upgrading for Better Multimedia

Chapter 13

Extra Vroom with Faster Graphics and Bigger Displays

Whether your computer is so new that you still have the packing boxes stashed in your den or it's been around long enough that some of the manuals have run off with your missing socks, a graphics and display upgrade could be one of the single best investments you can make in your system.

A new video card can deliver better 3D gaming performance and better speed for all applications. It also can provide features such as a TV-out port, video capture, support for pure digital LCD panels, and, if you have the desk space, support for a second monitor. Although these features have been around for awhile, system manufacturers often install low-end cards with outdated 3D chipsets that also lack support for advanced monitor features such as dual displays.

Ever since I switched to a dual-monitor/one-card setup in my office, my productivity has soared. Even if you don't do any *work* at home, a dual-display setup can do wonders for relaxation at the keyboard. You can surf twice as many web sites at one time, play a game and keep an eye on your email at the same time, and have more chat windows open at one time with more desktop space when you use two monitors. Whether you have room for just one monitor or are making the move to dual displays, today's monitors have larger displays, higher resolution, and better screen clarity than ever before.

It's a great time to upgrade your display and video card, and in this chapter, you learn how to upgrade both components as well as select the best combination of features for your needs. This chapter also helps you discover which computers block your move to better video and what you can do about them.

Ten Reasons to Upgrade Your Graphics and Display

Upgrading your graphics card requires a bit more work than other upgrades; after all, you need to make sure your system has an Accelerated Graphics Port (AGP) connector that supports the card of your dreams before you buy it. In addition, bringing home a big display can be a bit of trouble, especially if you have a small car. (The only way I was able to manage to squeeze my 19-inch monitor into my Ford Escort was to take it out of the box!) So, it might be tempting to skip these upgrades. However, if you find yourself nodding in familiarity as you read my top-ten list of reasons to upgrade, it's time to take the plunge.

1. You're tired of your current video's card support for high speed with low visual quality or low speed with high visual quality.

2. You already have a dual-display video card with nothing connected to the second display.

3. Whenever the kids use the computer, your monitor's so small that when they crank up the resolution the icons seem to disappear.

4. You bought a new digital LCD, but you need to use a clunky digital-to-analog adapter to plug it into your current graphics card.

5. Your monitor's highest resolution setting is so fuzzy you can't use it.

6. You'd like to have some room on your desk for something besides the monitor.

7. Your monitor is so dark when you play some DVDs that you're still not sure how the movie ended.

8. Your monitor is so dark when you play some games that you're always losing to the sniper/ninja/spy in the corner.

9. You're tired of slow frame rates that make your 3D game look like a cheaply made cartoon.

10. Your monitor's so small that when you watch a DVD, you have more letterbox border than movie.

Displays and Graphics 101

So, you're looking to upgrade your computer and you've realized that your trusty basic beige (or trendy black) sidekick spends a lot of time drawing pictures on the screen. Presto! You've discovered one of the biggest bottlenecks in the whole computing business: the computer has to take time away from its busy schedule to tell you what it's up to. It's easier to help your PC gain speed when you understand how video cards work.

The first PCs used display cards that could display fuzzy four-color text and graphics or could display sharp text but no graphics at all. Later models, including VGA, which every current video card emulates, could display both text and graphics. Although early video cards relied on the processor on the motherboard to control the display, later models began to move more and more of this responsibility to the chips on the graphics cards themselves.

Today, most graphics cards contain chips that can be described as graphics processing units (GPUs). The GPU on the graphics card does most of the work, but how fast it works depends in part on how quickly it receives signals from the computer. Thus, the choice of the right GPU and card interface has a big impact on your system's performance.

Starting in the late 1990s, 3D accelerators became common, freeing the CPU from the need to calculate the much more intricate appearance of 3D objects, shading, lighting effects, fog effects, gunshots, and explosions found in popular games such as *Quake III*, *Tribes*, and many others. Surviving the first round of a 3D game sometimes depends on how good a 3D accelerator you're using.

Although most recent video cards offer decent 2D acceleration, 3D acceleration with high image quality has been a lot harder to achieve. Breakthroughs in on-board memory and the development of the AGP slot were also needed to work along with the latest 3D accelerated chipsets to provide the high frame rates and realistic visuals that hardcore PC gamers demand. As you learn later in this chapter, many video cards originally provided by computer manufacturers skimp on 3D performance, making an upgrade a necessity for serious gaming, even on recently purchased systems. Can we blame the system makers for this one? Probably not. After all, all those basic, bland beige boxes look pretty much alike, don't they?

JARGON

A Crash Course in Video Standards and Terms

There are plenty of acronyms and other terms roaming around in video-card land. They don't bite, but they can be confusing. Here are some of the most common:

- **VGA**—Video Graphics Array is an analog video standard developed by IBM in 1987 that is still the baseline for today's video cards and displays. Resolutions start at 640×480 and go up; the number of colors ranges from 16 to over 16 million!

- **SuperVGA**—This is used by some to refer to 800×600 resolution, or by others to refer to any settings that exceed standard VGA (see previous entry).

- **UltraVGA**—This is used by some to refer to 1024×768 resolution or above.

- **Resolution**—Number of pixels in onscreen image, always listed as horizontal×vertical. The most popular setting for 17-inch CRT monitors today is 1,280×1,024. The higher the resolution, the greater the page size you can view without scrolling.

- **Vertical refresh rate**—The rate at which the display is refreshed with new information. Faster refresh rates reduce visible flicker, but too high a refresh rate on a low-quality display produces fuzzy text.

- **Color depth**—Refers to the maximum number of colors visible onscreen, expressed as a power of two. 8-bit color (2^8) equals 256 colors. 16-bit color (2^{16}) equals 65,536 colors. 24-bit color (2^{24}) equals over 16 million colors. The 32-bit color setting used on 3D cards actually displays 24-bit color while setting aside additional memory for the Z-buffer (an area of memory used to store 3D information). The maximum color depth possible varies with the video card's memory, resolution, and Z-buffer size selected.

- **Frame rate**—One of the measurements used to indicate a high-performance 3D card. This rate indicates the number of frames per second of 3D animation a card can show under specified conditions. Cards with faster 3D accelerator chips and high-speed components can provide faster frame rates than cards with lower-speed chips and components, but display color depth, game-specific display-quality settings, and system hardware such as RAM and CPU type/speed can also affect the frame rate.

- **AGP**—A high-speed slot especially for video, the AGP slot is from two to sixteen times faster than Peripheral Component Interconnect (PCI) slots. The additional performance of AGP makes it a natural choice for both high-performance 2D graphics such as photo and video editing and 3D graphics. Unfortunately, some low-cost systems don't have AGP slots.

So, how do you start improving your video card situation? I suggest you work in the following order:

1. Find out what you already have for video. Do you have an AGP slot? What speed is it? Are you stuck with PCI slots? Is your video card removable, or are you cursed with cheapjack integrated video? You might have already discovered this if you took the

"grand tour" of your system I suggested in Chapter 4, "Taking an Inspection Tour of Your System." If you skipped the tour, go back and take it. You might find out you're already in good shape video-wise, but until you get the details, you don't know the best way to fix any deficiencies in your system.

2. Evaluate your current video card, chipset, and monitor according to the feature list provided in this chapter. I name names, so if you're a fan of a particular video card, don't get mad—or get even—if I trash your favorite or rave about a card you can't stand. I don't own stock in any of these companies, and my comments are based on a combination of personal experience and lots—and I mean lots—of reviews from various sources.

3. Decide whether your current video is sufficient or needs to be upgraded. You're the only one who can make the call, but I promise to give you all the help I can by discussing the features you should be looking for.

4. Remove your current video (or disable it) and install the new card. The mechanics of "out with the old and in with the new" resemble other types of card upgrades, but video driver issues can put a few wrinkles into the situation. Learn whether you need to consider a motherboard upgrade first.

5. Learn how to evaluate your monitor and replace it if it's also not up to snuff. Although monitors all look pretty much alike on the surface, there are big differences inside— where it counts.

I wrap up the process by answering some of the most typical troubleshooting problems I've run into.

How Your Motherboard Affects Your Graphics Upgrade Options

Before you can get anywhere with a video upgrade, you need a place into which to install that upgrade. Based on the results of your "grand tour" investigation, you should now know where your current video is located. There are three major possibilities you might encounter, in order from best to worst:

*   **You have an AGP graphics card**—You can remove the old card and insert a better card.

*   **You have motherboard-integrated video with an open AGP expansion slot on your motherboard**—You can disable the on-board video and add a card.

*   **You have a motherboard-integrated video without an AGP expansion slot**— You can install a slow PCI video card, or opt for a motherboard upgrade that offers an AGP slot.

Figure 13.1 compares the rear of a system containing a graphics card with a system containing motherboard-integrated (built-in) video.

Figure 13.1

Rear view of a micro-ATX system with motherboard-integrated video (top) compared to an ATX system with a slot-mounted graphics card (bottom).

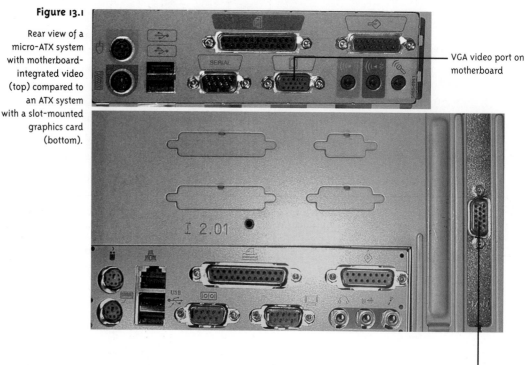

VGA video port on motherboard

VGA video port on graphics card

Although some micro-ATX systems feature both built-in video and an AGP slot, many do not. Most full-size ATX systems have AGP slots. Fortunately, if you're upgrading a recent system with a separate graphics card, you can remove the old card and plug in the new card. However, not all slots are alike when it comes to video.

AGP Versus PCI Slots

The two major standards for slots suitable for video cards are as follows:

- AGP
- PCI

Figure 13.2 demonstrates where an AGP 4x graphics card and a PCI graphics card can be installed on a typical system.

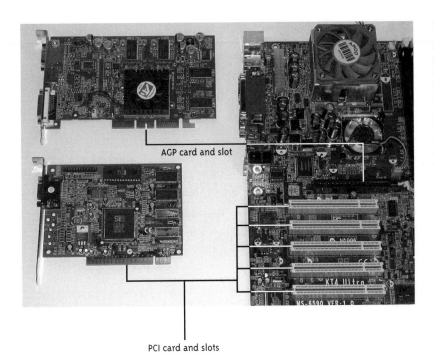

AGP card and slot

PCI card and slots

Figure 13.2

An AGP 4x graphics card (top left) can be installed only into an AGP slot (middle right), but a PCI graphics card (bottom left) can be installed into any open PCI slot (bottom right).

PCI slots have been around for over a decade, and their once-speedy 132MB/sec throughput for the 33MHz, 32-bit version used on desktop motherboards has been outstripped by the performance of AGP. See Table 13.1.

Table 13.1   AGP Standards

AGP Speed	Throughput	Difference Compared to PCI	AGP Version	Voltage
1x*	266MB/sec	2x PCI	1.0	3.3V
2x	533MB/sec	4x PCI	2.0	3.3V and 1.5V
4x^	1.06GB/sec	8x PCI	2.0	1.5V
8x#	2.12GB/sec	16x PCI	3.0	0.8V

*Not supported by current motherboard/graphics card designs.
^AGP 4x cards can run in AGP 2x mode if 4x is not supported by the motherboard.
#AGP 8x cards can run in AGP 4x mode if 8x is not supported by the motherboard.

Besides faster throughput, AGP has two other big advantages over PCI for video:

- AGP has a dedicated direct connection to the processor instead of sharing bandwidth with other PCI slot and motherboard devices.

- AGP can use onboard or motherboard RAM for handling 3D textures.

The advantages of AGP should make it obvious that PCI is obsolete for graphics card use. An open PCI slot should not be used for graphics unless your motherboard doesn't offer an AGP slot or if you prefer to implement a multiple monitor solution by installing two separate video cards. Although you can still buy PCI graphics cards, most mid-range and faster graphics chipsets no longer support the PCI slot, thus limiting your options.

MARK'S TIP SHEET: Stuck with PCI? Get a Motherboard Upgrade and Move to AGP!

A few years ago when AGP was new, there wasn't always a big difference between the performance of early AGP cards and PCI cards. Now, the difference is huge and will only be more pronounced as chipset makers continue to abandon PCI. If your motherboard doesn't have an AGP slot, considering squeezing a new motherboard with an AGP 4x or faster slot into your upgrade plans. Keep in mind that you can buy a motherboard with both an AGP 4x or 8x slot and built-in video if you want to save some dough now and still keep your options open.

AGP Slots and Voltage Standards

If your motherboard has an AGP slot, you can choose from a wide variety of features and chipsets on many different graphics cards. However, you need to understand that not all AGP slots and cards can be interchanged with each other. As Table 13.1 indicates, different AGP standards support different voltages. For this reason, the appearance of AGP slots has changed over time.

Figure 13.3 compares three different types of AGP slots with each other and with PCI slots.

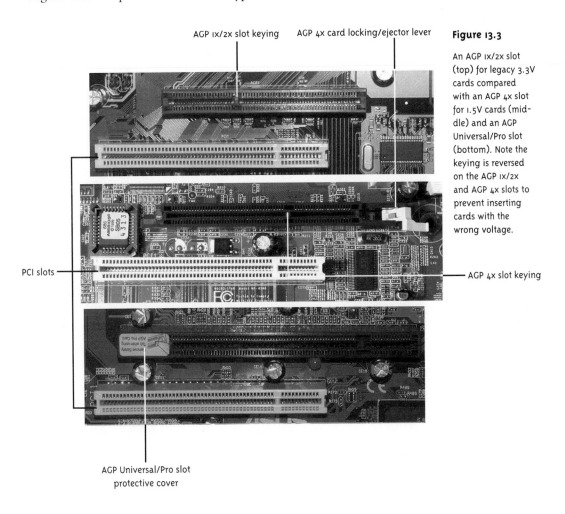

AGP 1x/2x slot keying   AGP 4x card locking/ejector lever

PCI slots

AGP 4x slot keying

AGP Universal/Pro slot
protective cover

Figure 13.3

An AGP 1x/2x slot (top) for legacy 3.3V cards compared with an AGP 4x slot for 1.5V cards (middle) and an AGP Universal/Pro slot (bottom). Note the keying is reversed on the AGP 1x/2x and AGP 4x slots to prevent inserting cards with the wrong voltage.

The AGP Universal/Pro slot shown in Figure 13.3 has a longer connector than either the AGP 1x/2x or AGP 4x slots. It is called a Universal slot because it isn't keyed; thus, it can accept both 3.3V and 1.5V cards. The additional length of the connector supports AGP Pro cards used in technical workstations. Because the AGP Pro section of the slot could damage non-Pro cards inserted into it, most motherboards that are equipped with a Universal/Pro slot block the Pro extension to prevent accidental insertion of non-Pro cards, as shown here.

Although most current AGP 4x and faster cards use a three-part connector (refer back to Figure 13.2) to support both legacy and current AGP slots, AGP cards with a two-part connector can be plugged into their native slot type or the AGP Pro/Universal slot only. If you are trying to install an older AGP card into a newer system, keep slot compatibility in mind.

ON THE WEB: Eliminating AGP Slot Confusion the ATI Way

ATI Technologies offers a terrific visual tutorial to the many slot and connector flavors used by AGP. See it at the "ATI AGP Graphics Card Implementation" page at www.ati.com/support/faq/agpchart.html.

CAUTION: STOP! LOOK! THINK!

AGP Is Not AGP—Details to Follow...
You won't see a headline like this in your local newspaper, but it's news to many PC users anyway—especially if your brand-new AGP card stubbornly refuses to work with your motherboard's AGP slot. Once again, a so-called standard proves to be anything but an airtight, "everything works with everything else" feature. How can you avoid getting burned when you try to match a new AGP video card with your AGP motherboard?

- Check the electrical requirements of the card versus what the motherboard provides to the AGP slot. Some of the newest motherboards, such as Pentium 4 motherboards based on Intel chipsets, require 1.5V AGP 4x/8x video cards.

- Make sure the slot supports the card speed you want to install.

Before you buy an AGP card for your system, or buy a new motherboard to work with your existing AGP card, check both vendors' web sites and third-party forums for compatibility issues. Also, make sure you install the latest motherboard chipset-specific drivers and card-specific drivers for best results.

Selecting the Chipset That's Best

If you've decided that it's time to replace your wheezing graphics card or comatose onboard graphics with a blazing AGP card, you have no shortage of solutions. Even though the number of high-performance graphics chip makers is smaller today than it was a few years ago, there are more cards from which to choose. Here's why:

- nVIDIA, as it has from the beginning, is strictly a graphics chipset maker. Any graphics card with an nVIDIA chipset onboard was produced and is supported by a third-party company.

- Matrox, as it has from the beginning, is strictly a graphics card maker that uses its own chipsets. Every graphics card with a Matrox chipset is built by Matrox.

- Since the late 1980s, ATI traditionally used the Matrox "only we build cards from our chips" model. However, starting in late 2001, ATI began to offer some, and later virtually all of its chips, to various third-party video card makers. Starting in late 2002, ATI began to take significant market share from nVIDIA in the chipset business, while continuing to make ATI-brand video cards as well.

As a result of ATI's joining the chipset business while maintaining its established graphics card business, you have about as many choices using ATI chipsets as you do with nVIDIA chipsets—especially if you shop at "white-box" component stores or online stores.

From the standpoint of performance, the race is between ATI and nVIDIA as of this writing. Matrox cards have excellent 2D image quality, but their 3D gaming performance is very poor.

It's impossible in the space available in this book to give you a comprehensive rundown of the nVIDIA and ATI chipsets on the market. Besides, if history is any guide, both nVIDIA and ATI will have introduced several new chipsets by the time you read this. Thus, the next section provides you with a checklist of significant features to look for along with examples of nVIDIA and ATI chipsets with these features.

ON THE WEB: Try Them? We Already Did!

Wondering how TechTV rates the current chipsets? Just ask! Type in the name of a recent chipset at the TechTV web site's search engine (http://cgi.techtv.com/search) to see articles and reviews that pit today's hottest 3D chips against each other. Type "video card" (don't forget to use the quotes) for hundreds of articles. We've got you covered with lots of information!

Key Features to Look For

The features you need in a graphics card are determined by how you use your computer and the amount of money you are willing to spend. From the standpoint of graphics cards, the major types of users fall into these categories. I bet at least one of these capsule descriptions describes you.

- **High-end gamer**—You need maximum 3D performance and hang the cost.

- **Mid-range gamer**—Your budget demands a balance between 3D performance and reasonable costs.

- **Casual gamer**—You don't live and die by computer games, but (without spending a lot of money) you need better 3D performance than the low-powered integrated graphics built into many computers.

- **Video producer**—You're far more interested in grabbing and editing video than in game playing.

- **The code or text jockey**—As long as you can see two displays at the same time, you're happy.

How do these shorthand descriptions translate into features? Table 13.2 sorts it out for you. See the following sections for more information.

Table 13.2 Key Graphics Card Features by User Type

User Type Feature	High-End Gamer	Mid-Range Gamer	Casual Gamer	Video Producer	Code/Text Jockey	Example Chipset(s)
DirectX 9.0 support	Yes	Yes	—	—	—	nVIDIA GeForce FX series ATI Radeon 9800 Pro, 9600 Pro
DirectX 8.0/8.1 support	Yes	Yes	Yes	—	—	nVIDIA GeForce Ti 4xxx ATI Radeon 9000, 9200
64MB of RAM	—	—	Yes	Yes	Yes	nVIDIA GeForce 4 MX ATI Radeon 9000
128MB or more of RAM	Yes	Yes	—	—	—	nVIDIA GeForce FX, GeForce 4 Ti ATI Radeon 9000 Pro, 9500, 9800 Pro

User Type Feature	High-End Gamer	Mid-Range Gamer	Casual Gamer	Video Producer	Code/Text Jockey	Example Chipset(s)
Memory bus and memory speed	Yes	Yes	—	—	—	For fastest memory bus and memory speed, look for high-end cards
Graphics chipset clock speed and number of internal pipelines	Yes	Yes	—	—	—	Low-end and mid-range cards use slower chipsets and chipsets with smaller numbers of pipelines
TV-out	Yes	Yes	Yes	Yes	—	Most current nVIDIA and ATI chipsets
Dual CRT or CRT/LCD display	Yes	Yes	Yes	—	Yes	nVIDIA GeForce FX, GeForce 4 Ti, MX ATI 9xxx Pro series
TV/video capture	—	—	—	Yes	—	ATI All-in-Wonder series and nVIDIA Personal Cinema series
Enhanced DVD playback	Yes	Yes	Yes	Yes	—	Most current nVIDIA and ATI chipsets

DirectX Support—Smarter Shading at a Price

If you're buying a new graphics card to improve your gameplay, you want to know how powerful the 3D effects features built into the chipset are. A card with high-quality 3D effects can create almost photographic renderings, while a card with a less sophisticated range of 3D effects creates images that are less compelling.

The major 3D chipset features that determine 3D image quality include hardware transform and lighting (T&L), vertex shaders, and pixel shaders.

A quick way to separate out the best from the rest is to find out which version of Microsoft DirectX they support. Microsoft DirectX is the driver technology Microsoft uses to run 3D games in Windows. To improve 3D visual quality, Microsoft has continually improved the built-in 3D rendering features included in each new version of DirectX, and video card makers have worked with Microsoft to incorporate those improvements into their hardware.

JARGON

Hardware transform and lighting (T&L)—The process of converting a 3D object into polygons (which are made of triangles) and placing the correct lighting effects across the surface of the polygons.

Vertex—The corner of a triangle in a 3D scene.

Vertex shader—Creates texture and other effects on the vertices in a 3D scene.

Pixel shader—Creates textures and other effects on the pixels making up a 3D scene.

Table 13.3 compares the 3D features of recent DirectX versions.

Table 13.3   3D Rendering Features by DirectX Version

DirectX Version Feature	7.0	8.0	8.1	9.0
Hardware transform and lighting	Yes	Yes	Yes	Yes
Programmable vertex and pixel shader	No	Yes	Yes	Yes
Enhanced pixel shader (more instructions and easier-to-use language)	No	No	Yes	Yes
Floating point pixel shader for more precision	No	No	No	Yes
Enhanced vertex shader (more instructions and flow control features)	No	No	No	Yes

As Table 13.3 shows, graphics chipsets that support DirectX 9 offer the most sophisticated 3D rendering effects available with any DirectX version.

Most 3D games on the market today support DirectX 8.0, but as time goes on, DirectX 9 support will become widespread. If you're even a casual gamer, I recommend you look for video cards whose chipsets support at least DirectX 8. DirectX 9 support was once confined to the higher levels of the nVidia and ATI lines, but can now be found in cards under $150.

Graphics Card RAM—More is Better for Resolution and Performance

The amount of RAM on the graphics card has a big impact on two factors important for game playing:

- Maximum screen resolution at a given color setting
- Performance

Today's graphics cards pack amounts of memory (64MB or more) that not long ago were regarded as more than sufficient for system memory. 3D graphics cards require much more memory than the 2D graphics cards used a few years ago because the memory on the card is used for many different kinds of data, according to The Tech Report's Geoff Gasior (www.tech-report.com):

- **Frame buffer**—The bitmap of what is seen on the screen at any given moment. You can calculate the frame buffer size by multiplying the horizontal pixels by the vertical pixels by the color depth and dividing the result by eight (the number of bits per pixel). For example, if you want to display 1,280 by 1,024 resolution at 24-bit color depth, you need almost 4MB of RAM on the video card just for the frame buffer. Here's the calculation: 1280×1024×24=31,457,280 bits; divide 31,457,280/8=3,932,160 bytes.

Both 2D and 3D cards use frame buffers, but the following memory-use factors are exclusive to 3D cards:

- **Back buffer**—The amount of RAM needed to create the next frame is equal to the frame buffer.
- **Z-buffer**—Stores depth information, and can be the same as the color depth or less. Most graphics cards compress the Z-buffer to save RAM.
- **3D programs**—The programmable vertex and pixel shader programs used by DirectX 8.0, 8.1, and 9.0-compatible graphics cards use memory; DirectX 8.1 and DirectX 9 programs are longer and contain more variables than DirectX 8 programs, so they need more memory.
- **Geometry data**—The greater the number of polygons in a scene, the greater the amount of RAM needed to display them.
- **Textures**—The amount of RAM used to store texture data varies widely. Although AGP supports the storage of texture data in main memory, using AGP card memory is much faster.

> **ON THE WEB: Deep Graphics Require Lots of RAM**
>
> To discover how much RAM your graphics card needs to display the color depth, resolution, and z-buffer depth you desire, see the "Memory requirements for 3D applications" page of the 3D WinBench web site at www.etestinglabs.com/benchmarks/3dwinbench/d5memfor3d.asp.

Low-end cards typically have 64MB of RAM, and mid-range and high-end graphics cards feature 128MB of RAM. Although older games such as Quake III show little effect with different amounts of RAM, newer DirectX 8- and DirectX 9-compatible games benefit from 128MB of RAM or more.

> **ON THE WEB: 64MB Versus 128MB at The Tech Report**
>
> Hats off to The Tech Report's Geoff Gasior for discovering the impact of graphics card memory sizing on performance. See his report at www.tech-report.com/etc/2002q3/graphicsmem/index.x?pg=1.

Other Chipset Design Factors

The internal design of the chipset is what specifies what level of 3D graphics the chipset can produce. However, a graphics chip vendor can create several different price levels for chips and cards with adjustments to the following:

- **Number of vertex and pixel shader pipelines in the chip core**—Low-end cards have fewer pipelines than mid-range or high-end cards; more is faster.

- **Memory bus width**—Low-end cards might have a 64-bit or 128-bit memory bus, while mid-range and high-end cards usually have a 256-bit memory bus; wider is faster.

- **Memory bus speed**—Measured in MHz, faster is better. Some vendors make comparisons more difficult by building different models with smaller amounts of faster RAM and larger amounts of slower RAM.

- **Memory chip type**—Square ball grid array (BGA) memory chips have smaller connectors and run faster, but are more expensive than the rectangular memory chips used on low-end cards.

- **Graphics chip core speed**—Measured in MHz; faster is better.

- **Anti-aliasing support**—Anti-aliasing smoothes the edges of on-screen objects, but it can slow down graphics display. More advanced cards offer higher-performance anti-aliasing, and low-end cards might use simpler and slower anti-aliasing technologies.

TV-Out and Dual Displays

Although multiple display support was once a rarity, all but the cheapest video cards now offer some type of multiple display support. However, make sure you understand the differences between which types of displays are supported by a particular card. In addition to the 15-pin VGA jack, today's graphics cards frequently feature one or both of the following:

- **TV-out**—The TV-out port has become a staple on almost all current graphics cards. It enables you to send your video display out to a TV or VCR's S-video or composite connector. Note that many low-cost graphics cards with dual-display support provide only VGA and TV-out ports.

- **DVI**—The digital video interface (DVI) supports digital LCD panels and is found on most recent mid-range and high-end graphics cards. However, because many LCD panels connect to the same 15-pin VGA port used by CRT monitors, graphics cards that have a DVI port are usually supplied with a DVI-to-VGA adapter so that dual displays can be supported even if both monitors use the VGA port.

Figure 13.4 shows the VGA, TV-out S-video, and DVI ports on the rear of a typical mid-range graphics card, along with the corresponding cable connectors.

Cards with TV-out or DVI ports have special driver software to enable you to select which display(s) are active.

Video Capture and Playback

Whether you want to capture video for editing and DVD creation or simply want to turn your computer into a digital video recorder so that you can watch your favorite TV shows whenever you want to, you can upgrade to specialized graphics cards that include TV and video input jacks and video capture software.

ATI makes the All-in-Wonder series (similar cards are available from some of ATI's manufacturing partners), and nVIDIA's manufacturing partners make the Personal Cinema series. ATI's All-in-Wonder cards are available in entry-level, mid-range, and high-end categories. The All-in-Wonder 9700 Pro shown in Figure 13.5 uses the same high-performance graphics chip used in the ATI Radeon 9700 Pro. The 9700 Pro has been replaced by an improved version known as the ATI Radeon 9800 Pro.

Figure 13.4

VGA, S-video TV-
out, and DVI ports
with matching cable
connectors (inset).

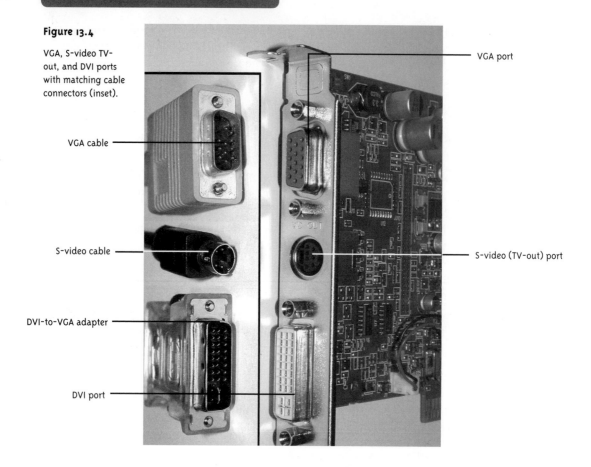

VGA cable

S-video cable

DVI-to-VGA adapter

DVI port

VGA port

S-video (TV-out) port

Figure 13.5

ATI's All-in-Wonder
9700 Pro combines
high-performance
3D graphics with a
full range of video
input-output, cap-
ture, and editing
features. Photo
courtesy of ATI
Technologies.

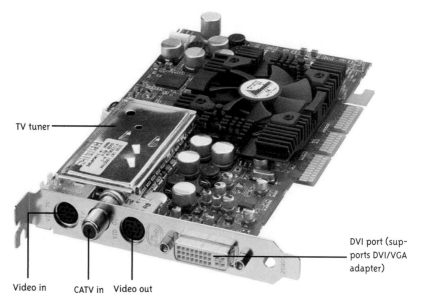

TV tuner

Video in   CATV in   Video out

DVI port (sup-
ports DVI/VGA
adapter)

nVIDIA's Personal Cinema series is based on nVIDIA's entry-level graphics chipsets: the latest models use the nVIDIA GeForce 4 MX chips.

Unlike ATI, which removes the dual-monitor display feature to make room for the connectors shown in Figure 13.5, nVIDIA's Personal Cinema uses an external breakout box to support audio/video input-output, as shown in Figure 13.6.

The ATI and nVIDIA products include software for video capture and editing, as well as TV recording and program scheduling. Consult the ATI and nVIDIA web sites for details.

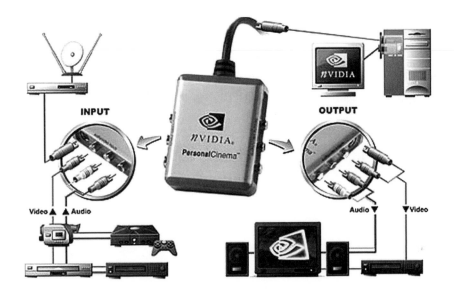

Figure 13.6

The nVIDIA Personal Cinema Digital Media Hub connects all types of home entertainment devices to the nVIDIA GeForce 4 MX graphics card at the heart of the nVIDIA Personal Cinema system.

ON THE WEB: Video Capture and Recording Your Way

Get more information on ATI's latest All-in-Wonder cards from the ATI web site at www.ati.com.

Discover the latest nVIDIA Personal Cinema features and manufacturing partners at the nVIDIA web site at www.nvidia.com.

Getting the Information You Need to Make an Informed Choice

With so many options available for your graphics card upgrade, it can be difficult to make a decision. Because these design factors have complex effects on card performance, the best way for you to determine which cards have the best performance for your needs is to review trusted benchmarking sources. In addition to TechTV's own reviews, I use the following to evaluate graphics cards and technologies:

- **Tom's Hardware**—www.tomshardware.com
- *MaximumPC*—www.maximumpc.com
- **Anandtech**—www.anandtech.com
- *PC Magazine*—www.pcmag.com
- **Extreme Tech**—www.extremetech.com
- *PC World*—www.pcworld.com

Out with the Old, In with the New

The process of upgrading your graphics card has the following major steps; these are covered in detail in the following sections:

1. Remove the old card and its drivers or disabling onboard video.
2. Install the new graphics card.
3. Install its drivers.
4. Configure the new graphics card.

Removing the Old Card

Before you open your system, take the electrostatic discharge (ESD) precautions described in Chapter 5, "Preparing for Your Upgrade." ESD can fry your expensive new video card, making it useless, so be careful.

MARK'S TIP SHEET: Shortcuts to Video Upgrade Success

Want to make your video card upgrade as easy and painless as possible? Try these tips:

- Before you shut down your system to start the upgrade process, set your video display type to plain old VGA. Why? Deep down inside, every whiz-bang video card on the market is still a VGA card. By telling the system you have a VGA card, you won't get any error messages when you switch one brand for another.

- If you forgot to take the preceding step and you're already booting up the system by the time you read this, press the Ctrl or F8 key and select Safe Mode from the Windows startup menu. Safe Mode runs the system with the usual VGA driver by default. Then, you can go into the Device Manager and delete the old video card from the device listing, restart your computer normally, and let it detect your new video card.

- If you're replacing built-in video with a "real" video card, make sure you follow the motherboard or system manufacturer's recommendations exactly. Some systems automatically disable onboard video the moment you pop a new video card into an open slot; others might require you to adjust a BIOS setting or jumper block on the motherboard. Do it wrong, and you might be without video when you restart.

- It usually makes more sense today to install a dual-head video card. But, if you prefer to add a second video card for dual-display support, check your current video card and proposed second card against the compatibility lists available at:

  - www.realtimesoft.com/ultramon—Also home of the inexpensive UltraMon multiple-monitor display program (a free trial is available).

  - www.digitalroom.net/techpub/multimon.html—Also features tips, tricks, and resource links.

Then, follow these steps:

1. Click Start, Settings, Control Panel, System, (Hardware tab in Windows XP), and click the Device Manager tab or button to open Windows' Device Manager. Then, select the existing video card and click Remove to take it off the list of installed devices.

2. Shut down your system and monitor.

3. Unplug your system and monitor.

4. Look at the rear of your system and locate the video cable running from the monitor; it's a heavy cable separate from the power cable. Unscrew it from the retaining bolts and remove the cable from your video connector. See Figure 13.7.

Figure 13.7

Although both the parallel cable and VGA video cable have thumbscrews, the video cable is smaller. On systems with motherboard-based video, the VGA port is on the same rear panel as the parallel port.

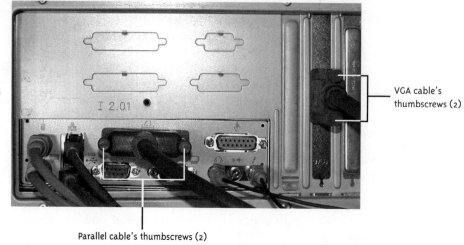

VGA cable's thumbscrews (2)

Parallel cable's thumbscrews (2)

5. Open the system (see Chapter 4 for details).

6. If you are not using an ESD ground wire, touch the side of the power supply to avoid ESD damage to your hardware.

7. Remove the screw holding your video card in place.

8. Label any cables running from your video card to other devices (such as a sound card or DVD decoding board) with a sticker, and then remove them.

9. Gently rock the card forward, then back, and then out (not side to side). If you are replacing an AGP card on a motherboard with an AGP locking lever (see Figure 13.8), be sure to unlock the card before trying to remove the card.

10. Place the old card on anti-static material such as an ESD mat you might have purchased with your ESD wristband, or a newspaper. Don't use aluminum foil or the outside of a computer anti-static bag. If you have a spare anti-static parts bag, put the card inside the bag.

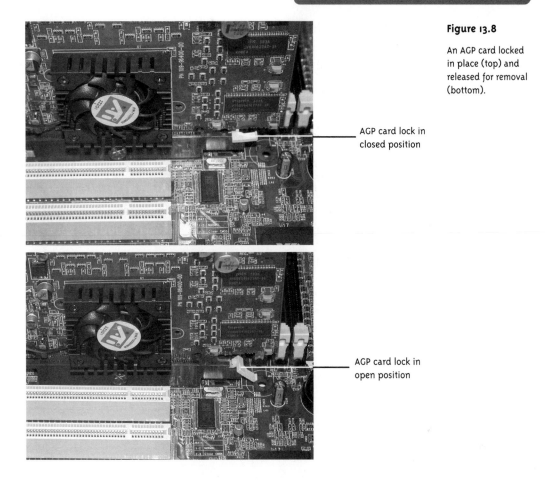

Figure 13.8

An AGP card locked in place (top) and released for removal (bottom).

AGP card lock in closed position

AGP card lock in open position

Installing the New Video Card and Driver Software

The installation of the new card is generally a mirror image of removing the old card. Any differences occur when you are:

- Installing a new card in a system that previously used motherboard-based video.
- Using a different slot for the new video card than the old one used.

Follow these steps to install your new card:

1. If necessary, remove the slot cover behind the expansion slot you want to use for the new video card.

2. Slide the video card straight down over the slot you plan to use.

3. Make sure the card's connectors are aligned exactly with the slot connectors and that the rear bracket is between the rear edge of the motherboard and the case.

4. Gently push the card into place with a slight front to back rocking motion. Push until the card's gold connectors are firmly inserted into the slot and the card bracket is firmly against the ledge at the back of the computer. See Figure 13.9.

Figure 13.9

A video card partly inserted into the slot (top) and fully inserted into the slot (bottom).

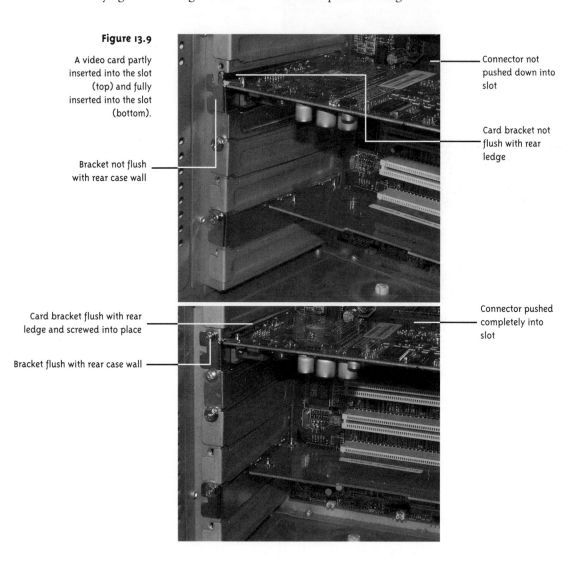

Connector not pushed down into slot

Card bracket not flush with rear ledge

Bracket not flush with rear case wall

Card bracket flush with rear ledge and screwed into place

Bracket flush with rear case wall

Connector pushed completely into slot

5. Use the screw you removed during removal of the old card or in Step 1 to fasten the card into place.

6. Make sure the card is tightly connected to the slot and the rear of the case.

7. Reattach the video cable from the monitor to the proper connector at the rear of the case. If the new card uses a DVI-I connector and the monitor uses the standard 15-pin VGA connector, connect a DVI-I to VGA adapter, such as the one shown in Figure 13.4, to the DVI-I port. Then, attach the cable, as shown in Figure 13.10.

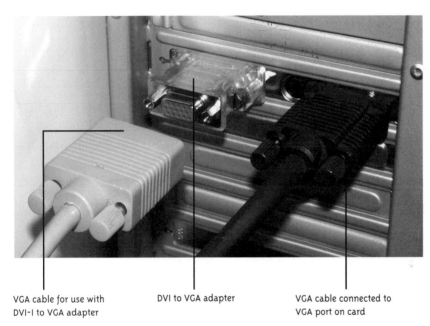

Figure 13.10

A DVI to VGA adapter (left) enables a dual-display video card to use two VGA-type monitors.

VGA cable for use with
DVI-I to VGA adapter

DVI to VGA adapter

VGA cable connected to
VGA port on card

8. Reattach the computer and monitor's power supplies to their power cables.

9. Turn on the monitor.

10. Turn on the computer.

11. Follow the manufacturer's instructions for installing the video drivers when prompted.

Configuring Your New Video Card

After your video card is installed, use the Windows Display properties to fine-tune its settings. You will normally want to adjust the following settings:

- Resolution
- Color depth
- Vertical refresh rate

To change these settings, use the Display properties sheet. To open it, you can do one of the following:

- Right-click the desktop (not an icon) and select Properties; click the Settings tab.
- Click Start, Settings, Control Panel, and then Display; click the Settings tab.

For details, see the "Fine-Tuning Your New Display and Graphics Card" section in this chapter.

A Bigger, Better Monitor Awaits

If you're looking for a more comfortable and faster computing environment, don't overlook your monitor. By replacing your 15-inch or smaller CRT monitor with a 17-inch (or larger) CRT monitor, you save untold amounts of wear on your directional arrows on your keyboard and reduce the odds of "mouse elbow." You also allow yourself to open more programs at once and avoid eyestrain while you use higher resolutions.

By combining a new monitor purchase with a dual-head video card, you can improve your productivity even more; use your new monitor as your primary monitor, and your old one as a secondary monitor. 17-inch CRT monitors have become the new standard display, and 19-inch CRT monitors offer a further improvement in screen real estate for not much more money. If you're short on desktop space, you can use a 15-inch LCD display in place of a 17-inch CRT, and a 17-inch LCD in place of a 19-inch CRT. A 15-inch LCD has about the same viewing area as a 17-inch CRT, and a 17-inch LCD has about the same viewing area as a 19-inch CRT.

Which one is right for you?

CRTs

Conventional "glass tube" monitors are also called *CRTs* for the Cathode Ray Tube used to display the onscreen image. CRT-type monitors closely resemble TVs in their basic construction, although they are built to a much higher standard for resolution and use computer, rather than TV, signals.

Both CRTs and TVs work by firing a stream of electrons at the inside of the picture tube to form the image. The speed at which the screen is painted with new data, from top to bottom, is referred to as the *vertical refresh rate* and is measured in Hertz (Hz), or times per second. Monitors are rated by their vertical refresh rate (which varies according to the screen resolution selected), the size of the picture tube (measured diagonally), and the dot pitch (the distance between each trio of red, green, and blue phosphor dots used to make the image onscreen).

JARGON

Become a Monitor Maven—Master These Terms

Vertical refresh rate—How fast the monitor redraws the picture on screen. Set this rate to be fast enough to avoid annoying flicker.

Picture tube size—Measured diagonally (corner to corner), it is about 1—1.5-inches smaller than the viewable area on a CRT monitor.

Dot pitch—The distance between each trio of red, green, and blue phosphor dots should be as small as possible; .25mm—.28mm is a satisfactory range for 14-inch to 17-inch screens. 19-inch and larger monitors should have dot pitches under .25mm. Larger distances make the image on-screen appear grainy.

The Ideal CRT's Features

The ideal monitor provides a big, sharp, clear, easy to view screen at any supported resolution and uses as little desk space as possible. What kinds of features should you look for in your search for the "ideal" monitor—or as close as you can come to it for your budget? See Table 13.4 for the details.

Table 13.4   CRT Monitor Features

Feature	Desirable	Acceptable	Not Acceptable	Notes
Screen Size (diagonal measure)	19-inch	17-inch	15-inch or smaller	The larger the screen, the higher the useful resolution in most cases.
Highest usable[1] screen resolution (19-inch)	1,600× 1,200 or above	1,280× 1,024 or above	1,024×768	Many monitors' highest resolution have refresh rates under 70Hz.
Highest usable[1] screen resolution (17-inch)	1,280× 1,024 or above	1,024× 768 or above	800×600	

continues

Table 13.4   Continued

Feature	Desirable	Acceptable	Not Acceptable	Notes
Tube type	Flat tube with short-neck design	Flat tube with standard neck design	Curved tube with standard neck design	Flat tube eliminates distortion and reduces glare common with curved screens.
Dot pitch (Aperture Grille Pitch)[2] 19-inch	.25mm (.24mm)	.26mm or .27mm (.27mm)	.28mm or above (same)	Finer dot pitch improves image sharpness.
Dot pitch (Aperture Grille Pitch) 17-inch	.26mm (.24mm)	.27mm (.25mm)	.28mm or above (same)	

[1] "Usable" is defined as a vertical refresh rate of 70Hz or higher; lower refresh rates cause excessive screen flicker.
[2] Aperture grille pitch is the distance between triads of vertical red, green, and blue phosphor strips used on some monitors in place of a shadow mask.

LCD Display Panels

Although LCD display panels are still two to three times more expensive than comparably sized CRTs (a 15-inch LCD panel is comparable in usable screen area to a 17-inch CRT), more and more space-conscious users are opting for them. A 15-inch or larger LCD panel needs less than eight inches of desktop depth, compared to 14 to 17 inches for a comparable 17-inch CRT display. LCD displays use far less power than CRTs, produce much less heat, and weigh far less (a 17-inch LCD panel weighs about 10 lbs, compared to 35–40 obs for a 17-inch CRT). So, what's not to like?

LCD displays have just one native resolution (normally 1024×768 in a 15-inch size or 1,280×1,024 in the 17-inch size), which is fine for office work or photo editing, but isn't always the best resolution for gaming or for web designers (who need to preview their pages at different resolutions). Although CRTs can adjust to many different resolutions without problems, LCDs must use scaling to display lower-resolution screens, sometimes with poor results. In addition, many low-cost LCD displays are designed to convert their internal digital signals to analog signals for use with ordinary video cards. This digital to analog conversion can cause the picture on-screen to shake or shimmer a bit. The newest LCD displays have a DVI digital input, but displays with the DVI connector are more common in the 17-inch and larger categories. LCD displays never flicker, so high refresh rates aren't necessary. However, most LCD displays have slower response times than CRTs, making them less suitable for game playing.

CRTs are a long way from becoming obsolete because they have several built-in advantages when compared to LCD displays, as Table 13.5 reveals.

Table 13.5	LCD and CRT Features Compared					
Display Type	Resolution	Graphics Card	Internal Signal Type	Viewing Angle	Refresh Rate	Notes
CRT	Adjustable from 640×80 up and sharp at various resolutions	Analog VGA (15-pin)	Analog	Wide	High	No signal conversion necessary
LCD	Fixed native resolution; can be scaled, but is not as sharp as native resolution	Analog VGA; DVI	Digital	Narrower	Low	Analog to digital signal conversion can cause display problems; software controls can help

The Perfect LCD Display Panel

If you prize the compact size, minimal depth, and energy requirements of an LCD screen, how can you make sure you get the best LCD display panel possible? Look for the following features:

- **Viewing angle of 150 degrees or more**—LCD panels don't allow as wide a viewing angle as CRTs, but you should be able to see the display clearly from one side.

- **Contrast ratio of 300:1 or higher**—CRTs have an average contrast ratio of 245:1, and the more you exceed this value, the crisper the display is. However, make sure the display also handles light and dark tones properly.

- **Pivoting feature**—Although some CRTs and display cards in the past have supported the shift of the display from its normal landscape horizontal mode to a vertical portrait orientation, the weight and bulk of CRTs has made this a rare feature. LCD panels are light and easy to swing, and this makes editing a long document even easier.

- **DVI connector**—When matched to a DVI-compatible video card, this provides for an all-digital display that avoids problems with pixel swim and jitter that are common when analog signals are converted.

> **JARGON**
>
> *Pixel swim*—The on-screen shimmer that results when the LCD display panel can't decide which of two adjacent cells should be turned on.
>
> *Pixel jitter*—Same as pixel swim. To minimize pixel swim/jitter, use the display controls provided with the LCD display, or switch to an all-digital LCD display and compatible video card.

Regardless of the display type you choose, you should try to see it in person before you plunk down your cash or credit card. Some displays look better on paper than they do in person.

Traps to Avoid

Avoid the following traps when you buy your next monitor:

- **CRT monitors with very low refresh rates at the resolutions you want to use**—Very low refresh rates at the monitor's highest resolution is a favorite trick of monitor makers who want to impress you with a "high-res" monitor at a low price.

   My rule of thumb is this: If the refresh rate isn't at least 70Hz at a given resolution, I'm going to ignore it. Thus, the many low-cost 17-inch 1,280×1,024 maximum-resolution monitors on the market whose refresh rates are 60 to 66Hz I call "1,024×768" monitors because that resolution has a very easy-on-the-eyes refresh rate above 80Hz in most cases. Another reason to discount the maximum resolution, especially on low-cost monitors, is the poor picture quality you often have at the maximum resolution. It's amazing to see how bad some monitors look at the maximum resolution and how much better the screen quality is just one notch down from maximum.

- **Curved-tube CRTs**—Flat tubes abound, even at moderate price points, and they're easier to use and more accurate. The curved-tube monitors are often also the ones with the useless maximum resolutions I mentioned earlier. Leave 'em on the shelf for somebody else.

Swapping Your Monitor

Installing a new display doesn't require that you open your system, thank goodness. However, you still have to crawl around on the floor to access cables. Here's how to make the process as painless as possible:

1. Open the Windows Device Manager and delete your current display (listed under the monitor category) from the list of devices.

2. Shut down the system and turn it off.

3. Turn off your old monitor and unplug it from power.

4. Remove the video cable from the back of your system.

5. Move the old monitor out of the way and put your new monitor in its place.

6. Attach the video cable from the new display to your computer's video connector.

7. Attach the power cable to the new display and then to an AC power source.

8. Turn on the display, and then the system.

9. Provide the driver disk or CD-ROM when prompted after the new display is detected by the system.

CAUTION: STOP! LOOK! THINK!

Don't Throw Your Old Monitor Away or Take It Apart

My favorite monitor recycling trick is to use it as a secondary display! A dual-head video card with Windows 98, Me, or XP makes it easy to run two monitors at once (Windows 2000 doesn't do as well with dual monitors).

If you're out of desk space or are already using two monitors, don't toss it out into the garbage. Check with your kids' school, your church, synagogue, mosque, or charity and see if they need a replacement monitor. As a last resort, look for a computer-recycling center near you that will let you drop off your foundling.

Never, regardless of your curiosity about the inside of a monitor, take one apart unless you are an expert TV or monitor repairman. Long after a CRT is turned off, the coils around the picture tube retain potentially *fatal* voltage. Curiosity killed the cat: Don't let it kill you.

Fine-Tuning Your New Display and Graphics Card

Although you can start using your new display and graphics card as soon as they're installed, you should take time to adjust them for the settings you prefer. By default, Windows uses low resolution settings and vertical refresh rates, and versions before Windows XP also use low color depth settings. Here's how to set up your display the way you want it.

Changing the Resolution and Color Depth

To change the color depth, click the Colors pull-down menu. Table 13.6 lists the meaning and suggested uses of the most common color options.

Table 13.6 Color Depth Settings and Uses

Color Depth Setting	Number of Colors On-Screen	Best Uses
16 colors	Same	Automatically selected by standard VGA or Safe Mode bootup with Windows 9x/Me; not recommended for normal use.
256 colors	Same	Use only when software or process can't run with more colors.
16-bit	65,536	Minimum needed for fairly realistic 3D gaming or photo viewing; some graininess will be visible in colors, but some games play faster in this mode.
24-bit	16.7 million	Realistic photo editing, but not as good for 3D gaming as 32-bit color. Use 32-bit setting if 24-bit setting not available.
32-bit	16.7 million	Provides the same number of colors as 24-bit, but is optimized for gaming as well as for photo-editing and business programs.

Generally, you should select 32-bit color if you have a 3D video card, 24-bit if 32-bit is not available, and use 16-bit color only if you can't select the resolution you want at 24-bit or 32-bit color.

To change the resolution, drag the slider to the resolution you prefer.

Table 13.7 lists the most common resolution settings, the minimum monitor size recommended for both CRT and LCD displays, and suggested uses.

After you select a new color depth and resolution, click OK. With most versions of Windows, your screen will change immediately to show you the results. Press Enter or Esc if you don't like the results on the screen.

Table 13.7 Resolution Settings and Uses

Resolution	Recommended CRT Monitor Size	Recommended LCD Monitor Size	Notes
640×480	14-inch	10-inch	Standard VGA resolution; normally used only in Safe Mode or VGA mode startup for troubleshooting
800×600	15-inch	12-inch	Super VGA resolution
1024×768	17-inch	15-inch	XGA resolution
1280×1024	19-inch	17-inch	UXGA resolution

Windows selects very conservative resolution and refresh-rate settings by default when you install a new display. To adjust the resolution and refresh rates to your favorites, do the following:

1. Right-click your Windows desktop to see the Display properties (or Properties) dialog box.

2. Click the Settings tab.

3. The main Settings screen enables you to adjust the color depth and resolution as covered earlier in this chapter. Click the Advanced button to displays the monitor type and video chipset Windows thinks your system is using (see Figure 13.11).

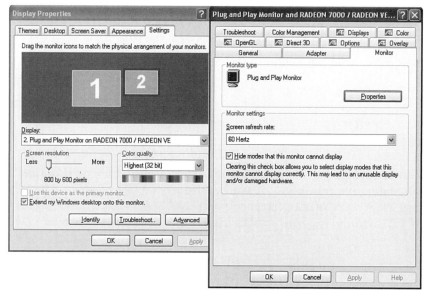

Figure 13.11

Click the Advanced button on the Settings dialog box (left) to display the multi-tabbed Advanced dialog box (right). The Advanced dialog box includes options with which you can change refresh rates (shown), video card or monitor drivers, and the features and performance of your video subsystem.

4. To adjust the vertical refresh rate, monitor or display type, or other display options, click the Advanced button. Depending upon the version of Windows, you use the Monitor tab (Windows XP, see Figure 13.11) or the Adapter tab to change the refresh rate. The Adapter Default setting used with Windows 9x/Me is very low and will usually cause on-screen flicker at 800×600 or higher resolutions when a CRT monitor is used. Use 72Hz–75Hz to reduce flicker; higher options may be available with some monitors. In Figure 13.11, the monitor being adjusted is an LCD display, so a 60Hz refresh rate is acceptable.

ANALYZE THIS

Video in Disguise

Both video card and display makers love to use the same hardware drivers for lots of different models, and, especially with displays, the name on the front of your display is frequently not the name you see listed on the Settings page. The monitor might not even be named, but be referred to as a Plug and Play monitor.

Should you be concerned? You should make a change only if the display is listed as something like Unknown Display or Standard Display; Windows doesn't permit you to select high refresh rates using these drivers because the display could be damaged. Check the video card or display vendor's web site for the latest drivers if you think that Windows is using the wrong driver.

Portable Particulars

Notebook and other portable computers have very limited display options compared to desktop computers:

- You can't upgrade the on-board video.
- You can't always run the on-board and external displays at the same time.
- Your resolution and color-depth options are more limited than they are on a desktop system.

How can you make the most of your portable computer's display, either when you initially buy your system or later? Try these tricks:

- **Project a comfortable image by selecting an external projector or monitor that matches the native resolution of your computer's LCD display**—The simultaneous-display feature of many notebook computers is designed to work only if the projector and internal display are both using the same resolution. If you want to see the same thing on your screen that's being transmitted to the crowd at your next meeting or training class, check the numbers on the projector before you buy. Most notebook computer screens run at 1024×768 resolution these days, so make sure your projector does too.

- **Look for portable computers that support Windows XP's DualView technology**—DualView enables the monitor connected to the external VGA port to be used as a true second display, just like the second monitor connected to a dual-head display card. However, you might need to install updated display drivers, and some portable computers simply can't support DualView.

Troubleshooting Your Graphics Upgrade

Whether your video upgrade requires major (internal) surgery or just a plug-unplug of a video cable, if anything can go wrong, it will—sooner or later. Here's help.

Help! I've installed a new video card and now my system won't boot!

There are quite a few potential causes for this one. Check the following:

- **Check the obvious first**—Did you reattach the display to power and to your new video card?

- **If your system was using built-in video, did you disable it correctly?**—If you need to manually disable built-in video and didn't do so first, your old and new video are fighting over who's in charge. Guess what? You lose.

- **Make sure you don't have a bare wire or screw touching the motherboard or any cards**—A short stops the system in its tracks.

- **Check again**—If you had to move or unplug and reattach any power or data cables to perform the upgrade, make sure you properly reattached everything.

Help! I'm getting video card errors after I installed my new video card!

The most likely cause of this error is failing to remove the old video card from the Windows Device Manager before removing the card itself. Start the system in Safe Mode, remove all video cards listed, and restart the computer normally.

To start the system in Safe Mode, press the Ctrl or F8 key during bootup until the system displays the Windows startup menu. Select Safe Mode from the menu. With Windows XP, select VGA Mode instead.

Help! My system can't find the video card or display drivers!

Use the Browse button during the driver installation to look for the drivers yourself; the driver files end in .inf. Check all folders on the installation floppy drive or CD-ROM for updated drivers for your video card. With a display, see if it needs special drivers or uses a generic plug-and-play driver.

Help! I can't select high resolutions or color depths, even though I know my video card has plenty of video RAM!

Odds are really good that Windows has selected the wrong video card driver. Use the Advanced button on the Display properties sheet (accessed by right-clicking the desktop) to select the correct video driver from the installation CD or floppy disk, or to use an updated driver you've downloaded.

Help! My CRT's display looks like a funhouse mirror when I change resolutions or refresh rates!

Use the front-panel controls on your monitor to adjust the horizontal and vertical screen size and position and to remove distortions. Save the changes into the monitor's non-volatile memory; the next time you switch to that resolution, your picture should remain steady.

Help! I decided to reuse an old PCI graphics card instead of buying a new dual-display graphics card and I can't get my system to recognize the new card.

Try the following:

1. It's easier to get good results with an AGP and a PCI graphics card. If you're trying to use two PCI cards, the computer can have problems determining which one is the primary card.

2. If you're using an AGP and a PCI card, restart your computer, open the BIOS setup program, and look for an option called Primary VGA BIOS. If this is set to AGP as in Figure 13.12, change it to PCI, save the settings, and restart your computer.

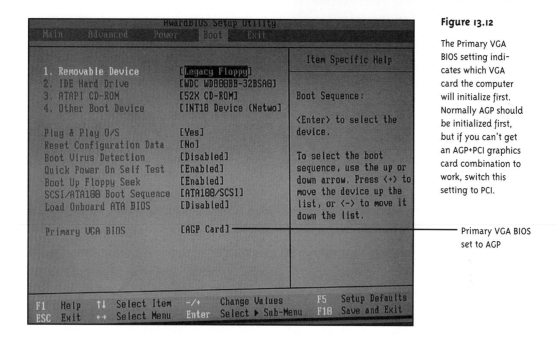

Figure 13.12

The Primary VGA BIOS setting indicates which VGA card the computer will initialize first. Normally AGP should be initialized first, but if you can't get an AGP+PCI graphics card combination to work, switch this setting to PCI.

Primary VGA BIOS set to AGP

3. Be sure to use the latest drivers available for both graphics cards. To obtain these, go to the card vendors' web sites.

4. Check the database of dual-display card installations at the UltraMon web site (www.realtimesoft.com/ultramon).

5. Consider buying a true dual-display card. Some AGP cards with VGA and DVI ports are available for as little as $100.

Help! I just went to the store to buy a new monitor and the salesperson recommends that I buy an extended service plan to go with it. Should I listen to the salesperson's recommendation?

As you know from Chapter 1, I'm not a big fan of extended warranties on computers because you can upgrade the components inside a computer and improve it if a component (such as a motherboard or video card) fails. A monitor is definitely *not* a user-serviceable component; touching the coils around the picture tube of a CRT-based monitor can kill you!

Getting an extended warranty make sense *only* in the following circumstances:

- *If* the monitor vendor doesn't already provide an instant-exchange service during the first year or so, when most failures take place.

  and

- *If* you can go to the store and swap for a replacement on the spot.

  and

- *If* the cost of the extended service plan isn't more than 25% of the cost of the monitor when new.

That's a dream plan. What about reality?

Some monitor vendors offer instant exchange programs during at least part of the warranty period, so an extended warranty duplicates the vendor's warranty. Most extended warranties make you wait while the monitor is sent back to a central repair depot for testing. In the meantime, you can't use your PC! Finally, although some extended warranties seem reasonably priced (you can get a three-year plan for an $800 LCD panel for $120 from one national vendor, which beats my 25% guideline), what about future price drops on monitors? In a couple of years from now, $120 might go a long way toward replacing the panel outright with a better model, and in the meantime, you can spend your money elsewhere. It's your choice, but for me, most extended warranties are primarily designed to pump up store profits instead of helping you, no matter what the salesperson says.

Chapter 14

PC Audio and More

Over the last fifteen years, PC audio has changed from an exotic oddity of interest to just a few game players to an integral part of practically every computer. However, sound card upgrades continue to be popular upgrades, even for computers with built-in audio. Why?

Today's audio user is far more sophisticated than computer users were a few years ago. It's no longer enough for audio to play back stereo sound from a CD or a simple game. Today's PC audiophile demands features such as surround sound, positional audio, compatibility with home theater equipment, and very high playback quality. Although a few high-performance motherboards with integrated audio meet these requirements, most computers need to upgrade to a sound card that has the features and audio quality demanded by today's games and multimedia products.

In this chapter, you discover:

- How to evaluate your current sound support
- How to upgrade it
- How to overcome problems with your sound system

Ten Reasons to Upgrade Your Audio Hardware

If your idea of high-quality sound is rolling up the windows on the car so that you can hear the radio better, it might be a tough sell to convince you that you need to upgrade your audio hardware. After all, something like 99 percent of the computers on the market include a sound card or motherboard-based sound already. However, maybe you can convince yourself you need to make a change, especially if you recognize yourself or your system in any of the situations in our top-ten list of reasons to look for better audio hardware.

1. You'd love to try surround sound, but you can't plug in more than two speakers and a subwoofer.

2. You're constantly losing deathmatches because you can't hear the enemies behind you.

3. There's enough snap, crackle, and pop coming out of your computer speakers to qualify your PC as an honorary breakfast cereal.

4. You have a wonderful home theater system, but your PC can't use it.

5. Your sound card is so old that it plugs into the last ISA slot on your motherboard.

6. When you bought your PC, you thought all audio was alike.

7. You'd like to hear the difference between indoor and outdoor scenes in your favorite games.

8. Your PC gets so slow when you play 3D games with sound effects that you always lose.

9. You're tired of 3D audio that sounds as if it came out of a Cuisinart.

10. You'd rather install a new sound card than return the 5.1 speaker set you got for your birthday.

If this top-ten list has helped you decide it's time to upgrade, it's also time to learn about PC sound and music standards so that you can find hardware that makes the most of the audio standards you care about.

Understanding PC Sound Standards

Whether you're playing a game or playing an MP3 file, PC sound is digitized sound. The quality of the sound card's digital audio playback features affects how high the sound quality is when you play pre-recorded audio. In addition, the quality of the digital audio recording features affects the sound quality you can achieve when you create your own digitized audio.

Here are the major PC sound standards, all of which use some form of digital audio:

- WAV
- CD audio
- 3D audio
- MP3
- Windows Media Audio (WMA)
- DVD soundtracks
- Musical Instrument Digital Interface (MIDI)

The following sections discuss each in turn.

WAV

WAV files are the basic digital audio type used on PCs since the first sound cards were introduced in the late 1980s.

WAV files are typically recorded at four different sampling rates (11KHz [kilohertz], 22KHz, 44KHz, and 48KHz), depending on the balance of quality and disk space usage desired. Higher sampling rates sound more realistic, but use more disk space. WAV files can also be recorded in mono (less space used) or stereo (more space used). 11KHz is sometimes known as telephone quality, 22KHz as radio quality, and 44KHz as CD quality. 48KHz is the sampling rate used by digital audio tape (DAT).

WAV files are used for the Windows event sounds played during startup and shutdown, and by programs (such as America Online's "You've Got Mail!"). You can create your own WAV files with the Windows Sound Recorder applet and the software bundled with most sound cards. You can also use numerous standalone commercial programs, such as Sonic Foundry's Sound Forge (www.sonicfoundry.com), Black Diamond Sound System's Music Master (www.soundlabs.com), Steinberg North America WaveLab (www.steinberg.net), and many shareware and freeware programs.

3D Audio

If you want to win, you need to hear and see the game environment as clearly as possible. Game players encounter a continuous stream of digitized audio that helps them hear allies and enemies, battles, gearbox ratios, musical clues, and much more.

Although early games simply used mono or stereophonic sounds, the rise of 3D graphics in gaming has been paralleled by the development of 3D audio, including 3D audio acceleration features in better-quality sound cards and sound chips. The simplest sound hardware uses special effects to simulate 3D sound with stereo speakers; more advanced sound cards feature jacks for four or more speakers, which provide extremely realistic 3D sound. However, 3D sound, like 3D audio, requires a lot from your system. If your audio is integrated into the motherboard chipset, 3D sound can slow down your system.

ON THE WEB: Can Your 3D Sound Help You Lose?

Check out Tom's Hardware's article "Sound Can Be Hazardous to Games" to see how slow onboard sound chips can slow down your 3D game performance. The article is at www6.tomshardware.com/game/20030405/index.html.

CD Audio

Untold numbers of home and business PCs double as wildly overpriced stereo systems that can also perform computing tasks. Or, to be more accurate, the stereo feature is free with the computer.

When a CD-ROM or similar optical drive is connected to the sound hardware, you can use the CD player software included with Windows or third-party sound programs to play CDs through the sound card's speakers. The same feature can be used to rip, or convert, CD audio into compressed file types such as MP3 and WMA.

MP3 and WMA

MP3 files are compressed audio that maintain nearly all the original sound file's quality, depending on the sampling rate used to compress the file. Winamp is the most famous of numerous MP3 creation and playback programs. You can read CD audio tracks (a process called *ripping)* with an MP3 creation program and encode the original audio into an MP3 file for storage on your hard drive or CD-R or CD-RW media. You can also download it to a portable audio player, such as those in Creative's Nomad series or SonicBLUE's RIO series. MP3 is the most popular compressed digital music standard used by PCs.

WMA is a rival sound compression format supported by Windows Media Player and by some portable players that also play MP3 files. WMA files often take up less space than MP3 files, and they are created through a similar ripping/encoding process by Windows Media Player and compatible programs.

READ THIS TOO: Reading Up on MP3s

Want to do more than just download MP3s? Get the big picture of what you need to become an MP3 maven from Ron White's *MP3 Underground* (Que, 2000).

The quality of both MP3 and WMA file playback is controlled by the sampling rate used to create the compressed file, not by the sound card. Higher sampling rates result in higher sound quality, but they do so at a cost of more disk space used.

If you want to create your own mix of digitized music, which format is better for you? The Microsoft WMA format, introduced about a decade after MP3 was developed, uses less storage space than an MP3 file of comparable quality and often sounds better than MP3. However, WMA is not as widely supported as MP3 on older portable audio players, and you may need to update some audio player programs to newer versions to get WMA support. It can also be more difficult to move WMA files freely from device to device because WMA supports a type of copy protection called *digital rights management*. The bottom line? Use WMA as often as possible, but remember than MP3 works with software and portable audio hardware that's never heard of WMA.

ON THE WEB: You Be the Judge

If you want to find out much, much more than you'd ever think to ask about all types of digitized sound, including *why* WMA is often better than MP3, check out CommVerge's multipart report "Continuing Codec Capers" at www.commvergemag.com/commverge/extras/P178673.asp.

Get the latest WMA and MP3 news and reviews from the TechTV web site. You'll find the MP3 super site at www.techtv.com/superguides/mp3/.

Search for "WMA" to find the latest news and reviews about the Windows Media Audio format.

DVD Movie Soundtracks

Although the sound card doesn't affect most types of digitized sound files, the quality of the sound you hear from a DVD movie definitely is. If you want to get as close as possible to movie-theater quality sound when you watch a DVD film, you need a sound card and DVD player that support Dolby Digital 5.1. You also need matching speakers. Sound cards with this feature use special output connectors called *S/PDIF (Sony/Philips Digital Interface Format)* connectors.

MIDI

MIDI is a distinctly different type of sound output. A MIDI file, instead of being a digitized recording of sounds, is a musical score that must be interpreted and played back by a sound card's MIDI synthesizer. In other words, the MIDI file contains musical notes to be played by specified synthesized instruments, and the MIDI synthesizer matches the notes to be played by each instrument with the correct synthesized instrument. MIDI music can be downloaded from a wide variety of web sites, and it is sometimes used on web pages that play music as you browse the page.

ON THE WEB: Ring Around the MIDI

If you're looking for MIDI files to download, check out the Original MIDI Ring, a collection of web sites that feature MIDI music and other MIDI information. Start your trek at www.ubikmusic.com/midiring/midiring.html.

Originally, most sound cards used a process called *FM synthesis* to play MIDI scores. FM synthesis imitated musical instruments, usually rather badly. *Wavetable synthesis,* which uses actual digital samples of different musical instruments, has replaced FM synthesis on sound cards during the last few years.

Because the size of the sample set and the number of simultaneous voices (each instrument is called a *voice*) can vary from card to card (more is better in both cases), the quality and MIDI features of a particular sound card have a big impact on MIDI playback. Although some early MIDI card used memory modules to hold sampled instruments, most cards today use a *soft wavetable* feature that borrows RAM from system memory to store samples.

Sound cards that feature wavetable synthesis make MIDI music sound much better than cards that use the older FM synthesis method.

Evaluating Your Current Sound Hardware

How good *is* your current sound hardware? That question can't be answered unless you first discover the following:

- How you use your sound hardware
- What features your sound hardware supports

Virtually all sound hardware today features some form of MIDI playback along with the capability to play WAV and other digitized sound files.

If you use your computer for the following uses, any PCI-based or built-in sound hardware solution is suitable:

- CD audio playback
- Simple sound recording using Sound Recorder
- Casual gaming
- Casual MIDI playback

However, if your audio needs are more demanding, the features built into your sound hardware must be more powerful to satisfy you. If they don't, it's time for an upgrade.

Onboard Sound Versus Sound Cards

There are differences between onboard sound and sound cards:

- The types of input and output jacks available
- The type of chip used to produce or playback digital audio
- The performance of the 3D audio acceleration
- The number of MIDI voices

Input and Output Jacks

Take a look at the audio jacks on your system to learn about the input and output features of your current audio hardware.

Figure 14.1 shows the jacks on the rear of a typical PC with integrated sound, and Figure 14.2 shows the jacks on a typical low-end PC sound card.

Game port/MIDI port (for joysticks and game controls)

Figure 14.1

The built-in sound hardware jacks on a typical low-priced PC. This particular PC has a C-Media sound chip on the motherboard, but many others integrate audio into the motherboard's chipset.

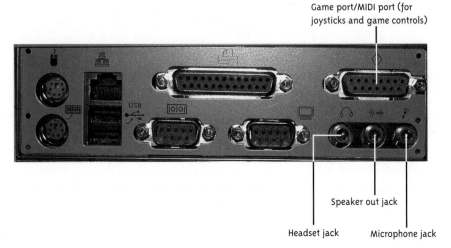

Speaker out jack

Headset jack   Microphone jack

Figure 14.2

The rear of a basic sound card with support for four speakers.

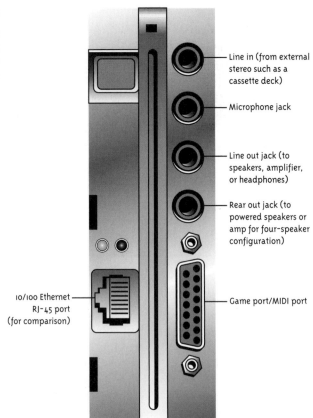

Line in (from external stereo such as a cassette deck)

Microphone jack

Line out jack (to speakers, amplifier, or headphones)

Rear out jack (to powered speakers or amp for four-speaker configuration)

10/100 Ethernet RJ-45 port (for comparison)

Game port/MIDI port

Most advanced sound cards have connectors such as S/PDIF (for digital audio such as DVD audio), digital DIN input/output (also for digital audio), and even MIDI in and MIDI out jacks. These connectors might be on the rear of the card or might be placed on a separate daughter card or external connector box. Hercules and Creative Labs are the major exponents of external connector boxes. These boxes include the Sound Blaster Live! Drive, the Audigy and Audigy2 Drive, and the Hercules Game Theater XP shown in Figure 14.3.

JARGON

S/PDIF—The Sony/Philips Digital Interface connector provides a way to transmit digital sound directly to or from a sound card without converting it to analog format. Many mid-range and high-end sound cards, PC speaker systems, CD-ROM, CD-RW, and DVD drives support this connector.

Digital DIN—A 9-pin digital interface used to connect multiple-speaker digital sound systems such as the Logitech SoundMan Xtrusio series, the Cambridge Sound Works DeskTop Theater 5.1 series, and others. This connector is used primarily by Creative Labs' SoundBlaster Live! 5.1, Audigy, and Audigy 2 sound cards.

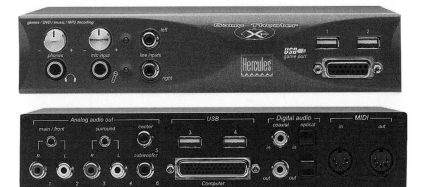

Figure 14.3

The Hercules Game Theater XP features a two-sided external rack with both basic (top) and advanced (bottom) audio I/O connectors. The rack connects to the Game Theater XP card with a proprietary cable. Photo courtesy of Hercules USA.

Because there are many ways to attach multi-speaker arrangements (four-speaker, Dolby Digital 5.1, and emulation of 5.1 with four speakers) on more advanced sound cards, be sure to check the sound card's instruction manual carefully for acceptable connection options and the sound mixer control settings needed for each speaker connection type.

> **READ THIS TOO: Do You Dig PC Sound? Dig This for More Information!**
>
> If you're ready to learn much, much more about PC sound standards and sound
> hardware, grab a copy of Scott Mueller's *Upgrading and Repairing PCs, 15th Edition*
> (Que, 2003).

A motherboard upgrade can also improve your audio output quality and options. Figure 14.4
shows the audio outputs available on the MSI KT4 Ultra motherboard I installed in
FRANKENPC (see Chapter 9, "Unlock Your System's Potential with Motherboard and
BIOS Upgrades," for details).

Figure 14.4

The MSI KT4 Ultra's
optional S-bracket
(center) adds four
and six-speaker
analog support
along with optical
and coaxial S/PDIF
digital outputs to
the standard two-
channel audio out-
put on the rear of
the system (left).

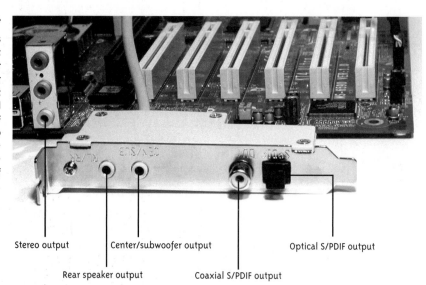

Stereo output   Center/subwoofer output   Optical S/PDIF output

Rear speaker output   Coaxial S/PDIF output

AOpen has developed a popular line of motherboards that incorporate a vacuum tube amplifier for warmer, richer, more realistic sound. Various models are optimized for different types
of music, and the standard vacuum tube can be replaced with a variety of models to further
customize the sound. Figure 14.5 provides an overhead view of the AX4GE-Tube model.

Figure 14.5

AOpen AX4GE-Tube motherboard. The vacuum tube amplifier is to the left of the PCI slots. Photo courtesy of AOpen America.

ON THE WEB: Back to the Future with TubeSound

Learn more about AOpen's TubeSound product line with these links:

- AOpen's TubeSound Technology brief explains the technical differences between the pioneering classical music and jazz-oriented AX4B-533 Tube motherboard and the newer rock/pop-oriented AX4GE/PE Tube series. The URL is www.aopen.com/tech/techinside/TubeComparison.htm.

- TechWare Labs provides a very detailed look at the audio quality of the AX4GE Tube-G motherboard at www.techwarelabs.com/reviews/motherboard/ax4ge_tube-g/.

Digging Beneath the Surface

Although you can learn a lot about the types of sound output your sound hardware can perform by examining its I/O jacks, you can't get all the details unless you dig a little deeper into the audio card's internal connectors and specifications.

All recent sound cards and motherboards with integrated audio feature four-pin connectors that work with the analog audio jack on the rear of optical drives. This enables the sound card to play audio CDs through your PC's speakers. However, to do so, the digital CD signal is converted to analog, which could cause noise and distortion during playback and CD ripping.

Most recent optical drives also have two-wire connectors that transmit digital audio straight from the CD to the sound hardware—if your sound card or motherboard has a matching jack. Many low-cost sound cards and motherboards with on-board audio don't have the two-wire CD digital jack. On these systems, you must use a program such as Windows Media Player to play your CDs digitally, and your CD ripping speed could suffer. Figure 14.6 shows how analog and digital CD audio cables attach to a typical sound card.

Figure 14.6

Analog (left) and digital (right) CD audio cables and jacks on a typical sound card.

If your sound card has provision for a daughtercard or external breakout box with additional input/output options, but you bought a model that didn't bundle these options, contact the vendor to see if you can purchase the daughtercard or breakout box separately. To see how to install these add-ons, see the "Installing Daughtercards and Breakout Boxes" section later in this chapter.

To discover the specifications for audio output, check your sound card's manual or look up the sound chip on the vendor's web site.

For MIDI output, research these issues:

- Number of voices (more is better)
- Number of MIDI channels (more is better)

For example, the Creative Labs Sound Blaster PCI512 supports 64 voices and 48 MIDI channels, while the Philips Acoustic Edge supports 64 hardware plus 512 software voices (total of 576) and 96 MIDI channels. The Philips card will provide better MIDI playback of musical scores you download or MIDI music used on some web sites.

For 3D sound, consider these issues:

- Number of 3D sound streams accelerated (more is better)
- Support for positional audio standards such as Creative Labs' EAX, Aureal's A3D, and Microsoft's Direct3D
- Ability to adjust card for speaker types, number of speakers, and 3D effects through the card's properties sheets

For sound recording, research these issues:

- 24-bit digital resolution and 96KHz or higher sampling provides more accurate conversion of analog sounds to digital format.
- A signal-to-noise ratio (SNR) of 100dB or higher means that you experience cleaner audio with less background noise.

Considering these factors, along with the analog and digital speaker outputs provided by your sound hardware, will help you find the best sound hardware for your needs.

ON THE WEB: The Reviews That Rule

Before you go blind reading sound card and speaker specifications from the vendors' own web sites, grab some reviews that help you to put the numbers in perspective. You might find these sources in particular to be very useful:

- **www.3dsoundsurge.com**—Part of the About network; it provides very thorough, detailed, technical information, news, and reviews.

- **www.computingreview.com**—User-written reviews about all types of hardware are available at this site. It has a similar flavor to Amazon.com's user-written book and media reviews.

- **www.tomshardware.com**—This is the English-language version of Europe's leading hardware news and reviews web site with detailed coverage of all types of computer hardware.

- **www.techtv.com**—Don't forget to search the TechTV web site for sound card news, reviews, and tips. Just use "sound card" for your search.

Upgrading to Better Audio

So, after reading the reviews for your current sound hardware, you've decided that it's time for a change? You'll find that today's sound hardware offers you more options than ever. Depending upon your hardware, you could do the following:

- Install a daughtercard or breakout box to improve I/O options with your existing sound card

- Connect an external audio device to improve audio quality and output options with any type of audio hardware, including motherboard-based, portable, and sound cards

- Replace your sound card or onboard audio with a sound card that has the features you need

- Replace your motherboard with a motherboard with better onboard audio (see Chapter 9 for details)

Which one is best for you? Use Table 14.1 to help you focus in on the best audio upgrade for your situation.

TABLE 14.1	CHOOSING THE RIGHT AUDIO UPGRADE				
Most Important Audio Use	**Reason You Want to Upgrade Your Audio**	**Current Type of Audio**	**Option One**	**Option Two**	**Option Three**
3D gaming	Slow 3D performance	Motherboard-based audio	Disable on-board audio and install sound card featuring fast 3D acceleration	N/A	N/A
3D gaming	Slow 3D performance	Sound card	Replace sound card with new model featuring fast 3D acceleration	N/A	N/A
3D gaming	Can't connect four or more speakers	Sound card	Check with vendor for daughtercard or breakout box with additional speaker options	Replace sound card with new model with fast 3D acceleration and six-speaker support	N/A
3D gaming	Can't connect four or more speakers	Motherboard-based audio	Purchase add-on ports for motherboard if available	Disable onboard sound and install sound card with fast 3D acceleration and six-speaker support	N/A
3D gaming	Can't connect four or more speakers	Portable computer-based audio	Install external sound processing unit such as the Creative Sound Blaster Extigy	N/A	N/A
Digital audio playback	Lack of digital I/O options	Motherboard-based audio	Purchase add-on ports for motherboard if available	Disable on-board audio and install sound card with digital I/O	Install external sound processing unit such as the Creative Sound Blaster Extigy

TABLE 14.1 CONTINUED

Most Important Audio Use	Reason You Want to Upgrade Your Audio	Current Type of Audio	Option One	Option Two	Option Three
Digital audio playback	Lack of digital I/O options	Sound card	Check with vendor for daughtercard or breakout box with additional I/O options	Replace sound card with new model with digital I/O	Install external sound processing unit such as the Creative Sound Blaster Extigy
Digital audio playback	Lack of digital I/O options	Portable computer-based audio	Install external sound processing unit such as the Creative Sound Blaster Extigy	N/A	N/A
Digital audio playback	Poor-quality audio playback	Motherboard-based audio	Install external sound processing unit such as the Creative Sound Blaster Extigy	Disable on-board audio and install sound card with high SNR (100dB or higher) and speaker/3D options as desired	Replace motherboard with AOpen TubeSound model
Digital audio playback	Poor-quality audio playback	Sound card	Replace current sound card with new model featuring high SNR (100dB or higher) and speaker/3D options as desired	Install external sound processing unit such as the Creative Sound Blaster Extigy	N/A
Digital audio production	Can't record 24-bit/96KHz audio	Motherboard-based audio	Disable on-board sound and install sound card with 24-bit/96KHz recording and digital I/O	N/A	N/A
Digital audio production	Can't record 24-bit/96KHz audio	Sound card	Replace sound card with model featuring 24-bit/96KHz recording and digital I/O	N/A	N/A

The following sections show you how to install daughtercards, external sound processing devices, and sound cards. See Chapter 9 for information on motherboard upgrades.

Installing Daughtercards and Breakout Boxes

With more and more interest in connecting computers to sophisticated 5.1, 6.1, and even 7.1 speaker setups and home-theater systems, it's easy to overlook the fact that some sound cards are almost ready to connect to better audio. The problem? You didn't buy the necessary *I/O* ports when you bought the sound card.

JARGON

I/O—Input/Output; any port that can receive (input) or send (output) signals.

White-box—Computer built from off-the-shelf components, usually by a local computer store.

If you have a Sound Blaster Live! or Audigy sound card from Creative Labs, these sound cards have a wide range of digital and analog I/O options built into the card. However, bulk-packed cards used by *white-box* PC builders and lower-cost versions sold at retail often don't include the daughtercards or breakout boxes needed to get access to the ports built into the card.

You can order the Optical Digital I/O 2 daughtercard from Creative Labs (www.soundblaster.com). It adds S/PDIF input/output and digital DIN speaker connectors to Sound Blaster Live! or Audigy sound cards, as well as additional features depending upon the I/O options on your sound card.

The Audigy Drive drive-bay mounted breakout box made for the Sound Blaster Audigy series can also be purchased from the Creative Labs web site. The earlier Live Drive can sometimes be purchased used from sources such as eBay (www.ebay.com). For other brands of sound cards, check with the vendors for upgrade options.

To install a daughtercard or internal breakout box, do the following:

1. Shut down the computer and unplug it.
2. Open the computer and locate the sound card.
3. Connect the data cables to the daughtercard or breakout box.
4. Install the daughtercard or internal breakout box into an open slot or drive bay.

5. Connect the cables for the daughtercard or breakout box to the sound card. Be sure to line up the cable connector with the correct pin on the sound card's interface (see Figure 14.7). Note that the Audigy Drive has two cables: a ribbon cable similar to the one used by the Optical I/O daughtercard and a round cable for the SB1394 port.

6. Connect power to the breakout box.

7. Plug in the computer and restart it.

8. Install drivers as needed.

9. After testing the breakout box, shut down the computer and close it up.

Figure 14.7

Connecting an Optical Digital I/O daughtercard to a Creative Labs sound card.

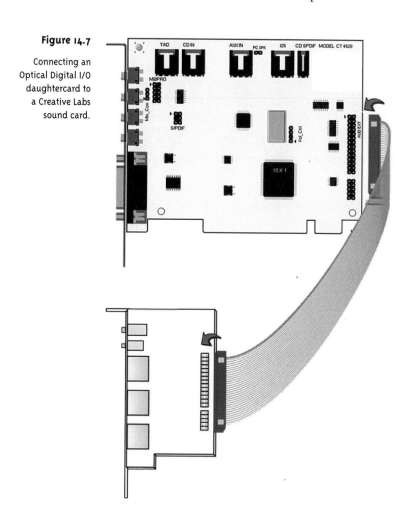

Installing a External Audio Processing Device

If your main reason to upgrade your onboard sound is to improve audio playback quality and output options, you don't need to open your computer to do it. This is especially good news if you have a notebook computer.

Instead of upgrading the sound card, replacing the motherboard, or just cursing your luck, you can plug a Sound Blaster Extigy external audio processor (see Figure 14.8) into any USB port on your computer. Extigy doesn't require a computer to work, so it can also be used to upgrade the audio output on a DVD set-top box, portable CD player, TV, or video game. After you install the driver software for the Extigy, it's ready to work with your PC.

Figure 14.8

Front view of the Creative Labs Sound Blaster Extigy. An additional S/PDIF port, analog and MIDI jacks, and the USB port are located on the rear of the unit. Photo courtesy of Creative Labs.

The Extigy has superb audio quality for playback from both PC and standalone analog and digital sound sources. However, if you want to create new recordings with DVD audio quality or speed up 3D gaming, you need a new sound card.

Installing a New Sound Card—Overview

The process of installing a new sound card includes the following steps:

1. Disconnect the speakers and other peripherals from the old sound hardware.
2. Remove the old sound card or disable onboard sound hardware.
3. Uninstall old sound software bundled with the hardware.
4. Install the new sound card and drivers.
5. Connect the speakers and hardware to the new sound card.
6. Configure the sound card for speaker configuration.
7. Check for proper operation (use diagnostics and play Windows sounds).
8. Install the new sound software.

Enjoy! Okay, so it might not always be this simple. Let's discuss this process a bit more in the next sections.

Removing the Old Sound Card

It's essential that you completely remove (or disable) the old sound hardware *and* its accessory software from your system before you add new hardware.

To remove a sound card, do the following:

1. Open the System properties sheet in the Control Panel, click the Windows Device Manager tab, and open the sound, video, and game controllers hardware category. In Windows XP, the Device Manager is found under the Hardware tab.

2. Select the listing for the sound card and click Remove. The Confirm Device Removal dialog box opens (see Figure 14.9).

3. After you click OK to confirm the device's removal, see if there are other devices you must remove. These might include:

   • Joystick/game port

   • MIDI interface

   • SoundBlaster emulation

   • Legacy audio drivers

4. If removing the entry for the sound card doesn't remove these entries, click each additional item, and then click Remove.

5. Before you shut down the system, uninstall the software provided with the sound card. After both the hardware and software are removed (as far as Windows is concerned), shut down the system.

6. Next, unplug speakers and other hardware from old sound hardware; don't forget to disconnect the analog or digital cable from the CD-ROM drive.

MARK'S TIP SHEET: Be Smart—Make Your Own Labels

Even though most recent sound hardware, speakers, and microphones are color-coded, there are several different (and incompatible) standards. If the component jacks aren't marked with symbols or text, make your own temporary tags and tape them in place. It's hard enough to crawl around behind your PC without needing to do it twice because you plugged the speaker into the microphone jack!

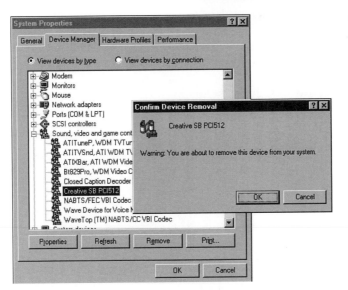

Figure 14.9

The existing sound card must be removed from the Device Manager to enable a new one to be installed without conflicts.

7. To finish the removal job, take the cover off the PC, unscrew the card, and take it out of the system. Set it down on an anti-static mat, inside a parts bag, or on some newspapers.

Putting Built-In Ports to Sleep

Systems with integrated sound require you to alter the BIOS configuration settings instead of removing a board.

To disable on-board sound, do the following:

1. Shut down the system.

2. Restart your computer and press the key displayed on-screen or listed in your user manual to enter the BIOS setup program.

3. Change to the screen used to configure built-in audio (this varies by system, but it might be I/O Device Configuration, Integrated Device Configuration, or something similar).

4. Select the Audio controller (see Figure 14.10) and disable it. On some systems, you might also need to disable legacy audio, game port, MIDI (MPU-401), and SB (Sound Blaster) devices as separate items. Check the motherboard manual for the details of the audio devices on your system.

Figure 14.10

BIOS configuration
screens for a typical
recent system with
on-board audio. The
audio controller
must be disabled
before a sound card
can be installed.

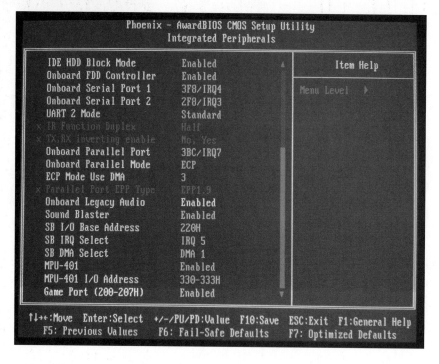

5. If the new sound card doesn't have a 15-pin gameport (refer back to Figure 14.1 to see an example), but you still use that type of controller, disable all settings except the game port.

6. Save the changes and restart the computer. Shut down the system after the memory test is completed.

In with the New

To install the new sound card, do the following:

1. Reuse the PCI slot used by the old sound card or remove a slot cover next to an empty PCI slot. If the old sound card used an ISA slot, and you are replacing it with a PCI slot, use the slot cover you remove from the PCI slot to close the ISA slot.

2. Slide the card into place and push it down firmly until it is solidly mounted in place. Lock the card into place with the screw removed from the slot cover or old sound card.

3. Reattach the speakers, microphone, and other hardware connected to the old sound card (such as the analog or digital audio jack from the CD-ROM drive).

4. Restart the computer and provide drivers as prompted.

5. Reboot the computer when prompted after installation; you should hear Windows startup sounds if your installation is correct.

6. Configure your sound card for correct speaker configuration (see Figure 14.11); you might need to open the Volume control in the system tray or select the device in the Multimedia properties sheet to access this configuration control.

7. Check for proper operation (use diagnostics supplied with the card, play Windows sounds, and so on).

8. Install new the sound software to support the card's special features (MIDI playback, sound recording, and so on).

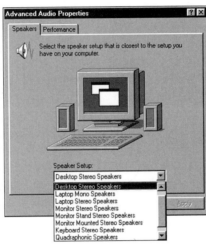

Figure 14.11

Sound cards default to the standard analog stereo speaker configuration. If you're using a different configuration, be sure to select the correct speaker configuration.

Upgrading Your Speaker System

If you use your PC's sound hardware primarily for playing CD audio for background music or for speech recognition, there's no need to add more speakers. However, if you're a 3D gamer or want to experience more realistic (and louder!) sound from your DVD movies or CD and MP3 collection, then it's time to add speakers. Of course, to do this, your system must have the right type of speaker jacks. If you are adding speakers to a low-end sound card, keep in mind that there's not much benefit in using high-end speakers with a low-end sound card.

Even if you don't need to add *more* speakers, you might want to install *better* speakers. You should install high-quality speakers in place of the low-end bundled speakers supplied with your computer if you upgrade to a high-end sound card. Otherwise, you won't get the full benefit of the sound card's superior sound quality.

If you want to evaluate your current speaker setup, you need to know how your speakers are arranged and how they connect to your current sound hardware. These two factors have a huge influence on how realistic your sound quality will be.

Speaker Arrangement

The simplest speaker arrangement of all is the two-speaker setup used by stereo sound cards. This setup uses a left channel and a right channel. Although advanced sound cards with support for positional audio standards such as EAX can improve the realism of sounds for gaming, this type of speaker setup is best for casual sound users only. A 2.1 speaker system adds a subwoofer (represented by the .1).

Many low-end and mid-range sound cards, as well as better motherboard-based audio, support four-channel audio. Four channel audio adds rear left and rear right speakers to the basic stereo configuration. A 4.1 speaker system adds a subwoofer.

High-end sound cards and motherboard-based audio support six-channel sound, also known as 5.1 audio. 5.1 audio adds a center speaker to the 4.1 speaker setup. Low-cost 5.1 speaker systems use analog speakers that depend upon Dolby Digital decoding built into the sound card or a software DVD player. Because Dolby Digital sound is converted from digital to analog, there is some loss of quality with these systems.

If you plan to use your speaker system for both PC and home theater use, look for digital 5.1 speaker systems that have a separate receiver that contains a Dolby Digital decoder. These speaker systems often have more power for better sound quality, especially at high volume. However, if you want 5.1 surround sound for gaming, check with the PC audio hardware vendor to determine which type of output (analog or digital) is supported for 5.1 gaming audio. Most current sound cards with analog and digital jacks output only stereo signals through the S/PDIF digital connector. If you want digital 5.1 gaming, your sound card needs to output a 5.1 signal through the S/PDIF port. Otherwise, you need to use analog speakers.

A few brand-new sound cards support seven-channel audio, also known as 6.1 positional audio or Dolby Digital EX. 6.1 positional audio has both front center and rear center speakers, and is otherwise similar to 5.1 audio.

7.1 positional audio is also available on a few high-end sound cards; it splits the rear audio signal used by 6.1 positional audio into two separate speakers. As with 5.1 setups, those that use digital speakers that contain hardware decoding provide better-quality sound than those that use analog speakers.

Figure 14.12 compares 2.1, 4.1, 5.1, and 6.1 speaker setups to each other.

F = Front
R = Rear
C = Center
FC = Front Center
RC = Rear Center
FL = Front Left
RL = Rear Left
FR = Front Right
RR = Rear Right
S = Subwoofer

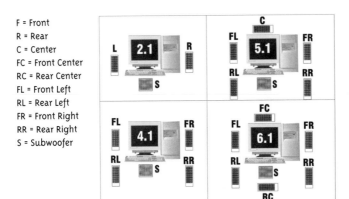

Figure 14.12

2.1, 4.1, 5.1, and 6.1 speaker setups all use subwoofers, but differ in the positions of primary speakers.

ON THE WEB: Understanding Surround Sound

AudioRevolution.com has an excellent article by Jerry Del Colliano on the differences in speaker setups and audio standards. Read it at
`http://www.audiorevolution.com/equip/surround/index.html`.

TechTV's tutorial, "DVD Audio Overview" is available at `http://www.techtv.com/ screensavers/answerstips/story/0,24330,2334015,00.html`.

Although both of these articles are primarily written for DVD home theater users, they are also useful resources for high-end PC audio users.

TechTV's "5.1 Surround Sound for the PC" helps you build your 5.1 configuration and place it in your room. Read it at `http://www.techtv.com/callforhelp/howto/ story/0,24330,3398555,00.html`.

Learn more about Dolby audio standards and how to play games that support Dolby audio from the Dolby web site at `www.dolby.com`.

By default, PC audio is configured to use a basic two-speaker stereo configuration, which also supports the subwoofer provided with a 2.1 configuration. If your PC came with speakers, chances are they were stereo speakers. If you want to use four or more speakers, you need to change the configuration of your audio with the Audio or Sounds and Audio dialog in Control Panel. Click the Advanced button in the Speaker settings section of the Volume tab and select your speaker type.

Analog Versus Digital Speakers

Analog speakers plug into the mini jacks you saw in Figures 14.1 and 14.2. These are best suited for adding a second set of speakers to enhance 3D gaming with more realistic directional sound.

Analog speakers work with any soundcard and are less expensive that digital speakers, but will limit the sound quality you hear with DVD movie soundtracks or other digital music/audio sources.

Digital speakers attach through either S/PDIF or digital DIN jacks, and are best suited for digital music and audio sources such as CDs or DVDs. Unlike analog speaker jacks, which connect directly to the speakers, S/PDIF jacks connect to a receiver that contains an amplifier and decoder. The receiver in turn connects to the speakers. Most decoders support Dolby Digital, and some also support Dolby Pro Logic II and Dolby Theater System. If you plan to use your speakers for both PC and home theater systems, support for Dolby Pro Logic II and Dolby Theater System decoding are important features to look for.

Digital speakers provide more accurate sound reproduction of digital audio sources than analog speakers, but cost more than analog speakers. Depending on the speaker system and the sound card's mixer settings, you can usually set up digital speakers for both DVD/digital music as well as gaming. Check your sound card's configuration options first.

CAUTION: STOP! LOOK! THINK!

Don't Buy Better Speakers Without Checking Your DVD Player Software
Although early DVD drives were shipped with hardware decoder cards, most recent systems use high-speed video cards and DVD player programs to decode and play back DVD movies. The DVD player program needs to support the type of speakers you want to buy; some don't support Dolby Digital 5.1 setups, or they might translate a 5.1 setup for use with four analog speakers (no subwoofer). Some DVD-equipped sound cards come with a player program with the right features, but if you prefer a different player program, make sure it's compatible with the speaker arrangement you want to use.

Sound Quality

As you learned in the preceding sections, sound quality is affected by speaker configuration, analog versus digital audio configuration, and how digital audio sources are decoded. It is also affected by:

- Speaker quality
- Speaker power

The following sections help you make the right decisions when you select your speaker upgrade.

Speaker Quality

Although a few high-end computers built for serious gaming or audio playback are already equipped with high-quality speakers, the low-cost speakers bundled with computer systems can't accurately reproduce the sounds your CD, MP3, and game collections are capable of producing. Bundled speakers often have poor-quality construction, limited frequency response, lack of power, and flat-panel designs that are optimized to save space on the desktop instead of producing great sound.

Multimedia and home theater speakers are more compact than traditional stereo speakers because they provide only high-range and mid-range audio. The low-range audio is directed to the subwoofer units. However, speakers of equal size can have drastically different sound quality.

Some of the speaker features to look for include:

- **THX-Certified system**—Speaker systems that are THX-Certified make an excellent choice for home theater systems because they support the Lucasfilm THX digital audio standard used in many recent films. See the THX web site (www.thx.com) for the latest list of certified speakers, sound cards, and computer systems.

- **Cone or planar-focus designs**—Traditional cone designs create relatively bulky speakers, but great sound. Monsoon's patented Planar Focus Technology looks like a conventional flat-panel speaker, but provides sound quality comparable to cone-design speakers. TechTV gave the MH-505 (www.monsoonpower.com) a four-star rating.

- **Solid speaker enclosures**—If you thump on the sides of a speaker enclosure, you should hear a thud. If you hear a ringing or rattling tone instead, the speaker enclosure isn't solid enough, and your audio will also be distorted by the rattling or ringing of the enclosure.

- **Cabling**—High-quality cabling with heavier insulation and gold-plated tips helps improve sound quality. If you're not happy with the sound quality of your current speaker set, try replacing the cables with Monster Cable or other high-quality cables.

Speaker Power

Speaker performance is measured in watts. The higher the wattage, the greater the power of the speaker system. However, there are many methods for measuring speaker power. The most accurate method is the (US) Federal Trade Commission's RMS (root mean square) method, which measures the output of each pair of speakers driven separately and the sub-woofer, and then adds the totals together. Thus, for a 5.1 speaker system, there are three measurements:

- Front pair
- Rear pair
- Subwoofer

The total is referred to as the Total RMS Power Rating. This is the highest amount of power the speaker system can deliver continuously. Other methods tend to exaggerate the actual power of the speaker system.

Connecting to Your Home Theater

Home theater systems can use either analog or digital audio connections. To connect your audio hardware to a home theater system's speakers, compare the output options on your hardware to your home theater's input options.

If your home theater system has digital speakers, you should use the S/PDIF digital output from your audio hardware to make the connection. Otherwise, use the analog connectors. See your audio hardware and home theater system manual for connector details before you purchase cables.

Selecting the Right Microphone

Most sound users are primarily concerned about sound *output*, but if you use video email, video conferencing solutions such as NetMeeting, voice chat during games, or voice-recognition software such as Dragon Naturally Speaking, you need to be concerned about sound input—specifically, microphones.

Most voice-recognition software comes with an acceptable headset microphone. If you need to replace it, be sure to check the hardware compatibility list for the voice-recognition software you use. Most sound cards are acceptable, but if you're tempted by a really cheap model, skip it; the distortion in cheap cards could make voice recognition less reliable than it already is. Keep in mind that voice recognition software such as Dragon Naturally Speaking, IBM Via Voice, and others require extensive setup and training before you can use them, and results are often disappointing.

You can also use headset microphones with video email and video conferencing. The standard headset microphones often support only monaural audio, however. If you want to hear music or your chatmates in stereo, upgrade to a stereo headset.

If you're concerned about how good your impression of a sportscaster or NASA rocket scientist is, you might prefer a boom microphone that sits on your desk or on top of your monitor. Boom microphones can pick up your voice from a foot away or more, so they can be positioned out of camera view. See Figure 14.13.

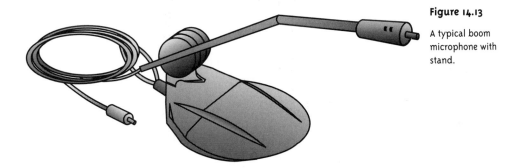

Figure 14.13

A typical boom microphone with stand.

Position the boom microphone so that it's pointed toward your mouth but is either at the edge of the picture or out of camera's view if you don't want the visual distractions. With NetMeeting and typical web cams, you can set the screen to mirror what the remote user will be seeing.

Regardless of whether you are broadcasting email greetings around the country, having a live chat with TechTV hosts, or dictating the great American technology novel, make sure that you use the wizards provided with the software to set up the volume level every time you use the software. Because of changes in room noise levels and microphone placement, you could get erratic results if you try to "set it once and forget it."

Microphone setup wizards, which set the volume, level, and boost controls, are even more critical if you are using a microphone built into a notebook computer. For best results, make sure you sit about the same distance from the screen each time you use the built-in microphone.

Troubleshooting Your Sound Upgrade

Feeling soundly thrashed by sound hardware problems? Been there, done that, and I'm back from the battlefield with help for you.

Chances are, the solution to a problem like yours is listed in the following sections.

Help! I've just decided to switch to digital speakers and now I can't hear anything.

Digital speaker configurations are tricky for two reasons:

- Some sound cards offer both a 9-pin DIN and a round S/PDIF connector.
- The default sound mixer settings assume you're using analog speakers.

First, make sure your sound mixer settings are adjusted correctly for your digital speaker output; look in the volume control in the system tray or the multimedia properties sheet for your sound card for these settings. They might be muted by default (if they are, you'll hear nada until you change the settings). Next, double-check the physical cable configuration to your speakers.

If you connected your optical drive to the digital (two-pin) connector on the sound card, you need to enable digital CD playback: In Windows 98SE, enable this setting through the Multimedia icon in Device Manager; click CD Music, select Enable Digital CD Audio for your drive, and click OK.

In Windows Me and XP, right-click on My Computer and select Properties to open the System properties sheet. With Windows Me, click the Device Manager tab; with Windows XP, click the Hardware tab, and then the Device Manager button. Right-click the optical drive, select Properties, click the Properties tab, and select Enable Digital CD Audio for this CD-ROM Drive (see Figure 14.14).

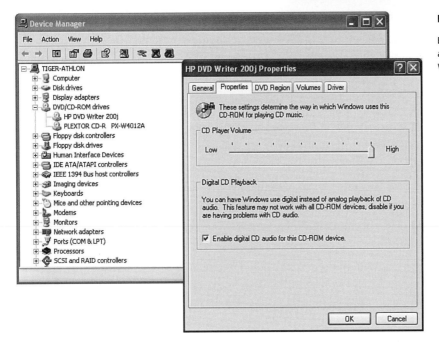

Figure 14.14

Enabling digital
audio playback in
Windows XP.

Help! My new sound card doesn't have a 15-pin game port. I just love my XYZ brand flight controller. What am I going to do?

First, if you're replacing motherboard-based audio with your sound card, see if you can disable the built-in audio and keep the game port, as discussed in the "Putting Built-In Ports to Sleep" section of this chapter. If this isn't possible or doesn't apply, look for a USB to game-port adapter that might be available from either your joystick vendor or a third-party vendor. Keep in mind that most of the new controllers on the market plug into the USB port, and that some users have reported compatibility problems with some devices when adapters are used with some games.

Help! I just added a new sound card to my system and everything's going to pieces. As soon as I try to play a sound, record anything, or do anything with the sound card, I get crashes and errors. What's wrong?

These are classic symptoms of a conflict between your new sound card and existing equipment. If you had on-board sound hardware and didn't disable it in the BIOS, crashes like this are certain to happen. If you *physically* removed your old sound card but didn't remove it from the Device Manager, your computer might be trying to install your sound card to other settings that are causing conflicts. If you used memory resident programs or drivers in the Autoexec.bat and Config.sys startup files with Windows 98 or 98SE for Sound Blaster emulation with your old sound card, you need to remove the references to the programs and drivers because they don't work with other sound cards.

Reboot your system in Safe Mode and remove all sound card-related listings for your new card as well as any old sound hardware listed. If you have on-board sound, be sure to go into the BIOS after you shut down the system and disable the sound. While you're looking at the BIOS, find an option for Extended BIOS Configuration Data and select the setting to discard the existing information and rebuild it. Look for references in the Config.sys and Autoexec.bat files to driver and program files used by your old sound card. Use a text editor such as Notepad to put the word REM before each line that is used by your old sound card. When you restart your computer, the system should redetect your new card and install it correctly.

Chapter 15

Digital Imaging and Video

I love digital imaging! Even if you've seen the same photos many times before, they take on new life when you see them onscreen. They seem to glow with an inner light. In addition, if you're famous for getting *almost* the best photo, scanners and photo-editing software give you a second chance to fix problems with cropping, color, and contrast correction. Faded photos? No problem! Dial back in the color that's left the building.

If you're new to photography, digital imaging gives you a choice: shoot film and digitize it when it's processed, or shoot digitally from the start. Thanks to the LCD preview screens found in most digital cameras and small inkjet and dye-sublimation printers, you can combine the thrill of instant photography with the immediacy of being able to email or print your pictures in a variety of sizes.

Digital imaging is no longer just for photos. Digital video (DV) camcorders combine the fun of filming family and friends at play with the ability to edit and title your work on a PC and create your own video CD or DVD.

In this chapter, I help you learn how to choose the best digital imaging hardware for your needs and bring that same see-it-now excitement to your computer.

Ten Reasons to Move to Digital Imaging and Video

You've seen the stacks of digital cameras, DV camcorders, and scanners at your local electronics store, and you've enjoyed other people's digital photo and video masterpieces, but you're still not sure you're ready to take the plunge. If you find your situation reflected in our top-ten list of reasons to try digital imaging and video, keep reading and learn how to turn your past, present, and future into pixels.

1. Your spouse is threatening to divorce you if you insist on dragging out the slide projector again.

2. You have a growing pile of undeveloped rolls of film.

3. You've been itching to make your own movies since you were a kid.

4. Just once, you'd like to hear somebody say to you, "I'm ready for my close-up."

5. Your photos are turning colors Kodak never intended.

6. You've already ordered your movie director's outfit.

7. You've taken too many photos of your thumb.

8. You're tired of saying, "The pictures aren't ready yet."

9. You like to know right away that you shot a great picture.

10. You like to know right away that you shot lousy footage (so that you can retake it).

Understanding Resolution

No matter what type of digital imaging you want to add to your system, you need to understand the impact that resolution has on the quality of your final results.

Resolution has slightly different meanings, depending on the context. When you consider a scanner's resolution, it is measured in *dots per inch (dpi)*. Digital camera and DV camcorder resolution is measured in *megapixels* (sometimes abbreviated as *MP*). Although the exact definition varies with the imaging device, one thing is constant: more is better.

If you're not completely sure how you will use photos you scan (or shoot) or video you capture, you should use the high-quality settings for your imaging device. You can always reduce quality (which shrinks image size) at a later point, but you can't add quality back into an image that was captured at low quality.

JARGON

Dots per inch (dpi)—Number of pixels (dots) per inch in a scanned image. The resolution used for scanning an image varies with the intended use: 72–96 dpi is suitable for use onscreen or on the web, but 300 dpi provides more detail for printed images. If an image will be cropped after scanning, the scan should be performed at a higher resolution.

Megapixel (MP)—A megapixel is one million pixels. The megapixel (MP) rating is calculated by multiplying the horizontal pixels by the vertical pixels used by a digital camera in its highest-quality setting. For example, a digital camera that captures 1,760 pixels horizontally and 1,168 vertically captures a total of 2,055,680 pixels. It would be referred to as a two-megapixel digital camera by some, and because totals are slightly rounded up by many vendors, it would be referred to as 2.1-megapixel digital camera by others. Low-end DV camcorders have less than one megapixel resolution, but mid-range and high-end models offer one megapixel or higher resolutions.

Selecting the Right Digital Camera

Digital cameras have become the instant cameras of the early 21st century. There are several reasons why:

- The small LCD displays present in all but the cheapest models enable you to see what the camera saw—just seconds after you take a picture. In addition, that same display lets you share your pictures immediately.

- You can transfer your pictures to a computer for emailing or archiving.

- Some of the latest inkjet printers have flash memory slots designed to give you the opportunity to print instant photos of your digital creations—without copying the files to a computer first! You don't need to fill up the flash memory card first, either; view or print just one or two pictures, dozens, or any amount in between.

CAUTION: STOP! LOOK! THINK!

Don't Throw Out Your Film Cameras Just Yet

Digital cameras are exciting and fun, but they aren't for everyone. Unless you're willing to slap down thousands of dollars (yes, you read that right) for a professional digital camera based on 35mm technology such as the Nikon D1H shown in Figure 15.1, you're limited to the zoom lens built into the camera and resolutions designed for 8×10-inch to 11×14-inch enlargements. You can find some digital cameras with manual exposure and focus controls, but they're rare. If you want maximum control for minimum cost, a mid-range 35mm single-lens-reflex (SLR) camera with interchangeable lenses is a better bet for now. Film-based SLRs are better for sports than any under-$1,000 digital camera, too, because they shoot faster and avoid annoying shutter and digital recording lag time.

If you want digital imaging plus the low cost of a film camera, you can get a CD with your pictures at developing time, or skip the prints to save money.

Figure 15.1

The Nikon D1-H
carries on the high-
performance profes-
sional digital SLR
tradition of the
Nikon D1 and uses
the same lenses as
Nikon F-series 35mm
SLR cameras. Photo
courtesy Nikon, Inc.

Like their film forbears, though, the profusion of digital camera models and brands available tends to make it difficult for many people to figure out what's best. The first step in picking the camera that's best for you is to understand a bit about how these cameras work.

How Digital Cameras Work

Digital cameras have many of the same features as film cameras:

- Autofocus lenses with zoom features
- Optical viewfinders
- Through-the-lens viewing (via the LCD preview/review screen)
- Automatic exposure

So what's different? The film!

Most digital cameras use a *charge-coupled device (CCD)* in place of the dark-brown filmstrips familiar to 35mm camera fans or the cartridges used by other camera types. The CCD records RGB (red-green-blue) picture data and has a specified sensitivity to light, typically equivalent to ASA/ISO 100-speed film. Because most film cameras use ASA/ISO 200, 400, or 800-speed film (larger ASA/ISO numbers indicate more sensitivity to light or "faster" film), digital cameras need more light than film cameras do to make a picture.

CAUTION: STOP! LOOK! THINK!

Variable ISO Settings Can Lead to Digital Disappointment
Some of the better digital cameras let you adjust the camera's ISO rating to a specific number (100, 200, 400, or 800). The idea is to optimize the rating for the lighting conditions, just as you would use different film speeds in bright light, dim light, or indoors. However, some cameras produce much poorer-quality pictures when higher ISO numbers are used. Try a few non-critical shots, evaluate the results on your monitor (at 100% or higher magnifications), and then decide if the faster "film" you get with playing with the ISO rating is worth the loss in quality you might see.

Megapixel Mania

The number of individual cells in the CCD determines its resolution, which is commonly rated in megapixels (each megapixel equals a million pixels). Think of your photo as being divided up into squares; the more squares used to make the final picture, the more true-to-life the picture is. The more cells (pixels) in your camera's CCD, the better. Table 15.1 breaks down the resolutions and intended uses of the digital cameras you can get for under $1,000.

Table 15.1 Megapixel Ratings and Suggested Maximum Print Sizes				
Megapixel Rating	**Horizontal Pixels***	**Vertical Pixels***	**Total Pixels**	**Suggested Print Size**
Digital webcam (VGA)	640	480	307,200	None
Typical 17-inch monitor	1024	768	786,432	N/A
1.0Megapixel	1152	864	995,328	up to 3×5 inches
2.1Megapixel	1760	1168	2,055,680	up to 5×7 inches
3.1Megapixel	2160	1440	3,110,400	up to 8×10 inches
4.0Megapixel	2272	1704	3,871,488	up to 11×14 inches
5.0Megapixel	2560	1920	4,915,200	up to 16×20 inches

*Some cameras might vary slightly from these values.

Of course, the CCD is only half of the story when it comes to replacing film. When the CCD receives the picture data, it needs to store it somewhere. Most digital cameras use flash memory storage for their film.

MARK'S TIP SHEET: Don't Buy Just Enough Resolution to Get By

It's tempting to cut corners when you buy a digital camera and buy one that has just enough resolution for the intended task. Don't do it! I can explain why you need to spend more money to get the right camera with just one word: cropping.

When you crop out that tree branch that's growing out of Aunt Millie's head or crop the half of cousin Derek that made it into the picture, your picture winds up using less of the resolution you started with. For example, if you took a picture with a 2-megapixel camera, and cropped out half the picture, what's the real resolution of the remainder? Just 1 megapixel, that's what! Print the cropped picture and you'll be looking at a jagged and fuzzy result (although it will still look OK onscreen).

Because even the greatest photographer (and over thirty years behind the viewfinder still doesn't put me in that league) needs to crop, you're going to leave part of the resolution behind every time you crop. Thus, if you want to have enough dots for sharp, clear print-outs, buy one megapixel higher than you think you need, if you can afford it.

The most common types of digital camera storage include the following:

- **Compact Flash***—The form of flash memory used by most cameras.

- **Smart Media***—A form of flash memory that's being replaced by xD-Picture Card.

- **Sony Memory Stick***—Guess who prefers this form of flash memory?

- **Secure Digital***—Used by some small-form-factor cameras.

- **1.44MB floppy disk***—Used on less-expensive Sony Mavica digital cameras (Sony also makes floppy disks).

- **120MB LS-120 SuperDisk***—Used on a few high-end cameras.

- **Mini CD-R**—Expensive but durable (non-erasable) storage used on a few high-end cameras.

- **Hitachi (IBM) Microdrive**—340MB–1GB miniaturized disk drive in a Compact Flash-sized case. It can be used in place of Compact Flash on many cameras; check with the vendor for compatibility.

*These forms of storage are pictured in Chapter 11, "Removable Storage to Go."

Keep in mind that the higher the megapixel rating of your camera, the fewer images you can store in a given storage device.

ANALYZE THIS

News Flash! How Flash Memory Works

Most digital cameras use *flash memory*, which is a very different type of memory than ordinary RAM memory; ordinary RAM loses its contents as soon as the system is restarted or the power is turned off. Instead of the capacitors or transistors used by ordinary RAM, flash memory uses cells. When voltage is applied to the cells whose contents are being changed, electrons move from their normal position to a different part of the cell, and stay there even when the power is turned off. This enables flash memory to store pictures when the camera is turned off, and enables you to move the flash memory card from your camera to a card reader for transfer.

Just as film comes in different exposure sizes, flash memory comes in different capacities (measured in megabytes). Most cameras come with flash memory cards that are very small and that can hold only a few pictures at the highest quality. I recommend you buy the largest flash memory card your camera can use so that you can take as many pictures as possible before erasing some or having to transfer pictures to your computer.

How Much Can You Store Before You Fill Up Your Media?

There are five factors that affect how much you can store in a given digital camera storage device:

- **The camera's resolution**—The higher the megapixel rating, the fewer the pictures that can be stored on the media.

- **The camera's quality setting**—High-quality pictures look better but uses more space than low quality because greater image compression reduces the quality of saved pictures.

- **The camera's resolution setting**—Most 2-megapixel and higher-resolution cameras offer two or more resolution settings. My 3Megapixel Nikon Coolpix 995 camera, for example, can be set for Full (2,048×1536, slightly over 3 million pixels) and four other resolutions down to VGA (640×480). I can store ten times as many photos on the same size media using VGA mode, but the images will be much less sharp.

- **The camera's image type**—Most low-end and mid-range cameras create *JPEG* (.jpg) files only, which use a form of compression that discards fine detail to save space. Some mid-range and high-end cameras can also store *TIFF* (.tif) files, which retain fine detail better than JPEG files, but use much more space. For example, I can store about 39 photos using the high-quality JPEG mode and using fine (highest-quality) resolution with my Nikon Coolpix 995 with a 64MB Compact Flash memory card, thanks to JPEG compression. For maximum sharpness when I shoot close-ups of equipment, I prefer to use the uncompressed TIFF file format; only six of these images fit on the same 64MB Compact Flash memory card.

- **The size of the media**—Most digital cameras are bundled with absurdly small flash memory cards. For example, my 3Megapixel Nikon Coolpix 995 was bundled with a 16MB Compact Flash memory card. At best quality settings using JPEG imaging, I can store about ten photos before it's time to change cards. The first upgrade I bought for this camera was a 64MB Compact Flash card! Although you can reduce quality or resolution settings to store more pictures, using a larger flash memory card lets you store more pictures without sacrificing picture detail.

Chapter 11 lists the typical size ranges available for the various types of flash memory cards used with digital cameras. Before you buy a larger card, check with the camera vendor to determine the largest size supported by your camera. Then, buy the largest card you can afford, or two or more smaller cards if their cost per MB is less than the largest card on the market.

JARGON

JPEG—Joint Photographic Experts Group, a lossy file format used by almost all digital cameras and scanners. Digital cameras can be adjusted to discard more detail to enable more photos to be stored in a particular amount of flash memory, or to discard less detail to improve quality but use more flash memory per photo.

TIFF—Tagged Image File Format, a lossless file format used by most mid-range and high-end digital cameras and scanners. TIFF files can be stored in a compressed format that does *not* discard data. However, both compressed and uncompressed files have more detail, but are much larger than JPEG files.

Essential Digital Camera Features

It's easy to get distracted by the whiz-bang features found on a lot of digital cameras. So much so that it's easy to forget that a digital camera has just one job…taking pictures!

So, what are the features you absolutely, positively must have? First, make sure you understand that a good digital camera costs some serious bucks: $400 or more. Thus, even though you use it along with your computer, you'd probably want to budget it as a home entertainment expense rather than a computer expense. After all, you want to have money left for other computer upgrades this year, right?

Tables 15.2 and 15.3 list the essential features you should look for, along with some handy extras you should consider if you have the bucks.

Table 15.2   Essential Digital Camera Features

Feature	Benefit	Notes
2-megapixel or better resolution	Can make decent digital prints.	The higher the resolution, the fewer the pictures that can be stored in a given amount of flash memory.
Close focusing (12 inches or less)	Enables easy close-ups of small objects.	Watch out for uneven lighting and use the LCD preview for accurate aiming.
Built-in LCD with preview and review options	Works like a single-lens reflex camera viewfinder to give you a more accurate preview of your picture; you have an instant view of the pictures you've taken.	LCD use reduces battery life substantially.
3x or better optical zoom	Gets you closer to distant subjects.	Avoid digital zooms; they enlarge the pixels.
Removable storage media	Lets you change "film" and keep shooting.	Compact Flash is the most popular type, but others are closing in on the king.
USB interface	Lets you transfer pictures to most recent PCs without using a card reader.	Using the camera to transfer pictures also reduces battery life; use this option only when a card reader isn't available.

Table 15.3 lists some useful features that can make life easier for you, but aren't essential to good photography.

Keep in mind that the picture quality is also affected by the quality of the lens the camera uses and by the adjustments you make when taking the picture. As with printers (see Chapter 21, "Output Unlimited with Printer Upgrades"), try to see samples before you buy or at least try the cameras in the store to see which one feels and works most comfortably for you.

Table 15.3   Useful Digital Camera Features

Feature	Benefit	Notes
Manual exposure control	Lets you adjust pictures while you shoot.	Makes getting better pictures easier; digital darkroom software can do only so much to correct pictures that are too dark or too light.
TIFF image capture option	Highest-quality pictures because no compression is performed on the image; use for prints and enlargements.	Uses much more storage space than the normal JPEG format; not necessary for web site use.
Video clip capture	Lets you capture short full-motion movies.	Quality and length of video clips are more limited than with a DV camcorder.
Image stabilization	Minimizes blurry pictures due to camera shake.	You can fix exposure or color problems with Adobe Photoshop, but you can't fix camera shake with any program.
Filter threads on lens	Filters can protect lens and enable special photo effects.	Keep filters clean to avoid degrading picture quality.
Wide-aperture lens	Lets you shoot good pictures in less light.	Use filters to protect these expensive optics.
3-megapixel resolution or higher	8×10-inch enlargements or larger.	Enables you to crop an image without losing detail.
Weather-resistant case	Lets you shoot in foul weather.	Check with the camera vendor for details. Look for cameras that meet IEC standard publication 529 IPX4, such as the Olympus Stylus Digital 300.

ON THE WEB: Click Your Way to the Best Digital Photo Gear

Wondering where to look for the latest digital camera, scanner, and photo-printer news, reviews, and tips? Send your browser to the Digital Cameras Superguide on the TechTV web site at www.techtv.com/superguides/digitalcameras/. Use the links to jump directly to help, reviews, and other topics.

You'll also find Zdnet's SuperCenters to be useful in your search: `www.zdnet.com/reviews/`. Click the links for digital cameras, scanners, and other products.

Wondering what other users think about digital photography equipment and software? Find thousands of reviews, buying guides, tutorials, and more at `www.pcphotoreview.com`.

User reviews are also the rule at `www.epinions.com`.

Traps to Avoid

The feature lists I've given you can help you get a better digital camera. But there are some "features" that you must absolutely avoid if you want to enjoy your digital photography experience:

- **No removable storage**—Cameras that don't offer some sort of removable storage should be called toys. In fact, some companies do market such low-end cameras to kids. Don't do this to yourself—get a grown-up camera that uses interchangeable storage and can keep shooting after you fill up the original storage device's capacity. With cameras without removable storage, you must dump the built-in flash memory's contents to the computer before you can take any more pictures. You'd better not go very far from home with a camera like this.

- **No support for rechargeable batteries or AC adapter**—Cameras that can't use any power source but alkaline batteries will send you to the poorhouse very quickly. If you're stuck with one of these, at least do yourself a favor and use the newer Ultra batteries made for high-drain applications.

- **No LCD preview**—Cameras that lack LCD preview screens force you to squint through a small optical viewfinder that gives you only a rough idea of the actual picture area. The closer you get to your subject, the more likely your camera will say "off with their heads" at picture time because of a nasty problem called *parallax*.

ANALYZE THIS

The Parallax View

What is parallax? It's the difference between the view that the camera lens has of the subject and the view that you have from a separate viewfinder. Parallax becomes a major problem if you're shooting within three feet of your subject because the viewfinder shows you a view that's considerably different than the picture-taking lens sees. Fortunately, most digital cameras give you an easy way to overcome the parallax problem: the LCD preview screen.

The LCD preview screen shows you the same view that you get when you take the picture, because it shows you what the camera lens sees. If you use a single lens reflex camera for film photography, you already know how valuable this is. If not, trust me; your days of cutting off heads are over. It's even worth buying rechargeable batteries to use this feature every time you shoot.

- **Digital zoom**—Whenever I look at a camera's features, I always ignore the digital zoom, although most digital cameras have a larger digital zoom ratio than optical zoom ratio. I never use the digital zoom because all digital zoom can do is magnify the pixels in the normal image. It might look okay through the small LCD preview window, but when you print out digitally zoomed images, the enlarged pixels detract from image quality.

ANALYZE THIS

Optical Zoom Versus Digital Zoom

The optical zoom feature found on many digital cameras uses a zoom lens, which is a lens that adjusts the magnification of the image it focuses onto the CCD at the rear of the camera. If you look at the inside of the lens elements of your camera while you press the zoom control, you can see the lens elements move closer or farther from each other.

Digital zooms, on the other hand, don't use the lens to magnify the image. Instead, the camera performs some calculations to enlarge the image after it strikes the CCD. Because the camera can work only with a fixed number of pixels in the image, it must magnify the pixels, and the end result is a more jagged, less sharp result when digital zooming is used.

Digital zooming is similar to what happens if you enlarge a small section of a film photograph in a photo editor. The picture isn't nearly as sharp as it would have been if the photographer had moved closer or used a zoom lens to capture just that part of the picture originally.

Selecting the Right Scanner

If you enjoy photography, you probably enjoy looking back on your life and hobbies through pictures. Although digital cameras provide the "See It Now!" excitement of instant photography and give you email and Internet-ready images, scanners enable you to bring the pictures of your life into the present.

After you've digitized your pictures, you can:

- **Print them**—You can use a high-quality inkjet or dye-sublimation photo printer or use a web-based or walk-up photofinishing service to get prints. Many camera shops and camera departments can print directly from your CD or flash memory card.

- **Crop them**—Put the attention on the subject you care about most.

- **Enlarge or reduce them**—Enlargements add impact; use reduced-size images in business cards.

- **Create panoramic views**—Create views from individual narrow-angle photos.

- **Store them**—Use CD-R, CD-RW, or recordable/rewritable DVD to create an image archive.

- **Create computerized slide shows**—Dazzling transitions and synchronized sound help guarantee that nobody nods off during the show.

- **Output them to videotape**—Use the TV-out jack on the rear of many recent video cards and computers to send photos to a videotape for use by the computerless.

- **Create books, web sites, and other publications**—Most of the photos in this book were shot with my digital cameras.

- **Post them online at a photo web site**—Send family and friends the URL and they can sit back and enjoy your work.

The list is endless!

In addition, during the digitizing process, you can correct the ravages of time and decay by doing the following:

- Intensify faded colors

- Reverse color shifts

- Increase or reduce contrast

- Retouch or crop out damaged areas

- Bring out hidden details

- Fix red-eye

Just as many photographers spend hours in the darkroom printing and manipulating their negatives, computerized photographers with scanners can spend hours transforming their old photographs—without a need for smelly chemicals!

How Scanners Work

Scanners also use a CCD, which makes them similar in some ways to digital cameras. The difference is the positioning of the CCD and what the CCD does with the image data.

A scanner is usually set up as a *TWAIN device* that is controlled by a photo-editing program such as Photoshop, Photo-Paint, or similar programs. Here's how it works:

1. You use the File, Acquire command in your software to start the scanning process.

2. When the scanner receives the Acquire command via the TWAIN software driver, the scanner is activated. Most types of scanner software create a preview image that you can use as a guide to the final scan. See Figure 15.2.

Figure 15.2

Adobe Photoshop
uses the File,
Acquire command
to launch a scan-
ner's control pro-
gram. After the
picture is scanned,
it is displayed in the
Photoshop work area
and the scanner
window is closed.
Photos from the
Soper/Christmas
family collection.

3. You select the image type (color photo, black-and-white photo, drawing, and so on), the scanning resolution, and the portion of the image you want in the final scan. You can also adjust contrast, brightness, color values, and other settings.

4. The scanner creates a final image based on the options you select.

5. After the scanning mechanism sends the picture data to the CCD for digitizing, the CCD transmits the data through the scanner's interface to the computer.

6. The TWAIN driver for the scanner passes the picture data to the photo editor. Now you can crop, rotate, and recolor away!

NOTE

Mark This Well—Twain Has Nothing to Do with TWAIN

Classic American Author Mark Twain has *nothing* to do with the TWAIN standard for imaging devices. Interestingly enough, the TWAIN working group (www.twain.org) mentions a connection with another famous 19th century author: Rudyard Kipling. His famous poem, "The Ballad of the East and West," contains the famous phrase "...and never the twain shall meet." According to the TWAIN working group, this phrase describes the difficulty of getting scanners and other imaging devices to work with computers before the development of the TWAIN standard. The oft-heard suggestion that TWAIN is short for "Technology Without An Interesting Name" is a high-tech urban legend.

Windows Me and XP also provide their own camera and scanner wizards, but I prefer to use the TWAIN interface because it provides more control over the scanning process.

MARK'S TIP SHEET: If Windows Me/XP Doesn't Recognize Your Scanner...

Windows Me introduced Microsoft's Windows Imaging Architecture (WIA) to provide a uniform way to control scanners and digital cameras. Windows XP has improved on WIA, but WIA depends on specific Windows Me or Windows XP drivers for the scanner.

If you've been using a scanner developed before Windows Me or XP, it might not have a WIA driver. The good news? It doesn't matter! As long as there's a TWAIN driver for the scanner, it will work in Windows Me or XP. The proof? I'm still using a 1997-vintage Epson Expression 636 scanner with a SCSI interface.

Scanner Types

There are several different types of scanners on the market, and each is designed to perform a specific task best. The scanner you buy should be one that:

- Is designed to work with the type of photo (print, slide, negative, large format, and so on) you prefer.
- Provides adequate image quality for both full-frame scans and close-up detail scans.
- Offers a high-speed connection to the computer.

Depending on your existing photo habits (and the photo collection you might already have on hand), you might find that more than one type of scanner is what you need.

ANALYZE THIS

Optical Versus Interpolated Resolution

When it comes to accurate scanning, optical resolution rules. Optical resolution is the actual detail that a scanner can detect—the higher the better. Flatbed scanners and some other types of scanners also feature a higher interpolated resolution value. Interpolated resolution seeks to fill in missing detail, but results can vary widely. Interpolated resolution should never be used on negatives or slides and is of limited use on prints (although it can be handy for adding detail to small areas you need to enlarge). When you compare scanners, always compare the optical resolution.

Flatbed—The King of Scanners

Ask to see a scanner at a computer store and you'll find yourself in front of a long line of scanners. All of them look like what you'd get if you removed the top of a copy machine, and their mechanisms are actually quite similar to a copier's in some ways.

Flatbed scanners move the CCD past the image being scanned to digitize it. Flatbed scanning mechanisms are simple, and recent advancements in CCD quality and lower prices put flatbed scanners into everyone's price range. Quite a few are available for under $100, and for under $200, there are some very good products.

Flatbed scanners are ideal for photos and documents and can work well with books. Some recent models even use a special hinged top that makes it easier to scan books without damaging the bindings.

Some flatbed scanners have a built-in transparency adapter, and others have a removable top that enables a transparency module to be attached. Because transparencies must be scanned with transmitted light rather than reflected light, special devices are required. However, because most transparencies are 35mm (24mm×36mm/1 inch×1.5 inches), the optical resolutions available with most flatbed scanners aren't high enough for good-quality scans. Because slides and negatives are very small, they should be scanned at 1,600 dpi or higher, compared to 300 dpi or higher for prints. However, flatbed scanners with full-size transparency adapters such as the Epson Expression 1680 Professional work well with larger-format negatives from press or view cameras (2.25 inches wide and larger). I've created three historic photo collection archives for libraries in Southern Indiana using such a scanner.

All-in-One Models Might Compromise Scan Quality and Features

All-in-one devices (which incorporate printer, scanner, copier, and sometimes fax features) are popular in small home offices where space is short and money is tight. Devices that have flatbed scanner/copier features can perform as well as low to mid-range standalone scanners. However, some of the scanners built into all-in-one devices still use the obsolescent sheet-fed scanning mechanism adapted from fax machines. A sheet-fed scanning mechanism pulls the document to be scanned past the CCD. This limits the maximum resolution and the accuracy of scanning, makes it difficult to scan documents that are smaller than letter size, and prevents the scanning of books, bulky items such as fabric, small 3D objects, and transparencies.

MARK'S TIP SHEET: Having It All with Just One Scanner

If you can afford only one scanner that has to scan prints, slides, and negatives at high resolutions, here are a few of my favorites:

- **Epson Expression 1680 Professional**—1,600×3,200 dpi and the ability to scan up to 8×10-inch transparencies, high-powered software, USB 1.1/SCSI ($1,149); FireWire version ($1,399) adds IEEE-1394 interface; www.epson.com.

- **Umax PowerLook 1100**—1,200×2,400 dpi, FireWire interface, and batch scanning ($900; $1,400 with PowerColor software); www.umax.com.

- **Canon CanoScan 9900F**—Amazing 3,200×6,400 dpi resolution, built-in 35mm and 4×5-inch transparency adapter, 48-bit color capture, fast USB 2.0/FireWire interfacing, and built-in dust and scratch removal ($400); www.usa.canon.com.

Slide/Transparency Scanners—Fine Detail at a Price

It can be easy to forget that when you are scanning a photograph that you are actually scanning a print made from a negative or a slide. You are not scanning the original, and this means that the resolution, tonal depth, and other available information is limited by the quality of the print with which you are working.

For maximum quality, it's best to scan the original slide or negative. Unfortunately, only the most expensive flatbed scanners have resolution that even approaches what you need to pull fine detail from the small 35mm negative or transparency. If you have a large collection of slides or prefer to scan the original negatives, you need a slide scanner.

A good slide scanner costs at least $500 to $1,000 or more, but it has an optical resolution of over 2000 dpi. The best slide scanners have resolutions of up to 4000 dpi.

Most slide scanners use a small holder that holds several negatives, but some slide scanners require you to load slides one at a time. Some newer models use a holder to let you scan several slides at a time.

Because you are scanning from the original image (the print is a copy), you can pick up fine detail that might not be present in even the finest print.

Portable Scanners Capture Photos Everywhere

If you need to carry a scanner with you everywhere for the most common scanning jobs, none of the preceding models is suitable: a flatbed scanner is too bulky and too fragile; ditto for an all-in-one model. Film scanners are relatively compact, but they can't be used for scanning documents.

Portable scanners such as the Visioneer Strobe XP100 (www.visioneer.com) and Ambir Technology TravelScan Pro and Visigo A4 (www.ambir.com) fit the bill for maximum portability in minimum size and weight. At 11 to 12 inches long and 12 to 13 oz. each with sheet-fed mechanisms, these scanners are about the size of a submarine sandwich, so they're easy to carry around. They draw power from the computer's USB port, so they don't require separate AC adapters.

These scanners do a great job of scanning documents and photographs, particularly the Visigo A4 (formerly called the TravelScan XP) and Visioneer Strobe XP100, both of which feature 600 dpi optical resolutions. Note that unlike a flatbed scanner or all-in-one device, sheetfed models like these can't scan books. Also note that at prices from $120 (TravelScan Pro) to $150 (Visigo A4 and Visioneer Strobe XP100), these scanners are more expensive than flatbed scanners with comparable performance.

Special Scanner Features Worth Looking For

To get the best results from your scanner, look for these scanner features:

- **Dual interface support for use with a variety of operating systems**—Although USB and IEEE-1394 dominate the PC and Mac worlds, more adventurous types who prefer Linux might find themselves locked out. A SCSI interface leaves the door open to using Linux or older versions of Windows.

- **Automatic document feeder (ADF)**—If you plan to use page-recognition software, an ADF will save you lots of time and trouble as it feeds sheet after sheet into your flatbed scanner. ADFs are also useful for scanning stacks of enlargements.

JARGON

Page-recognition software—Programs that can convert a printed page back into editable text. Better programs such as OmniPage can also scan the graphics and preserve the layout and use the same or similar fonts used in the original document. Page-recognition software is a great tool for turning older printed or typed documents into a storable, editable, searchable computer form.

- **Digital ICE automatic scratch and dust removal**—The Digital ICE feature found on some slide and transparency scanners is a lifesaver when you are scanning less-than-perfect media. Instead of the blurring of fine detail or tedious manual retouching you'd normally find necessary to hide or remove scratches and dust, Digital ICE scans the film surface and digitally removes dirt, dust, scratches, hair, and other debris from the final scan. Applied Science Fiction, Inc (www.appliedsciencefiction.com), creator of Digital ICE, also offers Digital ROC and Digital GEM for color reconstruction and grain reduction. See Applied's web site for details and to learn about scanners incorporating these technologies. Some Canon scanners incorporate proprietary technology designed to perform similar tasks.

- **True transparency adapter**—Although some flatbed scanners include a lid with transparency support, a true transparency adapter produces much better results with larger transparencies. This type of transparency adapter uses the same moving head technology that a flatbed scanner uses, but it places the scanning head above the transparency in a special cover that replaces the normal scanner cover. Another method that works well is a special drawer that slides out of the scanner. Although most flatbed scanners do not reach the resolution of a high-end dedicated slide scanner, these types of transparency adapters or drawers can provide results similar to the results you have with a dedicated slide scanner set for medium quality.

Selecting the Right DV Camcorder

DV camcorders use digital technology to record movies. Consequently, it's easier to work with DV camcorder-created movies than with the older 8mm and VHS-based analog technologies. You can transfer your DV movies direct to DVD, or edit them first.

There's no shortage of DV camcorders on the market, so how can you make sure you get the best one for your needs? Start by understanding the three different types of DV camcorders:

- Digital8
- MiniDV
- MicroMV

Sony invented all three standards (although many brands are now available), but they differ in many ways, including camera cost, size, blank tape cost, and how you capture and edit video.

> **ON THE WEB: DV Camcorders the TechTV Way**
>
> TechTV's digital cameras page features both still-image and DV camcorder reviews:
>
> www.techtv.com/products/digitalcameras/
>
> Use the TechTV search engine with DV camcorder to find more articles, reviews, news, and how-to's.

Digital8

Digital8, a digital adaptation of the Hi-8 analog camcorder format, is the oldest DV camcorder format. Digital8 camcorders are bulkier than MiniDV or MicroMV models, but you can use inexpensive Hi-8 tapes in your Digital8 camcorder and playback Hi-8 and 8mm tapes as well as Digital8 tapes with your camcorder. Digital8 performs compression on each frame separately.

Unlike analog camcorders, most Digital8 camcorders have an IEEE-1394 port (Sony calls it i.Link) for direct connection to your PC. Digital8 camcorders have 500 lines of resolution and capture about 460,000 pixels' worth of information when used in still-image mode. Digital8 camcorders with still-image capture can store still images on flash memory cards, but the relatively small amount of pixels means that the still photos are suitable for online or onscreen viewing only.

MiniDV

MiniDV and Digital8 camcorders can both capture footage that's better than analog camcorders, and both put up to 120 minutes on a single tape. MiniDV camcorders and tapes are smaller, but more expensive than Digital8 models. MiniDV camcorders also compress each frame separately.

MiniDV camcorders also include a FireWire (i.Link) port for connecting to a suitably-equipped PC. Low-end MiniDV camcorders capture about 680,000 pixels, but mid-range models achieve one-megapixel ratings and high-end models achieve two-megapixel ratings for sharper movies and still images. Figure 15.3 shows a typical mid-range MiniDV camcorder, the Sony DCR-TRV18.

Figure 15.3

The Sony DCR-TRV18 features still-image capture to Sony's own MemoryStick flash memory cards. Photo courtesy of Sony.

MicroMV

Sony introduced this newest and smallest DV format in early 2002. How much smaller is MicroMV than MiniDV? MicroMV cartridges are just one-third the size of MiniDV, and the cameras are tiny as well. However, small size doesn't mean low-quality results. Entry-level models have one-megapixel image sensors, and higher-level models have two-megapixel sensors for results comparable to MiniDV.

As with other DV camcorders, MicroMV models include an IEEE-1394 (i.Link) port to transfer movies to the PC. One major advantage enjoyed by MicroMV is the 64KB memory chip on each tape cartridge. This memory chip enables you to look at thumbnail images of the first frame of every sequence on the tape so that you can rewind or fast forward to the exact location.

Initially, MicroMV editing software was available only from Sony because MicroMV uses a different MPEG-2 compression scheme than other DV formats. However, some third-party products such as Pinnacle Systems' Pinnacle Studio 8 (www.pinnaclesys.com) and Ulead VideoStudio and MediaStudio Pro 7 (www.ulead.com) now work with MicroMV as well as other DV formats.

> **JARGON**
>
> **Movie Video Standards**
>
> *MPEG-2*—A standard developed by the Motion Picture Experts Group (MPEG) for compressed video that supports standard and HDTV output, MPEG-2 supports full-screen resolutions of 720×480 and 1280×720 along with CD-quality audio.
>
> *MPEG-1*—Another MPEG standard used primarily on PCs, MPEG-1 supports screen resolutions of 352×240.
>
> *QuickTime*—A movie standard developed by Apple that integrates audio and video. It's similar to AVI (Video for Windows), but not directly compatible.

The MPEG-2 file compression used by MicroMV works across 15 frames, retaining and compressing only the changed video information on frames 2 through 15. Because the compression technology is different than the frame-by-frame technique used by Digital8 and MiniDV, video-editing software must be updated to support this format. Sony provides a low-end, Windows-only movie editor with its cameras. Called MovieShaker, it can be used to mix MicroMV with Digital8 or MiniDV footage, and it enables video to be exported to AVI, MPEG1, or QuickTime formats for use with other editing programs.

How Key Features Affect DV Camcorder Pricing

Because DV camcorders can cost anywhere from around $400 up to $3,000 or more, they represent a major investment of your entertainment dollar. The price range is so wide because of the following factors:

- The quality of the lens, including its construction and zoom range
- The number and resolution of the CCDs used to capture the image
- The size of the camera

Lens Quality

One of the ways that camcorder makers can cut costs is with lower-quality optics. Although almost any DV camcorder has a lens good enough for capturing motion video, still-image capture and extreme wide-angle and telephone zooming make lens quality differences very apparent.

The easiest way to find superior optics is to look for DV camcorders that use lenses made by companies that specialize in photographic and video optics. Although some DV camcorder companies (Canon, for example) are famous for both cameras and lenses, other vendors use third-party optics on their mid-range and high-end cameras. For example, Panasonic entrusts their better camcorders' lenses to Leica, makers of the legendary Leica 35mm cameras. Sony's better camcorders rely on Carl Zeiss lenses, which have been used over the years by legendary German camera producer Zeiss-Ikon and currently by Kyocera's Contax line of 35mm SLR cameras.

Look for a 20× zoom ratio if you want to get exceptionally close to your subjects, but be sure to use a tripod or enable motion compensation in the camera to avoid camera shake.

Charge-Coupled Device Resolution

Most DV camcorders use a single-chip CCD image sensor, while high-end cameras use a trio of CCDs to capture red, green, and blue separately. The larger the diameter of the single-chip CCD, the higher the resolution and the better the image quality when comparable-quality lenses are used.

Low-end models often feature CCDs with 290,000 to 460,000 pixels, whereas midrange models have CCDs with 680,000 to 700,000 pixels. The best single-CCD models feature CCDs with one-megapixel (1,000,000 pixels) to two-megapixel resolutions. More pixels make for a sharper picture.

High-end cameras intended for use by serious videographers, the so-called "prosumer" models, replace the single-CCD design with a trio of CCDs. Each one captures one of the three primary colors (red, green, and blue), which are mixed to create the colors we see. Because each CCD is smaller than the megapixel-class CCD, special pixel-manipulation tricks are performed by many of these camcorders to increase image quality.

Camera Size

The smaller the camera, the more expensive it is. As you learned earlier, Digital8 cameras and tape are the bulkiest, MiniDV is smaller, and MicroMV is the smallest format of all. Within each family of cameras, less-expensive cameras tend to be bulkier than more-expensive models.

The extra research and development costs necessary to reduce optics and electronics in size get added to the cost of the camera. Keep in mind that a smaller camera is more likely to be used and taken with you, but if you get too small a camera, the controls could also be too small to use comfortably.

In recent tests of DV camcorders on the TechTV web site, Digital8 cameras weighed in at about 2 lbs, compared to 1.1–1.4 lbs for MiniDV camcorders. MicroMV camcorders weigh as little as 12 oz (3/4 of a pound).

Additional Features to Consider

Camcorders are loaded with features, some of which are more useful than others. Here are the features I think are most useful and why:

- **Comfortable zoom and camera controls**—Pick up the camera to determine if the controls are well-placed, and try the zoom to see if you can get smooth zooming from wide to telephoto.

- **Image stabilization**—Look for this feature if you don't want to lug a tripod around but want to show smooth video. For the best image quality (albeit at a higher price), look for optical systems; these use gyroscopes inside the lens to steady the image. Digital stabilizers control image shake with electronics and software. A digital stabilizer can reduce image quality, so look for a way to turn it off when you don't need it.

- **Special effects**—Some cameras have built-in special effects such as strobe, old-fashioned movie, monochrome, sepiatone, and transitions. They also might have special presets for specific lighting conditions, such as under fluorescent lights or while filming night sports. The presets for specific lighting help improve color and image quality under tricky lighting conditions, but special effects are less useful. Use them only if you also have plain video of the same scene and event.

- **Manual controls**—Overriding normal automatic modes can create better movies under difficult lighting conditions if you are an experienced videographer.

- **Battery life**—Lithium-ion batteries have longer life than the older NiCad and NiMH technologies, but it's also helpful to have a visual display of battery life appearing in the viewfinder. Be sure to compare the cost of spare batteries so that you can afford to have a spare in the charger.

- **Viewfinder and LCD design**—You might prefer to use a traditional viewfinder for some shooting jobs and the swing-out LCD display for others. Try them both, and make sure the optical viewfinder is easy to see into and has a flexible rubber boot to block the sun.

- **Interfacing to your computer**—Almost every DV camcorder has an IEEE-1394a port today. (Sony calls it an i.Link, whereas Apple calls it FireWire.) However, if you want to use your camcorder's digital still option, you might want to look for camcorders that also support flash memory cards for still-image capture. Some models also support USB interfacing (sometimes only for digital still transfer, sometimes for video transfer as well), but IEEE-1394a is much faster and is worth adding to your computer for the easiest and fastest video transfer.

- **Analog to digital transcoding**—If you have a collection of analog video tapes you'd like to convert to digital form, this feature enables you to transfer analog video into your camcorder and record a digital version. After a video is digital, you can edit it and do as many as 15 generations from the original tape before you see a noticeable picture quality loss.

- **Audio-in jack**—Look for cameras with this feature so that you can connect a separate microphone and put it closer to the action; the built-in microphones in most DV camcorders often pick up camera noise.

- **Night shooting**—Even if your DV camcorder has a built-in light, it might not be enough to give you great quality in the depths of night. To capture video way after dark, look for models that support zero-lux shooting.

- **Digital still mode**—Until recently, this feature wasn't worth using, because the 640×480 image size created by most older cameras was barely better than webcam quality. However, some of the newer midrange and high-end DV camcorders can capture megapixel or higher-resolution still images. Although you can do much better with a true digital camera, this is handy for occasional snapshots. For better image quality at any resolution, look for cameras that support progressive scan, which grabs two copies of the shot and combines them for extra sharpness (the same trick used by the now-discontinued Snappy still-image video capture device to improve picture quality).

> **JARGON**
>
> *Zero-lux*—Cameras with this feature can be used in complete darkness; the image is created with infrared light instead of visible light.

Connecting Your Imaging Device to Your PC

Digital cameras and DV camcorders don't require a PC to capture images and video, but you need to connect them to the computer at some point to retrieve the images and use them. Scanners, on the other hand, are useless without being connected to a PC. In this section, you learn how to determine if your computer is ready for the digital imaging or video device you want to use, and how to connect it to your computer.

Connecting Your Digital Camera to Your PC

Sooner or later, you'll need to unload the pictures from your camera to your computer. There are several ways to offload the pictures to free up your camera's flash memory for more pictures and make the images available for editing on your PC. In order of preference, here they are:

- Card readers
- PC Card adapters

- Direct USB connection

- Direct serial-port (called a *digital camera port* on some computers) connection

You need to purchase your preference of the first two options separately from your camera, but most cameras come with either USB or serial port connector cables (and sometimes they come with both).

Card Readers

A *card reader* is a small device (mine's about the size of a hockey puck) that attaches to the USB port (most use USB 1.1, but some are now optimized for the faster USB 2.0 standard) and has one or more slots for one or more types of flash memory devices. As I discuss in Chapter 11, as soon as you slide the flash memory card into the card reader, it shows up as a removable-media drive in Windows Explorer so you have immediate access to your photos.

Figure 15.4 shows how a typical card reader, camera, and flash memory device work together.

Figure 15.4

After you take pictures with your digital camera (1), you eject the memory card (2) and insert it into a card reader (3), which transfers it to the computer via a USB port. Photo Courtesy of SanDisk.

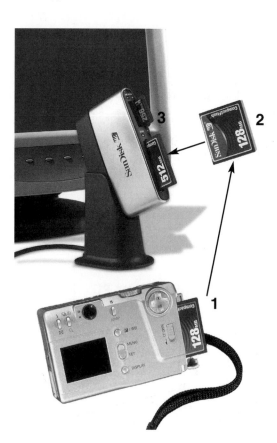

MARK'S TIP SHEET: Dealing with Balky Card Readers

USB card readers are supposed to be hot swap devices, meaning that you should be able to attach or remove the flash memory card without restarting your computer. Unfortunately, this doesn't always work.

If you find that your USB card reader causes problems when you insert or remove media, make sure that you have saved your work in any open applications before you insert or remove the media. Also, check with the manufacturer's web site to see if newer drivers are available.

Upgrading to Windows XP can also help, as it's more hot-swap friendly than other versions of Windows. Finally, make sure you're not displaying the contents of the flash memory card in My Computer or Windows Explorer when you remove it. Even Windows XP doesn't like this (you might need to close Windows Explorer or disconnect and reconnect the card reader), and earlier versions of Windows often crash.

I prefer card readers over other forms of data transfer because they don't use up your camera's battery power, you can use them on both desktop and notebook computers, and they can cost less than PC Card or floppy disk adapters. You can also buy multi-format card readers that support two or more flash memory types.

PC Card Adapters

Another battery-saving alternative to direct camera-to-PC transfer is designed especially for notebook computer users. A PC Card adapter enables your notebook computer's standard PC Card slot to read flash memory cards. See Figure 15.5.

A PC Card adapter is more compact than most flash memory card readers, but unlike flash memory card readers, PC Card adapters can be used only with notebook computers. Some adapters are designed for only one type of flash memory, but others support a variety of flash memory cards, such as the one pictured in Figure 15.5.

Figure 15.5

SanDisk's 4-in-1 PC
Card adapter works
with Compact Flash,
Memory Stick,
Secure Digital, and
Smart Media flash
memory cards.
Photo courtesy
of SanDisk.

USB Port

If you're trying to save money (in the short run), you can use the USB cable that came with your camera to transfer your pix directly to the PC. Your short-term cost savings will be eroded quickly by the need to replace your camera's batteries more often. You must turn on your camera to transfer data from your camera, and that uses power you'd probably prefer to save for taking pictures.

Serial Ports

The only good thing I can say about serial-port data transfers is that they work; however, this port is *30 times* slower than the USB 1.1 port, and even though some home PCs have labeled the 9-pin serial port as a *digital camera port*, that's no excuse for torturing yourself with slow data transfers and plenty of trips to the store for more batteries for your digital camera.

MARK'S TIP SHEET: Reduce Your Camera's Thirst for Electricity and Money—and Save the Environment!

Although digital cameras have eliminated the need for film processing and film purchase, they have other ways to sneak into your wallet and take your money. Whenever possible, use rechargeable batteries, rather than alkaline. Rechargeable batteries are good for the environment as well as your pocketbook because you can use them over and over again instead of throwing them away after a single use. You can use nickel metal-hydride batteries (NiMH batteries) or rechargeable alkaline batteries with many recent models. These battery types do not have the memory effect problem that the old nickel cadmium (Ni-Cd) batteries often did; if Ni-Cd batteries weren't fully discharged before recharging, they couldn't accept a full charge. If you need battery power immediately and can't wait for a recharge, use photo-grade or Ultra alkaline batteries in place of the normal models for longer life.

To save even more money when you're shooting indoors, look for the optional AC adapter available for many cameras. This is especially useful when you are using your camera (rather than a card reader or other device) to transfer pictures. Rechargeable batteries and AC adapters cost more than non-rechargeable ones do initially, but if you use your camera heavily, you will save a lot of money in the not-so-long run.

Connecting and Installing Your Scanner

The process of installing your scanner is similar to the process of installing any other device in that attaches to your computer through the same interface. With a plug-and-play Windows installation, you might provide the scanner driver after the scanner is detected, or you might need to install the scanning software first and then attach the scanner and restart the system. Check the scanner documentation for details.

Although some scanners include a SCSI or FireWire (IEEE-1394a) host adapter card, you don't need to install the bundled card unless you don't have the type of port already installed. Most scanners today are designed to connect to the USB 1.1 or USB 2.0 ports found in most recent computers. If the scanner requires you to add a separate interface card, you should install the card and make sure it is detected and is working according to the Windows Device Manager before you attach the scanner.

A scanner does not work within a photo-editing program unless its TWAIN driver is installed. Generally speaking, there is an option to test the scanner that can be run from the Windows Program menu. However, in most cases you need to use the File, Acquire option within the photo editor to start the scanner, as discussed earlier in this chapter.

With Windows Me and XP, as noted earlier, you can use the Scanner and Camera Wizard to scan images, but this tool lacks the options found in most TWAIN drivers.

CAUTION: STOP! LOOK! THINK!

Check the Drivers Before You Buy

Spec sheets and online descriptions for scanners don't always reflect the latest operating system and driver support. To find out if a particular scanner supports Windows XP or any other specific version of Windows, check the driver downloads section of the vendor's web site.

Checking for driver support before you buy a scanner or before you upgrade to a newer version of Windows can help prevent a mistake such as buying a scanner you can't use or causing your scanner to become obsolete after your Windows upgrade.

Connecting Your DV Camcorder

Almost every DV camcorder is designed to connect with an IEEE-1394 (FireWire) port on your computer. If you don't have this port already, plan to install one before you start working with your DV camcorder.

If your camcorder also has still-image capture, you might also need to connect it to a USB port or install a flash memory card reader to download the photos.

Troubleshooting Imaging Devices

Digital imaging is at the crossroads between photography and computers; for best results it helps to know and enjoy both fields. Here are some of the typical problems you might encounter as you explore digital imaging, along with solutions.

Help! I can save only a few pictures to my digital camera before I run out of space, but my friend with the same digital camera can take more pictures than I can. Why?

The number of pictures you can take with a digital camera is affected by the following:

- **The camera resolution and quality settings**—If you use the maximum quality and highest resolution settings so that your pictures are of the highest quality, you can store fewer pictures on each flash memory card. If your friend's camera is equipped with a larger flash memory card or uses lower quality and resolution settings, your friend will be able to take more pictures than you can without running out of space.

- **The amount of detail in each picture**—Digital cameras generally use a compression technique called JPEG. JPEG compresses similarly colored areas together and throws out varying amounts of detail at various quality settings to save more space. I noticed that when I used my digital camera to take pictures of equipment that pictures with a white background used less space than pictures with border-to-border detail. Why? The JPEG compression was able to compress the white space more than the areas of detail. So, if you took pictures of the same backyard in the winter when it was snow-covered and in the summer when it has different-colored flowers everywhere, the winter pictures would use less space than the summer pictures.

The simple solution to shooting more without sacrificing quality is buying a larger flash memory card. I recommend at least 128MB, or larger, if your camera (and your wallet) can do it. See the flash memory capacity charts in Chapter 11 if you're wondering which formats support the largest capacities.

Help! I'm saving money with rechargeable batteries, but I'm still running out of power at the worst possible times. Can you help?

Yes, I can—with a little help from you and your camera's instruction manual. To save battery power, make sure you are using the power saving features designed into your camera. Some of these include:

- Turning off the LCD preview after a short period of time. That little screen pulls a lot of power out of your batteries.
- Turning off the flash when you're outdoors.

Also, make sure you are fully charging your batteries when you use your recharger.

Help! I'm trying to shoot close-ups, but my pictures are fuzzy. I'm quite a bit farther away than the minimum distance listed. What's wrong?

There are two possible reasons you're having trouble:

- **You might need to turn on the close-focusing feature for your camera**—I missed this option myself for a while and was very annoyed with myself after I discovered my mistake. Push the closeup button to get obnoxiously close to your dog, your baby, or objects that won't care.

- **If you are close enough to block light from hitting the object, there might not be enough detail for the autofocus feature to work**—This is such a problem in my office that I use a floor lamp to add additional light before I shoot some close-ups.

Help! I just installed my scanner and it won't scan!

I've been there, done that. And I figured out a few of the reasons why you might be having problems:

- **Don't forget to reboot after you install the scanner**—Unless you're using Windows 2000 or Windows XP, a reboot is mandatory after you install almost any new hardware item.

- **You need to install the scanner driver manually**—If the scanner is showing up as an Unknown Device in Windows, it means that Windows knows it's there but can't figure out what it is. You might be able to use it anyway (scanner software doesn't always tell Windows what's up), but it's often better if you find the right driver and use the Driver tab in the Device Manager to install it. The Device Manager is part of the System properties sheet, which you can access from the Control Panel.

- **You forgot to turn on the scanner**—If a parallel-port scanner isn't on when you turn on the PC, you need to turn on the scanner and then restart Windows before you can use a parallel-port scanner. Sometimes you can use the Refresh option in the Windows Device Manager to gain access to a SCSI scanner that you turned on too late, but it doesn't always work. Don't worry about this with USB or IEEE-1394—they're hot-swappable.

- **The TWAIN drivers didn't get installed properly**—The easiest way to use most scanners is through the File, Acquire option of your graphics program, because the scanner brings the image back into your program's working area. However, if you don't see the scanner listed as a TWAIN device, this won't work. Reinstall the TWAIN driver and you should be back in business.

- **Incorrect SCSI device ID or termination**—SCSI is second only to IEEE-1394 for scanning speed, but it's the hardest interface to use. If you have two SCSI devices with the same ID, you can't use either one. And you must enable termination on the last SCSI device in the daisy-chain of devices. Miss either setting, and no scans for you! Read more about SCSI setups in Chapter 10, "Adding a Huge Hard Disk."

Help! My scans look terrific onscreen, but are tiny and look like garbage when I print them.

This is a classic sign of scanning at the wrong resolution. Typical monitors put just 72 to 96 dots per inch onscreen. Even low-cost inkjet printers can jam 600 dots or more into an inch. So, what looks great onscreen looks terrible and is much smaller when you print it out. Use a resolution of at least 240 dpi for scanning pictures you want to print; use higher resolutions if you are enlarging just a small area.

Help! I get stuttering video when I try to play back my DV clips.

Stuttering DV video clips can be caused by outdated DirectX software, outdated IEEE-1394 port drivers, and many other factors. Adobe's Troubleshooting Too-Fast or Stuttered Video Clips in Premiere 6.x has useful advice for Premiere users as well as for DV users in general. Find it at www.adobe.com/support/techdocs/29832.htm.

Help! My DV camcorder doesn't show up in Device Manager.

This problem could be caused by outdated or missing drivers for your IEEE-1394 card, your DV camcorder being shut off or going into a sleep mode, too long an IEEE-1394 cable being used, or other problems. Microsoft document #314873 provides a checklist for this problem. Search for it at http://search.microsoft.com.

Part V

Upgrading Connectivity

Chapter 16

Get Yourself Broadband— It's (Always) Going Fast!

One of the most frequent complaints I hear about faster computers is how little effect souping up the processor, video card, memory, and other components has on Internet speed. Those upgrades might help graphics-rich pages to display a bit faster, but they can't help speed up the soda-straw connection provided by the dial-up modem that so many computer users still rely on for an Internet connection.

If you want your online experience to be as supercharged as the rest of your computing experience is after performing the upgrades I describe in other chapters, you've come to the right place. Because Internet connections are about the only upgrade that costs you money month after month in service fees, it pays big time to learn how to get the most for your money.

Ten Reasons to Get Broadband

Because broadband is two to three times as expensive per month as a typical dial-up connection if you have just one phone line, it's a hard upgrade to justify for many users. One big benefit of broadband is that most types free up your phone line so you don't need a second line. And, the money you'd otherwise spend on that second line can be used toward the monthly cost of broadband. Need more reasons to make the move to broadband? Check out our top-ten list of reasons to switch. If you recognize yourself or your situation, keep reading.

1. You've been putting off updating your antivirus software because it takes so long to download.

2. You're furious when you can't call home after school because the kids are on the Internet.

3. You've only tried Internet radio once because the computer spent so much time trying to download the song that you got tired of waiting.

4. You're trying to sneak a CD burner into the office so that you can download those big service packs for your apps with a fast connection.

5. You're tired of losing online games so quickly that there isn't time to raise your blaster.

6. Your kids are tired of getting off the phone so that you can use the Internet.

7. You're the only person in your department who hasn't seen the new online-only movie trailer because it takes too much time to download.

8. Your connection's so slow, you're still trying to win your first eBay auction.

9. You're tired of ordering software on a CD because it would take three hours to download it to save five or ten bucks.

10. You unplugged your webcam because the connection's so slow that your friends think you're just a cheaply animated character on television.

Understanding Broadband 101

The best reason to upgrade your Internet connection is speed. Although today's 56Kbps dial-up modems are over 20 times faster than the 2.4Kbps modems used in the late 1980s, the online world has changed in ways that make that speed increase completely inadequate.

JARGON

bps—bits per second; the basic unit of measure used for communications. Kbps and Mbps are multiples of bps.

Kbps—Kilobits per second; each kilobit equals 1,000 bits, so a 56Kbps modem is capable of a top download speed of 56,000 bits per second. Dial-up modems are rated in Kbps or bps.

Mbps—Megabits per second; each megabit equals 1,000,000 bits. Some broadband services are rated in Mbps.

When I first went online, the Internet did not exist in its current form. People spent most of their time reading words and downloading tiny program files. There was no hyperlinking, no World Wide Web, and no graphical browser. You used your modem to dial up a distant computer's phone number directly. With rare exceptions, once you finished with that computer, you disconnected the call and made a separate call to access another computer's information.

Today, although people still read a lot of words on the Internet, it's a World Wide Web. You can go anywhere in the world at the click of a mouse and view full-motion video, download song files, download huge programs, send and receive video email greetings, and much more. Dial-up modems and the analog telephone system they connect to were never designed to cope with this richness of content. The more time you spend on the Internet, the more you need a better high-speed connection.

ON THE WEB: Getting Broadband the TechTV Way

With even the king of dial-up services, AOL, now pushing broadband, broadband Internet is here to stay. Check out these resources on the TechTV web site:

- The Screen Saver's Broadband page is your portal to understanding and installing broadband. See it at `www.techtv.com/screensavers/broadband/`.

- Read "Broadband FAQ" for help choosing cable, Digital Subscriber Line (DSL), or satellite:
  `www.techtv.com/callforhelp/features/story/0,24330,3318055,00.html`.

- Search the TechTV web site for "broadband" to find lots more help.

Comparing Dial-Up and Broadband Internet Services

Even though the device used to connect to a broadband Internet service is sometimes called a modem, it is really nothing like the modem you use to dial in to the Internet or to other computers today.

The many differences between high-speed and regular Internet connections include the following:

- **Speed**—The fastest regular connection is limited by FCC regulation to 53Kbps; cable modem service, the most popular high-speed Internet service available now, runs about 10 to 20 times that speed, or 500Kbps to 1Mbps. Some services run even faster.

- **Telephone line usage**—Unless you have a separate line for your dial-up connection, your regular modem prevents anybody from using the telephone, but most high-speed services either don't use telephone lines or can share the telephone line. So, you can talk to Aunt Millie and type an URL (web site address) at the same time.

- **Equipment required**—Virtually every PC is equipped with a 56Kbps modem designed for PC to PC and Internet connections. However, most broadband devices connect to a 10/100 Ethernet network port or a USB port. Almost every recent PC has one port or the other, but the broadband device must be purchased or leased separately.

- **Cabling required**—Your ordinary modem uses the same telephone lines that your phone does. Although DSL is a high-speed service that is also designed to use a telephone line, some types of DSL require a new phone line to be installed if the existing line doesn't provide high-enough signal quality to support DSL service. Other types of service use the same coaxial cable used by TV services.

- **Features**—Your conventional modem can send and receive faxes and can connect with computers that don't use the Internet. High-speed Internet service connects only to computers that are connected to the Internet. However, most libraries, banks, and other institutions that formerly used terminal emulation settings and direct dial-up phone numbers now have web sites instead.

- **Connection type**—Your conventional modem must dial a telephone number and takes as much a minute to establish a connection to the Internet. When you hang up the connection to make or receive a phone call, you must go through the same dial-up and connection process again. Most high-speed Internet service is instant-on; as soon as the computer finishes booting, you have a connection, and anytime you want, you can open your browser or email client and get the online information you need.

As you can see, it can make sense to switch to high-speed service if you use the Internet a lot or if you have only one phone line and you want to keep it freed up, but don't discard your existing modem unless you need to make room for the network card required for some new high-speed services.

Why 56Kbps Modems Can't Go Any Faster

Why do you need a high-speed Internet service that requires something different than the modem in your computer? Basically, the modem in your computer can go only about as fast as the telephone system enables it to go.

MARK'S TIP SHEET: Keep Your Modem? Sure, You Might Need It!

You don't need to keep your 56Kbps modem installed, or do you?

If you use your modem's fax send or fax receive features, keep it in your PC (a fax modem works like a printer that prints your document to the fax machine at the receiver's location).

What if your broadband service goes down? Some services provide a few hours of dial-up service free for use if you're away from your normal connection or if the broadband connection goes down. However, if your modem is missing, you can't use it.

If you have no free expansion slots for a network card but do plan to keep your modem, try these alternatives:

- Try the USB port for your broadband modem connection; many broadband devices and services support USB connections.

- Use an external modem to free up the PCI slot containing your modem.

- Use an Internet-based fax service such as eFax Plus (www.efax.com) or Faxaway (www.faxaway.com) to send and receive faxes so that you can remove your analog modem.

Keep in mind that your computer speaks in binary (0,1), but the telephone system is an analog system that can transmit different volume and tone levels. Modems are called modems because they *mod*ulate digital to analog data when sending data and *dem*odulate analog back to digital at the receiving computer.

Because of this conversion process, there's a calculation (called Shannon's Law after its creator, Claude Shannon) that determines the maximum speed at which analog modems can work. The actual speed limit is about 33,600bps. So, how is it that you can have a modem that downloads at speeds above 50,000bps? Many, but not all, phone systems enable a digital connection to be created between the telephone office's central switch (where the Internet connection is made) and your computer. This is how the so-called 56Kbps modem in your computer works. However, the faster connection works only one way (downloads) and your speed for sending information is no more than 33,600bps with modems that use the V.90 standard, the most common standard for 56Kbps modems.

What about V.92?

If you bought a modem in the last two years, or bought a computer with a built-in modem, it might actually support an improved version of V.90 called V.92.

V.92 has some great features, including the following:

READ THIS TOO: Bits, Bytes, and Baud

Check out the chapter on modems and Internet connections in Scott Mueller's *Upgrading and Repairing PCs* for much more about the technical details of standard, 56Kbps, and cable modems.

- Support for call waiting, enabling you to take a voice call without losing your Internet connection.
- Shorter connection times when you dial in to the Internet.
- Improved data compression so that you can receive more data in the same amount of time.
- Faster upload speeds to about 44Kbps (up from 33.6Kbps with V.90).

CAUTION: STOP! LOOK! THINK!

Get V.92? Not Until the ISP Gets It Too

Just about all the dial-up modems on the market support V.92. However, the reaction from most ISPs has been a big yawn with little movement to support its new features. With growing interest in broadband (even AOL is now pushing broadband), it's not likely that you'll ever see widespread support of V.92 features.

Fortunately, V.92 modems act like V.90 models if there's no V.92-specific support at the ISP's end. Wondering if your ISP supports V.92 features? Just ask—especially before you buy a new V.92 modem.

Instead of buying minor improvements in speed with V.92, spend the money on a dramatically faster broadband service.

The Hidden Costs of Sticking with a Dial-Up Connection

If you use the Internet for only a few hours each month, you might be satisfied with a dial-up connection that ties up your only phone line. But, if you come to rely on the Internet for breaking news and weather, entertainment, information, chatting, and so on, you want to have it available at all times.

If you stick with a dial-up connection, here's what it really costs to have an always-available connection:

- $15–20 per month for dial-up service
- $20–25 per month for an additional phone line

These figures can vary: Plug in the actual amounts you're paying now for online service and what your friendly local telco charges for the second line. Chances are you'll discover that our estimate of $35–$45 or more for a second phone line and your existing dial-up service should be very close to what you would actually pay.

By contrast, a typical cable modem or ADSL broadband connection is about $40 per month; this replaces your existing dial-up ISP. If you decide to lease the cable modem instead of buying it outright (I recommend buying a cable modem instead), add about $10 per month. Most DSL service plans bundle the equipment into the service fee per month. Again, costs might vary, but the typical $5 to $15/month difference between two phone lines and dial-up and broadband buys you broadband speed for uploading and downloading and keeps your phone line free. It's worth it!

The Contenders

Three major broadband services are worth considering, but there's no guarantee that you'll have more than one or two of these to choose from in your area:

- Cable modem
- DSL
- Satellite

There are two other types of broadband service that are not as widely available:

- ISDN
- Fixed wireless

ISDN, the original broadband Internet connection running at 64Kbps or 128Kbps, has been replaced by DSL (which is much faster and usually cheaper) in most markets. ISDN, like DSL, is provided in conjunction with your local telephone company (telco).

Fixed wireless, which uses direct line-of-sight microwave antennas to send and receive data, is offered primarily in rural or suburban areas by the same companies that provide wireless cable TV service. Because of the high infrastructure expense of fixed wireless and problems with line-of-sight, this type of service is not widely available. Developments of Wi-Fi (802.11-type wireless Internet) might supplement or even replace fixed wireless in the future.

ON THE WEB: When ISPs Compete, You Win!

Because broadband services aren't universally available yet, you can save yourself a lot of time by using a smart search engine to show you exactly what deals are available in your area.

The BestBuy broadband Internet search engine is available at `http://bbyinternet.getconnected.com/`.

Click the Broadband link at the Circuit City web site to learn about broadband and search for deals. Go to `www.circuitcity.com`.

The Broadband Compass web site is sponsored by Office Depot. Go to `www.broadbandcompass.com/`.

The broadbandreports.com search tool lets you specify more options than any other search engine, and lets you specify the technology you prefer. Go to `www.broadband-reports.com/psearch`.

Piggyback on Your Cable Network with a Cable Modem

In many cases, cable modem service is the fastest and most reliable Internet service that you can get, and it's available to millions of people who can't get its telephone-line–based rival, DSL. In fact, cable modems are the most widely used broadband option in the US. The reliability of cable modems is an irony to some because cable modem service comes from the same people who provide cable TV.

Turning a Cable TV System into Cable Internet

If you're wondering why *your* cable TV provider doesn't offer cable modem service, it's most likely that your provider has not yet switched to digital cable service. Although it is possible to provide high-speed download cable modem service through the old-fashioned all-coaxial cable network, you won't like it. All-coaxial cable modem service requires that you make your connection with a telephone modem. Using your old modem to tie up the phone line ruins one of the best reasons for broadband—being able to type and talk at the same time.

When a cable system switches to digital service, the additional capacity and speed provided by fiber-optic lines enables that system to provide cable modem service in the future. The cable company also needs to install the equipment necessary to connect to the Internet. However, if you see a digital service upgrade today, there's a fairly good chance you'll see cable modem service in the future.

There is one downside to cable modem service: You lose your choice of Internet Service Providers (ISPs). Unlike dial-up services, where you can connect through any company you like, the ISP used by the cable TV company is your ISP, like it or not.

MARK'S TIP SHEET: I Want My AOL and Broadband Too

If you love AOL, you don't need to leave it behind when you switch to cable modem service. AOL for Broadband lets you add AOL to any broadband service for about $10 a month. See the AOL web site (www.aol.com) for details.

How Fast Is Cable Modem Service?

The official answer to this question is this: "About 1.5 megabits per second (1.5Mbps)." I'd love to get service that fast. However, I gladly settle for the 500Kbps download service that I get on a routine basis. After all, that's 10 times faster than my dial-up service use to be. Some vendors now offer multiple speeds of cable modem service (fast and really fast), depending upon how much you want to pay per month.

My upload speed is also much faster than with my old dial-up service, making it easy to send big chapter files to my publisher as well as download chapters to revise.

Ordering and Paying for Cable Modem Service

The typical cable modem service costs about $40 a month plus the cost of the cable modem. You can buy a cable modem for a hundred bucks or less, so I recommend skipping the $10-a-month lease fee. Just be sure to find out if your provider prefers any particular brands. Most providers' networks are designed to use Cable Labs Certified cable modems (formerly called DOCSIS-compatible cable modems). Because this is an industry standard supported by most companies that make cable modems, you have a lot of choices.

> **MARK'S TIP SHEET: Grab a Broadband Deal at Your Local Electronics Superstore**
>
> Electronics superstores, such as Best Buy, Circuit City, and others, sell cable modems, but they also work with major broadband ISPs to provide special deals. You might qualify for a rebate, free installation, or some other special deal, so be sure to check the current deals before you order the service or buy your modem.

Cable modems connect to the Ethernet or USB port on your computer. They also connect to the coaxial cable that brings cable TV to your home.

To get cable modem service, contact your local cable company or check with the local stores that sell cable modems. In some situations, you might have two cable companies from which to choose. Even if you already have service from company A, you might get a better deal from company B, so it pays to ask.

Figure 16.1 shows how a typical cable modem and cable TV connection looks inside your home. You don't need to have both services, but many providers give you a price break if you do, and many even offer digital phone service that also uses the fiber-optic network.

DSL—Super Speed, but Service Can Be Less than Super

DSL service carries high-speed traffic over the same telephone line that brings voice traffic into your home, without interfering with your ability to make and receive phone calls. Unlike cable modem service, which can become slower when many users are connected at the same time in a neighborhood, DSL service isn't affected by how many users are connected in your neighborhood. In addition, DSL speeds can reach 768Kbps or faster.

Although DSL service has gotten steadily better since the horror stories of DSL provider bankruptcies of a couple years ago, the unevenness of DSL service and setup time still puts DSL behind cable modems in customer preference.

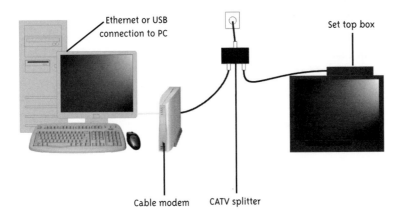

Ethernet or USB
connection to PC

Set top box

Cable modem

CATV splitter

Figure 16.1

Because cable
modem traffic uses
different cable
channels than cable
TV, a single coaxial
cable can bring
both TV and the
Internet into
your home.

In all too many cases, DSL service is still plagued with these problems:

- Technical problems with aging telephone lines can prevent high-speed connections.

- FCC regulations can make it difficult for telephone companies other than the original local telephone company to provide service in a regulated market.

- Slow or poor-quality installation and coordination of effort between DSL providers, the telephone company, and installers.

- DSL providers that quit and force you to scramble for replacement service.

There are good and bad DSL providers out there. Get a good one, and you can enjoy the advantages of DSL. Get a bad one, and you might wind up dumping DSL before it's even installed or wishing you'd tried something else.

How DSL Works

DSL requires your local telco (telephone company) to install special equipment at their central office. This equipment enables the telco to transmit DSL signals at a different frequency than your normal telephone signals so that the line can be shared between voice and data.

Most residential customers get Asymmetrical DSL (ADSL), which has faster download speeds than upload speeds. This type of DSL has monthly rates similar to cable modem service ($35/month and up) and speeds comparable to cable modem service. Some vendors offer several tiers of service, enabling you to find the right balance of speed and cost. ADSL is popular with telcos, too, because it can be installed by the customer and can use existing wiring to the home.

Business customers usually get Symmetrical DSL (SDSL). It requires new wiring to the location because it runs at the same speed for uploads as for downloads. SDSL is far more expensive than ADSL, and companies that specialize in one form of DSL often don't provide the other because of equipment differences.

ANALYZE THIS

Is My DSL Faster Than Yours? Distance Matters

Because of how DSL works with phone lines, the further your location is from the central office (CO or central switch), the lower your DSL performance. Most companies do *not* provide DSL if you are more than 16,000 *wire feet* (phone line distance, not crow-flies or driving distance) away from the CO. Special repeaters are needed to make the signal stronger to reach farther than 18,000 wire feet.

How Much Is DSL, and Where Can You Get It?

Even though DSL is provided through telephone lines, contacting your local telephone company might actually be the worst way to find out if DSL service is available to you. Although telcos provide DSL service, they also work with third-party vendors to provide DSL. However, if you contact the telco for information, you won't find out about any other DSL service offers than the telco's own; third-party deals might be better for you. In either case, special equipment must be installed at the phone company's central switch to enable DSL service to its customers.

You can use any of the broadband search services mentioned earlier in this chapter to find out if DSL service or an alternative is available to you. The most in-depth DSL coverage is available from my favorite DSL and broadband news and information site: Broadbandreports.com.

ON THE WEB: DSL and More, the Broadbandreports.com Way

Originally known as DSLreports.com, my nomination for the best single resource for all types of broadband information is now known as Broadbandreports.com.

Use Broadbandreports.com (`www.broadbandreports.com`) to discover which broadband ISPs provide consistently good service, which flunk the test, and which fall between these extremes. Get information about mergers, technology, legislation, tools, availability, and everything else you need to make an intelligent broadband choice.

DSL pricing for residential customers is usually around $40–$60 a month, including equipment. Pricing for business is usually much higher because of the differences in ADSL and SDSL service.

Satellite Internet

No matter where you live, if you can see the southern sky (if you're in the northern hemisphere), and especially if you already have a satellite dish for TV, chances are good that you can also use satellite-based Internet.

There are two choices for satellite-based Internet:

- **DirecWAY** (formerly DirecPC)—www.direcway.com
- **Starband**—www.starband.com

DirecWAY's been around longer, but for several years, it offered only a relatively clumsy system that used the high-speed satellite connection for downloading only and used a conventional dial-up modem for uploading. Starband introduced two-way service in late 2000, and DirecWAY brought its two-way service on line a few months later. Today, both services offer two-way satellite connections, freeing up your phone line. Table 16.1 compares typical download and upload speeds; speeds can be affected by signal strength, weather, and network conditions.

Table 16.1   DirecWAY and StarBand Service Comparison

Service	Download Speed	Upload Speed
DirecWAY	Up to 400Kbps	Up to 128Kbps
StarBand	150Kbps to 500Kbps	40 to 60Kbps

Notice that download and upload speeds can vary a great deal. This is due to the services' need to balance variable demand against the constraints of the amount of data that can be routed through the satellites.

From 22,500 Miles in Space to You—How It Works

Whether you choose DirecWAY or Starband, after the page request is received by the remote server, it is transmitted to the satellite company's broadcast facility, transmitted to the satellite, and then received by your dish, as shown in Figure 16.2. The same dish can be used for both satellite Internet and satellite TV.

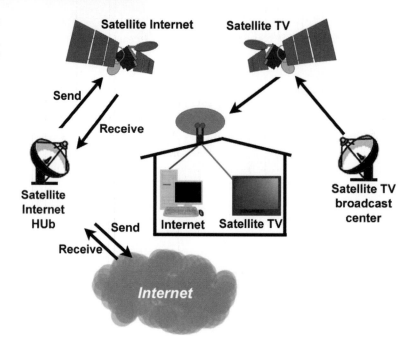

Figure 16.2

Satellite TV and satellite Internet services compared.

Limitations of Satellite Internet

The current crop of satellite Internet services use the satellite dish for fast downloads and slower uploads, thus keeping your phone line clear. However, you should still be aware that satellite Internet has some limitations, as compared to wired broadband services such as cable or DSL:

- Time lags involved in passing data through a satellite cause latency-sensitive services, such as gaming and voice over IP, to have relatively poor performance.

- Conventional router-based Internet sharing schemes can't be used because the satellite modem (receiver) is plugged directly into the computer's USB port instead of an Ethernet port, as is the case with DSL or cable modem. However, you can use Microsoft Internet Connection Sharing (ICS) to turn the computer connected to the satellite modem into a host that can act as a gateway for the other computers on the network.

- To enjoy business-related broadband features such as support for virtual private networks (VPNs) and large email or FTP uploads, you might need to look at a higher-cost business or telecommuter plan.

- Satellite broadband, unlike other broadband connections, can be adversely affected by bad weather conditions, just as satellite TV can be.

- DirecWAY's Fair Access Policy (FAP) will drastically slow down your system if you download too much information within a short period.

READ THIS TOO: Guiding You Through the Many Flavors of Internet Sharing

My book, *Absolute Beginner's Guide to Cable Internet Connections* (Que, 2002), is recommended reading for anyone who wants to share an Internet connection with any type of broadband device. It has separate chapters on Windows Internet Connection Sharing (ICS) for Windows 98, Me, and XP, as well as routers and third-party products. If you have a mixed Mac/Windows environment, this book is still useful as it also contains the specifics on how to share a connection with both types of computers.

Coping with DirecWAY FAP

DirecWAY's FAP has been one of the biggest complaints of users since DirecWAY was first introduced as DirecPC several years ago. Before you order DirecWAY, be sure to read the FAP at `http://two-wayupgrade.direcway.com/fap.html`. Note that a U.S. residential user who downloads more than 169MB of data within a four-hour time period (from 2:00AM to 5:00AM, the threshold increases to 225MB) triggers FAP limitations, which drops the download speed from its normal 200–400Kbps rate to under 50Kbps for as much as 8 to 12 hours. FAP limits are higher for business users. The DirecPC Uncensored web site provides a more detailed analysis of FAP, including information on how it differs between the European markets and the U.S. and Canadian markets.

ON THE WEB: FAP and FAP Help at Your Service

DirecPC Uncensored is a great unofficial resource for dealing with DirecWAY and DirecPC's foibles and improving its speed. Check out its FAP page (which also provides links to a downloadable FAPMON utility to help you measure your usage) at `www.copperhead.cc/fap.html`.

In addition to using a tool such as FAPMON to track your download usage, you should also consider downloading no more than 100MB at a time and then taking a break. Otherwise, FAP may kick in and drastically reduce your speed. Believe me, it's no fun watching a broadband service run slower than your 56Kbps modem used to. The best way to think of DirecWAY is to realize it is designed for fast surfing, not gigantic amounts of downloading.

What You Need for Two-Way Service

Both DirecWAY and StarBand require you to have a working USB port and Windows 98 or newer. Although the older one-way DirecPC service could be self-installed, the much stricter antenna aiming requirements needed to establish a two-way connection with a satellite 22,500 miles away require that both services be professionally installed.

One hidden benefit of two-way service is that if you already watch satellite TV, you can upgrade to a single dish that can pick up both DirecTV/DirecWAY or Dish Network/Starband services.

Speed, Pricing, and Availability of Satellite Internet

Both services have a basic monthly charge of just under $70 a month, but equipment and installation fees vary a great deal. Some dealers offer discounts if you also add satellite TV to your order. In addition, to help take the sting out of the high up-front cost of the satellite dish and professional installation, you can sometimes spread the cost of equipment across a multi-year contract.

Because the upfront and continuing costs of satellite Internet is higher than for cable or DSL Internet services, be sure to evaluate pricing plans and user opinions.

DirecWAY is available under a variety of brands and pricing plans. Here are the major vendors in the U.S. market. Contact them for the latest specials and service plans:

- **DirecWAY**—www.direcway.com
- **Earthlink Satellite**—www.earthlink.com
- **DirecWAY with DirecTV**—http://directv.direcway.com/
- **Agristar**—www.agristar.com
- **National Rural Telecommunications Cooperative (NRTC)**—www.nrtc.org

For StarBand, follow the buying links from the StarBand web site (www.starband.com) to its registered dealers.

CAUTION: STOP! LOOK! THINK!

Get the Straight Dope, Straight from the Users

Worried about getting FAPed? Wondering how good DirecWAY service *really* is? Wondering if StarBand is better? Before you dive into DirecWAY or StarBand, find out what its users think. You can subscribe to the `alt.satellite.direcpc` and `alt.satellite.starband` newsgroups with your newsreader (some email clients can do it, too). You can also search current and past content through `http://groups.google.com`.

One of the best news, tips, and gossip web sites for DirecWAY/DirecPC users is DirecPC Uncensored at `www.copperhead.cc`. If you're interested in StarBand, try `www.starbandusers.com`.

The Envelope, Please—Which Broadband Service Is Best?

Ever notice how the Academy Awards people no longer say, "The winner is…"? Now, they say, "The award goes to…". You know they didn't throw the finalists into a hat and draw a winner at random. Even though the Academy is reluctant to use the word "winner," there was a vote taken to choose the recipient of the Oscar.

Similarly, the broadband service you choose shouldn't be drawn out of a hat. Use this section to help you choose a winner—or at least narrow down the choices for further consideration.

Why Choose Cable Modems?

Cable modems make sense if you:

- Want a fast connection for uploading and downloading.
- Don't mind some variation in speed at peak usage times.

Why DSL May Be the One

Consider DSL if you:

- Have a local DSL provider with a good track record.
- Can achieve speeds as fast or faster than other broadband services available to you.

What Makes Satellite Internet the Best Choice

Consider satellite Internet if you:

- Can't get other broadband options.
- Can get two-way service.

- Don't mind paying high up-front hardware and installation costs.
- Want a single dish for Internet and satellite TV.

Making the Move to Broadband—The Process

The order and installation process is similar for all types of broadband service. Use this checklist as a guide to track your installation progress.

1. Decide which services are available in your area.

2. Determine the up-front and continuing cost of each service.

3. Select the service you want.

4. Determine the hardware and operating system requirements for your preferred service.

5. Contact the provider to arrange for installation.

6. Have the provider perform a site survey or wiring check, if needed, to verify that your location can handle the service.

7. Perform any upgrades (such as a network card, an operating system, and so forth) that you might need to make your system ready for broadband.

8. Wait for the installer (or watch for a DSL or cable-modem self-install kit to arrive).

9. Watch the installation process or install the kit yourself.

10. Make sure the installer tests the installation before leaving, or go online yourself to test the installation.

11. Store documentation and setup software in a safe place.

CAUTION: STOP! LOOK! THINK!

Don't Spend a Lot of Money to Get Ready for Broadband

You might be puzzled by the notion of selecting a broadband service and contacting the provider before you upgrade your system. Here's why it makes sense to choose the service first and get your computer ready later: Your location may not be suitable for the service you want.

That's right. Even if you've faithfully entered your zip code, address, telephone number, latitude, longitude, and GPS coordinates into the prequalification databases used by many broadband services, your particular address might still flunk out if you're trying to get DSL, satellite Internet, or wireless service.

Why might it flunk? DSL depends on the quality of the wire pair that runs between the DSL equipment at the telephone company's CO and your home or office. Because telephone networks have been cobbled together over the years with numerous changes made for the benefit of voice (not computer) data, homes and businesses next to each other could have completely different wiring quality levels. Save money by performing a DSL self-installation if that option is available, but make sure no money is due up-front before you have the service installed and make sure it works.

Last, note that satellite Internet depends on an unobstructed view of the southern sky (for users in the northern hemisphere) because of the geosynchronous (above-the-equator) location of the satellites used for Internet service. If your view of the southern sky is of a brick wall, you either need to pay extra for a tall tower to lift your dish out of the way of obstructions or try a different service. If you're not sure you can get the signal, contact an installer to see if you can get a site survey first before you pay for the equipment.

The bottom line? Don't pay any money for broadband until you know you can actually use the service. Then, and only, then, worry about your PC.

Self-Installing DSL

If DSL is installed by the telephone company, a special wall jack is usually provided as part of the service. This wall jack is electrically insulated from the rest of your telephone service to prevent interference with the high-frequency DSL signals.

However, in many markets that offer DSL, you can order a self-install kit. The self-install kit usually includes the DSL modem, setup software, and small devices called *microfilters*. Microfilters attach between your telephone, fax machines, and other telephone devices, and the wall jacks to block interference. This enables you to install DSL service yourself and prevent interference from affecting the signal. You need either a 10/100 Ethernet port or a working USB port to connect the DSL modem to your computer.

Figure 16.3 shows a typical DSL self-installation using microfilters. After the hardware is connected as shown, run the setup software provided by the DSL vendor to finish your installation.

Figure 16.3

The microfilter attached to the tele-phone (right) enables the DSL modem (left) to be plugged into the same jack without interference from the phone disrupt-ing DSL signals.

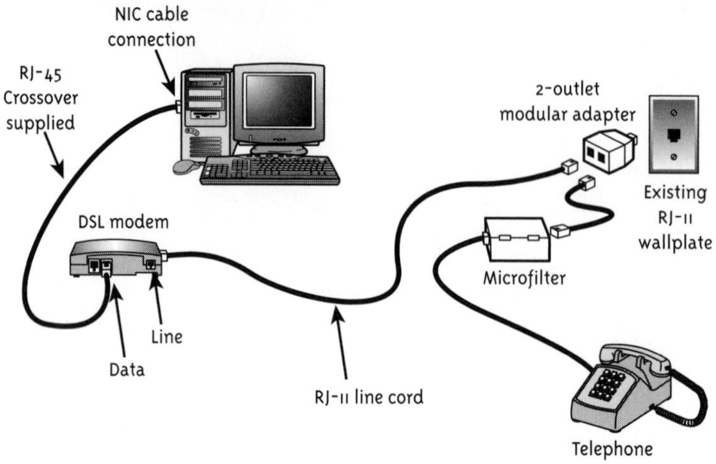

Self-Installing Cable Internet

If you already have cable TV, you might be able to self-install your cable modem service. Here's a brief description of the process. Cable modem vendors that provide self-install kits will supply additional information:

- Install a splitter on the existing connection to prevent cable TV signals from interfering with cable Internet connections. This splitter should be installed as close as possible to where the cable enters the home, and no other splitters should be installed between the splitter and your cable modem.

- Run new coaxial cables from the splitter to the existing TV or set-top box connection and to the location for the cable modem.

- Attach the cable modem to the coaxial cable and turn it on. This enables the cable modem to synchronize with the network (a process which takes several minutes).

- While the cable modem is synchronizing, install the setup program to configure your computer for cable modem service.

- Connect the cable modem to your computer via the Ethernet or USB port. After the cable modem is synchronized, open the web browser and surf the web.

Making Sure Your PC is Broadband-Ready

I have good news for you if you're considering broadband: Almost any computer built since 1998 is ready for it. All you need is a 300MHz or faster PC, 32MB of RAM, and Windows 98 or better.

The next issue is how you will connect your broadband Internet service to your computer. Broadband services don't use your existing modem. Instead, there are two basic ways that you can connect to most broadband Internet services:

- 10/100 Ethernet network card or port (see Chapter 17, "Share the Wealth with a Home Network," for information about Ethernet)
- A USB port (1.1 or 2.0)

The service is a little bit faster in some cases if you use Ethernet. However, if you don't have Ethernet already installed and don't have an open expansion slot, USB works in many cases, and some services use only USB ports.

Portable Particulars

Your notebook computer will have no trouble connecting to most high-speed services because most allow the USB port to be used as a connection. 10/100 Ethernet PC Cards for notebook computers are more expensive than PCI cards are for desktop computers, but they also work for most services except satellite Internet.

Adding Webcams and Other Enhancements

After you install your broadband equipment and activate the service, you're sure to see the Internet in a whole new light. It's faster than before and much more convenient because it's always on. Get even more enjoyment out of your faster connection with add-ons like these:

- **Webcam**—A webcam is a fun way to chat with family and friends, but it's painfully slow over a dial-up connection. USB models are easy to install, but be sure to choose one with a 640×480 or higher resolution so that you can enjoy a decent-sized chat window, even with a high-resolution screen.

- **USB hub**—Some systems have only two or three USB ports, so you might be running short after you install a broadband Internet device and a webcam. See Chapter 19, "Adding the Ports You Need for the Devices You Want," for details on how to install an internal USB hub or plug an external hub into an existing port.

- **Dual-display video card**—With an always-on connection, you might want to leave a browser or email window open all the time. A dual-display video card and an additional monitor make it easy; see Chapter 13, "Extra Vroom with Faster Graphics and Bigger Displays," for details.

- **Digital camera or scanner**—Whether you want to explore the great options available through online photofinishing or just want to email the grandparents your latest pix of the kids, digital imaging hardware helps you make the most of a fast Internet connection. See Chapter 15, "Digital Imaging and Video," for details.

Troubleshooting Your Broadband Connection

High-speed Internet is so terrific that when it doesn't work or can't be installed, you feel terrible. Here's how to keep the broadband joy flowing.

Help! The signal lights on the front of my broadband modem are blinking. What's wrong?

Depending on the modem, it might be nothing, or it could indicate you've lost connection with the network. A lot of modems have a blinking signal indicating they're receiving or sending data. That's okay. However, if the power or synchronize light is blinking, it could mean your modem isn't working or the network is down. Before you call for help, find the manual for the modem and find out exactly what the lights mean on your model. Then, learn how to reset the modem. Like any other piece of PC gear, an occasional reset can't hurt.

Help! Everybody at home wants to use my PC because I've got the fast Internet connection. Should I get an appointment book?

No, but getting something new is a good idea. If you have DSL or cable modem service, I'd get a router/switch combination. The router connects your home PCs to the Internet, and the switch shares the Internet (as well as shared drives and printers) at top speed. Chapter 17 has the details on how to create a home network so everybody can enjoy broadband Internet goodness.

If you're using satellite Internet, use a software-based solution such as Internet Connection Sharing (ICS), which is built into Windows 98SE and later versions.

Help! I used a program to tweak Windows Registry settings for my dial-up modem and got great speed. Since I installed broadband, however, my broadband modem acts like it's comatose. What do I do now?

Whenever you tweak the Registry for more speed for a dial-up modem, you've got to tweak it again when you replace the dial-up modem with a broadband modem because the Registry settings are different. If you don't, your speed will be abysmal. Use the same program you used before (such as TweakDUN, available online) to make the changes if your tweaking program supports broadband and your current version of Windows. If not, download a newer version. The latest version of TweakDUN is designed especially to support both dial-up and broadband connections.

NOTE

Tweak Away with These Great Downloads

Although TweakDUN was originally developed for dial-up networking with a regular modem, it can also useful for cable modem and other broadband users running Windows 95 through Windows XP. Download the latest version of TweakDUN from www.pattersondesigns.com/tweakdun/.

You can also download pre-defined Registry tweaks from www.speedguide.net. Use the tools at the Broadbandreports.com web site (www.broadbandreports.com/tools) to test your connection speed and quality and to change your settings.

No matter what program you use, be sure to back up your Registry first!

Help! I want to tweak my system, but I don't want to wreck my Windows Registry. I need an easy way to back up the Registry before I change it.

Great idea! Here are some ways to back up the Registry:

- Use the Registry, Export Registry File menu option in Regedit to save a .reg file that contains the entire Registry (Windows 9x/Me). You can merge this file back into the Registry with Regedit if you have problems later.

- If you use Windows 98, review Chapter 7, "RAM Your Way to Faster Performance," to learn more about its built-in Registry backup feature.

- Search the `http://support.microsoft.com` web site for the following articles on backing up and editing the Registry in the specified Windows version: Windows XP (322756); Windows 2000 (322755); Windows NT 4.0 (323170); Windows 95 (132332); and Windows 98/98SE/Me (256419).

Help! I think my browser's broken, but I'm not sure I want to put up with a huge download to get a replacement. Is there any way I can find out before I reinstall my browser again?

Your web browser, like any other software, can be broken by program file corruption, incorrect Registry entries, or missing plug-ins (the add-on programs that help your browser display multimedia content). Fred Langa (Windows guru and former stalwart of the now-defunct `WinMag.com` web site) has developed BrowserTune, an easy way (no downloading required!) to test your browser for proper operation and to make sure it's not slowing down your online experience. Try BrowserTune and check out Fred's great tech newsletters at `www.langa.com`.

Chapter 17

Share the Wealth with a Home Network

For years, computer pundits focused on networks in business, and for a long time, that made sense. After all, persuading computers built to be standalone islands of information to engage in trade with other computers wasn't exactly cheap—or easy. But, finally, it happened.

It's taken longer for the benefits of networking to penetrate the home and small office market. But, believe me, the "big guys" in networks have noticed how easy, how powerful, and how profitable home networking is. In the spring of 2003, Cisco Systems bought Linksys, one of the leading home networking vendors. Home networks work—and play—very nicely. Do you have one yet?

In this chapter, you discover that amazingly low equipment prices, basic networking features in recent Windows versions, and built-in network ports in a lot of recent systems have thrown the doors to the networking world wide open to just about everyone. In addition, unlike those who pioneered office networks, you don't need an IT degree or a living room-sized server to keep things working. You might not even need to run cables to connect your computers to each other.

Ten Reasons You Should Network Your Home

Why network? Here are ten serious and not-so-serious reasons to LAN (Local Area Network) it up:

1. Inviting your friends to a LAN party is "in."

2. Sharing your dessert is good; sharing your printer is better.

3. Sharing your printer is better; sharing your broadband Internet connection is best.

4. You can upgrade everybody's storage at the same time with a single storage device.

5. You can help the kids with homework without getting up from your chair.

6. If one PC breaks, other PCs can still get on the Internet.

7. If you think channel surfing is good, imagine channel and web surfing from your favorite easy chair.

8. Want to take your work outside on a lovely spring day? Grab your notebook computer and head for the deck.

9. Borrow the kids' printer instead of running out for ink or taking a floppy disk to their room. After all, they borrow everything from you.

10. Share your MP3 music folders and share the music all over the house.

CAUTION: STOP! LOOK! THINK!

Don't Think You Need to Share the Connection? Think Broadband

I just gave you ten reasons to install a home network, but for me, there's just one reason I needed to do it: broadband. If you have a high-speed Internet connection at your home or small business, it's foolish to connect it to just one PC. The network technologies you learn about in this chapter can help you share the connection with everybody at home or in your small office.

What happens if you don't share the connection? Everyone angles for an excuse to use the PC with the fastest Internet pipe—and you can't get much work done then.

Types of Home Networks

What is a network? Before your brain goes into overload picturing a scene where clipboard-toting engineers are wearing white coats and tending endless rows of reel-to-reel tapedecks, relax. A network is simply what you get when two or more computers are connected and share a resource such as a disk drive, a CD-ROM drive, a printer, the Internet, and so forth.

There are four ways to share resources between two or more computers:

- Ethernet
- Wireless
- Phoneline
- Powerline

A fifth method, Direct Cable Connection, is like a network in many ways but uses parallel, serial, or USB cables. It is much slower than the methods described here. You can learn more about Direct Cable Connection at the Parallel Technologies' web site (www.1pt.com); Parallel Technologies developed Direct Cable Connection for Microsoft.

ON THE WEB: Network with TechTV for More About Your Favorites

Search the TechTV web site (www.techtv.com) to find news and tips about all the popular networks.

The article "Set Up a Home Network" at www.techtv.com/screensavers/howto/ story/0,24330,3396863,00.html is a great place to start.

Which choices are best for you? Before you read my suggestions, you should first learn about each network type.

READ THIS TOO: More About Networking—At Any Level

This chapter is just an introduction to what you can do with networks at home. For more details, try the following books:

- Scott Mueller's *Upgrading and Repairing PCs, 15th Edition* (Que, 2003) has excellent coverage of the hardware side of both home and office networking.

- In addition, *Upgrading and Repairing Networks, Third Edition* (Que, 2003), by Scott Mueller and Terry Ogletree, is the book you need to learn all about office and corporate networking.

For overall coverage of networks that's just right for the home and small office, check out these reads:

- *How Networks Work, Sixth Edition* by Frank Derfler and Les Freed (Que, 2002).

- *The Absolute Beginner's Guide to Networking, Third Edition* by Joe Habraken (Que, 2001).

Fast Ethernet

The most popular forms of wired networks in the world are based on Ethernet. Ethernet comes in both wired and wireless versions. (I discuss the wireless version in Chapter 18, "Wireless Wonders.") The most popular wired version is known as 10/100 Ethernet, because it supports the 10BaseT 10Mbps standard as well as the later Fast Ethernet 100BaseT standard.

When connected to other 10/100 hardware, 10/100 Ethernet runs at 100Mbps (ten times as fast as original 10Base versions). It uses unshielded twisted-pair (UTP) cable. UTP cable resembles telephone cable, but has eight wires in four pairs and uses the RJ-45 connector, which is larger than the RJ-11 connector used by telephone cable. Figure 17.1 shows how a typical Category 5 UTP Ethernet cable compares to a telephone cable.

Snag protector on Category 5 UTP cable protects locking tab

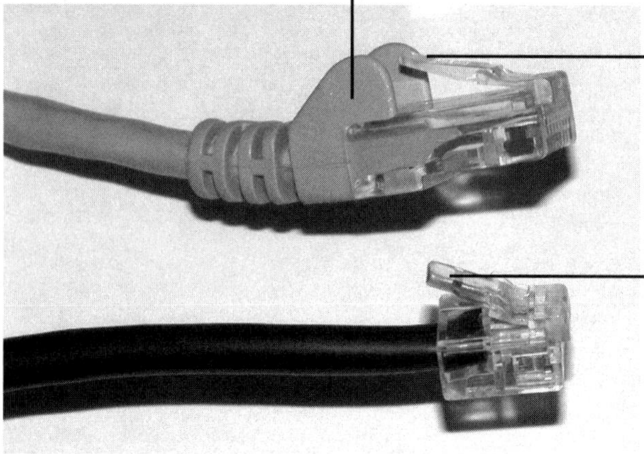

Figure 17.1

A Category 5 UTP cable (top) with an RJ-45 connector compared to a telephone cable (bottom) with an RJ-11 connector.

Locking tab on Category 5 UTP Ethernet cable

Locking tab on telephone cable

10/100 Ethernet is easy to buy and install; you can get boxed network kits from several vendors that contain the basic elements of a short-distance network.

What You Need for a 10/100 Ethernet Network

Here are the basics of a 10/100 Ethernet network:

- **One network interface card (NIC) for each PC if your computers don't have an onboard Ethernet port**—If you need to add a NIC, use a PCI card for desktop computers, a CardBus PC Card (PCMCIA card) for notebook computers, or a USB device if you want to move the port between computers. At 12Mbps, USB 1.1 ports are slower than 100Mbps Fast Ethernet. If you have USB 2.0 ports (they run at 480Mbps), look for USB 2.0 Fast Ethernet adapters.

- **One Category 5 (Cat 5) UTP cable for each PC**—This must be long enough to reach the hub, switch, or router.

- **One hub or switch with connections for all PCs on the network**—Switches are faster, but they cost more. 10/100 Ethernet runs at 100Mbps only if all cards and other devices on the network support 10/100 or Fast Ethernet (100Mbps only) standards. It also requires a hub or switch. If you are planning to use the network to share a broadband Internet connection, use a router with a built-in switch.

- **Windows network utilities and configuration**—Windows includes the network protocols needed to connect with other computers and the Internet, as well as utilities such as Ping and Winipcfg or Ipconfig to help you diagnose network problems.

JARGON

PC Card—Original version of the credit-card–sized add-on card for notebooks that was first called the PCMCIA card. Has a 16-bit wide data bus, which slows down data transfers.

PCI—Standard card type used in desktop computers.

CardBus—A 32-bit wide version of the PC Card slot; you can use 16-bit PC Cards with a CardBus slot, but CardBus can't work with 16-bit PC Card slots. CardBus slots are clearly labeled to help avoid problems, but you should know which type of slot your notebook computer has before you buy a network card.

Hub—Simplest connecting device used on an Ethernet network, it subdivides the bandwidth of the network among all devices connected to it.

Switch—Resembles a hub, but creates direct connections between sender and receiver and provides full bandwidth to each computer connected to it.

Router—Connects a LAN to the Internet or another network. Often combined with a switch.

Figure 17.2 shows you the hardware needed to build a typical Fast Ethernet network.

JARGON

Dongle—A proprietary connector that enables the narrow PC Card to connect to a standard-size cable.

Integrated—The 10/100 Ethernet port is built into the card, which has a wider-than-normal end.

ANALYZE THIS

10/100/1000—Backwards-Compatible Ethernet
Although some of the original Fast Ethernet hardware on the market would run only at 100Mbps, most Ethernet hardware on the market today is actually two types of Ethernet in one. It's called *10/100 Ethernet* because it can work with either older 10BaseT Ethernet or Fast Ethernet (100BaseTX) equipment. Dual-speed (10/100) cards, hubs, and switches adapt their speed to the speed of the other devices to which they're connected. Avoid Fast Ethernet (100BaseTX) network gear and go with 10/100 Ethernet.

continues

CONTINUED

The newest type of desktop network hardware, Gigabit Ethernet, is ten times faster than Fast Ethernet, but it also adapts to slower Ethernet speeds. For that reason, it is sometimes referred to as 10/100/1000 Ethernet. Although Gigabit Ethernet is faster than Fast Ethernet, it is supported primarily by large corporate networks at this time. Very little Gigabit Ethernet hardware is currently available for home and small office networks. Keep in mind that if you mix Gigabit Ethernet with 10/100 Ethernet hardware, the network runs at the speed of the slower hardware.

Figure 17.2

A 10/100 Ethernet network has a star arrangement (or star topology) because each NIC is connected to the central hub or switch. Equipment photos courtesy of Linksys.

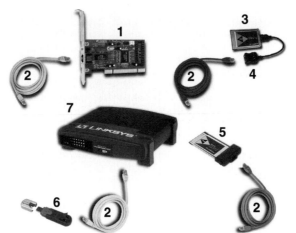

1. PCI 10/100 NIC
2. CAT 5 UTP cable
3. PC Card 10/100 NIC
4. Dongle to attach PC Card to cable
5. CardBus 10/100 NIC with integrated port
6. USB 2.0 10/100 Ethernet adapter
7. 10/100 switch

The Bottom Line on Ethernet and 10/100 Ethernet

10/100 Ethernet offers an overwhelming level of product support at very low prices; virtually any store that sells PCs also sells 10/100 Ethernet products. Many recent notebook and desktop computers now include built-in 10/100 networking, making potential costs even lower. The biggest gripe with Ethernet is those blasted Technicolor cables (you can also get them in neutral gray). They're hard to hide, and if you want professional-style installation with wall jacks, be prepared to spend some time and some bucks to pull your cables in and through walls.

- **Cost for a two-station network**—Under $100 for a hub or switch, two PCI network interface cards, and cables.

- **Cost to add additional PCs**—$20 to 25 per desktop (PCI card); $40 to 60 per notebook computer (PC Card or USB adapter); prices may vary.

- **Speed**—10Mbps (10BaseT); 100Mbps (Fast Ethernet); up to 200Mbps if full-duplex switch and cards are used.

- **Limitations**—Performance drops if more than 10 PCs are on a network, unless a Windows NT 4.0, Windows 2000, Windows 2003, or Novell NetWare server is used to share resources.

- **Best use**—All network uses, including Internet sharing and streaming audio and video.

Wireless Networks

"Cables? Cables? We don't need no stinkin' cables!" That's what you can say if you decide to use a wireless network. There are four varieties of wireless networks on the market; three are forms of wireless Ethernet. The fourth (Bluetooth) also supports keyboards, mice, DV camcorders, and other types of devices.

Wireless Ethernet networks are known by the names of the official standards (IEEE 802.11a, 802.11b, and 802.11g), but they are also known by various other names, including Wi-Fi (Wireless Fidelity), Wireless-A, Wireless-B, and Wireless-G.

The other major wireless network is called Bluetooth, and it's designed to support both PCs and other types of wireless information devices. You can even connect DV camcorders to your computer with a wireless Bluetooth connection!

Some notebook computers have wireless Ethernet NICs built in and some desktop and notebook computers have built-in Bluetooth, but in most cases, you need to add a wireless NIC to your computer to connect to a wireless network.

To learn more about the different types of wireless networks, see Chapter 18.

CAUTION: STOP! LOOK! THINK!

Whatever Became of HomeRF?

With the popularity of IEEE 802.11b and other types of wireless Ethernet, the HomeRF wireless networking standard lost out in the marketplace. The HomeRF Working Group was shut down in early 2003, but the HomeRF specification and additional HomeRF information is still available from www.palowireless.com.

Phoneline Networks

If you don't want to string wires all over the place and don't want to try wireless, you could use the voice and data network that's already installed in your home: the telephone line. You can use the existing wiring to carry both phone and network traffic at the same time without interference because the network uses different frequencies than normal telephone calls do. In fact, HomePNA network adapters have two jacks, one to connect the adapter to the telephone line and another for plugging a phone into the adapter.

HomePNA, the Home Phoneline Networking Alliance (www.homepna.org), is the trade group responsible for developing the HomePNA network standard now in version 3.0:

- HomePNA 1.0, the original version introduced in 1998, ran at just 1 Mbps (ten times slower than 10BaseT Ethernet); it used parallel and USB ports as well as add-on cards.

- HomePNA 2.0, introduced in 1999, runs at 10Mbps (the same speed as 10BaseT Ethernet). It is also the speed supported by DSL and cable modems for broadband Internet connections. Although HomePNA 2.0 runs too fast to use a parallel-port connection, it still supports USB connections as well as add-on cards.

- HomePNA 3.0, introduced in mid-2003, runs at 128Mbps, rivaling Fast Ethernet in performance. HomePNA 3.0 uses Quality of Service (QoS) analysis to determine what types of data are flowing on the network. QoS assigns a higher priority to streaming video and audio than to web pages, downloads, and other types of network traffic. Thus, it is a perfect match for the new breed of network-aware home entertainment audio and video devices reaching the market in 2003.

What You Need for a HomePNA Network

Because HomePNA computers communicate directly with each other, it's an easy network to set up. All you need is the following:

- **One HomePNA NIC**—PCI or PC Card or USB device; some computers also have built-in HomePNA 2.0 or 3.0 NICs. Figure 17.3 shows how a typical 10/100 Ethernet NIC compares to a HomePNA NIC.
- **HomePNA setup software**—Included with HomePNA NIC.

Options include the following:

- **Broadband bridge**—Connects between a broadband Internet (cable modem or DSL) connection and a HomePNA network for broadband sharing
- **Combo NICs**—PC Cards that support both 10/100 Ethernet and HomePNA 2.0 or 3.0 networks

Figure 17.4 shows a typical HomePNA 2.0 configuration using a broadband bridge.

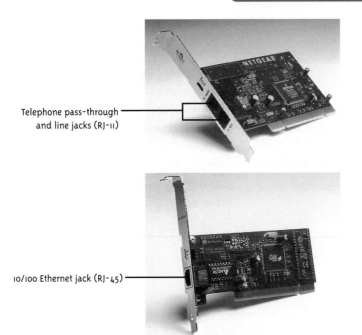

Telephone pass-through and line jacks (RJ-11)

10/100 Ethernet jack (RJ-45)

Figure 17.3

A typical HomePNA 2.0-based NIC (top) compared to a 10/100 Ethernet NIC (bottom). Note that the HomePNA NIC has two cable connections, compared to just one on the Ethernet NIC. Photos courtesy of Netgear.

1. PCI NIC with dual phone jacks to enable line sharing
2. Phone connected to second jack
3. Phoneline to wall jack
4. Wall jack
5. Baseboard or in-wall phoneline
6. USB adapter
7. Broadband bridge
8. CAT 5 cable between bridge and cable modem
9. Cable modem with Internet connection

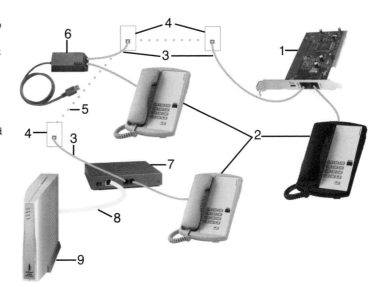

Figure 17.4

A typical HomePNA 2.0-based network with a PCI-based NIC, a USB network adapter, and a broadband bridge to the Internet.

The Bottom Line on HomePNA

HomePNA 2.0 is not much more expensive than Fast Ethernet, especially if you need only a few stations. It also has more-than-adequate performance for Internet line sharing and other networking tasks. Rewiring won't be needed in most cases, because HomePNA uses your existing telephone wiring. HomePNA 3.0 prices were not yet available as this book went to press, but they are expected to be comparable to HomePNA 2.0 hardware.

- **Cost for a two-station network**—Around $80 (desktop PCs with PCI cards).
- **Cost per additional PC**—Around $40 (PCI); around $70 (PC Card).
- **Speed**—10Mbps.
- **Limitations**—30 PCs per network.
- **Best use**—All home networking uses, including Internet sharing and streaming audio and video.

HomePlug

There's another network in your home besides the telephone lines: the electrical outlets found in almost every room of a typical home. The HomePlug Powerline Alliance developed the first successful standard for powerline networking, HomePlug 1.0, in mid-2001.

Although it took over a year for a wide variety of HomePlug network products to become widely available, you can now buy HomePlug network hardware from a variety of vendors, including Linksys, Phonex, Netgear, and others. Unlike HomePNA, which uses internal NICs as well as external USB devices, HomePlug adapters are external devices that connect to the USB and Ethernet ports found on most systems (see Figure 17.5). Because you don't need to open your computer to add it to a HomePlug network, HomePlug is one of the easiest networks to install. HomePlug can also be used to increase the range of a wireless network, as shown in Figure 17.6.

HomePlug 1.0 is no speed demon, but it's fast enough for a typical home network. Its rated speed is 14Mbps (12Mbps when plugged into USB 1.1 ports). Note, however, that real-world speed with current products is about 6Mbps when connecting to other PCs and about 2Mbps when connecting to a broadband Internet device. An improved HomePlug AV standard designed to run at 100Mbps with guaranteed bandwidth for multimedia devices was announced in the Fall of 2002, but the first HomePlug AV products are not expected until 2004.

Figure 17.5

A typical HomePlug network adapter. The Ethernet or USB cable from the computer connects to the bottom of the adapter. Photo courtesy of Netgear.

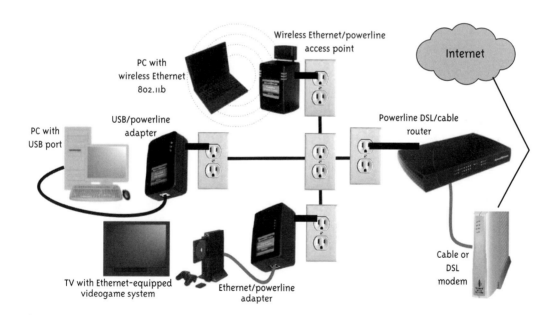

Figure 17.6

A typical HomePlug network that uses an Ethernet-to-HomePLUG adapter to connect to a router for shared Internet access.

The Bottom Line on HomePlug

HomePlug 1.0 is the most universally available and easiest-to-install network around because it works anywhere an AC outlet is present. However, because electrical interference causes performance to be about 60 percent slower than its rated speed, HomePlug 1.0 is the slowest home network currently on the market. It's fast enough for traditional network tasks, but it's not up to the task of delivering streaming video or audio in its current form.

- **Cost for a two-station network**—Around $80 (desktop PCs with PCI cards).
- **Cost per additional PC**—Around $45 (PCI); around $90 (PC Card).
- **Speed**—14Mbps (rated).
- **Limitations**—16 Windows-based PCs per network; not designed for use with Macs or non-Windows devices.
- **Best use**—Extending other types of networks.

My Favorites

Until the advent of HomePNA 3.0, there was no question that when it came to wired home networking, my first choice was 10/100 Ethernet. 10/100 Ethernet is ten times faster than HomePNA 2.0 and over twenty times faster than HomePlug in real-world performance. In addition, many recent systems already include an Ethernet jack.

Although HomePNA 3.0 is now about the same speed as 10/100 Ethernet, Ethernet still gets my top nod for its combination of performance, low hardware cost, and wide availability of hardware. However, if you need to run cable through walls, under floors, and so on, 10/100 Ethernet might not seem like such a good idea anymore.

HomePNA 2.0 or later is my second choice. If HomePNA 3.0 lives up to its specifications, it will be just about as good a choice as 10/100 Ethernet. Note that either flavor of HomePNA is a great choice if you don't want to worry about rewiring your home.

HomePlug is still quite a new product, but it's worth considering for networking and Internet sharing if you don't want to rewire. However, unlike HomePNA 3.0 and 10/100 Ethernet, HomePlug isn't fast enough for streaming audio and video.

ON THE WEB: It's Practically My Favorite Networking Site

My favorite "one-stop" web site for networking news, advice, tutorials, and reviews is EarthWeb's Practically Networked site at www.practicallynetworked.com.

Installing a Typical 10/100 Ethernet Home Network

In this section, I help you install and set up a typical Fast Ethernet network. You can choose either a preconfigured kit or build your own kit from the wide variety of network components on the market.

Hardware You Need

The easiest way to pick up the basics of a two-station network, if both computers are desktop computers, is to purchase a boxed network. Boxed networks are available from several vendors and make a good choice *if* you're not planning to share a broadband connection.

However, let's not kid ourselves. If you're tech-savvy enough to build a home network, you probably already have a broadband Internet connection or are busy shopping for one. The companies that make boxed network kits don't realize that yet, so skip the kit and make your own with this checklist:

- **Check your computers first for 10/100 Ethernet ports**—If your computer has an Ethernet port already, you've saved yourself $20 to $40 because you don't need to buy a NIC for that computer. Figure 17.7 shows typical Ethernet and USB port locations on desktop and notebook computers.

- **One 10/100 Ethernet NIC for each computer without a built-in Ethernet port**—Use a PCI card for desktop computers, a PC Card for notebooks, or a USB/Ethernet adapter for any recently manufactured computer if you want to freely move it between systems. Refer back to Figure 17.2.

- **One Cat 5 or better (such as Cat 5e or Cat 6) cable per computer**—Must be long enough to run between the computer and the router/switch. You can buy premade cables, but if you're planning cable runs over 100 feet, don't mind a bit of work, and want to save money, you can build your own cables. Building your own cables is also best if you need to run cables through walls.

Figure 17.7

A desktop PC (top) and notebook PC (bottom) with built-in 10/100 Ethernet and USB ports.

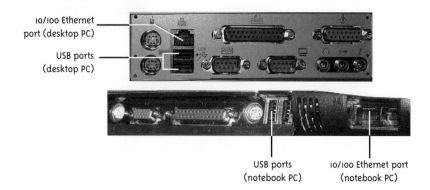

10/100 Ethernet port (desktop PC)

USB ports (desktop PC)

USB ports (notebook PC)

10/100 Ethernet port (notebook PC)

ON THE WEB: Do-It-Yourself Cabling Help Is a Click Away

If you want to build your own Category 5 network cables, check out the illustrated DUX Computer Digest guide at www.duxcw.com/digest/Howto/network/cable/index.htm.

The HomePCNetwork web site has an excellent illustrated tutorial on running wires through walls at www.homepcnetwork.com/index.htm?wireintro.htm.

• **One router with built-in switch for networking and Internet sharing**—By installing a router right away, your network is ready to share a broadband Internet connection. Sure, you could save a few bucks and use a switch instead, but you'll pay more in the long run. In addition, you'll need to set up an IP address manually for each computer if you don't use a router. Keeping track of IP addresses can be tough and creating the right type of IP address to avoid conflicting with public networks isn't easy for networking novices. For your peace of mind, get a router.

The router should incorporate at least four 10/100 Ethernet ports. If you want to host LAN parties, be sure the router also has an uplink port so that you can connect another switch to it if you need to connect more than four computers to it, now or later. In addition, make sure you have a power outlet nearby.

ANALYZE THIS

Skip Hubs Unless You Want to Skip Speed

Even if you decide to forego a router until you install broadband Internet, don't cripple your network by settling for a hub instead of a switch.

Switches and hubs are both designed to connect the different stations on a 10/100 Ethernet network to each other. What's the difference?

- A hub subdivides the total bandwidth (speed) of the network among the computers connected to it. For example, if you have a 10/100 Ethernet hub with four computers connected to it, your actual speed is just 25Mbps (100 divided by 4)! Use a switch and everyone gets the full speed of the network.

- Even better, most 10/100 switches and NICs now support a feature called *full-duplex*. Full-duplex means that your NIC can send and receive signals at the same time. If you have 10/100 NICs and a switch that supports full-duplex, multiply the speed of the network by two; it's a 200Mbps screamer!

- Switches used to be much more expensive, but they're now about the same price as a hub with the same number of ports. Hubs are now starting to show up in the clearance bins of some stores. Leave them there.

The Software and Configuration You Need

The software you need to create your network is included with Windows 95 and newer versions of Windows. Depending on the version of Windows you use, you might need to configure your network manually. On the other hand, Windows might provide a network wizard to do the heavy lifting for you.

If you have even one computer with Windows XP, you can use the Windows XP Network Setup Wizard to configure all the Windows PCs on your network. If the newest Windows version on your network is Windows Me, you can set up other Windows PCs on your network with the Home Networking Wizard setup floppy disk it creates during the network setup process.

The following steps assume that you're using a router to assign IP addresses to each computer on the network. Take it from somebody who's built networks both ways: routers make it easier, *much* easier.

If you don't want to fiddle around with configuring IP addresses for each computer on the network, you need to enable the DHCP Server feature in the router to provide IP addresses to the computers connected to it. See the "Adding a Router to a 10/100 Ethernet Network" section later in this chapter for more information.

JARGON

DHCP—Dynamic Host Configuration Protocol; a DHCP server that provides an IP address automatically. A router is usually configured to receive an IP address automatically from the DHCP server in the broadband Internet device. In turn, it uses its own DHCP server to provide IP addresses to computers connected to the router.

Setting Up a Home Network with Windows XP

Windows XP includes a network setup program. To start it:

1. Click Start.

2. Point to All Programs.

3. Point to Accessories.

4. Point to Communications.

5. Click Network Setup Wizard.

Then, answer the prompts onscreen to do the following:

- Specify what type of Internet connection you have.

- Provide a unique name for each computer.

- Provide a workgroup name.

- Specify whether to share any folders on the computer.

At the end of the process, you have the option to create a Network Setup disk for use with other computers, use the Windows XP CD as a setup disk for other Windows computers, or finish the wizard. Note that Windows XP automatically shares printers with other users.

READ THIS TOO: More, Much More, About Windows XP

If you want to dig deeper into home networking the Windows XP way, pick up a copy of *Special Edition Using Windows XP Home Edition, Bestseller Edition,* by Robert Cowart and Brian Knittel (Que, 2002). Bob and Brian cover wizard-driven and manual network configuration, Internet sharing, and advanced home networking features.

Setting Up a Home Network with Windows Me

Windows Me also includes a network setup program. To start it:

1. Click Start.

2. Point to Programs.

3. Point to Accessories.

4. Point to Communications.

5. Click Home Networking Wizard (HNW).

Answer the prompts onscreen to do the following:

- Specify what type of Internet connection you have.

- Provide a unique name for each computer.

- Provide a workgroup name.

- Specify whether to share the My Documents folder on each computer (Microsoft's recommended default location for the files you create); see Figure 17.8.

- Specify whether to share any printers connected to each computer.

At the end of the process, HNW creates a Home Networking Setup disk that you can use on other computers that run Windows 9x.

READ THIS TOO: Read More About Me (Windows Me, That Is)

If you want to dig deeper into home networking the Windows Me way, pick up a copy of *Special Edition Using Windows Me,* by Ed Bott (Que, 2001). Ed takes you through the process of network configuration with both wizards and manual settings, sharing an Internet connection and advanced home networking features.

Figure 17.8

Using Windows Me's
HNW to set up folder
and printer sharing.

Click this box to share the
My Documents folder.

Click this button to
set a password for
the My Documents
folder (if shared).

Clear this box to remove
sharing from printer(s).

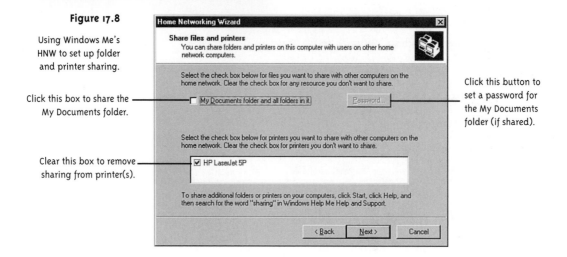

Setting Up a Home Network with Windows 98

If all you have is Windows 98 on your home network, setting it up is easy for you. Here's how:

1. First, install the network card and drivers. During this process, Windows also installs network protocols and software, so have your Windows CD handy.

2. After the installation, double-click the Network icon in the Control Panel.

3. You should see the following network components listed in the Configuration tab:

   - NetBEUI ->(network card name)

   - TCP/IP ->(network card name)

   - IPX/SPX ->(network card name)

4. If a network client is not installed, click Add, click Client, and then click Add again. In the next dialog box, click Microsoft and click the Client for Microsoft Networks, and then click OK. See Figure 17.9.

5. To install File and Print Sharing on computers whose resources you want to share, click Service, Add, Microsoft, and File and Print Sharing for Microsoft Networks.

6. Click the Identification tab and enter a unique name for each computer on the network. All computers must use the same workgroup name.

7. Click OK. Insert the Windows CD-ROM if prompted to finish the configuration. Reboot when prompted.

8. After rebooting, open the Network icon again on the system with resources you want to share. Click File and Print Sharing and select whether you want to share files, printers, or both.

9. Select the folder(s) and printer(s) you want to share; right-click the folder or printer, select Sharing, and set the access levels and passwords.

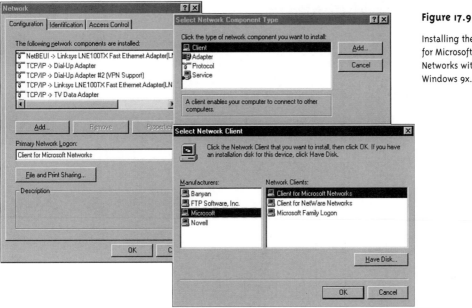

Figure 17.9

Installing the Client for Microsoft Networks with Windows 9x.

ON THE WEB: Configuring Networks the Hard Way

The Earthweb Practically Networked web site (www.practicallynetworked.com) offers several tutorials on manually configuring networks.

Installing HomePNA and HomePlug Networks

HomePNA and HomePlug networks are easier to configure than 10/100 Ethernet, in part because they were designed as home networks from the start and because these networks operate on a peer-to-peer basis. That is, they don't use a central hub or switch. To configure these networks, use the setup program provided with the network hardware on each computer on the network.

Cabling Do's and Don'ts

Your network is only as good as its weakest link: the cable. Stay out of trouble with these guidelines (★ indicates 10/100 Ethernet-specific guidelines):

- Don't use cracked, frayed, or damaged cables.
- If you decide to build your own cable, buy good tools that enable you to cut the cable and crimp the connectors without damaging them.★
- If you need to extend a Cat 5 cable, buy a Cat 5 cable coupler; they cost more than Cat 3 couplers, but they won't degrade the signal.★
- Don't run cable across a floor where it can be damaged.
- Electrical devices and fluorescent lights can interfere with network signals; route cables well away from them.

Adding a Router or Gateway for Easy Internet Sharing

As noted earlier in this chapter, I recommend including a router with a built-in switch as part of a 10/100 Ethernet network from day one to make setting up the network easier. However, a router isn't needed on a HomePNA or HomePlug network until you have a broadband Internet connection.

Adding a Router to a 10/100 Ethernet Network

If you already have a 10/100 Ethernet home network and decide to add broadband Internet access as described in Chapter 16, "Get Yourself Broadband—It's (Always) Going Fast!," you can buy a router with a single port and connect it to your existing switch, or buy a router with a built-in multiport switch as a replacement for your switch.

The router must be configured with the same settings as an individual computer would be to access the broadband Internet device. However, the router is configured through your web browser; you enter the router's IP address in the web address window of your web browser, provide the default username and password, and provide the information needed to set up your network. The information needed includes the following:

- The IP address used by your connection; use DHCP if your computer doesn't have a fixed IP address.
- The DHCP server settings, including enabling the DHCP server in the router and specifying the number of computers for which to provide IP addresses; this is also required if you install the router before you add broadband access.

Figure 17.10 shows a typical Linksys router configuration screen for DHCP services. By default, Windows is configured to receive an IP address from a DHCP server such as a router. If DHCP is not enabled, you must provide an IP address for each computer on the network in the network configuration for each computer.

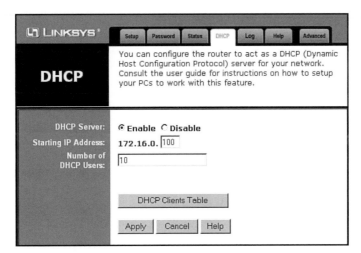

Figure 17.10

Configuring a Linksys router to provide automatic IP addresses for ten computers on the network.

MARK'S TIP SHEET: ISP-Specific Help for Home Networking

Many broadband ISPs provide home network setup information on their support web sites. You can also check the router vendor's web site for help.

After you connect the router to the network and configure it, rerun the Windows XP or Windows Me network wizards (described earlier in this chapter) to configure the network for shared Internet access. With Windows 98, set the TCP/IP protocol to use a server-assigned IP address instead of a specified IP address.

Adding a Router or Gateway to a HomePNA or HomePlug Network

Most routers for broadband Internet services, such as cable or DSL, are designed to connect through the Ethernet port found on typical broadband Internet devices. However, some multi-network routers support HomePNA as well as Ethernet. These routers include the 2Wire HomePortal 100 series.

Both HomePNA and HomePlug networks support Ethernet bridges, which enable a HomePNA or HomePlug network to be connected to an Ethernet network or Ethernet device such as a cable or DSL modem. See Figures 17.4 and 17.6 earlier in this chapter for examples.

Creating a Link Between Wired and Wireless Networks

Although wireless networks (see Chapter 18) are becoming extremely popular, they're not for everyone. It's more expensive to build a pure wireless network than any type of wired network, and wireless networks are generally slower than wired networks. Thus, you might want to create a mixed-media network, which uses both wired and wireless components for maximum flexibility.

Some of the devices you can use to create a mixed-media network include the following:

- **Network bridges**—A bridge is a device that connects two different types of networks so that they act as a single network.
- **Multi-function routers and gateways**—Routers and gateways that support more than one type of network can also be used as bridges.

Be sure to read the documentation for these devices carefully to make sure they support full network capabilities across all types of devices they support. The diagrams provided by many home network product vendors are very helpful in determining how to create a mixed-media network. For example, Figure 17.11 shows how Linksys HomePlug (powerline) and 10/100 Ethernet products can be used on a single network.

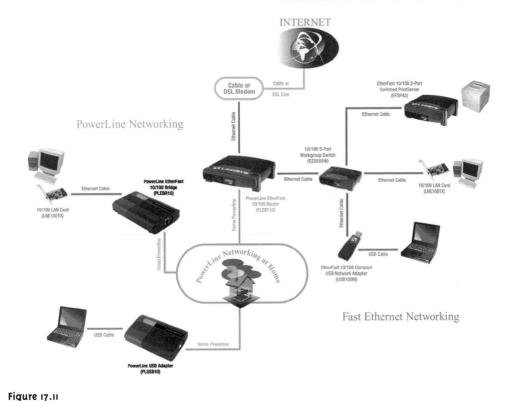

Figure 17.11

A mixed-media network featuring Linksys HomePlug and Ethernet devices. Diagram courtesy of Linksys.

Adding Digital TV and Audio to Your Home Network

Networks aren't just for PCs: You can now add digital TV recording devices from TiVo and ReplayTV, as well as streaming audio devices to your home network.

Adding Digital Video Recorders (DVRs)

Digital Video Recorders (DVRs) such as ReplayTV and TiVo enable you to set aside your VCR and record programs to hard disk for delayed viewing. They also support pausing live programs, so they've become very popular with TV sports and TV special event fans. DVRs are even more powerful when you add them to a home network.

ReplayTV models in the 4000, 4500, and 5000 series are ready to connect to a wired Ethernet network for sharing programs between devices. The new 5300 series models can also be connected to an 802.11b wireless network. Free ReplayTV Photo Transfer Software enables you to copy photos with Windows Explorer to a 5000-series ReplayTV DVR. ReplayTV also supports Internet sharing of recorded programs with other ReplayTV users.

A TiVo Series2 Digital Video Recorder (DVR) can be added to your home network if you buy the $99 Home Media Option direct from TiVo. It enables you to share TiVo recordings made with one TiVo with another, play music, and display photos from your computer on a TiVo; it also lets you use remote scheduling performed through TiVo Central Online to set up recordings when you're away from home. TiVo Home Media Option works with both wired and wireless Ethernet networks, using network adapters connected to the USB port on each Series2 DVR.

ON THE WEB: DVRs Unleashed Online

Learn more about the network-ready ReplayTV line of DVRs at www.replaytv.com.

Discover the Home Media Option and other TiVo features at www.tivo.com.

Search the TechTV web site for all kinds of ReplayTV and TiVo tips at http://cgi.techtv.com/search.

Adding Digital Music, Photo, and Video Players

An increasing number of home video and audio players are designed for use with home networks. The devices shown in Table 17.1 are among the first products on the market to enable you to share digital content hosted on your PC. See the vendor web sites listed for more information.

Table 17.1   Digital Music, Photo, and Video Players for Home Networks

Product	Digital Video	Digital Audio	Digital Photos	Network Type(s)	Notes	Web Site
CD30 C300	No	Yes	No	10/100, 802.11b wireless	Digital audio outputs; plays WAV, MP3, WMA	www.cd30.com
CD30 C200	No	Yes	No	10/100, 802.11b wireless	Plays WAV, MP3, WMA	www.cd30.com
CD30 C100	No	Yes	No	10/100	Plays WAV, MP3, WMA	www.cd30.com
HP Digital Media Receiver EW5000	No	Yes	Yes	10/100, 802.11b wireless	Remote control	www.hp.com

Product	Digital Video	Digital Audio	Digital Photos	Network Type(s)	Notes	Web Site
HP Digital Media Receiver EW5000	No	Yes	Yes	10/100	Remote control	www.hp.com
Prismiq MediaPlayer	Yes	Yes	Yes	10/100, 802.11b wireless via PC Card	Optional wireless keyboard	www.prismiq.com
Sony RoomLink PNCA-MR10	Yes	Yes	Yes	10/100, optional 802.11a wireless	Must be used with a Sony VAIO desktop PC	www.sonystyle.com

Controlling Access and Enhancing Security

Because of the low security provided by Windows home networking, a home network has to be a "trust-based" network. However, you still need to protect your information from intruders, especially when your network is connected to the Internet.

You should protect your home network and Internet connection in the following ways:

- Use firewall software such as Zone Alarm or Norton Internet Security on all computers connected to an always-on broadband Internet connection. These programs block unauthorized access to your computers and can also stop unauthorized programs from connecting to the Internet.

- If you need to connect to a virtual private network (VPN) at your corporate office, make sure your router or gateway supports VPN connections.

- With Windows 9x/Me, you can use passwords on shared folders or drives. To set or change a password on a shared folder or drive, do the following:

  1. Right-click the folder in Windows Explorer.

  2. Select Sharing.

  3. Next, specify the Access type. Use Read-Only for folders that can be read, but whose contents can't be changed or deleted. Use Full to allow files to be read, written, or deleted. Use Depends on Password to specify two levels of access, depending on the password used. See Figure 17.12.

  4. Enter the password(s) for Read-Only, Full, or both.

  5. Re-enter the passwords when prompted.

  6. Click OK.

  7. Tell other network users the password(s) you want them to use to access the folder.

Figure 17.12

Setting the pass-
word on a shared
drive in Windows
9x/Me.

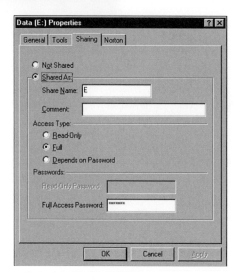

Windows XP Home Edition doesn't use passwords. Instead, it uses a feature called Simple File Sharing. Here's how it works:

- A Shared Documents folder is automatically set for sharing with other users of the same computer.

- A folder can be made private (accessed only by the user) if the drive is formatted with the NTFS file system.

- Other folders can be configured for full (read/write) or read-only access for other users of the same computer or other computers on the network.

- To share other folders with other users or other computers on the network, right-click a folder, click Properties, and then click Sharing to open a dialog box, as seen in Figure 17.13.

By default, the box Allow network users to change my files is checked. Clear it as shown in Figure 17.13 to make the folder read-only. Click Apply, and then OK to accept the changes.

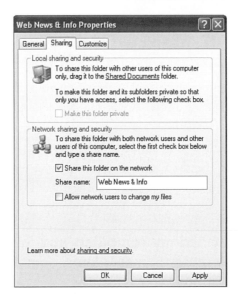

Figure 17.13

Setting a folder for shared read-only access in Windows XP.

ON THE WEB: Finding the Best Firewalls and Skipping the Rest

Ideally, your computer should be invisible to the rest of the Internet so you don't have any unwelcome guests dropping in on it. Find out how secure your computer is with the free Shields Up! Internet security test from Gibson Research, and also check out the latest recommendations on firewall software. Get started at www.grc.com.

Troubleshooting Your Home Network

Networking makes sharing internet access, peripherals, and files very easy—when it works. Some of the most typical problems network newcomers encounter are covered here.

Help! I found a great deal on a HomePNA 1.0 adapter, but now my HomePNA 2.0 network is ten times slower.

HomePNA 1.0 devices can be connected to a HomePNA 2.0 or 3.0 network, but the entire network has to slow down to HomePNA's 1Mbps speed to work. It's not such a great deal after all.

Help! I'm trying to install my NIC and the Windows 98 CD doesn't have the right driver. When I put in the driver CD that came with the NIC, the computer asks me for the Windows CD. What's the deal?

This is an all-too-common irritation with several versions of Windows, but there's nothing wrong with the system. During a NIC installation, Windows needs network files from its own CD as well as card-specific files that are usually on a CD or disk supplied with the card. The Windows installer assumes that the same folder name is used for the entire installation, which is seldom the case. Use the Browse button to change to the correct drive or folder if the system can't find the next file after you've changed the CD. Remember to wait a few moments after you insert the CD for the drive to spin up.

Help! I've just connected my computers and they're both complaining about duplicate computer names. I know something is supposed to be the same. What's wrong?

You've confused the *computer* name and the *workgroup* name. Each computer needs its own name, but the workgroup name needs to be the same for all systems on the same network. Change the name on one of the computers with a duplicate name, reboot it, and you're ready to share. The Computer Name is set through the Network properties icon in Windows 9x/Me, and through the Computer Name tab on the System properties sheet in Windows XP.

Help! A friend of mine told me about creating a two-station 10/100 Ethernet network without using a switch or router. Is this on the level?

Yes, your friend is right, but only partly. If you use a crossover cable that reverses some of the wire pairs, you can run the cable directly between the RJ-45 Ethernet ports on your computer without any problems. However, a crossover cable won't work after you add a router or switch to grow your network.

Chapter 18

Wireless Wonders

Want computing freedom? Disconnect the cables and switch to radio waves to carry your data. You don't need to be an Edison, a Bell, or a Tesla to do it. You just need to add one of today's wireless networking cards or USB adapters to your PC.

At home, at the office, or while waiting to catch a flight, wireless networking sets you free to chase information wherever you are. In this chapter, you learn about the leading wireless standards, what they're best used for, how to determine if your computer is already wireless-ready, and how to add wireless hardware to your desktop or portable computer.

Ten Reasons Wireless Connections Benefit You

Maybe your first exposure to wireless networking was watching those goofy "flying people" Windows XP commercials. Or maybe the idea of relying on something invisible to carry information makes you uncomfortable. Whatever the reason, if you're not sure that wireless networking is worth considering, look over my top-ten list of benefits. If you like what you see, keep reading.

1. If you must bring work home from the office, you'd rather work out on the deck than be cooped up inside.

2. It's fun to watch "Who Wants to be a Millionaire?" and look up the answers online while you relax in your recliner.

3. You don't need to cut holes in your walls to network your home if you go with wireless networking.

4. You can check your email while you wait for your (delayed) flight at many major airports.

5. You can connect your PDA to your computer and to your printer without wires.

6. Grab a cappuccino or a burger and surf while you snack at Starbucks or McDonalds.

7. Get out of the office, sit under a shade tree, and keep working.

8. You can add wireless networking to most types of wired networks, so you have the best of both worlds.

9. You can use the same wireless networking hardware at home and at the office.

10. You can use a wireless network in the same ways you use a wired network.

Types of Wireless Connectivity

Wireless networking has matured over the last couple of years. When I first began to research it, there were many different types of wireless networks. Some were based (more or less) on Ethernet and some were made for home use only. These early networks lacked uniform standards and sometimes required you to buy hardware from one company. It was a recipe for high prices and low satisfaction.

Today, although there are just a few standards that fall into two categories, there are more choices than ever. From low-cost hardware priced for home users to corporate-class hardware with airtight security, you're sure to find a budget-friendly solution that works well with others.

The major forms of wireless connectivity include the following:

- **Wireless Ethernet**—This family is based on various forms of the IEEE-802.11 network standard. The popular name for Wireless Ethernet is Wi-Fi, but Wi-Fi actually has three different flavors: 802.11b, 802.11a, and the newest member of the family, 802.11g. As you learn later in this chapter, it can be a bit tricky to interconnect these siblings. Wireless Ethernet can be used for all types of traditional network tasks, but its biggest appeal for home users is sharing an Internet connection without drilling holes in the walls or floors.

- **Bluetooth**—Unlike Wireless Ethernet, which is designed to build networks of several computers, Bluetooth is a one-to-one product that can also be used to connect peripherals such as keyboards, mice, PDAs, telephone headsets, and even DV camcorders. It has a short range and is sometimes simpler to set up than Wireless Ethernet.

Fortunately, you don't need to choose between these products. Both can be installed in the same computer and used for different tasks.

Discovering If You Already Have Wireless Connectivity

Until recently, if you wanted wireless networking, you needed to add a wireless network adapter to your computer. Fortunately, some notebook computer makers have begun to add the 802.11b flavor of Wi-Fi to their products through the use of built-in adapters or by using Intel's new Centrino technology. Centrino includes 802.11b Wi-Fi as part of its feature set, along with improved power management and a processor especially designed for portable computers. In addition, some motherboards from MSI (Micro-Star; `www.msicomputers.com`) and EpoX (`http://web.epox.com`) are Bluetooth-ready and might have the Bluetooth transceiver already installed. Thus, the odds, while still slim, are better than ever that you might already have either 802.11b or Bluetooth connectivity on your computer. Here's how to find out:

- Check the Windows Device Manager for Bluetooth devices. The Bluetooth adapter is displayed in the Network adapters section of the Device Manager, and other Bluetooth devices and protocols are listed separately. See `www.btsws.com/drivers/default.asp` for an example screenshot.

- Check the Windows Device Manager for Wi-Fi or Wireless Ethernet adapters. The adapter will be listed by name in the Network adapters category. You should also see a wireless network configuration utility icon displayed next to the time display in the system tray.

- Check the specifications for your computer at the vendor's web site.

Although a growing number of notebook computer already include Wi-Fi networking, you need to add a Wi-Fi or Bluetooth adapter to most computers if you want to enjoy the benefits of wireless networking.

Adding Wi-Fi/Wireless Ethernet Capability

There's no shortage of Wireless Ethernet hardware on the market, and there's also no shortage of confusion about the three different types of Wireless Ethernet available. Because of these factors, I recommend you follow this process in adding Wireless Ethernet capabilities to your computer(s):

1. Understand the differences between 802.11b, 802.11a, and 802.11g.
2. Determine which standard(s) you want to support.

3. Decide if you want an internal or removable solution.

4. Decide if you want to build a combo wired/wireless network or start from scratch with a wireless network.

5. Select the product(s) you need.

6. Install, configure, and enjoy!

The ABG Alphabet Soup of Wireless Ethernet Standards

The popular name for IEEE 802.11b Wireless Ethernet is Wi-Fi, a trademark of the Wi-Fi Alliance. Wi-Fi is short for "Wireless Fidelity," and the goal of the Wi-Fi Alliance is to make sure that different brands of 802.11-compatible hardware can connect and work with each other.

Unfortunately, although the first wireless network hardware to be tested for Wi-Fi certification was compatible with IEEE 802.11b, 802.11b was not the only wireless network with Wi-Fi-Certified hardware. IEEE 802.11a hardware, which uses a different frequency not directly compatible with 802.11b devices, can also bear the Wi-Fi-Certified mark.

Confused yet? It's going to get worse. A third flavor of IEEE 802.11 wireless networking, IEEE 802.11g, is expected to be supported by the Wi-Fi Alliance by mid-2003. Thus, by the time you read this chapter, it's likely that three different wireless Ethernet standards will fall under the roomy tent called Wi-Fi-Certified. Fortunately, 802.11g uses the same frequency as 802.11b, and can connect with 802.11b hardware.

Table 18.1 helps you sort out the differences in the standards.

It should also be noted that while the popular notion is that Wi-Fi equals Wireless Ethernet, it takes time for new products to be Wi-Fi Certified, and it's likely that some products might never achieve certification.

ON THE WEB: TechTV Helps End Wi-Fi Confusion

Be sure to search the TechTV web site (www.techtv.com) for information on Wi-Fi wireless networking. I recommend the following links to get started:

- "Digesting Wi-Fi Alphabet Soup" at www.techtv.com/freshgear/products/story/0,23008,3420324,00.html.

- "The ABGs of 802.11" at http://techtv.com/screensavers/answerstips/story/0,24330,2314275,00.html.

- TechTV also recommends the Wi-Fi networking links available at http://nocat.net/.

Table 18.1	IEEE 802.11-Based Wireless Networks				
IEEE Standard	**Maximum Speed**	**Wi-Fi Alliance Term**	**Number of Non-Overlapping Channels**	**Also Known As**	**Notes**
802.11a	54Mbps	5GHz band	12	Wireless-A, 5GHz	Dual-band hardware needed to connect with IEEE 802.11b networks; tri-band hardware needed to connect with IEEE 802.11b and 802.11g networks.
802.11b	11Mbps	2.4GHz band	3	Wireless-B, 2.4GHz	Dual-band hardware needed to connect with IEEE 802.11a hardware; standard 802.11b can connect with 802.11g hardware.
802.11g	54Mbps	(Not yet approved)	3	Wireless-G, High-speed 2.4GHz	Dual-band hardware needed to connect with IEEE 802.11a hardware; can connect with IEEE 802.11b hardware.

Products that have been approved as Wi-Fi Certified can bear marks similar to those shown in Figure 18.1.

What are the advantages of each type of network?

- 802.11b is the oldest and most widespread standard. As I mentioned earlier, 802.11b *is* Wi-Fi as far as the public is concerned. Consequently, public access points provided by hotels, airports, coffee shops, and the like support 802.11b standards.

- 802.11a, on the other hand, is used in many corporate wireless networks by businesses who appreciate the faster maximum speed and greater number of channels (more channels helps to reduce interference). 802.11a has a shorter maximum range than 802.11b, but can provide speeds that are five times as fast as 802.11b at a given distance.

- 802.11g is a classic compromise that provides the speed of 802.11a along with interoperability with 802.11b. Note that early 802.11g hardware might require firmware updates for complete compatibility with 802.11b hardware and Wi-Fi Certification after the final 802.11g standard is approved.

Figure 18.1

Wi-Fi-Certified marks for IEEE 802.11b, 802.11a, and dual-band (802.11b/a) hardware.

IEEE 802.11b

IEEE 802.11a

IEEE 802.11b/a

Choosing a Standard While Hedging Your Bets

All things considered, it would be very handy for everyone if there were a single Wireless Ethernet networking standard. There isn't, but you can hedge your bets by buying equipment that works no matter where you go.

To get the right stuff, ask yourself these questions:

- **Do you take a computer to a job or school location with a wireless network? Does the employer or school plan to install one in the near future? What standard(s) does it support?**—I suggest these questions first because you want to choose a standard for your home that also works with the environment you're in when you're away from home.

- **Do you travel frequently to large cities or through airports?**—Large cities, especially business-oriented hotels and airports as well as some cafes and coffee shops, have the highest concentration of wireless access points (WAPs) you can use (either free or for a daily or hourly fee). For these WAPs, you need 802.11b compatibility.

After you find out what the office or school is using and decide whether wireless access on the road is important, you can decide if an 802.11b-, 802.11a-, or 802.11g-based network is what you need at home. Table 18.2 provides some examples of how this information helps you make your decision.

Table 18.2 Example Decision Trees for 802.11 Wireless Networking

Work Network	School Network	Travel (Access Points)	Your Network Adapter Should Support
802.11a	802.11b	802.11b	Dual-mode (802.11b/a)
802.11b	802.11g	802.11b	802.11g (backwards-compatible with 802.11b)
802.11a	802.11g	802.11b	Tri-mode (802.11b/a/g)

MARK'S TIP SHEET: Wi-Fi Here, There, Everywhere? Tracking Down Hot Spots

If you're considering adding a Wi-Fi adapter to your computer for access to email and the Internet while traveling, here's how to find locations that offer access:

- The Wi-Fi ZONE web site has a location provider. See it at `www.wi-fizone.com`.

- John Dvorak (former host of TechTV's old *SiliconSpin* program) recommends `www.wifimaps.com`.

- YourWireless.net (`www.yourwireless.net`) has a directory of business-oriented Wi-Fi access points.

- Boingo offers fee-based access at over 1,200 sites; find them at `www.boingo.com`.

- EarthLink's Wireless High Speed Wi-Fi Service search page is located at `http://earthlink.boingo.com/search.html`.

- Airpath Wireless offers U.S. and international lookups at `http://isps.net/Directory/Default.aspx`.

To find more, use Google or other major search engines with the query text "hot spot," "Wi-Fi," and your city or state.

PCI, PC Card, or USB? Choosing the Right Adapter

After you decide which wireless standard(s) to support, you should consider what form factor to use for your wireless adapter (if you don't have one already built into your computer). There are three possibilities, as shown in Table 18.3 and illustrated in Figures 18.2 and 18.3.

Table 18.3   Wireless Adapter Form Factors

Network Adapter Form Factor	Compatible with Computer Type	Notes
PCI Card	Desktop computer	Some adapters are two-piece units that also feature a removable PC Card for use in a notebook computer; these are no longer in production.
PC Card (CardBus)	Notebook computer with CardBus slot	Easy to carry, but models without a retractable antenna must be ejected before the computer is stored in a carrying case.
USB adapter	Desktop or notebook computer with USB 1.1 or 2.0 port	Some models are bulky to carry, but can be switched between computers. Some models feature an adjustable antenna for better reception. Keychain-sized models are easy to carry, but might have limited range.

Figure 18.2 shows CardBus and PCI adapters along with a WAP; Figure 18.3 shows the extremes of USB-based wireless adapters.

Figure 18.2

PCI and CardBus wireless Ethernet network adapters and a WAP with integrated router. Photos courtesy of D-Link.

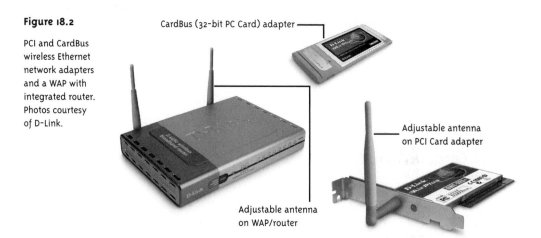

CardBus (32-bit PC Card) adapter

Adjustable antenna on PCI Card adapter

Adjustable antenna on WAP/router

ON THE WEB: TechTV Likes Wi-Fi; Let Us Tell You Why

Search the TechTV web site for "Wi-Fi" to track down reviews and tips on all types of Wi-Fi hardware—from access points to adapters.

Adjustable antenna on cable-connected USB adapter

Keychain-sized USB adapter; remove the cap to install the adapter into a USB port

Figure 18.3

Two types of USB wireless Ethernet adapters. The larger model has an adjustable antenna, but the smaller model can be stowed in a pocket or notebook case compartment. Photos courtesy of Linksys.

Pure Wireless or Combo Network?

After you choose the type(s) of network adapters you need, you need to determine how your computers will connect with each other at home. At offices, schools, and business travel locations, devices called WAPs are used to connect your wireless network adapter to the existing network. At home, you have more choices.

If you've never had a network before, you can create a pure wireless network by installing a WAP to transfer data between computers in *infrastructure mode*.

JARGON

Ad-hoc mode—Direct one-to-one connection between two wireless Ethernet clients.

Infrastructure mode—Wireless Ethernet clients connect through a WAP (similar to the switch or hub used in wired Ethernet).

However, a WAP without any additional features can't connect you to the Internet. You need a WAP with a built-in router or gateway (different vendors use different terms). As you learned in Chapter 17, "Share the Wealth with a Home Network," a router is a device that connects a local area network to another network, such as the Internet. Figure 18.4 shows how a pure wireless network can be used for Internet sharing.

Figure 18.4

A four-station pure wireless network with a shared Internet connection.

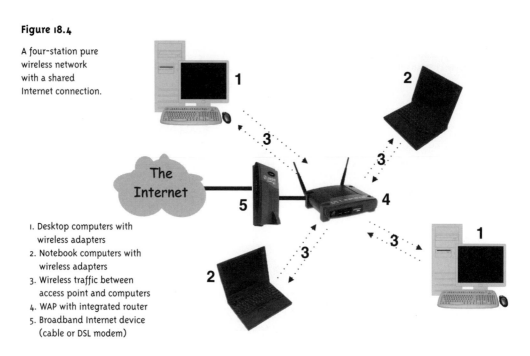

1. Desktop computers with wireless adapters
2. Notebook computers with wireless adapters
3. Wireless traffic between access point and computers
4. WAP with integrated router
5. Broadband Internet device (cable or DSL modem)

What if you already have a wired network? If it's a 10/100 Ethernet network, you can buy a single device that combines a WAP, a router, and a multiport switch to connect both networks to your broadband Internet device. You can also connect a WAP to your current wired network. If you have a HomePNA (phoneline) or HomePlug (powerline) network, you can use an Ethernet bridge to connect to a WAP/router/switch device. Figure 18.5 shows how a WAP with integrated router and switch can connect both wired Ethernet and wireless Ethernet networks to the Internet.

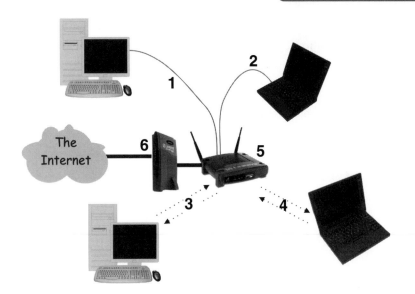

Figure 18.5

A combo wired and wireless Ethernet network with a shared Internet connection.

1. 10/100 Ethernet connection from a desktop computer
2. 10/100 Ethernet connection from a notebook computer
3. Computers with wireless Ethernet adapters
4. Wireless traffic to access point
5. WAP with integrated router and 10/100 Ethernet switch
6. Broadband Internet device (cable or DSL modem)

MARK'S TIP SHEET: Try Interacting with the Vendors

Some vendors of network hardware provide diagrams of how a particular device fits into a network. Review these diagrams carefully to plan your network before you buy and build it.

I also recommend that you download and read the manuals for the products you're considering. Some use wizards to help in setup and configuration, while others make you do a lot of the work. Ease of setup can help you decide which products to buy.

Accessories to Consider

It probably won't surprise you to learn that maximum range figures for wireless networks are wildly optimistic. If your home is a frame house, you should be able to use a single WAP/router device to handle all the computers. However, if your home has concrete or brick walls, or you want to use the computer out on the rear deck when the WAP's in the front office, you might need an additional access point. The additional one doesn't need any additional features because it will only relay traffic to the unit with the router and Internet connection.

As an alternative to a second access point, or possibly in addition to a second access point, you might need a signal booster or replacement antenna. If you suspect that range or building construction could be an issue, look for WAPs that can accept replacement antennas. Some access point vendors sell replacement antennas or signal boosters, or you can use third-party products.

ON THE WEB: Boosting Your Wi-Fi Range with TechTV

Check out Patrick Norton's article, "Extend Your Wi-Fi Range," at
`www.techtv.com/screensavers/answerstips/story/0,24330,3306273,00.html`.

Patrick recommends NetNimble for wireless antennas. Their new web site is
`www.netnimble.net`.

Buying Your Wireless Ethernet Hardware

Before you go to the store or shop online, complete a checklist similar to the one in Table 18.4.

Table 18.4   Wireless Network Shopping List Example

Product	Quantity Needed	Type	Preferred Brand and Model	Notes
CardBus network adapter	2	802.11g/a	XYZ G/A dual-band CardBus	One for each notebook computer for use at office and home
PCI network adapter	1	802.11g	XYZ G PCI desktop adapter	For use in a desktop PC
WAP/router	1	802.11g	XYZ G WAP/router	If model with switch is about the same price, get the one with a switch
WAP	1	802.11g	XYZ G WAP	Not needed unless you have problems with adequate coverage or speed with a single unit

The example shown in Table 18.4 lists 802.11g. I believe this will eventually be the best wireless Ethernet standard because it is as fast as 802.11a but can interconnect natively with 802.11b hardware. However, you should make sure that the 802.11g hardware you buy is Wi-Fi Certified or can be brought up to the final 802.11g standard with a firmware update.

Installing and Configuring Your Wireless Ethernet Network

You should install and configure the WAP for your wireless network before you install wireless network adapters. If the WAP is not available when the network adapters are installed, they will default to the *ad-hoc mode* instead of the infrastructure mode needed for Internet sharing.

If you are installing a WAP with an integrated router and switch in place of a router with an integrated switch, run the configuration utility on the currently installed router and write down the settings used for your current network. These same settings are needed for the WAP's router.

After you have recorded this information, unplug and disconnect the router/switch from the cable or DSL modem and connect the WAP/router/switch in its place.

Depending on the WAP, you might be able to connect a computer through a 10/100 Ethernet port to the WAP to run the WAP's configuration program or you might need to wait until you have a wireless network adapter connected to one of your computers.

MARK'S TIP SHEET: Why Sticking with One Brand Is Still Best

Although one of the virtues of Wi-Fi Certified hardware is the ability to mix and match brands, you could have problems setting up your wireless network if you need to use a wireless connection to configure your WAP. WAPs and adapters from the same vendor have matching default settings to make configuration relatively simple.

If you want to mix and match brands, make sure the WAP has a 10/100 Ethernet port so that you can plug in a computer and configure the WAP.

During WAP configuration, make sure you record the settings listed in Table 18.5. The same settings must be used on each wireless adapter, or you won't have a working network. The sample data is from a hypothetical network.

Table 18.5   Wireless Ethernet Configuration Settings Worksheet

Setting	SSID Name	Channel	WEP*	WEP Encryption Strength	WEP Key
Example	Myhome	3	Enabled	64-bit	12iu34nh59
Record your data here					
What the setting does	Names the network.	Specifies a channel for all stations to use.	If WEP is disabled, anybody can get on the network if they know the SSID; Windows XP can detect SSIDs.	Use the highest setting supported by both WAP and adapters for best security.	Use ten alphanumeric characters for 64-bit encryption; use 26 characters for 128-bit encryption.

*If all the hardware on the wireless network supports WPA, then WPA should also be enabled. See the devices' manuals for details. A firmware or driver update might be necessary for WPA support.

JARGON

SSID—Service Set Identifier, the unique name for your wireless network. By using different SSIDs, wireless networks near each other are kept separate. If you want to connect to a public WAP, you need to know its SSID.

WEP—Wireless Equivalent Privacy, the standard security feature built into Wi-Fi networking. WEP isn't air-tight, though, so the industry is moving to Wi-Fi Protected Access (WPA) as a replacement.

WPA—Wi-Fi Protected Access. A new security method for Wi-Fi networks based on the forthcoming IEEE 802.11i security specification. Instead of using a static key as WEP does, the key changes with each data packet sent. If some devices on a network support WPA but others do not, WEP is used instead. Firmware or driver updates are required for existing hardware to use WPA security, but new products might already include WPA security. By late 2003, WPA is expected to replace WEP in Wi-Fi-Certified products.

The physical installation of a wireless network adapter is very much like any other adapter installation. For a USB or CardBus adapter, the basic process works like this:

1. Read the instructions to find out when to install the drivers; sometimes you install the drivers *before* you plug in the card or adapter.

2. Install the drivers, if recommended, or go to Step 3.

3. Plug in the USB adapter or CardBus card and the system will prompt you for drivers, unless you already installed them.

If you are installing a PCI card into a desktop computer, the basic process works like this:

1. Read the instructions to find out when to install the drivers; sometimes you install the drivers *before* you shut down the computer and install the card.

2. Install the drivers, if recommended, or go to Step 3.

3. Shut down the computer and unplug it.

4. Take the ESD precautions outlined in Chapter 5, "Preparing for Your Upgrade," and remove the side panel or slide off the entire case.

5. Locate an unused PCI slot and remove the slot cover from the rear of the case.

6. Insert the card into the PCI slot and fasten it in place with the screw used to secure the slot cover.

7. Attach the antenna to the rear of the card.

8. Plug the computer into a power source and restart it.

9. Install the drivers when prompted (unless you installed them earlier).

After the network adapters are connected, they need to be configured. During configuration, use the same values you recorded in Table 18.5 so that your WAP and adapters can connect with each other. In addition, be sure to set the adapter for infrastructure mode.

After you complete the configuration process for the WAP and adapters, enjoy your network.

Protecting Yourself While Using Wi-Fi

Wi-Fi is designed to liberate networked computers from the tyranny of fixed locations; anywhere you can receive a compatible signal, you can connect to the network. However, if you don't take precautions, *anybody* with compatible hardware can also connect to your network and the valuable data contained there. It might not be the Great American Novel, but if you shop online, use home accounting software, or access password-protected sites, an unauthorized user on your wireless network could find a vast collection of data such as credit card numbers, bank account numbers, passwords, and more just waiting to be stolen and abused.

Don't think it can't happen to your network. "War driving," which involves intruders driving around with Wi-Fi-enabled notebook computers looking for unsecured networks, is a popular pastime. It's easy to find unsecured networks because almost all Wi-Fi adapters are configured to seek out and display the SSID values for networks they detect. All a war driver has to do is select the SSID to use, and they're on your network—*if* it isn't secure.

ON THE WEB: War Driving Exposed by TechTV

Learn more about war driving by searching the TechTV site (`http://cgi.techtv.com/search`) for articles on war driving: Enter "war driving" (include the quotes) into the search engine to find articles and links. Find more by doing a separate search for "wardriving."

War driving is so widespread that the *Doonesbury* cartoon featured it in its July 21, 2002 strip, in which ne'er-do-well Zeke Brenner thanks a suburban Wi-Fi user for free Internet access and tells him to keep an eye on his daughter's email. In the real world, don't expect anybody to thank you for free access if you don't secure your wireless network. Freeloaders might just borrow your Internet connection, but if they can find your data, some might grab it and run.

ON THE WEB: Unsecured Wi-Fi the Doonesbury Way

Follow this link to go directly to the *Doonesbury* war-driving cartoon:

`http://www.doonesbury.com/strip/dailydose/index.cfm?uc_full_date=20020721&uc_comic=db&uc_daction=X`

Note that although there's a search engine on the *Doonesbury* web site (`www.doonesbury.com`), you can also search the web for "Doonesbury" and "Wi-Fi" to find links to the cartoon.

A real-life Zeke might leave chalk markings behind on the curb to indicate to future freeloaders where "free" (unsecured) Wi-Fi access can be found. Learn more about the art and ethics of war chalking at `www.warchalking.org`.

Unfortunately, almost all Wi-Fi hardware uses a default setting that disables WEP security. Microsoft's line of Wi-Fi hardware was the first to enable WEP by default for greater protection. However, enabling WEP is just the first step in keeping your wireless network secure.

WEP is vulnerable to hacking for two reasons:

- **WEP uses a fixed-length encryption key that stays the same until the user changes it.** I recommend you change your WEP key periodically, especially if you discover your property's been war chalked to indicate how to access your network.
- **The length of the key, as Table 18.5 indicates, is tied to the security level of the hardware on your wireless network.** Many types of Wi-Fi hardware use 64-bit encryption (which uses a 10-digit key), but I recommend using hardware that supports 128-bit encryption because it uses a 26-digit key. A longer key is harder to break.

Wi-Fi Protected Access (WPA) will replace WEP in the official Wi-Fi standard by the end of 2003, but many vendors will have driver and firmware updates available before WPA is officially part of the Wi-Fi standard. I recommend that you install these updates for all the hardware (adapters and WAPs) on your wireless network and configure WPA to improve the security of your network. Keep in mind that if even one device on your network doesn't support WPA, you need to use WEP instead.

I also recommend that you make sure your router, whether it is built into your WAP or is a separate device, contains a firewall to block unauthorized intruders from accessing your network from the Internet.

A router that uses a feature called network address translation (NAT) provides some level of firewall protection, because the router doesn't disclose the actual IP address of the computers to the rest of the Internet. However, you get better security if the router also supports a feature called "stateful packet inspection," which remembers what types of requests were sent and allows only responses to those requests to be received by the network. The highest level of security combines a hardware firewall with stateful packet inspection with a firewall program, such as Zone Alarm Pro, and an up-to-date antivirus program.

Firewall programs (also known as personal firewalls) such as Zone Alarm Pro (www.zonelabs.com) can prevent any unauthorized programs from sending requests to the Internet. Modern antivirus programs such as Norton Antivirus (www.symantec.com) stop viruses, Trojan horses, and other types of nefarious programs received through email, infected disks, and other sources from taking over your computer and damaging its data or sending out data to remote intruders.

Even if you have a wired network, you should secure it with a router with a firewall, firewall software, and antivirus software.

Adding Bluetooth Capability

Although it's taken Bluetooth longer than wireless Ethernet to come to the market, a wide variety of Bluetooth hardware is now available. Although Bluetooth isn't afflicted with the fragmentation of semi-compatible standards (which is an issue that plagues wireless Ethernet), you still need to be careful to select Bluetooth hardware that works with the devices you want to use.

I recommend you follow this procedure to help ensure success:

1. Determine which devices you want to connect with Bluetooth.

2. Determine if the devices already have built-in Bluetooth hardware.

3. Verify that the devices you want to work together *can* work together.

4. Select the adapters.

5. Install, configure, and enjoy!

ON THE WEB: Bluetooth the TechTV Way

Check out tests, opinions, and reviews of Bluetooth products at TechTV's web site. In particular, read "Bluetooth Products With Bite" at `www.techtv.com/freshgear/ products/story/0,23008,3407392,00.html`.

Choosing the Devices You Want to Connect with Bluetooth

Bluetooth adapters are built for PCs, keyboards, mice, printers, Palm OS, and Pocket PC hand-held computers, and other devices. Before you start buying Bluetooth adapters, think carefully about how you want to use Bluetooth.

Bluetooth is designed to enable devices in a short range (up to 30 feet) to exchange data with each other. This data could be information passing to and from a PDA, to a printing device, and so on. If devices are already connected in a suitable way, you don't need Bluetooth.

Bluetooth makes sense if you want to establish communications between devices that aren't connected already. For example, if you'd like to print directly from your PDA, a Bluetooth card in a PDA and a Bluetooth adapter on the printer make it possible. Bluetooth also makes sense if you're trying to get away from cable connections for devices.

Bluetooth adapters for PCs are usually plugged into the USB port of a desktop computer or the CardBus slot of a notebook computer. Windows XP is the best operating system plat-form for trying Bluetooth because you get native Bluetooth support in Service Pack 1.

Discovering Built-In Bluetooth

Although PCs almost always need a Bluetooth adapter to connect to Bluetooth devices, an increasing number of devices (such as PDAs, printers, and smart phones) have built-in Bluetooth support. Check the instruction manual for your device or check the Bluetooth web site to see if your device is already Bluetooth-enabled.

ON THE WEB: Bluetooth, Officially Here

The official web site for Bluetooth products is www.bluetooth.com. The product lookup page is located at www.bluetooth.com/tech/products.asp. This lookup page also lists adapters for retrofitting existing products with Bluetooth, as well as products that include Bluetooth support.

Verifying Interoperability

Bluetooth is designed to work with both computers and electronic devices, some of which aren't all that intelligent. For that reason, Bluetooth's vision of all Bluetooth-enabled devices working together isn't yet a reality.

How can you increase the likelihood that PCs and other Bluetooth devices will work and play nicely together? Try these tips:

- Carefully read the FAQs and tech support notes at the adapter vendor web site *before* buying.

- If you already have Bluetooth-enabled devices, recheck the FAQs and tech support notes at the vendor web sites.

- Check third-party review sources, such as the TechTV web site (of course!; go to www.techtv.com), ZDNet (www.zdnet.com), *PC Magazine* (also available online at www.pcmag.com), Extreme Tech (www.extremetech.com), epinions.com (www.epinions.com), and Amazon.com (www.amazon.com) for product interoperability information and tips.

- Realize that some so-called "Bluetooth" implementations leave a lot to be desired. For example, Microsoft's Wireless Optical Desktop for Bluetooth has been criticized for requiring use of the proprietary transceiver packaged with the kit. This transceiver supports only a few of the dozen-plus Bluetooth connection types.

- Look for adapters that support Bluetooth as a server as well as a client. A Bluetooth server can share services with others, while a Bluetooth client cannot.

Buying the Adapters You Need

If you are connecting to existing Bluetooth-enabled devices, all you need to buy is a Bluetooth adapter for your computer. Because the Bluetooth standard continues to be improved (it's now at version 1.1), be sure you choose an adapter from a reliable company that offers good technical support and firmware upgrades when necessary. Many of the same companies that make wireless Ethernet devices also make Bluetooth adapters.

If you need to retrofit existing devices with Bluetooth adapters, make sure you verify device compatibility before you buy.

Installing and Configuring Your Bluetooth Network

After you connect the Bluetooth adapter to your computer and install the drivers, you need to enable Bluetooth support on other devices before you can continue.

The process of connecting your Bluetooth-enabled PC to other Bluetooth devices involves the following steps:

1. Discovering other Bluetooth devices with the Bluetooth software provided with your adapter.

2. Selecting a service provided by the device, such as file transfer, dial-up networking, information exchange, printing, information synchronizing, and so on.

3. Connecting to the service.

Typically, Bluetooth adapters for PCs use a Windows Explorer-type interface for discovering and listing Bluetooth devices and services provided by each device. See your adapter's instruction manual for details.

Protecting Yourself While Using Bluetooth

Bluetooth is designed to be an ad-hoc network, making and breaking connections as needed. If you don't want unauthorized people connecting with your Bluetooth-enabled computer, you can use the following methods to limit access:

- Turn off Bluetooth access to your computer and enable it only when you need to connect to other Bluetooth devices.

- Specify which devices in your office can use Bluetooth to connect with your computer.

- Enable security settings such as encryption and authentication. Note that some Bluetooth devices might not support all settings.

See your adapter's instruction manual for details.

Troubleshooting Your Wireless Connection

Wireless connections cut the cable, but don't necessarily cut the complexity of networking. Use the following tips to help keep your wireless connections working smoothly.

Help! I've bought a different brand of Wi-Fi adapter for my new PC, and I can't get it to connect to my existing network!

There are a lot of potential pitfalls you might have stumbled into. Here are the most likely possibilities:

- You bought the wrong type of Wi-Fi adapter. Keep in mind that Wi-Fi is really a blanket term for 802.11b, 802.11a, and 802.11g wireless networks. For example, if you bought an 802.11a adapter for an 802.11b or 802.11g network, it won't work.
- The default settings for the SSID, WEP, WPA, and channel might be different than for the rest of your network. Make sure the new adapter is set to use the same settings as the rest of the network.

Help! I already have a HomePlug powerline network, but the plug-ins in some of the rooms are away from where I'd like to work. Can I use Wi-Fi to get myself connected?

Yes, you can. The SpeedStream line of HomePlug network products from Siemens (www.speedstream.com) has a Wi-Fi access point that connects to the SpeedStream HomePlug network. No more cables across the floor!

Help! I have several Bluetooth devices, but my new Bluetooth adapter can't see any of them.

It's likely that Bluetooth is disabled by default on your existing devices. Read the instructions for each device to determine how to enable Bluetooth.

If the devices already have Bluetooth enabled, they might be configured to be non-discoverable to prevent access. The solution is to enable discovery on the device.

Part VI

Input This! Output That!

Chapter 19

Adding the Ports You Need for the Devices You Want

I don't care how much you spend on a new motherboard, new monitor, new printer, new anything—sooner or later, you'll want to add stuff to your computer. What kinds of stuff? Just look at the table of contents of this book. Whether it's a printer, a scanner, a digital camera, a webcam, a network adapter, a broadband Internet connection, a DVD burner, or a flash memory device—every one of these computer-refreshing upgrades needs to plug into some kind of a port. "No ports" means no digital goodness pouring into your system.

In this chapter, you discover what ports work with what devices and how to add more ports to your computer.

Ten Reasons to Add Faster Ports

Are you wondering if you need to add faster ports, such as a Universal Serial Bus (USB) 2.0 or a IEEE-1394, to your system? You can use this handy checklist to help you decide:

1. You're falling asleep waiting to burn a CD with your external CD-RW drive.
2. You just bought a digital video (DV) camcorder and you don't have any way to connect it to your computer.

3. You have so many USB peripherals that you think they're multiplying when your back is turned.

4. You're tired of crawling under the desk to unplug your scanner so that you can plug in your digital camera.

5. You're tired of crawling under the desk to unplug your digital camera so that you can plug in your scanner.

6. You don't want to open up your computer to add a bigger hard disk.

7. You don't want to open up your computer to add a rewriteable DVD drive.

8. You have a notebook computer you can't open up.

9. Every drive bay in your computer is full, and you're still short of space.

10. You have just one expansion slot left, and you want to make the most of it.

Did you recognize yourself or your system in this list? Read on to discover the solutions to your expansion woes.

Standard Port Types and Uses

Want to buy a new gizmo for your computer? It won't do much good to go shopping for one if you don't know how it will attach to your system. In this section, you learn about the ports found on typical systems and which devices work best on which ports.

Figure 19.1 shows the major built-in port types as they appear on the rear of a typical computer.

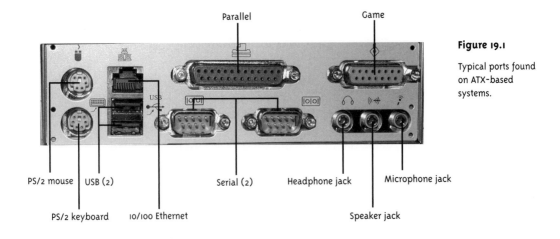

Parallel   Game

Figure 19.1

Typical ports found on ATX-based systems.

PS/2 mouse   USB (2)   Serial (2)   Headphone jack   Microphone jack

PS/2 keyboard   10/100 Ethernet   Speaker jack

The serial, parallel, PS/2 mouse, and PS/2 keyboard ports shown in Figure 19.1 are often referred to as legacy ports. Legacy ports received that name because they were used long before Windows became standard, are controlled by the BIOS chip on the motherboard instead of driver software, and work with any operating system, not just recent versions of Windows. These ports are being replaced by USB ports (also shown in Figure 19.1) and IEEE-1394 (FireWire) ports; in fact, some recent systems are known as "legacy-free" because they lack some or all of these legacy ports. Are legacy ports still useful? Find out in the following sections.

> **ON THE WEB: Port Tips Courtesy of TechTV**
>
> Search for your favorite port type at TechTV's web site (www.techtv.com), and you'll find reviews, tips, and tutorials on how to get more out of any port covered in this chapter.

Serial—Flexible But Slow

The serial port is also called the RS-232 port or COM port for the communications standard it upholds or the communications devices (such as modems) that connect to it. Some computers even feature a front-mounted serial port they call a digital camera port. Whatever you call it, there are two facts about the serial port that you can't ignore:

- It's very slow.
- It's basically obsolete.

The serial port was found on the very first IBM PC models built in 1981 (albeit as an add-on card), which means it's older that some of the people reading this book! Early versions had 25 pins in a DB-25 male connector, but the standard found on every recent system is nine pins, as shown in Figure 19.1.

Serial Port Uses—Past and Present

Over the years, the serial port has been used for a wide variety of add-on devices:

- **Printer interfacing**—Mainly used for label printers today; largely replaced by parallel or USB interfacing.
- **Direct PC-to-PC data transfer with programs such as LapLink**—Largely replaced by parallel, USB, infrared data transfer, or home networks.

- **Modem interfacing**—Being replaced by internal modems or USB external modems.

- **Digital camera data transfer**—Primarily on low-end digital cameras; USB or card readers used on better models.

- **Mouse and pointing device interface**—Replaced by PS/2 ports and now USB on most new mice and pointing devices.

- **Docking stations for Personal Digital Assistants (PDAs), such as those in the Palm or Handspring series**—Although some PDAs still use serial ports, most now use USB ports.

- **Shutdown notification for battery backup units**—Although some battery backup units still use serial ports, most now use USB ports.

It's an impressively long list, but in many cases, you'd need to be a PC old-timer to remember the last time you saw a serial port used for the particular task listed. The USB port has largely replaced the serial port for many tasks, meaning that even one or two serial ports in your system are more than enough.

Parallel Ports

The parallel port, also called the printer port or Line Printer (LPT) port, had few jobs in the early days of the PC revolution; most printers at the time used the slow serial port. However, as inexpensive dot-matrix printers fitted with user-friendly parallel ports flourished, so too did the fortunes of the parallel port.

What Parallel Ports Are Good For

After the bi-directional parallel ports hit the market in the late 1980s, the parallel port began to perform printer duties and the following:

- Direct PC-to-PC data transfer with programs such as LapLink or Direct Cable Connection

- Scanner interfacing

- Tape backup and removable-media drive interfacing

Although all these uses have remained popular until recently, the now-common USB port performs the same tasks with the newest printers, scanners, tape backups, and removable-media drives.

PS/2 Mouse and Keyboard Ports: Their Names Say It All

The PS/2 mouse port is for mice and similar pointing devices, while the PS/2 keyboard port is for keyboards. Period. End of discussion.

To learn more about using these ports or alternatives such as USB ports for input devices, check out Chapter 20, "Selecting the Best Input Devices."

Is It Time to Retire Legacy Ports and Devices?

Both the serial and parallel ports are referred to as legacy devices because these ports pre-date Microsoft Windows by many years. Just because USB (see the next section of this chapter) offers faster transfer rates than serial or parallel port modes, daisy-chaining, or hot-swap features, does it still make sense to buy or use serial or parallel devices?

Probably not anymore. Chances are you're using Windows 98 or newer versions of Windows. Any version of Windows from Windows 98 to Windows XP has excellent support for USB ports and devices. USB can do anything serial and parallel ports can do, and it does it faster and easier.

However, if you are thinking about using Linux (or perhaps already have a penguin-based system on your desktop), you might want to stick with parallel and serial devices. Linux distros based on Linux kernel 2.4.0 and above have built-in USB support. However, like most Linux device-driver support situations, the hardware manufacturers often don't provide the drivers for particular devices and aren't responsible for what happens with third-party open-source drivers written by members of the Linux community. My advice is to keep your options open: Buy printers and other devices that have both parallel and USB ports.

JARGON

Daisy-chaining—Connecting multiple peripherals to only one port, either by means of direct connection between devices or through a hub. Daisy-chaining is a technology used by SCSI, USB, and IEEE-1394 devices.

Hot-swapping—Removing and connecting a device without turning off the computer. Hot-swapped devices are recognized as soon as they're connected and can be used immediately.

Distro—Linux-speak for a specific customized variation of Linux, such as RedHat, Mandrake, and so forth.

If you find that you're dealing with a legacy-free system (a system without serial or parallel ports), but need to use serial and parallel devices, see the next tip for help.

MARK'S TIP SHEET: Using Legacy Devices in a Legacy-Free World

Worried about being stuck with legacy devices? You can still use parallel or serial devices in a USB world by installing the following devices:

- **If you have an empty PCI expansion slot, you can install a multi-I/O serial-parallel card**—This is cheaper than adapting a USB port to use these devices. However, if you are out of slots, or have a notebook computer, use the following options instead.

- **USB hubs with legacy ports**—These dual-purpose devices enable you to connect serial, parallel, or PS/2 devices through your legacy-free system's USB port. They can be useful for extending the useful life of legacy devices, but you need to make sure that the port supports the legacy device you have in mind. Legacy/USB hubs are far more expensive than USB-only hubs, so make sure you need the legacy-port support before you buy the hub.

- **Legacy-to-USB adapter cables**—Special cables enable you to attach your legacy device to a normal USB port or hub. Although these cables are expensive, the combined price of a special cable for a single legacy device and a standard USB hub is cheaper than the USB plus legacy device hub listed earlier. However, if you want to use different types of legacy devices, or more than one legacy device at a time, the USB hub plus legacy port solution makes more sense.

Keep these options in mind as more and more legacy-free systems (such as IBM's NetVista S40 series and legacy-free motherboards from various vendors) show up on desktops near you.

USB—Fast, Friendly, and (Almost) Free

One of the great benefits of recent Windows versions (Windows 98 and above) is their support for USB ports and devices.

The original version of the USB provides a top speed of 12Mbps. USB 2.0, which is a welcome case of a sequel being better than the original, runs at up to 480Mbps (!) and also works with all USB 1.1 devices.

USB ports of either speed have the following characteristics:

- The USB root hub, the term for the USB connection on the motherboard or add-on card, can handle up to 127 devices by means of daisy-chaining. A root hub supports two ports, so a computer with four USB ports has two root hubs.

- USB devices are designed to be hot-swappable, meaning that new devices can be recognized when attached to the USB port or USB hub while the power is on. The new devices can also be initialized immediately without having to reboot; similarly, USB devices can be moved from system to system without restarting the systems. Note that the original version of Windows 98 doesn't support hot-swapping, but Windows 98 Second Edition and newer versions of Windows do.

Most systems built since 1998 have working USB ports, although you might need to enable USB support in the system BIOS.

What the USB Port Does Well

Almost any type of external device can be attached to a USB port. The devices include the following:

- Scanners★
- Web cameras
- Flash memory card readers
- Flash memory keychain-sized storage devices
- Printers★
- Removable-media drives such as LS-120, Zip, CD-RW, and DVD★
- External hard drives★
- Game controllers
- Home networking and broadband connections
- Keyboards
- Pointing devices
- Analog modems
- Broadband Internet devices such as cable or DSL modems

★*Some devices in this category support the faster speeds of USB 2.0; check the device manual for details.*

MARK'S TIP SHEET: Why You Need USB 2.0 Ports Now

If you need to add USB ports to an older system and plan to use a lot of USB devices, skip USB 1.1 and go directly to a USB 2.0 card. This should be done regardless of whether you have any plans to get USB 2.0 devices. Here's why:

- USB 2.0 makes external hard drives and rewriteable CD and DVD drives practical. If you plug these drives into a USB 1.1 port, be prepared to take a lengthy nap during data transfers.

- USB 2.0 handles concurrent transactions (a fancy way of saying that more than one USB device can be transmitting at the same time) much better than does USB 1.1.

- USB 2.0 is ready for the latest USB devices and current USB 1.1 devices work better when attached to a USB 2.0 card! What's not to like?

If you don't have a USB 2.0 port, read the "Adding USB 2.0 Ports" section later in this chapter to learn how to join the USB 2.0 family. Because of the daisy-chaining inherent in USB, you can plug many devices into the same USB port with good results by using an external USB hub. See the "Adding Hubs and Converters" section later in this chapter for details.

If you bought your computer from mid-2002 to the present, you might have USB 2.0 ports already. The problem is that USB 2.0 ports look just like USB 1.1 ports. How can you tell which is which? By checking the following:

- Open the Windows Device Manager, and click the plus (+) sign next to the Universal Serial Bus Controllers category to expand it. Look for "Enhanced Host Controller" or "USB 2.0 Root Hub." If you see "Universal Host Controller" instead, the system has USB 1.1 ports.

- Check the specifications for your system. If your system has USB 2.0 ports, but Windows Device Manager identifies them as USB 1.1 devices, you need to do the following:

  - Enable USB 2.0 support in the system BIOS (see Chapter 4, "Taking an Inspection Tour of Your System," for typical BIOS screens).

  - Install USB 2.0 drivers for your motherboard or system.

Other Common Ports

Although USB ports can do almost anything, they're not alone on recent systems. Many recent computers contain these ports (they are also shown in Figure 19.1):

- **10/100 Ethernet**—Connects your computer to home or office networks and to broadband Internet devices such as cable modems. To learn more, see Chapter 16, "Get Yourself Broadband—It's (Always) Going Fast!," and Chapter 17, "Share the Wealth with a Home Network."

- **Game port**—Connects your computer to older game controllers. Most game controllers now use USB ports. To learn more, see Chapter 20.

- **Audio ports**—Connects your computer to speakers, headphones, and microphones (requires onboard audio). To learn more, see Chapter 14, "PC Audio and More."

High-Speed Ports You Can Add—And Why

In addition to USB 2.0, there are two other versatile high-speed ports that are candidates for adding to your system:

- SCSI
- IEEE-1394 (FireWire)

Read on to discover if you need the particular advantages of these ports.

SCSI

Small Computer System Interface (SCSI) is the longtime champion of versatility, working with drives, scanners, and other types of devices. However, it's rapidly losing its crown to IEEE-1394 and USB 2.0. Here's why:

- SCSI devices can use 25-pin connectors, two different types of 50-pin connectors, and 68-pin connectors. You need to know what connector type both ends of the connection use when you buy a SCSI cable. Otherwise, you might wind up with a box of expensive but useless SCSI cables, like me!

- A single SCSI host adapter card can handle up to seven or fifteen devices, depending on whether it supports a so-called "narrow" or "wide" version of SCSI. This seems like a lot compared to parallel or serial ports, but pales in comparison to USB or IEEE-1394.

- SCSI port and device speeds vary from as little as 10Mbps to as high as 320Mbps. However, SCSI scanners and CD-RW drives require only 20Mbps SCSI cards.

- External SCSI devices are connected to each other to form a daisy-chain, and the devices on each end of the SCSI daisy-chain must be terminated.

- Each device on a SCSI daisy-chain needs its own unique ID number.

Let's face it—installing even one SCSI device is like creating a small peripheral network on your desk. Adding two or more devices increases the odds of something going wrong.

JARGON

Daisy-chaining—Connecting multiple devices to a single port. SCSI devices have two ports. One is for the cable running from the SCSI host adapter to the device, and one is for running from the device to the next device in the daisy chain.

Device ID—A unique number that identifies each SCSI device attached to a host adapter. Internal SCSI drives use jumper blocks to set the device ID; external devices use a dial or switch to select the device ID.

Termination—SCSI daisy chains must have a terminator at each end of the daisy chain for proper signaling to take place. Internal SCSI drives use jumper blocks to enable or disable termination. Low-speed external devices use a selector switch, but drives and faster devices use an active (powered) terminator, which resembles the connector on a SCSI cable. The terminator is attached to one of the SCSI connectors, and the other SCSI connector is used to connect the peripheral to the host adapter or other SCSI peripheral.

Do you already have a SCSI port? It's doubtful unless you have added a hardware upgrade that included a SCSI card. Some older scanners made by companies such as Canon and HP often included a low-end SCSI card, but such cards were often designed specifically for scanners; if you want to add other SCSI devices, you need a better card. Although a few server-type motherboards have built-in SCSI ports, desktop computers seldom have built-in SCSI ports.

Should You Add SCSI to Your System?

Although adding a SCSI card made sense a few years ago, there's hardly any need to do it today. Although I have a SCSI removable-media drive and two SCSI scanners (and, of course, a SCSI card to connect them to my system), I bought these peripherals several years ago. Comparable devices today have USB 1.1, USB 2.0, or IEEE-1394 (FireWire) ports, which offer easier installation, comparable speeds, and greater versatility than most common forms of SCSI.

Remember that the only reason to add any type of add-on card to your system is to allow you to connect the devices you need. Because most SCSI drives and peripherals today are oriented to the server market rather than to the desktop market, most of us don't need the hassle that SCSI presents.

ON THE WEB: SCSI the TechTV Way

If you need to learn more about SCSI, search for SCSI on the TechTV web site (www.techtv.com) to discover a treasure trove of tips and reviews. For a quick tutorial on SCSI, look for the article "The SCSI Bible."

If you decide that you must install a SCSI interface, keep these facts in mind:

- There are many different SCSI standards and most cards support only a subset of the standards. If you buy a slow-speed card and later decide to add a SCSI device that supports a faster SCSI standard, it's off to the store with you to buy another SCSI host adapter.

- Some SCSI cards support only external devices, while others support both internal and external devices. If you're not sure what your future purchases will be, opt for a card that supports both types of devices.

- Adaptec, the leading vendor of SCSI cards, no longer sells cards in speeds under 160MBps. Their 19160 card is about $250, although scanners and removable-media drives work with 20Mbps cards. Third-party vendors such as SIIG (www.siig.com) offer 20Mbps and 40Mbps cards for well under $100.

- If you don't want to install a SCSI card to support a single SCSI device, consider using a SCSI-to-USB port adapter, such as Adaptec's USB2Xchange (see Figure 19.2). Similar devices are available for connecting a SCSI device to an IEEE-1394 (FireWire) port.

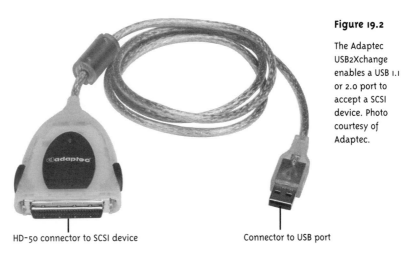

HD-50 connector to SCSI device

Connector to USB port

Figure 19.2

The Adaptec USB2Xchange enables a USB 1.1 or 2.0 port to accept a SCSI device. Photo courtesy of Adaptec.

CAUTION: STOP! LOOK! THINK!

Avoid SCSI Stupidity—Watch Out for Bundled-Card Bungles

The many different flavors of SCSI can be confusing. However, what's even worse is to fail to realize that using the wrong SCSI card leads to endless frustration. For example, trying to use the cheapjack SCSI cards supplied with scanners with SCSI hard drives usually leads to terrible throughput (at best), an inability to boot from the drive, and fiddling with expensive cable adapters to fit 68-pin and 50-pin devices and cables together. Remember this rule of thumb: OEM-provided SCSI host adapter cards are just barely good enough for the device with which they're supplied.

Not sure what your bundled card is fit for besides hosting the device with which it came? Look up the model on the manufacturer's web site—or at least look up the speed and see the jobs for which that type of card is best suited. It sure beats losing data!

IEEE-1394

IEEE-1394, better known to many folks under its Apple name of FireWire (and also called i.Link by Sony), competes with USB 2.0 for the title of newest, fastest, and potentially most flexible port developed for PCs.

In many ways IEEE-1394 resembles a mixture of the best features of USB and the older SCSI port:

- **Like USB, IEEE-1394 supports hot-swapping for easy installation and hubs for multiple-device support from a single port**—Each IEEE-1394 host adapter can support up to 16 devices per port, and typical host adapters feature up to three ports or more.

- **Like SCSI and USB 2.0, IEEE-1394 supports high data transfer rates**—Rates vary from 100Mbps up to 400Mbps with the current IEEE-1394a standard. (400Mbps is equivalent to 50MBps, which is 20 percent faster than Ultra 2 SCSI's peak rate of 40MBps.) The first IEEE-1394b devices were introduced in early 2003 and supported 800Mbps speeds (100MBps!). In the future, IEEE-1394b will reach speeds up to 3,200Mbps.

- **Like SCSI, IEEE-1394 requires less CPU attention than USB or IDE/ATA devices**—In fact, an IEEE-1394 port can connect directly with DV camcorders (which have very little in the way of computer brainpower) for data transfer. IEEE-1394 connections, in fact, need no computer at all, enabling direct device-to-device connections.

- **Like SCSI, IEEE-1394 also supports daisy-chaining of multiple devices without using an external hub**—Hubs are recommended when you want to use hot-swappable IEEE-1394 devices.

Unlike USB (but like SCSI), PCs featuring on-board IEEE-1394 ports are few and far between, although a small but growing number of new desktop and notebook PCs feature built-in IEEE-1394 ports. If your system lacks the port and you want to use IEEE-1394 devices, you need to add a card to your system. IEEE-1394, like USB, requires Windows 98 or newer versions of Windows.

MARK'S TIP SHEET: FireWire, i.Link, IEEE-1394? What's the Difference?

At one time, the term "FireWire" was reserved for Apple-compatible devices that had paid a license fee to Apple. However, the term "FireWire" is now essentially inter-changeable with IEEE-1394. IEEE-1394a and FireWire 400 refer to 400Mbps ports and devices. FireWire 800 is another name for IEEE-1394b ports and devices. i.Link is a Sony-specific term that refers to the 4-pin IEEE-1394a port (other vendors use the six-pin port). Various adapter cables enable you to use 1394a/FireWire 400 devices with FireWire 800/1394b ports and to connect four-wire devices to a six-wire 1394a/FireWire 400 port.

Why Add IEEE-1394?

Originally developed to make transfers of data from DV camcorders easier, IEEE-1394 also supports the following devices:

- High-performance flatbed scanners
- High-performance printers for graphics arts applications
- External hard disk, CD-RW, rewriteable DVD, and tape storage
- Networking
- Direct PC-to-PC connections
- Audio equipment
- Entertainment systems
- Set-top boxes for digital TV and video recording
- Digital video players
- High-performance web cameras

IEEE-1394 devices are not as common as USB devices, but many vendors are now rolling out external drives with connections for both ports. Windows 98 and above support IEEE-1394 ports and devices, but relatively few motherboards include 1394 ports at present. Consequently, it's increasingly likely that you will need to add a 1394 card to your computer at some point.

If you're wondering if you already have a 1394 port built into your computer (or already installed), look at Figure 19.3, which shows the typical appearance and locations of 1394 ports.

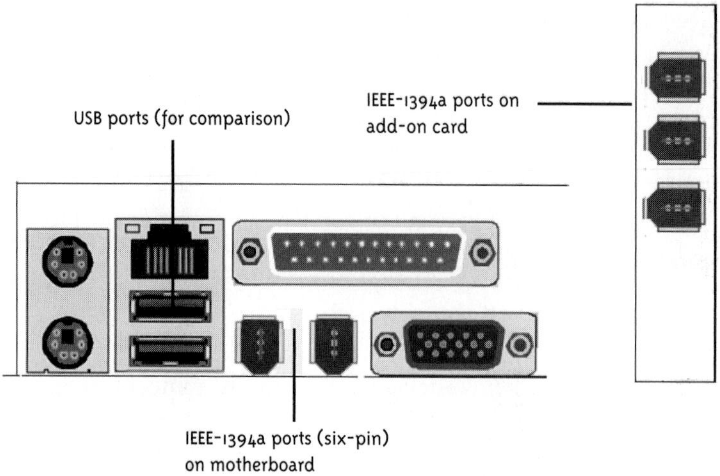

Figure 19.3

IEEE-1394a ports can be built into the motherboard (left) or into an add-on card (right).

USB ports (for comparison)

IEEE-1394a ports on add-on card

IEEE-1394a ports (six-pin) on motherboard

CAUTION: STOP! LOOK! THINK!

Don't Get Burned by FireWire

Before you rush out and buy an IEEE-1394 device, be sure to check the operating system compatibility for both the card and the device you want to use. For some reason, some IEEE-1394 devices work only with Windows 2000, Windows XP, and Windows Me, ignoring the device support that is also a feature of Windows 98. You're also likely to find some devices that ignore Windows completely for Apple's Mac OS, which is, after all, where the interface began its life.

Also, check the cabling type needed to connect to the device. The standard IEEE-1394 port is a six-wire connection, but DV camcorders and other self-powered devices use only four wires. Most IEEE-1394 host adapters come with a six-wire to four-wire adapter cable, and this is the time to use it.

Adding USB 2.0 Ports

Although almost every system on the market today has USB 1.1 ports, faster USB 2.0 ports are built into only a few of the latest systems. Fortunately, for about $30–35, you can add a multiport card to your desktop computer if you have an empty PCI slot (a multiport PC Card for a notebook computer will set you back about $60). You can also install a combo USB 2.0/IEEE-1394a (FireWire) card. See the "Adding IEEE-1394a Ports" section later in this chapter for more information.

READ THIS TOO

Not sure what a PCI slot looks like? Read Chapter 9, "Unlock Your System's Potential with Motherboard and BIOS Upgrades."

Figure 19.4 illustrates a typical USB 2.0 card for desktop computers.

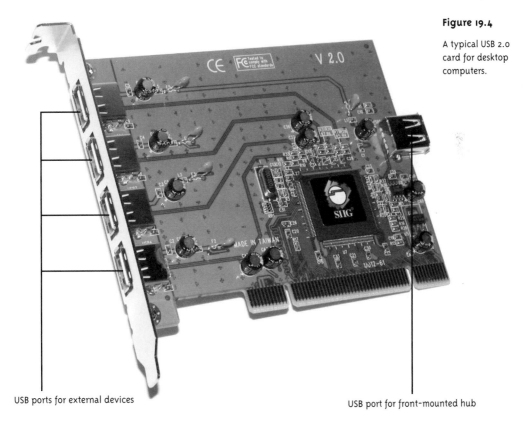

Figure 19.4

A typical USB 2.0 card for desktop computers.

USB ports for external devices

USB port for front-mounted hub

Note the front-mounted USB 2.0 connection in Figure 19.4. Later in this chapter, I show you how to connect a front-mounted USB 2.0 hub to this port to make attaching and removing USB 2.0 devices easy. Some USB 2.0 cards don't have this port, making it more difficult to use a front-mounted hub.

READ THIS TOO

See "Adding Hubs and Converters" later in this chapter for more information.

Installing the USB 2.0 Card in a Desktop Computer

Follow this procedure to install your card. The process is about the same with any recent version of Windows (98 or higher).

1. Shut down your system.

2. Disconnect the power cable from the outlet to cut all power to the system.

3. Use ESD protection equipment, such as a wrist strap and work mat, if available. (See Chapter 5, "Preparing for Your Upgrade," for details.)

4. Open your computer and locate an unused PCI slot.

5. Remove the slot cover; save the screw for use in reattaching the new card.

6. Insert the card into the slot.

7. Secure the card into place with the screw removed from the slot cover.

8. Reconnect the power cord and restart the computer.

9. Install drivers when prompted.

10. Restart your computer, if prompted.

11. Use your new ports!

Adding IEEE-1394a Ports

You can add IEEE-1394 ports to your computer by installing the following:

- A combo add-on card that has IEEE-1394 and USB 2.0 ports (refer to Figure 19.5).

- A SoundBlaster Audigy or Audigy 2 card (the SB1394 port on these cards is IEEE-1394a compatible), as in Figure 19.6.

- An add-on card that has multiple IEEE-1394 ports (refer to Figure 19.7).

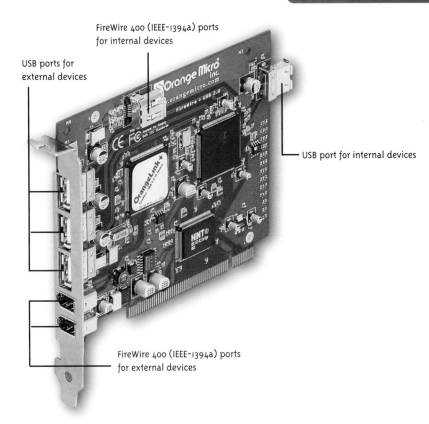

USB ports for
external devices

FireWire 400 (IEEE-1394a) ports
for internal devices

USB port for internal devices

FireWire 400 (IEEE-1394a) ports
for external devices

Figure 19.5

Orange Micro's
OrangeLink+ USB
2.0/FireWire combo
card for desktop
computers. Photo
courtesy of Orange
Micro, Inc.

The internal ports built into cards, such as in Figure 19.6, can be used to connect to front-mounted individual ports or to a multiport hub installed in a drive bay.

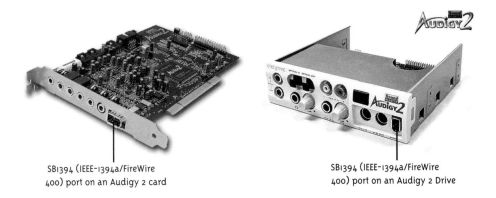

SB1394 (IEEE-1394a/FireWire
400) port on an Audigy 2 card

SB1394 (IEEE-1394a/FireWire
400) port on an Audigy 2 Drive

Figure 19.6

The Creative Labs Sound Blaster Audigy 2 features an IEEE-1394a-compatible port on the rear of the card (left). The Audigy 2 Platinum adds a front-mounted IEEE-1394a-compatible port as part of its Audigy 2 Drive breakout box (right). Photos courtesy of Creative Labs.

The Creative Labs Sound Blaster Audigy was the first sound card to incorporate an IEEE-1394a–compatible port (SB1394). The current Audigy 2 series continues this feature (see Figure 19.6). To learn more about audio upgrades, see Chapter 14.

With many different types of cards from which to choose, how can you make your best choice? You can make the best choice by using the decision grid in Table 19.1 to narrow down the possible choices.

Table 19.1 Choosing the Correct IEEE-1394 Card			
Available Types	**IEEE-1394 Only Card**	**Combo USB 2.0/ IEEE-1394 Card**	**Sound Card with IEEE-1394 Port**
You already have USB 2.0 ports.	Consider	N/A	Consider
You also need USB 2.0 ports.	N/A	Consider	N/A
You also need better audio features.	N/A	N/A	Consider

Installing an IEEE-1394a Card

The basic procedure for installing a card with IEEE-1394a ports is similar to the process used to install a USB 2.0 card. However, some cards also require you to connect a 4-wire power connector normally used for hard disk drives to the card to provide adequate power for the onboard ports (see Figure 19.7). You should perform this step after the card is physically installed, but before you reconnect the power and restart the computer.

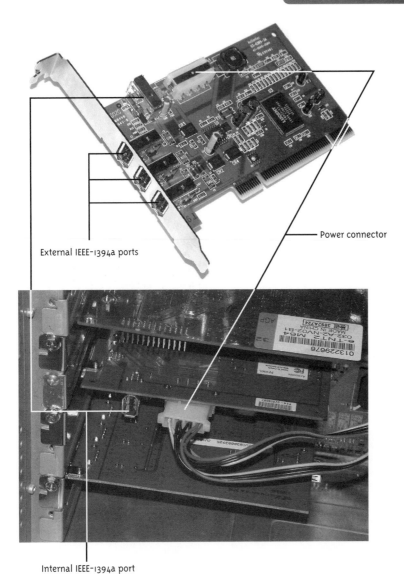

Figure 19.7

An Actiontec four-port IEEE-1394a card before installation (top) and after installation (bottom). Note the power connector.

Power connector

External IEEE-1394a ports

Internal IEEE-1394a port

Adding USB 2.0 and IEEE-1394 Ports to Your Notebook Computer

Most notebook computers have USB 1.1 ports built in, but don't have either a USB 2.0 port or a IEEE-1394 port installed. To add these ports to your notebook computer, you need to have an open Type II PC Card (PCMCIA) CardBus slot available. Most notebook computers have at least one Type II slot, and many have two stacked Type II slots; check your system documentation or vendor web site for details.

Because you might want to have a choice of USB 2.0 and IEEE-1394a ports for your notebook computer, I recommend a combo CardBus card such as the one shown in Figure 19.8. These cards are sold by SIIG, Orange Micro, and ADS Technologies, among others.

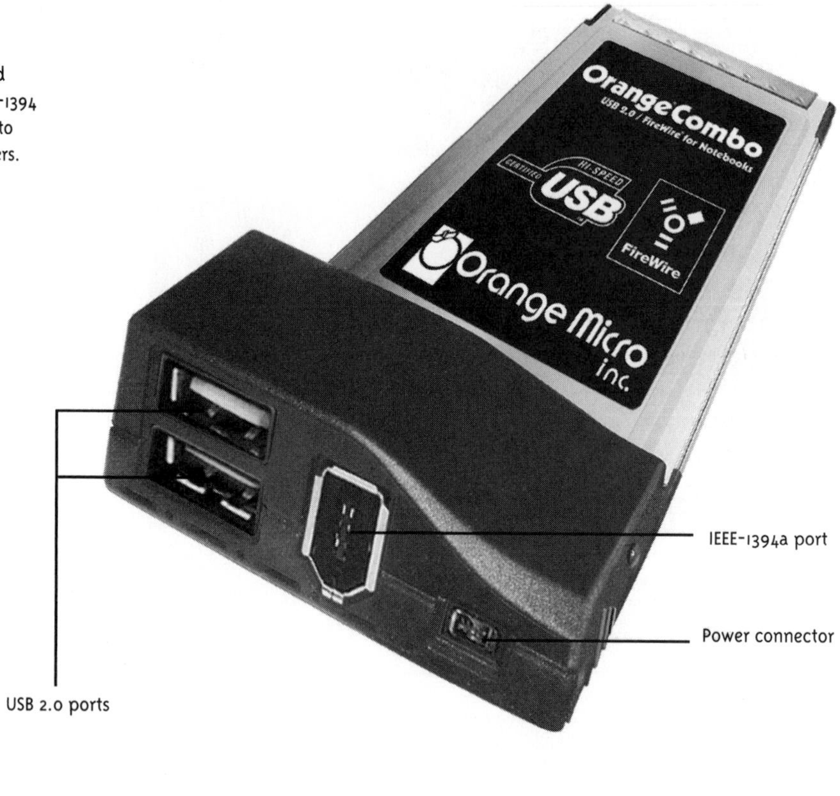

Figure 19.8

An Orange Micro OrangeCombo card provides both IEEE-1394 and USB 2.0 ports to notebook computers. Photo courtesy of Orange Micro.

IEEE-1394a port

Power connector

USB 2.0 ports

One important feature to keep in mind with any type of USB 2.0, IEEE-1394, or combo card for notebook computers is the need to plug the card into an AC outlet if you have bus-powered peripherals (peripherals that receive power through the USB or IEEE-1394 port).

> **ON THE WEB: A Shopping We Will Go (for Combo Cards)**
>
> Looking for combo USB 2.0/IEEE-1394a CardBus cards for your notebook computer? Check out these vendor sites:
>
> - SIIG (first to ship a combo card) at `www.siig.com`.
> - ADS Technologies at `www.adstech.com`.
> - Orange Micro at `www.orangemicro.com`.
>
> These vendors also carry combo cards for desktop computers.

To install one of these cards, simply slide it into the CardBus slot on your notebook computer and install the drivers when prompted. To remove the card, use the Eject or Safely Remove Hardware icon in the system tray (the icons next to the clock). When you reinsert the card, Windows recognizes it and installs the correct drivers automatically.

Specifying High-Speed Ports on Your Next Motherboard or Computer

If you're planning to install a new motherboard (see Chapter 9) or buy a brand-new computer, don't assume that your upgraded motherboard or new computer will already contain USB 2.0 or IEEE-1394 ports. While USB 2.0 ports have become more and more common since mid-2002, they are not yet a universal feature. IEEE-1394 ports are still relatively scarce as standard equipment.

It's cheaper (and saves slots) if the port type(s) you prefer are built into the motherboard instead of retrofitted to your computer at a later date. Follow the tips provided in "How to Read a Motherboard Ad" in Chapter 9 to help make sure you get the ports you want.

Adding Hubs and Converters

No matter how many shiny new USB 2.0 and IEEE-1394 ports you install, you won't have enough—or they won't be in the right place. Those of you who have already been doing the unplug-replug-unplug dance with your devices know full well what I mean.

The solution is simple for USB 2.0 users: Add a hub to your system. There are two types of hubs:

- **Self-powered hubs**—These use small AC adapters for power.
- **Bus-powered hubs**—No AC adapter needed here, folks; your computer's USB root hub (the USB port built into the computer) provides the power.

Avoiding the clutter of one more power cable might seem appealing, but don't fall for it. Self-powered hubs rule! They provide five times the power per port that a bus-powered hub does. Thus, power-sucking USB devices such as webcams (my Intel webcam requires the maximum 500mA of power used by any USB device) can work when attached to a self-powered hub, while they fail when attached to a bus-powered hub (these supply no more than 100mA per port). You can plug almost USB device into a self-powered hub; no more reading the fine print on the USB device for power usage information for you!

When you go shopping for a USB 2.0 hub, make sure that it's a USB 2.0 (Hi-Speed USB) hub; a USB 1.1 hub doesn't support the faster speeds provided by USB 2.0, and make sure you can attach it to a power source. Want to declutter your desk? Consider a hub you can slide into a drive bay. Figure 19.9 compares a typical USB external hub to a USB 2.0 internal hub from SIIG.

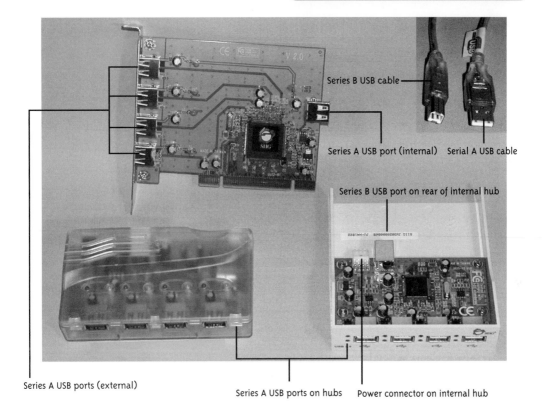

Series B USB cable

Series A USB port (internal)   Serial A USB cable

Series B USB port on rear of internal hub

Series A USB ports (external)

Series A USB ports on hubs   Power connector on internal hub

Figure 19.9

An external USB hub (left) connects to the USB external ports on a computer or USB card (center), while an internal USB hub (right) connects to the internal USB port.

Troubleshooting Your New Ports

Windows uses Plug and Play (PnP) to detect newly installed PCI cards in desktop computers. It uses a technology called Card and Socket Services to detect newly installed PC Card or CardBus cards in notebook computers. Most of the time, these installations go very well. However, occasionally, something goes wrong. Use this section to help debug any problems with your new USB 2.0 or IEEE-1394a ports; note that most of these methods can be used with other types of add-on cards as well.

If your new card is not detected, check the following:

- Make sure PnP is working correctly. See "Fixing Plug and Play Problems" later in this chapter for details.

- Make sure you attach a power lead to the card if required. As shown in Figure 19.7, some IEEE-1394 cards require power, as do some other types of cards. If the power lead is part of a Y-extender or splitter cable (divides one lead into two), make sure the extender is plugged into a power lead from the power supply.

If devices attached to the port are not detected, check the following:

- Bus-powered USB devices should be plugged into a root hub (port built into the computer) or a self-powered hub.

- Both USB and IEEE-1394 ports and devices need drivers. If the port isn't displayed by Device Manager (see Figure 19.10), the device using the port can't work either. Reinstall the drivers for the card and try again.

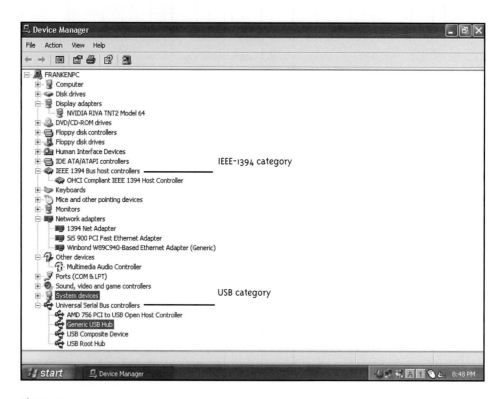

Figure 19.10

The Windows XP Device Manager on a system with IEEE-1394 and USB ports installed and working properly.

Fixing Plug and Play Problems

Normally, your new PCI card is recognized by the system and installed immediately. However, problems with IRQ sharing and assignments are the number-one reason PnP installations sometimes become nightmarish.

Try the following tips if you have problems getting your new card to be recognized by Windows:

- **Make sure that the Windows Device Manager shows only working devices—** Any unused listings or listings for removed, problem (yellow !), or disabled (red X) devices should be removed. To remove a device, select the device and click the Remove button.

- **Boot the computer in Safe Mode if you are using Windows 9x and make sure any listings for devices no longer on the system are removed—**Safe Mode enables you to see all previously installed devices, even if they are no longer present. If you see multiple listings for the same device, remove all but one of the listings. Listings for drives, video cards, or external devices that are no longer installed or attached should be removed with the Device Manager.

- **Make sure the chipset-specific device drivers are installed for your motherboard—**The Windows CD contains some of them, but others must be downloaded from the motherboard or chipset vendor.

- **Make sure IRQ steering is enabled in the Device Manager if you use Windows 9x/Me—**To check the status of IRQ steering, click System Devices, PCI Bus properties, and then the IRQ Steering tab. IRQ steering enables devices to share IRQs, a relatively scarce hardware resource (Windows XP performs this task automatically).

- **Make sure that the system BIOS is set to PnP Aware Operating System—Yes—**This enables Windows to set the IRQ and other hardware settings for each PnP card. This option, if present in your BIOS setup, is usually found in the Plug and Play menu. Activate your system's BIOS setup program at system startup to view or change BIOS settings.

- **Select level-triggered IRQs if the BIOS provides this option—**Level-triggered IRQs can be shared by PCI devices; some older systems don't enable sharing unless this option is set appropriately. This option is also found in the Plug and Play BIOS menu.

- **Use the BIOS option called Reset Configuration Data after you remove one or more cards from your system—**This forces the system to determine a new optimized hardware configuration when you restart the computer. This option is also found in the Plug and Play BIOS menu.

- **As a last resort, remove non-essential PCI cards (everything but video) from your system and install just the new card—**After it is recognized, install the other cards *one at a time*.

MARK'S TIP SHEET: Use This Driver—Now!

Sometimes PnP isn't perfect; it might install an old driver—or even the wrong driver—for your hardware. You can force the system to use the best driver by doing the following:

- Use the Add/Remove Hardware option when you install new hardware and select Have Disk instead of the default search for new hardware. Or, if the hardware is detected automatically when you restart the system, specify the location of the driver.

- Use the Update Driver button in the device's Properties sheet in the Device Manager. Again, set the search to look only in the location where the new driver is located.

- Download and uncompress the latest drivers for a device before you install the device; some add-on cards and devices sit around for quite awhile on store shelves and might not have updated software included. You may want to copy the drivers to a floppy disk for easier installation because Windows searches floppy disk drives for drivers by default.

Fixing Problems with PC Cards and CardBus Cards

Although PC Cards and CardBus cards are automatically detected by Windows, they *don't* use PnP installation. Instead, they use a feature called Card and Socket Services that is installed as part of Windows. If you plug in a PC Card or CardBus card, such as a USB or IEEE-1394 card, and your notebook computer doesn't recognize it, your computer's PC Card support might not be installed.

Open the Windows Device Manager (right-click My Computer, select Properties, Hardware, Device Manager) and check whether the PC Card (PCMCIA card) icon displayed. If you don't see it listed, your system can't recognize PC Cards. Check with your system vendor for instructions on how to enable PC Card support on your system; you might need to use the Add New Hardware wizard to detect your PC Card slot and set up the drivers.

After PC Card support is enabled, you should be able to install your card—provided your PC Card slot supports CardBus (for USB and IEEE-1394 and high-end SCSI cards).

Chapter 20

Selecting the Best Input Devices

Keyboards and pointing devices aren't the most glamorous computer upgrades around. Sure, it's fun to have a new joystick or game controller, but when you're working or surfing, don't overlook how much a better keyboard, mouse, or pointing device can do for your experience.

The perfect input device might not have been invented yet. But, if a better keyboard or mouse can make your hands more comfortable, help you avoid strain, and help you run your favorite programs more easily, that's close enough to perfect for most of us. In this chapter, I show you how to improve your computer experience through better input devices.

Ten Reasons to Upgrade Your Input Devices

There are a lot of people who put up with inadequate input devices through sheer inertia (the tendency of fingers resting on an input device to remain at rest). If that sounds a bit too much like you, check out the following list to see if you need to stop resting and start shopping for better ways to type, mouse, or play games:

- You just force-fed your keyboard a glass of Mountain Dew™.
- Your kid force-fed your keyboard a glass of Kool-Aid™—last week.
- You're tired of using Ben-Gay™ on your wrists after typing a few emails.

- You wonder where the "click-clack" went.
- You're tired of the keyboard keeping everyone awake at night because it's so noisy.
- Your keyboard is so worn out that you can't feel where the F and J keys are anymore.
- Your keyboard doesn't have a Windows key.
- Your mouse doesn't have a scroll wheel.
- You're still buying mouse-cleaning kits—and using them.
- Your keyboard has been named an official snack-food depository by an obscure government agency.
- Your new computer doesn't have a gameport, but that's the only place your old game controller fits.
- You're tired of lifting your hands off the keyboard to open your favorite programs.
- You're tired of losing death matches because your game controller is worn out.
- There's a key on your keeyboard that keeeeps sticking.
- You just installed a legacy-free motherboard and have just realized that there's no place to plug in your input devices.

Benefits of USB Input Devices

Although the PS/2 mouse and keyboard jacks weren't introduced until 1987, they reflect the "one jack, one job" design of most early PC interfaces. The PS/2 mouse port is for mice and pointing devices that emulate mice, such as touchpads and trackballs, and the PS/2 keyboard port is for keyboards. Similarly, the gameport found on many sound cards and on the rear of some systems with integrated audio is strictly for game controllers. Although so-called legacy-free systems are eliminating these separate jacks in favor of the more versatile Universal Serial Bus (USB) port, you shouldn't wait until your system no longer has these jacks to consider moving to USB.

USB input devices have the following advantages over PS/2 and gameport-based devices:

- **Hot-swap capability**—Unlike PS/2 devices, which require you to shut down the computer to connect or disconnect them, you can connect and disconnect USB input devices at any time with any recent version of Microsoft Windows (Windows 98 SE and above). Thus, if you share a computer with other users and each of you prefer different input devices, installing your favorite is as easy as unplugging one and plugging in the other.

- **Hub compatibility**—It's always been annoying to reach around to the rear of a system to reattach a loose input device. With USB input devices, you can plug them into a hub on the front of the computer (see Chapter 19, "Adding the Ports You Need for the Devices You Want") or on the desk.

- **Backwards compatibility with PS/2 ports**—Because there might be times when you'll need to use an input device (particularly keyboards and mice) with older systems, many (although not all) USB input devices also include PS/2 adapters (see Figure 20.1). When you shop for input devices, keep your options open by selecting hybrid devices that can plug into both port types.

All the input devices I use now are USB-based, and I love the convenience they provide. USB rules!

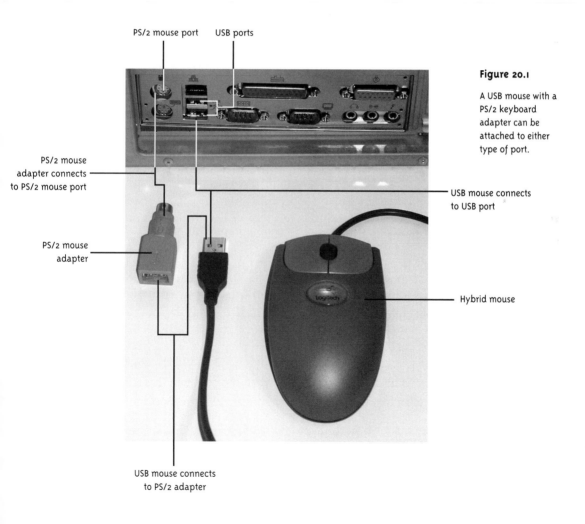

PS/2 mouse port   USB ports

PS/2 mouse
adapter connects
to PS/2 mouse port

PS/2 mouse
adapter

USB mouse connects
to PS/2 adapter

Figure 20.1

A USB mouse with a
PS/2 keyboard
adapter can be
attached to either
type of port.

USB mouse connects
to USB port

Hybrid mouse

Benefits of Wireless Input Devices

Do you like the convenience of instantly changing input devices by plugging or unplugging them? If so, you'll *love* skipping the wires altogether. Both leading and second-tier input device vendors now offer a wide variety of wireless mice, keyboards, mouse/keyboard bundles and game controllers. Although a few of these still use the older infrared (IR) technology, which requires a clear line of sight between input device and transceiver, most now use radio frequency (RF) connections.

What are the benefits of wireless input devices?

- **Greater user comfort**—You can put the keyboard in your lap and move your mouse without ever needing to flip the cables out of the way.

- **Better ergonomics**—The more comfortable your hands are, the less danger there is of repetitive strain injuries such as carpal tunnel syndrome.

- **Less cable clutter**—Although you still need to plug a transceiver into your computer, its cables can be routed out of the way. You don't need to worry anymore about snagging a keyboard cable on the picture of the kids or knocking over your can of Red Bull® with your mouse cable.

- **Greater distance between you and your screen**—If you're using one of those cool new Media Center PCs (the ones optimized for multimedia and DVD viewing), the normal two-foot distance between the monitor and your nose isn't far enough for optimum enjoyment of widescreen DVD entertainment. Conventional wireless input devices let you get as far as six feet away from your monitor or TV. Want to watch and control computer entertainment on a really big screen? Look for Bluetooth wireless keyboards and mice from companies such as Microsoft; Bluetooth has a range of up to 30 feet.

Figure 20.2 shows a typical wireless mouse and keyboard combo from Logitech and how the transceiver connects to the computer.

The transceiver shown in Figure 20.2 has two connectors, which is typical for a transceiver designed for wireless mice and keyboards. If the computer is a legacy-free computer, only the USB connector is necessary. However, in some cases when the computer has a PS/2 keyboard connector, it's necessary to attach the transceiver to the PS/2 keyboard port as well.

To discover why a system with USB ports might still need to use a PS/2 keyboard, read the next section of this chapter. It can save you a lot of headaches when you make the move to a USB keyboard—wired or wireless.

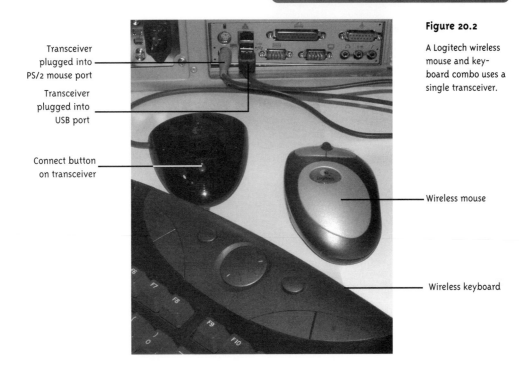

Transceiver plugged into PS/2 mouse port

Transceiver plugged into USB port

Connect button on transceiver

Wireless mouse

Wireless keyboard

Figure 20.2

A Logitech wireless mouse and keyboard combo uses a single transceiver.

Tweaking Your System BIOS to Enable a USB Keyboard

Although USB mice and keyboards plug into the USB port, they're treated much differently by the system BIOS chip on the motherboard. As you learned in Chapters 4 and 9, "Taking an Inspection Tour of Your System" and "Unlock Your System's Potential with Motherboard and BIOS Upgrades," the system BIOS controls built-in hardware, such as the ports on the motherboard. From the BIOS chip's standpoint, its primary task involving USB devices is to enable or disable the on-board USB ports.

After the system BIOS has enabled built-in USB ports, USB devices (printers, mice, and so forth) are controlled by device drivers loaded within Windows. USB devices don't work if you boot your computer to a command-line prompt to play an old game. Reason? The drivers haven't been loaded (they're not loaded until Windows starts). However, if you start your computer, let it boot into Windows, and then open up a command-prompt window and play an old game there, your mouse and other USB devices will work because their drivers were loaded by Windows first.

Here's how this relates to a USB keyboard. A USB keyboard isn't much use to you if it can work only after Windows starts. You couldn't activate the Windows troubleshooting menu or change settings in the system BIOS, because both activities happen before Windows is loaded. However, a USB keyboard can be used at all times if, *and only if,* the following are true:

- The USB keyboard is connected to a built-in USB port (not a USB port on an add-on card such as the one shown in Chapter 19).

- A BIOS setting called "USB Legacy Mode" or "USB DOS Mode" is enabled.

If you're wondering how you can enable this setting if you have a USB keyboard, congratulations! You've asked the prizewinning question—if your USB keyboard has a PS/2 adapter or if you're using a wireless keyboard with a transceiver configured as in Figure 20.2. To make the BIOS setting adjustment, connect the keyboard to the PS/2 port with the adapter.

If you have a USB-only keyboard, or if your PS/2 adapter is buried in a computer junk drawer someplace under the extra slot covers, drive rails, and an old floppy drive cable, you have a problem. You need to find that adapter (if you have one), or borrow a PS/2 keyboard from another computer. After you get a keyboard ready to connect to the PS/2 port, here's how to enable USB legacy support:

1. Shut down the computer and unplug it.

2. Attach the keyboard to the PS/2 keyboard port (it's the lower port on the rear of the system and is color-coded purple on many late-model computers).

3. Attach the power cable, turn on the computer, and press the key(s) to activate the BIOS setup program.

4. Move through the BIOS setup menu(s) until you locate the option for USB legacy support (see the top screen in Figure 20.3).

5. Set the USB Legacy option to Enable or Auto. If you cannot change its current setting and you don't have other USB devices, the USB ports might be disabled.

6. Locate the USB Function option and enable it (see the bottom screen in Figure 20.3), and then enable USB Legacy support.

7. Save changes to the system BIOS and shut down the computer.

8. Connect the keyboard to the USB port and restart the computer. You should now be able to access the system BIOS or activate the Windows startup menu. Install drivers if necessary for special keyboard functions.

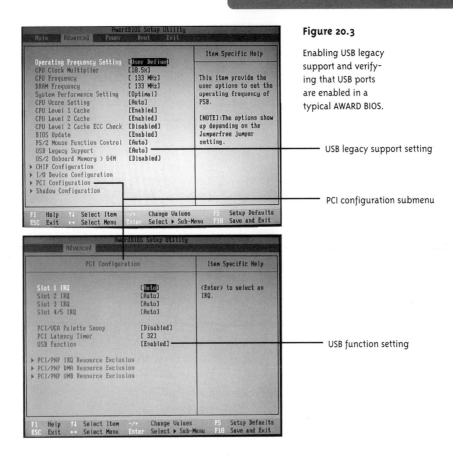

Figure 20.3

Enabling USB legacy support and verifying that USB ports are enabled in a typical AWARD BIOS.

— USB legacy support setting

— PCI configuration submenu

— USB function setting

Choosing the Correct Keyboard

If you want the same mediocre touch and feel and lack of spill-resistance that was the downfall of your old keyboard, any keyboard at your local computer emporium will do.

However, if you live and die by typing (like yours truly), and you want a built-in pointing device, ergonomic design, wireless capabilities, and other special features, raise your sights (and your budget) a bit.

Traditional flat keyboards are the least expensive, but some experts on ergonomics suggest that flat keyboards and rounded wrists aren't a very good combination. Split-key keyboards cost more, but many users swear by them after the initial period of adjustment. You can get split-key keyboards from many vendors, including Logitech, Microsoft, and many others.

If you prefer a wireless keyboard, these are available in both flat and split-key ergonomic models, but you will pay more for split-key wireless models. In most cases, you can buy a wireless keyboard and mouse bundle.

Many wireless keyboards and some wired keyboards now include dedicated keys that can launch email, web browsers, and media players. Because full use of these keys requires you to install software drivers, be sure that the keyboard's drivers support your version of Windows.

ON THE WEB: Looking for Keyboards in All the Right Places

Want more choices than you can find at your favorite walk-in store? Check out these online vendors:

- **Unicomp, Inc. (www.pckeyboard.com)**—Home of the IBM/Lexmark "buckling spring" capacitive-switch firm-touch keyboards, some of which also feature built-in IBM TrackPoint or trackball pointing devices.

- **KeyTronicEMS (www.keytronic.com)**—Developer of Ergo Technology keyboards, which offer five different levels of force across the keyboard, varying with the relative strength of each finger. Some models also feature a built-in trackball.

- **Ergonomic Resources (www.ergo-2000.com)**—Sells many different brands and models of ergonomic and click-type keyboards, including the Avant Prime and Avant Stellar (which revive the classic Northgate keyboard designs popular with many writers), as well as keyboards with integrated pointing devices and radical modular designs.

- **Cherry Corporation (www.cherrycorp.com)**—Manufactures specialized keyboards for card reader/fingerprint security systems as well as for standard home and office use. Cherry keyswitches are known for their durability.

- **Adesso (www.adessoinc.com)**—Manufactures keyboards with integrated Cirque Glidepoint touchpads as well as other input and I/O accessories.

Keep in mind that you can't try out the keyboard first if you order it online, so be sure to check the vendor's return policy. In some cases, you might pay only for return shipping and handling, but others might also charge a return or restock fee of $5 or more. To avoid disappointment, search the vendor's web site, epinions.com, or the web to find user reviews before you buy.

Choosing the Right Pointing Device

Pointing devices have undergone two amazing transformations in the last few years:

- Optical sensor technology
- Scroll wheels and buttons

If you're tired of losing mouse balls, opening the bottom of the mouse to clean the rollers, and looking for more responsive pointer action, an optical mouse is the way to go. An optical mouse replaces the normal ball and rollers used in traditional mechanical mice with an LED light source and a CMOS sensor that functions like a miniature camera, sensing motion and transferring the motion to the onscreen pointer without any moving parts. About the only way to confuse an optical mouse is to use a mirror or a repeating pattern as a mousing surface.

Although optical mice at one time commanded a premium price, they're now available at almost every price point from $20 on up. Almost all of Logitech's mouse line is now optical, as is most of Microsoft's line. Other major mouse vendors such as Kensington, Belkin, and IBM have also incorporated optical sensors into their mouse products.

Scroll wheels and buttons have been around longer, but if you're using an older mouse, you might not have these features yet. The ability to scroll through a long document or web page with just a flick of a wheel is a great labor and shoulder saver, and with many brands, you can also program the wheel to act as a programmable third mouse button. All optical mice also include a scroll wheel or button, and some deluxe mice also feature thumb buttons or additional finger buttons.

Figure 20.4 compares top and bottom views of a two-button mechanical mouse to a late-model optical mouse with a scroll wheel.

In addition to the basic issues such as sensor design and scroll buttons, you should also consider the following when you plan your mouse purchase:

- **Who will be using the mouse?**—If left-handers as well as right-handers will be using the mouse, consider ambidextrous designs similar to the optical mouse featured in Figure 20.4. However, if only right-handers will be using the mouse, the additional comfort of a right-hand mouse design and the additional buttons found on some models, such as the wireless mouse shown in Figure 20.2, might be worth the extra expense.

- **What size hands will be using the mouse?**—Typically, wireless mice are a bit larger than low-end mice. This is done to accommodate the extra electronics needed, and high-end wired mice with extra buttons are also a bit larger than low-end mice. For the greatest comfort, match the size of the mouse to the users' hands.

Figure 20.4

A typical mechanical mouse (left) compared to a typical optical mouse (right).

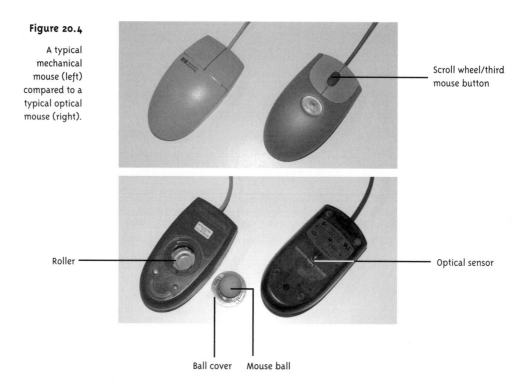

Scroll wheel/third mouse button

Roller

Optical sensor

Ball cover   Mouse ball

MARK'S TIP SHEET: In Search of Custom Mice

If you're a left-handed mouser, you don't need to settle for a mouse that's good for either hand. Contour Design (www.contourdesign.com) makes its PerfitMouse (also known as the Contour Mouse) in sizes from small to large for left-handed users as well as right-handed users (righties can also order extra-small and extra-large sizes). The PerfitMouse has three buttons and a built-in thumb rest.

- **Would an alternative pointing device be a better choice?**—Windows doesn't care if you're using a "real" mouse or another pointing device that emulates a mouse, but you might. If you're having chronic "mouse shoulder," you might want to look at alternatives such as trackballs, the 3M upright Ergonomic Mouse, the Cirque touch-pads, or integrated pointing devices built into keyboards.

ON THE WEB: Surf to a Mouse Alternative

Here are some of the vendors who make mouse alternatives:

Trackballs:

- Logitech (www.logitech.com)
- Microsoft (www.microsoft.com)
- Kensington (www.kensington.com)
- MicroSpeed (www.microspeed.com)

Touchpads:

- Cirque (www.cirque.com)
- Fellowes (www.fellowes.com)

Upright mouse:

- 3M (www.3m.com/ergonomics)

With the wide variety of mice and alternative pointing devices on the market, you should have little difficulty in choosing a good fit. However, before you plunk your money down, check the following:

- **Driver support**—Although a plain-vanilla mouse or pointing device emulates the Microsoft standard, you should install the mouse's own software to enable any additional features. Check the vendor's web site to verify support for your version of Windows, programmable features, and updates.

- **Warranty**—Although a warranty isn't as useful as it sounds (I can't wait for a repair, so I use my old device or buy a replacement while I'm waiting for a repair), it provides a useful gauge of the reliability of the product. Look for a one-year warranty as a minimum.

- **Durability**—Check out the display models at the store and see how well they're made. If the housing seems brittle or the construction quality is cheap, skip that model and look for another one.

- **Comfort**—The size, shape, button position, and force necessary to click the buttons all influence how comfortable a mouse will be.

Choosing the Right Game Controller

The versatile USB port is also the preferred port for game controllers on recent systems, replacing the venerable 15-pin gameport. This is a good thing, because if you're a serious gamer, you can really take advantage of the hot-plug capabilities of the USB port to change controllers as often as you boot up a new game. Wireless game controllers' radio receivers usually plug into a USB port as well.

The right game controller for you is the game controller that makes the most of your favorite game(s). Although you could play every game for the PC with a keyboard/mouse combo or a standard gamepad, you'll probably wind up losing the average death match or road race. Instead, add a front-mounted USB hub like the one shown in Chapter 19 and install your choice of controllers, like these:

- **Steering wheels**—Perfect for racing games.
- **Joystick**—Choose models with force feedback so that you can "feel" your aircraft in flight.
- **Gamepads**—Choose models with vibration feedback for more exciting action, whatever the sport.
- **Pedals**—Adds extra realism to racing, flight simulator, or flight combat games.
- **Diesel locomotive controller**—Play train simulators with a specialized controller.
- **Voice chat**—Coordinate your squad's attack or defense and conquer your online foes.
- **Wireless controllers**—These are perfect for relaxing with your favorite game on a big-screen TV or monitor.

If you look hard enough, you can find a specialized controller for almost any type of game you can play on a PC. Choose the USB connection, and you can interchange them freely.

ON THE WEB: Beyond Ordinary Game Controllers

Track down specialized controllers at these web sites:

- **Logitech (www.logitech.com)**—Wheels, joysticks, and gamepads.
- **Microsoft (www.microsoft.com)**—Wheels, joysticks, gamepads, and Game Voice chat.

- **CH Products** (www.chproducts.com)—Specialized flight controllers, such as sticks, pedals, and flight yokes.

- **Raildriver** (www.raildriver.com)—Train cab controllers for Microsoft Train Simulator, Auran Trainz, and model train layouts.

Installing Your New Input Devices

If you're opting for USB input devices, installing them couldn't be simpler, especially if you have already prepped your system BIOS for a USB keyboard. Follow this procedure for USB devices:

1. Some USB input devices require you to install the driver *first*. Follow the directions to do so before you connect the device.

2. Look for a USB port built into the computer for the USB keyboard; a USB port on a hub or add-on card will work fine for a USB mouse or pointing device.

3. Plug in the USB device(s).

4. Supply the driver when prompted unless you installed it earlier.

If you have decided to stick with PS/2 devices, follow this procedure instead:

1. Shut down your system and unplug it.

2. Crawl around on the floor under the table and locate the keyboard or mouse connector.

3. Carefully unplug the old keyboard or mouse.

4. Plug the new input device (and adapter if necessary) into the correct port.

5. Reconnect the system to AC power, restart it, and start using the new input device.

If you are installing a wireless USB input device, follow these steps:

1. Some USB wireless input devices require you to install the driver *first*. Follow the directions to do so before you connect the device.

2. Look for a USB port built into the computer for the receiver if you're installing a wireless keyboard with a USB receiver; a USB port on a hub or add-on card will work fine for a wireless mouse with a USB receiver. If your keyboard or keyboard/mouse receiver has a PS/2 connector, plug it into the PS/2 keyboard port to ensure that the wireless keyboard works even if USB Legacy mode is not enabled in the system BIOS.

3. Plug the receiver into the correct port(s).

4. Install the correct type of batteries into the input device. Most devices include batteries, but they might be of poor quality or have become stale, so have replacements available.

5. Supply the driver when prompted unless you installed it earlier.

6. If the receiver can't find the input device(s), follow instructions to synchronize the device(s) with an RF receiver or adjust the position of an IR receiver to establish a clear line-of-sight with the input devices.

If you are installing a wireless PS/2 input device, follow these steps:

1. Shut down your system and unplug it.

2. Crawl around on the floor under the table and locate the keyboard or mouse connector.

3. Carefully unplug the old keyboard or mouse.

4. Plug the receiver(s) for the new input device(s) into the correct port(s).

5. Install the correct type of batteries into the input device. Most devices include batteries, but they might be of poor quality or have become stale, so have replacements available.

6. Reconnect the system to AC power and restart it. Install any drivers requested by the system.

7. If the receiver can't find the input device(s), follow instructions to synchronize the device(s) with an RF receiver or adjust the position of an IR receiver to establish a clear line-of-sight with the input devices.

Useful Accessories

Regardless of the input device you choose, you might enjoy it even more with accessories like these:

- **Wrist rest**—Some keyboards include a built-in or removable wrist rest, but if your favorite doesn't, pick up a set for both mouse and keyboard. The gel-filled ones from various vendors are exceptionally comfortable.

- **3M Precise Mousing Surface**—Conventional mouse pads collect dirt that is redeposited on your mouse mechanism, and don't work well with optical mice. The Precise Mousing Surface series traps dirt and improves traction of conventional ball-type mice, and the Precise Optical Mousing Surface has a special light-reflective surface for better mousing—the optical way.

- **USB hub**—If you want to have more than one USB mouse or pointing device, add a powered hub to your system, as described in Chapter 19. A front-mounted or desktop hub also makes it simple to connect and disconnect mice and other USB devices as needed.

- **Y-mouse**—You can share a single USB or PS/2 mouse port or keyboard port between two devices with the unique Y-mouse series of adapters from P.I. Engineering (www.y-mouse.com). See Figure 20.5.

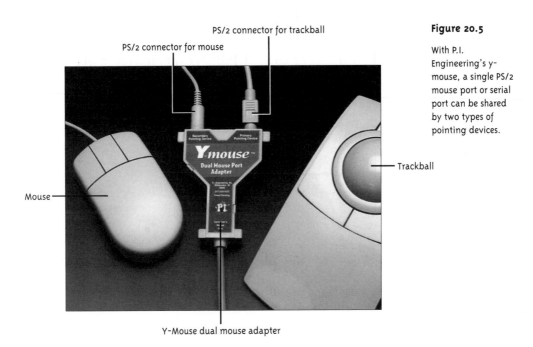

PS/2 connector for trackball

PS/2 connector for mouse

Mouse

Trackball

Y-Mouse dual mouse adapter

Figure 20.5

With P.I. Engineering's y-mouse, a single PS/2 mouse port or serial port can be shared by two types of pointing devices.

Troubleshooting Your New Devices

Use the following tips to help solve problems with your new input devices.

Help! I just bought a keyboard and mouse bundle to update my system, and now neither one works!

If you're using a PS/2-port wired keyboard and mouse, I bet you've mixed up the keyboard and mouse ports. Turn off the system, double-check your computer's instruction manual (the port label stickers on the back of the computer could be wrong or hard to read), and make sure each device is plugged into the correct port. Computers with ATX-type motherboards place the PS/2 mouse port above the keyboard port, but systems with proprietary mother-boards might arrange the ports differently. Color-coded mouse devices and keyboards can make life easier, but if you're using older products or have an older motherboard, the color-coding might not be present or could be wrong.

If you bought wireless devices instead, the receiver could be plugged into the wrong port, or there are a couple of additional possibilities:

- Infrared (IR) units need a clear line of sight between the receiver (which plugs into your computer) and the mouse or keyboard. Because coffee cups, sticky notes, and CD cases all tend to migrate in front of the usual receiver locations and block the signal, I prefer (and recommend) RF wireless devices.

- Radio-frequency (RF) devices sometimes need to be manually tuned to the same frequency, a process sometimes called *synchronization*. Press the Connect buttons on the transceiver, keyboard, and mouse to synchronize the devices. In addition, don't neglect the "wrong plug" problem I mentioned earlier. If you're using PS/2 keyboard/mouse port receivers, you can mix up wireless receiver plugs as easily as the cables that run all the way to the mouse or keyboard. Fortunately, USB-based receivers can use only a single connection to the computer if your system supports the USB Legacy option for the keyboard.

Help! I want to use my system's USB ports, but after enabling them in the BIOS, nothing's happening!

USB is terrific when it's already enabled, but getting it to work on systems where it's been taking an extended nap can be tough. Follow this procedure to solve problems with your USB ports:

1. Make sure you're using Windows 98 or newer; otherwise, the ports won't be recognized when you restart your computer.

2. See if the USB root hub is displayed in the Device Manager tab of the System Properties sheet (accessible from the Control Panel). If the listed hub has a red X (indicates the device is disabled) or yellow exclamation point (indicates the device has a conflict or driver problem) next to it, the root hub and the input devices plugged into it can't work until the root hub's problems are solved.

3. Click the USB root hub and select Properties to see what the difficulty is. If the device is disabled, select Enable Device on the General tab; when the device is enabled, the red X disappears.

4. If the device has a conflict or driver problem, use the Resources tab to see which device has a conflict. If there is no device conflict, download and install new motherboard driver software from the motherboard or system vendor's web site. In some cases, the motherboard driver software has its own installer, but in other cases you might need to use the Driver tab to install an updated driver. You should also run Windows Update to see if an updated USB driver is available.

5. If you are unable to resolve the conflict or install a new driver, find out if there's a BIOS upgrade or tech notes about your motherboard that can help you get the USB working.

6. If you cannot activate the USB ports on the motherboard, add a USB card instead of using the on-board ports, but note that an add-on USB card should not be used for keyboards. See Chapter 19 for details.

Help! The basic keys on my new multimedia keyboard work, but some of the special keys don't!

It's easy to forget that a multimedia keyboard needs special drivers if you want to use the additional keys. Install the drivers from the driver CD packaged with the keyboard, or download the latest drivers from the vendor's web site and install them. Then, follow the setup process for your keyboard and all those additional keys should be ready to save you time and effort. Figure 20.6 shows the Hot Keys setup menu for Logitech iTouch multimedia keyboards.

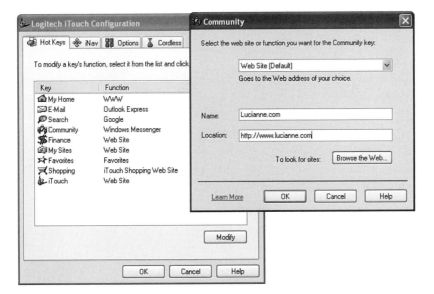

Figure 20.6

Modifying the default setting for the Community button on a Logitech iTouch multimedia keyboard.

Keep in mind that an input device won't work correctly if:

- The port used by the device is defective, disabled, or has a conflict.
- The port or the device itself doesn't have a working driver installed.

Chapter 21

Output Unlimited with Printer Upgrades

No matter how often people talk about the paperless office, or how advanced optical and network storage has become, you still need to make print-outs of your most important documents and photographs. A good printer can dazzle you with crisp, beautiful photo prints and sharp text, but a poor printer can undercut the quality of your work.

There's no need to settle for a poor-quality printer. Today's printers can print crisp, high-resolution black text at any size, make dazzling full-color photos, and even create specialized hard copies of your own business cards, labels, decals, T-shirt transfers, greeting cards, and much, much more.

It's still impossible to find a single printer that does every job equally well, but today's printers come closer than ever before. In this chapter, you learn how to choose and install the printer of your dreams.

Ten Reasons to Replace Your Printer

Years ago, printers were expensive, and a fair number of computers didn't have printers. Today, it's almost unheard of to have a computer without a printer next to it or accessible over a network. Nevertheless, just because you have a printer today doesn't mean you won't need (or want) a better printer tomorrow. Here are ten reasons to replace the printer you have with a better model:

1. No amount of cleaning or ink and toner replacement will produce a decent printout.
2. You're tired of waiting for output.
3. Your printer's idea of "high quality" isn't high enough.
4. The people at the office supply store laugh hysterically when you ask for ink or toner for your current printer.
5. The only place you can find ink or toner for your current printer is in the clearance bin.
6. Your vendor doesn't have Windows XP drivers for your printer.
7. Your printer lacks features you want, such as duplex printing, high-quality plain paper photo printing, and so on.
8. Your printer connects only to the parallel port, and your new system has only USB ports.
9. You're ready to ask for a second mortgage to pay for ink for your "low-cost" inkjet printer.
10. You're looking for better prints of your photos.

Alternatives to Replacing Your Printer

Although I've just given you ten reasons to replace your printer, you might prefer to try these upgrades and fixes first. They might stretch the life of your current printer a bit, or at least help you realize that you are absolutely, positively ready for a new printer.

CAUTION: STOP! LOOK! THINK!

Don't Fix It if It's Broken!
Remember the Great Depression? I don't, but my parents do. They learned to fix it up, use it up, wear it out, and make it do. It's still great advice for a computer user who likes to upgrade, rather than replace, a system. However, inkjet printers are a major exception to the rule. They're literally not worth fixing after the warranty period is over. Why? The labor costs will eat you for lunch, new models' print quality is higher and the cost is lower, and even in-warranty printers are usually discarded by the vendor and replaced rather than repaired. With inkjet printers, it's welcome to the world of disposable technology.

- **Install more memory in a laser printer**—Laser printers don't print the page until they receive all the data on the page. More memory minimizes the need to compress data to fit in the printer's memory, and it can also be used to hold part or all of an additional page to speed printing of multipage documents.

- **Install the latest drivers for your printer from the printer vendor's own web site**—Although your printer might work with the drivers Microsoft puts on the Windows CD, these drivers are typically bare-bones, lacking features found in the vendor's own enhanced drivers. How limited are the drivers on the Windows CD? Some don't even support the printer's maximum resolution! Go directly to the printer vendor's web site for the latest drivers.

- **In a pinch, try Windows 2000 drivers for your printer if Windows XP has never heard of it**—It's annoying how many companies don't provide support for perfectly good (and sometimes rather expensive) two- or three-year-old printers to run under Windows XP. Windows 2000 drivers often work, but if they don't, give your printer to somebody's who's still running Windows 98 or Me, and get shopping for a replacement.

- **Make sure you're using good ink and paper, especially with an inkjet printer**—It's amazing how badly an inkjet printer can print with incorrect combinations of paper and media, and how good it looks if you use the right settings. Make sure you use the right settings for your paper, and try using paper made especially for inkjet printers before you decide that your printer's trash. If you're using refilled or third-party cartridges, make sure they print as well as the originals do.

- **Buy higher-capacity ink cartridges if available**—Some Hewlett-Packard inkjet printers can use two sizes of ink cartridges. Generally, you should buy the larger cartridge for greater economy (it also helps prevent your running out of ink during a print job).

- **Clean the printheads in your inkjet printer**—If print quality has dropped, as compared to when the printer was new, use a cleaning sheet made for inkjet printers. If the printheads are removable (as with most brands except Epson), take them out and clean them or use the printer's own cleaning feature. If cleaning the printer and the printheads doesn't improve print quality, you're ready for a new printer.

So, if you've cleaned up and upgraded your old printer, but you still can't get the results you want, it's time to shop for a new one. What do you need to know to make sure you get the printer you want—and really need?

> **MARK'S TIP SHEET: Skip the Stockup Sales on Ink and Toner**
>
> If you work in an office, you probably get the same calls I do—somebody's always wanting to sell you a bunch of inkjet or toner cartridges. Be polite, but don't stock up unless you run your printer really hard. Here's why:
>
> - Ink and toner cartridges have expiration dates, just like groceries. The average Twinkie has a much longer shelf life than ink and toner do. If you don't use your consumables before they go bad, your print quality can suffer.
>
> - If your printer dies, you don't want to be stuck with a bunch of ink that fits only a few models, all of which are likely to be equally out of production.
>
> 'Nuff said. Just say no to stocking up beyond what you need for the next two or three months.

Understanding Printer Types and Technologies

Since the first IBM PC hit the market over twenty years ago, there have been five major types of printers developed for it and its numerous descendents:

- Daisy-wheel
- Dot-matrix
- Laser/LED
- Inkjet
- Dye-sublimation

However, you can't buy a daisy-wheel printer anywhere but a computer museum these days, and dot-matrix printers are basically confined to banks, warehouses, and other locations where their ability to create multipart forms is far more important than their relatively poor print quality or high noise levels while operating. At your friendly computer/electronics emporium, laser/LED, inkjet, and dye-sublimation printers compete for your printer dollar.

> **ANALYZE THIS**
>
> **Get It All in One Box**
>
> Multi-function devices (also called all-in-one devices) combine printing, copying, and scanning (and sometimes faxing). They use the same print mechanisms as inkjet and laser printers, but add a sheet-fed or flatbed scanner for scanning and copying. The latest models have print quality similar to their single-task printer siblings, and should be evaluated the same way. In this chapter, I concentrate on printer and copier features. In Chapter 15, "Digital Imaging and Video," I cover scanning features.

Inkjet Printers

Inkjet printers were introduced in the late 1980s, but they were not very popular for the first few years because of their high initial cost, demanding paper quality requirements (one early model from Hewlett-Packard had to use clay-coated paper!), and relatively low print quality. These early inkjet printers used only black ink and had maximum resolutions of just 300 to 360dpi. However, companies like Hewlett-Packard (with its long-lived DeskJet series), Canon (with its pioneering BubbleJet models), and Epson (whose Stylus Color series have made a lot of users forget that Epson ever made a dot-matrix printer) improved the original models by adding color, higher resolutions and plain paper support. Combine those improvements with much lower purchase prices, and it's easy to see how the inkjet printer has gradually become everyone's favorite first printer. Figure 21.1 shows you a typical inkjet printer.

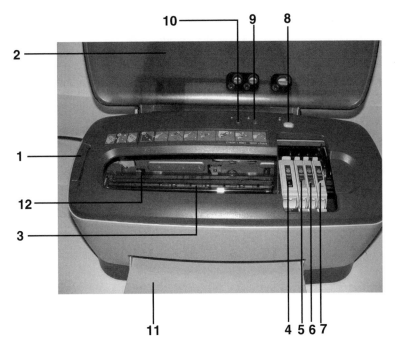

Figure 21.1

The features of a typical inkjet printer.

1. Printhead gap adjustment
2. Paper feed tray (behind dust cover)
3. Printhead support rod
4. Black ink cartridge
5. Cyan ink cartridge
6. Magenta ink cartridge
7. Yellow ink cartridge
8. Power switch
9. Paper advance
10. Ink cartridge cleaning/ changing control
11. Output paper tray
12. Printhead drive belt

Depending on the brand you buy, inkjet printers work in one of two ways:

- Thermal
- Piezo-electric

The *thermal* method was the method originally adopted (and still used to this day) by most inkjet printer makers, including Hewlett-Packard and Canon. This method heats the ink to a temperature of about 400° Fahrenheit, causing vapor bubbles to form inside the ink cartridge. The vapor bubbles propel the ink out of the ink cartridge through a multi-nozzle printhead and onto the paper. Canon's BubbleJet printers are named after this phenomenon.

The heat necessary to the printing process can be hard on the printhead, so both Canon and Hewlett-Packard's printheads can be removed from the printer for cleaning and replacement. Hewlett-Packard's printhead is an integral part of the cartridge, as is apparent from the printed circuit board on the side of Hewlett-Packard and compatible inkjet cartridges; Canon's printhead, on the other hand, uses replacement ink cartridge inserts. With the Canon cartridge, you can replace just the ink, or the ink and printhead, as needed.

Epson pioneered the *piezo-electric* method of inkjet printing, which is also used by Lexmark. This method uses a piezo-electric crystal inside the inkjet printhead. When electricity is run through the crystal, the crystal changes shape and forces the ink through the nozzles onto the paper. By eliminating the high ink temperatures of the thermal process, piezo-electric inkjet printers can use ink that is less prone to smear. In addition, the printheads can be built into the printer because they don't wear out from the use of heat.

Which printer type is better for you? Thermal inkjet printheads are much easier to keep clean, but piezo-electric inkjet printers have more durable printheads. Both types of printers are available in a wide range of prices.

Although some people would argue about technologies, what means more to most users than the method by which a printer makes the image on the page is how good that image is—and how quickly the printer can put the image on the page. Regardless of the print technology used, today's inkjet printers offer an impressive list of typical features.

Essential Inkjet Features

Inkjet printer models seem to change almost as frequently as magazine displays do. Thus, rather than cite models that might be replaced by other models in just a few weeks, I'm providing you with a list of essential features to look for, along with the reasons these features should be important to you.

- **1,200 dpi (dots per inch) or higher text and graphics resolution**—This resolution, especially on paper made for inkjet printers, means that one printer can handle all your correspondence and creative work, unless you opt for a photo printer. Photo printers can produce better image quality than a general-purpose inkjet printer, but at a cost of slow text-print speeds.

- **Separate ink tanks for each color**—It's frustrating to throw away a tricolor ink cartridge because you've used up one color, so get on the one cartridge per color bandwagon. General-purpose inkjets use cyan (C), Magenta (M), Yellow (Y), and Black (K), while photo printers might add photo (lighter) versions of magenta and cyan, and even a photo black for up to six or seven colors.

- **Ten pages-per-minute (or higher) rated speeds for text**—Get more done in less time, but remember that the vendors' idea of print speed isn't exactly realistic (it would be classified as fiction in the typical library).

- **Long print life**—Epson has pioneered longer print life by using pigment-based ink in some of its recent general-purpose and photo printers, but the latest printers with dye-based inks also feature improved print life. If you want to display your printouts, look for models with the longest estimated print life and follow the vendor's display instructions.

- **Low cost per page**—Although inkjet printers have a higher cost per page than laser printers, the cost per page can vary a lot depending on the size of the ink tanks and the size of the ink droplet used by the printer (measured in picoliters). Some printers have droplet sizes as small as two picoliters, so the print quality is better and less ink is used per printout. The inkjet and multifunction inkjet-based printers in *PC Magazine*'s November 2002 printer roundup (www.pcmag.com) have costs per page ranging from as little as 2 cents per page to as much as 11 cents per page.

Inkjet Printer Features Worth Considering

The features in this category are optional, and many of them apply especially to printing photos. However, if you're wondering which model to buy when two or three are similar, the presence of one or more of these features could be a tie-breaker.

- **Support for USB 2.0 ports**—Today's printers handle higher resolutions than ever before, which means that more data is flowing to the printer. Printers that support the extra speed of USB 2.0 help get the print job into the printer faster.

- **Support for roll paper and 4"×6" photo paper**—These options are very useful if you want to print banners and photos.

- **Consider wide format if you have a wide wallet**—If you find 8"×10" enlargements a bit small, look for larger-format printers from various vendors. They can (of course) also use standard paper sizes, but keep in mind that the extra size costs extra bucks.

- **Flash memory card reader**—This feature enables you to print without a computer, which helps make your digital camera a nearly instant camera. Be sure to verify the printer can read your camera's type of memory card; an adapter might be necessary.

- **Duplex printing**—Enables you to produce double-sided originals. Note that for best results you will want to use paper intended for double-sided printing.

- **CD/DVD printing**—If you create original projects with your rewriteable CD or DVD drive, printers with this feature let you print directly onto printable (blank white top surface) CDs and DVDs instead of using paper labels.

- **Network port**—Some inkjet printers are fast enough to be shared among multiple users. Although you can share a printer connected to a computer with other users, it might be more convenient to use a printer with its own network port. Such a printer can be positioned anywhere on the network. Depending upon the printer, you might have options such as 10/100 Ethernet, Wi-Fi wireless Ethernet, or Bluetooth for short-range wireless printing.

Laser/LED Printers

Laser printers use an electrophotographic process that somewhat resembles a copier mechanism. One of the major differences between copiers and laser printers is where the image comes from. Copiers transfer the image from a scanning mechanism to paper; laser printers translate print commands received from a computer into a printed page.

The "laser" in "laser printer" refers to the use of a laser beam to temporarily record the page you want to print onto the sensitized surface of the imaging drum inside the printer. This electrically charged image then attracts toner from the drum. At the same time, a sheet of paper receives an electrical charge with the opposite polarity; the paper then attracts the toner from the drum to form the printed image. A fusing mechanism bonds the image to the paper, and the printed sheet is ejected into the output tray. Figure 21.2 shows you the "inside story" of how laser printers work.

Because laser printers must receive the entire page into memory before printing any part of it, a laser printer is frequently referred to as a *page printer*. This term applies equally well to the LED printers manufactured by some vendors. LED printers use an LED array in place of a moving laser. The print quality and other details of the printing process are the same as those produced by a true laser printer.

There are three ways to control a printer:

- **PCL**—Hewlett-Packard's printer control language (PCL) is now in version 6. This is the most widely supported printer language for laser printers.

- **PostScript**—Adobe's page description language is now in Level 3. PostScript printers can handle more complex graphics and designs than PCL printers can.

- **Graphics Device Interface (GDI)**—It uses your computer's processor and Windows to create and image the page.

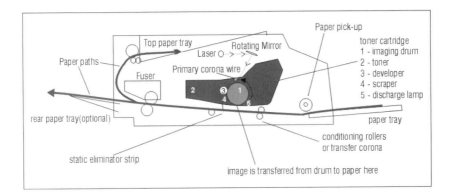

Figure 21.2

The interior of a typical laser printer that uses a replaceable toner cartridge/drum mechanism.

Some printers contain (or emulate) both PCL and PostScript languages and switch automatically to the language being sent to the printer.

A GDI printer can be very inexpensive and have very little memory because Windows and your PC do all the work. However, a GDI printer won't work at a command prompt or with Linux or other operating systems. I don't recommend GDI printers, and you can get a "real" printer with PCL and/or PostScript for not much more money.

Essential Laser/LED Printer Features

What should you look for in your next laser printer? I'd suggest starting with the features in this section:

- **600 dpi or higher print quality**—The latest mid-range and high-end models offer true 1,200 dpi print quality, but you may need to add a RAM upgrade to the printer to achieve this resolution with large graphics.

- **Choice of normal or straight-through paper path**—This gives you the option to use the straight-through paper path for business cards, envelopes, and other heavier-than-normal paper stocks.

- **Expandable RAM**—The more RAM in the printer, the faster that complex pages can be printed, and the greater the amount of graphics per page that can be printed.

- **PCL, PostScript, or emulations**—These printers are faster and can work with non-Windows operating systems.

READ THIS TOO: More on How Printers Print

If you can't live another minute without memorizing the six-step electrophotographic (EP) process used by the average laser printer or want to learn more about why color printers use four or six inks instead of 64 crayons, check out these books:

- In *How Computers Work, Sixth Edition* (Que, 2001), Ron White helps you visualize color printing and lots more about your PC.

- *Scott Mueller's Upgrading and Repairing PCs, 15th Edition* (Que, 2003) gives you the full scoop on the EP process, high-end color laser printers (the perfect way to spend two grand!), and lots more technical stuff on both inkjet and laser printers.

Laser Features Worth Considering

Beyond the essential features, other features you might look for, depending upon your needs, include the following:

- **Duplex printing**—Enables you to produce double-sided originals. Note that for best results, you will want to use paper intended for double-sided printing.

- **PostScript option**—If you're not sure you need the extra graphics pizzazz of PostScript immediately, but want to keep your options open, look for printers that can be upgraded to PostScript. This usually requires the installation of a so-called "personality" module (which might plug in where a normal memory module goes). Note also that PostScript printers require much more RAM than PCL printers, so be prepared for a RAM upgrade.

- **Multiple paper trays**—If you find yourself switching paper stocks, or between paper and envelopes or labels, look for printers that can use multiple paper trays.

- **Network port**—Many laser printers are fast enough to be shared among multiple users. Although you can share a printer connected to a computer with other users, it might be more convenient to use a printer with its own network port. Such a printer can be positioned anywhere on the network. Depending on the printer, you might have options such as 10/100 Ethernet, Wi-Fi wireless Ethernet, or Bluetooth for short-range wireless printing.

- **High-capacity paper tray**—It's annoying to put more paper in a printer by your desk; it's much worse than that to stroll down the hallway to find an empty output tray and a dozen jobs waiting for a networked printer to receive more paper. I strongly recommend using a big paper tray if you're going to network your printer.

Dye-Sublimation Printers

Dye-sublimation (dye-sub) printers work in a completely different manner than either inkjet or laser/LED printers. Dye-sub printers use a multicolored ribbon, but unlike dot matrix printers, controlled heat is used to transfer the image onto the paper, mixing colors in the process. Because dye-sub printers don't have a printhead, they produce true continuous-tone images. Thus, although the dpi of typical dye-sub printers is only 300–403 dpi, their actual image quality is comparable to inkjet printers with much higher rated resolutions.

While professional-level dye-sub printers are available in various large formats, most dye-sub printers for PCs (also known as digital photo printers) are designed to print on snapshot paper up to 4"×6", although a few are designed to print on paper up to 8"×10".

Dye-sub printers are 100 percent intended for use in printing photos. Unlike inkjet photo printers that can produce passable text in a pinch, a dye-sub is useless for any other task. However, if digital photography's your thing, you should consider a dye-sub printer.

Essential Dye-Sublimation Printer Features

If you're considering a dye-sub printer, there's only one reason to get it: great photo prints. Thus, this list of essential features is geared to help you achieve exactly that:

- **High image resolution**—Look for 300 dpi or higher resolutions; some older or low-end printers might have lower dpi, and they should be avoided.
- **Direct printing from your favorite flash memory type(s)**—You should be able to select your photos from a TV or built-in LCD display and print them without a computer, although you can connect a PC to almost any model.
- **Full 24-bit color**—Also described as 8-bits per color or 256 levels per dot, printers with this feature can produce over 16.7 million colors; 7-bits per color printers can produce only 2.1 million colors, which is a noticeable difference.
- **Protective overcoating**—Sometimes referred to as four-pass printing, this feature protects your photos from damage.
- **Borderless prints at your choice of sizes**—Some printers can't produce 4"×6" borderless prints, so you must settle for smaller borderless prints (3"×4") or borders on your larger prints.

Desirable Dye-Sublimation Printer Features

Beyond the basics, you might want to consider these additional features in your buying decision:

- **Direct printing from your favorite CD media**—Some dye-sub printers now feature a CD-ROM drive to enable you to print directly from a media CD without connecting the printer to a computer. Because the photos you want to keep will probably wind up on a CD-R or CD-RW disc sooner or later, this option (although expensive) could be useful.

- **Built-in preview display**—If you don't want to connect your printer to a TV or a computer to preview your images, consider models with a built-in display.

Selecting the Best Printer

In this section, I help you find the features that you'll find the most important on your next printer. You need to consider two major issues:

- How you plan to use the printer
- Major printer features

Because your printing needs are different from mine (not to mention my kids, my wife, and the folks down the hallway's printing requirements…), you need to determine the most important kinds of printing you do before you shop for a printer.

If you're a photographer, cross monochrome laser and LED printers off your list. If you're buying a printer for the kids to fool around with, you want to balance a reasonable up-front cost with ink prices that won't clean out your wallet. If you travel and don't want to borrow printers wherever you arrive, you want a lightweight printer. And so it goes. Once you decide how to use your printer, then its time to consider printer features such as:

- Interface type
- Up-front cost
- Consumables cost and cost-per-page
- Print quality
- Print speed

- Printer control language

- Available upgrades

- Long-term image stability

- Printer or multifunctional machine

- Space available for the printer

ON THE WEB: Printer Reviews Await You Online

Although there's no substitute, ultimately, for seeing actual printouts when you're buying a printer, save time and effort with online printer reviews and information at these web sites:

- `cgi.techtv.com/search`—Enter the words printer and review and select a date range to find reviews done the TechTV way.

- `www.pcmag.com`—Click the Printers link under the Product Guides section for reviews of inkjet, laser/LED, and dye-sub printers.

- `www.pcworld.com`—Click the Printers link under the Product Guides sidebar for reviews of inkjet, laser/LED, and dye-sub printers.

Printer Interfaces: Parallel Versus USB

The two major types of printer interfaces available today include:

- Parallel
- USB

Which one is best for you? If you plan to use your printer strictly with Windows 98, Windows Me, Windows 2000, or Windows XP, USB is probably your best bet. As you learned in Chapter 19, "Adding the Ports You Need for the Devices You Want," USB devices can be hot-swapped, plugged, and unplugged while the system is running. In some cases, USB printers are faster than parallel printers. However, if you plan to use your printer with MS-DOS, most versions of Linux, or older versions of Windows, you should choose a printer that has both USB and parallel interfaces. Remember that if you need to print screens or BIOS setup information before the computer starts, the USB port has not been initialized and a USB printer will not work.

Up-Front Cost

If you are on a tight budget, there is no question that inkjet printers get you printing for far less up-front cost than laser printers do. A good-quality (1,200 dpi or higher) inkjet printer can be purchased for between $100 and $150; most personal or small office laser printers cost between $300 and $500 or more, while color laser and LED printers are over $1,000. However, the price you pay upfront is only a fraction of what you ultimately pay for whatever printer you choose. You need to consider the cost of *consumables* as well.

Consumables Cost

The cost of consumables—items such as ink, toner, and paper—should be figured along with the initial cost of your printer. To determine the true cost of consumables, you need to know two factors:

- The cost of ink, toner, and paper
- The number of pages you can expect to print from an ink cartridge or toner cartridge

You can determine the second factor from either the manufacturer's suggested page count or from independent tests, such as those published in *PC Magazine* or *PCWorld*. These tests reveal that low-cost printers actually cost *more* in the long run than more expensive printers.

> **CAUTION: STOP! LOOK! THINK!**
>
> **Don't Be Penny-Wise and Pound Foolish**
> If you *really* want to save money on printing, spend more money on your printer. Really. Here's why.
>
> Tests by the folks at *PC Magazine* have proven that many inexpensive printers have the *highest* cost per page. The reason? Inexpensive printers often use small-capacity ink cartridges or toner cartridges. Low-cost inkjet printers in particular often use older printhead designs that use more ink per droplet, which makes low-capacity cartridges run out of ink even faster.
>
> Fortunately, today's latest models are much more thrifty than older models. Back in 2000, typical costs per page for inkjet printers ranged from 7 cents a page up to 31 cents per page. Today, typical costs per page range from just 2 cents per page up to 11 cents per page. If you're feeding an older printer with an insatiable appetite for print cartridges, changing to a newer model can reduce your cost per page *and* give you better printouts. It's a win-win deal!
>
> Even the best inkjet in cost-per-page calculations is an out-of-control spender compared to laser printers, which are incredibly frugal with your hard-earned money. The typical laser printer has a cost per page of well under a penny! You pay more upfront for a laser, but a whole lot less down the line. If you need text and lots of it, laser/LED printers rule! However, color lasers are very costly compared to their black-and-white siblings.

Inkjet Print Quality

You can measure print quality in two ways:

- **Print resolution**—With inkjet printers, this figure comes from the number of nozzles in the printhead and how tightly spaced they are. Some printers have different values for black and color printing because of differences in the printhead. Laser and LED printers have the same resolutions for black and color (if the printer has a color option).

- **How the printout looks**—This is affected by many factors, including print resolution, ink droplet size, color layering and blending technologies, nozzle shape, printhead technologies, and so forth.

At first glance, you might think that a higher resolution always results in better-looking printouts. Unfortunately, because of various issues including printhead design, paper choice, printer driver options selected, and other items, your eyes are the best way to determine the best output you can afford. However, you can use resolution statistics to rule out printers that cannot achieve the results you want.

Printers with resolutions under 1,000 dpi should not be purchased because their resolution is too low by today's standards to produce satisfactory output. For best results, choose inkjet printers with a resolution of at least 1,200 dpi and laser printers with a resolution of 1,200 dpi. Although you should still review actual print samples (either from demonstration printers at the store or by requesting print samples from the printer manufacturer), by ruling out printers with inadequate resolution, you can narrow down the possible choices.

With inkjet printers in particular, *how* the ink is placed on paper is just as important as the resolution in dpi of the printout. Generally speaking, the smaller the droplet of ink, the better. Droplets are measured in picoliters; the smaller the droplet, the better the print quality and the faster the print dries.

Another important factor is the number of ink colors that can be placed into an ink droplet. For example, the optional PhotoRet IV photo ink cartridge for several current Hewlett-Packard inkjet printers can place up to 32 colors in a single ink droplet, compared to 29 colors for PhotoRet III and only 16 colors for PhotoRet II printers.

You also need to judge print quality based on the paper type used for a printout. Especially with inkjet printers, the paper choice and print options used must match. To get the best results with photographs, you must use the heavier, more expensive, photo-quality paper and select special high-resolution photo-printing modes.

When you request print samples from the printer manufacturer, you see the printer in its best light, because the samples use the correct paper type for each print type. Although it might be more convenient to use the printer at the store for a sample, printers in stores are often supplied with the cheapest-quality paper, which does not produce satisfactory results in high-quality or photo output. If you can't create a sample printout at the store, ask to see a book of print samples.

Print Speed

When it comes to print speed, you're sure to want what I want: the fastest printer you can buy. However, figuring out which printer is the fastest is not always easy. Print speeds with laser and inkjet printers are measured in PPM (pages per minute). If you rely on manufacturer-supplied speed information, you are certain to be disappointed when you set up the printer and actually use it. This is because printer manufacturers typically use the most generous methods for estimating the speed of the printer.

Typically, the PPM speed is measured with black text pages, because printing graphics and colors is much slower. If possible, locate a review from a reliable source of printers you are considering and use their speed tests to determine which printer is faster; *PC Magazine*'s printer tests have been major factors in my printer choices over the years. Keep in mind that the following issues affect the speed of the printer:

- **Does the printer rely on the computer to create the page?**—Printers that use the computer to create the page are called GDI or *host-based* printers. These printers are very inexpensive, but tend to be slower than printers that use a true *page description language (PDL)*.

- **Is the printer connected to the parallel port or the USB port?**—If a parallel port is configured to use EPP or ECP modes, it is *slightly* faster than a USB 1.1 port. However, some printers are now optimized for USB 2.0 ports, which are much faster than either USB 1.1 or parallel ports.

- **How does the print quality selected and print options selected change print speed?**—Draft-quality printing is much faster than high-quality text or photo printing. Be sure to look at the print speed for the output quality you use most often.

JARGON

Become a Master of Printer Terms and Jargon

PPM—Pages per minute; how fast a printer prints is determined by the speed of its engine and the print mode selected.

Page Description Language (PDL)—The language the printer uses. The computer must use a printer driver that is compatible with the printer's PDL, or printouts will be gibberish.

Printer Control Language (PCL)—The PDL used by Hewlett-Packard LaserJet and most other laser printers that don't use PostScript.

Host-based—Printer that depends on the computer and operating system to create the page, rather than a PDL. Printers that use the Windows GDI to create pages are a type of host-based printer.

PostScript—A PDL used for laser/LED printers that has very powerful graphics features, but tends to be slower and is more expensive than PCL. PostScript printers also require more RAM than PCL printers.

RIP—Raster Image Processor, a program that enables a non-PostScript printer to print PostScript output. Often used by graphics professionals to allow low-cost printers to be used for proof copies of layouts and ads.

EPP—Enhanced Parallel Port, a high-speed bi-directional printer port mode that requires an IEEE-1284 printer cable.

ECP—Enhanced Capabilities Port, a high-speed bi-directional printer port mode designed for use with drives and scanners as well as printers. It also requires an IEEE-1284 printer cable.

Printer Language: Host-Based or PDL?

At one time, all printers used some form of PDL. A PDL is a language built into the printer that is used to control the printer. To print a page, your computer describes the page using the PDL's commands for font size, graphics, and font changes.

The most common PDL for laser printers is Hewlett Packard's PCL. Both Hewlett Packard and non-Hewlett-Packard laser printers typically use PCL 5. Laser printers used by graphic artists typically use PostScript instead of PCL because PostScript provides much more control over graphic output. However, printers with built-in PostScript are typically more expensive than printers with PCL or an emulation of PCL.

The situation is much different with inkjet printers. To help save money on an already-inexpensive product, most inkjet printer manufacturers don't use a true PDL in their least-expensive products. Instead, they use the host-based or GDI method of creating the page inside the computer. By leaving out the part of the printer that would normally *rasterize* the page (convert the page into dots) before printing, the cost of the printer can be reduced. However, GDI or host-based printing is suitable only for use with Windows. If you plan to use your printer with MS-DOS or with Linux, make sure you choose a printer that has a true PDL.

Available Upgrades

Most people don't think of printers as upgradeable devices, but some upgrades are possible for some printers. Some inkjet printers offer the following upgrade options:

- **Wider black printhead for faster printing**—Look for this option if an inkjet printer is your only printer. Note that some printers offering this option replace the color ink cartridge with the high-speed black cartridge, so you're back to the old cartridge-swapping days if you want to print color.

- **Six-color photo printing**—Compare the photo quality available with six-color printing to your printer's standard four-color printing before you decide if this option is useful.

- **PostScript *Raster Image Processor (RIP)***—If you use your inkjet printer to create proof copies for advertising, marketing, or publishing purposes, adding a RIP program to enable PostScript output is a very valuable, although expensive, option. A RIP converts PostScript commands into commands that can be understood by the printer. Some high-end inkjet printers feature built-in PostScript, which is faster than a software add-on RIP.

Some laser printers offer the following upgrade options:

- **Memory upgrades**—In my opinion, every laser printer needs a memory upgrade option. Unfortunately, many lower-cost laser/LED printers omit this option. Why is it important? If you try to print a page that does not fit within the laser's built-in memory, you receive an error message and your page does not print until you reduce the print resolution or simplify the page. How much memory do you need? Ideally, a 600-dpi PCL laser printer used to print complex graphics and photographs should have at least 6MB of RAM installed; a 1,200-dpi PCL laser printer used to print complex graphics and photographs should have at least 16MB of RAM installed. These values should be even higher for PostScript laser printers.

- **PostScript**—If you use your laser printer to create graphically complex printouts or proof copies, this is a very valuable, although expensive, option. Some printers enable you to upgrade to PostScript by plugging in a special personality module that contains a PostScript interpreter; this modules looks like a memory module and plugs into an empty memory socket.

ANALYZE THIS

RAM and Laser Printers

Laser and LED printers are page printers, and that means that the entire page has to fit into the RAM inside the printer. Although fonts and text use some memory, they don't strain even the minimal amounts of RAM found on low-end printers. However, when you throw graphics into the mix, you can have a big problem. Whether you're wanting to print a full-page table with all its gridlines, an illustrated brochure, or an 8×10 enlargement, graphics often require more RAM than might be present in your laser printer. Many laser printers today use data-compression techniques to try to print graphics-heavy pages, but the compression process takes extra time and doesn't always work.

If you try to print a graphics-rich page and the printer's error lights or LED display indicates an error, you've just had a close encounter with running out of laser printer memory. To work around the problem, use the properties sheet for your printer and reduce the graphics resolution to the next lower value, and then reprint the page. However, don't settle for lower resolution (and lower print quality) for long; get a RAM upgrade and use the full resolution of your printer.

Long-Term Image Stability

Traditionally, laser printer output has been considered to be more stable than inkjet printer output. There are reasons for this:

- Laser printer output is fused to the paper, making printouts water-resistant.

- Early inkjet inks, in particular, had very poor water resistance.

- Some inkjet printer ink/paper combinations react poorly to certain types of air pollution and can fade when exposed to bright light for protracted periods of time.

Epson now produces several printers that use pigment-based inks (known variously as DuraBrite or UltraChrome inks), which are designed to create printouts that can last up to 80 years on Epson papers, or up to 70 years on plain paper. By contrast, the latest Epson photo printers that use dye-based inks have an estimated print lifespan of up to 27 years. Whatever the estimated lifespan of the prints from your printer, prints need to be laminated or displayed behind glass to reach those estimated lifespans.

Printer Only or All-in-One/Multifunction

If you need a printer *and* either a scanner or a fax machine, you might want to consider a multifunction or all-in-one unit instead of an ordinary printer. These units combine copy/print or copy/print/fax capabilities into a single unit that can cost less and take up less space than the combined two or three devices would require.

Should you go the all-in-one route? A couple of years ago, I would have said "No way!" because of the severe compromises necessary to jam multiple functions into a single unit. I still recommend that you avoid all-in-one units that use sheet-fed scanners if you plan to use the scanner function frequently, and pass over units with text resolutions under 600 dpi.

However, a number of high-quality all-in-one units are now on the market from various vendors. Look for color print resolutions of 1,200 dpi or higher (if inkjet-based) or 1,200 dpi resolutions (if laser-based). Scan resolutions should exceed 1,000 dpi (optical). If you don't need fax capabilities, you can save money.

As with any printer, be sure to review print samples and reviews of features and limitations before you buy.

By considering all of these options and carefully examining the print quality of the prospective printers, you can find the perfect printer for your needs.

Space Available for the Printer

If you're trying to fit your printer into a tight spot in a small computer hutch, you should look carefully at how much space the printer requires. Start by comparing the printer's dimensions to the space available for the printer. If the model you prefer is too large, look for a smaller model or try to locate the printer elsewhere. Use a measuring tape at home and at the dealer's to check out the space available compared to the models you prefer.

If you're considering an all-in-one model, make sure there's clearance to add paper to the sheet-fed scanner or to raise the lid on the flatbed scanner portion of the printer.

If you want to use a printer with a straight-through paper path, such as an inkjet printer with a banner paper attachment or a laser/LED printer with an optional rear paper tray, make sure there's enough room to use the printer with these options enabled.

Installing Your Printer

As with any hardware device, the installation process requires both physical and software changes to your computer. Fortunately, it is not necessary to remove your existing printer drivers from your system before you install support for a new printer. This means you can switch between printers when necessary.

Pre-Installation Checklist

Before you install your new printer, use this checklist to make sure that you have what you need:

- **A printer cable**—Most printers do not include a printer cable. You need a USB Series A to Series B cable to attach your USB printer to the USB root hub or external hub. Be sure to specify a Hi-Speed USB (USB 2.0) cable if you use a USB 2.0 port and printer. You need an IEEE 1284-compatible printer cable to attach your parallel printer to your computer. See Figure 21.3 and Figure 21.4 for examples of these cables.

Centronics 36-pin port (to printer)   DB25M port (to computer's parallel port)

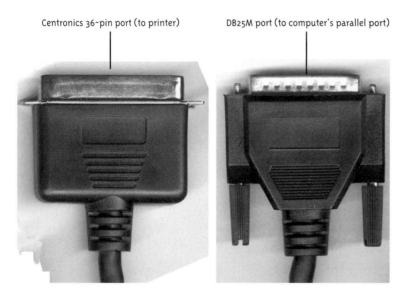

Figure 21.3

An IEEE-1284 parallel cable has a 36-pin connector that attaches to the printer and a 25-pin connector (right) that attaches to the computer's LPT/ parallel port.

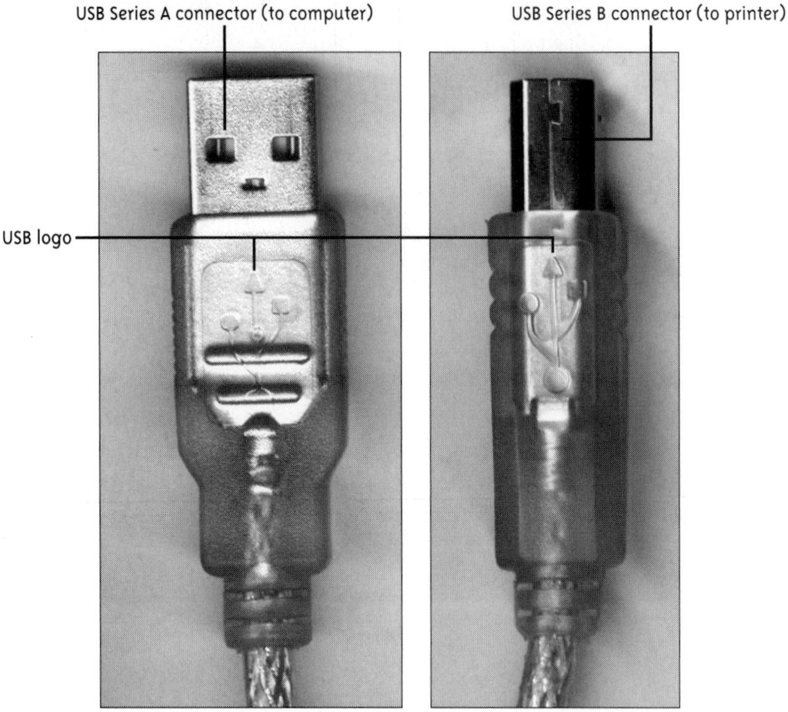

Figure 21.4

A USB Series A to Series B cable connects USB printers to a USB external hub or computer's built-in (root) hub.

USB Series A connector (to computer)

USB Series B connector (to printer)

USB logo

CAUTION: STOP! LOOK! THINK!

Cheap Cables Make for Poor Performance!

When you see the outrageous prices some stores charge for IEEE-1284 parallel cables ($20-30!), you might be tempted to dig around in your junk drawer for a leftover printer cable you salvaged from an old dot-matrix printer. Shop for a better price on cables if you want, but don't re-use an old cable.

What's the deal with IEEE-1284 printer cables? They're thicker than the old, cheap printer cables because they use all the wires to enable signals to come back from the printer as well as to go out to the printer. They have better insulation and use a twisted-pair construction to reduce interference. Your old printer cable doesn't have *any* of those construction advantages. In fact, if it's old enough, it won't even allow your printer to report back on its toner or ink levels. Wondering if you already have an IEEE-1394 printer cable? Check the cable itself for markings.

Bottom line: Your printer can't do its job without the proper cable.

- **Correct port configuration for parallel printers**—Most printers are designed to use either the EPP or ECP parallel port configuration; the same IEEE-1284 compatible printer cable works with either configuration. Select the appropriate port configuration in the system BIOS before installing your printer.

CAUTION: STOP! LOOK! THINK!

Why EPP and ECP? What's the Difference?

Although both EPP (Enhanced Parallel Port) and ECP (Enhanced Capabilities Port) are designed to support a maximum speed of about 2MBps, there are differences in the standards. EPP was designed primarily for printers, and ECP was designed to make it easier to daisy-chain another device, such as a Zip drive or scanner, with the printer. Both EPP and ECP modes use IRQ 7 (a hardware interrupt) that the normal printer port uses, but ECP also uses a DMA (Direct Memory Access) channel (either DMA 1 or DMA 3) to improve data transfer rates.

Check your printer manual (and the manuals of any other device that is daisy-chained with the printer) to see which mode is best for you.

- **Install the paper, ink cartridges, or toner cartridge and, if possible, use the printer's own self-test to make sure the printer works before you install it**—If the printer is unable to perform a self-test, there is no reason to install it; your software won't have any better luck persuading the printer to print. Pack it up and return it to the store for an exchange or refund.

The Installation Process

This section describes the printer installation process as it takes place in Windows XP, but the process is similar with other recent versions of Windows.

To install a parallel printer, follow these steps:

1. Shut down the computer and turn off the power.
2. Turn off the printer.
3. Connect the printer cable to the printer and to the parallel port on the computer. See Figure 21.5.
4. Turn on the printer.
5. Turn on the computer.
6. Provide the setup disk or CD-ROM supplied by the printer manufacturer when prompted for the printer driver.
7. Remove the setup disk or CD-ROM after the printer driver is installed.
8. Use the test print option at the end of the driver installation process; review the output to make sure that colors and graphics are properly printed. See the "What You Can Learn from the Printer Test" sidebar on the next page to learn how to troubleshoot your printer from this printout.

Figure 21.5

Attaching the parallel cable to the computer's parallel port (left) and the printer's parallel port (right). Thumbscrews and locking wires hold the heavy cable and connector in place.

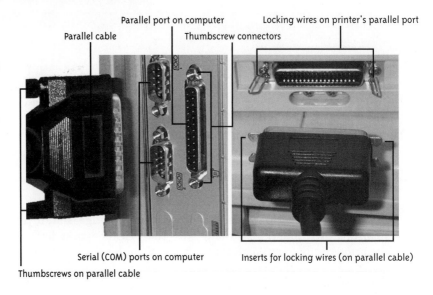

Parallel port on computer

Parallel cable

Locking wires on printer's parallel port

Thumbscrew connectors

Serial (COM) ports on computer

Thumbscrews on parallel cable

Inserts for locking wires (on parallel cable)

MARK'S TIP SHEET: What You Can Learn from the Printer Test

The Windows printer test sheet and the printer's own self-test tell you different things about your printer. Put them together, and you have excellent insight into your printer's features and what makes it print.

The Windows printer test sheet can be printed at the end of the printer installation process; you should do it to make sure the printer works! Here's what the test sheet shows:

- The Windows logo. If colors are missing or if the graphic is streaked or faded, you might have a toner or ink problem.
- The name of your printer.
- The printer model.
- The driver name and version number.
- Color support.
- Port name.
- The data format used by the printer.
- The driver files and versions used by the printer and their location.

The most useful self-tests are those performed by laser printers; to activate a printer's internal self-test, check the manual for which button(s) to press when you turn on the printer. Self-tests typically show the following:

- The PDL used by the printer (PCL, PostScript, or others)
- The amount of RAM on-board
- The number of pages printed since the printer was manufactured
- The fonts built into the printer

Use the Windows printer test and the printer's own self test to learn lots more about your printer—fast!

Follow these steps to install your USB printer:

1. Turn off the printer.
2. Connect the USB cable to the printer and to the USB port on the computer or hub. See Figure 21.6.

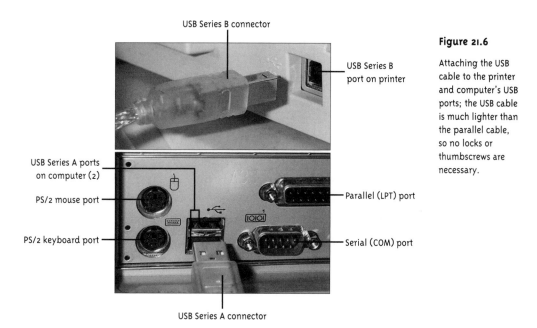

Figure 21.6

Attaching the USB cable to the printer and computer's USB ports; the USB cable is much lighter than the parallel cable, so no locks or thumbscrews are necessary.

USB Series B connector

USB Series B port on printer

USB Series A ports on computer (2)

PS/2 mouse port

PS/2 keyboard port

Parallel (LPT) port

Serial (COM) port

USB Series A connector

3. Turn on the printer.

4. Provide the setup disk or CD-ROM supplied by the printer manufacturer when prompted for the printer driver.

5. Remove the setup disk or CD-ROM after the printer driver is installed.

6. Use the test print option at the end of the driver installation process; review the output to make sure that colors and graphics are properly printed.

CAUTION: STOP! LOOK! THINK!

Read the Directions First with USB Printers!

Although most USB peripherals use an "install me now, then add the driver disk later" method of installation, printers sometimes follow the reverse order. This is because USB printers must set up a special USB printer port that is proprietary to the particular printer brand you're installing. Check the directions before you install the printer. If the drivers should go first, install them first, and then connect the printer!

Getting the Most from Your Printer

Now that you have a better printer, the task of getting better printouts is only partly completed. To make sure that you can get the most out of your printer, check out the tips and tricks in this section.

Selecting the Best Media

Although an inkjet printer is very inexpensive, purchasing the right type of supplies for the best print output isn't always so simple. Even though most inkjet printers offer a so-called "plain paper" option for routine printing, very inexpensive paper made for copiers tends to be too rough for good results. Use high-quality smooth paper when you need plain paper for routine printouts. For better results, use paper made especially for inkjet printer, and specify a brightness of 90 or above. Paper and media made especially for inkjet printers tends to cost more than laser paper, but the improvements in print quality are significant and worth it!

Selecting the Right Ink and Toner Cartridges

Some printers don't offer any choices: Ink is ink and toner is toner. However, if the model you select provides cartridge purchase or capacity choices, you can save money, time, and frustration by exercising these options:

- Save money by buying cartridges in two-packs if you buy ink or toner every few months. Because inkjet cartridges run out fairly quickly (especially if the inkjet printer is your only printer), having a backup is a good idea.

- Third-party or remanufactured inkjet or toner cartridges can save you a lot of money *if* they produce satisfactory print quality. Before spending a lot of money on third-party cartridges, try one to see if you like it.

- Choose high-capacity cartridges. Hewlett-Packard offers high-capacity ink cartridges for some inkjet printer models. They offer over twice the page count for less than twice the price. Hewlett-Packard also offers high-capacity toner cartridges for some laser printer models, offering 65 percent more toner for about 20 percent more cost. Not only do high-capacity cartridges save you money, but they also minimize the chances of running out of ink or toner in the middle of a print job.

- If you want to save even more money on inkjet printing, try a refill kit if they're available for your printer (most are available for Hewlett-Packard and Epson models). If you like the results, you can save a lot of money. However, keep in mind that if the refill kit uses a different formulation of ink than the original cartridge does, you could damage your printer and you won't get the same print quality the original cartridge produced.

Using Printer Options

The Windows printer properties sheet offers you a great deal of control over how your printer performs. You can view and change the printer options from the printer's properties sheet. Open the Printers folder from the Control Panel, right-click the printer, and select Properties. With most Windows programs, you can also access the printer properties sheet through the File, Print dialog box. Click Options or Properties to view and change the printer properties.

Although the exact options available vary according to the printer you use, the following are typical options you can expect to see frequently in Windows 98/Me:

- **General tab**—Click the Print Test Page button on this page to test your printer. Before I use an inkjet printer that hasn't been used for several days, I like to perform a print test to make sure that all of my ink nozzles are clog-free and working properly.

- **Details tab**—Use this tab to change printer drivers or to adjust principal settings for MS-DOS programs or network programs.

- **Sharing tab**—Use this tab to specify how to share your printer if you are on a network and have installed File and Print sharing software.

- **Color Management tab**—Use this tab to install color profiles for more accurate printing.

- **Graphics**—Use this tab to select the graphics resolution for laser/LED printers; text is always printed at the printer's maximum resolution. Reduce graphics resolution to enable pages to print if not enough memory is in the printer to print a page with large or complex graphics. You can also adjust other options such as lightness or darkness and dithering modes. I like to adjust these options if I'm creating an original to use for photocopying. I find that the best settings for a photocopyable original are different than what is needed for a final printout straight from the laser printer itself.

- **Paper**—Use this tab to select paper sizes and types and page orientation.

- **Main**—Inkjet printers use this tab to adjust overall (text and graphics) resolution, paper size and type, pre-configured print options (plain paper, photo paper, glossy photo paper, and so on), and customized selections of resolution, color settings, and text quality.

- **Fonts**—Laser/LED printers use this tab to select which font cartridges are installed (used on older models) and to specify special print options for handling scalable TrueType fonts.

- **Device Options**—Laser and LED printers use this tab to adjust the amount of on-board memory and memory handling. PostScript printers also use this tab to adjust PostScript-specific options.

JARGON

TrueType—A scalable font technology introduced in the late 1980s by Microsoft and Apple as an alternative to PostScript. Before TrueType and PostScript, each different point size (such as 12-point body text or 24-point subhead) was a separate soft font, which used up a lot of disk space and laser printer memory. TrueType fonts (and PostScript fonts) are outline fonts, which means that a single mathematical description of the font (a font outline) is used as the basis for any size font you specify. Some TrueType fonts are stored in the printer, but most are loaded from disk as needed. Many application programs, such as office suites or graphics programs, come with TrueType fonts, so you may have hundreds of fonts already, and you can always buy more!

Windows XP greatly reorganizes the printer properties sheets compared to Windows 98/Me. Here's how to navigate typical XP-style printer properties sheets:

- **General tab**—Click the Print Test Page button on this page to test your printer. Before I use an inkjet printer that hasn't been used for several days, I like to perform a print test to make sure that all of my ink nozzles are clog-free and working properly. Click the Printing Preferences button to select paper layout, print quality (resolution), and number of pages per sheet (you can print pages or more per sheet with many printers to save paper).

- **Sharing tab**—Use this tab to specify how to share your printer if you are on a network and have installed File and Print sharing software. With Windows XP Pro, click the Additional Drivers button to install drivers to let other users on the network use different versions of Windows while using this printer.

- **Color Management tab**—Use this tab to install color profiles for more accurate printing.

- **Ports tab**—Selects and configures the port to use for the printer.

- **Advanced tab**—Contains various settings, including access control by time, print priority, driver, new driver installation, spooler settings, handling of printed/spooled documents, printing defaults (sets defaults used by Printing Preferences button from General tab), print processor and data type sent to printer, and separator page.

- **Device Settings tab**—Use this tab to select paper sizes and types and page orientation. With laser printers, also sets printer memory size and font settings, as well as PostScript options on PostScript printers.

- **Utilities**—With inkjet printers, used to clean printheads, check/adjust alignment, and check ink levels.

Using Printer Utilities

The printer utilities provide the solutions you need to these annoying inkjet printer mini-mysteries:

- **The Case of the Neglected Printer**—Inkjet printers love attention; about the worst thing you can do to an inkjet printer is leave it on, day-in, day-out, and not print anything. Sooner or later, some of the tiny ink cartridge nozzles clog when the printer isn't used regularly. If you don't unclog them before you stick a sheet of $2 photo paper in the printer, wave good-bye to your money.

- **The Printer That Couldn't Print Straight**—Ever wonder how an inkjet printer can print huge fonts with a small printhead? It prints a part of the letter, advances to the next line, and then prints more and more until it's done. Precise alignment control is needed to make sure that every line starts at exactly the same place. A misaligned printer causes large fonts and straight lines to be printed crookedly.

- **The Puzzle of the Empty Cartridge**—The ink cartridge *looks* full, but how can you be sure before you print on expensive card stock or photo paper?

Printer utility functions typically include a print test that enables you to check nozzles for clogging, clean clogged nozzles, check the printer for alignment, and display current ink levels. Use the Utility menu to make sure your printer is working before you print photos, business cards, or use expensive media of any type. The Utility menu can be accessed through the properties sheet of most inkjet printers.

Upgrading the RAM on Laser/LED Printers

Laser and LED printers are called page printers because they print your document one page at a time instead of one line at a time (the way inkjet printers do). What needs to fit into a page printer's memory? All of the following:

- The TrueType font outlines required by the current page of the document to be printed

- The text in the current page of the document

- The graphics contained in the document

PostScript printers send PostScript-language descriptions of the entire page, which uses up even more printer RAM. The higher the graphics resolution of the printer, the greater the amount of RAM required to hold all the page elements. What happens if your printer doesn't have enough RAM to hold all the page elements? The printer displays an error message, you need to take the printer off-line and press the Page Eject button, and only part of the page is printed.

Running out of memory for complex pages is the most obvious reason to add memory to your page printer. However, there are other benefits, including the following:

- **Faster printing of text and graphics documents**—With more RAM in the printer, the printer spends less time trying to compress the data to fit in the RAM available.

- **Faster printing of multipage documents**—Because less time is required to process each page, the computer can pass each page of a multipage document to the printer faster.

The details of adding memory to a printer vary, but many printers use memory modules that are similar to those used in computers. Adding memory to your laser or LED printer is a very economical way to improve its performance.

How much memory is enough? I recommend the following:

- **600-dpi, PCL-, or host-based printers**—Upgrade to 6MB or more.
- **600-dpi PostScript printers**—Upgrade to 16MB or more.
- **1,200-dpi, PCL-, or host-based laser printers**—Upgrade to 16MB or more.
- **1,200-dpi PostScript laser printers**—Upgrade to 32MB or more.

You won't always need this much RAM, but upgrading your printer's RAM means you'll never need to worry about a printing error due to too little RAM, and you'll speed up printing as well.

Switching Printers

Depending on how your printers are connected, it can be very easy or very difficult to switch from one printer to another. In my office, for example, I have a laser printer and a high-resolution color inkjet printer. Obviously, I prefer to use the laser printer for text.

The inkjet printer is connected via USB, and the laser printer is connected to LPT1. I can access either printer over the network if I'm using another computer. Because the printers are not connected to the same port, all I need to do to use the printer I prefer is to follow this simple procedure within a Windows application:

1. Click File, Print.
2. Select the printer from the pull-down menu.
3. Make sure the printer is turned on and connected to the computer or to the network.
4. Choose the print options desired and start the print job.

When each printer was installed, I specified how it was connected to the computer (a one-time task), so I don't need to worry about sending the wrong type of print command to a printer.

I recommend a similar configuration to you if you want to have more than one printer installed: connect one to a parallel port, and the other to a USB port. If you're using older printers that don't have USB ports, you can purchase an inexpensive switchbox that enables you to share a single parallel port with two or more printers. I don't recommend the inexpensive switchboxes with the mechanical switch, because this type of switch can damage the parallel port on laser or LED page printers. Instead, buy a switchbox that uses an electronic switch and is compatible with the IEEE-1284 parallel-port standard. A typical auto switchbox set is shown in Figure 21.7.

Figure 21.7

A typical auto-switchbox kit that also includes file-transfer software. Additional cables are needed, depending upon whether the switchbox will be used to share two printers with one computer or two computers with one printer.

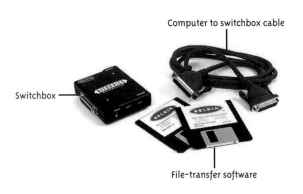

Computer to switchbox cable

Switchbox

File-transfer software

When you use a switchbox, you must make sure you have selected the correct printer in your software and selected the matching printer with the switchbox.

Sharing Your Printer with Another Computer

There are two major ways that you can share the wealth of the new printer with other users:

- Use file and print sharing over an existing network to make the printer available.
- Use an electronic switchbox designed to handle one printer and two or more computers. Such a reversible switchbox is shown in Figure 21.7.

Troubleshooting Your New Printer

Whether it's a brand-new or "new to you" printer you've installed, things can go wrong. Just ask Mr. Murphy if you don't believe me. Use this section to figure out the best solutions.

Help! I turned off my printer with the surge protector and now it won't print anything!

My ESP (extra sense about printers) powers tell me you're using an inkjet printer, and you've just discovered the best way I know of to ruin it before its time. What's wrong with using the master control on/off switch on a surge protector to turn your printer off along with everything else? Inkjet printers have *exposed* printheads when the printer is turned on. When you turn the printer off with its own switch, the printheads are capped to prevent their drying out. Turn off the power with a surge protector instead and they're left out to dry—literally!

Here's how to recover if you've been using the surge protector for a printer on-off switch. If you are using an Hewlett-Packard, Canon, or similar printer that incorporates the printhead into the ink cartridge, take it out of the printer and use an inkjet head cleaning kit (or alcohol on a swab). You can probably loosen the ink and finish the job by using the printer's own nozzle cleaning routine.

Epson printers are a tougher call. Because their printheads are built into the printer, you need to buy a special inkjet cleaning kit that has a clothlike sheet of media that you moisten with a cleaning solution. Run the printer with a small document using the cleaning sheet. Do this several times until you can see printing, and then use the printer's nozzle cleaning routine.

By the way, promise me you'll *always* turn off the printer before you touch the surge protector!

Help! My printer is spitting garbage instead of my resume!

I don't think anyone will hire a %&★&^%%$$, do you? Probably not, but with a bit of help from me, you might qualify as a printer tech.

I bet you just upgraded to a new printer that uses the same port as your old printer. When you don't change the default printer setting, your computer sends printer commands meant for the old printer to whatever is connected to the same port. The only way you can get recognizable text is if the two printers use the same PDL. When they use different PDLs, behold! You've just figured out a way to make pre-recycled paper!

Use the Printers or Printers and Faxes folder in the Control Panel to make your new printer the default printer. Right-click the icon for your new printer and select Set as Default. Now, the next time you print a resume, everyone (not just folks from Mars) will be able to read it.

Help! I just attached a USB printer to my computer and it won't print. I used a 10-foot USB cable because the six-foot cable recommended for the printer isn't long enough!

This is a job for (dramatic pause) USB Hub Man! Seriously, what you've encountered is why the printer vendor specified a six-foot cable to begin with. If a USB cable is longer than six feet, it might not carry signals properly between the computer and printer. My favorite solution (as you might have guessed) is to plug a self-powered USB hub into the computer and move it within six feet of the printer, and then plug in a six-foot cable to finish the connection. Take a look at Chapter 19 for a typical hub.

Help! I ran out of toner five minutes after the last office superstore in town closed for the night. My report is due first thing in the morning. Got any ideas?

OK, OK...maybe I overdid the "don't stock up too much" thing. But I never meant that you shouldn't have *any* spares on hand. I'm betting that when you said, "I'm out of toner," that what you *really* meant was this: "My printouts are streaking." That's different. Really.

What happens inside the garden-variety toner cartridge is that streaking takes place after the toner level in part of the cartridge drops below a particular level. You're going to run out soon, but as long as part of the printout still looks OK, you have enough toner for as many as 50 pages if you stop and do the following:

1. Hold or kill any print jobs; open the Printer icon in the system tray to see if any print jobs are running and use the menus there to stop them.

2. Turn off the printer. Laser and LED printers use high-voltage current to operate, and if you don't turn them off before you open them, it could hurt you. *Never* open a printer unless you unplug it first.

3. Take out the toner cartridge.

4. *Gently* swing it from side to side to redistribute the remaining toner.

5. Put it back in the printer.

6. Turn the printer on.

7. Print a test page. If the print quality is acceptable, print the rest of your documents.

8. Buy a replacement toner cartridge (and a backup cartridge) as soon as it's convenient.

Part VII

Upgrading System Stability

Chapter 22

Power Supply Upgrades

The power supply gets no respect. Nobody ever brags to their friends, "Hey, I have 450 watts of stabilized power in my system!" Instead, everybody's busy boasting about who's got the fastest CPU, who has the most RAM, or who has the biggest drive or most hard drives. If you need a tie-breaker, you might even talk about how fast your new rewriteable DVD drive is or check out the latest case mods to figure out who the new champion upgrader is—at least for this week. Most of this book is designed to help you win this bragging contest, but in this chapter we turn our attention to a component that *doesn't* help your system run any faster, doesn't crank out impressive benchmarks, and is practically invisible after you install it. If you read the chapter title, you already guessed—it's the power supply.

Ten Reasons You Might Need a New Power Supply

OK, if a power supply won't help your system run any faster, who needs it? If you find anything on the following list resembles your situation, you do. So, here goes:

1. You turn on the system and nothing happens, and after checking the input voltage, checking for shorts and grounds, and making sure your surge protector is still protecting, nothing happens.

2. The power supply is so hot that you're thinking about using it for a handwarmer next winter.

3. Your computer's locking up—frequently—even after you've checked the memory modules, CPU, and add-on cards for proper connections and cleaned out the gunk inside the case.

4. Your computer decides to take five by resetting itself.

5. You could grow corn and soybeans in rotation on the dirt attached to the power supply fan.

6. Your system's running very poorly since you installed a faster processor.

7. Your USB keyboard and mouse can't be recognized until you unplug and reattach them once or twice.

8. Your system crashes when you try to use your rewriteable CD or any DVD drive.

9. You've just replaced an older motherboard with a motherboard for a Pentium 4 processor.

10. There's smoke coming from the power supply.

Some of these reasons might make perfect sense to you now, while others might seem a bit mysterious. However, read on and you'll discover how a properly chosen power supply can solve all these problems.

Fast Facts About Power Supplies

Why worry about the power supply? Isn't that like figuring out who's got the best car on the basis of how many cup holders are on board? The power supply might not have the sex appeal of faster, bigger hard drives, 3D graphics, 24-bit audio, 3GHz CPUs, and DDR memory, but the power supply is in some ways even more important than the other components people prefer to talk about.

The power supply is so important because it converts that dangerous high-voltage AC power coming out of the wall socket into low-voltage DC current that powers your hard drives, your memory chips, your motherboard, and your CPU. Even though the typical modern PC has several cooling fans inside, the most important cooling fan is still the one inside the power supply.

The power supply can also be at fault when things go wrong with your system. A power supply that does not put out enough power or does not put out high-quality power that meets industry specifications can cause your system to lock up or crash. As our friend Murphy (you know his law) would have it, crashes usually happen at the worst possible time, such as when you're too busy to save.

As you learn in this chapter, power supplies differ according to their shape, their motherboard connections, and their size. In many situations, a power supply upgrade is the hidden element you need to get more reliable performance out of your system. In addition, if you decide that your system needs a new case, you normally get a power supply included with it.

> **READ THIS TOO: Powering Up Your Power Supply Knowledge**
>
> If you're in the market for much more technical detail about power supplies than we have room for in this chapter, pick up a copy of Scott Mueller's *Upgrading and Repairing PCs, 15th Edition* (Que, 2003). Scott provides complete details on all types of power supplies, voltage levels, form factors, testing, and sources.

Selecting the Right Power Supply

Ever tried going to an auto parts store to buy a car battery and have no idea which car it's for? Don't bother! Without details such as the model year and engine size, your search for a battery (or most any other car part) is futile.

Similarly, you need to know what type of power supply your system uses before you can buy a replacement. Power supplies are classified by form factor and wattage.

Form factor is a fancy term that is short for the shape, the size, and the doodads that connect the power supply to the motherboard. After you know the details about your current power supply's form factor, you can purchase a new power supply that will fit in your system.

Here are the three major types of power supplies you're likely to encounter in a system worth upgrading:

- **LPX**—Used with Baby-AT and LPX motherboards and a few early ATX motherboards.
- **ATX**—Used with ATX and NLX motherboards.
- **SFX**—Used with micro-ATX and flex-ATX motherboards.

You can tell them apart by the power supply case dimensions, by whether or not the power supply uses a switch, and by the motherboard connector type.

Shapes

Like everything else, power supplies have changed in shape since the first IBM PC was introduced over twenty years ago (in 1981, if you're curious). The 1980s-style power supply had a side-mounted switch that forced the user to reach to the rear of the machine to turn the system on and off. You could distinguish users of these machines from others because their right arms were longer than their left arms!

When low-cost systems with LPX motherboards were introduced in the late 1980s, a matching LPX power supply was developed. It was also known as the Slimline or PS/2 power supply. Although the connectors are different, ATX power supplies are the same shape as LPX power supplies. Both are 150mm wide and 86mm tall. The SFX-style power supply is much different in size and has two variations:

- Some SFX power supplies feature an external fan (as seen in Figure 22.1) that faces the CPU and helps cool it down.
- Other SFX power supplies have internal fans.

Figure 22.1 compares LPX, ATX, and SFX power supplies.

Switch Locations

The LPX/Slimline power supply uses a front-mounted switch; an extension cable from the power supply brings the switch to the front panel of the computer. Because different case types use different types of switches, you might need to remove the switch from your old power supply to attach it to the new power supply.

> **CAUTION: STOP! LOOK! THINK!**
>
> **It's Alive, It's Alive!**
> Most systems that use LPX/Slimline power supplies are obsolete, but if you find yourself working on one, *never* touch bare metal on the switch while the system is running or plugged in. The switch carries high-voltage AC current and can *kill* you. Be careful!

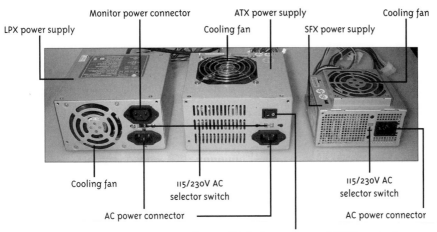

Monitor power connector   ATX power supply   Cooling fan

LPX power supply   Cooling fan   SFX power supply

Figure 22.1

Rear views of LPX (left), ATX (center), and SFX (right) power supplies.

Cooling fan   115/230V AC selector switch   115/230V AC selector switch

AC power connector   AC power connector

Power switch (not present on most ATX PS versions)

ATX and SFX power supplies don't need a switch; the motherboard is cabled to the front-mounted case power switch on the ATX and Micro-ATX systems. The motherboard passes power-on signals to the power supply, but no high-voltage current. Some ATX power supplies use a back-mounted toggle switch (as shown in Figure 22.1); this enables you to completely turn off the system when you service it.

Motherboard Power Connectors

The two major types of motherboard power connectors are:

- **LPX and earlier power supplies for Baby-AT, AT, and PC/XT motherboards that use a twelve-pin interface (two 6-pin connectors from the power supply)**—This provides 5V and 12V DC power, but not the 3.3V levels required by newer systems. Thus, motherboards that use LPX power supplies with 3.3V or lower-voltage processors must have a bulky voltage regulator circuit installed on the motherboard to adjust the voltage as needed.

- **ATX and SFX power supplies for ATX-series and NLX motherboards that use a twenty-pin interface with a single 20-pin connector from the power supply**—This connector provides the extra signals needed for power on/off and 3.3V power levels.

Figure 22.2 compares these two motherboard power connector types.

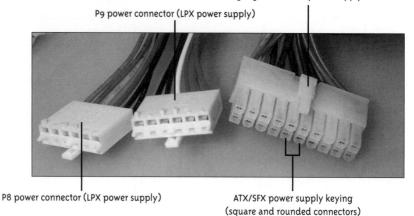

Locking lug on ATX/SFX power supply connector

P9 power connector (LPX power supply)

Figure 22.2

P8 (left) and P9 (middle) power connectors for LPX and earlier power supplies compared to ATX/SFX power connector (right). It's easy to reverse-plug P8 and P9, but doing so can damage or destroy your motherboard and power supply.

P8 power connector (LPX power supply)

ATX/SFX power supply keying (square and rounded connectors)

Power Supply Ratings

How big is your power supply? As you learned in Chapter 4, "Taking an Inspection Tour of Your System," power supplies are rated in watts, just like the light bulbs in any incandescent light fixture. And, just like light bulbs, computers get warm. How big a power supply do you need? The short answer is "it depends"—it depends on what is installed in your system and what you want to add later.

Typical LPX power supplies are 150 to 250 watts; the smaller units are typically found in desktop systems. Typical ATX power supplies are 250 to 450 watts. SFX power supplies top out at just 180 watts because of the small number of devices that can be installed in a micro-ATX or flex-ATX system.

Why Bigger Is Better

A power supply that is connected to devices that require more wattage than what's on board exhibit symptoms like overheating (ouch! I touched the power supply case) or spontaneous rebooting. This is what happens when the system performs a reset all by itself and you find yourself staring at the memory test and wondering where your data went. Spontaneous rebooting takes place when the motherboard's Power Good connection from the power supply is running above or below the correct voltage range.

Note that while power supplies are rated in watts, this is a conversion from the amperage levels used by different devices attached to (or built into) the computer. Each device uses one or more of these power levels:

- +3.3V

- +5V

- +12V

Some devices, such as USB ports, use only +5V, while others, such as an AGP graphics card, use +3.3V and +5V. Others, such as the motherboard, use all three voltage levels. And, as each device uses power, it puts a particular load (known as amperage, or amps) on that power level. To calculate the wattage used by any device, you need to know the voltage used and the amps used by each voltage. You should know that volts × amps=watts. If a device uses two or three voltage levels, add the wattage used by each voltage level to get the total.

One of the hidden dangers in a major system upgrade such as installing a faster processor, more RAM, an AGP video card (in a system that previously used integrated video), or a rewritable DVD or CD-RW drive is that each of these upgrades requires a huge amount of wattage. For example, each 128MB DDR memory module uses 10 watts of power, while a single AMD Athlon XP processor (2100+) can use almost 90 watts of power. A CD-RW drive uses about 16 watts.

ON THE WEB: Tom's Hardware

Tom's Hardware has performed an eye-opening test revealing the high wattage levels required by today's high-performance systems and the many inadequate power supplies on the market. Check it out at http://www6.tomshardware.com/howto/20021021/index.html.

How can you avoid overloading your system? Calculate the wattage used by each component and do some math.

Table 22.1 lists typical wattage requirements for today's most popular components and upgrades. This is a table I used to plan upgrades I performed on my production computer a couple of years ago. When I started, I had a 235-watt power supply. Would it still be big enough to handle the upgrades? Check out Table 22.1 for the details.

Table 22.1   Calculating Power Supply Requirements

	Wattage	Before Upgrade	After Upgrade	Notes
High-wattage AGP card	30	0	18	Will install in place of one PCI card
Typical PCI card	5	25 (5 cards)	20	Will remove one card and replace with AGP
Floppy drive	5	5	5	
10/100 NIC	4	4	4	
50X ATAPI	20	0	20	Additional drive CD-ROM
RAM	10 watts per 128MB	10	40	Replaced 128MB with 512MB
Ultra 2 SCSI PCI card	5	5	5	
IDE hard disk 5400RPM*	11	11	11	
Motherboard	30	30	30	
Athlon	45	18	45	Replaced CPU with faster Athlon
CD-RW	17	0	17	Added 12-10-32
Total wattage used		108	205	
70% of power supply maximum output ($235 \times .7$)		164.5	164.5	
Safety margin (70% of maximum minus total wattage used)	56.5 watts		No safety margin—within 30 watts of maximum	I need a power supply upgrade!

*7200RPM drives use about 15 watts

Before I started to perform the upgrades listed, my system required only 108 watts, a range well within the safe (70% of maximum) load that a 235-watt power supply can handle. According to Tom's Hardware, some power supplies miss their rated wattage by as much as 30%, which is why I like to allow a safety margin. However, the extra wattage consumed by CPU, memory, drive, and AGP card upgrades would drive this system to the edge of failure if the power supply wasn't upgraded first. Before I installed the AGP card and CD-ROM drive, I needed a power supply upgrade.

How big a power supply does this system need? To re-establish a safe computing margin, I needed to buy a power supply big enough to provide at least 205 watts at no more than 70% of its maximum rating, and a larger supply is better. A 300-watt power supply has a 70% rating of 210 watts, which would provide enough power for the rest of my upgrades, but provides no room for expansion. A 400-watt power supply has a 70% rating of 280 watts, which allows plenty of room for further expansion. 400 watts is the size I needed to be safe (and it's the size I wound up installing), even though the system would use only the wattage required for the installed equipment.

CAUTION: STOP! LOOK! THINK!

Run the Numbers Before You Upgrade

You can see that failing to run the numbers before making serious system upgrades is just plain dumb. Ever wonder why some of the upgrades you've made in the past didn't work so well? It could be that you just ran out of power. Check the specs for your equipment to determine the exact wattage rating for each card, memory module, CPU, and drive under the hood. If all you have is an amperage rating, multiply it by 115 (the voltage rating) to get the wattage. If the wattage factors for your existing system plus upgrades pushes past the safety factor, maybe you should upgrade the power supply before you throw a bunch of high-powered, high-wattage stuff under the hood. If you don't have exact values, use the values in Table 22.1 or see the Tom's Hardware report mentioned earlier to estimate your requirements.

How much bigger a power supply do you need? At least 50 watts more than the minimum needed to run everything at 70% capacity, and try to get 100 watts more if you can. The extra capacity doesn't use any more power than a smaller unit (which must be a comfort if you're tired of high utility bills!) and helps avoid system crashes.

Stay Safe—Beyond the Underwriter's Laboratory (UL) Ratings

Believe it or not, you can buy power supplies that aren't even UL rated, but why would you? The Underwriter's Laboratory (UL) rating is an essential *minimum* for choosing safe computer equipment. If you decide to save a few bucks by purchasing a power supply that lacks a UL rating, just remind yourself that the power supply receives fatal levels of AC voltage and is supposed to convert AC to safe, low-voltage DC. Are you *sure* you want to see how well a non-rated power supply does this?

But, it's a huge mistake to assume that every UL-rated power supply is the same. To find the differences between power supplies, look carefully at the (voltage) regulation and hold-time values for a given power supply. A better-quality power supply has lower percentage values for regulation (meaning that voltages varies less) and has a longer *hold time* (the length of time the system can run without AC power while a battery backup switches on).

Table 22.2 shows how a typical economy and premium power supply compare.

As you can see from Table 22.2, a low-cost power supply's power is of poorer quality. Who suffers if your system decides low-quality power isn't good enough? You do! And your equipment (not to mention your data) suffers right along with you. You can normally get this information from the vendor's spec sheet, so it pays to visit the power supply vendor's web site and poke around a bit before you buy a new power supply.

Table 22.2 Power Quality Comparison

	Regulation +3.3V	Regulation +5V +12V	Regulation −5 −12V	Hold Time
Economy power supply	5%	5%	10%	16ms
Premium power supply	1%	5%	5%	20ms

What You Must Know Before You Buy

Before you can buy a power supply, make sure you know the following:

- **Power supply form factor**—LPX, ATX, or SFX, and whether it's the SFX power supply with an external or internal fan.
- **Motherboard connector type**—LPX or ATX.

- **Current wattage rating**—A new power supply should be big enough to provide a safety margin in excess of the 70% maximum load recommended earlier. Go for at least 50 watts more than your original power supply, but buy whatever size you need to provide a safety factor with your current onboard equipment and any future upgrade you have in mind.

- **Special connector types needed**—Some motherboards designed for the Pentium III and Celeron CPUs need a 6-pin auxiliary power connector as well as the standard 20-pin connector. The Pentium 4 requires a special ATX12V connector as well as the standard 20-pin connector. See Figure 22.3 for examples of these connectors.

- **How many drive/device connectors are needed**—It's *much* better to buy a power supply with enough connectors for drives, case fans, and add-on cards that use additional power than to split one power connector into two with a Y-adapter.

If you don't know this information yet, stop and get it first.

Figure 22.3

ATX12V (left) or Aux (right) connectors are needed by systems running recent and current Intel processors.

CAUTION: STOP! LOOK! THINK!

Don't Get "Burned" by the Dell Difference

Be *very* careful if you're upgrading the power supply on a Dell computer built from September 1998 to the present. For some reason, Dell rewired the ATX power supply connector and motherboard power connector on many systems from this date onward; although you can still plug in a standard power supply into a system with the altered design, you'll literally fry it (or your system!) because the voltages are flowing to the wrong pins. Make sure you specify a *Dell-compatible* power supply if you have a Dell system that uses a non-standard power supply.

Wondering if your Dell has a non-standard power supply? Get the specs for your system from Dell's web site at www.dell.com. Dell computers that use a non-standard power supply have *no* 3.3 volt leads in the 20-pin power connector to the motherboard, while normal ATX power supplies have three. PC Power and Cooling (www.pcpowercooling.com) also offers a model-specific lookup for Dell models.

When you order your power supply, you can specify the wattage rating based on your calculations, or you might be able to use an interactive buying guide such as the one available at PC Power and Cooling (www.pcpowerandcooling.com).

ON THE WEB: Teaching an Old Power Supply New Tricks (or Vice-Versa)

Annoyed because your new Pentium 4 CPU wants a 4-pin auxiliary connector your current power supply doesn't have? Ticked off because your aging Baby-AT power supply failed and you're not ready to ditch it for an ATX machine just yet? Don't panic. PC Power and Cooling (www.pcpowerandcooling.com) has both types of adapters. You can make your existing 350-watt or larger power supply work with the P4 with the Pentium 4 ATX12V adapter (about $8). And, if the ATX power supply you buy has a rear-mounted switch, you can teach it to speak "LPX" for use with older systems with the ATX-to-AT conversion cable (also about $8).

CAUTION: STOP! LOOK! THINK!

Don't Touch That Power Supply's Interior!

There are two good reasons that power supplies are labeled "no user serviceable components inside":

- Reason #1: There are *no* user-serviceable components inside.

- Reason #2: The high voltage retained by the internal components can kill you while you search for a component you can fix.

Clear enough? Dead power supplies should be scrapped, not repaired. Buy a new power supply instead of opening up the failed power supply, or the power supply might not be the only thing that winds up dead.

Determining the Old Power Supply Is Dead or Defective

Because loose wires, screws, and defective hardware inside your computer can cause it to stop working and can even prevent it from starting up, you want to make sure your current power supply is dead before you replace it. Here are some tips to help you make sure your power supply is *really* dead:

- Follow the tips in Chapter 3, "Alternatives to Upgrades," for working with a "dead" system.

- Disconnect any Y-splitter cables (the cables that divide a single drive power connector to power two drives) and restart the system.

- Remove each add-on card (one at a time) and restart the system after you remove each card.

- Unplug each drive (one at a time) and restart the system after you unplug each drive.

- If the system starts after you disconnect a cable, card, or drive, that device is defective. I've seen defective PCI VGA cards and hard drives have dead shorts that will stop a system in its tracks.

Another way to determine if a power supply is dead is to attach it to a self-contained power supply tester (see Figure 22.4). If the LED glows, the power supply is working. If the power supply tests OK, but you can't start the computer, the wire leading from the front-mounted switch on an ATX-type system to the motherboard might be loose or connected to the wrong pins. Double-check the switch wire and you might solve your problem.

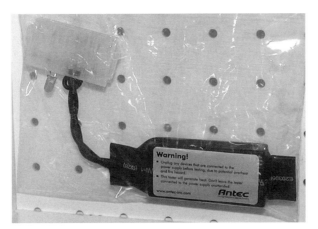

Figure 22.4

Antec, a leading power supply vendor, is one of several companies that produce a self-contained power supply tester like the one pictured here.

If the power supply starts the system, but you have crashes or other substandard behavior, the voltage levels on the power supply might be out of specification. Many recent systems have a BIOS screen that displays motherboard voltage levels and fan speeds (see Figure 22.5). If the voltage is out of specification, replace the power supply.

Figure 22.5

The Hardware Monitor screen in a typical recent BIOS lets you monitor voltage levels and cooling fan performance.

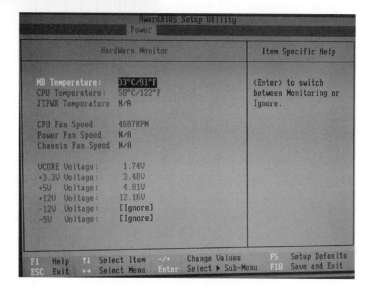

Table 22.3 provides the acceptable voltage levels for +5V and +12V.

Table 22.3   Acceptable +12V/+5V Voltage Levels

Voltage	Minimum	Maximum
+12V	+11.5V	+12.6V
+5V	+4.8V	+5.2V

When we compare these figures to those shown in Figure 22.5, we can see that this power supply is working within specifications.

The Replacement Process

When you've decided it's finally time to replace the power supply, you need to:

1. Purchase a compatible replacement (hopefully with a larger wattage rating).

2. Remove the old unit.

3. Compare the old unit to the new unit to make sure it fits.

4. Insert the new unit.

Now, the details.

ON THE WEB: Power Supply Help at Your Fingertips

The TechTV web site has lots of help for you on power supplies and power issues. Just search for "power supply" and you'll find plenty of articles, tips, and reviews. Go to www.techtv.com to get started.

If you're shopping for a new power supply, you'll find that the very best power supplies on the market are available from PC Power & Cooling, Inc (www.pcpowerandcooling.com).

If you're looking for less-expensive, yet high-quality alternatives, look into power supplies from Antec (www.antec-inc.com) and Enermax (www.enermax.com.tw); power supplies from these vendors have gotten good reviews at The Tech Zone (www.thetechzone.com) and other online extreme hardware review sources and are available from many vendors.

If you're buying a replacement power supply for a system using the AMD Athlon processor, be sure to check AMD's recommendations for power output in its "Builder's Guide," available online at www.amd.com/us-en/assets/content_type/white_papers_and_tech_docs/26003.pdf. (You will need Adobe Acrobat Reader to view this file.)

Out with the Old: Removing the Current Power Supply

Before you can remove the old power supply from your system, you need to:

1. Follow the ESD precautions listed in Chapter 5, "Preparing for Your Upgrade."
2. Unplug the power supply from AC current.
3. Disconnect the power supply from the motherboard.
4. Disconnect the drives from the power supply.
5. Disconnect auxiliary fans (case, CPU, drive bay, and so on) from the power supply.
6. Disconnect auxiliary power connectors on the motherboard.

MARK'S TIP SHEET: Easy Does It When You Disconnect Cables

When you remove the power cables from the motherboard, don't try to yank them straight out of the system. With the ATX/SFX 20-pin connector, squeeze the locking catch and then pull the connector gently upward. To remove the drive's power connectors, hold the drive and wiggle the connector gently one way, then the opposite way to release it. For details of the connectors and sockets, see Figures 22.5 and 22.6. With the LPX-style connectors, gently tug them until each one loosens. If necessary, you might need to lift them out at a slight angle to release plastic teeth from the locking mechanism on the socket.

Always hold the cables by the connectors to avoid strains on the cable.

Follow this procedure to remove the power supply:

1. Remove the side and top panels from the system to expose the power supply (they might slide off as a single unit or in separate pieces).

2. Remove the bolts that hold the power supply to the rear of the system (see Figure 22.6).

3. Slide the power supply toward the center of the system and lift it out of the system (see Figure 22.7).

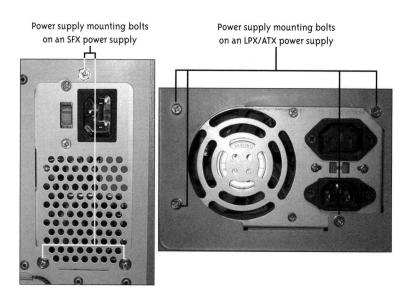

Power supply mounting bolts on an SFX power supply

Power supply mounting bolts on an LPX/ATX power supply

Figure 22.6

Before you can remove the power supply, you must remove the bolts that attach it to the system.

Figure 22.7

After sliding the power supply back into the case, lift it out of the case to remove it.

Installing the New Power Supply

The installation process is the reverse of the removal process:

1. Slide the power supply into the system; you might be able to place it on a tray built into the case or you might need to hold it while you attach the bolts.

2. Line the power supply up with the mounting bolts on the rear of the case.

3. Attach the power supply to the rear of the case; make sure you don't pinch the power or data cables during installation.

4. Attach the motherboard power connector from the new power supply to the mother-board (see Figure 22.8 and Figure 22.9).

5. Attach the drive power leads from the new power supply to the drives, the CPU (if necessary) and auxiliary fans, and any other devices that were connected to the old power supply.

6. Connect any auxiliary power connectors needed by the motherboard.

7. Double-check critical issues such as if the CPU fan is connected to the power supply and not to the motherboard; you can literally burn up today's high-speed CPUs in seconds if you don't have power running to the CPU fan.

8. Take a final look and plug in the AC cord.

9. Turn on the system and watch the monitor for the power-on self-test (POST), memory count, and other symptoms of a properly working power supply.

10. Close up the case only when you're sure it works!

Figure 22.8

Align the ATX/SFX power supply connector (top) so that the locking clip on the connector corresponds with the locking tab on the motherboard connector (bottom) before pushing it into place. The ATX/SFX connector is keyed with a mix of square and notched pins.

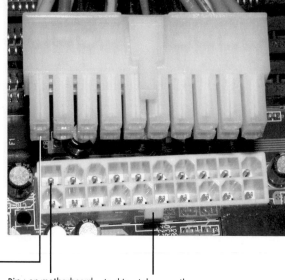

Pin 1 on power supply connector

Pin 1 on motherboard power connector

Locking tab on motherboard power connector

Figure 22.9

Align the black (ground) wires on LPX power supply connectors P9 and P8 to properly attach them to the motherboard. The keying mechanism does *not* prevent reversing the ground wires to the outside.

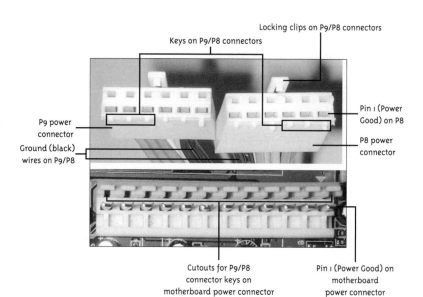

Keys on P9/P8 connectors

Locking clips on P9/P8 connectors

P9 power connector

Ground (black) wires on P9/P8

Pin 1 (Power Good) on P8

P8 power connector

Cutouts for P9/P8 connector keys on motherboard power connector

Pin 1 (Power Good) on motherboard power connector

MARK'S TIP SHEET: Catch Vendor Mistakes Before You Fry Your System

Vendors can (and do) send the wrong items sometimes, no matter how hard you work to describe exactly what you need.

Before you install the new power supply into the case, put the old one beside it and make sure they have the same connector type, are the same shape, and have mounting holes in the same place. If you have a Dell system, make sure you have received a Dell-compatible power supply if your system uses a proprietary model. If you have a problem, return the new power supply and exchange it for the correct type.

The Power Supply Protection Detail

What's the point of spending good money—and maybe spending a not-so-good time—buying and installing a new power supply if you risk losing it—and your system—every time a thunderstorm shows up? If you don't use good power protection equipment, you're risking all that hard work (and all the data you and your PC are making).

You should consider adding the following three types of devices to your system:

- A surge suppressor
- A battery backup unit
- A powerline tester

You should have a high-quality surge suppressor as a *minimum* power-protective device. If you can spare a little more money, give your PC the battery backup unit. This way, you can breath easier the next time the digital clock claims it's midnight at suppertime. To make sure that your home or office has correct wiring, use a powerline tester for a fast, low-cost check.

Surge Suppressor—Telling the Real Ones from the Fakes

A true surge suppressor is a device that can stop power *spikes* (temporary overvoltages) or *surges* (longer-lasting overvoltages) from frying your system. Surge suppressors don't do anything about lower-than-normal voltage levels (brownouts or dips in power); for that, you need a battery backup system. However, temporary power dips are often followed by surges, so your surge suppressor is still useful for protecting your system after the power returns to its normal level.

What's a fake surge protector? A multiple outlet unit that has no UL rating, or has only a *transient power tap* rating, even if the package calls it a surge protector. Don't be fooled! There are only two ratings that mean anything when it comes to stopping the overvoltages and power spikes that can kill your equipment:

- UL 1449 rating of 400V AC or less (lower is better)
- IEEE 587A let-through voltage rating of 100V or less

These standards measure surges differently, so don't panic over the differences between 400V and 100V—*unless* somebody bets you that electrocution isn't fatal. Trust me, it can be, so put down that bare wire. However, as far as your PC is concerned, if you can reduce a power spike that might have been thousands of volts down to a mere 400V or less, the power supply can handle the remaining excess voltage all by itself.

Several vendors make very good surge suppressors, including:

- Tripp-Lite (I've used their Isobar and Isotel series for years); `www.tripp-lite.com`
- APC; `www.apc.com`
- Belkin; `www.belkin.com`

These companies also make battery backup units, the second phase of system protection.

Nothing Lives Forever—Not Even Battery Backups

Battery backup units (also known as UPS for Uninterruptible Power Supply or SPS for Standby Power Supply) are now inexpensive enough for home and small-office use. PC users in California and anywhere else where power interruptions occur without warning already know how useful these devices can be. For the rest of us whose power (usually) stays on, here's how they work:

1. A small battery is charged by the power converter in the UPS system.
2. The UPS passes AC power through to the PC and watches for a power outage.
3. When/if the power goes out (I'm a pessimist, so let's say "when"), the UPS switches over to battery power and sounds an alarm to tell the user that it's time to shut down the system and call it a day (or a night). UPS systems equipped with serial ports or USB connections to your system and monitoring software can automatically shut down your system if you're not around. They then send a message though the network to all users, telling them to save their files and shut down before the battery runs out.

CAUTION: STOP! LOOK! THINK!

A Plague on Cheap Surge Protectors!

If you don't keep cheap surge protectors out of your home and office, they could plague you with catastrophic system damage.

I like to use the following criteria for choosing a surge protector:

- **High joule rating**—This is a measure of energy absorbed by the surge suppressor; the higher, the better.

- **Power filtration**—Some devices cause interference that can degrade the power signals and cause others to fail. Surge suppressors that provide separate filtered circuits help eliminate this problem.

- **Data line protection**—Every summer, computer retailers see sad-eyed people coming in to pick up a replacement estimate for their computer. Lots of them had surge suppressors, but their telephone lines weren't protected.

  Data line protection can now include RJ-45 (network/broadband Internet) and cable TV/cable modem (RG6 coaxial), as well as RJ-11 telephone. You can find surge suppressors for all types of data lines.

- **Protection indicator**—Many surge suppressors use a component called a *MOV* (*metal oxide varistor*) to stop surges. They eventually wear out. Better units use other types of devices to stop surges; but in any event, you want your unit to tell you when it needs to be retired. Some units are now designed to shut down and provide no power when their suppression capacity is exhausted. This is a feature worth looking for.

- **Wiring fault indicator**—A lot of homes and offices have incorrect wiring, and this can lead to computer crashes, lockups, and even equipment damage. Surge suppressors with these signal lights can tell you about ground or polarity problems before they hose your equipment.

- **Built-in GFI circuit**—Ground-fault indicator outlets (the ones with the test button) are commonly used in bathrooms and kitchens to prevent deadly short circuits. Some surge suppressors now have built-in GFI features to

It's important to remember that the typical run time for a UPS is only ten or fifteen minutes, a figure that varies according to the size of the battery and the drain imposed by the computers and accessories that use the battery.

To avoid premature rundown, plug only the CPU and monitor into the battery backup. Printers, especially laser printers, suck the life out of the battery very quickly. External drives, on the other hand, should be connected to the battery backup system *if* they are used for system backups.

Battery backup systems include their own surge suppression features to protect the CPU and the monitor, but printers and other equipment that aren't connected to the battery backup still need to be plugged into their own high-quality surge suppressors.

MARK'S TIP SHEET: Getting Your UPS Just Right

Most companies that sell UPS systems offer an interactive sizing and selection tool on their web sites. The process goes faster if you first make notes of the following:

- The current wattage requirement of your PC and monitor
- What operating system your PCs are using
- What network operating system (if any) your PCs are using
- Whether the PCs have serial or USB ports
- The amount of runtime you need to shut down your systems

Portable Particulars

If you fry the power supply in your notebook computer, you're either looking at a trip to the repair shop or a new unit; notebook power supplies aren't a user-replaceable item. Thus, it's even more important to keep from frying your portable's power supply.

To keep out of trouble, make sure you do the following:

- **Use an international (multi-voltage) power adapter if you travel outside North America**—If your adapter says 90~230V AC, it's got the right stuff to be happy anywhere you can plug it in. If not, buy one.

- **Switching power plugs doesn't switch voltage**—You can get adapter kits to change North American plugs into the wide variety of AC power connectors used around the world, but unless you can also adjust the incoming voltage, you'll fry your PC.

- **Your notebook computer needs surge suppression, too!**—However, you don't need to carry around a bulky unit if you're on the road a lot. Several companies carry small units perfect for the traveler, including RJ-11 phone line protection. You can also get an adapter for the wide variety of connectors used overseas.

Troubleshooting Power Problems

Power problems aren't fun, but is any PC problem fun? No, but at least you can use your PC to research other kinds of problems. However, if you can't get your PC to boot up, you're out of luck (at least until you can hot-wire your abacus). Use these tips to keep your power powerful and your voltage vital.

Help! I didn't get enough drive power connectors with my new power supply!

Before you toss the old power supply into the trash, make sure you've removed any Y-connectors for drives from the drive power leads. If you're still a couple short, buy some at the store. It's best to buy a power supply that has enough built in already. I've seen poorly made Y-adapters cause shorts that brought systems to a halt. If the wires on an adapter are thinner than the wires on the power supply, skip that one and look for an adapter with wires that are the same gauge as those used by the power supply.

Help! My motherboard can use either LPX or ATX power supplies. Which one should I buy?

Living in the past is never a good idea—especially when it comes to computers. Go for the ATX power supply and don't look back. As you saw earlier in this chapter, ATX provides a wider voltage range and is easier to install correctly. Since most of the systems I've seen with dual power connectors are pretty old at this point, ask yourself if this system is worth a new power supply.

Help! I'm concerned about my Dell system. How do I tell if it needs a Dell-specific or generic power supply?

Although some vendors offer listings of which models use the Dell-proprietary ATX power supply, it's always best to look at your specific system. Check Dell's web site (www.dell.com) and look up the technical overview for your system or open your system and look at the power supply wiring. Look in particular at the DC power connector detail. A standard 20-pin ATX/SFX power supply connector has orange wires for 3.3V power at pins 1, 2, and 11 and a gray power good line at pin 8. A Dell proprietary system's 20-pin connector has only one orange wire—pin 5 (Power Good)—and has no 3.3V power leads. No wonder mixing up a Dell motherboard or power supply with a standard device causes smoke!

Chapter 23

Winning Windows Upgrades

No matter how fast, how powerful, or how cool your system will be after you install the upgrades this book has helped you plan, those upgrades are nothing but a pile of circuit boards, metal, and plastic without an operating system (OS).

Your computer's OS is far more than the desktop you see when you boot your computer. It's the über-software, the program of programs, the big kahuna; simply put, it's the program that tells every other part of your computer what to do and when. Because the OS is intimately involved in the control of both your application software and your hardware, any realistic decision about whether you can install a particular upgrade must include taking a good hard look at how well your OS supports that hardware. You should also consider whether an OS upgrade will better prepare your system for new hardware.

You have three choices when it comes to OS upgrades:

- Get Redmond's latest (Windows XP)
- Stick with what you have (older versions of Windows)
- Try the penguin (some distro of Linux)

What's the best move, and how do you upgrade if you decide that now is the time? Let's find out.

Ten Reasons to Upgrade to a New Operating System

If you're wondering whether a new OS should be part of your upgrade plans, see if you recognize your situation in this checklist. If you do, it's time to make a move.

- You'd like your OS to recognize at least *some* of your hardware without resorting to driver disks.
- You want support for the latest 3D audio and graphics hardware.
- The Ctrl-Alt-Del keys on your keyboard are wearing out from bringing up the Task Manager to shut down a malfunctioning program.
- You reboot your computer so often that you've made it a part of your break and lunchtime routine.
- You're considering wireless networking.
- The software you'd like to try prefers (or demands) a newer version of Windows than the one you're using.
- Your hard disk has ten gigabytes or more of empty space just waiting for something useful to do.
- You want to manage your hardware better.
- You want better networking features.
- You want more control over your storage.

Should You Keep Your Current Operating System?

Even if you might have found an uncanny resemblance between your situation and some of the reasons to switch, you might be saying to yourself, "I just don't want to spend the money." I understand what you're saying. Maybe you don't need to upgrade—but maybe you do. To help you decide, it might help to review the features of pre-XP versions of Windows.

The Weakest Links—Obsolete Versions of Windows

If you're still using Windows 95, it's long since past time to give it up. It was already outdated a couple of years ago, and its lack of support for AGP video, USB, and lots of other goodies you want to add to your system make replacing it a no-brainer. Frankly, you should seriously consider upgrading any computer that's still running Windows 95.

Windows NT 4.0 looks like Windows 95, but it is really a distant ancestor of Windows XP. Windows NT 4.0 is as limited as Windows 95 in its support for the hot new hardware technologies you want (and need), although computers running Windows NT 4.0 are still showing up in schools and libraries courtesy of the Bill and Melinda Gates Foundation.

Windows 98 Clings to Life—For Now

Officially, Windows 98 is obsolete, but, in the immortal words of the Monty Python troupe, it "ain't dead yet!," especially if you want to play DOS and designed-for-Windows 9x (Windows 95/98-compatible) games. Windows 98 supports MS-DOS mode and direct booting to the MS-DOS prompt, making it better for DOS apps and games than Windows XP. Although Windows XP has a Program Compatibility Wizard to help run older software in a pseudo-Windows 98 environment, the real thing is always better if your software is particular about wanting the older version.

Until Windows XP was released, Windows 98 was the best small-business/home version of Windows around. Windows XP Home and Professional have better networking features and greater stability, but there are likely to be some Windows 9x games you might have a hard time running with XP, even with its Program Compatibility Wizard. The solution? When you install Windows XP, install it to a different partition on the hard disk so that you can choose which Windows to run when you start your computer.

Which Windows XP should you select if you want to move up from Windows 98? Choose Windows XP Professional if you use the third-party network drivers or connect to corporate networks that are running Windows 98. Choose either version if you use TCP/IP (Internet) networking only.

Eventually, Microsoft will stop supporting Windows 98, but in the meantime, if you have it and enjoy how it plays your games, keep it around.

Windows Me? Maybe for Thee, But Not for Me

Even though I helped Ed Bott with his *Special Edition: Using Windows Me* book (Que, 2001), I've never been a fan of Windows Me. Essentially, Windows Me is like a dumbed-down version of Windows 98 with DOS support removed and some new features added. Anything Windows Me can do, Windows XP (either version) can do better. In fact, some favorite Windows XP features such as System Restore, My Pictures slideshow folder, the Camera and Scanner Wizard, Windows Movie Maker, and the enhanced Windows Media Player are updated versions of utilities originally developed for Windows Me.

Choosing Your Next Operating System

Should you upgrade your OS before you install new hardware? It depends on the hardware—and the version of Windows you have now. Instead of mindlessly rushing out and buying the newest Windows version, you should find out exactly what benefits you get out of any particular Windows version *before* you rush out the door. This information might make you decide to stay put for a while, or might send you to your favorite computer emporium.

From an upgrader's perspective, there are four major reasons for buying a particular Windows version:

- Enhanced hardware support for existing and *new kinds* of hardware
- New features you really need
- Better system stability
- Support for new and improved software

If your current OS falls short in any one of these areas, it's time to shop for a new one.

Enhancing Support for New Hardware with Windows Upgrades

From hard disks to USB ports, different versions of Windows support hardware in different ways. As the following sections show, the newest versions of Windows provide the best and most seamless support for the newest hardware technologies.

Hard Disk Support the Windows Way

One of the most common computer upgrades, as you've already seen in Chapter 10, "Adding a Huge Hard Disk," is the hard disk. In addition, hard disk support is one of the clearest differences you can see between different Windows versions.

Table 23.1 compares hard drive support features among Windows 95, Windows 95B (OSR 2.x), Windows 98, Windows Me, and Windows XP.

Table 23.1	Windows Hard Drive Support Features				
Feature	Windows 95	Windows 95B	Windows 98	Windows Me	Windows XP
FAT32 (supports drive letters over 2GB)	No	Yes	Yes	Yes	Yes
FAT16 to FAT32 converter	N/A	No	Yes	Yes	Yes
Drives over 32GB	No	No	Yes	Yes	Yes
NTFS support	No	No	No	No	Yes

You're probably the king of cheapskates if you're still using Windows 95 on a computer you plan to upgrade. Give it up, already! As you can see from Table 23.1, Windows 95 chokes on hard drives over 32GB in size. It's time to move up. In addition, if you think you're fine if you're running Windows 98 or Windows Me, think again if you share a computer. The New Technology File System (NTFS) used by Windows XP is a much more robust file system than what Windows 9x/Me uses. If you choose Windows XP Professional, you can also encrypt files to keep them from being read by snoopers.

Go to the Head of the (New Hardware) Class

Need support for newer types of hardware than your system recognizes? It's time for an upgrade. Table 23.2 compares how the same versions of Windows support new types of hardware.

Table 23.2   Windows New Hardware Support Features

Feature	Windows 95	Windows 95B	Windows 98	Windows Me	Windows XP
USB 1.1	No	Yes*	Yes	Yes	Yes
IEEE-1394	No	No	Yes^	Yes	Yes
AGP	No	No	Yes	Yes	Yes
ACPI	No	No	Yes	Yes	Yes
DVD	No	No	Yes	Yes	Yes
USB keychain storage	No	No	Yes#	Yes	Yes
USB 2.0	No	No	Yes^	Yes	Yes

*Some late releases include USB drivers, but many USB devices require Windows 98 or above.

^Some products support only Windows 98 Second Edition.

#User must install drivers for USB storage devices.

Table 23.2 contains the newest, most exciting hardware developments of the last few years. Although the original USB 1.1 port has become a basic utility player with support for mice, keyboards, printers, and external floppy and Zip drives, its faster sibling, USB 2.0, is a super-star able to support high-speed external hard disks and CD/DVD burners. IEEE-1394 is the high-bandwidth rival to USB, providing a direct connection to DV camcorders as well as a fast interface for high-performance mobile disk storage and a high-speed connection to other PCs. AGP has helped 3D video become amazingly realistic by supporting high-speed frame rates and huge amounts of data on today's larger screens. ACPI provides interactive, all-encompassing power and peripheral management where users prefer to have it, within Windows. DVD support puts classic and brand-new movies on your desktop.

These new types of hardware all have one thing in common: Windows 95 can't handle them (with the exception of the poor and incomplete USB 1.1 support in late releases of Windows 95B).

Note that the level of support varies with the OS that you are using. Windows 98 can use these technologies, but only Windows 98SE and above fully support hot-plugging of USB and IEEE-1394 devices. In addition, although Windows XP can support most of these tech-nologies without installing additional drivers, earlier versions of Windows make you reach for the driver disk or CD before your new devices can get going. If you want to take full advantage of these types of hardware, again, a Windows upgrade might be in order.

CAUTION: STOP! LOOK! THINK!

Don't Upgrade the Hardware Before the Operating System
If you decide you need a new OS and your hard disk is large enough, make it upgrade priority #1! If the new OS isn't present when new hardware shows up, the hardware's installation won't be handled correctly. If you upgrade to Windows XP, its built-in drivers handle most newer types of hardware, making hardware upgrades very simple.

OS Upgrades Bring New Features

The most recent versions of Windows include so many new features that it would be difficult to do justice to all of them. Thus, in the comparison in Table 23.3, I've selected features that make the most difference to the upgrade-minded user in terms of system safety, networking, and AV support.

Table 23.3   Windows Feature Comparison

Feature	Windows 95	Windows 95B	Windows 98	Windows Me	Windows XP
Backup supporting most disk/tape devices	No	No	Yes	Yes	Yes
Automatic Registry backup	Limited	Limited	Yes	Yes	*
Automatic Registry repair	No	No	Yes	Yes	No
System Restore	No	No	No	Yes	Yes
Internet Connection Sharing	No	No	Yes^	Yes	Yes
Home Networking Wizard	No	No	No	Yes	Yes
Digital Camera and Scanner Wizard	No	No	No	Yes	Yes
DV editor	No	No	No	Yes	Yes
Multiple monitor support	No	No	Yes	Yes	Yes
Integrated CD-RW support	No	No	No	No	Yes
Auto detection of Wi-Fi networks	No	No	No	No	Yes

*Via System Restore Feature
^Windows 98SE only

As you can see from Table 23.3, Windows 98 and Windows Me clearly provide more safety features than Windows 95, but Windows XP beats them all. However, when it comes to home networking and AV features, Windows Me is better than Windows 98, and Windows XP is the best of all. In addition, Windows XP Professional, followed by Windows 98/98SE, is better than Windows Me for business networking.

As these comparisons make clear, a Windows upgrade provides enhanced hardware support, support for new types of hardware, and new features. These factors add up to a compelling case for a Windows upgrade, especially if you are still using Windows 95.

Operating System Upgrades for System Stability

I hate rebooting my computer, and I bet you do too. No matter how fast your hardware, rebooting your computer takes a few minutes out of your computing life and breaks up your work (or play). Let's face it: If you're not installing new hardware or a service pack, the only other reason to reboot a computer running Windows 9x/Me is because it's out of resources. These versions of Windows have a limited ability to track open windows and graphical objects such as icons, menu buttons and so on. The longer you run them, the lower the level of free system resources. Eventually, everything crashes (taking your next Great American Novel chapter or death match victory with it) unless you reboot your computer first.

If you're tired of rebooting your computer two or even three times a day, moving up to the latest Microsoft version (Windows XP) helps cure this problem because it's built on Windows NT/2000 technology, which can handle lots of open windows.

Operating System Upgrades to Support New Software

Even if support for better hardware and better stability haven't convinced you to upgrade your version of Windows yet, the next software purchase you make might be the factor that makes an upgrade a necessity.

Windows 95 is no longer supported by most new Windows business and utility programs, and the original version of Windows 98 isn't far behind. For right now, most Windows applications still work with Windows 98SE and newer versions, but if you're using older versions, be sure to check the operating system required for a particular software program before you buy it.

Keeping Your Current Version, Even If You Upgrade

After reviewing the previous sections, you might be ready to conclude that there's never a reason to turn down a Windows upgrade. However, you'd be wrong. If the OS installed in a particular system supports your hardware and you're satisfied with how it works, install the service packs suggested, but there's no need to upgrade.

However, if you want to keep your existing OS because it's good at playing games (Windows 98 is saying, "You talking about me?"), but you want to install a newer version because it's better for work (Windows XP gives a nod of recognition), you can do that too. Just be sure to have enough empty disk space available for the new OS, and install it as a dual-boot configuration.

XP's the One—But Which XP Is for You?

Windows XP ends the war between the "Windows is Fun!" fans (who like the game and multimedia support of Windows 9x/Me) and "Windows is Useful!" advocates (those white-coat IT guys who prefer Windows NT 4.0 and Windows 2000). Windows XP is a cross between the two distinctly different kinds of Windows, and it's designed to combine the fun of Windows 9x/Me with the stability of Windows NT and Windows 2000.

ON THE WEB: TechTV's Take on Windows XP

Check out our Windows XP Guide at `www.techtv.com/screensavers/supergeek/ story/0,24330,3337963,00.html` for fast access to news, reviews, and tips.

What about existing hardware and software? Microsoft has taken compatibility issues seriously in XP, including a compatibility mode feature that enables you to make XP pretend to be Windows 98, Windows NT 4.0, Windows 2000, or Windows 95 when you run a specified software title. In addition, although XP signals the death of DOS even more thoroughly than Windows Me did, Microsoft supports DOS gaming under XP, including SoundBlaster-compatible sound in a DOS box. If you're concerned about old game support under Windows XP, remember that you can always install it as a dual-boot operating system with your current version of Windows.

If you're not using Windows XP now, it's the logical upgrade if your current Windows version isn't stable enough or supportive enough of the latest technologies to satisfy you. Of course, that's not as easy a choice as it sounds. You have two versions of Windows XP you can buy:

- Windows XP Home Edition
- Windows XP Professional

To complicate matters, there are three different ways to buy each version:

- The cheap way
- The bundled way
- The expensive way

What's the difference? In the following sections, I'll help you figure out which options are best for you.

ANALYZE THIS

Buy a New PC to Get These Windows XP Versions

There are actually four different versions of Windows XP made for 32-bit processors such as the Pentium 4 and AMD Athlon XP, but two of them, Windows XP Media Center Edition and Windows XP Tablet PC Edition, are specially designed versions that are sold only with matching hardware. A Media Center Edition PC has multimedia and digital imaging hardware onboard (TV tuner, flash memory card reader, DVD drive, and so on), and a Tablet PC uses a stylus for data entry (although some models also have a keyboard).

There is also a 64-bit version of Windows XP made for (and sold with) systems that use the Intel Itanium processor for servers.

XP Home or XP Professional: Decisions, Decisions!

The choice between Windows XP Home and Windows XP Professional actually boils down to just two factors: money and office networking support. Unlike previous Windows choices (Windows 95 versus Windows NT 4.0, Windows 98 or Windows Me versus Windows 2000), choosing between the XP twins does *not* involve choosing between versions optimized for fun (9x/Me) or work (NT 4.0/2000). Both versions of Windows XP have a full boatload of fun and useful features, including the following:

- Scanner and Camera Wizard

- Windows Media Player

- Windows Movie Maker

- Unified Network Setup Wizard for dial-up, broadband, and home networking

- Windows Messenger

- Portable computer enhancements, such as DualView, ClearType antialiasing, and improved power management

- Enhanced drive and system management

- Automatic wireless Ethernet (Wi-Fi) configuration

- Internet connection firewall

- Internet Explorer 6.0

- Program Compatibility Manager (helps older programs run under Windows XP)

- Support for hyper-threading with Pentium 4 processors

So, what's the difference? Windows XP Professional adds the following major features to the common features of both products:

- Remote Desktop lets you access your desktop and run your PC from any other Windows-based PC

- Support for Windows NT/2000/2003 Server domain controllers and third-party networks such as Novell NetWare

- File and folder encryption

- File and folder access restrictions on a user-by-user basis

- Built-in, ten-user Internet Information Services (IIS) web server

- Multiple-processor support

- Multiple-language support

- Really useful Help and Support system, with fast access to both on-disk and online help resources

Essentially, Windows XP Professional is Windows XP Home Edition dressed up and ready to go to work. If you're considering a dual-processor motherboard, want remote support options, or think your computer might be venturing onto a corporate network, XP Professional is the better choice.

CAUTION: STOP! LOOK! THINK!

Checking Out Your System Before the Upgrade

Because Windows XP is a big departure from Windows 9x/Me, you should make sure your system and software can run Windows XP before you buy it. Download the Upgrade Advisor from `www.microsoft.com/windowsxp/home/howtobuy/upgrading/advisor.asp` to find out.

Unfortunately, the upgrade advisor is a hefty 50MB download. If you don't have a broadband connection, be prepared to spend some time downloading it, or check with your hardware and software vendors for compatibility information, patches and updated drivers needed for Windows XP.

The Upgrade Advisor also runs as part of the Windows XP installation process, but it's better for you to find out early if your hardware and software are ready for Windows XP.

If you've verified that your computer can run Windows XP, there's still the question of which version to buy.

The Cheap Way—Windows Upgrade Versions

The cheap way is to buy a Windows upgrade. The Windows upgrade is sold at retail stores and is less expensive than the full version. When you purchase this version, you also qualify for telephone support, which includes unlimited installation help and two incidents after Windows XP is installed. The major complaint about upgrade versions is that you need to provide proof of ownership of the previous version to install it onto an empty drive. Thus, don't make a Frisbee™ out of your old Windows CD or give it away. Sooner or later, you'll probably want to wipe out your drive and start over, and when you do, the upgrade version will prompt you for the old CD. By the same token, though, the upgrade version is designed to install over your previous version or into a separate partition so that you can run your choice of versions in a dual-boot configuration.

You can't upgrade Windows 95 or older versions or any server or evaluation version of Windows with a Windows XP upgrade CD. You can upgrade Windows 98, Windows 98SE, or Windows Me to Windows XP Home or Professional, but Windows NT 4.0 and Windows 2000 can be upgraded only to Windows XP Professional. Windows XP Home Edition can also be upgraded to Windows XP Professional.

The bottom line? Upgrade versions are designed to upgrade your system. If that's what you want to do—an upgrade version is the version for you.

The Bundled Way—Do-It-Yourself OEM Support

If you want a fresh start with Windows XP and don't mind shopping for a little bit of hardware, you can save a bit of money and get an OEM version of Windows XP.

Until recently, you would also get an OEM edition when you purchased a new computer,

JARGON

OEM—Original Equipment Manufacturer. An OEM version of Windows is intended for use as part of a new computer system.

but most computer vendors now supply only a crippled restore CD, or might just put the Windows .cab (compressed archive) files on a different partition of the hard disk.

ANALYZE THIS

Why I Hate Recovery CDs

I've hated recovery CDs since 1995 when companies like IBM first began to provide Windows 95 recovery CDs with their systems. My feelings haven't changed a bit, even though systems now come with newer versions of Windows, because the recovery CDs are now omnipresent and work the same irritating way.

The essential problem with the recovery CD business is that you no longer control the operating system; it controls you. The early versions of the recovery CDs had just one option: blow away your system and start over. I've often done the same thing myself. However, when I do it with either an upgrade or OEM version of Windows, the system might have different components on board (such as a new motherboard). Windows detects the new components and all is well.

On the other hand, if you use the system recovery CD, the system recovery rolls you back to the *original factory configuration* with a complete disregard for any new equipment on board. How bad can this be? An HP Pavilion system I had until recently had two Linksys network cards on board and an Adaptec SCSI host adapter in place of its original 56Kbps modem. The computer could not complete a system recovery until all three cards were removed from the system! Then, and only then, would the recovery process work. The cards had to be reinstalled after the recovery process was complete.

Give me a "real" version of Windows anytime. Basically, the system recovery versions (even the ones that refresh your configuration as opposed to nuking it) are worthless. If you're stuck in this situation, buy a CD-RW drive and a copy of Drive Image or Norton Ghost. Then, make your own recovery CD with what you have installed *now*. Make a new one whenever your hardware or installed programs change.

And, while you're at it, consider picking up an OEM or upgrade version of Windows that matches the Windows version you have installed so that you have complete freedom to work with your system.

If you've decided to buy a new PC (instead of souping up your old one) and are using this book to help you customize your new purchase, be sure to ask about the full Windows CD versus recovery CD issue before you pony up your plastic to make the purchase. Some users report that you might get a full Windows XP CD if you purchase the computer for business use rather than as a home computer. To find out, contact the vendor's corporate or business sales department or web page rather than the one for home users.

If you're creating a brand-new PC from components, you can buy a full OEM version of Windows. However, you need to shop at a local or online computer component stores, not your friendly appliance or office supplies/computer store.

If you want to buy an OEM version of Windows, you are required to buy hardware along with the OEM Windows product. Fortunately, the definition of hardware has also changed, and for the better. It used to be that you had to buy a motherboard or hard drive as a qualifying purchase; now, however, any (and I mean *any*) hardware will do. For example, Tiger Direct sells Windows XP Home and Professional OEM versions bundled with a CD-ROM audio cable. Although XP Home OEM is about the same price as the upgrade version, XP Professional OEM is about $30 cheaper than the upgrade version.

What are the benefits of an OEM version of Windows?

- **Install it on any system, any configuration**—Unlike the crippled recovery CD versions now supplied with most new computers, a full OEM version is like the upgrade version in its ability to be installed on a bare system with any configuration.

- **Lower pricing than retail full versions**—OEM full versions sell for prices comparable to or even lower than retail upgrade versions, a savings of as much as 50 percent off retail full-version pricing.

MARK'S TIP SHEET: On the Track of the Elusive OEM Version

Check out these sources for your hardware plus OEM version purchase of Windows XP:

- **Insight Components (formerly TC Computers)**—
  www.insightcomponents.com

- **Thompson Computer Warehouse**—www.tcwo.com

- **TigerDirect**—www.tigerdirect.com

Before you start salivating at the idea of saving some money, keep these potential drawbacks to the OEM version in mind:

- **OEM versions aren't designed as upgrade versions**—You can't use them as an upgrade version because the OEM version does a compliance check; if it finds an existing version of Windows, it stops the installation process. If you need to upgrade an older version of Windows, buy the upgrade version.

- **The OEM system manufacturer (you) is responsible for support**—OEM versions are cheaper because Microsoft isn't responsible for supporting the product. However, if you are comfortable with using the online Help and Support system rather than calling Redmond, Washington, doing without the ability to call Microsoft probably isn't a big deal.

CAUTION: STOP! LOOK! THINK!

Don't Throw Away Your Serial Number!

Retail Microsoft products put the serial number on the sleeve or jewel case containing the software. OEM software is different. Originally, the *Certificate of Authenticity (COA)* listing the serial number was shrinkwrapped inside the packet containing your Windows CD and OEM manual.

Microsoft now puts the COA on the *outside* of the packaging on the shrinkwrap itself. Don't throw away the shrinkwrap until you see whether the COA is there or inside the package. Remember—no COA, no install for you!

The bottom line is this: If you're building your own system or need a spare copy of Windows to support a system with one of those useless System Recovery CDs, this is the way to go.

The Expensive (But Flexible) Way—Full Retail Versions

If you need a Windows product that...

- Can be installed on any system configuration
- Does *not* require proof of previous ownership
- Can be installed either on a bare system or as an upgrade
- Makes you eligible for Microsoft telephone support (unlimited help with installation and up to two post-installation incidents)

...then you should buy the full retail version of Windows. Not surprisingly, the full retail version of Windows XP costs about twice what the typical upgrade costs. The bottom line is this: If you're really not sure what to do with Windows, this version lets you do it all.

Think Twice About the Penguin (Linux)

Although software and OS prices in real dollars are much lower than in the late 1980s (when a single office application, not a suite, cost $500!), outfitting your upgraded computer with a new operating system, office suite, graphic applications, and so forth can add several hundred dollars to the real cost of an upgrade if you stick with Windows and Windows-based applications.

If you're concerned about dollars and cents (and making sense of a tight budget), you might consider adding Linux to your system. If you have a broadband connection, you can download most of the popular distros (Linux-speak for versions such as Mandrake, SuSE, RedHat, and so forth) for free, or you can buy boxed versions that include a boatload of software for $30–$130, depending upon distro and included software.

ON THE WEB: Linux Online

TechTV puts the essential information about Linux together on its Linux Guide page at www.techtv.com/screensavers/linux/.

Other useful sites include the following:

- **JustLinux (www.justlinux.com)**—A site designed for those who "wanna learn Linux."

- **DistroWatch (www.distrowatch.com)**—Get the latest information about the many distros of Linux.

- **LinuxToday (http://linuxtoday.com)**—A categorized digest of Linux news.

- **The Linux Documentation Project (www.tldp.org)**—Your one-stop source for FAQs, how-tos, and guides to Linux.

Check them out before you get started.

Why is Linux (and Linux software) so inexpensive? It's based on a concept called "open source," which works like this: Developer A creates a program, which he can distribute. However, unlike conventional software, in which Developer B is sued (and put of out business) if she modifies Developer A's program, the open source concept permits her to modify Developer A's program *and* distribute it. Developer C (and Developer A) can build more improvements onto Developer B's work, and so forth.

> **ON THE WEB: Open Source Is Open for Your Inspection**
>
> Learn more about how open source works from the Open Source Initiative web site at
> www.opensource.org/.

If you decide to give a Linux distro a try, you need to realize that the world of Linux is much different than the world of Microsoft Windows, particularly when it comes to the following issues:

- **Where to get support**—Although the distro developer's web site will offer some answers, plan to spend time searching the web for the tougher problems you might encounter.

- **Where to get software drivers**—Although Linux is climbing in popularity, most hardware developers don't offer "official" drivers for Linux. Some offer links to third-party drivers, but in many cases, you will use a combination of the distro's bundled drivers and web searches to track down what you need.

- **Where to get applications**—There is no "one-stop shop" vendor for Linux applications as there is with Windows (can you say Microsoft?). Instead, think of Linux as the "anti-Microsoft," with lots of software from lots of vendors. However, if you choose one of the deluxe packaged distros, you won't need to spend hours downloading to get the programs you need because a lot of the top Linux programs are included on the distro CDs.

You need to be comfortable with the freedom and the extra responsibility of the Linux world to make using it a success.

One adjustment you *won't* need to make is how to run Linux. The days of Linux being strictly a mysterious command-line OS (think DOS with goofier program names) is long gone, thanks to the development of two graphical user environments (GUIs): GNOME and the K Desktop Environment (KDE). You still need to do some typing in a command window to run some types of procedures, but these GUIs provide you with a familiar environment for launching programs and managing files.

> **ON THE WEB: Getting the Latest Info on Linux GUIs**
>
> Get the latest information about GNOME at www.gnome.org.
>
> The latest KDE info is available at www.kde.org.

With easier installation than ever before and more choices in low-cost and free software than ever before, it might be time for you to try Linux. Because most games don't run under Linux unless you use a Windows emulator such as TransGamer (www.transgaming.com), I recommend you don't make Linux your sole operating system. Instead, use the boot managers available with most recent distros to configure your system so that you can launch the OS you prefer for a particular task when you start your computer.

ON THE WEB: Distro Central

Get the latest information and pricing for the leading Linux distros for home and small-office use direct from these official web sites:

- **Lindows**—www.lindows.com
- **Lycoris**—www.lycoris.com
- **Mandrake**—www.mandrakelinux.com
- **Red Hat**—www.redhat.com
- **SuSE**—www.suse.com
- **Xandros**—www.xandros.com

As you consider various distros, keep in mind that if your entire hard disk is occupied by Windows, you will need to do the following:

- Shrink the size of your Windows partition(s) with a tool such as Partition Magic (www.powerquest.com) or select a distro with its own partition-sizing tool.

- Install a larger hard disk and leave a portion of it unpartitioned so that it can be used by Linux.

The Windows XP Upgrade Process

Well, if you've read this far, you've probably been to the store, have a new Windows box stuck under one arm, and are ready to start the installation process. Just as I provided you with a number of (hopefully) thought-provoking options earlier in this chapter about *how* to buy your next version of Windows and *which version* to buy, I now want to help you decide *how* to install it.

Upgrade, Clean Install, or Dual-Boot?

As you learned earlier in this chapter, even with an upgrade version of Windows XP, you still have the option of performing a clean install to a bare drive instead of replacing your existing Windows installation. You can also install Windows XP in a dual-boot configuration. Table 23.4 compares what happens when you select each of these options.

Table 23.4 Install Methods Comparison					
Install Option	Start from Windows	Start with Windows CD (boot)	Retain Existing Programs, Data, and Settings	Avoid Problems with Existing Programs and Settings	Location of Installation
Upgrade	Yes	No	Yes	No	Windows folder
Clean install	No	Yes	No	Yes	Bare drive
Dual-boot	Yes	No	*	Yes	Unpartitioned free space on hard disk

* Does not affect current programs, data, and settings, but software will need to be reinstalled for use with the new operating system

Which installation option is the best? Here's my advice:

- **When to upgrade**—If you have a healthy system now and you don't want to keep your old version of Windows, an upgrade will probably go well and will enable you to get back to work within an hour or so.

- **When to clean install**—If your current configuration has problems and you don't mind reinstalling your software and your data (after backing it up, of course), do a clean install. Depending on how much software you need to reinstall, your system could be down for much of the day.

- **When to dual-boot**—When you want to use both your existing and new operating systems on the same computer and you have an empty drive or free disk space large enough for the new OS and programs, do a dual-boot. Depending on how much software you need to reinstall to the new operating system, your system could be down for much of the day.

Before You Upgrade Checklist

As you learn later in this chapter, it's easier than ever to upgrade to Windows XP. However, what if something goes wrong? Especially if you're upgrading (or performing a clean install) on your one and only system, you'd better have a safety net. Here are my suggestions on how to get ready for problems.

1. Make sure your system meets the minimum requirements for the version of Windows to which you want to upgrade. Meeting the recommended requirements is better. The most common problems are not enough RAM and not enough hard disk space, but Windows XP also checks for CPU speed. Figure 23.1 shows a system running Windows 98 that needs a larger hard disk before upgrading to Windows XP. See Chapter 10 for details of how to install the new hard disk and copy your current drive's contents to the new hard disk before continuing with the upgrade.

Figure 23.1

This Windows 98 system has only 832MB free on the C: drive and has no other hard disk installed. Windows XP requires a *minimum* of 1.5GB of free space.

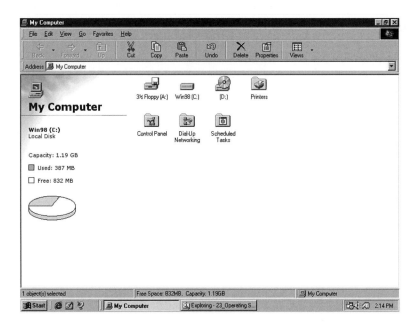

2. Make sure you have new Windows version-compatible drivers for all your system's components. If you did your homework in Chapters 4 and 5, "Taking an Inspection Tour of Your System" and "Preparing for Your Upgrade," and made a report of your system's configuration, you are ready to go to Microsoft's Hardware Compatibility List web site (www.microsoft.com/hcl/default.asp) and check your equipment's compatibility with the new version of Windows.

3. Go directly to the vendors' web sites and download the drivers you need or might need. Don't assume that Windows XP will properly identify every device during installation. Network cards, modems, and video cards could cause problems. Devices that have just been introduced are not supported by the drivers on the Windows XP CD. When you download new drivers, copy the driver files for each device to its own folder to make them easier to use during installation.

4. Make backups of your boot drive. Even though there's an option to reverse the installation, making your own backup is a better idea. I recommend you use a CD-RW drive and a drive imaging program such as PowerQuest's DriveImage or Symantec's Norton Ghost (also part of Norton System Works Professional).

5. To free up space if you're marginal on free disk space, delete all leftover files made by disk-repair tools: *.CHK (made by ScanDisk), *.NDD (Norton Disk Doctor), and *.TMP files with dates older than the current date; use Find or Search to locate these files. You should also delete *your browser cache* (the files viewed by your browser) if you need a bit more space. With Internet Explorer, click Tools, Internet Options, and then Delete Files. With Netscape, click Edit, Preferences, Advanced, Cache, and then Clear Memory Cache.

6. Make sure your drives (C: and above) are all in tip-top shape by running ScanDisk. If you have Norton Utilities/System Works or SpinRite, use these programs to test your drives instead of using ScanDisk; they're better than ScanDisk is at detecting problems.

7. Update your anti-virus program and signature files, and then scan your system and your backup media for viruses; you don't want to back up a virus you might restore later.

8. Disable anti-virus software; it might be launched at startup in Autoexec.bat, run in your Startup group, or launched through the Registry. The latest versions of antivirus software can disable all of these startup options for you, but older versions might require you to make manual changes to shut them off.

9. Disable anti-virus settings in your BIOS. These might include "Write-protect boot sector" and "Anti-Virus boot sector."

10. Record network and dial-up networking settings such as the following in case you need to recreate them after the installation:

   • TCP/IP configuration settings

   • Dial-up networking phone numbers and login procedures

   • Usernames and passwords

MARK'S TIP SHEET: WINIPCFG—A WINning Way to Network Information

Run WINIPCFG from Start, Run to see the TCP/IP network settings you use for your system; select the network adapter you use for details. The basic display shows your system's IP address. Click More Information to see Gateways and DHCP or WINS servers. Click the question-mark box to the left of the IP Configuration title bar for the program and select Copy to transfer the information to the Clipboard. Then, paste it into Notepad or a word-processing document for safekeeping. See Figure 23.2.

If you're upgrading from Windows 2000 or Windows NT 4.0, run IPCONFIG instead to view this information.

Figure 23.2

WINIPCFG information (left) after being pasted into Notepad (right).

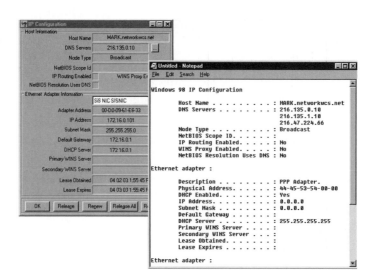

11. Back up your data; it's easier if you store your files in the My Documents folder or a separate drive.

12. Install more RAM if you were planning to anyway; it will help the installation to go faster.

13. Check for BIOS upgrades for your system and install them *before* you start the upgrade process. If you don't, your system might not have ACPI support, and you won't be able to use this more advanced, better form of power management.

14. Run the Upgrade Advisor software you can download from the Windows XP web site or select Check system compatibility from the Windows XP opening menu. Make any necessary changes to your system (such as uninstalling programs or downloading updated drivers) before installing Windows XP. See Figure 23.3.

Note that both Windows XP Home Edition and Windows XP Professional use the same Upgrade Advisor program you can download from the Microsoft web site when you select the Check system compatibility option. However, because Windows XP Home and Windows XP Professional share the same code base, a program or device that won't work with Windows XP Professional won't work with Windows XP Home Edition either.

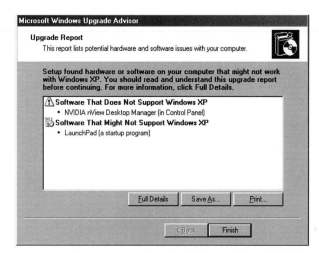

Figure 23.3

The Windows XP Upgrade Advisor displaying warnings about currently installed programs that will not or might not work with Windows XP.

MARK'S TIP SHEET: On the Track of a New BIOS

Be sure to recheck the coverage of BIOS upgrades in Chapter 9, "Unlock Your System's Potential with Motherboard and BIOS Upgrades," to learn where to go for a BIOS upgrade.

Replacing Older Versions of Windows with Windows XP

To start the Window XP upgrade process if you want to replace your old version of Windows, do the following:

1. Insert your Windows XP CD into the CD-ROM drive while your old version is running.

2. Unless you've disabled AutoRun, the Windows XP splash screen is displayed. Choose Install Windows XP, Perform additional tasks, or Check system compatibility.

3. If you haven't used the Windows Upgrade Advisor on this system, click Check system compatibility. You can run the advisor (Figure 23.3) or go to the compatibility web site.

4. After completing the Upgrade Advisor check (if necessary), click Install Windows XP.

5. Select Upgrade (the default setting) to change your installed version of Windows to Windows XP, which enables you to use your existing software and settings without reinstallation.

6. Read the license agreement, click I accept, and click Next to continue.

7. Enter the product key from the back of the CD package and click Next to continue.

8. The installation process begins; a display on the left side gives an estimate of how long the process will take until completion. The computer restarts several times during the process.

9. At the end of the process, the Welcome to Microsoft Windows dialog box is displayed. You can use it to activate your copy of Windows and set up users.

10. After you complete the steps listed in the Welcome dialog box, the Windows XP desktop is displayed.

CAUTION: STOP! LOOK! THINK!

Take 30 Days to Think About It

If you've installed Windows XP on a system that is marginal (slow processor, small hard disk, and so forth), you can remove it if you find it's not performing satisfactorily. Open the Add/Remove Programs icon in the Control Panel to locate the uninstall program. However, if you want to install Windows XP on another system without hassles, *don't* activate it until you're sure you're happy. Windows XP doesn't need to be activated until 30 days have passed from the install date, so take your time and think it over.

Installing Windows XP as a Dual-Boot Configuration

If you want to continue to use your older version of Windows, such as Windows 98, but have the ability to run Windows XP, you need to install Windows XP in a dual-boot configuration. Because Windows XP uses a different Windows kernel, Registry, and can use the NTFS file system, it should be installed to either:

- Empty (unpartitioned) space on your current hard drive
- A separate hard drive

In either case, Windows XP sets up its own boot manager to allow you to choose the version you want when you boot the system.

CAUTION: STOP! LOOK! THINK!

Don't Install a Three-OS System Without a Real Boot Manager
Microsoft's boot managers are designed to cope with only Microsoft OSs (surprise, surprise!). If you're also considering dropping some form of Linux on your system, you need to install a commercial boot manager first. Two very good choices include the latest version of PowerQuest's excellent Partition Magic program (8.x), which includes the BootMagic program (www.powerquest.com), and System Commander 7 from V Communications, Inc. (www.v-com.com), which also includes both partitioning and boot management features. Both can cope with all types of boot-management combinations not possible with the Microsoft-included utilities and can adjust and reallocate disk space between operating systems without data loss.

Preparing to Install Windows XP to Dual-Boot

Unlike Windows 9x/Me, which aren't designed to run on hard disks other than C:, Windows XP can cope with any hard disk letter. On my system, which also has Windows 98SE and several other drive letters used for data, temporary files, and creating CD images, Windows XP uses drive J:!

Windows XP creates its own hard drive letter during installation when you install it to unpartitioned space on your hard disk. If your current Windows installation has 20GB or more free space on the drive, use Partition Magic or System Commander to shrink the existing disk partition so that Windows XP can use some of the empty space (I recommend at least 15GB or more) for its installation. If not, you can install a second hard disk and use it for Windows XP, or follow the procedure given in Chapter 10 to copy your existing Windows installation to a larger drive so that there's plenty of space for Windows XP to use.

MARK'S TIP SHEET: Making a Lean, Mean, Dual-Boot Machine

You need to install the software you want to use with Windows XP after you install or Windows XP on its own disk partition. Install only the programs you have to use with this version of Windows; you'll probably be amazed at how few programs you need to install.

The Dual-Boot Installation Process

After you have verified you have sufficient space on an installed hard drive for Windows XP, you're ready to install Windows XP in a dual-boot configuration. There are more steps involved than with an upgrade (replacement) installation because Windows XP doesn't use existing settings.

> **ON THE WEB: TechTV Helps You Do the Dual-Boot**
>
> The process of installing Windows XP to dual-boot with Windows 98/Me is almost identical to the process used with Windows 2000. Check out TechTV's overview of the process, "Windows Tip: Give Your Computer the Dual Boot," at www.techtv.com/ screensavers/windowstips/story/0,24330,3338930,00.html.

Follow this process:

1. Insert your Windows XP CD into the CD-ROM drive while your old version is running.

2. Unless you've disabled AutoRun, the Windows XP splash screen is displayed. Choose Install Windows XP, Perform additional tasks, or Check system compatibility from the splash screen.

3. If you haven't used the Windows Upgrade Advisor on this system, click Check system compatibility. You can run the advisor (Figure 23.3) or go to the compatibility web site.

4. After completing the Upgrade Advisor check (if necessary), click Install Windows XP.

5. Select New Installation (Advanced) and click Next.

6. Read the license agreement, click I accept, and click Next to continue.

7. Enter the product key from the back of the CD package and click Next to continue.

8. Click the Advanced Options button on the Setup Options screen.

9. Click the box I want to choose the install drive letter and partition during Setup. Click OK.

10. Click Next.

11. Update the Windows setup files if prompted.

12. After the computer restarts, a blue and white text display appears. Setup loads driver files.

13. Press Enter when prompted to continue Setup.

14. Select unpartitioned space for the installation; Windows XP changes this space to the next available partition number during formatting.

> **MARK'S TIP SHEET: When 0 Equals 1**
>
> The Windows XP installation program refers to your first hard disk as Disk 0 and the second hard disk as Disk 1. If you want to install Windows XP to the second hard disk, be sure to choose Disk 1.

15. Select the file system to use for Windows XP. If you don't want your old version (9x/Me) of Windows to access the drive, or you want to use advanced features such as compression or encryption, select NTFS. If you want your old version of Windows to access the XP drive, select FAT32. If you tested the drive before starting the install procedure, choose the Quick method. Otherwise, choose the regular format (the regular format takes a long time).

16. After formatting the empty space, Windows XP continues the setup process, copying files and launching the Windows XP Setup Wizard. Click Next to continue.

17. Click Customize to change regional and language options, Details to adjust text input languages, or Next.

18. Enter your name and organization. Click Next.

19. Windows XP generates a computer name. Change it and click Next, or click Next to keep it.

20. Verify or change date and time settings. Click Next.

21. When prompted for network settings, select Typical if you are networked with other Windows 2000/XP users and click Next. Then, skip to step 24. Select Custom if you want to access shared resources on a Windows 9x/Me computer. Click Next.

22. If you select Custom and have an IEEE-1394 adapter, it can be used as a network adapter. If you don't plan to use it to connect to other computers, clear the checkboxes for network components and click Next.

23. Clear the checkbox next to QoS Packet Scheduler on the Ethernet adapter configuration screen; leaving this feature enabled slows down connections to Windows 9x/Me shared resources. Click Next.

24. The setup process continues. When the computer reboots, select Microsoft Windows XP to complete the Windows XP installation. Select Microsoft Windows to run your old version.

25. At the end of the process, the Welcome to Microsoft Windows dialog box is displayed. You can use it to activate your copy of Windows and set up users.

26. After you complete the steps listed in the Welcome dialog box, the Windows XP desktop is displayed. Restart the computer if prompted to complete installation of some devices.

After Windows XP is installed in a dual-boot configuration, you need to install any applications you want to use with Windows XP. In most cases, applications you use with Windows 98/Me will also work with Windows XP, but utility programs such as Norton Utilities/System Works, antivirus programs, and disk management programs might need to be upgraded to an XP-compatible version.

Installing Windows XP on an Empty Hard Disk

If you don't want to retain any trace of your previous version of Windows, or if you have built a computer from components, you can install Windows XP to an empty hard disk. This resembles the process used to install Windows XP in a dual-boot configuration, but with the following differences:

1. You must use the Windows XP CD-ROM to boot your computer.

2. If you use the Windows XP upgrade version to perform the installation, you must insert a Windows CD from one of the eligible versions when prompted to prove your eligibility to install the upgrade version.

During the installation process, Windows XP will do the following:

- Create disk partition(s) and format them
- Prompt you for various configuration options

At the end of the process, the Windows XP desktop appears. You can then install your favorite applications.

ON THE WEB: Getting Help with Other Dual-Boot Situations

If you've already installed Windows XP and then realized you'd like to dual-boot Windows 98/Me, or you'd like to create some other type of dual-boot configuration, visit the Windows XP Dual Boot Tip Page at www.winxpfix.com/page5.htm.

Troubleshooting Your Windows Upgrade

A Windows upgrade can be a piece of cake, giving you little more to do than watch those annoying Microsoft ads during the install process. Or, it can be a disaster. I'm hoping your experience is more like the former, but if you're experience is coming out like a disaster movie script, check out the solutions below. Don't forget that if you purchased a retail version of Windows that Microsoft provides unlimited installation support. Here's hoping you don't find out how many times "unlimited" might be!

Help! I can't find my XYZ brand video card on the Windows Hardware Compatibility List (HCL). Do I really need to buy another card—I've had this one for only a month!

The HCL doesn't do a really good job of distinguishing between videocard brands and models and chipset brands and models. It's very likely that your video card chipset is listed as compatible, and this is all you really need to worry about. nVIDIA-based cards, for example, can run with either "generic" nVIDIA drivers or brand-optimized drivers, but a lot of the smaller companies don't customize the drivers much…if at all. Now that ATI also sells chipsets to various vendors as well as making ATI-brand video cards, you could encounter the same issue with ATI chipsets. As with nVIDIA-chipset cards, some vendors of video cards based on ATI chipsets don't modify the drivers much at all.

To find out what chipset your card uses, check in the Windows Device Manager. Then, check the chipset against the HCL, or go to the card manufacturer's web site (best option) or chipset manufacturer's web site to see if drivers are available. Keep in mind that Windows 2000 and Windows XP prefer digitally signed drivers (drivers that have been approved by Microsoft).

Help! I just booted from my Windows XP upgrade CD to install Windows on my Windows Me system, but the setup program can't find my original Windows installation. I didn't get a Windows CD with my computer (just the .cab install files on the hard disk), so how do I prove that I own Windows Me?

It sounds as if you're wanting to replace Windows Me with Windows XP, or install Windows XP so that it can be a dual-boot installation. In either case, you *don't* boot from the Windows XP CD. Instead, start Windows Me normally, and then insert the Windows XP CD to start the installation process. See the sections "Replacing Older Versions of Windows with Windows XP" or "Installing Windows XP as a Dual-Boot Configuration" in this chapter for details.

Help! I just finished installing Windows, but I've been reading about security patches and fixes I need to apply. What's the easy way to keep my new installation up-to-date?

Microsoft created Windows Update to keep Windows working properly in an almost automatic fashion. Windows Update compares your installed Windows XP program files and drivers to its database of the latest patches, updates, fixes, and new drivers available from Microsoft, and provides a list of the updates you need. Windows XP can even download and install them automatically for you if you prefer.

To start Windows Update with Windows XP, click Start, Control Panel, Windows Update. Windows Update is also part of Windows Me and Windows 98/98SE. With these versions, click Start, Windows Update.

When you start Windows Update, Microsoft might prompt you to install an updated Windows Update component on your system before Windows Update can work. After Windows Update starts, it creates a list of Critical Updates and Service Packs (including important security and stability fixes), Windows program updates, and Driver Updates. Most of the time, you should install Critical Updates as soon as they become available. However, Microsoft's Service Packs (which bundle together all the critical updates previously released and might add additional features) are notorious for having problems in their initial release. So, you might want to wait until a Service Pack has been tested before you install it.

ON THE WEB: The Windows Experts to Check for the Latest News

When I wonder if a Service Pack or Critical Update is worth installing or if I should wait, I check these resources:

- **Brian Livingston's BriansBuzz**—The longtime InfoWorld magazine columnist now has his own Windows newsletter. Subscribe at www.briansbuzz.com.

- **Stu Sjouwerman's WinXPNews**—Stu's the author of *The Windows XP Power Pack* (Que, 2003); check out the site and the newsletter at www.winxpnews.com.

- **Woody Leonhard's Woody's Windows Watch**—One of a series of Windows and Microsoft Office newsletters from the co-author of *Special Edition Using Microsoft Office XP* (Que, 2001) and author of many other books on Windows and Microsoft Office; check out the site and the newsletters at www.woodyswatch.com.

Part VIII

Upgrading for Portability

Chapter 24

Upgrading to Mobile Information Devices

If you're tired of running back to your office to transcribe notes, addresses, phone numbers, or other information from a notepad back into your computer, or if you want to take some computing firepower on the road, there's never been a better time to add mobile information to your system.

Devices such as notebook computers, PDAs, smart phones, and Tablet PCs might not seem like PC upgrades, but because they enable your "home base" PC to work harder for you, they are.

In this chapter, discover why you should consider mobile information devices, which type(s) of mobile information devices are the best upgrades, and what your upgrade options are if you already have a notebook computer or PDA.

Ten Reasons to Go Mobile

Not sure you want to get away from your favorite PC? We'll see about that. Here are our top-ten reasons you might be ready to look at going mobile. If you recognize yourself, keep reading.

1. You're tired of transcribing handwritten notes into your PC after a meeting.
2. Your kids have PDAs and you don't.
3. You'd like to replace the legendary "cocktail napkin" brainstorming session with something that's more up to date.
4. Your home "office" is the kitchen table after the homework is done, so you need the smallest computing device you can find.
5. You're tired of dragging your PC all over the country when all you really need is email access.
6. You want to have all the sales information you need for the next presentation in the palm of your hand.
7. You'd rather write with digital ink than worry about washing that important phone number off your hand.
8. You're on your wireless phone so much that you figure it should know a few things by now.
9. Showing off pictures of your kids on a full-color PDA screen is beyond cool.
10. Using a PDA that's also a phone means there's one less thing to forget in the morning.

Your Mobility Options

If you're looking to make your digital life more mobile, there are four major types of devices that can do it for you:

- Notebook computers
- PDAs (Personal Digital Assistants)
- Smart phones
- Tablet PCs

Each has unique advantages, so the question is, which one is right for you? To find out, take a look at the following:

- Form factors
- Features
- What you give up
- What you gain

ON THE WEB: Mobile Product Reviews Are Just a Click Away

TechTV's Mobile Computing page is the perfect place to start exploring for reviews and news about PDAs, smart phones, and other mobile gear. See it at `www.techtv.com/products/mobilecomputing/`.

How Form Factors Affect Options

What do you give up when you consider mobile information devices? A lot of the answer to that question depends on the form factor of the device you're considering.

JARGON

Form factor—Size and shape of a particular item or category of devices.

If you're thinking about adding a notebook computer to your arsenal, you're not giving up much at all. Today's notebook computers have good keyboards, large screens, and high-speed I/O ports so that you can add the devices you want. They also have large hard drives and CD-RW or DVD drives.

The biggest single feature that's different about other types of mobile information devices is how you input data. Depending on the device you choose, you might do one of the following:

- Work a small keyboard with your thumbs.
- Learn a stylized type of handwriting for recognition.
- Create hand-written and hand-drawn documents that can be turned into computer-readable data.

Sometimes, you can add a classic QWERTY keyboard to a mobile device, or specify a model with a keyboard, but most of these devices aren't designed for heavy data entry. Instead, they are meant to provide portable access to information you created with your desktop PC.

Notable Reasons to Get a Notebook

Not long ago, choosing a notebook computer required a huge sacrifice in computing power. Not anymore. Whether you opt for a compact modular model or a beefy desktop replacement, you can tote a lot of computing power around with you wherever you go.

Today's notebook computers can do most of the same jobs you once needed a desktop computer to do, thanks to advances in networking, high-speed ports, and onboard storage. Wi-Fi wireless networking (see Chapter 18, "Wireless Wonders") is included in many recent notebook computers and can be retrofitted to others. Wi-Fi makes networking and Internet access cable-free and available in thousands of locations around the world. Hi-Speed USB (USB 2.0) ports (see Chapter 19, "Adding the Ports You Need for the Devices You Want") open the door to high-speed external drives and other peripherals. Built-in rewriteable CD and DVD drives enable notebook computers to handle data, music, and movies with ease.

Although notebook computers can't be upgraded in the same way as desktop computers, you have a lot of choices when you make your initial purchase:

- For less than $1,500, you can get a 20GB or larger hard disk, DVD/CD-RW combo drive, USB 2.0 ports, 15-inch color LCD display, and 10/100 Ethernet. Computers in this price range are excellent buys for basic portable office productivity. However, they often use low-performance processors, such as Celerons, and use integrated video, so they're not the best choices for multimedia.

- For less than $2,500, you can get more compact and lighter models. Some are thin designs that use external drives, while others use detachable modules for the DVD or CD-RW drive. Most models in this price category feature integrated wireless networking and a separate graphics controller for faster display and better 3D graphics. Some models in this price range also feature interchangeable drive bays and batteries. Most of these computers feature faster processors such as the Pentium 4 or new Pentium-M. Figure 24.1 shows a typical mid-range notebook computer, the Gateway 600.

- Models above $2,500 can feature rewriteable DVD drives, 60GB hard disks, Ultra XGA (1,280×1,024) displays, wireless networking, and the other features available in lower-priced models.

Figure 24.1

The Gateway 600 series features modular drives, an IEEE 1394 port, TV-out, S/PDIF digital audio out, hard drives from 30GB to 60GB, and your choice of a combo CD-RW/DVD drive or a rewriteable DVD-RW drive. Photo courtesy of Gateway.

What's your best choice? If you're looking primarily for a computer to carry in the car or plop down at your kitchen table when you're away from the office, a low-priced model will do very well. However, if you're going to be running through an airport, the large form factor, weight (typically seven pounds or more), and relatively short battery life found in typical low-priced models might not be the best choice.

ON THE WEB: Value Notebooks the TechTV Way

Check out Hahn Choi's head-to-head comparison in "Best Value Notebooks" at
`www.techtv.com/freshgear/products/story/0,23008,3398089,00.html`.

Move up to the middle price range and you can reduce the strain on your shoulder and get greater customization and battery life. Note that drives built for notebook computers with interchangeable drive bays are usually sold only by the notebook computer vendor and cost much more than internal drives sold for desktop PCs.

High-end models offer practically everything found in a leading-edge desktop computer, but they cost much more. However, if you need to perform digital video editing, photo editing, or other types of high-intensity computing away from your desk, these models might be worth it.

ON THE WEB: The Notebook Computer Contenders

For the latest products, check out the leaders in notebook computers at their web sites:

- **HP/Compaq**—www.hp.com
- **IBM**—www.ibm.com
- **Toshiba**—www.toshiba.com
- **Gateway**—www.gateway.com
- **Dell**—www.dell.com
- **Fujitsu**—www.fujitsu.com
- **Sharp**—www.sharpsystems.com

PCWorld's Notebooks Product Guide includes its Top Notebook Computers page with monthly rankings, prices, and reviews. Get started at www.pcworld.com.

PC Magazine's Notebook Product Guide lists recent reviews and First Looks at new products. Go to www.pcmag.com to get started.

Why Pick a PDA?

If your major concern is information *access* rather than information *creation*, a PDA could be the right choice. After all, you wouldn't lug around a file cabinet of customer contacts if all you needed was an address book. Similarly, you don't need to haul around a seven-pound notebook computer if all you need is the ability to look up information.

A PDA does have some ability to input information, thanks to support for stylus input and optional keyboards for some models. However, the real advantage of a PDA is convenient access to important email, documents, and other data without hauling around a notebook computer.

There are two major flavors of PDAs worth considering:

- Palm OS-based models
- Microsoft Windows CE-based Pocket PC models

Although Pocket PC models might appear, at first glance, to be the obvious choice as a side-kick to a Windows PC, the popular Documents to Go program from DataViz enables Palm OS-based handhelds to access Word, Excel, Adobe PDF, and other types of popular data files.

You can buy a PDA for as little as $100 or for as much as $600 or more. What are the differences?

- **Display type**—Palm OS models with low-resolution (160×160) monochrome displays enable you to get a PDA for around $100. Crank up the resolution to 320×320 and add contrast as Sony CLIE models (also Palm-OS-based) do, and the price rises to $200 or more. Full color starts at around $250–$300. Pocket PC handhelds are full color, as are some high-end Palm OS systems. Check color depth if you want to display photos. 16-bit (65,536-color) screens do well with photos, but some displays support a lot fewer colors. Figure 24.2 shows a typical PocketPC, the HP iPAQ h1910, with a 16-bit color screen.

- **Memory**—The memory in a PDA supports both data and programs. Palm OS programs are smaller than PocketPC programs, so a Palm OS PDA needs less RAM to be useful. Palm OS devices with less than 8MB of RAM are marginal for heavy use, as are PocketPC models with less than 32MB of RAM. Even if you choose a model with much more RAM than these minimums, you should look for models with expandable memory. Otherwise, you could eventually run out of room for additional programs or data storage.

Figure 24.2

The HP iPAQ h1910 is a lightweight PocketPC with a full-color screen and digital music play-back capabilities. Photo courtesy of HP.

- **Memory expansion**—Low-end PDAs often leave out memory expansion, but mid-range and high-end models usually offer this feature. For the best deals, look for models that support standard flash memory types such as SD (secure digital), MMC (multimedia card), CF (compact flash), or memory stick instead of proprietary cards used only with certain PDA models.

- **Processor speed**—As with desktop PCs, PDAs are also seeing increases in processor performance. The fastest PocketPC models use the 400MHz or faster Intel XScale processor (older models used the StrongARM processor), and the fastest Palm OS models use 200MHz or faster processors, compared to the 33MHz or slower models used in low-end and older models.

- **Input options**—Every Palm OS or PocketPC uses a stylus for inputting data, but if you'd rather have a keyboard, a few models feature a built-in model you work with your thumbs.

ON THE WEB: Put Your Stylus Away and Type into Your PDA!

If you need heavy-duty input, you can use various keyboards, such as the Pocketop wireless PDA keyboard, the Flexis FX-100, and the Think Outside Stowaway.

Check out TechTV's review of the Flexis FX-100 at `www.techtv.com/products/mobilecomputing/story/0,23008,3367609,00.html`. Our reviewers chose it as a finalist for TechTV's 2002 Best of CES. Flexis comes from Man & Machine; see their web site at `www.man-machine.com/`. Figure 24.3 shows the Flexis FX-100 in action.

The compact foldable Stowaway keyboard from Think Outside is also a TechTV favorite. Check out our review at `www.techtv.com/freshgear/products/story/0,23008,2425631,00.html` and the Think Out web site at `www.thinkoutside.com`.

Figure 24.3

The Flexis FX-100 works with Palm OS and PocketPC PDAs (top); it can be rolled up for convenient storage (bottom). Photos courtesy of Man & Machine.

- **Onboard features**—Some advanced PDAs now feature 802.11b (Wi-Fi) wireless Internet, Bluetooth wireless networking, built-in digital cameras, music playback, and other features. Some features add bulk as well as expense, so choose only the features you really expect to use.

With many models available from many different vendors, now's the time to consider a PDA.

Why a Smart Phone Could Be a Smart Decision

If you need a PDA and a phone, or text messaging and a phone, or anything else and a phone, maybe what you want is a smart phone. A smart phone can send and receive data (such as text messages) as well as voice messages.

Until recently, smart phone services were oriented to business uses, but most cellular-phone providers now offer text-messaging service as a low-cost option with some plans. If you want more than just text-messaging, some smart phones also offer voice recording, full-color screens, Palm OS or Pocket PC PDA features, and more.

Although a basic smart phone with text messaging can be had for less than $50, adding full-blown PDA features to a smart phone puts the resulting device in the same price range as a high-end PDA.

Some of the PDA/smart phone hybrids we've reviewed favorably include the following:

- **Handspring Treo 180, 270, 300 series**—Palm OS 180 and 270 models support GSM cellphone networks such as Cingular and T-Mobile, while the 300 model supports Sprint. See www.handspring.com for details. Figure 24.4 shows the full-color Treo 270 and monochrome Treo 180 models.

- **T-Mobile Sidekick**—Proprietary email, messaging, web browsing, and AOL Instant Messenger, plus basic organizer features. Also known as the Danger hiptop. See www.danger.com and http://t-mobile.com for details.

- **T-Mobile Pocket PC Phone Edition**—Microsoft Pocket PC plus full telephone features. See http://t-mobile.com for details.

- **Kyocera 7135**—Palm OS, 16-bit color screen, SD/MMC memory expansion, GPS, and lots of other features for the Verizon network. See www.kyocera.com for details.

ON THE WEB: Smart Reviews of Smart Phones

Find TechTV's full reviews of smart phones at the following locations:

- "Review: Handspring Treo" at www.techtv.com/products/consumerelectronics/story/0,23008,3353619,00.html.

- "Handspring Treo 270 and 90" at www.techtv.com/news/computing/story/0,24195,3387181,00.html.

- "Best All-in-One Cellphone/PDAs" at www.techtv.com/freshgear/products/story/0,23008,3402702,00.html.

Figure 24.4

The Handspring Treo 270 (left) and Treo 180 (right) feature Palm OS. Photo courtesy of Handspring.

When Tablet PCs Are the Right Prescription

If you're looking for a device that offers the power of a notebook computer, the use of a stylus, and more options than a PDA, that device is here now. It's called the Tablet PC. As with the Pocket PC, Microsoft provides the software, and leading computer vendors provide the hardware.

Unlike Pocket PC, whose dependence on Windows CE and non-PC processors sometimes makes for compromises in features, performance, and compatibility, Tablet PCs run a modified version of Windows XP Professional called Windows XP Tablet PC Edition.

Because Tablet PCs are a high-tech replacement for a legal pad, Tablet PC Edition adds new applications to the basic feature set found in Windows XP Professional:

- Tablet PC Input Panel provides complete-sentence handwriting recognition.
- Windows Journal stores diagrams as well as text.
- Sticky Notes is a digital storage area for jotting down reminders, phone numbers, and all the things you'd stick on the edges of your desktop computer's monitor.
- Speech-to-text conversion (a feature borrowed from Office XP) provides an alternative to handwriting recognition.

The result of these design changes is that Tablet PC Edition is designed to work with a stylus, instead of being adapted to work with a stylus as with previous generations of Windows-based portables. If you also want to use a keyboard for heavy-duty text entry, look for convertible models, such as the Compaq Tablet PC TC1000 shown in Figure 24.5, that also include keyboards.

Figure 24.5

The Compaq Tablet PC TC1000 from HP is a convertible model that can be used with a keyboard or stylus. Photo courtesy of HP.

Because Tablet PCs are designed to be used the way you would carry a paper notepad, they're smaller and lighter than traditional notebook computers, weighing in at just three to four pounds on average. As a result, many models don't include features such as optical drives. If you prefer a model without a built-in drive, I recommend looking for models with USB 2.0 or IEEE-1394 ports so that you can connect with high-speed CD or DVD burners.

Wireless networking based on Wi-Fi is another must-have feature, although some models omit it. We also prefer models that have docking stations, which can provide ports and other features at your desk you can leave behind when you go back to the field.

Because they feature lightweight designs, stylus-compatible screens, and other innovations, Tablet PCs are comparable in price to mid-range notebook computers. Most models sell for between $2,000 and $2,300.

ON THE WEB: TechTV Takes on Tablet PCs

Check out these reviews and stories for more information:

- "Roundup: Windows XP Tablet PCs" at `www.techtv.com/freshgear/products/story/0,23008,3411155,00.html`.
- "First Look: Windows XP Tablet PC Edition" at `www.techtv.com/news/products/story/0,24195,3406620,00.html`.
- "First Look: Gateway Tablet PC" at `www.techtv.com/news/products/story/0,24195,3415569,00.html`.

Which Way to Mobility Is Best for You?

With four distinct choices for carrying and getting information while you're on the run, you're in an enviable situation. However, which choice is best for you?

If you want to replicate your office or home-office computer experience away from your normal PC, a notebook computer is far and away the only choice. If you're in the mood for gaming as well as getting some work done, choose a model with high-performance 3D graphics based on recent ATI or nVIDIA mobile chipsets. Choose a Tablet PC with a keyboard if you want to have the option to use handwritten notes and diagrams in your work.

If you're more concerned about staying organized instead of creating reams of new information when you're away from your PC, get a PDA. If it doesn't include Documents to Go, order a copy no matter which operating system your PDA has. It is the best PDA software for working with popular data types away from your normal PC.

A smart phone with text messaging keeps you in the loop even in a "no talking" zone, but if you want to stay organized and can have only one device to carry around, make it a combination smart phone/PDA.

Making the Most of Your Existing Mobility Devices

If you already have a notebook or PDA, it might not be everything you had in mind. It might be missing features or capabilities. Although you can't upgrade these devices as freely as you can a desktop PC, upgrades are possible to the following:

- Memory
- Storage
- Input/output

In the following sections, you learn what you can do to make your current notebook computer or PDA smarter and more powerful.

Upgrading Your Existing Notebook

There are some things you *can't* do with a notebook computer:

- You can't make it lighter (unless you take out the battery or drives).
- You can't replace the processor.

However, you *can* upgrade the following:

- Memory
- Storage
- Ports
- Connectivity
- Input/output devices

Memory Upgrades

A memory upgrade for a notebook computer has hidden benefits over the same type of upgrade for a desktop computer. Both types of computers gain faster performance, especially when moving to 512MB or more of RAM from lesser amounts with Windows XP. However, a notebook computer will usually see its battery life improve when you install a memory upgrade. Here's why: Any computer running Windows can use virtual memory (disk space set aside for a swapfile) when real memory runs short. Disk drives use more power than RAM, so a lack of RAM causes more disk access, lowering battery life.

As noted in Chapter 7, "RAM Your Way to Faster Performance," RAM upgrades for notebook computers are now primarily done with SO-DIMM modules instead of the proprietary modules used previously. This means that a notebook memory upgrade is less expensive today than in the past. You still need to check compatibility before you buy, but the memory you buy can come from a wider variety of vendors. To learn more about memory upgrades, see Chapter 7.

Upgrading Storage

External hard drive, removable-media, and optical storage solutions covered in earlier chapters (Chapter 10, "Adding a Huge Hard Disk", Chapter 11, "Removable Storage to Go," and Chapter 12, "A Burning Desire for Better Optical Drives,") can be used with your notebook computer if it has the right ports. However, external hard disk storage adds weight and bulk and, unlike other types of storage for portable computers, you might have an alternative.

You can replace the internal hard drive in most recent (and not-so-recent) notebook computers with kits from vendors such as SimpleTech (www.simpletech.com), Apricorn (www.apricorn.com), and others. To make the data transfer process simple, look for drive-cloning devices provided by these vendors. These kits plug into the PC Card slot on your computer to transfer data from the existing drive to the new drive. Some kits enable the old drive to be used as a secondary drive after the drive is replaced with a new drive.

> **ON THE WEB: Upgrading a Notebook Hard Drive the TechTV Way**
>
> As an alternative to using a cloning device or commercial kit, Patrick Norton covers the complete do-it-yourself process with "Upgrade a Laptop Hard Drive" at www.techtv.com/screensavers/answerstips/story/0,24330,2315390,00.html.

If your computer is designed with an interchangeable drive bay, check with the computer vendor for options.

Upgrading Ports

If you just bought your notebook computer, you probably have USB 2.0 ports and you might even have an IEEE-1394 port as well. However, only a year or so back, these ports were uncommon, and a lot of otherwise-capable notebook computers don't have these ports. If you're trying to add external storage to your notebook computer, you need USB 2.0 or IEEE-1394 ports.

Until a few months ago, you could find CardBus (32-bit PC Card) upgrades that provided one port type or the other. Fortunately, dual-mode chipsets have hit the market and many vendors now provide both functions in a single card. See Chapter 19 for details and sources.

Upgrading Connectivity

The development and rapidly growing use of wireless Ethernet technologies is one of the greatest boons to portable computer and PDA users. Having integrated 802.11b support saves your PC Card/CardBus slot for other types of expansion, and it's easy to add the appropriate adapter to your system so that you can surf the web when you're away from home. See Chapter 18 for details.

Upgrading Input/Output

If you're away from your desk with your notebook computer, you don't need to give up the ability to print or scan documents. Lightweight inkjet printers such as the Canon i70 weigh four pounds or less and feature print quality and resolutions comparable to full-size inkjet printers. Thermal transfers printers such as the Pentax PocketJet II use specially-coated paper, but never need ribbons or ink cartridges. USB-powered lightweight scanners such as Visioneer's Strobe XP100 (11 ounces) and Pentax DSmobile USB (12 ounces) can digitize photos and convert single-sheet documents into readable text with the page-recognition software bundled with the scanners.

Use the USB ports on your notebook computer to add other types of I/O devices as needed, including input devices and flash memory card readers. Some printers can also be used with PDAs, although you might need to add an optional IrDA or Bluetooth adapter in some cases.

ON THE WEB: Lightweight I/O for Your Notebook Computer

Check out the Canon i70 and its older lightweight siblings at www.usa.canon.com.

Learn more about the Pentax PocketJet II printer and the Pentax DSMobile USB scanner at www.pentaxtech.com.

Discover more information about the Visioneer Strobe XP100 at www.visioneer.com.

Upgrading Your Existing PDA

Many people "upgrade" their existing PDA by replacing it, sometimes after it takes one too many knocks (my son Ian is now on his third one). As I suggested in the opening chapter of this book, replacing a broken or lost item is the perfect opportunity to get a better one.

However, if your PDA keeps ticking no matter what type of a licking you give it, take a close look at it. You might find ways, including the following, to make it work better for you:

- Upgrading memory
- Adding new features

Upgrading Memory/Storage

As I discussed earlier in this chapter, the memory in a PDA works much harder than in a PC. A PDA's memory is used for program storage, data storage, and workspace. Although some low-end PDAs don't have any provision for user-installable memory upgrades, most mid-range and better models do.

Most recent PDAs use one or more of the flash memory cards discussed in detail in Chapter 11, "Removable Storage to Go." However, even if your PDA uses a non-standard expansion interface, such as the Springboard slot used on some Handspring Visor models, you might still be able to use an adapter to add standard memory. Expansys (www.expansys.us) offers two MemPlug converters for Handspring Springboard slots. One is for Sony Memory Stick, and the other is for SD or MMC cards.

Adding Features

Some PDAs that have SD slots also support SDIO devices. SDIO (secure digital I/O) is a new variation on the standard SD interface that enables the slot to support various types of I/O devices. For example, SDIO devices are already available to add Bluetooth wireless short-range networking and 802.11b (Wi-Fi) wireless networking. More uses are coming.

The IR (infrared) port on the PDA can be used for keyboards as well as for data transfer to other computers. Check with your PDA vendor for additional options for your device.

Why the Best Upgrade Might Be a New Model

Whether you have a notebook computer or a PDA, your upgrade options are much more limited than with a desktop computer. If you need one of the following:

- A better display
- A faster processor
- Support for SDIO or memory expansion not already present

…The best upgrade is a new computer or PDA.

Troubleshooting Your Mobile Information Device

A mobile information device can be a great enhancement to your productivity, but if something goes wrong, it becomes a detriment instead of an enhancement. Here are some tips to make moving to your preferred mobility device as painless as possible.

Help! I want to use my favorite documents with my PDA, but it can't read them.

Some PDAs don't include software that supports your favorite applications. Try the programs in Chapter 25, "Upgrading Your Portable's Connection with Your PC," to improve your PDA's ability to work with your favorite types of files.

Help! My notebook computer has Windows XP, but it won't support dual displays. When I plug in a monitor, I see the same desktop on both displays.

Windows XP features DualView, an adaptation of its built-in multiple-display technology that can enable some notebook computers to handle a monitor as if it's plugged into a dual-display adapter. DualView capabilities depend upon the notebook computer's having hardware support for DualView. Check with the computer vendor before you buy to see if DualView is supported on a particular model. If you already have a notebook computer, look for a driver update that might enable DualView. Keep in mind, though, that without hardware support, DualView won't work.

Help! My smart phone is a great phone and PDA, but it can't connect to the Internet! Any ideas?

There are quite a few possible reasons why you can't connect to the Internet. Here are the ones I'd check first:

- **Make sure you have signed up for Internet access for your phone.** Some mobile phone providers bundle Internet access with compatible phones, while others require you choose an ISP. This is particularly true if your smart phone works as a dial-up rather than an always-on connection.

- **Your signal strength may be too low for Internet connection, although you can make voice calls.** Check the signal strength indicator on your phone and move to a location with a better signal.

- **Check your dial-up number if you use a dial-up ISP.** With the explosion in new area codes, many ISPs of all types are adding and changing dial-up numbers to keep up with changes in area codes. Make sure you're using a valid dial-up number, and ask for a list of alternatives.

- **Check your GPRS configuration.** A GPRS phone can't connect to the Internet if the configuration is wrong; contact your provider for the correct settings.

- **Make sure your smart phone is set to the correct mode.** Many smart phones require you to select the correct mode for the task you want to perform. For example, Handspring Treo smart phones require you to select Handheld Mode when you use the PDA features, and Wireless Mode when you use the phone or Internet features. Select the right mode and try again.

- **Your Subscriber Identity Module (SIM) card is not connected tightly, damaged, or missing.** Phones and smart phones used with GSM networks use SIM cards. The card can be swapped to another phone so that the card user is properly billed for activity. If your smart phone uses a SIM card, remove it and make sure it is not damaged. Insert it tightly. If your smart phone's SIM card is missing, contact the wireless provider for help.

Help! I have a Tablet PC with Office XP installed, but Office XP can't recognize my handwriting.

You need to install the Microsoft Office XP Pack for Tablet PC. It's a free download from the Microsoft web site (www.microsoft.com/office/tabletpc/), which enables Word, Excel, PowerPoint, and Outlook to recognize handwriting. It also enables Microsoft Journal to work with Outlook.

Chapter 25

Upgrading Your Portable's Connection with Your PC

Whether you're an old hand at mobility or have just added one of the devices discussed in Chapter 24, "Upgrading to Mobile Information Devices," to your life, getting information back and forth between your mobile technology and your PC isn't always as simple or fool-proof as it ought to be. Whether you're looking for a better hardware solution or smarter software to get your desktop and your portable devices talking to each other, this is the right place to start.

Ten Reasons to Improve How Your Devices Share Information

Maybe you've never had a problem with your computer and mobile information device communicating. However, after you read my top-ten list of reasons to look at upgrades, you might realize you could improve your connection. I don't think you should change things that aren't broken, but if your connection's on the fix-up list, keep reading.

1. You think "file synchronization" is an obscure Olympic sport.
2. You're never quite sure where your information is.

3. You connect your PDA to two computers, and the cradle is always at the wrong computer.

4. You can't carry your most important information because it's in the wrong format for your mobile device.

5. You're sick and tired of trying to remember which format to use to save files so that they work on your mobile device.

6. Your new desktop computer doesn't have a serial port, so you can't plug in your PDA.

7. You'd like to pull the latest data from your PC no matter where you are.

8. You're tired of reaching under the desk to plug in your PDA.

9. The software you use most on your PC can't communicate with your PDA.

10. You can't transfer documents between systems without terrible things happening in the process.

Upgrading to Better Synchronizing Software

If you use a PDA along with a desktop or notebook computer, you need to make sure the latest data, such as updated documents and new or revised contact information, is transferred between computers. File-synchronization software is designed to automate the task of comparing files and information and transferring the latest files and information between computers.

If your PDA is still using its original software, you could be limiting your file-synchronization options. For example, the latest version of Palm Desktop software (4.1) now supports quicker transfers of programs, multimedia content, and other files, and it has a photo viewer. If it's been a while since you upgraded your software, check with your PDA vendor for an update.

Advantages of Third-Party Synchronization Programs

One of the major tasks performed by file-synchronization programs is to transfer contact data between email and organizer programs run on your PC and your PDA. However, sometimes, the file-synchronizing software supplied with your PDA doesn't support the applications you want to use. For example, you might prefer Outlook Express (the free email client bundled with Internet Explorer) instead of Outlook (the information manager plus email client bundled with Microsoft Office). Or, you might use less-common platforms such as smart phones or PDAs that don't run Palm OS or Pocket PC/Windows CE.

If you use Windows 2000 or Windows XP on your desktop and notebook computers, you can use a built-in Windows feature called "offline files" to perform file synchronization. However, if you use earlier versions of Windows, this feature is not available.

In situations like these, consider using a third-party synchronization utility. Here are some of the leaders.

Intellisync

Intellisync version 5.x supports Outlook and Outlook Express as well as Lotus Notes, Lotus Organizer, Palm Desktop 4.x, Microsoft Exchange, Microsoft Schedule Plus, ACT!, and Novell GroupWise, and it enables you to map fields in different databases to each other to prevent data loss. Intellisync supports PalmOS, PocketPC, and Windows CE-based devices, and a free 30-day full-version trial is available from Pumatech (www.pumatech.com).

CompanionLink

If you use ACT! or GoldMine software, CompanionLink offers several file-synchronization tools that can work with Outlook, Lotus Notes, and Palm Desktop. These programs offer many enhancements over the synchronizing tools supplied with other programs such as ACT! PalmPilot Link or GoldMine's bundled PDA support. Learn more at www.companionlink.com.

XTNDConnect PC

If you use a Sony Ericsson mobile phone or a Casio Personal Organizer, you should consider XTNDConnect PC from Extended Systems (www.extendedsystems.com). A single application works with those platforms as well as PalmOS and PocketPC to synchronize with your PC. It supports Microsoft Outlook, Lotus Notes, Lotus Organizer, ACT!, Ecco Pro, GoldMine, and Palm Desktop.

P.I. Protector Mobility Suite

Some types of file synchronization for PCs require you to load software on both systems. P.I. Protector Mobility Suite puts the software inside the device that contains the data: your USB flash drive or other removable storage device.

P.I. Protector Mobility Suite handles *one-way* or *two-way file synchronization* and stores Outlook Express email and web browsing content, such as cookies and favorites on the removable storage device. It works with desktop, notebook, or Tablet PCs running Windows 98 Second Edition or later. Get more information from Imagine Lan, Inc. (www.imaginelan.com).

LapLink Gold 11 Classic and TrueSync

Long before local area networks were common, LapLink enabled PC users to transfer files between computers with a specially designed serial or parallel file transfer cable. LapLink Gold 11 (www.laplink.com) still provides PC-to-PC file transfer features with its specially designed serial, parallel, or USB cables, and also provides file synchronization and remote control features. LapLink Gold 11 supports all 32-bit versions of Windows, from Windows 95 through Windows XP.

LapLink also produces TrueSync, which provides *multi-point* data synchronization for PC-based information managers such as Lotus Notes and Microsoft Outlook to Palm OS, Pocket PC, and Nokia and Ericsson wireless phones.

JARGON

One-way file synchronization—Files are transferred from the source computer to the target computer; used when all data files on one computer are newer than the files on the other computer.

Two-way file synchronization—Files are compared on both computers, and the newest files are transferred in both directions as needed; used when some data files on each computer are newer than the files on the other computer.

Multi-point file synchronization—Synchronization takes place among all connected devices at the same time.

Cradles, Cables, and Your PDA

Your PDA is practically useless unless you can attach it to a PC for a periodic topping off of its information fuel tank. However, changes in technology and shortsighted decisions by original vendors can be frustrating. The following sections can help you deal with making the best connections between your PDA and your PC.

Moving to USB

Time is running out for the classic serial-port synchronizing cradle used by many PDAs. In fact, if you buy a thin and light notebook computer as your primary PC, switch to a legacy-free PC, or install a legacy-free motherboard, your serial port cradle's time will be up because the serial port is usually missing from these computer designs. The serial port is the oldest and one of the slowest ports found in the PC, and USB ports have replaced it for just about every use.

If you want to try (or *must* switch to) USB for your older PDA, here are your options:

- Replace your serial-port cradle with a USB cradle.

- Add a USB adapter kit to your existing serial cable.

- Add a serial port card to your PC.

- Use the serial-port cradle with another PC you want to use with your PDA and buy a USB cradle or cable for your primary PC.

- Buy a universal (USB/serial) cradle for your PDA.

I recommend getting a USB or universal cradle if you plan to keep your PDA for a while and getting the less-expensive USB adapter kit if you're considering moving to a better PDA.

ON THE WEB: Expansys to the Rescue

If you're not happy with the cradle, cable, or other options available from your PDA vendor, the Expansys web site has lots of problem-solving devices to choose from for all major platforms used by mobile devices (Pocket PC, Palm OS, Psion, Symbion, Linux, and Tablet PC). See it at www.expansys.us.

Syncing in More Than One Place

A cradle is a handy place to keep your PDA if you're always working with the same PC. However, if you're on the go, you might be checking email at the office, at home, and in a hotel in the same week. You *could* buy an extra cradle for each PC, but that's a lot of expense for something you use occasionally. In addition, a cradle's just one more bulky thing to pack. Even if your PDA normally uses a cradle, you can often get a more compact file-synchro-nization cable. The cable is small enough to pack, and if you're worried about whether to get a USB or serial-port model because you don't know what you'll be plugging into next, vendors such as Expansys offer universal cables for most popular PDA models.

Worried about keeping your PDA's battery charged up when it's away from its normal charging/synch cradle? You can get a Sync-and-Charge cable that can recharge the PDA through your PC's USB port while syncing the units.

Solving File-Format Frustrations

If you work with more than just calendars and to-do lists, you need to transport documents of various kinds back and forth between your primary PC and your mobile device. Whether you're dealing with the PC–to-PDA and back again round-trip, or the seemingly simpler desktop-to-laptop-to desktop round-trip, problems with file conversions along the way can wreck your documents and your nerves.

The following sections help you make sure your documents survive the trip, no matter which end they start from.

From PC to PDA and Back with Documents to Go

File-synchronization programs handle transporting calendar and email message files between PDAs and PCs. However, if you work with a PC on a day-to-day basis, you do much more than schedule appointments or read email. You create letters, memos, spreadsheets, and presentations. You might create (and you certainly look at) Acrobat PDF files. In addition, just because you're away from your desk with a PDA doesn't mean you don't need to use the documents you create on your PC wherever you are.

If you have a Palm OS PDA, the need for software that can help you view, use, and revise common file formats created on a Windows or Mac OS computer is obvious. What's not so obvious is that Pocket PC users also need third-party software support. Reviews have demonstrated that the applications Microsoft bundles with Pocket PCs, such as Pocket Word and Pocket Excel, fall well short of perfection when working with files created by their full-size siblings or when sending modified files back to the PC. With either type of PDA, you need to make changes and create new documents as well as view existing documents and get the new or revised documents back to the PC without data or format loss.

Although Pocket Word and Pocket Excel fall short, Documents To Go from Dataviz (www.dataviz.com) works very nicely. Documents To Go is available in three editions:

- **Standard**—Word processing and spreadsheet; bundled with some Sony PDAs.
- **Professional**—Adds support for PowerPoint presentations from Windows PCs; bundled with some Palm PDAs.
- **Premium**—Adds support for email from Outlook, Outlook Express, and Lotus Notes; PDF (Acrobat) support; pictures; and charting from Excel spreadsheets.

Although the dominance of Microsoft Office means that many users of Documents To Go will be working with Word, Excel, and PowerPoint documents, many additional file formats are supported. WordPerfect, plain text, AppleWorks, ClarisWorks, WordPro, Quattro Pro, and Lotus 1-2-3 are supported by the word processing and spreadsheet applications. The email client also supports many popular file types as attachments. Figure 25.1 shows a sample screen from the word processing module.

A 30-day trial is available, and users of bundled versions are eligible for upgrade pricing.

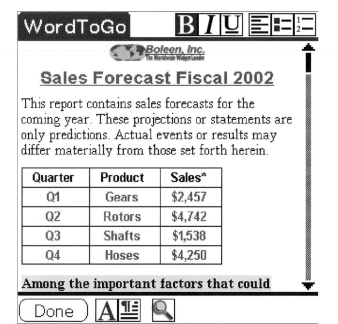

Figure 25.1

Documents To Go's word processing module supports the display of embedded graphics. Screenshot courtesy of Dataviz.

ON THE WEB: Documents To Go Goes the Distance

Walter S. Mossberg's Personal Technology column for the *Wall Street Journal* tested Documents To Go against Pocket PC. See the results at:

http://ptech.wsj.com/archive/ptech-20030206.html

Jason Johnson prefers Documents To Go for an overall Palm OS office suite, but also finds other office suites have strong individual components. Read the review at:

http://www.palmtipsheet.com/html.texts/tipsht36.html#palm-office

Links to other reviews are available on the Dataviz web site.

Coping with PC-to-PC Document Woes

At first glance, it might seem easier to transfer files between two PCs than between a PC and a PDA. However, this isn't always the case. If you don't have an *exact* match for the following, your documents could be mangled during the trip:

- Same application
- Same version
- Same file format

Although many PCs have been bundled with Microsoft applications in recent years, one frequent problem is that Microsoft keeps fiddling with its file formats. Although the difference between Word XP and Word 2000, for example, isn't enormous, Word XP to Word 97 (or back again) can cause plenty of problems.

If you don't have exactly the same application on both your home and traveling systems, try the following:

- If one system uses a newer version of Microsoft Word than the other, use the Tools menu's Save dialog box to disregard features introduced after the version of Word on the other system; if you need additional fixes, use the Tools menu's Compatibility tab to make additional adjustments.

- If the computers use different applications, use a common file format such as Rich Text Format (.rtf), or look for a low-cost way to add the preferred application to one computer or the other. For example, if you want to standardize on Microsoft Word, buy a copy of Microsoft Works Suite (not Works) for each computer that lacks Word. Some vendors are now shipping WordPerfect, which (unlike Word) has used the same file format for several versions. If you prefer WordPerfect, you can get it as part of WordPerfect Family Pack. Or, if you prefer to use Quattro Pro and other Corel office applications as well as WordPerfect, get WordPerfect Office.

Even if you have the same applications on both computers, watch out for the following problems:

- **Missing file conversion filters**—If you save a file in a format the other computer can't read, the target computer can't use it. Use the Custom Installation option to select the same import/export filters for both computers. I prefer to install all the filters, just to be on the safe side.

- **Missing fonts**—If you stray away from the safety (and boredom) of Courier New, Arial, and Times New Roman and select fonts on one system that aren't on the other computer, your documents will be converted to the nearest matching font. Page breaks and other formatting will be clobbered in the process.

- **Different or missing printer installations**—Windows applications format the document according to both the fonts and the printer installed. Some programs, such as presentation applications, might not work properly if a printer isn't installed. Even if one of your computers is never connected to a printer, install the drivers for your default printer and set it as the default so that your documents will match on both computers.

Troubleshooting Your Portable's Connection to Your PC

Whether you use a PDA, notebook computer, or Tablet PC to carry your digital life with you, getting information between your preferred portable device and your PC isn't always trouble-free. Try these tips to make the connection work as smoothly as possible.

Help! I want to use Offline Files, but I keep getting an "out of disk space" error when I select the network share with the files I want to transfer to my notebook computer.

When you set up Offline Files to work with a particular set of files, they are copied to your computer from the network. Then, when you synchronize with the server containing the files, changes are copied back to the server. If you have limited space on your notebook computer's hard drive, you should create a collection of files you work with most often and store them in a special folder instead of trying to use an existing shared folder. For example, if I selected the "My Documents" folder on my desktop for offline access with my notebook computer, over 16GB of files would need to be transferred to the notebook computer! However, if I create a network share folder with just my email and current projects, it might require only one or two GB of space.

Help! I'm trying to synchronize data with my Palm OS device, and half the time it doesn't work.

HotSync failures can happen for a variety of reasons:

- You might have an application that has crashed on your Palm; reinstall it.

- You might have open entries in your To Do List or Memo Pad; save them and try the HotSync process again.

- The program that provides the conduit (connection) between the Palm OS device and the PC might be corrupted. Reinstall it.

See the TechTV web site article "Alternatip: Stop That Awful Synching Feeling on Your Palm" (`www.techtv.com/screensavers/answerstips/story/0,24330,2440711,00.html`) for more tips.

Help! I'm looking for software to synchronize my smart phone with my computer, but I don't want to spend a lot of money.

Don't overlook the software bundled with the phone. Many phones include synchronization software; if your phone didn't include it, check with the vendor web site to see if you can download it.

Glossary

Terms in *italics* are also in the glossary.

2-megapixel Refers to digital cameras with a charge-coupled device (CCD), which has approximately two million pixels. Resolution is approximately 1,536×1,024 pixels.

24-pin Dot-matrix printhead type that creates good NLQ (Near Letter Quality) printing.

286 First CPU used in MS-DOS systems to allow more than 1MB of RAM.

3-megapixel Refers to digital cameras with a CCD having approximately three million pixels. Resolution is approximately 2,048×1,536 pixels.

32-bit disk access Windows disk access that bypasses the ROM BIOS for speed; optional in Windows 3.x; a standard feature in Windows 9x/Me/2000/XP.

32-bit file access Windows for Workgroups 3.11 disk cache that replaces Smartdrv.exe; a standard feature in Windows 9x/Me/2000/XP.

386 First CPU to allow upper memory blocks and EMS memory with EMM386 memory manager; available in 32-bit (DX) and 16-bit (SX) versions.

486 First CPU with built-in math coprocessor (DX versions) and cache RAM (all versions).

586 CPUs roughly equal to Pentium-class; also used by AMD and Cyrix for CPUs that could be used to upgrade 486 systems to Pentium 75MHz performance.

6x86 VIA (originally Cyrix) Pentium-class CPU (also known as MII).

8086 16-bit sibling of the 8088; used by some compatible systems such as Compaq.

8088 Original chip used in IBM PC and PC/XT; has 8-bit data bus and 1MB RAM limit.

9-pin Dot-matrix printhead type with high durability and good multipart form printing but poor NLQ printing.

10/100 Ethernet Ethernet cards, hubs, and switches that support either 10Mbps (10BaseT Ethernet) or 100Mbps (Fast Ethernet) standards.

10/100/1000 Ethernet Ethernet cards, hubs, and switches that support 10Mbps (10BaseT Ethernet), 100Mbps (Fast Ethernet), and 1000Mbps (Gigabit Ethernet) standards.

10BaseT Ethernet A form of 10Mbps Ethernet that uses Category 3 or Category 5 unshielded twisted-pair (UTP) cables connected to a hub or switch.

AC Alternating Current. It is lethal at household voltage levels and must be converted to DC for use in computers.

access point Device on a Wi-Fi network that provides a connection between computers on the network. Can be combined with a *router* and a *switch*.

ACPI Advanced Configuration and Power Interface. It controls how peripherals, BIOS, and computers manage power and is supported by Windows 98/Me/2000/XP and replaces APM.

active-matrix LCD screen using a transistor for every pixel. This type of screen provides a bright, wide viewing angle.

active partition Hard disk partition that can be used to boot the computer; must be formatted with the /S option to be bootable in MS-DOS or Windows 9x; only primary partitions can be active.

ActiveX Microsoft technology for interactive web pages; used with Internet Explorer.

active heatsink A *heatsink* with a fan. Active heatsinks were originally introduced to keep processors cool, but are also being used to cool the 3D accelerator chips of most high-performance video cards and the North Bridge chips on many recent motherboards. An active heatsink is usually powered by a motherboard power connector or a spare drive power connector.

address bus Bus used by CPU to access memory by its hexadecimal address.

Administrator Windows NT/2000/XP Professional term for the manager of a given computer or network; only users in the Administrators group can perform some management tasks.

ADSL Asymmetric Digital Subscriber Line. A form of *DSL* that enables faster downloads than uploads. Can be provided over high-quality existing phone lines and is well-suited for residential and small-business use.

AGP Accelerated Graphics Port. This high-speed dedicated video slot or circuit can use system memory for 3D textures. It comes in 1x, 2x, 4x, and 8x speeds.

allocation unit size Minimum amount of disk space a file actually uses; varies with FAT type and disk size; also known as *cluster size*.

AMD Advanced Micro Devices; one-time second source for Intel 286-486 CPUs now makes advanced CPUs. Current models include Athlon XP (comparable to Pentium 4) and Athlon 64 (new 64-bit processor architecture). Also made Athlon, Duron, K6, and K5 processors.

AMR slot Audio Modem Riser slot; a small slot designed to handle a riser card that supports motherboard's built-in audio and modem capabilities. AMR slots are frequently found on recent motherboards, but the actual riser cards are hard to find.

analog Infinitely variable; opposite of digital. VGA is an analog display technology.

APM Advanced Power Management. It is supported by most recent BIOS and Windows 3.1/9x/Me/2000/XP. Most recent system use ACPI power management instead.

application program Program used to create, modify, and store information. Microsoft Word, Adobe Photoshop, and Corel Draw are all application programs.

archive attribute Indicates file has not yet been backed up; automatically set when a file is created or modified.

ARCNet Attached Resource Connection Network. This early coaxial-cable network was used to replace IBM 3270 terminals that used the same RG-59 cable; it is now obsolete.

AT Advanced Technology. IBM's first 286-based PC.

ATA AT Attachment. A series of standards for IDE drives and devices.

ATAPI   AT Attachment Packet Interface. A term used for CD-ROM and removable-media drives that can connect to an IDE interface.

AT commands   Commands used to control modems; they are sent by telecommunications programs such as Windows' HyperTerminal. ATDT 555-1212 (uses tone dialing to call 555-1212) is an example of an AT command.

Athlon   First AMD processor to use a non-Intel slot (Slot A); later used Socket A and reached speeds up to 1.4GHz. Replaced by Athlon XP.

Athlon XP   AMD's newest CPU with top speeds exceeding 2GHz; replaced the original Athlon and uses the 462-pin Socket A.

ATX   Advanced Technology Extended, an advanced motherboard and power supply design; motherboard is wide with two rows of I/O ports on rear of system to the left of the expansion slots; power supply uses a 20-pin connector. ATX has become the standard for PC motherboards since it was introduced in 1996. See also *flex-ATX* and *micro-ATX*.

AUI   Attachment Unit Interface. This 15-pin connection on 10Base5 Ethernet cards is now obsolete.

auto-detection   IDE hard disk setup procedure that allows system to query drives for geometry at startup; can also be used with some BIOS setup routines.

auto-ranging   Multimeter option that allows meter to select correct voltage range.

B-size paper   11×17-inch paper; the next size up from A-size paper used in Europe (similar to 8.5×11-inch U.S. letter size).

Baby-AT   Motherboard that uses the same mounting holes but is physically smaller than the IBM AT (Advanced Technology) motherboard.

backup   Making a copy of a file for safekeeping, especially with a special program that must be used to restore the backup when needed; backups may be compressed to save space. Full backup backs up the entire contents of the specified drive or system; a differential backup backs up only the files that have changed since the last full backup.

base memory   Also known as *conventional memory*; memory between 0–640KB used by MS-DOS.

bayonet   Mounting method used to attach ARCNet and Thin Ethernet cables to cards or T-adapters.

beep code   Power On Self-Test (POST) audio error messages.

binary   Numbering system used to store computer data; 0 and 1 are the only digits.

binding   Configuring network hardware with protocols it will use.

BIOS   Basic Input Output System. It controls and tests basic computer hardware at the beginning of the boot procedure.

bit   1/8 of a byte; 8 bits equals 1 byte; many devices send/receive data in bits.

block mode   IDE disk access method that reads multiple sectors before an IRQ is issued.

blog   Short for weblog. A journal created by one or more writers and posted on the web, a blog usually has short paragraphs added on a daily or weekly basis that discuss current topics of all types with links to other web sites for more information, and similar or contrasting points of view on the topic.

blogger   Creator of a blog. See *blog*.

blogging   The process of creating a blog. See *blog*.

Bluetooth   A short-range wireless networking standard that supports non-PC devices such as mobile phones and PDAs, as well as PCs. Bluetooth uses the 2.45GHz frequency with a range up to about 30 feet. Data transmission runs at 1Mbps or 2Mbps, depending upon the version of the technology supported by the devices.

BNC   Bayonet Neil-Concelman. This barrel-shaped connector is used for Thin Ethernet and ARCNet Coaxial cable and T-adapters.

boot   Starting the computer. A warm boot is restarting the computer without a reset or shut-down. A cold boot is shutdown or reset before startup.

boot disk   Disk (usually a floppy disk) with operating system files needed to start the computer.

boot sector   Starting location of operating system files on a floppy disk or hard disk.

boot sequence   Procedure followed by system during the startup process; also called bootstrap-ping.

bootlog.txt   A hidden file created by Windows 9x/Me in the root directory of the boot drive, it stores all startup events and can be used to troubleshoot startup problems.

Broadband Internet   Internet connections with rated download speeds in excess of 100Kbps. Most common types include *cable* and *DSL*, but ISDN, fixed wireless, and satellite Internet services are also broadband services.

browser   Program that interprets HTML documents and allows hyperlinking to web sites.

BSOD   Blue Screen of Death. This is a fatal system error in Windows 2000 and XP that stops the system from starting; it is also called a stop error, and is named after the blue back-ground and the white text error message. Blue screens can also appear in other versions of Windows, although Windows 2000 first made the term popular.

buffer   A special holding area for data before the data is transferred to the destination device. CD-RW drives use RAM buffers to store data being written to CD-R media by a disk-mastering program.

buffer underrun   Error condition during CD-R mastering in which the drive empties the CD-RW drive's buffer and can't finish mastering the disc. The media must be discarded. New drive features such as BURN-proof can pause a drive's writing operation and enable it to continue after the buffer is refilled. See *burning a coaster*.

buffered memory   Memory that is isolated from the memory controller in the chipset by extra components on the memory module. Buffered memory is often used on mother-boards with more than three SDRAM or DDR SDRAM slots or systems designed to handle a very large amount of memory.

burning a coaster   An unsuccessful attempt to create a CD-R with a mastering program; usually caused by a buffer underrun, but can also be caused by defective media.

BURN-Proof   Sanyo's technology for pre-venting buffer underruns on CD-RW drives.

bus frequency   The actual clock speed of the system bus; it is multiplied by a given factor to calculate the bus speed. In typical system BIOS setups on recent systems, the bus frequency needs to be selected so that the BIOS can cal-culate the correct bus speed for the processor. For example, an Athlon XP with a bus speed of 333MHz has a bus frequency of 166MHz (the processor performs two operations per cycle). A Pentium 4 with a bus speed of 800MHz has a bus frequency of 200MHz (the processor per-forms four operations per cycle). See *bus speed*.

bus-mastering High-speed data transfer used by advanced IDE interfaces and some add-on cards.

bus mouse Mouse that plugs into a 6-pin port on an add-on card, now obsolete.

bus speed Also called front-side-bus or FSB speed; this is the speed at which the CPU addresses the memory and motherboard components. Common bus speeds on current systems include 333MHz (recent Athlon XP processors), 400MHz (early Pentium 4 and Celerons based on the Pentium 4 design), 533MHz (newer Pentium 4s). Note that the bus speed of these processors is not the same as the *bus frequency*. See *bus frequency*.

bus topology Network topology in which all systems share a common cable.

byte One character; the basic building block of data storage; 8 bits equals 1 byte.

C-shaped paper path Cross-section of the paper path used by some inkjet laser printers; the paper is pulled through the printer and returns to an output tray on the same side of the printer as the input tray.

cable select Method of IDE configuration in which a special cable indicates which drive is master and which is slave. 80-wire ATA data cables are designed to use cable select.

cache A holding place for information to allow faster access than normal; used for drives (disk cache) and memory (Level 1, Level 2 caches).

cache hit Data in cache.

cache miss Data not in cache. It must be retrieved from next cache level, normal storage, or RAM location.

Card and Socket Services See *CSS*.

CardBus 32-bit version of PC Card/PCM-CIA slot used for fast network interfacing, USB 2.0, and IEEE-1394 ports.

carpal-tunnel syndrome A common type of Repetitive Strain Injury (RSI) affecting the wrists.

Castlewood Orb A high-capacity removable-media drive available in two capacities (2.2GB and 5.7GB) and a variety of interfaces. Developed by Castlewood Systems, Inc.

Category 5 The most common type of unshielded twisted-pair cabling used for networking and signaling applications. Category 5 (CAT 5) cabling supports 10BaseT, Fast Ethernet, and Gigabit Ethernet. However, Gigabit Ethernet uses all four wiring pairs in Category 5 cable, while the others use only two pairs. You can use Category 5E (CAT 5E) or Category 6 (CAT 6) cables in place of CAT 5 to provide an extra margin of signal quality.

CAV Constant Angular Velocity. CAV is the method used by low-cost CD-ROM and similar optical drives to read data. CAV drives spin the media at a constant speed, and as a result, reach their maximum x-speed ratings only at the outer edge of the media. P-CAV drives combine CAV and CLV technologies for more speed.

CD-R Recordable CD. Contents of CD-R can be added to but not changed.

CD-ROM Standard optical drive. Most can read CD-R media, but they require MultiRead capability and a UDF reader program to read CD-RW media.

CD-RW Rewriteable CD. The contents can be changed. A CD-RW drive can also use CD-R media.

Celeron   Economy version of Pentium II, Pentium III, or Pentium 4 processors; older models were available in Slot 1 or Socket 370 form factors, but the most recent models use Socket 478.

Centronics   A double-sided edge connector originally made popular by the early Centronics parallel printers. Currently used for parallel ports in printers (36-pin version) and for older narrow SCSI external devices (50-pin version).

CGA   Color Graphics Adapter. This was the early digital video standard with 320×200 4-color or 640×200 2-color modes.

channel   Pathway between two devices, as in DMA channel.

character printers   Term for printers that output one character at a time, such as dot-matrix, inkjet, and obsolete daisywheel printers; also called *line printers*.

chip   Ceramic shell containing miniaturized computer circuits and connectors.

chipset   A group of chips that perform support functions for a motherboard (such as memory controllers, I/O, PCI and ISA bus controllers) and replace the large numbers of separate chips once used for these tasks. Chipsets normally contain anywhere from one to three chips, including the North Bridge, South Bridge, and Super I/O chips (see separate entries for details). A motherboard's processor and memory compatibility and other features are determined by the chipset it uses.

CHS   Cylinder-Head-Sectors per Track. CHS refers to the standard hard-disk geometry specifications that must be specified in the system BIOS for IDE drives. The user can enter the values manually, but most recent systems can autodetect the correct values.

clean boot   Booting system without device drivers; also refers to starting a system with an uninfected floppy disk for virus detection.

client   Computer that uses shared resources on network.

client/server network   Network using dedicated servers such as Novell Netware or Windows Server 2003.

cluster size   See *allocation unit size*.

CLV   Constant Linear Velocity. A method used by more expensive CD-ROM and similar optical drives to read data. CLV drives vary their rotational speed depending upon what part of the media is being read by the laser. As a result, speed ratings across the media are more consistent.

CMOS   Complimentary Metal-Oxide Semiconductor. Refers to low-power chip design; it's also a common term for Real-Time-Clock/non-Volatile RAM chip (RTC/NVRAM).

CNR slot   Communication Network Riser slot. The CNR slot is a successor to the AMR slot and is designed to provide a standard motherboard connector for a small card with modem, Fast Ethernet networking, and audio capabilities.

coast   Time period that a computer's power supply can continue to run without AC power flowing to it; the coast time for typical PC power supplies is longer than the switchover time from AC to battery backup power.

COAST   Cache on a Stick. This is the standard pipeline-burst cache module used on some early Pentium systems; it resembles a SIMM but uses a different type of connector.

coaster   An unusable CD-R disc, usually the result of a buffer underrun during mastering. See *burning a coaster* and *buffer underrun* entries.

coaxial   Cable with solid inner conductor and metal mesh shielding.

cold boot   Starting a system from power-down or with reset button; memory count and other hardware tests are performed.

collating   The process of holding a page in the memory of a laser or LED printer and printing multiple copies before receiving and printing the next page; activated by the print options in the application being used to print the document.

color depth   The number of colors that can be displayed on-screen, often referred to in powers of 2. Common values include 8-bit (2^8 equals 256 colors), 16-bit (2^{16} equals 65,536 colors), and 24-bit (2^{24} equals 16,777,216 colors). The 32-bit color depth settings on 3D video cards provide the same color depth as 24-bit color, but uses the extra 8 bits for 3D drawing functions.

COM port   Serial port.

combo card   A PC Card (PCMCIA card) that combines two functions, usually network and modem.

combo slot   Two slots grouped together so that only one at a time can be used; typically used for PCI and ISA slot types.

Compact Flash   Popular flash-memory storage standard used by digital cameras. It can be attached to desktop and portable PCs by means of a card reader or PC Card adapter.

compact installation   Windows 9x/Me installation option that does not load optional accessories to save disk space.

Config.sys   Text-based configuration file used by MS-DOS and Windows 9x to load 16-bit device drivers and set up the system.

consumables   Collective term for paper, media, ink, and toner used by various types of printers. The true long-term cost of a given printer must take into account the cost per page of the consumables used by the printer.

continuity RIMM   A device resembling a normal RDRAM RIMM module but containing no on-board RAM. A continuity RIMM must be used to fill any empty sockets on motherboards, which use RIMMs for proper handling of memory signals. For example, if you use two RIMMs on a motherboard with three RIMM sockets, the third socket must have a continuity RIMM installed, or the motherboard won't work.

continuous tone   Original photographs contain tones from blacks to white; laser printers convert these to digital form for printing.

Control Panel   A Windows feature that sets Windows hardware options. It can be accessed from the Start or Start, Settings menu in most versions of Windows.

cool-switching   Windows use of Alt + Tab keys to move from one active program to another.

copy-protection   Methods of preventing software from being duplicated or used without the developer's permission. Old methods included using the original floppy disk at all times to run the program and using an install program that rendered the original floppy disk useless after installation. Current methods include the use of a *dongle*, which must be attached to the serial or parallel port of a computer before the program can be run or deliberately damaging a section of the program CD-ROM so that it can't be duplicated.

CPU   Central Processing Unit. The computational "brains" of the computer, such as Pentium 4, Athlon XP, and so on.

CQ   Correspondence Quality. This is the best print option on some 9-pin dot-matrix printers.

CRT   Cathode Ray Tube. A monitor's picture tube, a large vacuum tube that displays information.

CSS   Card and Socket Services. This software enables computers to interchange PC Card (PCMCIA) devices.

custom installation   Windows 9x/Me installation option that provides maximum control over setup process.

cycle   Refers to alternating current sine wave; 50Hz (cycles per second) is the European/Asian standard; 60Hz is the North American standard.

cylinder   Part of hard disk geometry; all the tracks are in a vertical row.

CYMK   Cyan Yellow Magenta Black. Refers to a four-color model for graphics and printing; these are the ink colors used by most inkjet printers and might sometimes be referred to as CMYK when used to describe printer colors; compare to RGB (Red, Green, Blue), a three-color model used for on-screen graphics.

DAE   Digital Audio Extraction. The process of converting tracks from a music CD to a digital format such as MP3 or WMA at faster than normal 1x analog speeds. Many recent CD-ROM and CD-RW drives have high-speed DAE rates to make the production of digital audio more efficient. A DAE rate of 24x, for example, means that a CD audio track that takes 4 minutes (240 seconds) to play at normal 1x speed can be converted to digital format in 10 seconds!

daisy-chaining   Connecting multiple devices through a single port; used by EPP and ECP parallel-port modes, SCSI, and USB ports.

daisywheel   Obsolete typewriter-style fully formed character printing.

data bus   Carries data between devices on the motherboard.

data mirroring   A type of RAID (Redundant Array of Inexpensive Drives) configuration in which one drive is an exact copy of the other. As the first drive's contents change, the second drive's contents are changed in exactly the same way to create an automatic, immediate backup. This technique is used by RAID Level 1.

data striping   A type of RAID configuration in which two drives are used as a single logical unit. By writing to two drives at once, disk performance is increased, but if either drive fails, all data is lost. This technique is used by RAID Level 0.

DB-9   9-pin D-shaped external cable connector used primarily for serial ports (DB9M) and for old video standards such as EGA, CGA, and monochrome (DB9F).

DB-25   25-pin D-shaped external cable connector used for parallel port (DB25F) and some serial ports (DB25M). F stands for a female connector (with holes) and M stands for a male connector (with pins).

DC   Direct Current. Low-voltage is used by the motherboard; high-voltage is used in some printers. DC must be converted from AC.

DCC   Direct Cable Connection. This is a temporary "mini-network" used by Windows 9x/Me/2000/XP to connect to computers through server or parallel ports for data transfer; it can also be used with IR ports, which emulate serial ports. XP calls this Direct Parallel Connection when parallel ports are used.

DDR SDRAM   Double-Data-Rate SDRAM. A faster form of SDRAM used by many high-performance video cards and motherboards.

debug startup options   /d: startup options used by Windows 9x for troubleshooting.

decimal   Base-10 numbering system used for ordinary calculations.

dedicated server   Computer used strictly to provide shared resources, such as Novell NetWare, Windows NT Server, Windows 2000 Server, or Windows Server 2003.

defragment   Reorganizing the files on a drive to occupy contiguous sectors to improve retrieval speed; an integral part of Windows 9x/Me/2000/XP.

degauss   To demagnetize a CRT display. Degaussing removes color fringing and distortions onscreen. Some monitors automatically degauss the CRT when the monitor is turned on, and others offer a degaussing button or menu option to degauss on demand.

desktop   Windows 9x/Me/NT/2000/XP location for shortcuts; Windows 3.1 location for program groups.

desktop PC   A computer that sits on the top of the desk, instead of on the floor (tower style). Usually has fewer drive bays and fewer expansion slots than a tower PC.

detlog.txt   A Windows 9x/Me hidden file that records the results of the hardware detection performed when Windows was first installed. If a Windows installation fails, use detlog.txt to see which hardware may not have been detected properly.

device driver   Program used to modify an operating system to support new devices.

device ID#   Method of indicating different devices attached to a SCSI host adapter; each device must use a unique device ID#, which is set on each device.

Device Manager   Windows 9x/Me/2000/XP portion of system properties sheet used to view and control device configuration. These include IRQ, DMA, I/O port address, memory address, drivers, and other configuration options.

DFP   Digital Flat Panel. This early standard for LCD display panels for desktop PCs was superseded by the current DVI standards.

DHCP   Dynamic Host Configuration Protocol. Provides IP addresses as required; allows a limited number of IP addresses to service many devices that are not connected at the same time.

digital   Data that is stored or transmitted as zeros (off) or ones (on).

digital rights management   Also known as DRM. This refers to storage devices such as Secure Digital flash memory cards or to file formats and programs such as *WMA* (created by Windows Media Player), which allow the creator of digital content to control how the content is used and where it is played back.

DIMM   Dual Inline Memory Module. This high-speed, 168-pin memory module is used in Pentium II, Pentium III, Celeron, Athlon, and Duron systems.

DIP   Dual Inline Pin. A rectangular chip with legs on long sides only. Design used for the system BIOS chip on some motherboards.

directory entry   A directory (folder) or file allocation unit in use by a file or folder; all file systems have limits on the maximum number of directory entries per drive, and FAT16 has a limit of 512 entries in the root directory.

disk cache   A section of RAM that holds data passing to and from a hard or floppy drive to speed up disk operation. Windows 9x/Me/2000/XP all feature integrated disk cache.

DMA   Direct Memory Access. High-speed transfers between devices and RAM that bypass the CPU.

DNS   Domain Name System. Translates domain names into IP addresses.

docking station   Allows notebook computers to use devices not built-in, such as standard PCI or ISA cards, external CD-ROM drives, and others; requires a proprietary, dedicated external bus connector.

domain   Windows Server term for a group of computers that share resources and use a common user account; a server called the domain controller stores the Active Directory data used to manage the domain.

domain name   Unique alphanumeric identifier for web sites.

dongle   Removable connector that allows a PC Card (PCMCIA device) to use cables too thick to plug directly into the card; also refers to copy-protection devices attached to serial ports or parallel ports to allow software to run.

dot-matrix   A printing method using a printhead with one or more columns or print elements to create the image; usually impact, using an inked ribbon.

dpi   Dots per inch. The resolutions of a printer, scanner, or monitor are commonly defined in dpi. Higher values provide sharper images and text, but use more memory or disk space to store.

DRAM   Dynamic RAM. The slowest type of RAM, which requires frequent electrical refreshes to keep contents valid.

driver   See *device driver.*

DSDD   Double-Sided Double Density. A type of floppy disk media.

DSHD   Double-Sided High Density. A type of floppy disk media holding more than DSDD due to a different magnetic coating.

DSL   Digital Subscriber Line. A type of broadband Internet service that uses telephone lines to carry Internet traffic at speeds as high as 768Kbps or more while allowing you to use your phone for normal functions at the same time. Two major types of DSL are ADSL and SDSL. See those entries for details.

dual-boot   Operating system installation that allows you to run the previous operating system as an option; both Windows 98/Me and Windows XP can be installed in a dual-boot configuration.

dual-scan   An advanced type of passive-matrix LCD screen that splits the screen into two sections. It is better than passive-matrix, but it gives a slower and narrower viewing angle than active-matrix. Now obsolete.

DUN   Dial-Up Networking. This is the Windows 9x/Me term for using a modem to connect to other computers.

duplex   A communication method that enables data flow in both directions. *Full-duplex* allows simultaneous send and receive at the same speed. *Half-duplex* allows alternating send and receive.

Duron   A now-discontinued low-cost version of Socket A AMD Athlon; has 128KB of Level 1 cache and 64KB of level 2 cache.

DVD   Digital Versatile Disk. High-capacity replacement for CD-ROM.

DVD-RAM   A rewriteable DVD standard developed by Panasonic and supported by the DVD Forum. A few of these drives also support DVD-R write-once media.

DVD-RW   A rewriteable DVD standard developed by Pioneer Electronics and supported by the DVD Forum. These drives also support DVD-R write-once media.

DVD+RW   A rewriteable DVD standard supported by the DVD+RW Alliance, and sold by HP, Philips, Sony, and other vendors. Most of these drives also support DVD+R write-once media.

DVD±RW   Refers to drives that support both DVD-R/RW and DVD+R/RW media. Sony was the first company to produce this type of drive.

DVI   Digital Video Interface. Replaces DFP as the standard for support of LCD displays on desktop computers. DVI-D is for digital displays only; DVI-I supports digital and analog displays.

ECC   Error Correcting Code. Advanced memory that can correct errors and requires special chipsets. It is used primarily in servers.

ECP   Enhanced Capabilities Port. A high-speed IEEE–1284 parallel port option that uses IRQ, DMA, and I/O port address settings; good for daisy-chaining different devices.

EDO   Extended Data Out. A faster version of DRAM used on some older Pentium systems and video cards.

EEMS   Enhanced Expanded Memory Specification. This nonstandard version of EMS memory was used by some AST memory boards but is now obsolete.

EGA   Enhanced Graphics Adapter. It provided 640×350 16-color digital graphics but is now obsolete.

EIDE   Enhanced IDE. Marketing term for major features of ATA-2 version of IDE.

EISA   Enhanced Industry Standard Architecture. This 32-bit version of ISA slots is obsolete, but might be found in older servers.

email   Electronic mail. The contents of email can include text, HTML, and binary files. Email can be sent between computers via an internal computer network, a proprietary online service such as AOL or CompuServe, or via the Internet.

EMS   Enhanced Memory Specification. Paged memory used by some MS-DOS programs; it can be created with Emm386.exe with the RAM option or by specifying the amount of EMS memory to create. It is now obsolete.

enhanced Int13h support   BIOS feature required to support drives over 8GB (over 16,384 cylinders by 16 heads by 63 sectors per track).

EP   Electrophotographic. The process by which a laser printer creates a page.

EPA   Environmental Protection Agency. Federal, state, and local organizations that set standards for safe disposal of products, including computer consumables such as batteries and cleaning supplies.

EPP   Enhanced Parallel Port. A high-speed IEEE–1284 standard that uses an IRQ and an I/O port address.

Epson ESC/P2   Enhanced version of the escape sequence-based printer language used for dot-matrix and inkjet printers by Epson and other vendors.

ergonomics   The study of the usability of hardware and software products with an eye to comfort and efficiency.

ESD Electro-Static Discharge. High-voltage but low-amperage electric discharges between items with different electric potential; harmful to equipment but not to people. ESD can damage or destroy computer components, even if the ESD discharge level is too low to feel. Also called static electricity.

ESDI Enhanced Small Device Interface. Obsolete hard disk interface standard using two cables; primarily for drives over 100MB.

Ethernet Network that uses an IEEE 802.3 access method.

executable file .exe file; a machine-readable program file that can be run in any area of memory or any type of program file, including .com and .bat files.

expansion board Also known as *add-on card* or *add-on board*.

expansion slot A motherboard connection used for add-on cards; ISA, PCI, and AGP are typical types.

extended partition A nonbootable hard disk partition that can contain one or more logical DOS drives.

external command A command-prompt command that is actually a separate program.

Faraday cage Anti-static equipment bags that have a metal-coated outside surface.

Fast Ethernet A 100Mbps version of Ethernet that runs over Category 5 or better-quality UTP cables. Most Fast Ethernet hardware supports full-duplex operation for an effective speed of 200Mbps. Fast Ethernet hardware that is also compatible with 10BaseT is called *10/100 Ethernet*.

Fast SCSI A version of SCSI with double the transfer rate of SCSI-2; up to 20MB per second.

FastDisk Also known as *32-bit disk access,* an optional high-speed disk access method introduced by Windows for Workgroups 3.11. FastDisk used a special driver that was added to the System.INI file. FastDisk is the ancestor of the 32-bit disk access features found in Windows 95 and later versions.

FAT File Allocation Table. The part of the hard disk or floppy disk that contains pointers to the actual location of files on the disk.

FAT16 FAT method used by MS-DOS and Windows 95; also supported by Windows 98/Me/NT/2000/XP; allows 65,535 (2^{16}) files maximum per drive and drive sizes up to 2GB (NT/2000/XP also support FAT16 drive sizes up to 4GB).

FAT32 FAT method optionally available with Windows 95 OSR2.x, Windows 98, Me, 2000, XP. It allows 2^{32} files maximum per drive and drive sizes up to 2TB (terabytes).

fatal error Error detected during POST that prevents the system from starting; Phoenix, AMI, IBM, and MR BIOS use beep codes to indicate most fatal errors.

fault tolerance Technology that allows a defective component to fail without destroying data. RAID 1 and RAID 5 are examples of fault-tolerant technologies, because they allow one drive to fail without wiping out the data stored in the drive array.

FC-PGA Flip-Chip Pin Grid Array. A processor chip design developed by Intel that moves the processor core to the top of the chip, away from the motherboard. This enables better heat transfer to the heatsink attached to the processor. Both FC-PGA and PPGA processors use the same Socket 370 interface, but the processors' pinouts are different. Thus, some older Socket 370 motherboards can't use FC-PGA chips.

FDISK   MS-DOS and Windows 9x/Me hard disk preparation program.

fiber-optic   Network cabling using photons rather than electrical signals to transfer information.

file attachment   Text or binary data such as pictures, music files, and other types of data files that are sent along with an email message.

file attributes   Controls how files are used and viewed and can be reset by the user. Typical attributes include hidden, system, read-only, and archive; Windows 2000 and XP also use compressed and encrypted attributes when NTFS file system is used.

file extension   Up to three-character alphanumeric after the dot; indicates file type such as .bat, .exe, .doc, and so on.

file system   How files are organized on a drive; FAT16, FAT32, and NTFS are popular file systems supported by various versions of Windows.

firewall   A network device or software that blocks unauthorized access to a network from other users. Software firewalls such as Zone Alarm or Norton Internet Security are sometimes referred to as *personal firewalls. Routers* can also function as firewalls.

FireWire 400   Apple's name for IEEE-1394a high-speed serial connection (also known as *i.Link*).

FireWire 800   Apple's name for IEEE-1394b high-speed serial connection.

firmware   "Software on a chip" such as BIOS.

Flash memory   Memory device that uses electricity to change its contents, but does not require power to maintain its contents; widely used for BIOS chips and for digital camera and digital music storage. Sometimes referred to as Flash ROM.

FlexATX   Smallest ATX-family form factor for motherboards, it is narrower and shorter than microATX. FlexATX motherboards are often used in so-called small form factor systems that might have only one or two expansion slots, or no expansion slots at all.

floppy disk   Low-capacity removable media used by 3.5- and 5.25-inch floppy disk drives.

FM synthesis   Low-cost, low-fidelity method used on some sound cards for playing MIDI files by simulating the sound of different instruments.

font   A particular size, shape, and weight of a typeface. 12-point Times Roman Italic is a font; Times Roman is the typeface.

forced hardware   Hardware that is normally plug-and-play (allowing changes to the hardware configuration as needed) and has been manually set to use fixed resources; not recommended in most cases but might be necessary for compatibility with older programs which expect a device such as a sound card to use a particular configuration.

form factor   The physical shape, size and mounting arrangement of computer components such as a motherboard or power supply. A replacement for an existing component must have the same form factor as the original device.

form feed command   Ejects current page from the printer; can be software-driven or uses a button on the printer.

format   Can refer to document layout or the process of preparing a floppy disk or hard disk for use.

FORMAT   MS-DOS and Windows 9x/Me program to prepare a drive for use; hard disks must be FDISKed first.

FPM   Fast Page Mode. Type of DRAM used on most SIMMs.

FQDN   Fully Qualified Domain Name. Similar to UNC naming, but uses the domain name or IP address of the server rather than its network name.

frame rate   How quickly still images are displayed on-screen to simulate movement, usually measured in FPS (frames per second). Values below 30fps will cause noticeable jerkiness in viewing streaming media. Much higher frame rates are desirable for gaming for more realistic and responsive gameplay.

FSB   Front-Side Bus. The speed at which the processor communicates with memory. See *bus speed*.

FSR   Free System Resources. Windows 9x/Me measurement of the lowest of system, user, or GDI heaps.

FTP://   File Transfer Protocol. File transfer to or from a special server site on the World Wide Web.

fuser   Hot roller assembly in a laser printer that melts toner to paper.

gateway   Access point that allows a network (such as a LAN) to access another network (such as the Internet).

GB   Gigabyte. 1 Billion bytes.

General Protection Fault   See *GPF*.

generic driver   Device driver that provides minimal functions for a hardware device. The Generic/Text-only printer driver in Windows prints text but no fonts or graphics.

geometry   Term for the arrangement of sectors per track, cylinders, and heads on BIOS-controlled hard disks such as IDE/ATA. The manufacturer's recommended geometry is typically found on a label attached to the drive.

Gigabit Ethernet   A 1000Mbps version of Ethernet that runs over fiber-optic cable and can also use Category 5 or better grades of UTP copper cable for short-distance runs. See also *10/100/1000 Ethernet*.

GPF   General Protection Fault. A frequent type of illegal operation in Windows 9x/Me, GPFs are caused by clashes between two programs wanting the same memory space. It is common with Windows 3.1/9x/Me due to cooperative multitasking's weak memory barriers and is often caused by programs running incorrect DLL driver files.

GUI   Graphical User Interface. User interface with features such as icons, fonts, point-and-click commands; Windows and MacOS are popular GUIs.

hard drive   Storage device with rigid, nonremovable platters inside a case; also called *hard disk* or rigid disk.

hardware   Physical computing devices.

hardware profile   Windows 9x/Me/2000/XP feature that allows the user to store multiple hardware configurations and select the desired configuration at boot time.

head   Reads and writes data in a drive.

header   Beginning of a document, an email message, or a file.

header cable   Cable used on Baby-AT motherboards to route PS/2 mouse, USB, parallel, and serial port signals from the rear of the computer to the actual port connections on the motherboard. The header cables are often attached to brackets that can be used in place of empty expansion slots.

heatsink   A metal or plastic series of fins on a CPU or dot-matrix printhead used to dissipate heat quickly; CPUs normally use a heatsink equipped with a fan (called an *active heatsink*). A heatsink without a fan is also called a passive heatsink.

hexadecimal   Base-16 counting system used in computers for memory addresses and I/O port addresses.

hidden attribute   File attribute that makes a file invisible to the default Windows Explorer view or to the DIR command.

high-level format   Type of format performed by Windows Format program on hard drives and floppy drives; rewrites file allocation tables and root directory but doesn't overwrite existing data on the rest of the disk surface.

Hi-Speed USB   Another term for USB 2.0.

HomePNA   The Home Phoneline Networking Alliance network standard. A series of network standards that use existing phone lines to connect computers into small networks.

HomeRF   The HomeRF network standard. A radio-frequency home networking standard developed by the HomeRF Working Group, Inc. This working group was disbanded in early 2003 and this type of network is now obsolete.

host adapter   SCSI or IDE drive interface; may be incorporated into motherboard or located on a card.

host-based printers   Printers that use the Windows GDI, rather than a printer language, to control printing.

hot-swappable   Devices that can be attached and removed while the computer is running. The most common hot-swappable devices for PCs use PC Card, USB, and IEEE-1394 connectors.

HTML   Hypertext Markup Language. A standard for markup symbols that allow hyperlinking, fonts, special text attributes, graphics, and other enhancements to be added to text files for display with web browsers such as Microsoft Internet Explorer and Netscape Navigator. The official source for HTML standards is the World Wide Web Consortium (W3C), but both Microsoft and Netscape have added proprietary features to the HTML dialects they understand.

HTTP://   Hypertext Transfer Protocol. The basis for hyperlinking and the Internet; it is interpreted by a web browser program.

hub   Central connecting point for UTP-based forms of Ethernet. A hub broadcasts messages to all computers connected to it, and subdivides the bandwidth of the network among the computers connected to it. See *switch*.

icon   Onscreen symbol used in Windows to link you to a program or routine.

IDE   Integrated Drive Electronics. Popular 40-pin hard disk interface. See *ATA*.

IEEE   Institute of Electrical and Electronics Engineers. Sets standards for computer, electrical, and electronics devices.

IEEE 587A   Standard for surge protection devices.

IEEE 802.x   Series of IEEE networking standards used as the basis for Ethernet, Token Ring, and others.

IEEE 802.11a   A wireless Ethernet standard that uses 5–6GHz radio signals and provides performance at rates from 6Mbps up to 54Mbps. It is not compatible with other 802.11-based wireless networks unless dual-band access points are used. It is also known as *Wi-Fi* 5GHz band.

IEEE 802.11b   A wireless Ethernet standard that uses 2.4GHz radio signaling for performance from 2Mbps to 11Mbps. It is compatible with 802.11g-based wireless networks, but not with 802.11a-based networks unless dual-band access points are used. It is also known as *Wi-Fi* 2.4GHz band.

IEEE 802.11g   A wireless Ethernet standard that uses 2.4GHz radio signaling for performance up to 54Mbps. It is compatible with 802.11b-based wireless networks, but not with 802.11a-based networks unless dual-band access points are used. Wi-Fi certification for 802.11g devices is expected in mid-2003.

IEEE-1284   Standard for parallel printer interfaces.

IEEE-1394   A series of standards for high-speed serial interface, also known as FireWire or i.Link.

i.Link   Sony's term for *IEEE-1394a* or *FireWire 400* ports.

illegal operation   Windows 9x/Me term for a wide variety of problems that cause programs to stop running prematurely; use Dr. Watson to record the system condition and to troubleshoot these problems.

in the wild   Term for viruses found outside virus labs.

INF file   Windows 9x/Me/2000/XP hardware installation file type.

INI file   Windows configuration file type, used more often with Windows 3.1 but still used with Windows 9x/Me.

initialization string   Series of commands sent to a modem by a telecommunications program to configure the modem; sent before the modem is dialed to make a connection.

inkjet printer   Popular non-impact printer type.

install   Process of making a computer program usable on a system, including expanding and copying program files to the correct locations, changing Windows configuration files, and registering file extensions used by the program.

integrated port   Ports such as serial, parallel, USB, floppy, IDE, keyboard and PS/2 mouse that are built in to most recent motherboards. Some motherboards also integrate sound and video to reduce costs. Integrated ports make systems less expensive but require motherboard replacement when ports fail.

Intel   Leading manufacturer of CPUs, chipsets, and other PC components. See Intel's web site at www.intel.com.

interface   Connection between two devices.

Interlink   MS-DOS file transfer program using serial or parallel ports with LapLink-style cables.

internal command   Command-prompt command that can be used as soon as the system is booted without other files; stored in Windows 9x/Me's Command.com or Windows 2000/XP's Cmd program.

Internet   The world-wide "network of networks" that can be accessed through the World Wide Web and by Telnet, Archie, and other utilities.

I/O   Input/Output.

I/O port address   Hardware resource used to transfer data between devices; major resource used by Windows 9x to detect hardware (see *Detlog.txt*) during installation.

IPX/SPX   Internetwork Packet Exchange/Sequenced Packet Exchange. The standard network protocols used by Novell NetWare versions 4.x and earlier.

IR Infrared. Type of port common on portable computers and found on some desktop computers. This type of port is used for short-distance file transfer via DCC or for printing to IR-equipped printers and is normally configured as a serial port. Being replaced by *Bluetooth*. See *Bluetooth*.

IRQ Interrupt Request Line. 0–15; used by CPU to receive and send signals to hardware devices needing or requesting attention.

ISA Industry Standard Architecture. 16-bit version of the expansion slot originally created for the IBM PC; now obsolete.

isopropyl alcohol A type of alcohol used as the principal solvent in many specialized computer-cleaning kits.

ISP Internet service provider. A company that provides individuals and businesses with access to the Internet through dial-up, DSL, cable modem, wireless, or LAN connections.

Java A programming language developed by Sun Microsystems for use on a wide variety of computers; it is widely used in web browsers for animations and interactive features; it requires special files called Class Libraries to be added to the web server.

JavaScript A programming language that can be embedded in HTML files for simple, non-graphic calculations and interactive features.

Jaz A now-discontinued Iomega high-capacity removable drive and media.

K5 An early AMD Pentium-class CPU; replaced by the K6 family.

K6 AMD's highly successful Pentium-class chip. Now discontinued.

Kb Kilobit (1,024 bits).

KB Kilobyte (1,024 bytes).

Kbps Kilobits per second. Often used to rate modems and broadband Internet connections.

KBps Kilobytes per second. Often used to rate parallel port performance.

known-working Computer or component that has been tested and is known to work correctly; not the same as "new."

LAN Local Area Network. A network in which the components are connected through network cables; if a router is used, the network is a WAN. See also *WLAN*.

landscape mode Print mode that prints across the wider side of the paper; from the usual proportions of a landscape painting; this mode is usually slower than the default portrait mode because the fonts and graphics must be rotated; this mode is controlled by the application performing the print job.

LapLink Popular MS-DOS and Windows file transfer program and cable standard; Windows Direct Cable Connection and old MS-DOS Interlink programs can use LapLink cables.

LARGE Award BIOS disk option for translating drives over 528MB; not the same as LBA mode.

large disk support Windows 9x/Me FDISK option that, when enabled, allows you to create FAT32 drives; also called large drive support.

laser printer Type of nonimpact page printer.

LBA Logical Block Addressing. A popular method for translating hard drive geometry to allow drives over 528MB to be used by MS-DOS and Windows.

LCC Leaded Chip Carrier. Early method for packaging 286 CPUs; chip was held in place by a hinged cover and wire retainer.

LCD   Liquid Crystal Display. Type of screen used on portable computers and on flat-panel desktop displays.

legacy   Technology that predates modern standards. ISA slots, PS/2, serial, and parallel ports are typical examples of legacy technologies.

legacy USB support   BIOS option that enables USB keyboards to work outside of Windows in command-prompt and BIOS setup modes.

Level 1 cache   Memory cache located in CPU core.

Level 2 cache   Memory cache located outside CPU core; can be on CPU assembly (Pentium II, Celeron 300A and above, Pentium Pro, Athlon, Duron) or motherboard (Pentium, K6 family, and so on).

line-draw graphics   Also known as box-draw characters; these are used with many MS-DOS batch files and programs to create shapes onscreen. They may be inserted with Alt + number pad entries if PC-850 or IBM character set is in use. In Windows, use the Character Map utility with a fixed-pitch font such as Courier New to create boxes and lines in your text documents.

line feed   Advances paper to next line; button found on many dot-matrix printers.

line printer   Printer that prints one line of characters at a time. Refers to printers such as inkjet and dot-matrix; also called *character printers*.

Lithium-Ion battery   Abbreviated as Li-Ion; advanced battery technology used by many notebook computers. These batteries provide long battery life without any memory effect, so that a partly discharged battery can be recharged completely.

local drive   A drive letter that is built into or directly attached to your own computer, such as hard, floppy, IDE, USB, SCSI, or IEEE-1394 drives. Network drives that have been assigned drive letters (mapped drives) appear as local drives in the My Computer view of the system in Windows.

logging   Recording events during a process, such as in Windows' Bootlog.txt file, used to record Windows startup events.

logical drive   Drive letters that reside within a disk partition, especially within an extended partition; a single physical drive can contain two or more logical drives.

loopback plug   A device that attaches to a parallel or serial port for diagnostic testing; routes output lines to input lines. This is a common option for third-party diagnostic programs such as CheckIt and AMIDiag.

low-level format   Type of format performed by the FORMAT command on floppy disks if the /U option is used; rewrites disk sector markings and deletes all prior disk information. This is performed at the factory on IDE/ATA hard drives and must be performed on SCSI hard drives during initial configuration.

LPT   LinePrinTer. A parallel port.

LPX   Low-profile version of power supplies using the 12-pin motherboard connector or a nonstandard type of motherboard with a riser card.

LS-120   Formal name for SuperDisk drives and media; drive uses 120MB floppy disks and can also read/write standard 3.5-inch media.

LS-240   Formal name for second-generation SuperDisk drives and media. These drives read and write to 240MB floppy disks, as well as original 120MB SuperDisk media and standard 3.5-inch media. LS-240 drives can also reformat standard 1.44MB floppy disks to hold 32MB of data.

macro   A series of commands that can be stored inside a spreadsheet or word-processing file to automate certain operations; some viruses exploit the macro feature of Microsoft Word or Excel.

macro virus   A virus that uses Microsoft WordBasic or VBA commands to infect Microsoft Word or Excel documents; can be used to damage or destroy files or drive contents.

mapped drive   Using a drive letter as a short-cut to a network resource; optional with UNC-aware operating systems such as Windows 9x/Me/NT4/2000/XP, but necessary for MS-DOS programs to use network drives.

master   The first drive in logical sequence on IDE cable, determined by master/slave jumpers on each drive. When the 80-wire ATA/IDE cable is used with *cable select* settings, the drive on the black connector is master.

mastering   The process of creating a CD or DVD with a program such as Easy CD/DVD Creator or Nero Burning ROM. These programs and others write large amounts of data to the media with disk at once or track at once methods, instead of the *packet writing* method used by *UDF*.

math co-processor   Also known as FPU. Used for floating-point math computations performed by spreadsheet and CAD programs, it is now part of 486DX and all newer CPUs.

matrix   Describes the arrangement of the pins in the printhead of a dot-matrix printer or the nozzles in the printhead of an inkjet printer. The smaller the pins or nozzles and the more closely they are positioned to each other, the better the print quality.

MAU   Media Attachment Unit. Connects 15-pin port (AUI) on 10Base5 Ethernet cards to Thick Ethernet cable. It is now obsolete.

Mb   Megabit. One million bits.

Mbps   Megabits per second. Often used to describe speeds of networks and broadband Internet connections.

MB   Megabyte. One million bytes.

MBps   Megabytes per second. Often used to describe speeds of IDE and SCSI storage devices.

MBR   Master Boot Record. Pointer in first sector of a drive indicating where operating system files can be found; can be attacked by viruses.

MCGA   MultiColor Graphics Array. 320×200 256-color or 640×480 2-color subset of VGA used on low-end IBM PS/2 computers.

MDA   Monochrome Display Adapter. Nongraphics digital "green-screen" monochrome display standard.

media   Anything used to carry information, such as network cables, paper, floppy disks, and so on.

memory address   Hardware resource used by some add-on cards for RAM or ROM chips.

memory bank   Memory bits equal to data bus of CPU; might be one or more memory modules.

memory module   Memory chips on a small board, such as COAST, SIMM, and DIMM.

microATX   A reduced-size version of the *ATX* motherboard form factor. MicroATX motherboards support up to four expansion slots; most support no more than three. Most microATX motherboards have integrated audio and video.

Microsoft Knowledge Base   Online collection of Microsoft technical articles used by Microsoft support personnel to diagnose system problems. Can also be searched by end users by using the http://search.Microsoft.com web site.

MIDI   Musical Instrument Digital Interface. A standard for recording musical scores used by electronic keyboards and most sound cards.

milliseconds   ms. One thousandth of a second; used to rate storage or Internet access times; smaller is faster.

Mini-ITX   A very compact motherboard design developed by *VIA Technologies* for use in low-power computing appliances. Mini-ITX motherboards have one or two PCI expansion slots, integrated video, audio, and 10/100 Ethernet as well as *legacy* ports, but use surface-mounted VIA C3 or Eden processors instead of removable processors.

MMC   Microsoft Management Console. The Windows 2000/XP utility used to view and control the computer and its components. Disk Management is a component of MMC.

modem   Short for Modulate-Demodulate, this device converts digital computer information into analog form and transmits it via telephone system to another computer.

Molex   A type of rectangular power connector used on hard drives and optical drives; features two clipped corners for positive keying.

monitor   TV-like device that uses either a CRT or an LCD screen to display activity inside the computer. Attaches to the video card or video port on the system.

motherboard   Also known as system board or planar board. A circuit board that has expansion slots or riser card, CPU, memory, and chipset that fits across the bottom of a desktop PC or along one side of a tower PC.

Mount Rainier   A specification for CD-RW and DVD+RW drives that supports background formatting and defect management. Mount Rainier support is not yet standard in current operating systems, but is expected to be added to future version of Windows. See www.mt-rainier.org for additional information.

mouse   Pointing device that is moved across a flat surface; older models use a removable ball to track movement; most recent models use optical sensors.

mouse elbow   Similar to tennis elbow; RSI (Repetitive Strain Injury) due to excessive mouse usage.

MP3   A compressed digitized music file format widely used for storage of popular and classical music; quality varies with the sampling rate used to create the file. MP3 files can be stored on recordable or rewriteable CD or DVD media for playback and are frequently exchanged online. The process of creating MP3 files is called *ripping*.

MPEG   Motion Picture Expert Group; creates standards for compression of video (such as MPEG 2) and audio (such as the popular MP3 file format).

ms   See *milliseconds*.

MSAU   Multistation Access Unit. A hub-like device used on Token Ring networks to connect computers; the "Ring" refers to the token passing inside the MSAU between stations. Also known as MAU.

MS-DOS alias   8.3-type filename created from long filename in Windows 9x/Me for use at an MS-DOS prompt or for older systems. Windows NT/2000/XP use a slightly different method to create MS-DOS alias names.

MS-DOS prompt   Onscreen location where commands can be typed; normal prompt lists current drive and folder (directory).

MSDS   Material Safety Data Sheet. Information sheet for consumable products listing safety information.

MSDOS.SYS   In Windows 9x/Me, a text-based configuration file that sets up options for boot management and system startup.

multimeter   A device used for multiple electrical tests, including AC and DC voltage, continuity, Ohms, and others.

multiplier   Also called clock multiplier, this is the number of times faster the CPUs internal speed is when compared to its bus speed. For example, a 3.06 GHz Pentium 4 has a bus speed of 533MHz and a multiplier of 5.75 (533×5.75 equals 3060MHz or 3.06GHz).

MultiRead   A standard for CD-ROM and DVD drives that can also read CD-RW media.

MultiRead2   A standard for DVD-ROM drives that can also read CD-RW and DVD-RAM media.

nanoseconds   ns. One billionth (one thousand millions) of a second; common measurement for DRAM chips and modules; a smaller ns rating equals faster RAM.

NetBEUI   Microsoft's version of Net BIOS: a simple, nonroutable network protocol used for Windows 3.1x/Windows 9x/Me networking.

network   Two or more computers that are connected and share a resource such as hard disks or printers.

network drive   Drive or folder available through the network; usually refers to a network resource that has been mapped to a local drive letter.

nibble   4 bits.

NIC   Network Interface Card.

NiCD battery   Nickel-Cadmium battery. Rechargeable battery technology once popular for portable computers.

NiMH battery   Nickel Metal Hydride battery. A battery technology used today primarily on low-cost notebook computers; it can be used to replace NiCD batteries for longer battery life per charge.

NLQ   Near Letter Quality. The best print quality available from 24-pin dot-matrix printers.

NLX   A compact motherboard standard that allows fast replacement of a defective motherboard, it uses a riser card mounted at the end of the motherboard nearest the power supply.

nonparity   Memory that has data bits only.

North Bridge   The chip in a chipset that connects the processor bus to high-speed buses such as memory, PCI, and AGP slots.

NOS   Network Operating System. Software that allows a PC to access shared resources; might be part of a regular OS or might be an add-on.

ns   Nanoseconds.

NTFS   New Technology File System. The native file system used by Windows NT, Windows 2000 and Windows XP; the Windows 2000/XP version is called NTFS 5.0. All NTFS versions feature smaller allocation unit sizes and superior security when compared to FAT16 or FAT32.

null-modem   Serial cable that crosses send and receive lines to allow two PCs to communicate directly with each other without a modem. LapLink, Interlink, and DCC serial cables are null-modem cables.

NVRAM   Non-Volatile RAM. A motherboard chip that stores BIOS configuration information, also known as a CMOS chip.

objects   Items that can be viewed or configured with Windows Explorer, including drives, folders, computers, and so on.

OEM   Original Equipment Manufacturer. These products are sold to system builders, not at retail. Might lack some features of the retail version, such as bundled software.

OEMSETUP   Automatic Windows 9x/Me setup option included on the boot floppy disk supplied with OEM versions of Windows 9x/Me on CD-ROM.

optical   Storage such as CD-ROM, and so on, which uses a laser to read data.

OS   Operating system. Software that configures and manages hardware and connects hardware and applications. Windows XP is an OS.

OSR   OEM Service Release. Updates to the original version of Windows 95. OSR1 can be downloaded; OSR2.x must be purchased with hardware.

overclocking   Speeding up a computer by increasing the multiplier and/or bus speed used by a CPU past its rated limits; can create faster systems but can also cause system crashes.

overload   Using devices that draw more wattage than a power supply is rated to provide.

packet writing   A method for writing data to an optical disc in small blocks (packets). This method is used by *UDF* programs. Packet-written media requires a UDF reader, unlike media created with a *mastering* program, which can be read without any additional software.

page description language   PDL. The commands used to define the page's layout, contents, fonts, and graphics before it is transferred to a laser or LED printer. Leading PDLs including HP PCL (Printer Control Languge) and Adobe PostScript.

page printer   Laser and LED printers; printers that must receive the entire page before transferring it to paper.

paper bail   Spring-loaded arm with rollers running in parallel with the platen on dot-matrix printers to hold a single sheet of paper in place.

paper path   Route paper takes through a printer; straight-through paths have fewer jams.

parallax   The difference in view between the camera lens and a separate optical viewfinder on digital and film cameras. Parallax can cause objects at close shooting distances to be cut off or cropped incorrectly. Use the LCD display found on most digital cameras to avoid parallax errors.

parallel   Data-transfer method used to send 8 bits or multiples of 8 in a single operation; used by parallel port, IDE, floppy, SCSI, and memory devices.

parity   RAM error-checking method that compares checksum from 8 data bits to parity bit; system stops if values don't match.

partition   Section of a hard disk set aside for use by an operating system.

partition table   Area near the beginning of the hard disk storing disk geometry used to prepare drive, operating system(s) in use on drive, and partition start/end positions.

passive-matrix   Now-obsolete early LCD display technology that uses one transistor for each row and each column of the display. Compared to active-matrix, passive-matrix displays have slow screen response, are dimmer, and have a narrow viewing angle.

password   A word or combination of letters and numbers that is matched to username or resource name to enable the user to access network resources or accounts.

path   Series of drives and folders (subdirectories) that are checked for executable programs when a DOS command is issued or drive/network server and folders used to access a given file.

PC Card   Newer name for PCMCIA technology; credit card-sized devices inserted into a notebook computer for networking, modem, memory, and I/O expansion.

PCI   Peripheral Component Interconnect. A high-speed 32-bit or 64-bit expansion bus developed by Intel in 1993 that is standard on all Pentium II and newer systems.

PCL   Printer Control Language. Hewlett-Packard's printer language that is used on most LaserJet printers and many DeskJet printers. It is widely emulated by other laser printer makers.

PCMCIA   Personal Computer Memory Card International Association. Original name for PC Card technology; see PC Card.

PDA   Personal Digital Assistant. A hand-sized computer that provides date book, notepad, and limited application software features. The Palm and Handspring series (which run PalmOS) and the PocketPCs (which run a version of Windows CE) are popular examples of PDAs.

peer server   Client PC that also shares drives or other resources on a Windows network.

peer-to-peer network   Network in which some or all of the client PCs also act as peer servers.

Peerless   Iomega's now-discontinued modular removable-media drive system.

Pentium   First Intel CPU with 64-bit data path.

personal firewall   Software that blocks unauthorized access to a computer with an Internet connection. Can also be configured to prevent unauthorized programs from connecting to the Internet. The free Shields Up! service at Gibson Research (`http://grc.com`) tests the protection provided by personal firewalls and recommends specific products.

PGA   Pin Grid Array. Chip connector widely used for CPUs. It uses rows of pins projecting from bottom of chip to attach to sockets; variations are currently used for Celeron, Pentium III, Pentium 4, AMD Athlon XP, and Athlon 64 CPUs.

phantom directory   A problem with floppy drives in which the drive fails to detect a disk change and keeps the FAT from the original disk in memory, resulting in data loss if the new disk is written to using the old disk's FAT. Problems with line 34 (changeline support) are the cause of phantom directories.

photon   Light measurement corresponding to the electron; used by fiber-optic cables to transmit data.

physical drive   Same as hard drive or hard disk; all physical drives must be partitioned and high-level formatted before they can be used by Windows.

piezo-electric   An inkjet printing technique in which ink is forced through the printhead by the activation of a piezo-electric crystal.

PIF file   Program Information File. A file that provides special instructions to Windows on how to run a particular MS-DOS program; manually created with Windows 3.1, automatically created when program is run in Windows 9x/Me/2000/XP.

PIO   Programmed Input Output. A series of IDE interface transfer standards (modes 0–4) for data flow that runs through the CPU. It has been replaced by faster UDMA modes.

pinfeed   A simplified version of a tractor feed that uses pins fixed to either end of a platen to pull paper past the printhead of a dot-matrix printer; unlike a tractor feed, a pinfeed mechanism cannot be used with labels or other narrow paper stock.

pipeline-burst   An advanced form of memory caching that sends a continuous stream of data (pipelining) in a single operation called a burst.

platen   The rubber roller in a dot-matrix printer that is used for paper feed of single sheets.

PLCC   Plastic Leaded Chip Carrier. A common chip package used for 286 CPUs and the BIOS chips on some recent systems. The square chip has metal leads on all four sides that make contact with flexible-metal leads in the socket.

PnP   Plug and Play. A Windows 9x/Me/2000/XP technology for using the operating system to detect and configure add-on cards and external devices such as modems, monitors, scanners, and printers. PnP hardware can be moved to different resource settings as needed to make way for additional devices.

pointing stick   A pointing device used as a mouse replacement; it is integrated into some portable and desktop keyboards and responds to finger pressure. The best-known version is the IBM TrackPoint.

port replicator   Provides a single connection for serial, parallel, I/O, and video cables for portable computers; the port replicator is connected to the external devices, and is then connected to the portable computer through an external proprietary expansion bus or through a USB port.

portable   A computer you can carry around and use with battery power; the most-popular type is the notebook computer.

portrait mode   The default print option that prints across the short side of the paper; it gets its name from the usual orientation of portrait paintings and photographs.

POST   Power On Self Test. BIOS test of basic hardware performed during cold boot.

POST diagnostic card   ISA or PCI card that displays hexadecimal POST codes. It is useful for finding POST errors that are not reported by beep codes or onscreen error messages.

PostScript   Adobe's printer language optimized for elaborate graphics and text effects; used on many laser and inkjet printers used in graphics arts.

POTS   Plain Old Telephone System. Regular copper-wire telephone system that uses modems to connect one computer with another; distinguished from ISDN or DSL telephone systems.

power management   BIOS or OS techniques for reducing power usage by dropping CPU clock speed, turning off monitor or hard disk, and so on during periods of inactivity.

PPGA   Plastic Pin Grid Array. The PGA variation used by Socket 370 Celeron CPUs.

PQFP   Plastic Quad Flat Package. Surface-mounted technology used by 386SX CPUs as standard package.

primary partition   Hard disk partition that will become the C: drive on a single-drive system. It can start the system when formatted with /S option and must be set as active with FDISK or other disk-partitioning program before it can be used to boot the system.

printer language   Rules for printer commands issued by the printer driver; popular languages include PostScript, HP PCL, and Epson ESC/2.

print spooler   Program that stores and manages print jobs on disk and sends them to the printer; an integral part of Windows.

printhead   Printer component that places the image on paper using pins and ribbon or inkjet nozzles.

program group   Windows 3.1 collection of icon shortcuts; can be created when a program is installed or by the user.

properties sheet   Windows method for modifying and viewing object properties.

proprietary   Opposite of standard; refers to technologies that are used only by a single vendor. For example, a particular proprietary memory module fits only a few models of notebook computers made by a particular vendor.

protocol   Common language used by different types of computers to communicate over a network.

proxy server   Web server that sits between actual server and client PC and sends a copy of the actual content to the PC; used for filtering of content and security.

PS/2   IBM series of computers introduced in 1987. It replaced IBM PC and AT. Models 50 and up introduced Micro Channel Architecture, an unsuccessful attempt to make PCs easier to maintain and service. Term also refers to round 6-pin mouse and keyboard ports originally introduced by the IBM PS/2 series but still widely used.

pull tractor   Tractor-feed mechanism that's located after the printhead in a dot-matrix printer; it pulls the paper past the printhead and requires the user to waste a sheet of paper to tear off a print job.

push tractor   Tractor-feed mechanism that's located before the printhead on a dot-matrix printer; it pushes the paper past the printhead and makes zero tear-off printing possible.

QWERTY   The standard arrangement of typewriter keys is also used by most English or Latin-alphabet computer keyboards; name derived from the first five letter keys under the left hand.

RAID   Redundant Array of Inexpensive Drives. Various technologies for using a two or more SCSI or IDE drives as a logical unit (array) for improving speed, fault tolerance, or both. Some motherboards have ATA or Serial ATA RAID 0 (data striping) or RAID 1 (data mirroring) capabilities on-board. For RAID 0+1 (striping and mirroring) or RAID 5 (advanced striping with parity checking), dedicated SCSI, Serial ATA, or ATA/IDE host adapter cards must be used.

RAM   Random Access Memory. Memory whose contents can be changed.

RDRAM   Rambus Dynamic RAM. A high-speed narrow-channel (8-bit) wide memory technology designed to work with 1GHz+ processors better than other memory technologies such as SDRAM or DDR SDRAM. RDRAM is supported by some Intel chipsets for the Pentium III and the first Intel Pentium 4 chipsets, but is two to four times more expensive than DDR SDRAM. Most tests do not show a clear-cut practical advantage to RDRAM over DDR SDRAM.

read caching   A method of disk caching that uses RAM to hold data being read from disk; data being saved to disk goes straight to disk instead of being held in RAM. Windows uses read-caching for floppy and removable-media drives by default to avoid data loss from disk changes.

read-only   Storage that is protected from changes.

read-only attribute File attribute used to protect a file from unauthorized changes; cannot be overridden or altered and can be deleted only by explicit user override.

read-write caching A method of disk caching that uses RAM to hold data being saved to disk as well as data being read from disk for faster performance. Windows uses read-write caching for hard drives by default.

Recovery Console Special Windows 2000/XP command-line mode used for restoring damaged systems; can be launched from the Windows 2000 or XP CD-ROM or can be installed as a boot option.

Recycle Bin Windows holding area for deleted files, allowing them to be restored to their original locations; can be overridden to free up disk space.

refresh rate Rate at which electron guns in the monitor's CRT repaint the picture onscreen; also called vertical retrace rate. It is measured in Hz (Hertz); 1Hz = 1 time per second.

register size CPU's internal data pathway in bits.

registration Windows process of matching file extensions with compatible programs.

Registry Windows 9x/Me/2000/NT/XP structure that stores information on programs and hardware installed on the system and user configuration settings. For example, the Windows 9x/Me Registry is stored in two files: system.dat and user.dat in the \Windows folder; Windows 2000/XP Registry is stored in the \WinNT\System32\Config or \Windows\System32\Config folder.

REM Remark. Use at the beginning of any statement in Config.sys or Autoexec.bat to prevent the statement from being processed during system startup; the semicolon (;) is used for the same purpose on .INI files used by Windows.

removable-media Any drive whose media can be interchanged; floppy disk, CD-ROM, optical, and tape.

repeater Amplifies a network signal to enable it to run over longer cable than normal; hubs or switches also act as repeaters.

Repetitive Strain Injury See RSI.

replicate Make a copy.

resistor Used on networks and drives to indicate "end of bus."

resolution The number of dots per inch (dpi) supported by a display, scanner, or printer. Typical displays support resolutions of about 96dpi, while printers have resolutions of 600dpi to as much as 2,400dpi. Bitmaps should be scanned or created to suit the different resolution requirements of the target device. A low-resolution bitmap works well on-screen but won't print well because printers have higher resolution than displays.

ribbon cable Flat cable used to connect drives to interfaces.

RIMM Rambus Inline Memory Module. A high-performance memory module using Rambus DRAM (RDRAM). RIMMs use serial instead of parallel data transfers. Used primarily by some recent Intel and SiS-chipset motherboards for Pentium 4 processors.

ring topology Logical arrangement of computers in a circle; permission to transmit it is passed from one computer to the other; used by token-ring networking.

RIP Raster Image Processor. Converts line-draw (vector) graphics into bitmap (raster) graphics for printing. RIPs are built into laser and LED printers and some high-end inkjet printers. RIPs can be added in software or firmware form to lower-cost inkjet printers to enable them to print PostScript output.

ripping   The process of converting CD Audio tracks into digital music formats such as MP3 or WMA.

riser slot   A motherboard slot used for special types of motherboard support cards (as opposed to standard slot types such as ISA, AGP, or PCI). Riser slots are used on LPX motherboards for the riser card used for add-on cards, and on more recent motherboards for AMR and CMR cards.

RJ-11   Standard telephone cable connection use by modems and fax units.

RJ-45   UTP network cable connection used by 10BaseT and Fast Ethernet.

ROM   Read Only Memory. Memory whose contents cannot be changed.

root directory   Top-level folder on a drive that stores all other directories (folders); the root directory of C: drive is C:\. Sometimes referred to as a root folder.

router   Device that routes data from one network to another. Often integrated with wireless *access points* and *switches*.

RS-232   Standard serial port for PCs.

RSI   Repetitive Strain Injury. Injuries that occur because of repeating the same movement again and again.

RTC   Real Time Clock. Keeps time in a PC; is part of the so-called CMOS (RTC/NVRAM) chip.

S-Video   High-quality video standard used in many recent VCR and DVD products for input and output of video signals. Many recent video cards with TV output also feature S-Video jacks.

safe format   Default floppy disk format for MS-DOS; allows floppy disk to be unformatted.

safe mode   Windows troubleshooting startup mode; runs the system using BIOS routines only.

sampling rate   Frequency at which analog sound data is stored for digital conversion; a higher sampling rate produces better quality but also larger .wav files.

SCAM   SCSI Configured Auto Magically. An auto-configuration technique supported by many SCSI hard drives and SCSI interface cards designed for use with hard disks.

Scanreg   Windows 98/Me utility that checks the Registry for errors automatically at boot time or upon request; replaces a damaged Registry with the backup copy.

SCSI   Small Computer System Interface. A flexible interface usable for hard and optical drives, scanners, and other devices. Narrow SCSI interfaces enables daisy-chaining of seven devices to a single port. Wide SCSI enables daisy-chaining of up to fifteen devices to a single port.

SDRAM   Synchronous DRAM. Fast RAM that is synchronized to the motherboard's clock speed; current types include 66MHz, 100MHz, and 133MHz.

SDSL   Synchronous DSL. A type of DSL connection in which upload and download speeds are the same. SDSL connections are marketed to business rather than to home users and almost always require a newly installed circuit to the location and professional installation. See also *DSL* and *ADSL*.

SECC   Single Edge Contact Connector. Connector type used by Slot 1-type Intel Pentium II CPUs.

SECC2   Improved SECC connector used by Slot 1 type CPUs.

sector   512-byte structure, which is the basic storage unit for drives; the sectors arranged in a concentric circle on the media's surface are called tracks.

SEPP   Single Edge Processor Package. Bare-card type CPU package for Slot 1 used by early Celeron CPUs.

serial   Data-transmission technique that sends a single bit at a time at various rates; used by RS-232, USB, Serial ATA and IEEE-1394 interfaces.

Serial ATA   Also known as SATA, this version of *ATA* uses thin data and power cables to transmit data serially at rates of 150MBps or higher. SATA uses the same commands as ATA. Some recent motherboards have built-in SATA host adapters, but you can also add an SATA or ATA/SATA host adapter card to existing systems.

server   Computer that shares drives and other resources over a network. Peer servers can also be used as workstations; dedicated servers provide services to other computers such as file, print, email, and so on.

SETUP   Normal Windows 9x/Me installation program for OS and applications.

SGRAM   Synchronous Graphics RAM. A variation on SGRAM used by advanced video cards.

shadowing   A method for speeding up ROM access by copying ROMs in upper memory area to RAM, which "shadows" the same area.

share–level   Type of network access used by peer servers. A separate password is required for each shared resource; no central list of users is maintained.

shared resource   A drive, printer, or other resource available to more than one PC over a network.

shortcut   A Windows 9x/Me/2000/XP icon stored on the desktop or in the \Windows\Programs folder with an .lnk extension; double-click the icon to run the program or open the file.

SIMM   Single Inline Memory Module. 30-pin or 72-pin memory module with edge contacts used on 386 through Pentium-based systems.

single sheets   Individual sheets of paper such as copy, laser, inkjet paper; the most common form of printer paper used today.

SIP   Single Inline Package. SIMM-like memory module with 30 projecting pins rather than edge contacts. Used on a few 286-based and 386-based systems, it never became popular and is now obsolete.

slave   Second drive to be accessed on IDE cable; set with master/slave jumpers.

Slot 1   Slot used for Intel Pentium II, early Celeron, and some Pentium III CPUs.

Slot A   Slot used by early AMD Athlons; not compatible with Slot 1.

slot cover   L-shaped metal cover attached to rear of system in place of card brackets when cards are not inserted into every expansion slot.

Smart Media   A type of flash memory used by some digital cameras; requires a card reader or PC Card adapter to be compatible with portable and desktop computers.

socket   Square or rectangular motherboard connector used for processors or other removable chips such as BIOS chips.

Socket 370   370-pin square socket used by most Pentium III and all socket-mounted Celeron CPUs.

Socket 423   423-pin square socket used for the initial releases of the Pentium 4 processor.

Socket 478   478-pin square socket used for current releases of the Pentium 4 processor. It is also used by the Celeron processors based on the Pentium 4.

Socket 5   320-pin square socket used by Pentium 75 through Pentium 133 processors and the OverDrive processors made to replace those models.

Socket 603   603-pin square socket used for Pentium-4 based Xeon processor.

Socket 7   321-pin square socket used for Pentium 75MHz through 200MHz Pentium, all MMX Pentium, and Pentium-class processors such as the Cyrix MII and the AMD K6 series. Features a voltage regulator module (VRM) on the motherboard to adjust voltage for newer processors.

Socket 754   754-pin square socket used by the Athlon 64 processor.

Socket 8   387-pin rectangular socket made for the Pentium Pro processor. Can be adapted to Celeron-based processors via third-party adapters.

Socket A   462-pin square socket used for the latest versions of AMD Athlon, all Athlon XP, and all AMD Duron CPUs.

SODIMM   Small Outline DIMM. A type of DIMM module used in certain portable computers.

software   Instructions that create or modify information and control hardware; must be read into RAM before use.

South Bridge   The chip in a motherboard chipset that connects the PCI bus to the slower ISA bus. Newer South Bridge designs also perform the tasks of the *Super I/O chip*.

spam   Unsolicited email. Named after (but not endorsed by) the famous Hormel lunchmeat. Many email clients and utilities can be configured to help filter, sort, and block spam.

SPGA   Staggered Pin Grid Array. PGA variation used on Pentium and pin-compatible CPUs.

SPS   Standby Power Supply. Correct term for so-called UPS battery backup systems that switch from AC power to DC power when the AC power fails.

SR   Service Release. Microsoft term for updates to Microsoft Office, Internet Explorer, and so on.

SRAM   Static RAM. RAM based on transistors; requires electricity far less often; too expensive and bulky to use as main RAM, but popular for use as Cache RAM.

ST-506   Improved variation of the ST-412 hard disk interface invented by Seagate Technology; original hard disk interface for IBM PC/XT and AT; uses two cables for data and signals but is now obsolete.

standby   Power saving mode in which the CPU drops to a reduced clock speed and other components wait for activity.

standoff spacer   Plastic or brass device that attaches between motherboard and bottom or side of case for installation.

star topology   Network topology in which a central hub is connected to individual workstations with separate cables. This topology is used by Ethernet networks that use *UTP* cables. Wireless networks also use this topology, but substitute a wireless access point in place of a hub, and radio waves in place of cables.

start page The web page that is first displayed when you open a web browser; can be customized to view any web page available online or stored on your hard disk.

startup event File loading and other activities during the startup of Windows.

static electricity See *ESD*.

storage Any device that holds programs or data for use, including hard disks, floppy disks, CD-ROM drives, and so on.

STP Shielded Twisted Pair. A version of UTP used for Token Ring and sometimes Ethernet that uses metal shielding to protect against interference.

straight-through paper path Paper path available as an option with most laser printers to allow labels and heavier stock to go straight through the printer without being curved around rollers.

subsystem Portion of a computer that performs a particular task; the printer subsystem, for example, contains the printer, cable, port, printer driver, and BIOS configuration settings.

SuperDisk Marketing name for the LS-120 and LS-240 floppy drives and media.

Super I/O chip Part of the motherboard chipset that controls I/O devices such as serial and parallel ports, USB ports, the floppy controller, the keyboard, and the mouse port. May be integrated with the South Bridge in newer chipsets.

surge protector Device that absorbs high-voltage events to protect equipment from damage.

suspend Power-saving mode that shuts down monitor and other devices; saves more power than standby.

SVGA Super VGA. May refer to 800×600 VGA resolution or to any VGA display setting that uses more than 16 colors or a higher resolution than 640×480.

swapfile Area of a hard disk used for virtual memory; Windows 9x/Me/2000/XP uses a dynamic swapfile (called a paging file in Windows 2000/XP) that can grow or shrink as required.

switch Network device that sets a direct path for data to run from one system to another; can be combined with a *router* or wireless *access point*; faster than a hub because it supports the full bandwidth of the network at each port, rather than subdividing the bandwidth among active ports as a hub does.

switchbox Device that enables several external components to share a single serial, parallel, or other type of port or might allow several computers to share one printer.

system attribute File attribute used to indicate if a file or folder is part of the operating system; boot files are normally set as system and hidden.

system bus Motherboard wire traces carrying data, power, control, and address signals to components and expansion slots.

System Monitor Windows 9x/Me standalone utility (built into the Performance tool in Windows 2000/XP) that monitors the performance of different portions of the computer; can be customized.

System Restore A feature built into Windows Me and Windows XP that allows the user to revert the system back to a previous state in case of a crash or other system problem. System Restore points can be created by the user and are created automatically by Windows when new hardware and software is installed or by a predefined schedule. When you restore the computer to a previous state, no data or program files are erased, but registry entries for drivers, hardware, or programs created after the restore point are lost. Thus, you might need to reinstall a device or program after you use a system restore point.

T-adapter Connects to rear of 10Base2 Ethernet card to allow RG-58 cable to be attached in a bus configuration.

TAPI Telephony Application Programming Interface. Windows method for interfacing with modems and other telephony devices; allows system to interface with POTS, PBX, videophones, and others by interfacing with their TAPI drivers.

TCP/IP Transmission Control Protocol/Internet Protocol. The Internet's standard network protocol that is now becoming the standard for all networks.

temp file Temporary file. A file created to store temporary information such as a print job or an application work file. It may be stored in the default TEMP folder (such as \Windows\Temp) or in a folder designated by the application. Temp files may use the .tmp extension or start with a ~ (tilde).

terminator Device attached to the end of a daisy-chain of SCSI devices or the end of a bus-topology network such as 10Base2 Ethernet. Removing the terminator causes device or network failure.

token ring IBM-designed network based on IEEE 802.5 standard.

toner cartridge A one-piece unit containing toner, developer, and an imaging drum. It is used in many laser printer models and is sometimes referred to as an EP cartridge.

topology The arrangement of cables in a network.

touchpad A pressure-sensitive pad that is used as a mouse replacement in some portable computers and keyboards; can also be purchased as a separate unit.

Tracert The Windows version of the Traceroute command; used to track the routing between your computer and a specified IP address or server.

tractor-fed paper Paper with perforated edges; used by printers with tractor-feed mechanisms.

TrackPoint An IBM-designed pointing device that is integrated into the keyboards of portable computers made by IBM and is licensed by Toshiba and other firms. Also referred to as a pointing stick, it resembles a pencil eraser that is located between the G and H keys; the buttons are located beneath the spacebar.

tractor-feed Paper feeders that push or pull paper with perforated edges past the printhead on dot-matrix printers; uses tractor-fed paper.

Travan An Imation-developed development of the QIC-80 and QIC-Wide tape drive standards. Travan drives use a .315-inch wide tape. Current Travan designs support 20GB storage (2:1 compression) and 40GB storage (2:1 compression).

Trojan horse Program that attaches itself secretly to other programs that usually has a harmful action when triggered. It is similar to a computer virus but cannot spread itself to other computers, although some Trojan horses can be used to install a remote control program that allows an unauthorized user to take over your computer. Antivirus programs can block Trojan horses as well as true viruses.

TSR   Terminate and Stay Resident. Program that stays in memory to provide system services or hardware support such as Mouse.com; usually found in Autoexec.bat on MS-DOS and Windows 3.1 systems; Windows 9x/Me usually have 32-bit drivers that replace TSRs, and Windows 2000 and XP do not use 16-bit drivers at all.

TWAIN   Technology developed by the TWAIN Working Group to provide a standard interface between scanners and digital cameras and imaging programs. Launch the TWAIN driver for your imaging device in your program, acquire (scan or download) the image, and the image is retrieved into your application. TWAIN is *not* an acronym.

Type I slot   Thinnest PC Card slot; seldom used for devices.

Type II slot   Medium-thickness and most common PC Card slot; Type II slots can be used as a single Type III slot. Common Type II devices include modems, network interface cards, combo cards, SCSI and USB cards, and newer ATA-compatible hard drives.

Type III slot   Thickest PC Card slot. Common Type III devices include older ATA-compatible hard disk drives; a Type III slot can also be used as two Type II slots.

typeface   A set of fonts in different sizes (or a single scalable outline) and weights; Times New Roman Bold, Bold Italic, Regular, and Italic are all part of the Times New Roman scalable typeface.

typical installation   Windows 9x/Me and application software installation option that should install the features needed by most users.

UART   Universal Asynchronous Receive Transmit. The hardware "heart" of a serial port or modem; modems that lack a UART depend on the OS to operate.

UDF   Universal Disk Format. A standard for CD-RW, CD-R, and rewriteable DVD drives to drag and drop files to compatible media using a method called *packet writing*. Currently, UDF support requires an add-on program such as DirectCD, InCD, or others that are supplied with CD/DVD mastering programs. Eventually, *Mount Rainier* support will enable UDF support without add-on software.

UDMA   See Ultra DMA. Fast data-transfer methods for IDE drives; bypasses the CPU.

UL-1449   Underwriter's Laboratory standard for surge protectors.

Ultra DMA   UDMA. Improved method for DMA transfers between ATA/IDE drives and memory. UDMA uses error-checking to assure reliable data transfer at burst transfer speeds up to 100MBps.

Ultra SCSI   Various types of faster SCSI with transfer rates of 20MB–40MB/second.

Ultra VGA   UVGA. Another name for 1,280×1,024 display resolution.

UMA   Unified Memory Architecture. Memory is shared between the system and video circuit; reduces video cost but reduces performance.

unbuffered memory   Memory that interfaces directly with the chipset's memory controller. Unbuffered SDRAM memory is used by most PCs.

UNC   Universal Naming Convention. Allows network clients to access shared resources without the use of mapped drive letters or port redirection.

unconditional format   Floppy disk format option that rewrites sector markings and destroys existing data.

undelete   MS-DOS utility program that can retrieve "deleted" files still on the system; can be run as a TSR to improve chances of file retrieval. Windows 9x/Me/2000/XP's Recycle Bin performs a similar function.

underclocking   Reducing motherboard speed and/or clock multiplier below correct values to slow down CPU; usually a result of incorrect system configuration. Can also be done deliberately to permit a newer processor to run at a speed compatible with an older system.

unerase   See *undelete*; this Norton Utilities program performs the same task as undelete.

unformat   Reverses safe format of floppy disk or hard disk; cannot be used if new data has been copied to the drive.

uninstall   Process to remove Windows programs from the system; Windows 3.1 programs usually require a separate utility; Windows 9x/Me/2000/XP programs usually include this option.

Universal Disk Format   See *UDF.*

upgrade   Replacing an old version of software or hardware with a new version.

upgrade version   A version of a program (such as Windows XP) that requires proof of ownership of a previous version before it can be installed.

upper memory   Also known as *reserved memory*. Memory addresses between 640KB and 1MB set aside for ROM and RAM used on some add-on cards; empty spaces can be used as UMBs by Emm386.exe.

UPS   Uninterruptible Power Supply. Term for battery backup that uses battery at all times to power system; sometimes referred to as *true UPS* to distinguish them from SPS units (also employer of friendly driver in brown outfit who delivers computer products).

URL   Uniform Resource Locator. The full path to any given web page or graphic on the Internet. A full URL contains the server type (such as `http://`, `ftp://`, or others), the site name (such as `www.selectsystems.com`) and the name of the page or graphic you want to view (such as bookstore.html). Thus, the URL `http://www.selectsystems.com/bookstore.html` displays the bookstore page on the author's company web site.

USB   Universal Serial Bus. High-speed eventual replacement for older I/O ports; requires Windows 95 OSR 2.1 or above; Windows 98/Me/2000/XP recommended for best results, since many devices won't work with Windows 95's USB support. USB 1.1 has a peak speed of 12Mbps. USB 2.0 has a peak speed of 480Mbps; USB 2.0 ports also support USB 1.1 devices. USB 2.0 devices can be plugged into USB 1.1 devices, but run at only USB 1.1 speeds.

user-level   Network security used by Novell NetWare or server versions of Microsoft Windows; server keeps a list of users and rights/permissions; a single password provides access to all resources the user is allowed to access.

username   Used with a password to gain access to network resources.

utility program   Program that enhances day-to-day computer operations but doesn't create data; most Windows versions includes ScanDisk and Defrag utilities among others.

UTP   Unshielded Twisted-Pair. Most common type of network cable; uses RJ-45 connectors.

VA   Volt-Amps. A common way to rate battery backup units.

VBA   Visual Basic for Applications. Microsoft's application development language used with Microsoft Office. VBA is also used by many email-borne viruses, such as ILOVEYOU, because VBA scripts can be run by Microsoft email clients such as Outlook and Outlook Express.

VCACHE Virtual Cache. Windows for Workgroups 3.11 optional 32-bit disk cache driver; standard feature of Windows 95 and newer versions.

VESA Video Electronic Standards Association. Trade group of monitor and video card makers that sets video standards for resolution, color depth, and digital displays.

VESA BIOS extension TSR program supplied with many VGA cards to allow standard video drivers for MS-DOS games to work with different brands of video cards; some VGA cards have a built-in VESA BIOS extension.

VESA Local Bus 32-bit extension of ISA bus used on many 486 and a few early Pentium systems; developed for video cards, but also used for IDE and SCSI interfaces. Also called the VL-Bus, it is now obsolete.

VFAT Virtual File Allocation Table. Windows for Workgroups 3.11 optional 32-bit file access driver; standard feature of Windows 95 and later versions.

VGA Video Graphics Array. First popular analog video standard; basis for all current video cards.

virtual domain A portion of a physical web server; appears as a separate web server to the user and is accessed with a unique domain name.

virtual memory Hard disk space used as a supplement to RAM; also known as swapfile or paging file.

virus Computer program that resembles a Trojan horse that can also replicate itself to other computers.

VL-Bus See *VESA Local-Bus.*

VMM Virtual Machine Manager. Windows 9x and later versions uses VMM to provide multi-tasked services known as virtual machines to each running program, making each program think it has the entire computer at its disposal.

volt Measurement of AC or DC electrical power.

voltmeter Device that measures AC or DC electrical power; often integrated into a digital multimeter (DMM).

VRAM Video RAM. RAM used on some older high-end video cards; can read and write data at the same time.

WAN Wide Area Network. Network that spans multiple cities, countries, or continents. Network sections may be linked by leased line, Internet backbone, or satellite feed; routers connect LANs to WANs and WAN segments to each other.

warm boot Restarting computer with software; no memory or hardware testing.

watt Measure of heat used to rate power supplies.

WAV A non-compressed standard for digital audio. Most recording programs for Windows, such as the Microsoft Sound Recorder, can create and playback WAV files. However, WAV files are very large, and are usually converted into other formats for use online or for creating digital music archives.

wavetable Method of playing back MIDI files with digitized samples of actual musical instruments.

Wide SCSI 16-bit version of SCSI interface.

wide-carriage Dot-matrix printer equipped to handle wide tractor-fed paper.

Wi-Fi The name for IEEE-802.11a, 802.11b, or 802.11g Wireless Ethernet devices that meet the standards set forth by the Wireless Ethernet Compatibility Alliance.

wildcard Character used to replace one or more characters as a variable in MS-DOS DIR, Windows 3.1 File Manager; enhanced in Windows 9x/Me/2000/XP Find/Search, Windows Explorer. ★ = multiple characters ? = single character.

Winmodem US Robotics term for modems that lack a UART chip and use Windows for data handling.

WINS Windows Internet Naming System. Method used by server versions of Windows to dynamically match NetBIOS computer names to their IP addresses (NetBIOS name resolution).

wireless network General term for any radio-frequency network, including Wi-Fi and others. Most wireless networks can be interconnected to conventional networks.

WLAN Wireless local area network. Instead of wires, stations on a WLAN connect to each other through radio waves. The IEEE 802.11 family of standards guides the development of WLANs.

WMA Windows Media Audio. This is the native compressed audio format created by Windows Media Player. WMA files provide similar quality to *MP3* files but use smaller file sizes. Unlike MP3, WMA files support *digital rights management*.

word length Number of bits in characters sent via serial port. 8-bit word length is used in PC-to-PC communications; 7-bit word length is used to communicate with mainframe computers.

WordBasic Microsoft Word's macro language.

WRAM Window RAM. Modified version of

VRAM used on a few older video cards.

write-protect Storage area that cannot be changed. Sliders on floppy disks are used to write-protect the contents, and motherboard options are used to write-protect many FlashROM BIOS chips to protect them from unauthorized upgrades.

WWW World Wide Web. The portion of the Internet that uses the Hypertext Transfer Protocol (http://) and can thus be accessed via a web browser such as Microsoft Internet Explorer, Netscape Navigator, and others.

XCOPY MS-DOS and Windows command-line utility that copies groups of files into RAM and then to disk for faster transfers than COPY. This utility can also create folders during the copying process; when run with the Windows GUI in memory, it offers many additional features.

XMS Extended Memory Standard. Standard for managing memory above 1MB; Himem.sys turns extended memory into XMS memory.

XVGA Extended VGA; commonly refers to 1024×768 display resolution.

Y-adapter A splitter that converts a single drive power connector into two power connectors.

Y-Mouse A series of keyboard, mouse, and pointing device connectors made by PI Engineering (www.y-mouse.com), enabling uses to connect two different keyboard or pointing devices to a single port.

ZIF Zero Insertion Force. PGA-type sockets that have a lever and clamp mechanism to allow 486 and newer chips to be inserted and removed without tools; Socket 3 and above are ZIF sockets.

zero tear-off Dot-matrix printer feature that allows the user to remove a printout without wasting a sheet of paper; requires a push tractor.

Zip Iomega Zip is a popular removable-media drive using 100MB, 250MB, or 750MB proprietary media; also refers to the PKZIP format for compressed archive files.

ZV Zoomed Video. Special PC Card slot type equipped to support full-motion video with appropriate MPEG cards.

Index

Symbols

+12 voltage levels, 682
+5 voltage levels, 682
1.44MB floppy disks, 482
10/100 Ethernet, 540, 548, 597
  adding routers, 556-557
  installing, 549
    hardware requirements, 549-550
    software requirements, 551
  installing for home networks
    on Windows 98, 554
    on Windows Me, 553
    on Windows XP, 552
120MB LS-120 SuperDisk, 482
137 GB ATA barrier, 298
15-pin VGA cables, 44
16-bit, 124
20-pin ATX power connectors, 114
200 RPMM Ultra SCSI hard
  drives, 302
3.5-inch drives, 111
30-pin SIMM, 172
3D accelerated cards, 50
3D audio, 447-448
3D graphics cards, 20
3D sound, 457
3M Precise Mousing Surface, 628
4-pin ATX12V connectors, 114
40-wire cable, optical drives, 396
5.25-inch drives, 111
50% rule, 25
56Kbps modems, 516-517
6-pin auxiliary power connectors, 114
64-bit wide memory bus, 199
80-wire cables, optical drives, 396

A

A+ Certification, 55
AC adapters, digital cameras, 487
AC voltage switches, 28
AC97 audio, 254
Accelerated Graphics Port. *See* AGP
access points for wireless
  networks, 575

accessing BIOS/CMOS, 142
accessories to input devices, 628-629
accessors for WAPs, 575
active heatsinks, 32
ad-hoc mode, 573, 577
Adaptec SCSI card 29160N, 303
adapter kits, installing ATA/IDE,
  315-316
adapters
  Bluetooth adapters, buying, 583
  host adapters
    installing SATA, 320-321
    for SCSI hard drives, 327
    troubleshooting, 344
  IDE host adapters, motherboards, 239
  PC Card adapters, 503
  for power supplies, 680
  true transparency adapters, 495
  Wi-Fi adapters, troubleshooting, 585
  wireless adapters, form factors, 571-573
  wireless network adapters,
    installing, 578
  Y-adapters, 34
Add a Scheduled Task, 68
adding
  Bluetooth hardware, 581-582
  converters, 610-611
  digital music players to home
    networks, 560
  Dr. Watson to Windows startup
    group, 60
  DVRs to home networks, 559-560
  hubs, 610-611
  IEEE-1394 ports to notebook
    computers, 608-609
  IEEE-1394a ports, 604-606
  photo players to home networks, 560
  routers
    to 10/100 Ethernet networks, 556-557
    to HomePlug networks, 558
    to HomePNA networks, 558
  SCSI hard drives, 302
  USB 2.0 ports, 603-604
    to notebook computers, 608-609
  video players to home networks, 560
  Wireless Ethernet, 567-570

Adesso, 622
ADF (automatic document feeder),
  scanners, 494
ADR (Advanced Digital Recording),
  366-368
ADR2, 367
ads about motherboards, reading,
  252-254
ADSL (Asymmetrical DSL), 523
Advanced Digital Recording (ADR),
  366-368
Advanced view, Dr. Watson, 61
age of computers
  calculating effective age of, 23-25
  deciding to upgrade, 22-23
  reducing system's effective age, 24-25
AGP (Accelerated Graphics
  Port), 246
  expansion slots, 104
  motherboards, 246-247
  slots, 104-106
all-coaxial cable modems service, 521
all-in-one devices, 79
  printers, 636
  scanners, 492
  versus printers, 652
alternatives to replacing printers,
  634-635
AMD Athlon XP, 213
AMD Athlon, 212-214
AMD processors, Socket A, 213
American Megatrends (AMI), 267
American National Standards
  Institute (ANSI), 289
AMI (American Megatrends),
  267-268
AMR (Audio Modem Riser), 253
analog speakers versus digital
  speakers, 470
analog to digital transcoding, DV
  camcorders, 501
analog video capture hardware, 156
ANSI (American National Standards
  Institute), 289
antistatic electronic cleaning
  cloths, 31

X-Y-Z

www.informit.com

YOUR GUIDE TO IT REFERENCE

New Riders has partnered with **InformIT.com** to bring technical information to your desktop. Drawing from New Riders authors and reviewers to provide additional information on topics of interest to you, **InformIT.com** provides free, in-depth information you won't find anywhere else.

Articles

Keep your edge with thousands of free articles, in-depth features, interviews, and IT reference recommendations— all written by experts you know and trust.

Online Books

Answers in an instant from **InformIT Online Books'** 600+ fully searchable online books.

POWERED BY

Safari

Catalog

Review online sample chapters, author biographies, and customer rankings and choose exactly the right book from a selection of over 5,000 titles.

New Riders

ww.newriders.com